SCHOOLING SEX

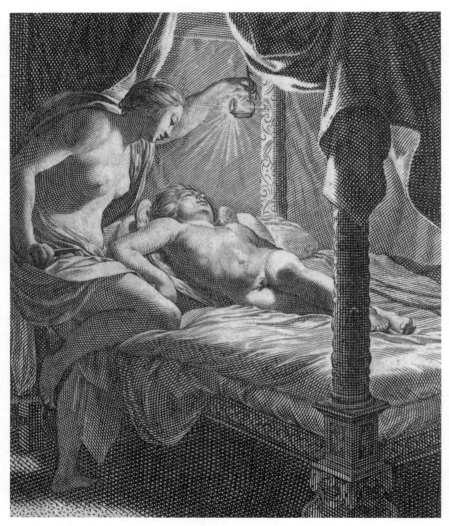

Claude Mellan after Simon Vouet, *Psyche Contemplates the Sleeping Amor* (detail)

SCHOOLING SEX

Libertine Literature and
Erotic Education in Italy,
France, and England
1534–1685

JAMES GRANTHAM TURNER

OXFORD
UNIVERSITY PRESS

OXFORD

UNIVERSITY PRESS

Great Clarendon Street, Oxford OX2 6DP

Oxford University Press is a department of the University of Oxford.
It furthers the University's objective of excellence in research, scholarship,
and education by publishing worldwide in

Oxford New York

Auckland Bangkok Buenos Aires Cape Town Chennai
Dar es Salaam Delhi Hong Kong Istanbul Karachi Kolkata
Kuala Lumpur Madrid Melbourne Mexico City Mumbai Nairobi
São Paulo Shanghai Taipei Tokyo Toronto

Oxford is a registered trade mark of Oxford University Press
in the UK and in certain other countries

Published in the United States
by Oxford University Press Inc., New York

British Library Cataloguing in Publication Data

Data available

Library of Congress Cataloging in Publication Data

Turner, James, 1947–
Schooling sex : libertine literature and erotic education in Italy, France, and England,
1534–1685 /c James Grantham Turner.
p. cm.
Includes bibliographical references and index.
1. Erotic literature, French–History and criticism.   2. Erotic literature, English–History
and criticism.   3. Erotic literature, Italian–History and criticism.   4. European
literature–Renaissance, 1450–1600–History and criticism.   5. European literature–17th
century–History and criticism.   I. Title.
PN56.E7 T87 2003   809'.933538'09409031–dc21   2002192591

ISBN 0-19-925426-5

1 3 5 7 9 10 8 6 4 2

Typeset by SNP Best-set Typesetter Ltd., Hong Kong
Printed in Great Britain
on acid-free paper by
Biddles Ltd, Guildford and King's Lynn

Discite grammatici cur mascula nomina cunnus
Et cur femineum mentula nomen habet
                              (Johannes Secundus)

She that takes pious Precepts for her Rule,
Is thought by some a kind of ill-bred fool;
They would have all bred up in *Venus* School.
    (Sarah Fyge, *The Female Advocate* (1686), 7)

The School of Venus, or the Ladies Delight Reduced into Rules of Practice
            (title of an English translation of *L'Escole des filles, c.*1676)

Preface and Acknowledgements

How did Casanova learn the 'theory' of sex? Why did male pornographers in the two centuries before the marquis de Sade write in the characters of women? Why are the female genitals gendered masculine and the male feminine? What happens when philosophers take sexuality seriously and sex-writers present their outrageous fantasies as an educational, philosophical quest? What forms of sexuality emerged in an age of scientific and intellectual revolution? These are some of the questions raised and answered in *Schooling Sex*, the first full history in English— perhaps in any language—of the 'libertine literature' identified in David Foxon's classic 1965 bibliography and brought to a wider public in Lynn Hunt's influential essay collection *The Invention of Pornography: Obscenity and the Origins of Modernity, 1500–1800*.[1]

Libertine literature aspires to write the scriptures of a new religion: in the beginning was the flesh, and the flesh was made word. But these are not *mere* words. Though libertines sometimes disparage 'discourse' and dismiss virtue as 'nothing but language', in fact they revere the arousing power of rhetoric and the sensuous immediacy of what Montaigne called 'words of flesh and bone'.[2] In the dialogue of instruction and seduction language is not merely discursive but performative and gestural, calling into play the body it recounts. Montaigne's deepest meditation on sexuality revolves around an erotic passage in Virgil, and it is from that essay that I derive my idea of sex as a 'discipline', ambiguously situated between Nature and Art.

My subject is the idea of sexual education in all its ramifications, from the simple instructional dialogue to the complex aspirations of the 'philosophical libertine', seeking to transform erotic passion into an advanced experimental system. The heart of the book is a series of readings in those major texts that formed the libertine or 'hard-core' canon; starting with Italian authors like Pietro Aretino, the courtesan-philosopher Tullia d'Aragona, the pederast-professor Antonio Rocco, and the renegade aristocrat Ferrante Pallavicino (beheaded by the papal authorities in his twenties), it moves on to the seventeenth-century classics *L'Escole des filles* and *Aloisia Sigea*, the text that defined sexual 'theory' for Casanova.[3] The last flourishes

[1] (New York, 1993), esp. chapters by Paula Findlen, Joan DeJean, and Margaret Jacob; Randolph Trumbach's essay reviews my earlier articles on libertinism.

[2] *Essais*, III. v ('Sur des vers de Virgile', 851.'665; see Abbreviations below for citation system.

[3] I should point out that I deal only with *sexual* libertinism, which overlaps but cannot be equated with the religious, intellectual, and literary experiments studied in René Pintard, *Le Libertinage érudit dans la première moitié du XVIIᵉ siècle* (Paris, 1943), Giorgio Spini, *Ricerca dei libertini: La teoria dell'impostura delle religioni nel Seicento italiano* (1950; rev. edn., Florence, 1983), Gerhard Schneider, *Der Libertin: Zur Geistes- und Sozialgeschichte des Bürgertums im 16. und 17. Jahrhundert* (Stuttgart, 1970), Hugh M. Richmond, *Puritans and Libertines: Anglo-French Literary Relations in the Reformation* (Berkeley and Los Angeles, 1981), Joan E. DeJean, *Libertine Strategies: Freedom and the Novel in Seventeenth-Century*

of Italian Renaissance pornography form an essential and hitherto unexplored link in the transmission of key ideas to France and England—the replacement of the trickster-whore by the domestic-affective mistress, the cultivation of extreme sexuality as *summum bonum* and 'sublime' aesthetic masterpiece, the rhetorical construction of desire, the 'lascivious genius' of the writer, the naturalness of 'unnatural' perversions, the performative mutability of gender, and the centrality of the ephebe or 'Ganymede' as a figure of universal longing. I explore not only the core works themselves but their readers (real and imaginary, hostile and friendly), reconstructing a context that includes some of the most important male and female writers of the period: in France, Montaigne, Descartes, Scudéry, and Molière; in England (where the influence of these forbidden texts extended just as deeply) Jonson, Milton, Cavendish, Wycherley, and Oldham. The final chapters pay close attention to the Earl of Rochester and Aphra Behn, who embroider significantly on libertine themes; in the final chapter I show that Behn proclaims a new passion-centred conception of literary value and defines a new form of female desire compatible with sublimity or greatness. To introduce the whole study, I begin by analysing two scenes from the most famous memoirs of the seventeenth and eighteenth centuries, in which Pepys and Casanova first encounter these formative erotic dialogues.

A few isolated moments from this literature and its reception-history have come under intense scrutiny. The passage in Pepys's diary that describes his arousal by *L'Escole des filles*—the kernel from which much of this book evolved—has been quoted and discussed in every imaginable forum from *The History of Private Life* to *The Times Literary Supplement*, from the legal history of pornography to the general theory of subjectivity.[4] But nobody has analysed the entire genre of erotic literature in detail, nor answered Foxon's call to study the 'intellectualization'[5] of sex—and I would add the eroticization of the intellect—that began in the Renaissance, blossomed in the seventeenth century, and left its mark on later voluptuaries like de Sade and Baudelaire. I read these faux-pedagogical works as imaginative artefacts and consequential documents, utopian fantasies and ideological weapons in the conflict over gender and social decorum. Yet in a perverse way they *are* formative, as I prove with parallels from contemporary educational reformers and with evidence of how they were transmitted, interpreted, emulated, and prosecuted. (Several of my authors were imprisoned or executed, a measure of how dangerous these writings were thought to be.) Pedagogical treatises including Comenius' *Great Didactic* and Milton's *Of Education* give a central role to the 'simple, sensuous, and passionate', while Milton persistently associates Eros and education, insisting that true virtue necessitates reading even hard-core authors like Aretino. Education-scenes

---

France (Columbus, Oh., 1981), and the ongoing series ed. Antony McKenna and Pierre-François Moreau, *Libertinage et philosophie au XVII*ᵉ *siècle* (Saint-Étienne, 1996–   ). This sexual focus explain why I deal with the influence of Lucretius but not of Epicurus.

⁴ For specific examples, see Introd. nn. 3, 6, 7 below.

⁵ *Libertine Literature* (see Abbreviations below), p. ix ('sex became to some extent intellectualized') and cf. p. v, where Foxon 'point[s] the way for someone else to write that book'.

in dramas like Jonson's *Epicoene* associate all kinds of transgressive, artificial, 'hermaphroditic' sexuality with the College of Women; in contrast, Margaret Cavendish, Duchess of Newcastle, satirizes male efforts to eroticize women's higher education in her comedy *The Female Academy*, from which I derive models for reading male-authored sexual fiction. In particular, I relate the libertine text to two issues hotly debated in mainstream discourse of the period—the relation between cognition and corporeal desire, and the role of women in the educational revolution.

My literary and intellectual history of carnal knowledge began, appropriately enough, with Adam and Eve: *One Flesh: Paradisal Marriage and Sexual Relations in the Age of Milton* (Oxford, 1987, 1993) explored clashes between the idealization and denigration of sexuality in the Genesis tradition that culminated in *Paradise Lost*. Even when I concentrated on biblical commentary and epic, I emphasized the shaping influence of scurrilous and libertine writings by what Milton called the Sons of Belial, and in more recent work I reverse the perspective and place the wicked text at the centre. *Libertines and Radicals in Early Modern London: Sexuality, Politics and Literary Culture, 1630–1685* (Cambridge, 2001) focused on 'popular Libertinism' and on 'pornography' in the literal sense, the sexually explicit discourse of prostitution and its application to social institutions and political events. There I read sexually explicit satire as a deliberate attempt to confront and neutralize women's efforts to establish their own institutions—an attempt that frequently unravels, either by paying an unintended tribute to women's achievement, or by feminizing the norms that supposedly serve as a touchstone.

This concern with the fabrication of female agency continues in *Schooling Sex*, which uses some of the same texts—*The Whores Rhetorick, L'Escole des filles, Venus in the Cloister, The Parliament of Women*—but with a different emphasis. The preoccupation with the courtesan ceases to drive hard-core writing after Pallavicino's *Retorica delle puttane* (1642), vanishing completely in Rocco's homoerotic *L'Alcibiade fanciullo a scola* (published 1651), but the most influential works emanating from France increasingly focus on female intellectual and sexual education. Libertine dialogues like Nicolas Chorier's *Aloisiae Sigeae Satyra Sotadica* (translated as *L'Academie des dames* and *The School of Love*) spoke through learned female personae and even claimed to be female-authored, a claim swallowed by male readers like Oldham who felt 'outdone' by women in 'both acting and describing lust'.[6] Among the many women writers I bring in to confront the male-dominated libertine tradition are the sixteenth-century polyglot Aloisia Sigea of Toledo, supposed author of Chorier's scandalously explicit dialogue, and the seventeenth-century feminist Sarah Fyge, who objects that men want all women 'bred up in Venus' School' (epigraph, above): the full title of the English translation of *L'Escole—The School of Venus, or The Ladies Delight Reduced into Rules of Practice*—suggests that her fears were justified. These writings by French and English contemporaries of Molière, mingling scandalous eroticism with Cartesian physiology and the

---

[6] Ch. 7, sect. 2 below.

'philosophie de l'honnête homme', clearly react against the *salon*, the *femme savante*, the alleged hegemony of *préciosité*. But they succeed—perhaps unwittingly—in creating a powerful and sometimes sublime image of libido released from moral constraint and fuelled by intellectual curiosity.

These hard-core writings are formed into a canon by citation, translation, 'traduction', imitation, clandestine printing, and manuscript circulation, in a host of texts that range from the famous to the utterly obscure. In each case my discussion is fuller than any yet in print, and some of my discoveries have never been discussed or even published: the infinitely perverse third part of Chorier's *Aloisia* (never translated into English), the original full edition of *L'Academie des dames* (which survives in a single copy, ignored by most scholars), vanished English translations transcribed from legal archives, unpublished manuscript poems on 'heroic' pornography, the unique burlesque drama *Sodom and Gomorah* (different from the better-known and less extreme *Sodom*), together with similar obscene texts in French like *La Comédie galante de Monsieur de Bussy* or *La Bibliothèque de l'Arétin*, and brilliantly amoral defences of Rochester, in which *L'Escole* and Chorier become critical touchstones and sexual arousal becomes a theoretical model of literary excellence. (My central texts are identified in the list of Abbreviations below.) Some of the primary materials that I first encountered in manuscript or rare early editions have now become available in modern editions, though their scholarly value varies alarmingly. French reprints from the 'Enfer de la Bibliothèque Nationale' (prominently reviewed by Robert Darnton in the *New York Review of Books*)[7] subtract from the sum of knowledge by presenting faulty abridged texts as authoritative, unlike the excellent recent editions of Aretino, Pallavicino, and Rocco. I bring to this newly visible literature a badly needed textual expertise, which allows me to reveal its full complexity and interrelation for the first time—particularly since the most advanced of all these hard-core texts is in Latin, the language of international science and uninhibited sexual speculation.

This is not so much a philosophical or theoretical book as a practical history, though Lucretius, Ficino, Bacon, Hobbes, and Spinoza play cameo roles and Descartes appears at many turns, interacting with his great patroness Christina of Sweden, grounding erotic myth in a detailed physiology of arousal, explaining the lover's cognition as a product of pumping fluids and 'opening' vessels. I confront sexual writing directly rather than seeking cryptic evidence for a general conception of sexuality, and I use neither a psychoanalytic nor a Foucauldian vocabulary. But I do address issues that are of increasing interest to philosophers and theorists. Like my seventeenth-century libertines, recent philosophy brings gender back into reason (Genevieve Lloyd) and takes the passions seriously, critiquing the narrow

---

[7] 22 Dec. 1994, 65–74; the problem of bad editions is acute in the case of Chorier and the *Academie*, the most important libertine texts of this period (see Ch. 7 nn. 32, 49, 62–4, 66, 68 below). Garbled fragments of my core texts have even appeared on the Internet, ostensibly for female consumption; for example, www.womenzerotica.com/erotica/erotica/dialogue.html displays a passage stolen from Donald Thomas's 1972 partial transcription of a 1745 translation of *L'Escole*, ascribing it to Pepys's 1668 diary and claiming that it illustrates 'The Rennaissance' (*sic*).

view of Descartes that emphasizes his dualism at the expense of his theory of the passions as a mode of thought that 'straddles' and questions the mind–body divide (Susan James).[8] Academic conferences now answer Iris Murdoch's call for 'a philosophy in which the concept of love can once again be made central'.[9] In France, the connection between *philosophie* and the boudoir has never really been broken, and with a few exceptions[10] most theoretical speculations on *l'amour* have been French; even the staunchly British Roger Scruton adopts a neo-Sartrean existential tone in *Sexual Desire* (1986). My book provides the first chapter in this history of critical reflection on sexual passion. Chorier and his contemporaries envisage a bold new fusion of desire and reason, coining phrases like *ingeniosa libido* and 'speculative lust'. Writing in drag as a female author, Chorier speaks through sexually emancipated intellectuals who affirm that 'everything cedes to educated desire' or *erudita libido*.

Schooling Sex reconstructs the 'ars erotica' that Foucault declared missing from the West, the classic 'discourse on sexuality' that Foucault speculated about but never studied. These scenes of illicit self-formation throw light on how arousal affects subjectivity (and how both can be simulated), how sex can be at once natural and constructed, how discourse and figuration themselves become the object of desire. I have certainly been influenced by the older feminist critique of sexual politics, but the more I analyse the distribution of power within these dialogues the less convincing I find the male dominance they ostensibly serve. When Wycherley's famous rake and trickster Horner shocks his audience by mentioning 'Bawdy Pictures, new Postures, [and] the second Part of the *Escole de Filles*', he convinces them that he is a eunuch who 'hates Women perfectly', that the lewd book must be a compensation for genital deficiency. Rochester's *Imperfect Enjoyment* re-enacts those moments in Chorier when men as well as women 'dissolve' into sexual fluids, experiencing orgasm 'at every pore' rather than in one organ; despite much boasting of physical prowess with women and boys, the phallus comes across as not only unreliable but insensible, impotent (as Chorier calls it in Latin) even when it is working properly. As in Johannes Secundus' famous question about the grammatical gender of the genital organs—featured in many of my key texts and cited as an epigraph above—representing sex not only violates decorum but inverts agency: fictitious 'women' begin by subjecting themselves to the phallus, but soon talk themselves into the dominant position. I would claim more affinity with the new academic-feminist reading of pornography: Linda Williams provides the useful term 'hard core'[11] and

[8] Lloyd, *The Man of Reason: 'Male' and 'Female' in Western Philosophy* (1984); James, *Passion and Action: The Emotions in Seventeenth-Century Philosophy* (Oxford, 1997), esp. 106–7. Recent books on the passions include those of Philip Fisher and Martha Nussbaum.

[9] Brown University, 20–1 Apr. 2001.

[10] Cf. Alan Soble (ed.), *The Philosophy of Sex: Contemporary Readings* (2nd edn., Savage, Md., 1991), Robert M. Stewart (ed.), *Philosophical Perspectives on Sex and Love* (New York, 1995), or Linda LeMoncheck, *Loose Women, Lecherous Men: A Feminist Philosophy of Sex* (New York, 1997); Arnold Davidson adopts a strict form of Foucauldianism, disallowing any use of the word 'sexuality' that does not conform to the master's chronology, in 'Sex and the Emergence of Sexuality', *Critical Inquiry*, 14 (1987), 16–48, expanded in *The Emergence of Sexuality* (Cambridge, Mass., 2001).

[11] *Hard Core: Power, Pleasure, and the Frenzy of the Visible'* (Berkeley and Los Angeles, 1989; expanded edn. 1999).

a model for the meticulous analysis of abject material; Laura Kipnis demonstrates 'that within the staged, mythic world of pornography a number of philosophical questions are posed, though couched in a low idiom . . . questions about what men are (and aren't), what women are (and aren't), questions about how sexuality and gender roles are performed, about class, aesthetics, utopia, rebellion, power, desire, and commodification'.[12]

'Queer' history and theory has been particularly influential in bringing new texts to light and using them to posit the artificiality of the heterosexual norm, revealed as construction or performance. *Schooling Sex* certainly contributes an unprecedented close reading of Rocco's *L'Alcibiade fanciullo*, linking it to other little-known sodomitic texts and showing that its conception of beauty and nature migrates into the heterosexual mainstream. I explore the widespread association between 'ingenious lust' and 'Sodomy', male and female. I suggest that 'queer' eroticism underlies the (mainly) heterosexual tradition studied in the following chapters, that *L'Escole des filles* and its successors pursue the same goal as *L'Alcibiade*: an aestheticized, voluntary, Epicurean sexuality, an *amour philosophique* removed as far as possible from animal 'necessity'. I emphasize the persistence of the Sapphic theme in Chorier's Latin original—giving lesbianism an empowering history, a founding ancestress, and a classificatory vocabulary—and show how deeply this is cut in later French adaptations. But I aim to avoid the binary division into straight and queer. There is a danger even among sophisticated social constructionists of tacitly installing modern, Western homosexuality as the privileged norm in place of 'compulsory heterosexuality'. For example, I show that the pederastic woman, who penetrates young men with her enlarged clitoris, was frequently evoked in ancient and early modern discourse, and yet this phenomenon escapes the attention of modern historians because it eludes their categories; even the best of them discuss clitoral hypertrophy solely in terms of sex between women, imposing a kind of homonormativity.[13]

Instead I offer a new map of early modern desire, with different polarities and different conceptions of which forms of lust constitute the great perversion that defines all others: *iconophilia* or Pygmalionism, where the erotic object is desired *qua* artefact, irrespective of sex and age; *logophilia* or arousal by narrative; *spermatophilia* or excessive emphasis on ejaculation as the sole source of pleasure (even when issues of contraception and procreation are swept under the table); castratism or sexual fascination with the eunuch (illustrated from *L'Escole des filles*, from medico-legal treatises, and from satires on opera); *heteropaedophilia*, where a mature woman takes the active role with an *ephebe* or Ganymede, a labile youth ambiguously poised between male and female. Even well-worn concepts like sodomy and 'nymphomania' emerge from this book in a new light. My frontispiece,

[12] *Bound and Gagged: Pornography and the Politics of Fantasy in America* (1999), p. viii; James Atlas, 'The Loose Canon: Why Higher Learning has Embraced Pornography', *New Yorker*, 29 Mar. 1999, 60–5, interviews both Williams and Kipnis.

[13] Cf. Katherine Park, 'The Rediscovery of the Clitoris', in David Hillman and Carla Mazzio (eds.), *The Body in Parts* (1997), and Judith C. Brown, *Immodest Acts: The Life of a Lesbian Nun in Renaissance Italy* (New York, 1986), 17–19.

which I later evoke to illustrate a particularly intimate scene in Chorier's *Aloisia Sigea* (Fig. 11 below), can also serve as a paradigm or emblem of the whole project. Mellan and Vouet show Psyche exploring the mysterious sleeping body of her boy-husband Amor, just at the moment that her forbidden light displays him. She is at once the Soul in quest of the truth of Sex—driven by the 'compulsion de vérification' or 'force d'enquête jamais apaisée' that Claude Reichler finds at the heart of libertine Eros[14]—and the well-fleshed woman of libertine fiction, actively discovering the *ephebe* subject to her gaze.

Reichler's 'unappeasable urge to enquire' or 'insatiable need to know', expanding on Michel Foucault's *volonté de savoir*, has been an influential idea. But my model is more the close reading of the second and third volumes of Foucault's *History of Sexuality* than the brilliantly suggestive yet sketchy first volume, really a set of maxims in the tradition of his near-namesake La Rochefoucauld. Conceptually, I emphasize the libertines' aspiration to *connaître* rather than *savoir*, aesthetic and hedonist connoisseurship rather than the confessional, power-oriented knowledge that preoccupied Foucault. As my epigraph from Secundus suggests, I am fascinated by the paradoxical interactions *between* language and embodiment rather than the dominance of discourse over all. The mere *fact* of sex's inseparability from language can no longer be classed among marvels; since I began work in this field, I have watched Foucauldian discursive constructionism evolve from a daring innovation into a new orthodoxy. The time is long past when ritual invocation of his name could substitute for rigorous argument and deep research.[15] Foucault was quite right to insist that the historian of sexuality must confront the difficult relation of discourse and power, but he also exemplifies its problems. His working assumptions may have undermined his theoretical positions. Foucault wittily compares 'our' compulsive sexual curiosity to Diderot's *Les Bijoux indiscrets*, where Mangogul's magic ring reveals the illicit sexual lives of every woman in the Court, producing an authentic, unmediated voice from beneath their skirts.[16] Whereas hitherto the 'discourse of sexuality' has been as coercive and tendentious as Mangogul's use of his ring, he goes on, the new historian must make *the ring itself* speak—a solution that prolongs the discourse-as-liberation model that he is supposed to have demolished.

My subject is not the simple knowledge of sex—a topic nicely covered by Roy Porter and Lesley Hall in *The Facts of Life: The Creation of Sexual Knowledge in Britain, 1650–1950* (1995)—but how sexuality comes to be a 'discipline' or body of knowledge. The title *Schooling Sex* nods towards my colleague Thomas Laqueur's *Making Sex: Body and Gender from the Greeks to Freud* (1990), though obviously I choose to study a smaller period more intensively. (The same ambitious time-frame characterizes Jonathan Dollimore's *Sexual Dissidence: Augustine to Wilde, Freud to Foucault* (Oxford, 1991).) All kinds of historical studies have been useful, notably

[14] *L'Âge libertin* (Paris, 1987), 55; cf. my 'The Culture of Priapism', *Review*, 10 (1988), 2–13.

[15] Cf. my *Sexuality and Gender in Early Modern Europe* (Cambridge, 1993), pp. xv–xvi, and my review of the *Journal of the History of Sexuality*, inaugural issue, in *Modern Philology*, 91 (1993–4), esp. 406–8, 410–11.

[16] *La Volonté de savoir* (Paris, 1976), 101.

Reichler's *L'Âge libertin*, Yves Citton's book on impotence, Laura Coci's editions of *La retorica delle puttane* and *L'Alcibiade*, and early work in the history of education by Roger Chartier and Dominique Julia.

Surprisingly few literary studies of sex and gender have tackled these libertine texts directly, however. Two US dissertations on the French erotica (by Ruth Larson and Anne Menke) have yielded only a handful of articles, while special issues of *Œuvres et critiques* and *L'Esprit créateur* have necessarily treated the subject in a fragmentary way. After Foxon's *Libertine Literature in England*, works like Peter Naumann's *Keyhole und Candle* (1976), Roger Thompson's *Unfit for Modest Ears* (1979), and David Frantz's *Festum Voluptatis* (1989) offered reliable bibliographical data and detailed plot summaries. On the English side, Restoration libertinism has inspired some important essays, and Warren Chernaik's book on sexual freedom (Cambridge, 1995) deals well with the Hobbesian and Lucretian underpinning of Behn, Wycherley, and Rochester. The French social context is convincingly reconstructed in Ian Maclean's *Woman Triumphant: Feminism in French Literature, 1610–1652* (Oxford, 1977) and Joan DeJean's *Tender Geographies: Women and the Origins of the Novel in France* (New York, 1991).

Several recent books confront some aspect of my core texts when pursuing a related theme or setting the scene for their work on the later eighteenth century. Ian Moulton's *Before Pornography: Erotic Writing in Early Modern England* (New York, 2000) deals with Aretino's *Ragionamenti* and *Il marescalco* (in relation to Jonson's *Epicoene*). Elizabeth Wahl gives careful scrutiny to the lesbian passages in Chorier that also feature in my 'Sapphic' reading (*Invisible Relations: Representations of Female Intimacy in the Age of Enlightenment* (Stanford, Calif., 1999)). Carolin Fischer's *Éducation érotique: Pietro Aretinos 'Ragionamenti' im libertinen Roman Frankreichs* (Stuttgart, 1994) emphasizes the 'critique of society and Church' in texts like *L'Escole des filles*, adopting a somewhat literal, Enlightenment-Whiggish approach influenced by Robert Darnton. Jean-Marie Goulemot's *Forbidden Texts* (Philadelphia, 1994)—originally entitled, after Rousseau, *Ces Livres qu'on ne lit que d'une main*—theorizes about the effects sought by publishers and readers of similar writings in eighteenth-century France, though (as one reviewer pointed out) he does not address the crucial question that I place at the centre, why should the sexual education of a young woman be the main libertine theme? Why should a title like *Thérèse philosophe* (or *L'Escole des filles*) be so 'enticingly oxymoronic'?[17] Mitchell Greenberg's *Baroque Bodies* (2001) relates *L'Escole* and *L'Académie* (in a fragmented text) to a psychoanalytic reading of the 'classical' or 'absolutist' body. Drawing quite different conclusions, Joan DeJean offers a detailed reading of *L'Escole* and its publication, a key episode in *The Reinvention of Obscenity: Sex, Lies, and Tabloids in Early Modern France* (2002).

[17] Madelyn Gutwirth, *Eighteenth-Century Studies*, 30 (1997), 333: 'Why should the *déniaisement* of the girl . . . be the core erotic plot?' Goulemot's stress on the novel's single-minded voyeuristic perspective and monovocal instructional mode hardly applies to the 17th-century texts discussed below, whose dialogue form makes them performative rather than narrative.

Several Sade-dominated studies of the French eighteenth century do pay some attention to the seventeenth. I differ from them by resisting teleology. Though I do occasionally draw parallels with Fanny Hill or *Les Liaisons dangereuses,* I would not agree that (in Lynn Hunt's terms) the invention of pornography must be tied to the origins of modernity: these are not texts 'before their time', but instead *constitute* their time, expressing a restless and contradictory Eros more like the 'Baroque' evoked in Julia Kristeva's interpretation of Don Juan.[18] (Though I bring in texts written between 1534 and 1685, the white-hot core of libertine literary production is 1642–60, the age of the Fronde in France, warfare and unrest in Europe from Sweden to Naples, the regicide and revolution in England, and papal repression in Italy that led to the capture and execution of Pallavicino.) Jean-Pierre Dubost pinpoints the central issue as 'Eros and Reason', but provides only a cursory reading (using the wrong texts), impatient to elevate de Sade into the be-all and end-all of libertine discourse.[19] Peter Cryle's *Geometry in the Boudoir: Configurations of French Erotic Narrative* (1994) brings a much-needed theoretical awareness to this literature, and begins to take seriously the formation of a libertine canon, its relation to *ars erotica,* and the educational-cognitive dimension of postures and techniques. He draws on the Italian predecessors as well as the French 'classics' up to *Vénus dans le cloître,* my latest example, but (like many other scholars) bases these readings on corrupt texts and inaccurate translations. Jean Mainil's *Dans les règles du plaisir: Théorie de la différence dans le discours obscène romanesque et médical de l'Ancien Régime* (Paris, 1996) takes its title from *L'Escole des filles* (called an 'obscene novel' despite the dialogue form) and discusses at length many passages that originate in Chorier, though limiting himself to an abridged version of the French adaptation. Mainil explores the paradoxes of gender difference in libertine and medical texts, interpreting them as unrelievedly phallocratic and marital, and arguing in consequence that they render female pleasure 'impossible'; my reading, in contrast, emphasizes the play in these dialogues and their destabilizing effect on what I call 'phallepistemic' certainties.

One scholar in this field stands out, and I would like to acknowledge her first. Lise Leibacher-Ouvrard's articles on *L'Escole* and Chorier have become indispensible over the years, and many points in this book grow out of a long-running and friendly dialogue with her. When her work appears in book form it will complement, or more truthfully supersede, the French portions of *Schooling Sex.* (I should add that Leibacher-Ouvrard tackles many interesting *libertins* who did not achieve international canonicity and who are therefore neglected here, notably Pierre-Corneille Blessebois.) Secondly, I would have liked to thank David Foxon for helpful advice and shared material over three decades; I am sorry that he died before seeing this distant reflection of his teaching.

---

[18] *Histoires d'amour,* Folio Essais edn. (Paris, 1983), 251–63.
[19] *Eros und Vernunft: Literatur und Libertinage* (Frankfurt, 1988), ch. 3.

Many other individuals have helped with perceptive comments, useful references, copies of work in progress, or general encouragement. I would like to thank Ann Banfield, Richard Best (who taught me *Les Femmes savantes* in 1961), Gordon Braden, Dennis Burden, Dympna Callaghan, Alison Conway, Joan DeJean, Margaret Doody, Cobi Feingold (an early and perceptive critic), Amy Greenstadt, Lorna Hutson, Richard Luckett, Wendy Motooka, Nicholas Paige, Joanna Picciotto, David Robinson, Ingrid Rowland, Alison Shell, Randolph Trumbach, Elizabeth Wahl, and John Wing. Martha Pollak has watched over this project in sickness and in health.

My research has been helped over the years by grants from the John Simon Guggenheim Foundation, the American Council of Learned Societies, and the National Endowment for the Humanities (including fellowships at the Newberry and Folger Libraries), and by a President's Research Fellowship in the Humanities from the University of California. I would like to acknowledge the helpful staffs of the Bodleian Library and Trinity College Library, Oxford; the British Library, the Victoria and Albert Museum Library, the Greater London Record Office, and the Public Record Office, London; the Bibliothèque nationale de France, Paris (Richelieu and Tolbiac), and the Château de Chantilly; the Biblioteca Apostolica Vaticana, Rome; the Herzog August Bibliothek, Wolfenbüttel; the Österreichische Nationalbibliothek, Vienna; the Bancroft Library, Berkeley, the Huntington Library, San Marino, the Kinsey Institute Library, Indiana University, the New York Public Library, the Library of Congress and the Folger Shakespeare Memorial Library, Washington, DC, the University of Chicago and the Newberry Libraries, Chicago. The Pepys Library of Magdalene College, Cambridge, and the university libraries of Nottingham, Leiden, and Michigan have kindly sent microfilms or other bibliographical resources. Among all these collections, by far the most important are the Private Case of the British Library and the Enfer de la Bibliothèque nationale.

A few passages have been published in articles or delivered as lectures and conference papers, though they have been thoroughly revised. For these chances to work up some of my examples in preliminary form, I would like to thank the University of Tulsa Center for the Study of Women's Literature, the McMaster Association for 18th-Century Studies, the History of Consciousness Program of the University of California, Santa Cruz, the University of Wisconsin, Madison, the University of California, Los Angeles, the Modern Languages Association Division on Seventeenth-Century French Literature (particularly session organizers Abby Zanger and Joan DeJean, again), and my own department at the University of California, Berkeley, for inviting me to give the Charles Mills Gayley Lecture. For earlier publication opportunities I am grateful to Margaret Doody (again) and Gerald Maclean, and to the editors of *Notes and Queries, Œuvres et critiques* (guest editor Kathleen Clark), *Studies in Eighteenth-Century Culture*, and *Papers on French Seventeenth-Century Literature*.

At Oxford University Press, I would like to thank Sophie Goldsworthy and the expert advisers she brought in (Colin Burrow, Paul Hammond, and a reader who remains anonymous). I keenly regret that Kim Scott Walwyn, the publisher of *One Flesh*, did not live to see the appearance of this volume.

For permission to publish illustrations I am grateful to the Bibliothèque nationale de France (both Estampes and Imprimés), the Pepys Library, Magdalene College, Cambridge, the British Library, the British Museum Department of Prints and Drawings, and the Bodleian Library, Oxford.

J. G. T.

Contents

PART II

LIBERTINE CANONIZATION: RECEPTION-HISTORY AND THE EROTICS OF LITERARY RESPONSE

List of Illustrations

Abbreviations and Principal Works Cited

This checklist identifies the core texts of libertine literature studied below, the main bibliographic resources necessary to study them, and the principal canonical writers brought into their reception-history. Here and throughout the notes, the place of publication is conventionally omitted for books published in London.

Academie	Jean Nicholas(?), *L'Academie des dames, divisée en sept entretiens satiriques* ('A Ville-Franche, chez Michel Blanchet', 1680), BL PC 31.b.30; a partial translation of Chorier's *Satyra*, with some additions. *Academie* (*sic*, without accent) refers to the original text, known only from this surviving copy; to avoid confusion, citations from later abridgements (some of which revive the *Académie des dames* title with added accent) are given in full
Alcibiade	See Rocco
Aloisia Sigea	See Chorier
Aretino	Pietro Aretino's *Ragionamenti* are cited by dialogue number and page from *Sei giornate*, ed. Guido Davico Bonino (Turin, 1975), followed [in brackets] by the corresponding page in Raymond Rosenthal's translation, *Aretino's Dialogues* (New York, 1971), reissued with epilogue by Margaret Rosenthal (New York, 1995). (*Ragionamento della Nanna e della Antonia* (1534) is designated as 'I' and *Dialogo nel quale la Nanna . . . insegna a la Pippa* (1536) as 'II', with small roman numerals for the dialogues internal to each.) Aretino's sonnets on the *Modi* exist in several versions; unless otherwise specified I cite them by number from the appendix of Bette Talvacchia, *Taking Positions: On the Erotic in Renaissance Culture* (Princeton, 1999). See also *Puttana errante*
Behn	*The Works of Aphra Behn*, ed. Janet Todd (Columbus, Oh.). Vol. i: *Poetry* (1992); vol. ii: *Love-Letters between a Nobleman and his Sister* (1993); vol. v: *The Plays, 1671–1677* (1996); vol. vi: *The Plays, 1678–1682* (1996). Plays will give act and scene before the page number
BL	British Library, London. Shelfmark included for printed works of extreme rarity, generally in PC (i.e. Private Case)
BnF	Bibliothèque nationale de France, Paris. Shelfmark included for printed works of extreme rarity, generally in Enfer
Chorier, *Adversaria*	Nicholas Chorier (1612–93), *Adversariorum de Vita et Rebis Suis Libri III*, ed. and tr. Alcide Bonneau, in Isidore Liseux (ed.), *La Curiosité littéraire et bibliographique*, 3rd ser. (Paris, 1882). Citations from these Latin MS memoirs include the volume number in the *Curiosité* series
Chorier, *Satyra*	*Aloisiae Sigeae Toletanae Satyra Sotadica de Arcanis Amoris et Veneris* ('Aloisia Sigea of Toledo, *Sotadic Satire about the Secrets of Love and Venus*'), ed. Bruno Lavagnini (Catania, 1935). All references to Chorier's Latin text will consist of the page number from Lavagnini's

edn., checked against other 17th-century edns., notably British Library, PC 30.i.3 (Lyons?, *c*.1665?), clearly earlier than that of 'Amsterdam, 1678'. (Later editions emphasize the name of the supposed translator from Spanish into Latin, Jan van Meurs or Johannes Meursius, 1579–1639.) For the convenience of readers using other edns. (e.g. those of Isidore Liseux), I add the dialogue number when applicable, before the page. All translations from the *Satyra* (or *Aloisa Sigea*) are mine, but it has been translated accurately into French, by Alcide Bonneau in *Les Dialogues de Luisa Sigea*, ed. Liseux (Paris, 1882), and by André Berry, *Satire sotadique de Luisa Sigea de Tolède* (Paris, 1969). For English versions, 1684–1745, see Chapter 7, section 3 below. More recent translations into English, inept and partial (omitting the crucial seventh dialogue) were published in 1890 (Paris, after Bonneau's French) and 1974 (Lawrence, Kan., tr. from the original Latin by Donald A. McKenzie).

Coci	Laura Coci, editor. See Rocco, *Alcibiade*, and Pallavicino, *RP*
CPW	See Milton
CW	*The Country-Wife*. See Wycherley
DNB	*The Dictionary of National Biography*
Donne	Cited by poem and line from John Donne, *The Elegies and the Songs and Sonnets*, ed. Helen Gardner (Oxford, 1965)
Dryden	Cited from *The Works of John Dryden*, ed. Edward Niles Hooker, H. T. Swedenberg, et al. (Berkeley and Los Angeles, 1956–). The California edn.
École des filles	See *Escole*
Escole	Author unknown (Claude Le Petit?), *L'Escole des filles, ou La Philosophie des dames, divisée en deux dialogues* (1655; 1668), ed. Pascal Pia (Paris, 1969); this edn. includes full transcripts of the 1655 trial documents, which indicted the two publishers, Michel Millot and Jean L'Ange, as authors. The old-spelling title *Escole* denotes this particular work (sometimes catalogued as by Millot), to distinguish it more readily from works with a similar title that seem intended to be confused with it. Citations will be by page from this edition (abbreviated as 'Pia'); where necessary, Pia's text is modified by readings from the earliest surviving exemplars, BnF Enfer 112 ('Paris', 1667) and BL PC 29.a.16 ('Fribourg, Chez Roger Bon Temps, 1668'). Pia's introduction, and the forematter of *L'Escole* itself, is paginated in upper-case roman numerals; to help place quotations from the main text, I have added a dialogue number before the arabic page number. Except when citing *The School of Venus* (see following) all translations are my own.

The English translation *The School of Venus* (first mentioned in a John Oldham MS datable to 1676–7) survives only in two prosecution documents, of 1680 and 1745, which transcribe selected offensive passages; in the few cases that they overlap, the wording is the same in both. The shorter and earlier document (cited as 'Middx.') is Greater London Record Office, Middlesex Session Roll MJ/SR 1582, recognizance 1. Fuller extracts (but only from the first 71 pages of the book) are found in the King's Bench trial records of 1745, KB 28/176/148. All citations from this document, abbreviated 'KB', will include (in quotation marks) the pages of the lost printed version whenever they are specified in the margins of the extracts it quotes. The full title page, cited mechanically in each article of the KB indictment, ran: *The School of Venus or the Ladies delight reduced into Rules of Practice being the Translation of the French L'Escole des Filles in two dialogues between Frances a Marryed Lady and Katy a young maiden adorned with Twenty four curious plates designed from Aretenez's postures Discite Grammatici cur Mascula Nomina Cunnus et cur Femineum Mentula Nomen habet.*

The KB extracts have been (partially and inaccurately) transcribed in the introduction to Donald Thomas's modern English translation, which also uses the title *The School of Venus* (New York, 1971); citations will use the abbreviation 'Thomas'

Foxon	David Foxon, *Libertine Literature in England 1660–1745* (New Hyde Park, NY, 1965); reprints articles originally in the *Book Collector* (1963)
Garasse	François Garasse, SJ, *La Doctrine curieuse des beaux esprits de ce temps, ou pretendus tels, contenant plusieurs maximes pernicieuses à l'Estat, à la Religion, et aux bonnes Mœurs, combattue et renversee par le P. François Garassus* (Paris, 1623)
Jonson	Cited by page number (with act and scene for the drama and vol. for other texts) from *Ben Jonson*, ed. C. H. Herford, Percy Simpson, and Evelyn Simpson (Oxford, 1925–63)
KB	King's (or Queen's) Bench, English law court, documents in the Public Record Office, London. See *Escole*
Lavagnini	See Chorier
Le Petit, *Œuvres*	*Les Œuvres libertines de Claude Le Petit, parisien brûlé le 1ᵉʳ septembre 1662*, ed. Frédéric Lachèvre ([Paris], 1918). Other works by Le Petit, including his commendatory poem for *Escole*, are cited in the notes below
Love	See Rochester, *Sodom*
Lyons	See *Sodom*
Meursius	See Chorier, *Satyra*
Middx.	Middlesex County Records. See *Escole*
Millot	See *Escole*
Milton, Columbia	*The Works of John Milton*, ed. F. A. Patterson et al. (New York, 1931–8). The Columbia edn. (used for Latin prose citations)
Milton, *CPW*	*The Complete Prose Works*, ed. Don M. Wolfe et al. (New Haven, 1953–82). The Yale edn.
Milton, *PL*	*Paradise Lost*, cited by title and line
Modi sonnets	See Aretino
Molière	Cited by act, scene, and line (for verse), from *Œuvres complètes*, ed. Georges Couton, Bibliothèque de la Pléiade (Paris, 1971)
Montaigne	Cited by essay number and page in *Œuvres complètes*, ed. Albert Thibaudet and Maurice Rat, Bibliothèque de la Pléiade (Paris, 1962), followed by the corresponding page in *Complete Works*, tr. Donald M. Frame (Stanford, Calif., 1957)
OED	*The Oxford English Dictionary*, 2nd edn., on CD-ROM

Oldham, MS	Oxford, Bodleian Library, MS Rawlinson Poet. 123; autograph working drafts of poems by John Oldham (1653–83), later bound into a volume
Oldham, *Poems*	*The Poems of John Oldham*, ed. Harold F. Brooks with the collaboration of Raman Selden (Oxford, 1987)
Pallavicino, *RP*	Ferrante Pallavicino (1615–44), *La retorica delle puttane, composta conforme li precetti di Cipriano, dedicata alla Università delle Cortigiane più Celebri* (1642). Cited from the scholarly edn. of Laura Coci (Parma, 1992), which includes full biographical and bibliographical details; where necessary I have replaced Coci's lightly modernized text by the reading of two early editions, 'Cambrai' (1642) and 'Villafranca' (1673), adding the date for identification. For a partial adaptation in English, see *WR*
Pepys	Cited by entry date from *The Diary of Samuel Pepys*, ed. Robert Latham and William Matthews (Berkeley and Los Angeles, 1970–83)
Pia	See *Escole*
PL	*Paradise Lost*. See Milton
Puttana errante	Prose dialogue attributed to Pietro Aretino, the work most commonly meant when 17th-century authors refer to 'Aretino'. The earliest surviving text, a 16th-century MS now in Chantilly, is entitled *Il piacevol ragionamento de l'Aretino. Dialogo di Giulia e di Madalena*, and edited by Claudio Galderisi, introduction by Enrico Rufi, foreword by Giovanni Aquilecchia (Rome, 1987). The title *Puttana errante* (stolen from a poem by Lorenzo Venier) was given to this 'Dialogue of Giulia and Madalena' in later, printed versions, e.g. *La puttana errante, overo Dialogo di Madalena e Giulia, di M. P. Aretino* ([Leiden, c.1668]), Bodleian Vet. 33 f.304, which also switch the names of the teacher and the pupil Citations will give the page from the Galderisi edn., followed by the Bodleian *Puttana errante*
Ragionamenti	See Aretino
RCH	David Farley-Hills (ed.), *Rochester: The Critical Heritage* (1972); includes contemporary biographical and critical essays, notably Robert Wolseley's 1685 preface to *Valentinian*
Rocco, *Alcibiade*	[Antonio Rocco (1586–1653)], *L'Alcibiade fanciullo a scola*, D. P. A. (written c.1630, published 'Oranges, 1652'), cited from the scholarly edn. of Laura Coci (Rome, 1988). A French translation was published in 'Amsterdam' (Brussels), 1866, and two extracts in English are included in Byrne R. S. Fone (ed.), *The Columbia Anthology of Gay Literature* (New York, 1998), 151–6
Rochester	Cited by page number from *The Works of John Wilmot, Earl of Rochester*, ed. Harold Love (Oxford, 1999). Includes works unreliably attributed to Rochester (1647–80). See also *RCH*, *Sodom*
RP	*La retorica delle puttane*. See Pallavicino
School of Venus	See *Escole*
Sodom	Anonymous burlesque verse drama (c.1672–8), cited from Rochester, *Works*, ed. Harold Love (Oxford, 1999); both versions (the shorter entitled *Sodom and Gomorah* and labelled A by Love) are included in Love's 'Appendix Roffensis' of works once attributed to Rochester but

	unlikely to be by him. My readings have been checked against Princeton University Library, MS AM 14401 and *Rochester, Complete Poems and Plays*, ed. Paddy Lyons (1993); where relevant, the Lyons page number will *follow* the citation from Love's edn. of the longer B text. (This is for the reader's convenience, and in no way implies that I accept his ascription to Rochester.)
Thomas	Donald Thomas, *The School of Venus*. See *Escole*
Vénus	[Jean Barrin?], *Vénus dans le cloître, ou La Religieuse en chemise, entretiens curieux par l'abbé du Prat* (1683), expanded in successive edns. from 3 to 6 dialogues. All citations from *Vénus* are from the *Réimpression de l'édition de Cologne, 1719*, ed. B. V[illeneuve?], Le Coffret du Bibliophile (Paris, 1934), checked against earlier edns.) and preceded where necessary by the dialogue number
	Two English translations are identified by short title and date: Oxford, Bodleian Library, Don. f. 537, *Venus in the Cloister, or The Nun in her Smock, Done out of French* (1683), and the translation published by Curll, BL PC 25.a.93, *Venus in the Cloister, or The Nun in her Smock* (1725)
Wolseley	See *RCH*
WR	Adaptor unknown, *The Whores Rhetorick, Calculated to the Meridian of London, and Conformed to the Rules of Art* (1683); partial translation of Pallavicino's *RP*, with additions from Aretino's *Ragionamenti*
Wycherley	Drama cited by act, scene, and page from *The Plays of William Wycherley*, ed. Arthur Friedman (Oxford, 1979); *The Country-Wife* (1675) is abbreviated *CW*
Wycherley, *Works*	*Complete Works*, ed. Montague Summers (1924)

Introduction
Sex Talks
Libertine Texts and Erotic Philosophies

... secret *whoredom, self pollution*, speculative *wantonness*, men with *men*, women with *women*, as the Apostle speaks, *Rom.*1. At this day, all the world shall see and hear these privy pranks, then the Books shall be opened.

(Thomas Shepard, *The Sincere Convert* (1664), 58)

I was a sort of philosophick libertine, and pursued pleasure for the sake of demonstration; I paused, I reasoned, I made critical reflections on every enjoyment; I proposed something beyond gratifying a low and sensual inclination; mine was a deliberate search after happiness.

(Elisabeth Singer Rowe)

Two scenes of reading define the scope and material of this book. Discovered in the most famous memoirs of the seventeenth and eighteenth centuries, they frame my enquiry into the educational and philosophical implications of libertine literature, and identify the texts that I will read most closely in the following chapters: *L'Escole des filles, ou La Philosophie des dames* (1655) and *Aloisiae Sigeae Satyra Sotadica de Arcanis Amoris et Veneris* (*c*.1660). Though the publication-history of these erotic dialogues was established decades ago by the great bibliographer David Foxon, his call for a deeper study of the 'intellectualization' of sexuality in the mid-seventeenth century[1] has gone largely unanswered, despite the vast surge of interest in the 'discourse of sexuality' provoked by Michel Foucault's *Volonté de savoir* and by feminist critiques of pornography. *Schooling Sex* attempts to answer that call, and in particular to enquire why the idea of female education—the conjunction of *école* and *filles*, *philosophie* and *dames*—should generate such a frenzy of composition.

The first scene is by now the most familiar episode in the history of what Lynn Hunt calls the 'invention of pornography'. On the morning of Sunday, 9 February 1668, Samuel Pepys appears to have been in two places at once: 'Up, and at my chamber all the morning and the office, doing business and also reading a little of *L'escolle des Filles*.' His entanglement with this quintessential libertine text—'a mighty lewd book, but yet not amiss for a sober man once to read over to inform himself in the

---

[1] Preface, n. 5 above; for Foxon's *Libertine Literature*, Pepys's diary, and other frequently cited texts, see Abbreviations above.

villainy of the world'—had begun in a more public setting, a respectable bookshop in the Strand. Expecting an urbane French conduct book to share with his wife, he began browsing but discovered it to be 'the most bawdy, lewd book that I ever saw, rather worse than *putana errante*—so that I was ashamed of reading in it' (13 Jan. 1668). Nevertheless, he returned a third time four weeks later to 'that idle, roguish book, *L'escholle des Filles*', buying it surreptitiously 'in plain binding' (8 Feb.), and on the following Lord's Day he took his pleasure of it in full, starting in the morning while simultaneously doing 'business' in his home office, finishing it the same night after a day of music-making with friends:

> We sang till almost night, and drank my good store of wine; and then they parted and I to my chamber, where I did read through *L'escholle des Filles*; a lewd book, but what doth me no wrong to read for information sake (but it did hazer my prick para stand all the while, and una vez to decharger); and after I had done it, I burned it, that it might not be among my books to my shame; and so at night to supper and then to bed. (9 Feb. 1668)

Like many other historians of sexuality I will take my cue from this now-famous passage, where Pepys splits himself into a 'sober man' and a priapic rogue, and assures us repeatedly that his object is 'to inform himself'. I will concentrate more on the French text than on Pepys, but I will bring to libertine literature questions derived from its reception-history: what representations of sex as discipline, what opportunities to 'school' or 'inform himself', did Pepys find in this 'escolle des Filles' or 'School for Girls', which he stalked, captured, and devoured with such intense arousal and shame?

Throughout this bibliophiliac affair Pepys sees the book as a lively quasi-human agent, shuttling between active and passive, subject-formation and object-lesson. Like the 'lascivious' books banned by the Council of Trent (Ch. 1 n. 84 below), the 'mighty lewd book' actively 'teaches' rather than merely presenting or narrating. *L'Escole des filles* is not just a text that must be 'read with one hand'—as Rousseau reported a lady friend saying—but a text that pursues the reader, that 'makes him discharge', that forces him to define reading as a dirty deed ('after I had done it, I burned it'). Such a book actively 'disgraces' and 'shames' the company it keeps. When Pepys tries to place *L'Escole* in a conceptual library, he imagines it as a strolling adventuress or 'wandering whore' ('rather worse than *putana errante*') scandalously intruding into the orderly, well-bound, official collection that will carry his image into history: he resolves to buy it in plain wrapper, and to burn it the moment after enjoyment, so 'that it may not *stand* in the list of books, nor among them, to disgrace *them* if it should be found' (8 Feb. 1668, my emphasis). 'Stand' is precisely the word he uses for his own erection the following evening, as he reads the libertine text by the fireside. Paradoxically this book about female sexuality—the dialogue of the ingénue and her young married cousin, initiating her into the 'facts of life' and the pleasures of adultery—invades Pepys with what Donne called a 'masculine persuasive force',[2] experienced as a quality of the text rather than the reader. If this school of *filles* can 'stand' as well as give him pleasure, then it 'informs' by a kind of active penetration.

---

[2] Elegy XVI, 'On his Mistris', line 4.

L'Escole allows Pepys to enjoy a kind of sex without owning to a sexual relationship. In the act of writing up his response he can preserve the memory and file it away, evoking it and distancing it, categorizing and controlling it according to its literary genre. Even before reading *L'Escole*, its innocuous title and frontispiece (Fig. 4 below) had made Pepys speculate about the kind of book it might be and the kind of 'school' it might create; he had already placed it in an imaginary scene of domestic industry and mutual enlightenment, since he first identifies it as 'the French book which I did think to have had for my wife to translate' (13 Jan. 1668). To weave themselves common interests, the Anglo-French couple had been reading *Le Grand Cyrus* together (in English), luxuriating in Madeleine de Scudéry's vision of educative community under female leadership; Pepys clearly hoped that *L'Escole* would extend this cultural project. After discovering its genital content and shameless philosophy of female hedonism, he switches to a different didactic tradition—the Italian 'pornographic' canon that I explore in the earlier chapters of this book. When he declares it 'rather worse than *putana errante*', we see him expertly gauging the French book according to its power to arouse and its relation to previous authorities; *La puttana errante* was a sixteenth-century dialogue of courtesanal instruction, recently republished and passing as an authentic work by the celebrated Pietro Aretino, gathering and codifying every known sexual posture. Now Pepys extends the calibrating, mapping process to the new libertine text, using this *Wandering Whore* as the standard to measure its 'badness'.

I propose to take the teaching, 'informing' role of early modern erotic discourse seriously, not by endorsing its liberating message or comparing it to more recent pornography, but by confronting 'bad' texts like *L'Escole des filles* with the educational theories and practices of their own period. Critical readings of this passage in Pepys have tended to emphasize the inadequacy of the didactic claim, the secrecy of the writing, the 'tremulous' and 'private' corporeality manifested in what is often read as the first authentic account of the male response to pornography. Historians of French culture give this fragment of English diary a privileged place in a 'history of private life' otherwise almost entirely Gallic; as if it exemplifies the Foucauldian episteme in action, Pepys's embrace of *L'Escole* becomes an originary moment, a sudden eruption of modernity.[3] Scholars of England paint a grimmer picture. Roger Thompson finds Pepys's account 'profoundly inhibited and uncomfortable, . . . tantalised, drunkenly horrified',[4] while Bridget Orr relates it to 'anxiety about regulating female discourse' (plausibly linked to the emergence of women writers in England), as well as to the critique of pornography and the 'origins of the scopic

---

[3] Cf. Roger Chartier in vol. iii of *Histoire de la vie privée, De la Renaissance aux Lumières*, ed. Chartier, tr. Arthur Goldhammer as *A History of Private Life*, iii: *Passions of the Renaissance* (1989), 143–4; Keith Thomas, 'Behind Closed Doors', *New York Review of Books*, 9 Nov. 1989, 18; Joan DeJean, 'The Politics of Pornography: *L'École des Filles*', in Lynn Hunt (ed.), *The Invention of Pornography: Obscenity and the Origins of Modernity, 1500–1800* (New York, 1993), 110.

[4] *Unfit for Modest Ears: A Study of Pornographic, Obscene and Bawdy Works Written or Published in England in the Second Half of the Seventeenth Century* (1979), 210 (cited in turn by Roy Porter and Lesley Hall in *The Facts of Life: The Creation of Sexual Knowledge in Britain, 1650–1950* (1995), 18 (and for the *Escole* passage cf. 91).

regimes of modernity'.[5] Francis Barker, determined to impose a nineteenth-century model of the repressed 'bourgeois', finds the utmost significance in 'the guilty sexuality which the passage takes such pains not to speak'.[6] Far from falling silent, however, we have seen that Pepys explicitly records in racy Franco-Spanglish that *L'Escole des filles* 'caused my prick to stand all the while, and to ejaculate once' (*una vez to decharger*).[7]

Looking more closely, we can see that the phrasing and even the orthography of this notorious diary entry play a complex, teasing game of secrecy and display. Like the Parmesan cheese Pepys buried during the Great Fire, the sexual allusions are concealed in order to be found and relished again. In the passage describing his arousal the faltering syntax encloses his sex in a double binder, a parenthetical 'but' clause nesting inside another 'but' clause. It is encoded, first by the shorthand, then by the lingua franca of European vocabulary, and then by the schoolboyish habit of adding nonsense-syllables to certain words; thus he turns *belly* into 'benleri', *did* into the prosthetic 'dild', and *pleasure* into 'plelesonure', putting the lesson back into it. When Pepys's pen came to record his adventures with *L'Escole* it wrote, not the bold 'prick', but the bashful 'primick'.[8] Yet this encryption never inhibits the flow of Pepys's sexual discourse, and the codes themselves prove quite legible, the French and Spanish words easily accessible. As Fig. 1 shows clearly, the key words 'L'escholle des Filles' and 'decharger' are written in longhand, and blaze forth from the page of shorthand. Rather than concealing, Pepys's polyglottism adds colour and worldly sophistication, injecting a self-conscious and performative tone into the private space of the diary. Here as elsewhere, his linguistic practices bring Court culture and European geography into the microcosm of the body.[9] Pepys would be surprised to learn that he had 'banished' sex to a 'secluded domain, . . . a silent bedroom'.[10] Sex talks. But for Pepys and others it talks in an excited babble of immigrant tongues: in his libertine novel *Les Bijoux indiscrets* Diderot slips into English to describe the sexual exploits of a coarse but vigorous sea captain; conversely, the Clerk of the Royal Navy uses Mediterranean languages to describe the warmer regions of his body. He does not 'deny' his sex, as Barker insists, but dresses it up, with a baguette under its arm and a little sombrero on its head.

Schooling Sex follows this hint in Pepys by exploring the intersection of formative texts and articulate readers in Latin, Italian, French, and English. Chapter 1 starts by

---

[5] 'The Feminine in Restoration Erotica', in Clare Brant and Diane Purkiss (eds.), *Women, Texts and Histories, 1575–1760* (1992), 199.

[6] *The Tremulous Private Body: Essays in Subjection* (1984), 62; Barker uses not the diary itself but a doubly censored text, a selection made for schoolchildren from the prudish Victorian edition (which I recall as an English O-Level text in 1960, my first encounter with this passage). Bowdlerized versions still circulate, e.g. in the sound recording read by Kenneth Branagh and in the French translation by Renée Villoteau, *Journal* (Paris, 1987), 389.

[7] Words that have now been quoted in the most venerable journals, e.g. *TLS* 13 Jan. 1995, 15 (letter from Michael Paffard).

[8] I am grateful to Dr Richard Luckett, Pepys Librarian, Magdalene College, Cambridge, for advice on transcription; for a specimen of garbling, see note to 31 May 1667.

[9] Cf. p. 13 below (Italian proverb about Charles II's *cazzo*) and my 'Pepys and the Private Parts of Monarchy', in Gerald MacLean (ed.), *Culture and Society in the Stuart Restoration: Literature, Drama, History* (Cambridge, 1995), 98.

[10] Barker, *Tremulous Private Body*, 2.

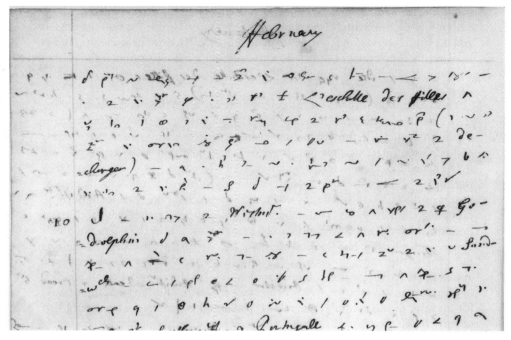

1. Samuel Pepys's diary for 9 February 1668

pondering Montaigne's concept of sexual knowledge as a 'discipline born in the blood' as well as learned from books, and subsequent readings will sample all the relevant 'disciplines'—a term I take to mean an organized body of knowledge as well as a punitive technique. The discourse of sexuality comprises theology and canon law, the philosophy of mind and body, medical teachings on generation and its discontents, as well as those pedagogic texts that raise the question of gender, like Jan Amos Comenius' *Magna Didactica* or the many debates over *l'éducation des filles*. The centre of each chapter, however, will remain those books like *L'Escole des filles* for which 'pornography' would be an understandable anachronism. Except when talking literally of *pornographia*—the graphic representation of prostitutes studied in my previous book *Libertines and Radicals*—I would rather identify these sixteenth- and seventeenth-century texts as 'explicit' or 'hard-core'. In early modern terms these books are categorizable as 'mighty lewd', or in Montaigne's phrase 'impertinently genital in their approaches'—a term that applies both to the adventures of his youth and to the arousing texts he studies in old age, which remain firm and 'masculine' when he himself has grown soft.[11] This crude anatomical 'impertinence' places them beyond the pale and guarantees their circulation in a clandestine economy: Pepys might have called *L'Escole des filles* an 'idle, roguish book' (an indulgent

<hr />

[11] *Essais*, III. v, cited in Patricia Parker, 'Virile Style', in Louise Fradenburg and Carla Freccero with Kathy Lavezzo (eds.), *Premodern Sexualities* (1996), 211.

half-condemnation at most), but he still consigned it to the flames; in France both author and text are sentenced to burning for offences 'against the honour of God and the Church, and quite contrary to good morals and Christian discipline', and in England the bookseller is indicted for publishing a 'nequissimum scandalosum vitiosum et illicitum librum', horribly corrupting the young male subjects of Charles II.[12]

This 'corruption' involves more than the mere intention to arouse, which in some circles constitutes the definition of pornography. Quite apart from the naive intentionalism of such a definition, arousal is an ephemeral phenomenon that scarcely endures a second, critical reading. Pepys only managed 'una vez to decharger', and then pitched *L'Escole* into the fire; all the texts analysed below survive because they were detained for further questioning, either in gentlemen's libraries or in prosecutors' records. Textual arousal may lead to nefarious acts, as the enemies of pornography insist, but in Pepys's case the crime was book-burning rather than rape. In this period arousal did not constitute scandal *per se* or contravene the essence of literature as understood in late Renaissance theory: as we shall see in Chapter 2, on Ferrante Pallavicino's 1642 *Retorica delle puttane* (or 'Whores' Rhetoric'), all the liberal arts aimed to stir the passions of the beholder, and—as Horace insisted—the author or narrator must seem to experience the passion herself. The danger of these books for the seventeenth-century reader like Pepys, and their interest in the twenty-first century, lies in their capacity to confuse boundaries, to introduce foreign bodies, to associate polymorphous language and sexual practice, and to organize this Babel under a libertine-hedonist philosophy 'contrary to good morals and Christian discipline'—in short, to form an erotic-didactic counter-discipline.

My second example of 'impertinently genital' reading takes place early in the following century. The 11-year-old Giacomo Casanova sits at the dinner table, eager to prove himself in the company of five auspicious adults: his patron, his tutor, his mother, an English man of letters, and the aristocratic rake-poet Giorgio Baffo, a 'sublime genius . . . in the most lubricious of genres'.[13] The Englishman initiates a conversation that resembles Baffo's sonnets in being at once decorous in form and priapic in content. To test the boy's educational progress, he asks him to expound a famous couplet by the sixteenth-century poet Johannes Secundus, on the distribution of power in sex and language:

> Discite grammatici cur mascula nomina cunnus
> Et cur femineum mentula nomen habet.[14]

Tell me, grammarians, why [in Latin] *cunt* is a masculine noun and *prick* is a feminine noun.

He thus flaunts the names of the genitals in the face of a cleric, a minor, and a widowed matron, relying on her presumed ignorance of Latin to create an intimate

---

[12] Ch. 3 n. 13 below; *The School of Venus*, Middx. prosecution (see Abbreviations above).

[13] Jacques Casanova de Seingalt, *Histoire de ma vie*, Édition intégrale, i (Wiesbaden, 1960), 9.

[14] For the whole epigram, see Secundus' *Opera*, ed. Petrus Scriverus (Leiden, 1619), 141; in the original, the *cunnus* achieves masculine status because it can perform 'indefatigably' and 'endlessly'.

circle of masculine initiates, fellow-sharers in a tradition of literate eroticism and 'lascivious erudition' stretching back to the Renaissance. As in the sexual joking analysed by Freud, the woman is both evoked and excluded—though Baffo did ease the situation by whispering the true meaning into the mother's ear. Paradoxically, however, this triumph of masculine wit raises questions about precisely what it seeks to confirm: male supremacy and the congruence of language and sexuality. Casanova's improvised answer—which inspired the English visitor to shower him with warm embraces and a pocket-watch—declares (in metrical Latin) that *cunnus* is masculine because the masculine gender must always be assigned to the dominant party: 'the slave must always bear the master's name' (22–3).

How did Casanova acquire this literary-erotic expertise, this knowledge that allowed him to promote his own sex even while declaring the absolute dominion of the female? The tutor assumes, naively, that his pupil has displayed a purely philological skill, all the more brilliant because innocent of sexual knowledge. But Casanova did in fact know the subject matter, at least 'in theory, . . . having already read Meursius, in secret, precisely because he had forbidden it me'. Didactic discipline generates its own opposite. Casanova's tutor obediently follows the dictate of the Council of Trent, which allowed adults to read 'elegant' classical erotica but insisted that 'they must not be read by boys for any reason'; the teacher identifies his rival, the 'book that teaches lascivious matters', in the very act of prohibiting it.[15] The precocious 'boy'—on the threshhold of adolescence and already the object of the Englishman's leading questions—has read a book that confers a complete theoretical knowledge of sex, a book which would be so familiar to the presumed reader that a single word can explain the whole matter: 'Meursius'.

Casanova was quite typical in assuming that the forbidden work of 'Meursius' (also ascribed to 'Aloisia Sigea') would give him a 'theoretical' grasp of the entire sexual realm. (Part II will trace the complex reception-history of this high-libertine text, its evocation as touchstone of elegance and *ne plus ultra* of immorality.) Even more than *L'Escole des filles*, this encyclopedic work achieved a classic status which allowed it to be cited in Enlightenment narratives of subject-formation. In Diderot's *Bijoux indiscrets*, for example, the courtier Sélim describes how he passed through various educational stages meant to be typical of an aristocratic youth, each stage associated with a particular kind of text. His first erotic experience, like Gargantua's in Rabelais or the future Louis XIII's at the French court, is created by the nursemaids who fondle and 'take liberties' with him; he then enters the male world by studying the classics of Greek and Roman erotica with his tutors; next he learns various masturbatory 'gentillesses de collège' from his father's pages; and finally 'reading *Aloysia*, which the pages lent me, gave me every possible inclination to perfect myself. I was then fourteen.'[16]

---

[15] H. J. Schoeder (ed.), *Canons and Decrees of the Council of Trent* (1941), 548; by Casanova's time Chorier's work hid under the textbook title *Joanni Meursii Elegantiae Latini Sermone*, which echoes the Council's permission to read 'lascivious and obscene' classics *propter sermonis elegantiam*.

[16] *Œuvres*, ed. André Billy, Bibliothèque de la Pléiade (Paris, 1951), 177 (ch. 44); for Diderot's proposal of a bust in honour of 'Meursius', see my Epilogue.

Casanova and Sélim were formed by the same book, Nicolas Chorier's *Satyra Sotadica* (subtitled 'On the Arcana of Love and Venus'), supposedly written by a woman intellectual of the sixteenth century, Aloisia or Luisa Sigea of Toledo, and then allegedly translated from Spanish to Latin by the Dutch scholar Johannes Meursius. 'Aloysia' and 'Meursius' both serve to identify this double-authored work, female in content and Latin in form. In Casanova and in Diderot, homoeroticism and the sharing of the text comprise equivalent and successive stages in masculine initiation: at the dinner table the Englishman and the schoolboy embrace over 'Meursius'; in the 'college' below stairs, the male servants and their young master enjoy each other with 'Aloisia', not now in élite Latin but in the translation *L'Académie des dames*—an ironic title since it is boys and not 'ladies' who use it as their school. Unlike Pepys, who reads in solitude 'to inform himself in the villainy of the world' and who ends by ejaculating and burning the book, these Italian and French readers enjoy their textually provoked eroticism collectively and then proceed to model their lives on the expanded sexual possibilities represented in the pages of 'Aloisia'. The book of sex thus provides both the stimulus and the means 'de se perfectionner', to complete the self-fashioning of the courtly seducer, the *honnête homme*, the heroic libertine.

What *would* the adventurous young man have found in this classic treatise on the 'Secrets of Love and Venus'? Paradoxically, the book that mothers must not see concerns female rather than male sexual awakening, the 'free' discourse of women passing those secrets among themselves and thereby forming the sexuality of the younger generation. As we shall see in Chapters 3 and 4, Chorier's *Aloisia Sigea* builds upon but transcends the form of *L'Escole des filles*, for which critics have coined the unwieldy but accurate term 'pseudofeminocentric'. A series of dialogues between Octavia and her older cousin Tullia begins with the simplest description of the genitals and proceeds, in good didactic fashion, through all the complications of lesbian, marital, and extramarital sex; Octavia may be tongue-tied and ignorant at the beginning, and the earlier dialogues may take place wholly within the marriage-bed, but by the end she finds herself describing incredibly complex perversions in a tone of sophisticated philosophical appreciation. Obviously these enlightened and autonomous 'women' have been fabricated by a male author for a male readership; as in Casanova's dinner conversation, text and reader form a mutual masturbatory circle, playing with their models of the *cunnus* in front of a mother who must stay out of the picture. But the puppets disobey. Narrative authority is gendered female, libertine mothers take command, men appear more as objects than subjects, and the phallus, at first a 'sceptre', 'sword', or 'battering ram', becomes sometimes a 'female slave', sometimes a 'queen', 'heroine', or 'empress'—extending the grammatical conundrum set up by Secundus. Indeed, the Latin text has already rehearsed the Secundus connection and schooled Casanova in his impromptu answer: the lines quoted by the Englishman, articulating the paradox of 'masculine' cunt and 'feminine' prick, are printed as a colophon in all editions of Chorier's work. One translation of *L'Escole des filles* even blazoned them on the title page—an epigraph not only suggesting the élite appeal of Latinity but defining the quintessence of what the reader might learn in *The School for Girls* or *The Ladies' Academy*.[17]

In Chorier's simulation of the female philosophical libertine—taken as the genuine work of Aloisia Sigea by some seventeenth-century readers—true pleasure increasingly derives, not from heroic priapism, but from 'erudita libido' or educated desire, encyclopedic knowledge, conceptual refinement, the expert control and deployment of images. The seventeenth-century French author has thus transformed the Italian discourse of prostitution, launched in Aretino's 1534 *Ragionamenti* and refined in Pallavicino's *Retorica delle puttane* (Chapter 2 below). The whore-trickster becomes the 'woman of pleasure', consciously raising her sexuality to the status of art, and the salty street-dialogue of Aretino becomes the Latin of high-libertine 'theory'. *L'Escole des filles* had already softened and tamed the discourse of illicit sexuality by what I call the 'domestic turn', confining it to the vernacular, heterosexual exploits of the *bonne bourgeoise*; Chorier reinvests this libertine domesticity with the perverse sophistication of Secundus and his ancient Roman masters.

For Casanova, Secundus and Chorier together form a mutually defining couple, whose interaction constitutes both the 'theory' and the history of sexuality. Libertine literary history could almost be described as a set of variations on Secundus' epigram, and the three-way encounter of these authors certainly defines the limits of my period. I trace the paradoxical interchanges of language, education, and sexuality from the humanist age of Secundus to the Cartesian epoch of Chorier, and from there to the dawn of the eighteenth century. The age of Casanova and Diderot will be revisited only briefly in my Epilogue, but this book will follow the reading of Chorier with detailed case studies of his reception and invocation in the generation following, in erotica such as *Venus in the Cloister* (1683) and in libertine-inclined authors such as John Oldham and John Wilmot, Earl of Rochester (Chs. 6–8 below).

Secundus' question (and Casanova's answer) pose a 'theoretical' challenge even today, if we take *both* gender and language seriously. According to 'Natural Philosophy' masculinity derived from essential and innate features of dominance. According to grammatical laws the gender of the word determined the nature of the thing and its place in the hierarchy. (As we shall see in Chapter 1, every schoolboy learned that 'the masculine gender is more worthy than the feminine'.) How then can biology and grammar diverge, assigning the feminine gender to the most masculine part, the Empress Mentula? Secundus' witty epigram locates one crucial place where they fail to correspond, and sends them into a spin by defining the phallus as the quintessentially female attribute. In the French adaptation of Chorier Secundus' paradox receives a fresh twist, reminding us that education in language constituted an important gateway to élite masculinity. The author of *L'Academie des dames* (1680) incorporated Secundus' line into his own epigram, proposing that any sexual 'grammarian' unable to answer the opening question—precisely

[17] Ch. 3 n. 33 below.

the question that the Englishman poses to the pre-adolescent Casanova—should be castrated on the spot, refused physical entry to the category of manhood.

My subject, then, is the educational fantasy in sexual writing, or what I call the erotic-didactic nexus, as it evolves towards the idea of philosophical libertinism. In some circles *Éros philosophe*[18] is considered a purely eighteenth-century phenomenon, but titles like *La Philosophie des dames* (the second and more outrageous part of *L'Escole des filles*) show that it belongs very much to this period. My analysis of the 'schooling' element in seventeenth-century hard-core discourse, and the formative claims made by its real and imaginary readers, defines a crucial moment in the literary history of gender and the intellectual history of the body. The title of *L'Escole/La Philosophie* in translation, *The School of Venus or The Ladies Delight Reduced into Rules of Practice* (c.1676), suggests both the effect sought by libertine discourse and the methodology appropriate to study it: the libertine text must be understood as an ideological 'school' and a performative script, encouraging the translation of 'theory' into 'practice', while at the same time 'reducing' the fiction of female subjectivity to a set of male-ordered 'rules' for procuring 'the ladies delight'—in effect defining the entire purpose of ladies *as* delight. As early as 1686, the militant feminist Sarah Fyge accused men of wishing to have all women brought up 'in Venus' School', a phrase that serves both as a title for the erotic-didactic text and as a euphemism for the brothel.[19]

Putting women in their places, for 'pornographers' and their feminist critics alike, seems to have been the principal task assigned to these 'mighty lewd books'. Many of the texts studied below must strike the reader as grossly and aggressively misogynist, 'offensive' in every sense; as we shall see in Chapter 5, Horner in Wycherley's *Country-Wife* (1675) only has to mention *L'Escole des filles* for observers to conclude that 'he hates Women perfectly'. In the following analysis, however, I devote less attention to the hostility of these works and more to the disobedience of their female characters, to the cracks and slippages revealed in the gendering process, and to the countervailing work of women authors. As Secundus' paradox suggests, linguistic dominance confers 'masculine' authority on the hyper-feminine narrator and preceptor. Conversely, the male author feminizes himself by impersonating and expropriating the discourse of sexuality, what Montaigne calls the 'flux de caquet' or stream of midwives' babble—applying the term to his own writing.[20] As Oldham pungently remarks, emulating Aloisia Sigea puts him in the position of a 'Secretary' to the vulva (Ch. 6 below), acknowledging her power to dictate the 'Arcana of Venus',

---

[18] The title of an essay collection by François Moureau and Alain-Marc Rieu, on *discours libertins des Lumières* (Paris, 1984), in which only the article by Rosy Pinhas-Delpuech (11–20) deals with the 17th century; the same chronological assumption is shared by Catherine Cusset (ed.), *Libertinage and Modernity*, special issue, *Yale French Studies*, 94 (1998).

[19] *The Female Advocate, or An Answer to a Late Satyr against the Pride, Lust and Inconstancy of Woman* (1686), 7; cf. *The London-Bawd* ('4th edn.', 1711), 113 ('The House which I now keep . . . goes under several Denominations: Some call it *The School of Venus*') and D. A. Coward, 'Eighteenth-Century Attitudes to Prostitution', *Studies on Voltaire and the Eighteenth Century*, 189 (1980), 386 n. 38 ('Académie de Venus').

[20] Ch. 1 n. 70 below.

to shape the sexual 'discipline'. The articulate pornographic heroine unravels ancient binary classifications like active/passive, strong/weak, culture/nature, and even female/male; as Aretino proposed and *The Whores Rhetorick* repeated, 'A Whore is a Whore, but a Whore is not a Woman'.[21]

In a further complication, Wycherley's Horner suggests that mastery of the canon might be a hollow victory at best, since his triumphant flaunting of the illicit book, with its supposedly privileged view of the secret desires of externally virtuous women, is designed to convince bystanders that he is a eunuch (Ch. 5, sect. 2 below). In this alternative view, representation compensates for deficiency and verbal misogyny expresses only an inability to please women. Indeed, the libertine remains profoundly uncertain whether language is a mediating force or an obstacle between physical desire and rational self-consciousness, an accessory to seduction or a substitute for it. As Wycherley's contemporary the Earl of Mulgrave lamented, lovers 'fall into discourse' when 'action' fails.[22] Molière's Dom Juan likewise declares that 'Tous les discours n'avancent point les choses; il faut faire et non pas dire' (discourses don't carry things forward; we must *do*, and not *say*). Nevertheless, his classic account of the pleasure he takes in methodical seduction, 'day by day' and 'step by step', ends with an admission that language was the whole point: his passion collapses after conquest because 'there is nothing more to say'.[23]

Though women's writings form only a small proportion of the total discourse on sexuality, and the immodesty of the subject restricts them still further, the presence and relevance of female authorship was felt strongly in the 'pornosphere'. With the obvious exception of the homoerotic *Alcibiade fanciullo a scola* (Ch. 2, sect. 2), all the core erotic texts discussed below purport to capture the true voice of women. Diderot's fantasy of the *bijou indiscret*, the talking vulva that cannot lie, suggests that in sexual matters the female voice was considered immediately truthful, exempt from the problems of discourse. Chorier even invents an elaborate fiction to ascribe the maternity of his *Satyra Sotadica* to the historical figure Aloisia Sigea (1522–60), in the spirit of other learned forgers who claim to have discovered the intimately sexual letters of Cleopatra herself; to create a 'learned lady' erudite in nothing but sex he must simulate the real-life achievement of women humanist intellectuals. As we shall see repeatedly, canon-forming citations and allusions to these core texts likewise link them to known female authors: *Erotopolis* constructs a courtesans' reading-list that includes *The School of Venus* and the novels of Madeleine de Scudéry, the same association that led Pepys to buy *L'Escole des filles* for his wife to translate;[24] the facetious 1684 *Parliament of Women* refers to 'the Queen of *Navars* Novels' and Margaret Cavendish's *World's Olio* as it reviews books for the new national curriculum—though in the end it entrusts the entire task of subject-

---

[21] Ch. 2 n. 38 below.   [22] Ch. 6 n. 73 below.

[23] *Dom Juan*, II. iv, I. ii ('forcer pied à pied toutes les petites résistances qu'elle nous oppose . . . lorsqu'on en est maître une fois, il n'y a plus rien à dire'); for the problem of language, see my 'Lovelace and the Paradoxes of Libertinism', in Margaret Anne Doody and Peter Sabor (eds.), *Samuel Richardson: Tercentenary Essays* (Cambridge, 1989), 70–88, esp. 74.

[24] (1684), 59–60, more fully cited in Ch. 5, sect. 1 below.

formation to three texts only, decreeing 'that *Aloysia Sigea*, *L'Eschole de fils*, and *Peter Aretines* discourses be translated, and fairly Printed for the Particular good of the Female Common-weal' (102, 80, 136–7). *Schooling Sex* reads these male-oriented and male-consumed female impersonations against the grain, with the help of women's own *prise de parole*.

It is not my intention to present an essentialist, unified voice of 'female' authenticity, but rather to sample multifarious discourses. Against the fabricated sex-and-theory queens of libertine fiction, ancestors of Fanny Hill and Thérèse Philosophe, I will set Marguerite, Queen of Navarre, and Margaret Cavendish, Duchess of Newcastle (both cited in the faux-feminist *Parliament of Women*), Marie de Gournay, Lucy Hutchinson, Louise Bourgeois, Marie de Sévigné, Aphra Behn, Jane Barker, and others. Reversing Pepys's association with Scudéry, I link *L'Escole des filles* and its ilk to contemporary educators like Anna Maria van Schurman and Françoise de Maintenon, and to the *femmes fortes* explored in Ian Maclean's *Woman Triumphant* and Joan DeJean's *Tender Geographies*. As well as austere sixteenth-century humanists like Sigea, I bring in courtesan-authors like Veronica Franco and Tullia d'Aragona—whose version of philosophical Eros I discuss at length in Chapter 1—and feminists like Moderata Fonte, who define love as the 'female' subject par excellence and extend sympathy to the transgressive woman. Many other women are cited from manuscripts or legal records, or evoked as sources of cultural influence like the *salonnières* Catherine de Rambouillet and Julie de Montausier, Wycherley's preceptors during his teenage years.

Rather than leaving the boys alone together, then, I crowd them with citations from the women they impersonate, some necessarily brief, some analysed at length. I show Queen Christina of Sweden influencing Descartes's turn to the philosophy of passion, which in turn was expropriated for the 'Cartesian erotics' of *L'Escole des filles* and the *Satyra Sotadica*. From Sarah Fyge I derive the idea of coercive enrolment in 'Venus' School', and hence the idea of reading texts as institutions. From Margaret Cavendish, and especially from her 1662 comedy *The Female Academy* (Ch. 1 below), I learn to interpret the sexualization of women's philosophy and women's education as a reactionary, defensive move. More broadly, I trace the cultural influence of women's creativity even in the details of pornography: scandals surrounding the composer Barbara Strozzi bring out the erotic fascination of castrati (Ch. 2, sect. 1); the 'knowing hand' of the painter Artemisia Gentileschi appears in the masturbatory fantasies of *La Philosophie des dames* (Fig. 7, Ch. 3).

Unlike earlier studies of libertinism and philosophy—Dale Underwood on Hobbes and Lucretius in the English Restoration, Warren Chernaik on sexual freedom in Behn and Rochester—*Schooling Sex* takes its cue from titles like 'The Ladies' Philosophy' to ask, what is at stake in this impersonation of the *femme savante libertine*? What does the erotic canon defend against? Is 'The Ladies' Academy' really a School of Men? To place men in the pupil's role provoked a certain disquiet: education should remain a high-cultural preserve, sexuality a baser 'natural' domain where men instinctively play the active part without needing instruction, where anatomy replaces knowledge as the agent of destiny. To reveal the libertine as

'Learned' (in both senses), to show sex 'taught' by books rather than conveyed in the blood, to 'read' men as if they were themselves texts, makes all too visible the constructedness of masculinity. Behn makes this explicit in her critique of libertine inconstancy: if man's desires 'like lightning flash and are no more', this comes not so much from innate character as from 'a fatal lesson *he has learn'd*, | After fruition ne're to be concern'd'.[25] This 'discipline' is born, not 'in the veins'—as Montaigne put it—but in the pages of 'mighty lewd books', of the kind that informed Pepys and Casanova.

Making sex speak has always seemed problematic. The Judaeo-Christian legacy of shame imposed an embarrassed silence, and yet for the Christian the sexual has always been irreducibly cognitive bound up from the start with knowledge however carnal. As St Augustine put it, the sexual drive 'rubescit videri' ('blushes to be seen'), but still 'appetit sciri' ('hungers to be known').[26] Augustine found an epistemic component in sexuality itself, and other Church Fathers gave lust a kind of creative, authorial power, a capacity to 'assume all forms' like Proteus and 'fashion all things' like an artist; in our period, devotional writers feel the need to warn off corrupt readers 'whose lust is all their book'.[27] The texts that make up what I call the hard-core curriculum act out this 'appetite-to-be-known' in their didactic and initiatory scenarios, starting with inchoate but intense longings and ending with 'erudite' mastery of all the tricks in the book. Libertine education evolves through all the stages of the conventional school, from practice to theory, from basic grammar to intermediate rhetoric and then to advanced 'philosophy', taught in a 'college' or 'University of Love'. This progression or graduation is clearly spelled out in titles like *The Practical Part of Love* and *The Female Academy* (Ch. 1 below), *La retorica delle puttane* (Ch. 2), *La Philosophie des dames* (Ch. 3), *The School of Love* and *L'Academie des dames* (Ch. 7).

If it is not to seem merely facetious, libertine 'philosophy' must establish some real intellectual credentials while at the same time abandoning the conceptual hierarchy that separates genital sexuality from the higher faculties of language and cognition. Plato had pushed this separation to an almost comic extreme: the unsatisfied womb may become a raging animal and the penis, worse still, is by its very nature a brute beast 'deaf to reason'.[28] (Compare Pepys's diagnosis of Charles II, '*Cazzo dritto non vuolt consiglio*', the stiff prick wants no counsel.[29]) Nevertheless, some Renaissance philosophers like Tullia d'Aragona attempt to reconcile physical desire with Platonic love-doctrine (Ch. 1, sect. 1 below). Plato powerfully embodied the idea of Eros as Gnosis, a fit subject for the Academy, an esoteric doctrine leading by 'steps'

[25] Ch. 8 n. 47 below; cf. my discussion of Behn in 'The Culture of Priapism', *Review*, 10 (1988), 30–1.

[26] Cf. my *One Flesh: Paradisal Marriage and Sexual Relations in the Age of Milton* (Oxford, 1987, 1993), 47.

[27] Clement of Alexandria, *Paedagogus*, ii. i, *Opera Graece et Latine*, ed. John Potter (Oxford, 1715), i. 250–1; George Herbert, 'The Church Porch', line 12.

[28] *Timaeus*, 91b–c, cited by Montaigne (just before the 'discipline' passage) and explicated by Constance Jordan in 'Sexuality and Volition in "Sur des vers de Virgile"', *Montaigne Studies*, 8 (1996), 68–9.

[29] 15 May 1663.

to a higher initiation and divulged by a female speaker (the prophetess Diotima in the *Symposium*). Though often interpreted as merely 'anti-Platonic', seventeenth-century libertinism retains much of the Platonic hierarchy when it exalts the most intense sexual experience, when Antonio Rocco's *Alcibiade fanciullo a scola* (*c*.1630) equates the superiority of homosexual love with the 'diletto dalla conoscenza' that distinguishes us from animals (Ch. 2, sect. 2), when *L'Escole des filles* uses the same terms for heterosexual pleasure outside the constraints of marriage (Ch. 3), or when Chorier makes conceptual figuration and Protean 'metamorphosis' the primary source of desire in a text ostensibly devoted to physical passion (Ch. 4). Even Milton, a fierce defender of virtuous Eros against the libertine opposition, assigns physical consummation a cognitive and heuristic role. Not only does he give Adam and Eve a full sexual life in Eden—the subject of my earlier book *One Flesh*—but he declares that '*by*' this wedded love all other human relationships 'first *were known*' (*Paradise Lost*, IV. 751–7, my emphasis).

Less idealistic philosophies of sex could be derived from Lucretius and Lucian, Descartes and Hobbes. Lucretius' *De Rerum Natura* provided a profoundly contradictory model, quite apart from the fact that his teachings ran counter to Christian orthodoxy; the great poetic authority on Epicurean atomism sounded oddly ambivalent about pleasure, which (in its refined form) constituted Epicurus' *summum bonum*. Book I celebrates 'sweet Venus' as a cosmic, social, and aesthetic force, invoking her simultaneously as the procreative spirit that arouses all animals in the spring, as the calming influence over Mars that re-establishes prosperity and harmony in civil-war Rome, and as the seductive 'charm' or *lepor* that he implores for his own poem. In book IV, however, he paints a picture of 'our Venus' so vivid and disturbing that Lucy Hutchinson, the first English translator of the full *De Rerum Natura*, declared it fitter work for a midwife.[30] Human sexuality is represented either as joyless procreation or as futile frenzy.

Like Plato (and Descartes later), Lucretius describes sexual intercourse as the attempt to unify two bodies—but his explanation is wholly material and atomistic. Perception and desire both spring from the physical image, the hollow, gauzy simulacrum that peels off from the object, enters through the eye, and combines with the brain of the perceiver. Lovers long to incorporate each other like food—hence all the frantic rubbing and biting—but they are doomed to perpetual frustration: 'all is in vain, for they can rub nothing off, nor penetrate, nor pass with their whole body into another.'[31] As later philosophers infer, 'sexual relationships' are impossible and 'sexual techniques'—the postures and attitudes taught in all the books studied below—are nothing but 'ornaments, dissimulations, inadequate compensations for

---

[30] *Lucy Hutchinson's Translation of Lucretius: De Rerum Natura*, ed. Hugh de Quehen (Ann Arbor, 1996), 139; Hutchinson omits precisely the passages that Dryden selected for his own pleasure, adding extra sexual details (cf. n. 31 below).

[31] *De Rerum Natura*, IV. 1110–11 ('nequiquam, quoniam nihil inde abradere possunt | nec penetrare et abire in corpus corpore toto'); Dryden translates as 'bodies cannot pierce, nor be in bodies lost' and adds 'all the instruments of love' to the hands and teeth in the feeding frenzy, as if the penis were also a devouring organ (iii. 58–9).

this blockage'.[32] Lucretius bequeathed both an art of erotic description and a scientific enquiry into its material processes, which in turn influenced Virgil's *Georgics*—an even more prestigious poem that encapsulates in quotable form the sexual origin of consciousness ('mentem Venus ipsa dedit', 'Venus herself gave the mind') and the uniformity of the procreative urge in all creatures ('Amor omnibus idem', 'love is the same in all'). We shall find these concepts and these phrases in learned speculations on sex from Montaigne (Ch. 1 below) to Rocco (Ch. 2) and Chorier (Ch. 4).

Lucian's satirical perspective on Socratic love helped to offset the Renaissance emphasis on Platonic purity. (Lucian's *Dialogues of the Hetairai* also influenced Aretino and subsequent adaptors of the woman-to-woman dialogue, after they were translated as *Piacevoli ragionamenti* in 1527.) As we shall see, both Rocco and Chorier propose the 'prurient Socrates' as a role-model for hedonistic philosophy, and both give a prominent place to the *Erōtes* then thought to be by Lucian, which calmly compares the pleasure-claims of heterosexuality and paedophilia while inclining towards the latter. When Rocco (in the persona of Alcibiades' love-struck tutor) praises those 'few' whom Nature has made 'speculativi' and 'of a philosophical spirit', who entirely 'flee' all connection with women (*Alcibiade*, 73), he summarizes the argument most fully laid out in pseudo-Lucian: marriage is a biological necessity, associated with the earliest and crudest stages of civilization, whereas 'love for males is a noble duty enjoined by a philosophic spirit. Anything cultivated for aesthetic reasons in the midst of abundance is accompanied with greater honour than things which require for their existence immediate need, and beauty is in every way superior to necessity' (*tou anagkaion to kalon kreitton*).[33]

This equation of 'philosophic' desire with élite homosexuality persisted. Tullia d'Aragona, speaking from her position in the genteel demimonde of Florence, uses *Socratici* as a familiar term for pederasts, and 200 years later Voltaire uses *amour nommé socratique* the same way, wondering why 'an infamous assault against nature should nevertheless be so natural'.[34] Montesquieu describes men of previously orthodox 'taste' succumbing to *amour philosophique* when they fall in love with beautiful *castrati* actors—his main example being an Englishman on the Grand Tour,[35] like the one who plied the boy Casanova with gender-confusing quotations from Secundus. The transsexual eunuch, the product of theatrical and surgical art, evokes a language of 'philosophy' and 'taste' that overrides the normative disposition.

Among modern philosophers, Descartes is the one cited most frequently in the following pages, mainly because his uncompromisingly physical explanations of

---

[32] Jean-Claude Milner, *Le Triple du plaisir* (Paris, 1997), 36, a ref. I owe to Ann Banfield, who notes that Jacques Lacan, in *Le Séminaire*, xx: *Encore, 1972–1973* (Paris, 1975), repeatedly asserts that 'il n'y a pas de rapport sexuel', apparently alluding to the impossibility of devouring the body of the Other (26).

[33] Loeb Classical Library *Lucian*, VII, tr. M. D. Macleod (1967), ch. 33 and cf. chs. 39 ff., 51.

[34] *Dictionnaire philosophique*, ed. Béatrice Didier ([Paris], 1994), 79; for d'Aragona and 'Socratic' pederasty see Ch. 1, sect. 1 below.

[35] Travel notes for 1729, *Œuvres complètes*, ed. Roger Caillois, Bibliothèque de la Pléiade (Paris, 1985), i. 679.

amorous passion gave such rich opportunities to libertine writers who might reject his severe dualism. Erudite pornographers like Chorier naturally rejoiced in Descartes's theory of the body driven by surges of hot fluid (the animal spirits) and commanded by a tiny bud of flesh, the pineal gland. Cartesian ideas as well as body-images flourish throughout this literature. In *L'Escole des filles* as well as in *Dom Juan*, 'method' becomes a key term in the language of sexual technique, the 'step-by-step' advance of carnal knowledge 'by an orderly effort', according to 'a set of certain and easy rules'.[36] In Pallavicino's *Retorica delle puttane* as well as in Descartes's letters to Queen Christina and *Les Passions de l'âme*—the late treatise influenced by her questioning—the most extreme and intense forms of love are given a 'heroic' or sublime status, increased rather than diminished by excess (Chs. 1–2). Descartes recognizes that Nature 'represents' erotic *jouissance* as 'the greatest of all the goods that humanity can possess',[37] and his contemporaries express the same concept more directly, finding the supreme good in 'fucking': *L'Academie des dames* declares that 'le souverain bien | Ne consiste qu'à foutre bien' (Fig. 16 below); *The Whores Rhetorick* imagines women who 'place their chief happiness, their *summum bonum* (as I have heard a Philosopher speak), in gratifying their carnal and obscene desires' (213). Even the *cogito* is adapted to give ontological force to *coitus*, anticipating the modern phallocentrist's creed *je bande donc je suis*.[38]

The relation between Cartesian erotics and libertine sexual fiction, I suggest, cannot simply be explained as parodic mockery. Not coincidentally, they both emerged at a crucial turning point in intellectual history, when the passions and the material body came under the closest scrutiny. Philosophia could always be embodied *allegorically* as a female power, enthroned upon Nature—putting it firmly beneath her as it raises her to eminence—and served by muscular ephebes who raise the banner of 'causarum cognitio', the understanding of causes (Fig. 2). This is Raphael's icon in the Vatican Stanze, made visible in seventeenth-century France in a large-scale engraving. In the age of Descartes the allegorical body of philosophy became literal; emotions, appetites, and even the machinery of the aroused body became primary objects of systematic study, while advanced programmes of sexual enlightenment claimed to be distinguished by *connoissance de cause*, as we shall see in Rocco and *L'Escole* itself. Jacqueline Lichtenstein has even discovered a feminization of philosophy in France, under the influence of the *salons*, and illustrates it with the Raphael–Audran engraving of *La Philosophie*.[39]

As Susan James concludes from her study of emotion from Descartes to Spinoza, 'the fundamental categories of activity and passivity' become 'increasingly precarious' in this period; *L'Escole des filles*, which teasingly displays the motto *Agere et pati* on its title page, confounds those gendered categories still further by placing the

---

[36] *Regulae ad Directionem Ingenii*, rule 4, and cf. *Discours de la méthode*, esp. part 2 ('peu à peu comme par degrés').

[37] *Les Passions de l'âme*, art. 90.

[38] Cf. Georges Falconnet and Nadine Lefaucheur, *La Fabrication des mâles* (Paris, 1975), 30, Erik Rémès, *Je bande donc je suis: Roman* (Paris, 1999), and Ch. 3 n. 75 below.

[39] *La Couleur éloquente: Rhétorique et peinture à l'âge classique* (Paris, 1989), 'Ouverture', esp. 2.

2. Benoît I Audran after Raphael, *La Philosophie*

woman on top at every juncture (Ch. 3 below). Theories of the divided, multiple soul give way to a new conception of *desire* as 'the central appetitive force which enables us to stay alive and governs all our actions'.[40] This idea of an all-explaining and 'all-encompassing' master-drive—which Hobbes and Spinoza both call *conatus*, and Hobbes himself translated as 'endeavour'—is entirely congruous with the obsessive devotion to sexual desire in libertine literature, where the appetite for carnal knowledge translates into an escalating narrative drive towards ever greater complexities and transgressions. As I show in Chapter 4, *conatus* is a key word in Chorier, the most important erotic writer of the period and the chief supplier of 'theory' to

---

[40] James, *Passion and Action: The Emotions in Seventeenth-Century Philosophy* (Oxford, 1997), 291.

Casanova. The new, unified notion of desire revives Augustine's theory of Love as the impulse from which all other passions derive, and it seems no accident that the two most extreme libertine poets, Claude Le Petit in France and the Earl of Rochester in England, also versified St Augustine.[41]

Conceived in this grand theoretical way, passion and desire break down the mind–body distinction, thereby weakening all conceptual structures based on that separation. Sexual ethics, whether hedonist like Rochester's or ascetic like Spinoza's, could now be derived from internal examination of embodied passion rather than from external authorities like law or Scripture. Even Descartes, in James's interpretation, encourages the view that despite his dualism 'thinking is in general passionate', that 'the body thinks'.[42] Erotic literature rushes to provide the practice for this theory. Throughout the libertine canon, in all its languages, we will encounter phrases like 'ingenious lust' or 'erudite libido'.[43] The result is a dizzying synthesis of sex and knowledge, desire and connoisseurship, that undermines Foucault's distinction between *ars erotica* and *scientia sexualis* and anticipates modern coinages like 'pornology' or 'erotography'.[44] Even comic versions of this synthesis—when Chorier describes the penis as a little philosopher or derives *cunnus* from the same etymological root as *cognition*—convey real ideas through intellectual humour or *serio ludere*, as Chorier himself insists (Ch. 4 below). Before our period, reason was generally conceived as a 'Princess' aloof from the passions and fiercely opposed to them by definition; after our period, no less a philosopher than David Hume could declare that reason 'is and only ought to be the slave of the passions'.[45] The texts studied below—the hard-core dialogues that excited Pepys and Casanova, as well as poems like Rochester's 1676 *Satyr against Mankind* that define 'right reason' as a device to keep up the pleasures of sense—play a crucial role in this transformation.

Hobbes's account of the restless and insatiable *conatus* sounds very much like Lucretius' description of intercourse; though Hobbes substituted power for sex as the unattainable goal, many contemporaries switched them back again. It is easy to sense Dom Juan looming up behind the principle that 'Felicity is a continuall progresse of the desire, from one object to another, the attaining of the former being still but the way to the later.'[46] Many literary historians have traced similarities between Hobbes, Rochester, and the stage-libertines of English drama.[47] Instead I would emphasize Hobbes's radical nominalism, which swept away the notion of an essential difference between love and lust, making it all the more thinkable to study

[41] See my *One Flesh*, ch. 2, esp. 42 ('my weight is my love'); for Augustine in Le Petit and Rochester, see Chs. 3 n. 116 and 6 n. 57 below.

[42] *Passion and Action*, 97, 106.

[43] See Killigrew, *Comedies and Tragedies* (1664), 458, and Chorier, *Satyra*, VII. 220.

[44] Coined by Gilles Deleuze (Ch. 4 n. 90 below) and Jean-Pierre Dubost (Ch. 4 n. 53), respectively.

[45] Thomas Wright, *The Passions of the Mind in General* (1601–24), ed. William Webster Newbold (1986), 95 (a ref. I owe to Amy Greenstadt); Hume, *Treatise on Human Nature*, II. iii. 3.

[46] *Leviathan*, ch. 11.

[47] See, among many others, Thomas H. Fujimura, *The Restoration Comedy of Wit* (Princeton, 1952), Dale Underwood, *Etherege and the Seventeenth-Century Comedy of Manners* (New Haven, 1957), and Warren Chernaik, *Sexual Freedom in Restoration Literature* (Cambridge, 1995), ch. 1, 'Hobbes and the Libertines'.

genital desire and sexual practice with the philosophical attention previously given to Platonic Eros. Hobbes applies Virgil's biological maxim 'Amor omnibus idem' to the whole of human sexuality, not just to women as Montaigne had done, and he insists on its cognitive dimension:

The appetite which men call *Lust*, and the fruition that appertaineth thereunto, is a *Sensual* pleasure, but *not onely* that; there is in it also a delight of the minde. . . . The name *Lust* is used where it is condemned; otherwise it is called by the general word *Love*: for the passion is one and the same indefinite desire of different Sex, as natural as Hunger.[48]

This collapsing of a time-honoured dichotomy became so familiar that John Dunton, commenting on one of Rochester's most obscene poems, can airily refer to '*Love* or *Lust* (for Philosophers make no great distinction between 'em)'.[49]

Hobbes's 'bold but also bald'[50] mechanistic theory reminds us that seventeenth-century science—that is, 'Natural Philosophy'—revived several systems based on the material stratum, whether Baconian empiricism, Epicurean atomism, or the left-wing Aristotelian physiology taught at Padua (explicitly evoked by Rocco to defend the naturalness of homosexual desire). Bacon equated Cupid with the atom, an association followed by several Stuart writers eager to link courtly eroticism with Epicurean theories of matter and pleasure.[51] Conversely, innumerable passages in libertine prose and verse equate sexual experiment with 'science', and though the intention is sometime facetious it concurs with the arguments of serious moralists eager to stamp out such reading matter. John Evelyn, Fellow of the Royal Society, draws on 'experimental' evidence when he warns his soon-to-be-married son against 'lewd postures', 'un-natural figures', and 'speculative Lusts'—a phrase that conjures up an entire programme of cognitive-erotic transgressions, acted out in front of mirrors.[52] (We have seen that both the Venetian libertine and the American preacher associate *speculative* sex with homoerotic experiment.[53]) In a sense Pepys, another stout member of the Royal Society, puts empiricism into action when he pursues *L'Escole des filles* as 'a sober man' in search of information, and he does find the book at the shop of John Martin, official printer to that organization; at about the same time, Robert Hooke turns his microscope on spermatozoa generously provided by himself. The historian Margaret Jacob plausibly sees

[48] *Humane Nature, or The Fundamental Elements of Policie, Being a Discoverie of the Faculties, Acts, and Passions of the Soul of Man, from their Original Causes* (1650), 106–7.

[49] *Petticoat-Government, in a Letter to the Court Ladies* (1702), 18; for an attempt to reinstate the love/lust distinction on cognitive grounds, see J. Martin Stafford, 'On Distinguishing between Love and Lust', *Journal of Value Inquiry*, 11 (1977), 292–303.

[50] James, *Passion and Action*, 136.

[51] Cf. Reid Barbour, *English Epicures and Stoics: Ancient Legacies in Stuart Culture* (Amherst, Mass., 1998), ch. 1 *passim*, esp. 23, 28, 34–7.

[52] Letter to John Evelyn, junior, endorsed by recipient 'From my Father 1680', BL MS Evelyn, Correspondence, vol. 13, letter number 1526 (I am grateful to John Wing, librarian of Christ Church, Oxford, for permission to examine this manuscript when it was still in private possession). W. G. Hiscock, *John Evelyn and his Family Circle* [1955] 122–3, partially transcribes the letter and dates the wedding to February 1680.

[53] p. 15 and epigraph, above.

L'Escole, L'Academie des dames, and their eighteenth-century progeny as 'materialist pornography', where male and female characters alike become hard particles propelled by appetite, colliding and combining according to the newly discovered laws of dynamics.[54]

Schooling Sex offers a more precise point of contact between (pseudo)didactic erotica and natural philosophy—via the 'educational revolution' that inspired new colleges, teaching orders, and curricula. Seventeenth-century educational theory posited direct, sensuous knowledge as the basis for acquiring complex ideas: Comenius insisted that children should encounter the world 'ad vivam autopsian', by living sense-impression, and reformulated the entire sensible world as a set of graduated steps to the universal wisdom he called Pansophia. But how can pupils learn about the passions? How could the live interior be experienced without an autopsy in the medical sense, which becomes vivid for the spectator only when the subject herself is dead?

Educational reform yoked together many different techniques for intensifying perception and rendering the world *ad vivum*, for exploring both the body and the soul, and each one finds its 'pornotropic' or sexualized equivalent in the clandestine erotic text. Graphic illustration and rhetoric aim to bring the referent 'as if before the very eyes'.[55] Science invents ways to dilate and inspect the living interior as well as to dissect the dead. Various religious practices transfer these discursive and corporeal technologies to spiritual introspection. Devotional writers particularly encourage female truth-seekers to 'leaf through their inner book to apprehend the word made flesh', and one of them, analysed by Nicholas Paige, conceives the 'interior' as a physical space where Love holds the subject captive: 'the very word *intérieur* ravishes' his disciple, who in turn exhorts others 'to enlarge and dilate their interior incessantly'.[56] The single word *dilate* belongs equally in the rhetorical, medical, and devotional mode.

The close relation of Eros and natural philosophy is emblematized in another seated figure engraved after a high Renaissance model, from Charles Estienne's 1545 treatise on dissection (Fig. 3). This disquieting image literally combines scientific and libertine representation, because the figures are taken directly from erotic images engraved by Jacopo Caraglio. In this case the seated figure is hermaphroditic; the body (as Bette Talvacchia has shown) is borrowed from an ephebic Bacchus in the original *Loves of the Gods*, with female head and genitalia added.[57] The posture, the setting, and the added diagrammatic markings all suggest or point towards the pudenda, yet paradoxically obstruct the actual anatomical purpose since the organ in question is barely visible. The sensuous head and suggestive left hand

[54] 'The Materialist World of Pornography', in Hunt (ed.), *Invention of Pornography*, 157–202.
[55] Ch. 2 n. 6 below; Dubost briefly sketches a link between Loyolan spiritual exercises, *L'Académie des dames*, and the *ante oculos* effect of rhetoric, in 'Libertinage and Rationality: From the "Will to Knowledge" to Libertine Textuality', in Cusset (ed.), *Libertinage and Modernity*, 63.
[56] Jean Aumont cited Ch. 1 n. 46 below, Jean-Joseph Surin cited Ch. 3 n. 23; for rhetorical and genital associations, see Patricia Parker, '*Othello* and *Hamlet*: Dilation, Spying, and the "Secret Place" of Woman', *Representations*, 44 (Fall 1993), 60–95.
[57] *Taking Positions: On the Erotic in Renaissance Culture* (Princeton, 1999), 177–9.

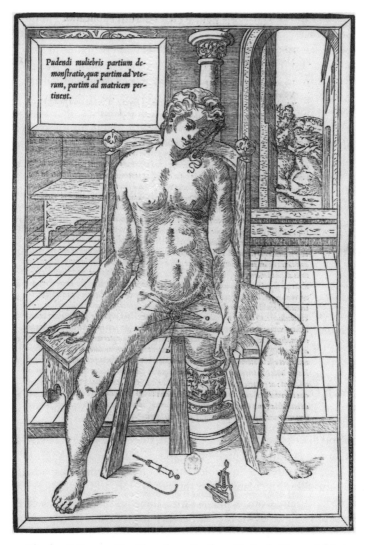

Pudendi muliebris partium de-
monstratio, quæ partim ad vte-
rum, partim ad matricem per-
tinent.

3. Charles Estienne, *De Dissectione Partium Corporis Humani* (Paris, 1545), 287

hint at erotic rather than obstetric self-exploration, and the author even apologizes for his 'confusing' and 'indecent' illustration.[58] It may seem far-fetched to claim that this image comments on the difficulties of inferring interior knowledge from external genitalia, except that the objects in the foreground explicitly raise that issue: the

[58] Charles Estienne, *La Dissection des parties du corps humain* (Paris, 1546), 312, 313, amplifying his own *De Dissectione Partium Corporis Humani* (Paris, 1545), 288 ('ne quis impudicam picturam calumnietur').

syringe inserts without seeing, the hook brings matter to light but at the risk of injury or death, whereas the speculum—also known as 'the miroure or beholder of the Wombe'[59]—allows precisely the *viva autopsia* that Comenius placed at the core of all education. Even today the speculum is used by sex-positive performance artists such as Annie Sprinkle and (metaphorically) by feminist theorists, most notably Luce Irigaray. In the seventeenth century the name of this inward-gazing instrument—literally, a mirror—links it to instructional titles such as John Sadler's *The Sicke Womans Private Looking-Glasse, wherein Methodically Are Handled All Uterine Affects, or Diseases Arising from the Wombe* (1636). I will argue that shockingly vivid representations of sexual arousal—or what Evelyn calls 'speculative lust'—likewise serve as a speculum, erotic-educational rather than gynaecological.

The libertine text turns all these devices back into flesh, matching their speculative power 'to the life'. *La retorica delle puttane* teaches how to combine verbal and sexual intensification, creating an illusion of *sviscerato affetto*—literally, emotion that draws the guts out—while remaining secretly unmoved. The French initiation-dialogues drop the trickery and give special educative force to the experience of arousal, which constitutes the whole point of living, the supreme manifestation of life, and therefore the readiest means to bring the truth of the body *ad vivum*. *L'Escole des filles* proposes a 'hieroglyphic' mode of analysing the sex act, based not on biology but on 'reciprocal mutation', each lover 'figuring herself' the other and so being 'reassured' that exterior gesture signifies inward affect (Ch. 3 below). Chorier's *Aloisia Sigea* puts this theory into practice, inventing a 'Sapphic' seduction-dialogue where words, eyes, hands, and genitals cooperate to arouse the pupil, so that she 'sees everything hidden in the depths of my viscera as if it were placed before my eyes' (Ch. 4 below). The educator tries to seduce and to *educe*, drawing out the aroused body first visually and then literally, by gesture, exclamation, and ejaculation of seed.

Physical and discursive at the same moment, this erotic version of *viva autopsia* is contrasted to the speculative method of male 'ridiculous adolescents' (Chorier, *Satyra*, III. 44), who infer the invisible truths of female sexuality from glimpses of the exterior and fill in the blanks with their own fears and prejudices about insatiable 'learned' women. Considered as satire, these texts aim to replace Pansophia with Pornosophia, to discredit the *femme savante* in favour of the mistress exclusively 'sçavante et spirituelle en amour' (*Escole*, p. XLIX). But they also critique masculinist ideology and perceptual shortcomings, offering a counter-programme of sensory enlightenment that is in fact quite congruous with the system-building ambitions of the seventeenth century.

The relation between hard science and my hard-core curriculum is therefore an intimate and dialectic one. Didactic sexology and titillating description converge: titles like *The School of Venus, Aloisia Sigea*, and *Sodom* are frequently cited, and even sold, alongside ostensibly medical works like *Aristotle's Problems, Culpepper's Midwife*, Meibomius' *De Flagrorum Usu in Re Veneria* (*The Venereal Use of Flogging*),

---

[59] A.M. (tr.), *The Frenche Chirurgerye* (Dort, 1597), fos. b3ᵛ, c2ᵛ (incorrectly cited in *OED*, s.v. 'speculum' 1); cf. Jacques Guillemeau, *Les Œuvres de chirurgie* (Paris, 1598), 138, 152 ('Mirouër').

Claude Quillet's georgic poem *Callipædia* or 'How to Make Beautiful Children', Venette's *Tableau de l'amour conjugale*, or Sinibaldi's *Rare Verities* (discussed in Chapter 1 below).[60] Chorier's section-title *Fabrica* evokes Vesalius' anatomy, and his main title *The Arcana of Love and Venus* taps into the desire for 'books of secrets' and instruction in 'how to do it'.[61] Meanwhile, the greatest biologist of the century turned to generation after his triumphant work on the circulation of the blood. An utter failure from the point of view of modern science, William Harvey's *Exercitationes de Generatione Animalium* shares crucial features with the erotic texts studied below. Harvey deepens the mystery of gender by declaring, on grounds of experimental observation, that nothing whatsoever passes from the male to the female at conception; on the other hand, his passionate belief in the creative power of the blood—site of his own famous discovery—leads him to ascribe almost magical properties to the male sperm 'concocted' from it. Despite his attack on other scientists who pursue fictional ideas rather than empirical observation, Harvey can only imagine fertilization as a 'plastic art', an 'immaterial Idea' that sparks conception in the brain-like tissue of the uterus just as the artist translates a concept into an image.[62] This profound interfusion of cognitive and genital functions is precisely what Harvey shares with the libertine text. In *La retorica delle puttane*, in *L'Alcibiade*, in *L'Escole des filles*, and in *Aloisia Sigea*, we shall see the same presentation of the 'idea' as the key to physical arousal, the same simultaneous erasure and exaltation of the male seed, the same ambiguous treatment of the female as an autonomous, self-manifesting agent and as a mere accessory to the male.

Harvey explores conception in birds rather than pleasure in humans, of course. But even here some covert resemblances slip in. The scientist and the eroticist both pursue the hidden *arcana* of sexuality, and both produce narratives of desire that promote the arousing power of narration. When Harvey isolates the hen so that she can only hear the cock's crowing, she 'trembles with a kind of gentle horror' just as if she had actually copulated—vivid proof of the discursive construction of sexuality? Similarly, the dialogists of *L'Escole* and *Aloisia* describe their own orgasmic response to the descriptions they are sharing: 'ma cousine, je descharge!' In Rocco and in Chorier these discursive pleasures blend with physical provocation, as dialogue turns into action ('take away that adulterous finger!'). Harvey likewise caresses his experimental subjects and softens their '*Uterine Orifice*' with his 'gentle finger', producing a stream of *gaudiis indiciis* or pleasure-indicators, 'murmurs, cries, and gesticulations' that 'express the delightful sweetness of Venus'. Even the 'exceeding large *Yard*' of his ostrich matches the pornographic script.[63]

---

[60] For allusions, advertisements, and prosecution evidence, see nn. 79, 82, and Ch. 7, sect. 3 below; Foxon, 6, 13–14; Porter and Hall, *Facts of Life*, chs. 1–3 *passim*.

[61] Cf. William Eamon, *Science and the Secrets of Nature: Books of Secrets in Medieval and Early Modern Culture* (Princeton, 1994), and Rudolph M. Bell, *How to Do It: Guides to Good Living for Renaissance Italians* (1999), ch. 2.

[62] (Amsterdam, 1651), preface *passim*, 143–4, 295, 557–8 (tr. Martin Lluellin, *Anatomical Exercitations Concerning the Generation of Living Creatures* (1653), 263–5, 542–3).

[63] 42, 10–14 (Lluellin, *Anatomical Exercitations*, 76, 20–3), *Escole*, II. 141, Chorier, *Satyra*, IV. 72; cf. Thomas Laqueur, *Making Sex: Body and Gender from the Greeks to Freud* (1990), 142–8, esp. 146.

In Donne's 'A Lecture upon the Shadow' the expert amorist promises to read 'a Lecture, Love, in love's philosophy', words that impressed Julia Kristeva so much that she displayed them (in English) as the epigraph to her book *Histoires d'amour*. But Donne's conception of philosophy requires that he and his lover 'Stand still'— the arresting opening words of his poem—in order to apply it with the proper detachment. In contrast, I show a kind of sexual philosophy in action, immersed in the phenomena of arousal. Just as Evelyn feared, the higher cognitive faculty mingles with animal and irrational lust, while reason transforms sex from a fixed routine or natural instinct into a fabulous opportunity for experiment and invention, what Chorier called *ingeniosa libido* or *erudita libido*. This school of 'venerian speculation'[64] competed vigorously with the official idea of philosophy, and education, as a victory over bodily impulse and animal desire.

Competing conceptions of the philosophical life underlie seventeenth-century representations of sexuality, and their opposition can be felt, I hope to show, in even the most scandalous and frivolous texts. Molière's *Les Femmes savantes* allows only two possibilities for the woman, the absurd anti-corporeality of the *précieuses*— 'Mariez-vous, ma sœur, à la philosophie'—and the stifling domesticity proposed by the *bon bourgeois* husband, apparently endorsed by the playwright:

> Former aux bonnes mœurs l'esprit de ses enfants,
> Faire aller son ménage, avoir l'œil sur ses gens,
> Et régler la dépense avec économie,
> Doit être son étude et sa philosophie.[65]

Forming her children's minds according to good morals, running her household, supervising her staff, and regulating her expenses economically, should be woman's study and philosophy.

But libertinism proposed a third way, making philosophy itself sexual, and vice versa. The Restoration rake celebrates 'this quick-sighted Philosophical Age wherein whoring is improv'd to a liberal Science', a comic version of the 'besoin de savoir insatiable', the 'tactical rationality introduced into sexual relations', that for Claude Reichler constitutes the libertine era.[66] Even within the same comedy, 'philosophy' can serve as a vehicle and as an impediment to sexual self-realization. In Vanbrugh's *Provoked Wife* (1697), the suffering spouse blames 'old foolish Philosophers' for loading women with 'fine notions of Virtue' that prevent her from taking a lover. Below stairs and in a different accent, meanwhile, the French maid evokes philosophy to justify complete sexual abandon: Lady Fancifull asks with exaggerated horror, 'Why sure you wou'd not sacrifice your Honor to your Pleasure?'; Mademoiselle replies 'Je suis Philosophe.'[67] The idea of cognitive and erotic co-

---

[64] John Davies, *A Scourge for Paper-Persecutors, or Papers Complaint . . . with a Continued Inquisition against Paper-Persecutors, by A.H.* (1624), 3.

[65] I. i. 44, II. vii. 573–6; Roger Chartier and Dominique Julia, 'L'Éducation des filles', in Chartier, Julia, and Marie-Madeleine Compère, *L'Éducation en France du XVI᷉ au XVIII᷉ siècle* (Paris, 1976), 232, compare an almost identical passage in Fénelon's *Traité de l'éducation des filles*.

[66] Francis Fane, *Love in the Dark* (1675), 14; Reichler, *L'Âge libertin* (Paris, 1987), 59.

[67] *The Complete Works of Sir John Vanbrugh*, i, ed. Bonamy Dobrée (1927), 117 (1. i), 123 (1. ii); for an earlier version of this point, see my 'Culture of Priapism', 18.

development—shocking in Evelyn's 'speculative Lusts' and amusing in Vanbrugh's *soubrette philosophe*—mutates into Elisabeth Singer Rowe's surprisingly sympathetic portrait of the 'philosophick libertine', who 'pursued pleasure for the sake of demonstration', who paused, reasoned 'made critical reflections on every enjoyment' in a 'deliberate search after happiness'.[68]

Finally, we should ask what set this libertine-didactic philosophy in motion? Through what cognitive and material channels did it flow, and what conditions in the republic of letters allowed *libido* to become 'erudite'? Language clearly played a large if paradoxical role. La Rochefoucauld implies a certain scorn for those who can only feel desire if they have heard it constructed in language, as if Dom Juan and his followers were right to promote *faire* over *dire* and 'action' over 'discourse' (p. 11 above): 'Il y a des gens qui n'auraient jamais été amoureux s'ils n'avaient jamais entendu parler de l'amour.'[69] ('There are people who would never fall in love if they hadn't heard love talked about.') But he does at least recognize the constitutive power that his near-namesake Foucault would later elevate to a paradigm, and many contemporaries went further. Chorier ultimately promotes the pleasures of discourse and figuration over the *nausea* of physicality (Ch. 4 below), and Maucroix—who described the sensational effect of Chorier's dialogue as it 'ran through Paris'—produced his own libertine twist on linguistic constructionism: 'f..tez donc, les Belles, f..tez | la vertu n'est que du langage!' 'fuck, darlings, fuck, virtue is nothing but language!'[70]

To be most effective, sex talk had to be codified in book form. The apocalyptic preacher might trust that when 'the Books shall be opened' all speculative lusts will cease, but back in the Old World it was precisely Books that disseminated them. The very form of the book invoked the intimate crevices of the body, an analogy that still appeals to poets today.[71] Already in the sixteenth century, moralists and gossip-mongers fantasized over the transforming power of 'Aretino' and his kind: the modern girl 'is so nouseled in amorous bookes . . . that she smelleth of naughtinesse even all her life after', contaminated as if by whore's milk;[72] advanced vice manuals 'translated out of Italian into English, sold in every shop in London', teach 'new school points' for the bedroom, 'not fond and common ways to vice, but such subtle, cunning, new, and diverse shifts . . as the simple head of an Englishman is not able to invent'.[73] (By 1584 the London printer John Wolfe could also run up authentic-looking editions of the Italian originals.) It is true that sexual writings we might categorize as pornographic were assimilated to the genre of mock-praise.[74] Far more commonly and persistently, however, they were given a dreadful

---

[68] *Letters Moral and Entertaining* (1733), 2nd pagination, 157–8, in *Friendship in Death*, facsimile ed. Josephine Grieder (1972).

[69] *Maximes*, number 136.   [70] Ch. 7 nn. 1–2 below.

[71] Cf. Ch. 1 n. 76 below ('the two-leaved book') and Robert Pinsky, 'Book', *Three Penny Review*, 87 (Fall 2001), 4.

[72] Edward Hake, cited in Helen Hackett *Women and Romance Fiction in the English Renaissance* (Cambridge, 2000), 43.

[73] Roger Ascham, *The Schoolmaster* (1570), ed. Lawrence V. Ryan (Ithaca, NY, 1967), 39, 67–9.

[74] Sir John Harington, *The Metamorphosis of Ajax* (1596), ed. Elizabeth Story Donno (1962), 63–4, equates his scatological mock-encomium with Aretino's *Ragionamenti* and '*Puttana errante*' as well as Erasmus' *Praise of Folly*.

power to fascinate and corrupt. 'Loose Aretine flames' provoke widows to copulate with passive boys or 'smooth-faced catamites, . . . as if a woman should a woman wed'.[75] Pepys still cites *La puttana errante* as the benchmark for judging *L'Escole des filles*,[76] and Evelyn's warnings against 'unnatural figures' and 'lewd postures' do not even need to name their author as Aretino.

The core post-Aretine texts that form the body of this book—listed for convenience in the Abbreviations above—achieved a similar notoriety in the seventeenth and eighteenth centuries. Their authors were banished (like the aristocrat Rochester), burned in effigy, or even executed at an early age: Claude Le Petit was burned at the stake for sodomy and obscenity, and the highly cultured Ferrante Pallavicino—recruited by Richelieu to establish an academy for the study of Italian literature—was captured and beheaded by the papal authorities.[77] Once in print these books were intermittently seized, prosecuted, and incinerated, either publicly by the executioner or privately by furtive consumers like Pepys.[78] Key books such as *The School of Venus, Sodom,* and *Aretinus Redivivus* have vanished completely, except for manuscript copies and selections transcribed into prosecution records; others survive in one single exemplar. (In each case I cite afresh from the original document, undoing the damage caused by defective modern reprints.) At the same time, however, drama and criticism constantly named these notorious titles, booksellers flaunted them openly, and collectors listed them in their libraries, the best set belonging to John Hoyle, the libertine friend of Aphra Behn.[79] In France, copies of *L'Escole* were traced to courtiers and ministers; in Holland and England, visitors saw them in the shops.[80] Even the outrageous *Alcibiade fanciullo*— imitated in libertine literature but not directly cited—appeared in multiple editions, entered élite libraries, and was regularly denounced in learned bibliographies for celebrating 'the art of sodomy'.[81] Latin classics like Chorier's *Aloisia Sigea* had an excellent survival rate in gentlemen's collections; the Bodleian copy of Meibomius on flagellation came from the library of Lord Baden-Powell, author of *Scouting for Boys.*

[75] Thomas Middleton, cited and analysed in Ian Frederick Moulton, *Before Pornography: Erotic Writing in Early Modern England* (New York, 2000), 158; my terms for this perversion, common throughout the hard-core curriculum and its analogues, are *epheberasty* and *heteropaedophilia.*

[76] Pepys does not record buying this prose dialogue (identified in Abbreviations above); he may have read it after 1 July 1663, when he confessed that 'I do not to this day know what is the meaning of this sin [buggery, amply described in *La puttana errante*], nor which is the agent nor which the patient,' but this may express ontological rather than physiological confusion.

[77] Laura Coci, *RP*, introd.

[78] For details see Le Petit, *Œuvres*, pp. xxv–xliii; Coci, *RP* introd.; Foxon, 7–18, 31–3; and Anne Sauvy, *Livres saisis à Paris entre 1678 et 1701* (The Hague, 1972), *passim.*

[79] Ch. 5 n. 6 below; cf. Foxon, 9 (one bookseller stocks up with 'some *Escole des filles, Aloyisiae Zigaeae Amores* etc.' only to be closed down the following year) and 'The Compleat Auctioner', BM Personal and Political Satires, 1415 ('*c.*1700'), openly displaying 'Aretines Post[ures]', 'Play of Sodom', Rochester's 'Poems', 'Culp Midw.', 'Arist[otles] Mast[erpiece]', 'Tulliae Octav', 'Sch: of Venus'. Thompson, *Unfit for Modest Ears*, 203–5, tabulates libertine and bawdy books in English libraries pre-1700.

[80] Pia, p. XXI; Foxon, 9; Wijnand W. Mijnhardt, 'Politics and Pornography in the Seventeenth- and Eighteenth-Century Dutch Republic', in Hunt (ed.), *Invention of Pornography*, 297.

[81] See Coci's introd. and textual note to *Alcibiade*, esp. 9 n. 7; it also appears in the late-18th-century list of confiscated books cited by Marchi (Epilogue n. 29 below).

Montaigne's contrast between masculine book-learning and the 'discipline' of Nature—to which I now turn, at the threshold of Chapter 1—raises the fundamental question, who reads these texts and for what purpose? Montaigne assumes that men are the primary consumers of eroto-didactic literature, and identifies as its real concern the male need for sexual instruction, for self-fashioning through 'study'; nevertheless, its principal subject is female learning. Titles like *The School of Venus or The Ladies Delight Reduced into Rules of Practice* remind us that, ever since Nanna trained her daughter Pippa in Aretino's *Ragionamenti*, most pornography took the form of an initiatory dialogue between two women. Imaginary reception-scenes assume that women themselves read and apply these texts. Thomas Carew's 'Rapture' imagines Lucretia 'studying' the works of Aretino, transforming herself into a product of his text, and Restoration dramatists imagine women secretly compiling their own didactic library, lining their studies with *Aristotle's Problems*, '*Lescholle de Files*, a pretty French book', and '*Annotations upon Aretines Postures*, three Excellent Books for a Ladies Chamber'.[82] The emphasis falls on the first element in Montaigne's oxymoron, 'the schoolmaster Nature'—though the *maître* wears drag in every version except the openly homosexual *Alcibiade*. In her indignant feminist counterblast *The Female Advocate* Sarah Fyge contrasts the virtuous woman, self-constructed by 'Rule' and 'Precept', to the slanderous image projected by libertines and satirists, fashionably seductive, sexually advanced, and therefore sexually defined. Echoing the title of the *Escole* translation, Fyge points out that the ostensibly hedonist-naturalist woman is equally 'reduced to rules of practice', equally confined by a didactic institution, and rather more coerced to conform to male interests: 'They would have all bred up in *Venus* School.'[83]

---

[82] *The Poems of Thomas Carew, with his Masque Coelum Britannicum*, ed. Rhodes Dunlap (Oxford, 1949), 52; John Learnerd, *The Rambling Justice* (1678), 51 (IV. vi).

[83] n. 19 above.

PART I

Erotic Education and the (Hard)Core Curriculum

Sex as Discipline

The Idea of Erotic Education

Allons à cette heure estudier des frases d'*Amadis* et des registres de Boccace et de l'Aretin pour faire les habiles; nous employons vrayement bien nostre temps! Il n'est ny parole, ny exemple, ny démarche qu'elles ne sçachent mieux que nos livres: c'est une discipline qui naist dans leurs veines, *Et mentem Venus ipsa dedit*, que ces bons maistres d'escole, nature, jeunesse et santé, leur soufflent continuellement dans l'ame; elles n'ont que faire de l'apprendre, elles l'engendrent.

(Montaigne, 'Sur des vers de Virgile')

Now let's go and study the fine phrases of *Amadis de Gaule* and the registers of Boccaccio and Aretino, to make ourselves clever and proficient lovers; that's a really good way to spend our time. There is no word, no example, no move that women don't know better than our books; it's a discipline born in their bloodstream—*the mind was created by Venus herself*—which those good schoolmasters, Nature, Youth, and Health, are continually breathing into their soul; women don't have to learn it, they engender it.

T H E disciplining power of erotic discourse—the power of *L'Escole des filles* to 'inform' Pepys, the power of Chorier's *Satyra Sotadica* to give Casanova his 'theory' and to 'perfect' Diderot's worldly hero—obliges us to read it as more than titillating fantasy or withering satire. Without minimizing its priapism and misogyny, I propose to call its bluff by treating it as *institution* as well as representation. As my Introduction showed, libertine promoters and feminist opponents agreed in regarding these texts as 'Schools of Venus' and handbooks of 'speculative lust'. Chapters 2 to 4 will move on to a detailed study of this 'schooling' effect in the two foundational French dialogues, *L'Escole* in Chapter 3 and Chorier in Chapter 4, and in two Italian works that French *libertin* discourse emulates: Ferrante Pallavicino's 1642 *Retorica delle puttane* ('The Whores' Rhetoric'), the last and most sophisticated of the courtesan-training texts that derive from Pietro Aretino's *Ragionamenti*, and Antonio Rocco's 1650 *Alcibiade fanciullo a scola* ('Alcibiades as a Schoolboy'), the exclusively homoerotic seduction-dialogue which I propose as a model for the rethinking of 'Nature' in heterosexuality. In this chapter I will establish the cultural and ideological work performed by the sex-as-education trope.

I bring together many kinds of evidence—feminist dialogues by Moderata Fonte and Margaret Cavendish, pedagogical treatises including Milton's *Of Education*, medical and philosophical enquiries into sexual love—to contextualize hard-core literature. Section 1 looks at sixteenth-century Italian sexual discourse, contrasting the influential dialogues of Aretino, literally 'pornographic' since they are spoken by prostitute characters, with the erotic philosophy of an authentic courtesan, Tullia d'Aragona. I am particularly interested in the transmigration of erotic learning from the underworld of prostitution to the domestic sphere, to the marriage-bed and the schoolroom. Serious scientists like the papal physician Sinibaldi incorporate jocular salacity into their treatises; educational theorists like Comenius and Milton conceive learning itself in sensuous, erotic terms, or even argue for the benefits of pornography (section 2). Later sections extend the trope to higher education, juxtaposing misogynist and feminist accounts of the 'Female Academy'. The Aretinesque conceit of the 'College of Whores' or 'University of Love' mutates into Ben Jonson's satire against the Collegiate Ladies—gendered as 'hermaphrodites' for presuming to claim cultural as well as sexual authority (section 3). The final section shows how the idea of erotic education was reappropriated by *femmes savantes* and absolutist feminists in the turbulent mid-seventeenth century, with particular focus on Queen Christina of Sweden and Margaret Cavendish, Duchess of Newcastle.

Montaigne's comments on the futility of reading Aretino form a suitably slippery threshold for this enquiry. 'Now let's go and study the fine phrases of *Amadis de Gaule* and the registers of Boccaccio and Aretino', he exhorts his fellow-men ironically, 'to make ourselves clever and proficient lovers; that's a really good way to spend our time. There is no word, no example, no move that women don't know better than our books; it's a discipline born in their bloodstream.' Citing the proverbial *mentem Venus ipsa dedit* from Virgil's *Georgics* (III. 267), the stockbreeders' maxim that 'the mind was created by Venus herself', Montaigne proposes a deep polarity between male 'ability' (clumsily acquired by time-wasting study) and female sexual understanding, 'which those good schoolmasters, Nature, Youth, and Health, are continually breathing into their soul; women don't have to learn it, they engender it.'[1] He reveals desire as a bookish construction, anticipating La Rochefoucauld and Foucault, but at the same time he maintains the old gendered polarization of female nature and male culture: men 'learn' their sexual know-how and women 'engender' theirs. (How different from Marguerite de Navarre, where Nature—the 'maistre d'escolle bien secret'—kindles desires in both the male adolescent and his widowed mother that lead directly to their unnatural coupling.[2]) Montaigne's backhanded praise of women's 'natural' capacities rests upon an assumption of male creativity; 'books' may be futile, but they are still '*our* books', a masculine cultural achievement that women undercut by mere instinct. His wry paradox asserts the superiority of female 'Nature' in much the same way that he praises the wisdom of cannibals and animals.

At this point in Montaigne's long, fluid, Protean essay on sexuality, the dichotomy

---

[1] *Essais*, III. v. 834–5/652; see Constance Jordan, 'Sexuality and Volition in "Sur des vers de Virgile"', *Montaigne Studies*, 8 (1996), 69, 70 n. 9.

[2] *Heptaméron*, III. xxx.

of Nature and Culture still dominates the explication of gender; he reverses the value assigned to each, but still places the 'engendering' female in one category and the 'learning' male in the other. The entire ideological apparatus of patriarchy rested on this polarizing identification of Nature with the feminine and Culture with the masculine: we shall see that, whenever educational theory turns into a contest between the sexes, women's 'natural impertinencies' are accused of preventing self-transformation through education, and their physiological 'Sex' is assumed to imprison their souls—though men are somehow exempt from this determinism (Ch. 3, sect. 5 below). But representations of the libertine *institutrice* (the common theme of Aretino, Pallavicino, *L'Escole des filles*, Chorier, and their successors) strain this dichotomy to the breaking point, since 'Venus' becomes a complex technology of pleasures and postures rather than a 'natural' instinctive urge, and since it is the female voice (albeit ventriloquized) that transmits the knowledge and assumes the authority. Elsewhere in his encyclopedic essay, Montaigne himself places sexuality firmly in the category of Culture. He deplores the military arts that glorify death and destruction, and calls for an equivalent artistic elaboration of sex, prolonging its simple pleasures by transforming them into the successive chambers of a palace or the hierarchic 'degrees' of philosophic initiation.[3]

Montaigne's idea of cultivated priapism derives from Aretino, suggesting that his 'studies' in that lewd author were far from fruitless. In a letter justifying Giulio Romano's *Modi* and the obscene sonnets he wrote to accompany them, Aretino had likewise argued that we should cover the mouth and hands with shame, since they commit so many foul deeds, and display the penis proudly as a cap-badge or pendant jewel, organizing public festivals in honour of the genitalia.[4] The libertine textbook, scandalously showing-and-telling what should never be revealed, carries out Aretino's injunction. But Aretino's foundational letter brings up a further ambiguity: is libertine discourse purposive, or is it (as he said of his 'lascivious sonnets') a *trastullo d'ingegno*, a playful exercise of wit, fuelled by the same 'spirit' that inspired the original *Modi*? Everyone cites the Horatian formula that writing must instruct as well as please, but when the *dulce* is so scandalous how can it be *utile*? And if the didactic prevails, what kind of school does 'Nature' set up? A phrase like 'The School of Venus' enacts the same dramatic irony that Molière exploits in *L'École des femmes* and *L'École des maris*: a school run *by* husbands, or a school *for* husbands to learn by their mistakes? an attempt to indoctrinate future wives against their amorous 'Nature' (which fails precisely because they learn their desires from the list of prohibitions), or a textbook on how to outwit a repressive guardian and find true love? Is libertine representation a *parody* of teaching, mocking the very idea of intellectual development or self-transformation in a creature so 'naturally' depraved as woman, or is it an *act* of teaching, a 'register' (as Montaigne put it) of what every participant in the game of love must learn?

[3] III. v. 856–60/669–72, esp. 860/672 ('Il y a des degrez en la jouyssance').
[4] Pietro Aretino, letter to Battista Zatti, *Lettere*, ed. Francesco Erspamer (Parma, 1995–   ), i. 656 (also in *Ragionamenti*, II. iii. 312–13 [325–6]).

1. 'A DISCIPLINE BORN IN THE BLOOD'? PIETRO ARETINO, TULLIA
   D'ARAGONA, AND THE EROTIC 'ACADEMY'

In his remarks on the 'registres d'Aretin' Montaigne redefined earlier Italian erotic literature as an educational resource, at least for those males who need textual 'discipline' because they lack the address that comes 'naturally' to women. In Aretino's *Ragionamenti* themselves, however, the eroto-didactic synthesis is frequently replaced by burlesque of intellectual pretension and satire against the prostitute. Didactic language proliferates in the first day's dialogue—when Nanna recounts her own learning experience in a feverishly sensual convent—and on the fourth day, when she instructs her daughter Pippa in what she calls the 'arte puttanesca' (after pondering, like a good Renaissance mother, what mode of life to prepare her for).[5] The essence of the 'courtesan's art' (to be as whorish as possible in bed and as refined as possible in public) is drummed into Nanna by an overbearing *maestra*, and she in turn *ammaestra* (or 'mistresses') her own protégée. In the opening nunnery-sequence the fiction of female-to-female transmission is compromised when Aretino inserts a male instructor, the young monk who slips Nanna a manual of postures and who teaches her 'to put her finger on one place in the pussy that brings up the feeling at a stroke'—a remarkable arrogation of knowledge to the male, a full decade before the first medical account of the clitoris and the controversy over who 'discovered' it.[6] Once this patent author-surrogate disappears, Nanna's pedagogic authority seems to grow unchallenged. But it grows in direct proportion to her comic vulgarity and contempt for educational improvement.

Aretino locks his magisterial bawd-narrator securely into the grotesque lower stratum, letting her transmit 'arts' only if they are clearly labelled 'puttanesca', suitable for the avowed 'whore' rather than the culturally privileged 'honourable courtesan' or mistress. When Pippa encourages Nanna to 'open a school' her mother replies positively: 'il puttanesimo ha tanto ingegno', whoring has so much 'brilliance' or 'genius' of its own, that even without a master you learn more in eight days than in the whole of your previous life. Nanna then sets out a course of advanced '*puttanismo* studies' that includes a veneer of literary cultivation (Ariosto, Petrarch, Boccaccio) and training in demure refinement, every blush and glance to be practised in front of a hand mirror.[7] Procuring is likewise imagined as a discipline with its own 'school' and doctoral programme, graduating 'witches and poetesses' as well as mistress-bawds like Nanna herself. In practice, however, Nanna belittles the poetic paraphrases and rhetorical figures that other courtesans use to suggest their

---

[5] Cf. Stanley Chojnacki, '"The Most Serious Duty": Motherhood, Gender, and Patrician Culture in Renaissance Venice', in Marilyn Migiel and Juliana Schiesari (eds.), *Refiguring Woman: Perspectives on Gender and the Italian Renaissance* (1991), 133–54, esp. 148–9.

[6] *Ragionamenti*, I. i. 19 [24], 46–7 [52], I. ii. 67 [73] ('un luogo al volpone', literally 'fox'), II. i. 168 [175]; cf. Katherine Park, 'The Rediscovery of the Clitoris: French Medicine and the Tribade, 1570–1620', in David Hillman and Carla Mazzio (eds.), *The Body in Parts: Fantasies of Corporeality in Early Modern Europe* (1997), 176.

[7] *Ragionamenti*, II. i. 184–5 [192], 224 [233]; for different uses of the mirror in Aretino and Pallavicino, see Ch. 2 n. 33 below.

educated refinement, equating such ornament with sexual perversion and insisting on the crude, earthy vocabulary of *cunt, prick*, and *fucking*. This anti-Petrarchanism emerges especially when she speaks as an agent of male desire: if she were a man, she explains to Pippa, she would look for firm flesh and lively embraces, rather than a knowledge of Petrarch and Dante, for a 'honeyed' tongue rather than a 'learned' one (*una lingua melata, e non adottorata*).[8] Aretino's mock-didactic apparatus only serves to strengthen the barricade between the sensuous *melata* and the intellectual *adottorata*. The libertine discourse of the following century, in contrast, will try to fuse the two.

Aretino's imitators modify this heavy insistence on *puttanismo* in one important respect. For the most part the instructional format is still fenced off by the cordon of explicit prostitutional language, often announced in the very title (*Tariffa delle puttane di Venegia* or 'Price-List of Venetian Whores', *La puttana errante* or 'The Whore Errant'). When the *Tariffa* calls a two-shilling harlot 'Vice-Rectoress of the College', or when Pallavicino dedicates his *Retorica delle puttane* to 'La Università delle Cortegiane più Celebri',[9] they widen the gulf between the sex worker and her client (a separation more confident than in Aretino himself, the self-taught plebeian who shares much with the prostitutes he caricatures). But alongside this branding of the *puttana* we can glimpse a tendency that will not fully emerge until *L'Escole des filles* in 1655: what I call the 'domestic turn', away from prostitutional trickery towards a kind of homely idyll of sex-for-sex's-sake.

In the pseudo-Aretine dialogue later known as *La puttana errante*, the best-known pornographic discourse before *L'Escole* and the benchmark that Pepys cites to evaluate the 'lewd book', this intermittent domesticity appears in the setting (an artisan's country home), in the vocabulary (genitalia as noodles or pieces of firewood), and in the action. Impromptu coupling takes place with aunts and cousins, sometimes up against the heroine's sleeping mother; after growing up in this household, the heroine sets up an easygoing ménage where she lives with her scholar-lover in complete 'domestichezza'.[10] In the sonnets that circulated under Aretino's name, too, the mock-lecture format alternates with this more domestic *mise en scène*. A young mother rocks the cradle or suckles her child while her lover offers his own 'milk', tries to match her rhythm, and even addresses her as 'Mummy'.[11] (Aretino's Nanna records the male habit of crying 'mammina, mammotta e mammetta' at the moment of orgasm, but never develops this household observation into its own scene.[12]) In a more sophisticated variant on the domestic turn, Alessandro

---

[8] II. iii. 305 [317] ('ne la scuola de la ruffiania si sono addottorate . . . le negromantesse e le poetesse'), I. i. 38 [43–4], II. ii. 192 [200].

[9] Antonio Cavallino?, *Tariffa* (1535), ed. Guillaume Apollinaire (Paris, 1911), 58; Pallavicino, *RP* title page.

[10] *Dialogo di Giulia e di Madalena*, 65, 75, 81, 89, 91; *Puttana errante*, 10, 17, 21, 28 (see Abbreviations for details of this work).

[11] *Sonetti lussuriosi di M. Pietro Aretino* ('Venice, 1556', but in fact an 18th-century reprint), Vienna, Österreichische Nationalbibliothek, BE 5 X 69, sonnets 15 ('Il putto poppa, e poppa anche la potta') and 16 ('Sta cheto, bambin mio, ninna, ninna . . . Mammina, a vostra posta compir~'); cf. *Modi* sonnet 15.

[12] *Ragionamenti*, II. i. 172 [179].

Piccolomini's *Rafaella* or *Della creanza delle donne* (1540), the techniques of pleasure and deception are used to prepare, not for a career of public *puttanismo*, but for
discreet affairs under the cover of marriage. Though not explicitly hard-core,
Piccolomini's refinement of the Aretine scenario—the experienced bawd initiating
the nubile younger woman—makes a crucial step towards the clandestine but
non-prostitutional sexuality of *L'Escole des filles* and *Aloisia Sigea*.

Aretino defended his erotic writings as a *jeu d'esprit*, meant only to celebrate his own
arousal and display his own *ingegno*, but in France they were subsumed into the didactic paradigm. Montaigne, as we have seen, assumes that men read Aretino to extract lessons in sexual 'ability' (even though the text itself almost exclusively shows
women teaching women). Joachim Du Bellay anticipates this double gender-focus
in his verse monologue 'La Vieille Courtisanne': the speaker claims to know 'everything that Aretino teaches', to 'put into practice all the secrets discovered in his book'
(like Du Bellay himself, who borrows heavily from Aretino's *Ragionamenti*), but she
uses this erotic training to establish her house as 'a public school of *honnesteté*',
obligatory for all young men who wished to learn 'how to entertain the Ladies'.[13] Du
Bellay's assumptions about the formative role of the Roman courtesan exactly
match those of the memoirist and gossip-monger Pierre de Brantôme, who traces
many of his didactic anecdotes to his friendship with 'La Greca' in Rome, and describes her shaping and polishing the oafish Frenchmen who come to her 'school'
for instruction more than for pleasure.[14] Brantôme derives from his Italian sojourn
and from Italian writers like 'Aretino' the idea of sex as a 'school of secrets', located
on the border between the discursive and the corporeal, and symbolized by the in-
terlacing of tongues in the kiss.[15]

Brantôme's response to Aretine education remains deeply divided, particularly
when the domestic turn breaches the prostitutional cordon that keeps illicit sexuality in its own underworld, categorically distinct from marriage. He reserves his
strongest shock and fascination for wives who bring the 'figures of Aretino' into the
marriage-bed and aristocratic ladies who take on the teaching role of the courtesan,
becoming *sçavantes en amours* and 'well able to give lessons to others'.[16] In numerous anecdotes the 'book of figures' gives access to the secret world of female desire.
The aristocratic suitor feels sure that he will eventually succeed with a certain 'belle
et honneste dame', knowing that she owns 'un Arétin en figure' in her *cabinet*—
knowing, moreover, that 'her husband knows and has seen it and given his permission' (26). The libertine connoisseurship shared by husband, wife, and lover will
guarantee access to her inmost 'cabinet', to the leaves of her private book; her clan-

---

[13] *Œuvres poétiques*, ed. Henri Chamard, v (Paris, 1923), 162, 170.
[14] Cf. *Le Cabinet satyrique* (1618), ed. Fernand Fleuret and Louis Perceau (Paris, 1924), i. 267–73, 'Regrets d'une jeune courtisanne grecque sur l'impuissance d'un vieil courtisan françois'. Instructional res-
idence with an Italian courtesan, and boasting of expertise in postures and perversions, is documented
in the case of one English aristocrat; see Alan Nelson, *Monstrous Adversary: A Documentary Biography of
Edward de Vere, Seventeenth Earl of Oxford (1550–1604)* (Liverpool, forthcoming).
[15] Pierre de Bourdeille, abbé de Brantôme, *Les Dames galantes*, ed. Maurice Rat (Paris, 1947), 32–4, 328.
[16] Ibid. 329.

destine acquisition will give him the purchase he requires. 'Nature' and 'Art' conspire in these case histories, but Brantôme varies his estimate of their relative contribution. At one point he remarks that we hardly need erotic books and pictures nowadays, since wives can learn all the techniques in their 'escholes de marys'—anticipating Molière's comedy of the same name. Elsewhere, however, he pretends to devalue both kinds of didactic art. 'Le livre et la pratique'—the 'Aretine' book and the practical lessons given by previous men—work together to help the adulterer's cause, but the principal didactic-formative authority is neither masculine nor artificial: rather, 'Dame Nature is the best mistress of all the arts.'[17] Brantôme approximates the attitude struck in Montaigne's comment on the futility of male erotic self-fashioning, except that here Nature is gendered female too, a teaching Dame rather than a *maistre d'escole*.

Already in the sixteenth century, then, we see that French visions of Italy conjured up the figure of the libertine *institutrice* presiding over the erotic academy. This semi-fictional character—guardian of the *ars erotica* that Foucault thought vanished in the West—'forms' the uncouth males who come to her from barbarian countries, controls their sexual initiation, and transmits the 'secrets of the school of Venus'—which evolve rapidly from the simple 'facts of life' into an esoteric tradition of pleasure heightened by connoisseurship, Eros raised to a philosophical quest, cognition and arousal interfused, Nature transformed by Art, sexuality transmuted into the source of culture and cultivation. Aretino had coupled *ingegno* with sexual erudition, but under the oxymoronic label *puttanismo*; the suffix 'ism' suggests a philosophical school or organized body of knowledge, but the *puttana* drags it down to the unthinkable. In the next generation the ribald bawd-trickster evolves, first into the *cortegiana honesta*, and then into the *grande dame galante*, explored ad infinitum in Brantôme's salacious anecdotes and later in Chorier's dialogues. In all the cases considered so far, however, the narrative of female didactic supremacy is undermined by the obvious fact that males actually write the script. Brantôme's La Greca exists only as a trace within his manuscript, an authority but not an author. Du Bellay's fictional 'Old Courtesan' is further framed and distanced by her current decrepitude; she is now an object-lesson in a 'Philosophy' of dissuasion, rather than the subject or creator of a philosophy of Eros—even though her house once resembled a 'public school' where élite males received essential training in *honnêteté*.[18]

The tables are turned in those rare cases where 'public women' countered the degradation of *puttanismo* by memorializing themselves in art. When Du Bellay departs from his Aretine model and (briefly) makes the courtesan's house '*quasi* comme une escolle ouverte | D'honnesteté' (170), he seems to echo the praises lavished on the non-fictional Roman philosopher Tullia d'Aragona; the Florentine authorities

[17] Ibid. 27, 30–1; Peter Cryle, *Geometry in the Boudoir: Configurations of French Erotic Narrative* (1994), 25–6, seems to believe that Brantôme refers to the canon exemplified by *L'Escole des filles* and Chorier's *Satyra*, both written many decades after his death.

[18] *Œuvres poétiques*, 181 (this warning against the courtesan is more useful than any other 'doctrinale Philosophie').

exempted her from wearing the courtesan's uniform because of her 'poetry and philosophy',[19] and the humanist Lattanzio Benucci declares that noblemen, literati, and
cardinals flock to her house '*as if* to a universal and honoured Academy' (my emphasis). Reversing the usual gendered priority of writer and speaker, the real-life
Benucci makes this tribute in a fictionalized dialogue scripted and published by
d'Aragona herself, the 1547 *Della infinità d'amore.*[20]

D'Aragona's status as cultured courtesan provoked widely polarized responses.
She is treated with great (if circumscribed) respect as the interlocutor of Sperone
Speroni's 1537 *Dialogo d'amore*, where a character with her name expresses philosophical, aesthetic, and erotic ideas that she would later endorse in her own *Infinità*,
giving them to the speaker Tullia. The joy of love, for example, coexists with reason
but can only attain full perfection when joined to a physical experience. The
painterly beauty of Titian, and the writerly vividness of Aretino, serve Tullia as
models of this transfigured embodiment, which reverses the conventional relation
of active and passive by making the beloved a kind of painter who creates herself
in the lover.[21] On the other hand, her authority in Speroni's dialogue is reduced by
disagreement and interruption, which has led one critic to argue that he dismisses
her with contempt.[22] Actual insults target d'Aragona's literary prowess and
courtesan experience in the most degrading terms; the *Tariffa delle puttane di
Venezia* presents her as a vulgar whore who 'washes chitterlings in the Helicon of her
own urine'.[23]

Tullia d'Aragona's own contribution to the Renaissance philosophy of Eros
deliberately recalls, and modifies, the foundational moment of the genre in
Plato's *Symposium*: Socrates learned the central mysteries not from Alcibiades or
Aristophanes but from Diotima, and Tullia constitutes herself as the modern
Diotima (though she also resembles Socrates himself in her teasing professions of
ignorance (27/66) and her expression of intellectual verve through amorous
play). D'Aragona treats her male predecessors quite respectfully, synthesizing Plato,
Aristotle, Marsilio Ficino, Leone Ebreo, and Benedetto Varchi (her interlocutor in
this dialogue), but her gender and her courtesan's 'experience' give her a distinct
privilege. Tullia is quite decorous in her self-references, but she clearly articulates
the irony of asking 'a woman like me' to define love, insists on her word being taken
as truth if not 'alla autorità' then 'alla sperienza', a greater authority than any
'philosophers' reasoning', and overrides Varchi on the grounds of her greater prac-

[19] Fiora A. Bassanese, 'Private Lives and Public Lies: Texts by Courtesans of the Italian Renaissance',
Texas Studies in Literature and Language, 30 (1988), 299, records a pardon for d'Aragona countersigned
by the Grand Duke 'Fasseli gratia per poetessa'.

[20] ed. Alessandro Zilioli (Milan, 1864), 90 ('come ad una universale e onorata Accademia'); *Dialogue
on the Infinity of Love*, ed. and tr. Rinaldina Russell and Bruce Merry (1997), 109 (subsequent refs. will give
the original page followed by the corresponding passage in the tr., even when I use my own version).

[21] As Mary Pardo shows in 'Artifice as Seduction in Titian', in James Grantham Turner (ed.), *Sexuality
and Gender in Early Modern Europe: Institutions, Texts, Images* (Cambridge, 1993), 57–8, 86 n. 8.

[22] Janet L. Smarr, 'A Dialogue of Dialogues: Tullia d'Aragona and Sperone Speroni', *MLN* 113 (1998),
204–12, esp. 205.

[23] 54 ('mezzo palmo di budello | Lava pisciando il Fonte d'Helicona'); her literary reputation did sur-
vive into the following century, her *Rime* being re-edited in 1693 (Naples, ed. Antonio Bulifon).

tical knowledge of sexual love—which he is too ready to dismiss as 'vile and sordid'.[24] She certainly endorses the Platonist hierarchy of two kinds of Aphrodite—one 'lascivious' and popular, the other celestial and cognitive—but she refuses to divorce the higher Love from corporeality. Whereas Plato's Diotima proposed 'steps' that lead upward and away from corporeal and individual love, the Tullia-character argues that the fully embodied soul, the *composto* of mind and flesh, is actually nobler than the soul alone (26/65).

Countering the usual Aristotelian model of active male form and passive female matter, Tullia persuades Varchi that the (conventionally passive) 'loved one' is not only nobler than the (conventionally active) 'lover', but is in fact the true agent.[25] (Perhaps these theories gave Brantôme the sense that Italian training encourages women to take the initiative in bed?) Her rigid distinction between mere animal 'desire' and a higher love derived from 'reason' starts to unravel even as she expounds it, since the key words *ragione* and *desiderio* show up in both categories: each kind of love has its own 'reason' (61/89), and the higher form culminates in 'the transformation of oneself into the object of one's love, with the desire that she be converted into oneself' (*desiderio che el'a si transformi in lui*, 62/90). How then does this mutual transformation take place? Strict Platonists (and their *précieuses* descendants) claim that union can only occur in the 'spiritual' faculties of sight and mind, untainted by the material body: impertinently genital texts like *L'Escole des filles* will discover 'metamorphosis' and 'mutual exchange' in the most advanced postures (as we shall see in Chapter 3). Tullia opens the way to both developments. She concedes the superiority of sight and *fantasia*, but insists that corporeal, sexual union is needed to homogenize with the love-object 'as much as possible'. And here she encounters a split or cavity in the philosophical heritage that would resonate well into the following century. Like the libertines later, d'Aragona tries to reconcile Platonic Eros—a special kind of love that raises adepts above the animal stratum, the fusion of two separated halves of a primal being—with an embodied materialism borrowed more from Lucretius than from Aristotle. The higher, honourable love is infinite precisely because its devotees 'desire' the total fusion of body as well as mind, but Lucretius reminds us that 'bodies cannot penetrate one another'. True *desiderio*—the word is openly used—can therefore 'never arrive at its goal'.[26]

Varchi's final question for Tullia involves her even deeper in nuances that weaken the disciplinary attempt to separate good and evil love. Given that gross carnal lust ends the moment it has achieved its purely physical goal, how does she explain the continual and intensified desire of lovers after consummation? Lucretian impossibility only provides part of the answer. Tullia adds new, worldly considerations that clearly derive from her own incarnate 'experience' rather than from bloodless

---

[24] 31/68, 35/71, 39–40/75; it is difficult to agree with Smarr's assertion ('A Dialogue of Dialogues', 209, 210) that Tullia distances herself from her courtesan status.

[25] *Infinità*, 23/63, 33/70, and cf. 87–8/106–7; this reversal of the active/passive dichotomy was prefigured in Speroni's Tullia.

[26] 62/90; though they do not cite the common source in Lucretius, IV. 1110 ff., the notes to the Russell–Merry edn. show that Leone Ebreo provides the closest source for d'Aragona's readmission of corporeality (and simultaneous recognition of its impossibility).

theory. After the first enjoyment the goal becomes not primal union but *exclusive possession*—which seems to be equally impossible—and the inevitable jealousy spurs ever greater feeling. Even without this stimulus desire expands into addiction: 'they want that delight one more time, and then another, and so on down the line' (*di mano in mano*). The 'vulgar and lascivious' kind of Eros turns out to be just as infinite in its own way, not narrow and brutish but spacious and multiplex; Tullia admits that it has its own breadth or *larghezza*, its own *gradi* or 'steps'. And the boundary of the two kinds seems quite permeable: in lovers of the right temperament the lascivious can cause, and evolve into, the 'amore onesto e virtuoso' (just as the higher can regress into the lower or 'the domestic into the wild').[27] In these brief but suggestive explanations d'Aragona conceptually maps the internal architecture of obsessive sexuality, the space within which libertinism will build.

Tullia's philosophical rehabilitation of lust extends even to the borders of the unnatural. The longest section in the dialogue, and the testing-ground for all theories of embodiment, hierarchy, and visual beauty, is Tullia's interrogation of Varchi on the subject of 'Socratic' love between older and younger men. If we define her goal as an erotic-didactic synthesis, a courtesan's philosophy freed from the taint of *puttanismo*, then we can appreciate the problem she inherited from her predecessors: the most powerful literary models for the conjunction of Eros and Logos, the linkage of cognitive expansion with advanced sexual pleasure, were either 'Aretine'—heterosexual but low and 'pornographic'—or 'Socratic' and homosexual. D'Aragona sharply denounced the whorish obscenity of Aretino's *Ragionamenti* (despite her friendship with the author),[28] but could not wholly align herself with the intellectual defence of élite homoeroticism, beginning with the *Symposium* itself and Ficino's influential commentary. The prestige of this Socratic model prompts Varchi to introduce it as an alternative for Tullia to ponder, but its sodomitic notoriety prompts Tullia, in reply, to grill him especially hard about its corporeal implications.

    Both the historical and the fictional Varchi insisted on the 'pure' version of Socrates' love for Alcibiades and Plato's for the pupils of his Academy, admitting that they were indeed 'amantissimi' ('lovers to the maximum extent', 70/96) but denying them any physical consummation and thus distancing them from the institution of pederasty flourishing in contemporary Florence. But a strong countertradition in the Renaissance (as in the ancient world) asserted that Socrates' 'straight pederasty' really did involve physical enjoyment. In Castiglione's *Courtier*, for example, Cesare questions whether Alcibiades' bed was an appropriate site to demonstrate chastity in the middle of the night, and why, if the beauty of wisdom is the sole object, philosophers should seek it exclusively in gorgeous adolescents.[29]

[27] 80/102, 82–3/103–4.
[28] Cf. the preface to her narrative poem *Il meschino*; Aretino's allusion in *Lettere*, i. 295, suggests some familiarity and grudging respect between him and d'Aragona.
[29] Giovanni dall'Orto, ' "Socratic Love" as a Disguise for Same-Sex Love in the Renaissance', in Kent Gerard and Gert Hekma (eds.), *The Pursuit of Sodomy: Male Homosexuality in Renaissance and Enlightenment Europe* (New York, 1989), 46 (citing Castiglione, *Cortegiano*, III. xlv); for the unchaste Socrates, see 40, 44, 46, 49, 60–1, Juvenal, II. 10 (which openly calls the *Socratici* 'cinaedes'), and Lucian (Ch. 4 n. 15 below).

Montaigne assumes that physical consummation takes place in the 'noble Socratic coupling of body and mind', an 'exchange' of sexual favours for 'philosophical and spiritual intelligence'—a bargain that in old age he dearly wishes women would strike with *him*.[30] This corporeal reading of Platonic Eros produced its own libertine tradition, celebrating rather than denying sodomy, most fully realized in Rocco's dramatization of Alcibiades' seduction by his tutor, and later adopted as a model for heterosexual hedonism in Chorier—where the 'prurient Socrates' is often cited as a model of lascivious wisdom (Ch. 4, sect. 5 below).

For a century before Rocco raised the schoolmaster to high-libertine status the sodomitical pedant/pederast had been the butt of conventional satire, but in Varchi's case the 'Socratic' reputation had some documentary basis. His love-poems to young male pupils were so ardent that they embarrassed their recipients (as we learn from their own letters) and prompted accusations that he took only handsome pupils and 'stuck his lofty and deep knowledge directly into their brains'.[31] Tullia seems thoroughly familiar with the subculture of the *Socratici* and with the issues raised by the rumours against Varchi. She praises the nobility of Plato's vision—indeed, demands why it should not be adopted for heterosexual love, anticipating Montaigne. But at the same time she presses Varchi to admit the corporeal, erotic component. In particular, she asks why only beautiful, nubile young men should inspire this purely intellectual desire in philosophers.[32] In wishing to corporealize 'Socratic' love—and promote it to the paradigm of all Eros, irrespective of gender—Tullia emulates and goes beyond her major source Ficino, who had at least recognized that in philosophical circles 'those who associate with males have intercourse with them in order to satisfy the urge of their genital parts'. Ficino can downplay this 'natural' sodomitical conjunction because, according to his Platonic theory, 'the genital force of the soul has no power of cognition'.[33] At moments in Tullia d'Aragona, and at greater length in her seventeenth-century libertine successors, this separation of the cognitive and the sexual will break down.

2. EDUCATIONAL THEORY MEETS THE 'PORNODIDASCALIAN' TEXT

Montaigne's naturalistic praise of women's sexual cognition—'une discipline qui naist dans leurs veines'—plunges us into the central preoccupation of libertinism,

---

[30] Most of Montaigne's comment in *Essais*, III. v, on the 'noble harde Socratique du corps à l'esprit'—which I render as 'coupling' (literally the leash that couples hounds together) and Frame translates as 'exchange', since the woman 'buys' philosophy at the price of her 'thighs'—is written in the margin as an afterthought (875/684).

[31] Dall'Orto, 'Socratic Love', 54–9; Francesco Grazzini ('Il Lasca'), *Rime burlesche* (Florence, 1882), 29–30, esp. 29 ('poi che'l vostro sapere alto e profundo | ficcate lor s" tosto nel cervello').

[32] 72/97. Though Ficino (and 'daily' observation) is her main source, d'Aragona may also be responding to the end of the Speroni dialogue in which she herself had been featured and perhaps snubbed; as Smarr suggests ('A Dialogue of Dialogues', 206) 'the final image of the perfect lover as Ganymede, raised from earthly to divine love, might well make a woman feel insecure'.

[33] *Commentaire sur le Banquet de Platon: Texte du manuscrit autographe*, ed. and tr. Raymond Marcel (Paris, 1956), 229, a passage that uses the word *natura* three times.

at the intersection of philosophical, juridical, medical, and political discourses on gender and reason. Platonic theory like Ficino's recognized the genital-procreative urge as a function of the soul, but explicitly denied that any cognition was involved; Montaigne, like his libertine followers, conceives desire as a mental force (however compromised by the body). He canonizes his tribute to female ingenuity by citing Virgil's 'mentem Venus ipsa dedit', but what kind of 'mind' does Venus give? Since Virgil's phrase actually refers to the uncontrollable mental impulses of mares in heat, we must further ask: what kind of humanity does this naturo-didactic trope ascribe to the subject of arousal? Given these animalistic associations, in what way can sex be a *discipline*? How does the 'blood'—code name for other blood products like spirits and sperm—participate in education or 'engender' knowledge of itself?

Libertine 'schooling' texts exploit a contradiction developing within pedagogic theory itself, between discipline as curbing and discipline as fostering, between education as quelling the passions and education as developing the senses. Virtue is inevitably defined as the goal (for boys as well as girls), but theorists assign widely differing roles to the body as vehicle or obstacle in its achievement. Unorthodox thinkers like Leone Ebreo and Tullia d'Aragona modify Platonic theories of Eros-as-Gnosis to readmit corporeal love. As we shall see in the case of Comenius and Milton, the most idealistic educational theorists of the seventeenth century defined the senses as the origin of all knowledge and the passions as the essential component in salvation and enlightenment. In contrast, traditional masculinists and progressive feminists alike identified the body and its passions as the enemy of true education, the raw and tainted natural stratum that must be subjugated and transformed. One of the militant speakers in Moderata Fonte's *Merito delle donne*, for example, attacks those men who deny women basic education by pointing out that it is illiterate serving maids and ignorant plebeian women who give in to their lovers, whereas *scienza* teaches self-control, 'love of virtue', and the strength to 'abstain from temptation'.[34] A century later, Vanbrugh would update this assumption to comic effect (Introd. above): the suffering but virtuous wife bridles her desire by asserting 'philosophy', while the maid runs after pleasure because she is a *philosophe*—no longer driven by mere ignorance but by an alternative, libertine quest for 'knowledge'.

Though Fonte refutes the masculine slander that opening the mind inevitably opens the legs, she still chooses sexual transgression as her example of temptation. For women, as male pedagogues never tire of pointing out, one site alone served as synecdoche for the entire body and soul: sexual chastity was the supreme virtue without which all the others counted for nothing. (Juan Luis Vives's influential treatise on women's education, which spells out this doctrine with shocking clarity, goes into such detail about the dangers of unchastity that a courtesan could use it as her training manual.[35]) The gallant version of this reductive vaginocentrism taught that

---

[34] *Il merito delle donne* (1600), ed. Adriana Chemello (Venice, 1988), 168; *The Worth of Women*, ed. and tr. Virginia Cox (1997), 236–7.

[35] *The Education of a Christian Woman: A Sixteenth-Century Manual*, ed. and tr. Charles Fantazzi (2000), 64–172, and cf. Elaine V. Beilin, *Redeeming Eve: Women Writers of the English Renaissance* (Princeton, 1987), esp. 6.

women had a unique sensibility and expertise in matters of Eros—an idea as old as Plato's *Symposium*, where Socrates purports to have learned everything from the prophetess Diotima, and revived in d'Aragona's courtesan philosophy. Fonte herself unwittingly contributes to this sexual constriction of women's role; the all-female gathering dramatized in *Il merito delle donne* devotes the entire first day of their symposium to the qualities of lovers and husbands, confirming the traditional idea of the *gyneceum* as a 'Court of Love debating its finer points.

Assuming that Fonte's dialogue drew some attention as a work 'authenticated' by her gender, it may even have stimulated the libertine interest in exploring the educational development of transgressive women; though her feminist characters embrace a refined 'Platonic' model of Eros they seem fully cognizant of, and surprizingly sympathetic to, the 'other' kind of woman who openly solicits men or indulges those passions that render men inferior—referring not just to courtesans but to all women who take lovers (88–90). The author's gender and respectability (stressed in the forematter of this posthumous publication) would reinforce the notion of *Amore* as the 'female' subject par excellence, even though subsequent discussion ranges into law, politics, rhetoric, and science. By an irony that flourished under the double standard, libertinism assumed exactly the same vaginocentric definition of woman's essence, purpose, and talent, even though it celebrated what the virtuous school deplored. As we shall see in Chapter 4, Chorier's *Satyra Sotadica*—the most advanced and explicit dialogue of the seventeenth century, which claims to be written by a virtuous sixteenth-century woman author like Fonte herself—justified the fiction of female authorship by asserting that 'women are more capable of depicting these matters'.

To be 'born in the bloodstream' sexual consciousness must be seen as an extra-cognitive, physiological process, a precipitate of humours and concoctions, natural and therefore fundamentally immutable. Education can only hasten or delay this biochemical development. In this model Nature is conceived as a *force* (rendering certain restraints futile or pathological), though concomitantly it is also assumed to be a *limit* (rendering certain aspirations impossible). One English nobleman, for example, informs his son that women cannot be educated at all, except in the 'feminine' realm of sexual attraction and home economics: girls mature early in 'outward carriage, making small progress in any learnings after, saving in love, a little craft and a little thriftiness'.[36] Once again we see compliment and insult merge. The assumption of an exceptional sexual-domestic gift carries a heavy price tag: women's supposed aptitude for 'love' justifies their exclusion from every other part of the educational process, on 'natural' grounds.

Though libertinism and patriarchy are consonant in many ways, the libertine fixation on consummated sexuality unsettles the epistemological dichotomy of masculine 'apprehending' and feminine 'engendering'. If knowledge is 'born in the blood' then it must be transmitted by a kind of infusion or contagion. As long as this

---

[36] Henry Percy, ninth Earl of Northumberland, MS treatise dated 1609, cited in Anthony Fletcher, *Gender, Sex, and Subordination in England 1500–1800* (1995), 365.

transmission takes place between women alone—the master narrative of the libertine dialogue, culminating in the lesbian initiation-scenes of Chorier's *Satyra*—masculinity need not be implicated. But in a more arrogant variant of Montaigne's 'natural' education, carnal knowledge is engendered by the act of generation itself. (Mind or *mens*, in a Latin etymological pun, comes from the *mentula* or penis.) Donne's youthful elegy against a young mistress who has abandoned him after he has trained her, for example, combines this phallo-didacticism with a carelessly blasphemous reinterpretation of the Eden myth: 'I planted knowledge and Life's Tree in thee.'[37] According to this implantation- or infusion-model—often ascribed to pederastic philosophers like Varchi and Rocco, justifying their infatuation with a prize pupil—seduction *is* education, penetration *is* indoctrination; the *mentula* becomes the tree of life and knowledge, the agent of enlightenment, or (if we recall Secundus' point about its grammatical gender) the disciplining schoolmistress.

Montaigne offers us the starkly gendered polarity of blood or books, and Donne presents his own phallus as the best instrument for planting knowledge. In the history of libertine literature, however, the book is by far the more potent organ of instruction. We might even say that libertinism *begins* in a library. The Jesuit François Garasse's massive attack on the obscene poetry of Théophile de Viau, for example, did far more to constitute *libertinage* as a coherent stance or philosophy than any writing by those he attacks; Father Garasse needs his enemies to seem formidable and unified, and thus homogenizes libertine ideas as well as libertine subject matter into a prophetic 'Library'. The *Parnasse satyrique*, *Quintessence satyrique*, and similar anthologies of lewd lyric had rehearsed a repertoire of transgressive gestures, but Garasse's maniacally thorough taxonomy organizes them into an anti-Christian conspiracy, a methodical discipline with its own literature. This 'Bibliothèque des Libertins' binds the most disparate materials into a curriculum of canonical texts, grouping modern *satyriques* with ancient hedonistic philosophers and Renaissance materialists—though Garasse follows the Council of Trent in exculpating those classical eroticists who 'slide sweetly in by favour of their beautiful inventions'.[38]

The educational function of the libertine text may be inscribed into its very title. When Caspar von Barth turned one of Nanna's instructional dialogues into Latin, endowing it with the prestige, freedom, and internationalism of the classical language, he coined the learned-sounding Greek name *Pornodidascalus*—a parallel to *Erotodidascalus*, Barth's title for a collection of amorous verse.[39] The use of Greek confers an intellectual aura and prepares the sexual discourse to take its place among other disciplines rooted in the body, medical and legal. Barth anticipates

---

[37] Elegy VII ('Nature's lay Ideot, I taught thee to love'), line 26.

[38] *La Doctrine curieuse des beaux esprits de ce temps* (Paris, 1623), 781–2, 1016–17; for Trent see n. 84 below, and for Garasse and Théophile see Joan DeJean, 'Une autobiographie en procès: L'Affaire Théophile de Viau', *Poétique*, 4 (1981), 431–48, esp. 441, and Louise Godard de Donville, 'L'Œuvre de Théophile de Viau aux feux croisés du "libertinage"', *Œuvres et critiques*, 20/3 (1995), 185–218.

[39] *Pornodidascalus, sive Colloquium Muliebre Petri Aretini . . . Addita Expugnato Urbis Romae* (Frankfurt, 1623), in BnF Y² 12498–9 bound with *Erotodidascalus* (Hanover, 1625); cf. also *Pornoboscodidascalus*, Barth's Latin translation of Rojas's *Celestina*.

later pseudo-scientific coinages like 'pornography', and prefigures some of that term's ambiguity: *didascalus* firmly defines its central purpose as instructional, but *porno* presents the same problems as titles like 'The School of Women', confounding the subject and the object of teaching. Does the reader learn *about* prostitutes and thus how to avoid them, or is he (she?) implicated in a kind of teaching that *resembles* prostitution, a hard-core representation that itself constitutes an illicit act?

The medical discourse of sexuality also shares in this 'Pornodidascalian' author-effect. The English translator signs the name 'Erotodidascalus' to his popular abridgement of Giovanni Benedetto Sinibaldi's magisterial, Greek-titled *Geneanthropeia sive De Hominis Generatione*, and he even recruits the august Italian author (professor of medicine and personal physician to the Pope) as a 'Pornodidascalian'[40]—exactly the word that Barth uses to identify the mixture of forbidden instruction and illicit pleasure in Aretino's dialogue. This is not so much a desecration as a recognition that serious educational purpose can coexist with 'pornographic' entertainment, according to the Horatian principle of *utile et dulce* that Sinibaldi himself cites in his preface. Even in the original, the learned medical treatise defends its right to treat the subject of generation humorously ('jucunde') and to 'arouse' the reader erotically; indeed, works on this topic cannot succeed *nisi pruriant*, unless they excite.[41] Early modern sexology, in its erudite form as well as in popular 'how to' books, included vast amounts of material shared with contemporary erotica: salacious anecdotes, historical genealogies of deviant practice, biographies of famous sexual overachievers, and casuistic explorations of what one of Sinibaldi's sources called 'Medico-legal Questions'.[42]

Sinibaldi's encyclopedic *Geneanthropeia* lists the great sexual inventors of antiquity and devotes a whole chapter to 'bizarre', 'upside-down', and 'contraceptive figures' like the woman climbing on top of the man ('De Venere pendula, aliisque Veneris inconcinnis, infoecundisque figuris'), part of a section on the thousand different 'figurae' possible in copulation (cols. 841–2). The author of the English pocket edition, *Rare Verities, the Cabinet of Venus Unlocked and her Secrets Laid Open*, conveys this 'pornodidascalian' expertise in the most concise way possible: by displaying his knowledge of Aretino. Erotodidascalus ranks 'Aretine' with the same courtesan-authors of antiquity that Sinibaldi (like Brantôme before him and Chorier later) places at the head of his historic genealogy: '*Cyrene* invented twelve several wayes to delight her lovers, but of late times *Aretine* found out two and fourty, which he calls his Postures.' Translating the chapter on 'fantastical venereal postures', he cuts through several pages of learned commentary with the all-explanatory sentence 'See more in *Aretines* Postures.'[43]

[40] *Rare Verities* (1658), fo. A6.
[41] (Rome, 1642), title page, fo. ¯5; for the classical texts used in this preface (some retained in the English abridgement) see Ch. 4 n. 19 below.
[42] Cf. Paolo Zacchia's *Quaestiones Medico-legales* (1621–30), frequently cited in Sinibaldi.
[43] 31–2, 65; for Cyrene, the Greek courtesan called *dodecamechanos* or 'twelve-tricks' (and mentioned in Aristophanes), see Sinibaldi, *Geneanthropeia*, col. 241, and Ch. 4, sect. 4 below (Chorier).

The preface to *Rare Verities* articulates many questions endemic to the erotodi-dascalian project, in the form of objections from a friend of the editor that are then turned into publicity for the book's appeal. Moralistic readers can denounce the book's obscenity in public, but they will enjoy it privately, caught up in a solipsistic arousal that comes as much from their own brain as from the images on the page: 'their fancies immerg'd in its luxurious imbracements commit adultery with their own Chimeras.' Perhaps the book tends 'rather to incite an itching or titillation whereby women's may be disposed to conception, than to stir up the conception of learned men's brains'? Perhaps the author compromises his own masculinity, like the man who dressed as a woman (and shaved off all signs of his sex) to steal the se-crets of the all-female Bona Dea ceremonies (an exemplum also found in the origi-nal treatise). Perhaps putting sex into discourse, even in the guise of a responsible physician, inevitably violates female space or (as the subtitle promises) 'unlocks the Cabinet of Venus and lays open her secrets'.[44]

Alternatively, now that arcane Latin knowledge has been reduced to a small ver-nacular handbook, women could discover 'titillating' truths about their own bodies hitherto unknown to them, and this might empower them to excess, making every woman not only a *sage femme* but an anatomy professor of herself. Like that other self-help compilation *Aristotle's Problems*, access to these *Rare Verities* could make 'every Lady a Peripatetick, and sworn Philosopher'. The friendly objector describes this imaginary, intimate self-application in some detail: now that the book can be bought on the open market, chambermaids may 'roll over your pages' while scruti-nizing their own labia to see if they match the chapter on signs of virginity.[45] The self-help book becomes a kind of speculum. Literalizing a trope used by the most serious religious conduct-writers of the period, he invites girls to 'research their interior' as if it were a book, to 'leaf through their inner book to learn about the in-carnate word'.[46] And the body of *Rare Verities* does indeed select passages to interest a 'chambermaid' curious about her own sex. Reading the chapter on the clitoris, for example, she (he?) would find herself part of the ebb and flow of the seasons, chang-ing sex as easily as putting out buds: 'It is somewhat longer in the Summer than in Winter; for by reason of the heat, it inlarges it self, nay many times it issueth out, metamorphosing the woman into a man.'[47]

Despite this 'titillating' faux-concern with female self-discovery, Erotodidascalus and his friend argue most urgently for male concerns. They make explicit what Montaigne assumes in his comment on Aretino, that it is 'artificial' men, rather than 'natural' women, who need instruction in the 'facts of life' and who 'expect to find them in some exterior, perhaps written or printed body of exper-

---

[44] *Rare Verities*, fos. B7, B6ᵛ, B4, and title page (and cf. the idea of the author as Venus' picklock, B1ᵛ, B3); Sinibaldi, *Geneanthropeia*, cols. 154, 237–4.

[45] B4ᵛ–5 (cf. B7, attacking hypocrites who 'will tell you it is the spawn of *Aristotles Problems*'), B6ᵛ; the author himself evokes 'the longing Chamber-maide' on fo. A7.

[46] Pierre Coton, 1609 ('aidez moy en l'exacte recherche de mon interieur'), and Jean Aumont, 1664 ('feuilleter votre livre intérieur où on apprend la parolle incarnée'), cited in Ruth Ellen Larson, 'Women, Books, Sex, and Education in 17th-Century French Literature', Ph.D. dissertation (Yale, 1991), 44–5.

[47] 55, accurately translating *Geneanthropeia*, col. 536.

tise'.[48] Male readers competent to search the full Latin text of *Geneanthropeia* would find abundant answers to their worries: how to reduce the size of an over-large penis; how the seed is generated from the blood and spinal fluid; whether copulation can occur without love, and if so whether infertility can be caused by emotional estrangement (cols. 328–30, 578–609, 15). The preface to *Rare Verities* attacks the learned élite for keeping such useful knowledge locked away in a classical language, as if they want to make Englishmen so ignorant of generation 'that when they are married, they must be forced to come to them to be taught the way of copulation' (fos. A5ᵛ–6). Far-fetched as this sounds, in one well-documented case an English poet and intellectual actually did consult the Latin original during a bewildering marital crisis, when his wife left him one month after their wedding without having conceived. John Milton transcribed into his personal commonplace book Sinibaldi's opinion that loveless copulation was 'infertile' as well as 'cold, unpleasant, noxious, feral, and revolting'; whereas Sinibaldi adduced this as further justification for treating the subject 'jocundly', Milton uses it to insist that the innocent party trapped in such 'monstrous fetters' deserves a divorce.[49] *Rare Verities'* image of the clueless newly-wed matches Milton's thinly veiled self-portrait in the divorce tracts—the idealistic but inexperienced young man, fatally subject to errors in the realm of Venus.[50]

Educational theory of the mid-seventeenth century confronted issues of embodiment, gender, and sensory learning quite directly. As we shall see throughout this book, these issues raged most intensely in debates over women's education, reflected in the acrimonious definitions of women's 'philosophy' in Molière's *Femmes savantes* and in the hypersexual dialogues of *L'Escole des filles* and *L'Academie des dames*. But we can already trace their pressure in the best-known writings on general education, in the Europe-wide campaign for educational and social reform led by Jan Amos Comenius, and in Milton's responses to Comenius. In *Of Education* and other revolutionary pamphlets that address the political and personal crises of 1642–5, Milton even gives an essential educational role to the *pornodidascalia*.

Though he sneers at Comenius' new textbooks[51] and clings to the notion that classical literature can provide most of the knowledge a boy needs, Milton's programme closely matches Comenius' belief that the key to pedagogy was the apprehension of the concrete, material world, sequenced according to the natural development of the child and leading to the spontaneous, unforced 'flow' of wisdom. Comenius' personal motto, inscribed in a circle around an emblematic natural landscape, defines both the process of education and its product, the

---

[48] Herbert DeLay, '"Dans les reigles du plaisir . . .": Transformation of Sexual Knowledge in Seventeenth-Century France', in Wolfgang Leiner (ed.), *Onze Nouvelles Études sur l'image de la femme* (Paris, 1984), 15 (argues that *L'Escole des filles* 'transforms both man and woman' this way).

[49] Columbia edn., xviii. 160 (*CPW* i. 414), citing Sinibaldi's 'frigida, insuavis, infoecunda, noxia, ferina, foeda' (col. 15).

[50] See my *One Flesh: Paradisal Marriage and Sexual Relations in the Age of Milton* (Oxford, 1987, 1993), ch. 6.

[51] *CPW* ii. 364.

sensuous apprehension of concrete particulars and their conversion into a well-rounded, peace-loving, philosophical subject: 'omnia sponte fluant, absit violentia rebus'; 'may everything flow spontaneously, may violence be banished from everything!' He asserted throughout his work—in didactic theory, in proposals for universal 'mother schools' offering the same curriculum to boys and girls, and in textbooks like the *Orbis Sensualium Pictus*—that 'nothing in the intellect was not previously in the sense', that 'exercising' and even 'exciting the senses' lays the foundation for all wisdom and right action, that successful education must begin with 'reductio intelligibilis ad sensuale', that the pupil learns best when she (or he) experiences the object vividly, directly, and individually (*ad vivam autopsian*), uniting the physical and the cognitive into a single intense moment that remains imprinted in the consciousness.[52] Comenius' concept of 'living autopsy' or 'vivid self-witnessing' irresistibly suggests the reader of *Rare Verities*, exploring the leaves of her interior book. But the gendered implication of sensuous self-exploration evidently troubled him. Though he insisted on giving full educational access to males and females alike ('whether in Latin or in the national vernacular'), he hedges his radicalism nervously by citing a string of misogynist commonplaces against the woman teacher and the *erudita*. Like Montaigne, he himself becomes *eruditus* in sexual literature, citing Juvenal VI and a translation of Euripides that echoes the Virgilian line *Venus ipsa mentem dedit*: 'I hate learned women, because Venus herself gives them greater astuteness.' Rather than refuting these slanders like a good humanist, Comenius concedes their point and limits women's education to texts that inculcate domestic duties and make no appeal to 'curiosity'—that is, texts that fail according to his own pedagogy of discovery and 'excitement'.[53]

Milton's *Of Education* likewise insists on a 'solid' and physically grounded pedagogy, since 'our understanding cannot in this body found it selfe but on sensible things', and thought must begin with what is 'most obvious to the sence'. 'Orderly conning over the visible' provides the practical 'method' of attaining a wholly utopian goal—what Comenius called *Pansophia* and Milton 'an universall insight into things', which might even 'repair the ruin' of the fall from Eden. This Comenian 'reduction of the intelligible to the sensual', combining with a distinctly Miltonic belief in the educative role of the passions, explains the extraordinary prominence given to his own art. Future leaders will complete their schooling with rhetoric (for the public speaking required of them) and its inescapable companion, the 'more simple, sensuous, and passionate' art of poetry.[54]

For Milton, the educative 'exercise of sense' particularly involves the subjective senses, the emotions, and the erotic drive that according to Plato can be trained into a love of higher knowledge. Though *Of Education* ignores the question of schooling

---

[52] See *Didactica Magna*, in *Opera Didactica Omnia* (Amsterdam, 1657), esp. ch. 28 (on the Mother School, defined as an 'Excitatorium Sensuum', col. 171), and my 'The Visual Realism of Comenius', *History of Education*, 1 (1972), 116–17, 120. In Beckett's *Malone Dies* the (pseudo)Aristotelian phrase *Nihil in intellectu nisi prius in sensu* is taught to a parrot, who cuts it off after the first three words.

[53] *Didactica Magna*, cols. 43–4 (ch. 9).

[54] CPW ii. 364–9, 374, 404–6; the introd. and notes to this Yale edn. list resemblances to and differences from Comenius.

for girls and never specifically addresses the place of sex in the curriculum, the autobiographical passages in his political tracts—prompted by accusations of debauchery—assign a crucial role to erotic reading in his own education. His awakening began with Ovid's erotic elegies, whose explicitly sexual 'matter' is conveyed in a coy-seeming euphemism ('what it is, there be few who know not') which actually echoes the most erotic moment in Ovid's *Amores*; after Corinna has stripped naked and come to bed, 'Cetera quis nescit?' 'Who doesn't know the rest?'[55] Initiation into Ovid provided Milton with a literary model 'most agreeable to nature's part in me'; indeed, 'I was so allur'd to read, that no recreation came to me better welcome.' He then devoured the entire erotic-chivalric canon before moving on to Plato's *Symposium*, extracting useful lessons 'so that even these books which to many other have bin the fuell of wantonnesse and loose living, I cannot think how unlesse by divine indulgence prov'd to me so many incitements' to the love of virtue. Vice would lead from there to the 'bordelloes'—precisely the accusation that Milton's enemy had brought—and Virtue leads to the sage and serious doctrine of virginity, but both processes use the same 'fuel' and both start with 'allurement' and 'incitement'.[56]

Milton's expropriation of Socratic Eros, the last item in this self-designed curriculum, recurs whenever he tries to define the intersection of cognition and desire. Diotima's teaching in the *Symposium* provides the model of true marriage in *The Doctrine and Discipline of Divorce*, an oxymoronic 'intelligible flame' or 'rationall burning' (*CPW* ii. 251–3). His panegyric to wedded love in *Paradise Lost*—uttered over the copulating bodies of Adam and Eve in Eden and thus unmistakably sexual—praises it for being 'founded in reason' (the criterion used by Tullia d'Aragona and Leone Ebreo to readmit physical love) and for making 'known' all subsequent social bonds (IV. 751–7). When Milton deals with education directly, he transfers the properties of Eros to the desire for Gnosis itself: in a highly emotional verse letter to his tutor, he identifies their relationship first with the love of Socrates and Alcibiades, then with that of Odysseus and Penelope (reversing the active–passive roles by casting himself as the epic hero); in *Of Education*, he claims to produce 'infinite desire' in his pupils, 'enflaming' them with the love of learning and 'infusing into their young brests' a 'noble ardor'—an imagery of warmth and fluid injection that would sound quite familar to Varchi, Rocco, and their enemies. He goes further in stretching the meaning of 'sense', declaring young men 'of a more delicious and airie spirit' the 'wisest' and potentially the most responsive to the new emphasis on 'solid things' rather than empty words. Here and throughout his campaign to form a revolutionary élite, Milton makes it clear that his principal hope lies with those voluptuaries and libertines ('those especially of soft and delicious temper') whose senses are keener and therefore easier to awaken.[57]

---

[55] I. v, line 25, and cf. *Ad Patrem*, lines 90–2, for a striking imitation of Ovid's poem, when the nude Scientia visits Milton for a 'kiss'.

[56] *CPW* i. 889–91 (*Apology for Smectymnuus*).

[57] Elegy IV, 'Ad Thomam Iunium (Thomas Young)', lines 23–4, 55–6; *CPW* ii. 376–7, 385, i. 817–18 (*Reason of Church Government*).

In *Areopagitica*, itself an educational treatise as well as an attack on censorship, the necessity of passion is fully theorized and the Montaignean confrontation between the male reader and Aretino becomes an explicit theme. Milton defends 'the benefit which may be had of books promiscuously read', since not only is 'the knowledge and survay of vice' absolutely 'necessary to the constituting of human vertue', but the true adept must know 'the *utmost* that vice promises to his followers' (II. 516–17, my emphasis). Though 'promiscuous' reading need not necessarily mean sexual writing,[58] he explicitly posits 'objects of lust' as necessary stimulants for tempering the 'passions' implanted by God, and he even gives concrete examples of lascivious texts that prove the uselessness of censorship and the canonical status of the offensive: the 'wanton' poems of Ovid (which first 'allured' Milton and 'fuelled' his love of imaginary women), the *Satyricon* of Petronius, the hedonistic teachings of 'that libertine school of *Cyrene*' (499, 518, 495). (Though Milton refers to the philosophical school he must also have known, from Aristophanes and Sinibaldi if not from Brantôme, that the courtesan Cyrene taught 'twelve techniques' of coupling and was recognized as the direct ancestor of Aretino's 'postures'.) Their modern equivalent is 'that notorious ribald of *Arezzo*, dreaded, and yet dear to the Italian Courtiers' (518)— that is, Pietro Aretino himself, the original Pornodidascalus, the touchstone of outrageous extremity, the founder of a new 'libertine school'.

Areopagitica's argument for eroticized reading reshuffles the key terms in Montaigne's account of the eroto-didactic moment: now futility is associated with 'severest discipline', the misguided attempt to create virtue by 'banishing objects of lust' rather than cultivating them under control, and 'the registers of Aretino' are brought forward as an example of the depraved but vital discourse that must remain freely available to an élite readership. Now temperance is 'born in the bloodstream', since Milton conceives reading in physiological terms, as a homoeopathic agent 'provoking' antibodies and 'working' within to produce chastity rather than libertinism. Milton includes Aretino among 'the heathen writers of greatest infection, if it must be thought so, with whom is bound up the life of human learning',[59] and thus allows Aretine pornography into the category of educational literature, however toxic. And he confirms this intellectual designation when he describes Aretino and Petronius sharing with their fellow-courtiers 'the choisest delights and criticisms of sin' (518)—meaning not hostile critiques but sin evaluated, selected, and enhanced by critical intelligence. 'Choicest delights' arranged according to a libertine canon of taste correspond precisely to what is alluring about the Bible itself, which 'describes the carnall sense of wicked men not unelegantly'.[60] 'Criticism' allows the cognitive and the erotic to meet in Milton's mind, just as they meet in the seducer imagined by Ben Jonson:

[58] But Milton certainly uses it in this sense (496); 'passion' likewise has its sexual meaning already, here as in *PL* VIII. 530–1 (Adam recounts that on his wedding night 'here passion first I felt, | Commotion strange').

[59] ii. 518; Aretino can be included among 'heathen Writers' because, for the ultra-Protestant Milton, the term included 'modern *Italy*' (I. 812). For Milton's 'ethics of confrontation' see my *One Flesh*, ch. 5.

[60] 517; Milton uses *elegant* in its etymological sense of selection or choice, an essential process because 'reason is but choosing' (527).

> some yong *Frenchman*, or hot *Tuscane* bloud,
> That had read ARETINE, conn'd all his printes,
> Knew every quirke within lusts laborinth,
> And were profest critique in lechery. (*Volpone*, III. vii. 78)

Areopagitica thus anticipates Claude Le Petit's address to the 'Critique qui fais l'esprit fort | En matière de fouterie',[61] and Elisabeth Singer Rowe's more refined 'philosophick libertine', who 'made critical reflections on every enjoyment' (Introd. above).

'Choicest delights and criticisms of sin'—the programmatic enhancement of pleasure to the superlative degree—are virtually synonymous with 'the utmost that vice promises to his followers', essential for any student who wants to avoid superficial or childlike knowledge. 'fugitive and cloister'd vertue unexercised and unbreathed' (ii. 515). Discursive and cognitive boosting of Eros—precisely the goal of the hard-core curriculum studied below—may even enter the ideal marriage: in one of his divorce tracts Milton argues that 'the deed of procreation . . . of it self soon cloies, and is despis'd, unless it bee *cherisht and re-incited* with a pleasing conversation'.[62] Libertines make better husbands, Milton concludes, because their 'bold accustomings' give them sexual experience and wisdom (II. 249); Petronius, Aretino, and their progeny offer a vicarious version of this bold accustoming, a graduated and controllable discipline of sex. Hostile readers turned this commitment to the educational value of virtual carnal knowledge back on Milton himself, branding him 'a great agent for libertinism', deriding his divorce tracts as a Bible of promiscuity. One Restoration satirist, commenting on exactly the 'ribald of Arezzo' passage in *Areopagitica*, declared that 'the more modest *Aretine*, were he alive in this Age, might be set to School again, to learn in his own Art of the *Blind Schoolmaster*'.[63] The radical educational reformer now finds himself thrust into the role of Montaigne's 'schoolmaster Nature', the doctor of sex.

3. 'HERMAPHRODITICAL AUTHORITY': JONSON'S *EPICOENE* AS
   UNIVERSITY OF LOVE

Once sexual education migrates from the category of Nature to the category of Art—from 'discipline born in the blood' to 'choicest criticisms of sin'—it can be structured by the idea of *graduation*. The 'steps' of Platonic initiation (an idea given to the powerful if fictional female preceptor Diotima) are expropriated for the facetious equation of advanced sexual expertise with higher education, an area of achievement almost exclusively reserved for élite males. European universities occasionally admitted female prodigies like Anna Maria van Schurman, made to sit

---

[61] *Œuvres*, 107, 'Au lecteur critique'.   [62] *Colasterion* in *CPW* ii. 740 (my emphasis).
[63] John Warly, *The Reasoning Apostate* (1677), cited in George F. Sensabaugh, *That Grand Whig Milton* (1952), 51; Richard Leigh, *The Transproser Rehears'd* (1673), 136–7. Both refs. are gathered in Christopher Hill, *Milton and the English Revolution* (1977; New York, 1979), 109, 453–4.

in a cubicle at the University of Utrecht to screen her from the male students,[64] and
the private academies of Italy, despite their intensely homoerotic (and homosexual)
culture, extended membership to stars like the actress-author Isabella Andreini or
the composer Barbara Strozzi.[65] (The official academies of France, meanwhile, were
rigidly excluding women, as a reaction against their cultural hegemony in those private gatherings that we call *salons* but which contemporaries often called 'colleges'
or 'académies'.) A few women did achieve eminence in learning or pedagogy at court
rather than in college: queens like Elizabeth of England or Christina of Sweden
might have expected sycophantic praise for their erudition, but even the relatively
obscure Aloisia Sigea of Toledo received a papal eulogy for her expertise in classical
and biblical languages, taught classics to the Portuguese royal family, and was
praised by Guillaume Postel for 'surmounting' the achievements of both sexes—an
exercise in sublimity cruelly fulfilled in the following century when Chorier made
her the author of the most extreme pornography yet written.[66] Small in number but
highly visible, intellectual women formed a strong irritant that explains the enduring popularity of the erotic 'Female Academy' trope, which culminates but does not
conclude in Pallavicino's dedication of *La retorica delle puttane* to 'the University of
the Most Celebrated Courtesans'.

The notion of a 'Chair' or 'Academy' of Eros reaches back through a long history
in which the facetious and the serious are inextricably braided. Praise of Tullia
d'Aragona as the presiding genius of something 'like a universal and honoured
Academy' (sect. 1 above) undoes decades of sneering at the courtesan's intellectual
ambitions, but evokes that tradition in the act of undoing it. When Montaigne's heir
Marie de Gournay insists that in antiquity philosophers like Diotima and Aspasia
taught 'cathedralement et souverainement sur tous les hommes', she reverses a
satiric tradition going back to the Old Bawd in the *Roman de la Rose*, who has
learned so much in a lifetime of 'practice' that she feels she 'could teach theory from
an endowed Chair'.[67] De Gournay's remarks stimulated a growing interest in the
history of women's philosophy, yielding two entire books by 1700, but at the same
time provoked a pornotropic reaction; the second part of *L'Escole des filles*, we recall,
bears the title *La Philosophie des dames*.[68] In the faux-feminist continuation of the
popular *Caquets de l'accouchée* (in which a male voyeur-narrator pretends to have
infiltrated the birthing chamber, and reports the uninhibited *caquet* or 'chatter' of
the midwife and her all-female company), a 'woman who understands philosophy'

[64] *Whether a Christian Woman Should Be Educated, and Other Writings from her Intellectual Circle*, ed.
and tr. Joyce L. Irwin (1998), 5; Constance Jordan records a similar screening arrangement in the 20th
century, in 'More from "The Other Voice" in Early Modern Europe', *Renaissance Quarterly*, 55 (2002), 263.

[65] Cf. *Lettere di Isabella Andreini padovana, Comica Gelosa, et Academica Intenta* (Venice, 1612); Strozzi
was closely involved with the Venetian Unisoni and Incogniti, who included the author of *L'Alcibiade
fanciullo* (cf. Ch. 2 n. 47 below).

[66] See Odette Sauvage's edn. of Aloisia Sigea, *Dialogue de deux jeunes filles sur la vie de cour et la vie de
retraite* (Paris, 1970), 17–23, and for Chorier, Ch. 4 below.

[67] *Égalité des hommes et des femmes, Grief des dames, suivis du Proumenoir de Monsieur de Montaigne*,
ed. Constant Venesoen (Geneva, 1993), 42; Jean de Meung cited in Coci, *RP* p. liv.

[68] Gilles Ménage, *Historia Mulierum Philosopharum* (Lyons, 1690); Laurent Bordelon, *Theatre
philosophique . . . seconde édition augmentée des Femmes philosophes* (Paris, 1693).

formally argues for women's equality or superiority, repeating almost verbatim de
Gournay's comments on women's invention of the arts and their exalted role in
Plato and Socrates. The context, however, collapses this discursive and intellectual
self-assertion back into the comic-erotic. This protest against the *Caquets* itself continues those pamphlets: set in an enclosed women's bath-house and carefully
guarded against the voyeur's eye (though the female narrator claims an equal right
to bathe naked in the river), the titillating act of representation clearly violates this
space and constitutes the intrusion she fears.[69] Satire against the new feminist
'philosophe' revives the ancient topos of the Bona Dea, the all-female ritual that the
curious spy must witness even at the cost of shedding his manhood.

Male authors evidently felt compelled to don female disguise and penetrate, in
imagination, that inaccessible world behind the façade of virtue, where women supposedly generate and transmit the truths of sex. Men wanted to regard *themselves* as
the controlling source of all knowledge, the worldly authorities who inscribe their
expertise on the blank and innocent female; in Aretino, the young woman even
learns about her own clitoris from a male instructor (n. 6 above). Montaigne undermined this attitude, pointing out how men earnestly strive to learn the arts of
love from Aretino while women know them 'in their blood', taught by 'the schoolmaster Nature'. Obsession with intimate female-to-female instruction makes male
discourse a *caquet* too, and again Montaigne had recognized this: after losing himself in the endless sexual speculations of 'Sur des vers de Virgile', he finally describes
his own essay-writing as 'un flux de caquet'.[70]

By adopting an austerely virtuous self-presentation, most women authors
and educators aim to distance themselves equally from the cultured courtesan
and from the slanderous male assumption that linguistic prowess or fluency
necessarily meant a breach of chastity. The courtesan had long been associated with
'public' discourse, sometimes facetiously and sometimes seriously—as we have
seen in the case of Tullia d'Aragona, who assumes the leading role in discussions
within her own 'Academy' (and publishes the result). Patricia Parker evokes this
association to explain why women were debarred from learning rhetoric in
school, and Bridget Orr—trying to account for the female-to-female format of
pornography—relates it to 'a traditional masculine fear of mobile and public
femininity which would threaten order and property', a fear that led to the bridling
of scolds as well as the discouragement of authorship.[71] If female mastery of
language was equated with sexual incontinence, then conversely the sexuality of
the 'loose woman' was conceived as itself a kind of rhetoric—an idea pungently

---

[69] 'E.D.M.', *La Responce des dames et bourgeoises de Paris au Caquet de l'accouchée* (1622), in *Les Caquets
de l'accouchée: Recueil général, suivi de L'Anti-Caquet, des Essais de Mathurine et de La Sentence par corps*
(Paris, c.1890), 185–200, esp. 191–6; cf. Domna Stanton, 'Recuperating Women and the Man behind the
Screen', in Turner (ed.), *Sexuality and Gender in Early Modern Europe*, 247–65.

[70] III. v. 875/684; for *caquet* (and other gendered terms for soft or hard language) in Montaigne, see
Patricia Parker, 'Virile Style', in Louise Fradenburg and Carla Freccero with Kathy Lavezzo (eds.),
Premodern Sexualities (1996), 201–22, esp. 215.

[71] 'The Feminine in Restoration Erotica', in Clare Brant and Diane Purkiss (eds.), *Women, Texts and
Histories, 1575–1760* (1992), 199, citing Parker's *Literary Fat Ladies*.

expressed by Ulysses in Shakespeare's *Troilus and Cressida*. Reeling from Cressida's kiss, he exclaims

> There's language in her eye, her cheek, her lip—
> Nay, her foot speaks; her wanton spirits look out
> At every joint and motive of her body.

Bodily 'joints' become 'motives' of seductive eloquence; the gesture of sexual openness becomes a powerful kind of authorship, when Cressida and her peers 'wide unclasp the tables of their thoughts | To every ticklish reader' (IV. v. 55–61). *Satyrique* poetry offered this trope in a still more reductive form: 'Madame, your cunt is a splendid and erudite school; open it to the public free of charge, and you will make it even more famous than the religious Lycée.'[72]

Feminist educational polemic confronted this corporealization or envagination of women's intellectual ambitions. Paradoxically, while Comenius sought to base a didactic revolution on the material objects of the *Orbis Sensualium Pictus*, and while Milton devised a regenerative curriculum that gave pride of place to the 'simple, sensuous, and passionate' art of poetry, women called for a more purely intellectual and spiritual approach. Their own writings proposed new forms of celibacy, a willed asexuality or (in Astell's case) a secular nunnery, as the only solution to the all-pervasive sexualization of their sex.[73]

The equation of organized sex and public articulation or methodized language produced 'ticklish' meanings for each step of the curriculum, leading from Grammar and Logic to the higher discipline of Rhetoric. The University of Love trope flourished in the era of *L'Escole des filles* and *La retorica delle puttane*. Such jesting was encouraged by the Renaissance tradition of *serio ludere*, and by the affective, physiological terms used to characterize the scaled progression through the disciplines. Milton's *Of Education*, for example, describes the movement from logic to rhetoric as the opening of a hand, and emphasizes the affinity of rhetoric with the palpable and emotive aspect of poetry; the two arts differ only in degree, poetry being 'lesse suttle and fine, but more simple, sensuous and passionate' (*CPW* ii. 403).

However trivial, mock-institutional satires on the 'University of Love' reveal the process of disciplining sexuality, organizing the bewilderingly 'female' realm of the senses according to a single epistemic principle. The Spanish satire *Universidad de amor y escuelas de el interes*, for example, purports to show how women would run their own institution of higher learning: despite an impressive range of faculties (literature, logic, music, rhetoric, medicine, military science, fencing and riding schools) they only teach one subject—the extortion of money from the gullible male.[74] The French adaptation by Claude Le Petit, the libertine author most closely

---

[72] 'Ravery [Madame in 1619], votre con est brave et docte école', in *Le Cabinet satyrique*, ed. Fleuret and Perceau, i. 114.

[73] DeJean, *Tender Geographies: Women and the Origins of the Novel in France* (New York, 1991), 105–6, cites 'Le Triomphe de l'indifférence', a MS dialogue (contemporary with *L'Escole*, and apparently female-authored) in which two women argue for an absolute renunciation of love.

[74] By 'Antolinez de Piedrabuena' (Zaragoza, 1642), variously attributed to Salvador Jacinto Polo de Medina (BL) and Benito Ruiz (BnF), fos. 6, 6ᵛ–7, 8, 8ᵛ, and *passim*.

associated with *L'Escole des filles*, tries to vary this monomania by embroidering the sexual details, giving us not one but two enclosed systems of obsessive reiteration. The Salle des Fortifications crawls with Shandean puns on the depth of the *fossé* and the width of the breach, the Manège applies Pluvinel's famous riding manual to *chevaucher* in the sexual sense, while the School of Arms teaches the correct 'posture' for parrying thrusts 'inside, outside, on top and underneath'. Le Petit expands the original grammar-jokes in a direction suggested by Secundus: a 'beautiful little school-girl' examined on the question 'What gender is My Prick' ('M . . . V . . . cuius generis') replies in Latin 'feminini, Magister', explaining (with a respectful bow) that it earns the feminine gender because it has had 'so many women'.[75]

Throughout the literature of clandestine sexuality, in fact, narratives ostensibly about scandalous female self-fashioning reveal their covert preoccupation with masculine 'schooling'. In the English porno-biography *The Practical Part of Love* (1660) the mock-educational sequences—catechism, 'bawdy Lecture', excruciating puns on grammar—are introduced 'for the benefit of Female Students' (26). But in the more advanced sections, when the training proceeds from grammar school to the 'University of Love' (as in the two parts of *L'Escole des filles*), the description of intense but narrow research seems to portray male obsession rather than female self-discovery. The University Library features a single, well-worn volume with only two red-edged leaves; like the 'tables' of Cressida's thoughts, this 'two-leaved book' signifies nothing more nor less than the vulva itself, as if women's entire education could be reduced to that body part.[76] But advanced study in this female 'University' turns the most devoted men into equally one-dimensional beings. When the prostitute's clients get to 'Physicks' in their graduate programme they 'dive into the *deep mysteries* and *Secrets* of *Nature*, even losing themselves in the search thereof, in the caverns and hollows of the Microcosme; nay they even blind themselves in poring on their ——— *Book*' (34–5).

The most famous inter-articulation of sexual and grammatical meaning was Johannes Secundus' epigram 'Discite grammatici cur mascula nomina cunnus' ('Tell me, grammarians, why *cunnus* is a masculine noun and *mentula* is a feminine noun'), which the young Casanova, fresh from his reading in Chorier, cleverly reinterprets for the benefit of his English visitor: 'the slave must always bear the master's name' (Introd. above). But this kind of linguistic and grammatical humour flourishes wherever cracks open up between languages and bodies, grammatical gender and the human clefts or appendages that supposedly anchored gender difference in the physical realm. It is particularly reserved for 'unnatural' states of dissonance between conventional categories and personal desires: titles like *Hic Mulier* associate the assertive or 'masculine' woman with unthinkable solecism, while the

[75] *L'Escole de l'interest et l'Université d'amour* (Paris, 1662), 39, 49 (Le Petit's narrator offers the wrong answer 'n[e]utrius generis' and is then corrected by the 'belle Escolière', who 'would have liked to have the question in the middle of her belly'), 101–2, 105, 109 (comparison with the corresponding episode in the *Universidad de amor* shows that Le Petit has added each of these details).

[76] 40; cf. Le Petit, *Université d'amour*, 135 and for the slang phrase 'two-leaved book', not in *OED*, *The Poems of Thomas Carew, with his Masque Coelum Britannicum*, ed. Rhodes Dunlap (Oxford, 1949), 157–8.

counterblast *Haec Vir* accuses the foppish male of femininity;[77] undergraduate rumours about Milton's sexuality, which earned him the title *Domina* or 'Lady', are denounced as bad grammar and bad logic, giving feminine gender to what should
properly be masculine and failing to recognize that his femininity is accidental
rather than intrinsic.[78]

In sixteenth-century comedy the stock figure of the pedant-pederast, the schoolmaster too interested in his boys, brings on paroxysms of genital-grammatical punning.[79] In a crude but much-interpreted scene of Shakespeare's *Merry Wives of
Windsor*, the Welsh schoolmaster grills 'William Page' on the 'focative case' (IV. i).
In Giordano Bruno's *Candelaio*, the pedant invites his favourite pupil home to
'exercise' yet once more the adverbs *infra, in retro, ante, coram, a tergo, intus et extra*
(underneath, backwards, in front, face to face, from behind, inside and out), anticipating Le Petit's *Université d'amour* and Donne's heterosexual invitation to bed:
'Licence my roaving hands, and let them go, | Before, behind, between, above,
below.'[80] *Double entendre* runs in a different direction when he is arrested by the
police and tries to establish the respectability of his profession; inextricably, every
explanation of gender sounds like an admission of guilt. As he rattles off basic grammar he soon reaches the common gender (male and female together, as his interrogator exclaims) and the '*epicenum*, where neither one nor the other sex can be
distinguished'—a category immediately applied to himself. When he substitutes
'virile' for 'masculine' they see him (quite rightly) as enforcing a sense of 'what ladies
lack' and flaunting the *membrum virile* in front of his class of little boys. When he
protests that he really means 'the kind that goes with males' (*il geno che conviene a
maschi*) they whack him again because 'this is a women's thing'. He is female precisely because he is so male, *una cosa da femine* (despite his exclusive fixation on
boys) because his Logos reveals him determined by his Eros. As he is locked up for
professing 'the art of kid-shearing' he utters the intellectual's lament that 'verba
nihil prosunt', 'words avail nothing'—but in fact it is words that have landed him in
gender trouble.[81] Paradoxically, the pederast's verbal mastery renders him female by
making him equivalent to the learned lady, who *must* be incontinent because her
mouth has been set free.

Since access to Latin and Greek marked an important rite of passage forced upon
(and jealously reserved for) boys, we could read sexo-grammatical bawdy as in-
sider's play, a schoolboyish desacralizing of authority which nevertheless confirms
the sense of belonging to an élite. But humour need not destroy the possibility
of constructing sexuality as a field of knowledge: the trope also functions as what
Foucault called a *dispositif*, an epistemic sorting machine, categorizing and

---

[77] *Hic Mulier, or The Man-Woman, and Haec-Vir, or The Womanish-Man* (1620).

[78] Prolusion VI, Columbia edn. xii. 240.

[79] Cf. Leonard Barkan, *Transuming Passion: Ganymede and the Erotics of Humanism* (Stanford, Calif.,
1991), esp. 57–69.

[80] *Œuvres complètes*, i: *Chandelier (Il candelaio)*, ed. Giovanni Aquilecchia and Giorgio Bárberi
Squarotti, tr. Yves Hersant (Paris, 1993), 181; cf. 249 (a list of sexual postures include 'retoncunno', i. e. *retro
in cunno*, and Donne, Elegy XIX, lines 25–6.

[81] *Candelaio*, 279–83 (iv. xvi).

hierarchizing the truths of sex. When women are granted their own college (as in the title *L'Académie des dames*) we must recognize some triumphalist jeering at their exclusion from Latinate education and the techniques of self-presentation that went with it. On the other hand, constructing the higher disciplines as a *cosa da femine* makes them available for feminist appropriation: Moderata Fonte's *Merito delle donne*, for example, makes hay with both grammar and rhetoric, combining high hilarity with sharp analysis. Women must learn Latin as the gateway to all disciplines, but still men's grammar would differ from women's: their agreements are always wrong, they only know the passive form of *Amo*, 'their appetites know no parentheses', they recognize only masculine and neuter, accusative, dative, and ablative—whereas nominative, genitive, and vocative belong to women alone (139–40). Fonte's parody of rhetoric, an improvised but highly ornate address that reduces the all-female audience to laughter, rapidly modulates into aggrieved eloquence: 'Do not despise us, do not abandon us; consider that you are men because we are women' (133).

In its masculinist default mode, mock-educational humour sets up a roadblock on the frontier of Latinity, to police the crucial moment when boys leave the mother school and the maternal stage. As Bruno's pedant explains, vernacular language comes from the nurse whereas Latin weans or 'unboys' his pupils, an act for which he coins the ugly verb *dispuerascere* (75). It was at the start of their Latin course that boys would be spoon-fed the ideology of gender that Secundus and Casanova twist so elegantly: 'the Masculine gendre is more worthy than the Feminine, and the Feminine more worthy than the Neuter' (the undistinguishable Epicene having no stable place in this hierarchy).[82] Excluding girls apparently let boys realize their worthiness', but the presence of Latin-trained women like Aloisia Sigea, Elizabeth Weston, Anna Maria van Schurman, or Lucy Hutchinson, the first English translator of Lucretius' *De Rerum Natura*, provoked a reaction rather like the dirty joke analysed by Freud, at once inviting and banishing.[83]

Latin led not only to the professions but to a neoclassical world of bisexual sophistication and discursive freedom. The classical manner could suspend even the severest censure: the Council of Trent, vehemently prohibiting all books that 'professedly teach lascivious and obscene matters', made allowances for ancient erotica on account of their 'elegance and propriety of language'.[84] It was in Latin that Casanova read Chorier and played variations on Secundus, that the Chancellor of

---

[82] William Lily [et al.], *A Shorte Introduction of Grammar* (1567), fo. C5; cf. Elizabeth Pittenger, 'Dispatch Quickly: The Mechanical Reproduction of Pages', *Shakespeare Quarterly*, 42 (1991), 404.

[83] Cf. Hutchinson, *Memoirs of the Life of Colonel Hutchinson, with a Fragment of Autobiography*, ed. N. H. Keeble (1995), 14–15 (anxiety and 'emulation' provoked by her Latin skill), and Martha Moulsworth, 'Memorandum' (10 Nov. 1632), in *My Name Was Martha: A Renaissance Woman's Autobiographical Poem*, ed. Robert C. Evans and Barbara Wiedemann (West Cornwall, Conn., 1993), 5 ('Lattin is not the most marketable maraidge mettall').

[84] H. J. Schoeder (ed.), *Canons and Decrees of the Council of Trent: Original Text with English Translations* (1941), 547–8 (my tr.); cf. Paula Findlen, 'Humanism, Politics and Pornography in Renaissance Italy', in Lynn Hunt (ed.), *The Invention of Pornography: Obscenity and the Origins of Modernity, 1500–1800* (New York, 1993), 55

Florence wrote a mock-rhetorical address to the whores of Rome,[85] that the future Calvinist leader Théodore de Bèze wrote Catullus-like poems about the 'little slit' of a lady and the problems of satisfying his boyfriend and his mistress at the same time,[86] and an Anglican bishop expounded the pleasures of procreation.[87] Expert Latin forgery reconstructed the letters of Mark Antony and Queen Cleopatra, consulting a gynaecologist on how to diminish her lust and improve his.[88] Maria Thynne jokes in coded Latin about her husband's 'frequent rising',[89] and in language almost as garbled Bruno's schoolteacher reveals his taste for the 'rosy little lips and sweet little tongues' of boys (*roseorum labellulorum, lingulae blandulae*), and defines his ideal pupil as the 'appository of the fruits of my erudition and receptacle of my doctrinal seed', the young sapling or wand (*virga*) that he likes to 'bend' or 'erect'.[90] If women were learning to read about such polymorphous pleasures, they must be fenced out.

The grammar-joke and the Female Academy intertwine and expand in Ben Jonson's *Epicoene* (1609), whose superficially disparate plots are tied together by the associa-tive logic of libertine discourse. The full title of the comedy, *Epicoene, or The Silent Woman*, yokes together the indistinguishable gender and the unattainable ideal of masculinism: according to conventional misogyny, when women escape the mas-culine bridle and form an autonomous society they release a flood of *caquet* or noisy babble, which in turn signals their uncontrolled promiscuity; female silence would be just as oxymoronic or freakish as what Bruno called the '*epicenum*, where neither one nor the other sex can be distinguished'.[91] The title thus announces two double-headed creatures, and the action supplies a series of further monsters (even though the 'silent woman' turns out to be neither). Multifarious representatives of 'unnat-ural' sexuality—sodomite, hermaphrodite, eunuch, dominatrix, contraceptive expert—parade through the play, all of them (directly or indirectly) linked to the 'College of Women' that Jonson weaves into the picture with some violence. *Epicoene* gains in coherence if these scattered images of deviation are seen as permutations of a common trope, connected and interchangable elements of one controlling conceit—the sexual academy or structured 'College' of transgression.

---

[85] Leonardo Bruni's reconstruction of Heliogabalus' speech was reprinted in edns. of the *Scriptores Historiae Augustae* and added to Chorier's *Satyra* in the Elzevier edn. (Amsterdam, 1757).

[86] *Juvenilia*, ed. Alexandre Machard (Paris, 1879), *Epigrammata*, LXXIV (on an unnamed lady's *rimula*), XC (his love for Audebertus and Candida); for the later notoriety of these early poems, see Montaigne, III. v. 867/678, and Garasse, 780–1, 1016.

[87] Samuel Parker, *Tentamina Physico-Theologica* (1665), 99–108.

[88] See Ingrid D. Rowland, 'The Letters of Cleopatra and Marc Antony to Quintus Soranus: A Seventeenth-Century Forgery and its Motives', in Margaret M. Miles (ed.), *Cleopatra: A Sphinx Revisited* (Berkeley and Los Angeles, 2004), forthcoming (I am grateful to the author for a pre-publication draft); this text by Melchior Goldast (not to be confused with the real work of Cleopatra the Gynaecologist, Ch. 3 n. 125 below) was reprinted in all edns. of Chorier's *Satyra*.

[89] *Two Elizabethan Women: Correspondence of Joan and Maria Thynne*, ed. Alison D. Wall (Devizes, 1983), 37.

[90] *Candelaio*, 75–7, 115.

[91] p. 56 above; cf. Jonson's own definition in his grammar treatise, 'the *Promiscuous*, or *Epicene*, which understands both kinds, especially when we cannot make the difference' (viii. 507).

Variations of the 'epicene' are manifested in virtually all the play's subthemes, which seem at first only arbitrarily connected. The main plot involves the baiting of Morose, a one-dimensional 'humour' character who cannot abide noise and is treated to a series of farcical scenes involving trumpets, drums, and *caquet*; meanwhile the 'Female College' of independent ladies features in several satirical set pieces (on cosmetic artifice, on usurpation of male cultural privileges) but contributes little to the action. In Jonson's version, this serviceable trope berates women simultaneously for seeking education (in political science, divinity, or mathematics) and for imposing their own erotic definition of pedagogy, substituting sexual connoisseurship for true knowledge of the woman's duties.[92] The title-character Epicoene joins these strands by simulating, in quick succession, a mute submissive fiancée for Morose (who wants to marry to spite his nephew), an articulate, 'Amazonian' *femme forte* (who drives her new husband to distraction and gains admission to the College), and a seducible female for the pseudo-libertine fops who boast her favours. All these projections collapse in the closing moment of the drama, when this quintessential 'woman' is revealed as a boy in disguise.

Jonson's 'Female College' synthesizes classical and sixteenth-century representations of deviant sexuality and women's collectivity, and anticipates in miniature the *Wunderkammer* of unnatural lust in the more elaborate 'schooling' texts of seventeenth-century libertinism. Two of Jonson's Italian sources, however, raise an alternative if equally epicene model of 'collegiate' sexuality—the all-male relationship of master and youth. Bruno's pedant-pederast survives in *Epicoene* only in fragmented form, despite the flaunting of his favourite gender in the title; his comic Latinity has been transferred to another kind of 'woman's thing', the hen-pecked husband Captain Otter, while his taste for boys is reserved for the gentlemanly hedonists who drive the plot, manipulate the fortunes of Morose, and recruit the audience to their cause. Here Jonson borrowed less from Bruno than from the notorious Pietro Aretino himself, the universal 'register' of masculine self-fashioning.

In Aretino's comedy *Il marescalco* (*The Court Stable-Master*) the equally morose and eccentric protagonist is likewise trapped in marriage despite his characteristic aversion, tormented by aristocratic wits, and then released when the bride turns out to be a boy. But in Aretino the main character's 'humour' is an aversion to women *tout court*, and especially to the literate, creative (and therefore libertine) Renaissance woman that the duke pretends to force upon him in an arranged marriage; the Marescalco cringes at the very thought of his fiancée publishing her own poetry and enjoying Giulio Romano's hard-core engravings, *I modi*.[93] Jonson splits off this positive image of cultural autonomy and turns it into the grotesque Collegiates, revealing that he shares rather than repudiates the Marescalco's repulsion. It

[92] Cf. Ann Rosalind Jones and Peter Stallybrass, 'Fetishizing Gender: Constructing the Hermaphrodite in Renaissance Europe', in Julia Epstein and Kristina Straub (eds.), *Body Guards: Cultural Politics of Gender Ambiguity* (1992), 104 ('women eager *not* for education but for extravagant entertainment and multiple adultery', my emphasis).

[93] Pietro Aretino, *Teatro*, ed. Giorgio Petrocchi (Verona, 1971), 72. For parallels between the two comedies see *Ben Jonson: Volpone and Other Plays*, ed. Lorna Hutson (1998), p. xxxi, and Ian Frederick Moulton, *Before Pornography: Erotic Writing in Early Modern England* (New York, 2000), 211–19.

is the learned lady's confidence as a literary critic that earns her the insult 'hermaphrodite', and in his epigrams Jonson assails a woman writer in equally sexualized terms: in this acid cocktail of misogyny, homophobia, and writerly jealousy the female rival 'forces' her Muse with 'Tribade lust', inspired by a gender-levelling 'Epicoene fury'.[94]

Read as a palimpsest, Morose's neurotic dislike of 'noise' overlays and corresponds to the Marescalco's intense preference for boys, which generates and unifies the plot of Aretino's comedy; once the unwelcome bride is revealed as a handsome ephebe, the stable-master lives happily ever after. Suppressing this fairytale ending and converting Morose into a Malvolio-figure excluded from the comic finale, Jonson inverts the Marescalco's inversion. But Aretino's vision of the homoerotic ménage still appears at moments in *Epicoene*, showing through Jonson's overpainting. Morose's homophonic sequestration resembles the closet as a homophobe might imagine it: 'all discourses but mine owne afflict me', and he communicates with his subservient all-male entourage through a 'trunk' or tube.[95] Only seconds earlier one of the pseudo-libertines had been dismissed as a 'wind-fucker', so the audience is alert for analogies between folly and diverted sexuality, and for parallels between the different suitors of Epicoene. (Clerimont's ambiguous compliment to these 'wind-fuckers' also makes them hermaphrodites; told that 'you carry the feminine gender afore you' (v. i. 252), *they* think that they sweep the ladies off their feet but the audience sees the vulva appended to their front.) Jacobean decorum would not permit Morose to avow an 'Italian' preference on stage, but in his desperation to dissolve the marriage he does publicly declare himself 'no man' (v. iv. 265), incorrigibly impotent. His pretence neatly reverses that of the airy priapists, who boast of their affairs with Epicoene-as-woman and are then exposed as either liars (the obvious interpretation) or sodomites, as if they have been enjoying her qua boy all along. The fictional hypersexuality of the wind-fuckers and the fictional asexuality of Morose are further linked by comparison with the Marescalco, who likewise invents a medical condition in a vain attempt to get out of marriage. By confessing 'sono aperto' (87)—literally, 'I am open'—he disables himself from the active role in any kind of relationship, referring not to a hernia (the usual interpretation) but to the state of the lifelong catamite or the over-age boy prostitute: 'a Coach with 6 Horses could drive through my Arse-hole.'[96]

These glimpses of the sodomitic subculture become explicit at a crucial point in *Epicoene*. The happy union of man and boy—Aretino's concluding device—appears at the structurally opposite moment, in Jonson's opening tableau. The gentleman-hero Clerimont enters in the process of getting dressed, with his 'Boy', preparing to sing a song—musical talent being highly regarded in catamites, as the old bawd explains in Pallavicino's *Retorica delle puttane* (p. 82 below). When True-wit comes upon this scene he identifies it immediately: 'here's the man that can melt away his time ... between his mistris abroad and his engle at home' (I. i.

---

[94] 'An Epigram on the Court Pucell' (*Underwood*, xlix. viii. 222); cf. *Forest*, x (107).
[95] II. i. 177 (all citations from *Epicoene* give the act, scene, and page from Herford and Simpson, vol. v).
[96] Vatican MS Capponiano 140, *Dialogo intitolato la cazzaria*, 'Parte Seconda', fo. 93ᵛ.

165). The 'engle' or ingle means the passive partner in sodomy, the boy lover, the ultimate reward in Aretino's comedy and perhaps in Jonson's too.

This relaxed exposition-scene gives the audience a tantalizing flash of the boy-actor's talents, anticipating the Protean abilities of Epicoene herself, the 'gentleman's son' mysteriously 'brought up' for the last six months by another member of their circle, Dauphine—presumably in the same hothouse atmosphere that True-wit so expertly recognizes in Clerimont's 'soft lodging'. Clerimont's 'engle' vanishes from the plot after scene i, and the same actor might well have doubled as Epicoene. Clerimont's heterosexual mistress also disappears as a motif, and his final line in the play echoes this pederastic opening: when True-wit reveals the disguise-plot he simply remarks 'a boy', words that the actor can endow with the appropriate mixture of surprise and relish.[97]

The two gentlemen also use the first scene to establish two competing models of epicene sexuality. True-wit imagines Clerimont slipping easily 'between his mistress and his ingle', enjoying a 'soft', polymorphous erotic world in which men and woman compete for the boys. Something of this gender-bending excitement must have prevailed in the playhouse where all the parts were played by spectacular boys. Jonson himself alludes to the transsexual glamour of the boy-actor in his first play for the Blackfriars company, bringing onstage three high-spirited 'Children' who identify themselves as 'fine engles', and again when he makes Volpone boast of his amorous and thespian success with the 'ladies' when, as a young man, he played Hadrian's lover Antinous in a masque for Henri III; he also took special pride in acting as a tutor to Nathan Field, the probable star of *Epicoene*.[98] (Traces of this erotic charge can still be felt in Pepys, for whom Edward Kynaston, the last of the boy-actors, became by turns 'the prettiest woman' and 'the handsomest man in the house'.[99]) In these cases the fluidly theatrical youth appeals to women as well as men. Clerimont and the Boy, however, collude in a harsher and more exclusive attitude, closer to that of Aretino's Marescalco (or the schoolmaster in Rocco's *Alcibiade*, as we shall see in Chapter 2). They bond—musically and discursively—by rehearsing misogynist commonplaces, and particularly by emphasizing their physical disgust at women concealing their 'unsound' faces with greasepaint and plaster. The song ('Still to be neat') turns out to be not a serenade but a diatribe, and its anti-cosmetic obsession is echoed throughout the play, not only by Clerimont but by True-wit.[100]

---

[97] v. iv. 269–70; Clerimont does express some interest in heterosexual pursuit at iv. i. 219, when he rescinds his earlier insult about Lady Haughty's autumnal face, but this is clearly a feint to encourage a new plot-twist in which Dauphine makes love to all the Collegiates.

[98] *Cynthia's Revels*, induction, 40, *Volpone*, iii vii. 82; cf. Richmond Barbour, ' "When I Acted Young Antinous": Boy Actors and the Erotics of Jonsonian Theater', *PMLA* 110 (1995), 1006–22, and Mario DiGangi, *The Homoerotics of Early Modern Drama* (Cambridge, 1997), 67, 73–7.

[99] 7 Jan. 1661; cf. Thomas A. King, 'Displacing Masculinity: Edward Kynaston and the Politics of Effeminacy', in Andrew P. Williams (ed.), *The Image of Manhood in Early Modern Literature: Viewing the Male* (1999), 119–40, esp. 127–9.

[100] See I. i. 167–8 (lifted from Ovid's *Ars Amatoria*), ii. ii. 182 (from Juvenal), ii. vi. 197, iv. i. 219–20 (Ovid again), and cf. Morose's jeer at Lady Centaur's face-paint (iii. vi. 215) and Otter's exposé of how his wife comes apart (iv. ii. 225–6, from Martial; Jonson plagiarizes most when he attacks borrowed finery.

Clerimont's 'engle' acts as the link, sexual and dramatic, between the central wit-characters (plotting to obtain their desire and fortune by tricking Morose) and the Collegiate Ladies, who form a separatist community devoted to pleasures conventionally reserved for the élite male. As 'Epicoene' the juvenile lead conceals his true gender from even the most expert observer (since the audience is never let into the plot), but as 'Boy' he belongs in a different grammatical category, the gender that William Lily called 'commune of two'.[101] The ambiguous ephebe, between boyhood and manhood—or as Clerimont jokes, 'above a man' as well as 'under a man'—can pass freely into the all-female household, where he is treated as an erotic plaything, kissed, tumbled on the bed, and invited to dress in women's clothes (I. i. 165). Thus the homoerotic space of the first scene, the 'soft lodging' where wits and ingles co-habit, projects an image of an equivalent women's room; where we might see a variety of different houses (a *salon*, a place of seduction, or a women's refuge) Jonson evidently sees only the 'College'.

To confirm the association between pubescent sexuality and singing Clerimont warns the boy that he might find his 'voyce' or testicles strewn in the rushes on 'my ladies' floor (I. i. 165). Active and independent women must become castrators in Jonson's masculinist view, but their goal is not to suppress sexuality (as nineteenth-century psychology might have supposed) but to enhance it. Jonson's classical source, Juvenal's malignant satire on the excesses of Roman women, provides not only the general link between erudition and promiscuity—the learned woman demands that her husband 'lie with her' in Latin and Greek—but specific instances of her taste for well-endowed slave boys, selected for their impressive genitals and then castrated to preserve them at the height of adolescent potency.[102] True-wit returns to this epheberastic theme in his tirades against the Collegiate Ladies, who presume not only to keep up with the news, buy expensive fashions, discuss theology, criticize contemporary writers (including Jonson himself), and learn mathematics, but to 'kisse a page, or a smooth chinne that has the despaire of a beard'—evidently a male privilege like all the others.[103] At the very end True-wit returns us to the beginning by predicting that the boy Epicoene—'brought up' in secret by Dauphine, and now enlightened by the truths he has gathered from the female enclave—will become a sexual 'visitant' like the polymorphous 'Boy' in scene i (v. iv. 269–71).

By analogy with castration, Jonson associates the Collegiate Ladies with all kinds of artificial sexual interventions. They change their bodies into mechanisms by applying every known cosmetic device, committing what Clerimont's song calls the 'adulteries of art'. They make their own eunuch playthings (as Juvenal explains, to avoid the need for 'abortions'). Like the 'tribade' rival in Jonson's epigram they incur the hint of lesbianism, setting up house with a 'she-friend or cosen' (II. ii. 181). When Morose declares his impotence they assert their 'authority' in another way, eager to

---

[101] *Shorte Introduction of Grammar*, fo. A6.

[102] Juvenal, VI. 191 (*Epicoene*, II. ii. 181), 366–78 (followed immediately by lines on women's inordinate love of singing voices); for later Juvenal echoes see below, Ch. 3, sect. 4 (eunuchs in *Escole*) and Ch. 4 n. 51 ('concumbunt graece' in Chorier).

[103] II. ii. 182, echoing the *desperatio barbae* of Juvenal's eunuchs (VI. 367).

search his genitals for physical proof—so constituting themselves as the 'jury of matrons' or midwives whose intervention in impotence and paternity trials caused
more anxiety than reassurance.[104] The Academy clusters round Epicoene on her
wedding day to teach 'the colledge-Grammar', usurping the traditional mother's
role to transmit more libertine facts of life: how to rule her husband and extort expensive luxuries, how to visit '*China* houses' for shopping and assignations, how to
maintain affairs with multiple lovers in complete 'securitie'. Translating attitude
into physiology at every opportunity, Jonson spells out the secret discipline that
allows graduates of the College to operate with impunity:

EPICOENE (now Mrs Morose). Have you those excellent receits, madame, to keepe your
selves from bearing of children?
HAUGHTY. O yes, Morose. How should we maintayne our youth and beautie, else?[105]

Jonson's female 'College', the grotesque counterpart to the normative homosocial
gathering of boys and men, thus embodies the utmost that an advanced degree in
carnal knowledge might mean: doubling or eliding genders, confounding active
and passive, separating pleasure from procreation, 'fucking' the wind (or their
neighbour's ingle), 'searching', probing and snipping, altering the 'natural' body and
the deference that goes with it.

All these attempts to uncouple destiny from anatomy, for Jonson, constitute a
single act of sexual and political transgression—the assertion of 'hermaphroditical
authority'. The Collegiate Ladies' ambition to form independent judgements on literary matters, a prime function of the *salon*, automatically turns them into genital
freaks: in his remarks to Clerimont and his ingle in the opening scene, True-wit
brings out the accusation of dimorphism precisely to attack their critical faculty, as
they 'crie downe, or up, what they like or dislike in a braine or a fashion, with most
masculine or rather *hermaphroditicall* authoritie'.[106] Tribade, Epicoene, and hermaphrodite thus become major figures in Jonson's campaign to cry down the
female brain, and from Jonson they pass into the common stock of literary insult.
Edward, Lord Denny, called Lady Mary Wroth a 'Hermophradite in show' for
having written prose fiction, and she calls him a 'Hirmophradite in sense' for thinking so.[107] Aphra Behn was likewise declared a hermaphrodite for having 'neither Wit
enough for a Man, nor Modesty enough for a Woman'.[108]

---

[104] v. iv. 265; for impotence trials see Katherine Eisaman Maus, *Inwardness and Theater in the English Renaissance* (1995), 128–57 (130, 145–57 on *Epicoene*), and Pierre Darmon, *Le Tribunal de l'impuissance: Virilité et défaillances conjugales dans l'Ancienne France* (Paris, 1979).

[105] III. iii. 204, IV. i. 219, IV. iii. 227–9 (yet another detail lifted from Juvenal (VI. 595–7)).

[106] I. i. 167; contrast IV. vi. 246, when the College makes a topical allusion to 'the *french hermaphrodite*' to disparage excessively neat men.

[107] Wroth, *Poems*, ed. Jacqueline A. Roberts (1983), 32–4 (discussed in Jones and Stallybrass, 'Fetishizing Gender', 102).

[108] 'A Session of Poets' (*c*.1688), in Behn, *Oroonoko*, ed. Joanna Lipking, Norton Critical Edition (New York, 1997), 190.

4. INTELLECTUAL WOMEN, CARTESIAN PASSION, AND MARGARET CAVENDISH'S *FEMALE ACADEMY*

One can hardly overestimate the social and cultural upheavals of the eighteen years during which all the key texts of libertinism appeared, from the *Retorica delle puttane* in 1642 to the *Satyra Sotadica* in 1660. For many observers this turmoil was epitomized by disorderly eruptions of female agency—powerful regencies, religious and political initiatives by women, the emergence and eclipse of *femmes fortes* like Queen Christina, Madeleine de Scudéry, and the duchesse de Montpensier, whose *frondeuse* activism and subsequent retreat into fiction have been linked by Joan De-Jean to the emergence of the novel. By a paradox more apparent than real, this gendered apprehension produced not only a surge of 'porno-political' satires against the female academy,[109] but more serious appreciations of women's intellectual power (exemplified in Descartes's exchanges with Christina and Elizabeth of Bohemia), appreciations which nevertheless retain an erotic charge. Eulogy and satire mirror one another, high and low manifestations of the same sexualizing trope. My case studies will be Queen Christina as patron of erotic philosophy and founder of academies, and Margaret Cavendish as author of imaginary philosophical institutions; male efforts to eroticize women's higher education are particularly well articulated in her comedy *The Female Academy*.

The libertine woman–woman dialogue offers a kind of negative template of the female educative community. While new orders of teaching Dames were organizing schools and colleges throughout France, the mother-figure in *L'Academie des dames* plays 'la Maitresse et la Gouvernante' by fingering and flogging all the girls in her play-group.[110] Pierre Le Moyne's *Gallerie des femmes fortes* saw intellectual development diminishing the 'boundaries which separate' the sexes; *L'Escole des filles* defines the developing woman exclusively by those boundaries.[111] Madeleine de Scudéry's *Le Grand Cyrus* proposes a utopian commune of women joined in 'conversation', criticizes an educational system that forms them only for trivial 'galanterie' or menial household service, and—through her autobiographical character Sapho—particularly blames those women who have internalized male gender definitions, who scoff at her indifference to beauty or her refusal to define herself as 'wife to her husband, mother to her children, and mistress to her slaves'.[112] *L'Escole* seems to uphold this reform, by creating autonomous 'conversing' women who reject submissive identity and the confines of marriage, but in fact collapses Scudéry's critique by reducing their concerns to precisely the male-oriented *galanterie* she detests.

---

[109] e.g. *A Discoverie of Six Women Preachers* (1641), 6 ('I have declared some of the female Academyes, but where their University is I cannot tell; I suppose that Bedlam or Bridewell would be two convenient places for them'), *Newes from the New Exchange, or The Common-Wealth of Ladies* (1650), 2 ('an Academy').

[110] i. 109 (see Abbreviations above for details of this unique text, and Ch. 3 nn. 156–8 below for teaching orders).

[111] Ian Maclean, *Woman Triumphant: Feminism in French Literature, 1610–1652* (Oxford, 1977), 138.

[112] DeJean, *Tender Geographies*, ch. 2 *passim*, Maclean, *Woman Triumphant*, 139, 154.

The *femmes savantes* of Europe, thrown into prominence by the events of the mid-century, were perceived as interconnected and equivalent, and they prompted not just porno-political or Moliéresque mockery but serious eulogy and a fervent desire for patronage and approval. The English Parliamentarian Simonds D'Ewes, for example, enters into a triangular correspondence with Schurman and Bathsua Makin (tutor to the royal children) in which Schurman herself gives an erotic tone to the intellectual passion that bonds them: in the free medium of Latin she responds warmly to his enthusiasm for Makin, reminding her admirer—in language that recalls Milton's rapturous claims in *Of Education*—how 'you were upon that account inflamed with an incredible desire of having conference with me' (*incredibili accensum fuisse nos alloquendi desiderio*).[113] In classicizing epistles designed as much for the republic of letters as for the individual recipient, Schurman eulogizes not only Makin but Marie de Gournay and Elizabeth of Bohemia.[114] Princess Elizabeth and Queen Christina were Descartes's most significant patrons and correspondents, not only inviting him to their courts (killing him by exposure to the Stockholm winter, according to malicious gossip) but changing his philosophical agenda by the questions they posed. He urges his two princesses to communicate with each other, just as Simonds D'Ewes had linked Schurman and Makin.[115] Pierre-Daniel Huet, the founder of French novel criticism, compares Schurman to Scudéry and Christina,[116] just as the English revolutionary Hugh Peters links Schurman, Mary Cary, Elizabeth, and Christina as trophies of female virtue, in contrast to the alluring worldly woman with her 'naked Breasts' and 'black Patches'.[117]

Christina herself, though violently inconsistent on the subject of female educability, cultivated exceptional women in *both* the categories that Peters uses to define the 'daughter of God', seeking out both the famous intellectual (van Schurman) and the famous courtesan (Ninon de Lenclos).[118] In her patronage, as in the cultivated eccentricity of her personal behaviour, she combined the *libertine* and the *érudite*, bodying forth the association that runs through even the most idealistic praise—

[113] *Opuscula, Hebraea, Graeca, Latina, Gallica*, ed. Friedrich Spanheim (Leiden, 1648), 218, and cf. Clement Barksdale, *The Learned Maid* (1659), 48.

[114] *Opuscula*, 69 (citing Gournay's *Égalité* in a letter to Rivet), 281–7, 300–3, 318–20; *Whether a Christian Woman Should Be Educated*, 44, 55, 57–71.

[115] Jean-François de Raymond, *La Reine et le philosophe: Descartes et Christine de Suède* (Paris, 1993), 74, and Erica Harth, *Cartesian Women: Versions and Subversions of Rational Discourse in the Old Regime* (1992), 69–77, esp. 71.

[116] *Mémoires*, ed. Philippe-Joseph Salazar (Toulouse, 1993), 86–7.

[117] Preface to Cary's *A New and More Exact Mappe or Description of New Jerusalems Glory* (1651), fos. a2–3; cf. Sue Wiseman, 'Unsilent Instruments and the Devil's Cushions: Authority in Seventeenth-Century Women's Prophetic Discourse', in Isobel Armstrong (ed.), *New Feminist Discourses* (1992), 183, and *DNB* for Peters's embarrassing overtures to Queen Christina.

[118] Susanna Åkerman, *Queen Christina of Sweden and her Circle: The Transformation of a Seventeenth-Century Philosophical Libertine* (Leiden, 1991), 103, 301–3, and cf. 288 (a maxim in which Christina characterizes 'le sexe feminin' as a 'defaut de la nature' but then crosses out the last three words); in *Ouvrage de loisir, ou Maximes et sentences*, after several sweeping statements about women's unfitness to rule, she declares that 'temperament and education' create all the difference between the sexes (Maxim VII. 30, in Johann Arckenholtz (ed.), *Memoires concernant Christine, reine de Suede*, ii (Amsterdam, 1751)).

the shadowy presence of the erotic 'other woman' in all conceptions of female intellect. Even in a formal eulogy of Christina that sets her at the head of an army of virtuous scholars and queens, Ezechiel Spanheim feels compelled to bring in counter-examples like Sappho and Sempronia, who confirm the equation of women's learning and creativity with sexual or political enormity.[119]

Christina's questions for Descartes placed the traditionally feminine subject of erotic passion at the centre of philosophy. Even before wooing him to Sweden she presses him repeatedly to determine what love is, whether the 'natural' experience of desire applies to the love of God, whether love or hate does greater damage when it slips out of control, why the most intense form of love is felt for a particular individual. Descartes's analysis is careful to distinguish (rational) *amour* from (corporeal) *passion* on a theoretical level, but his language and his illustrations collapse that distinction; love is by definition 'a passion that makes us join willingly with some object' irrespective of its scale or value, an experience of merging into a single whole, an *inclination secrète*, an irresistible 'force' that flourishes independently of any rational sense of the individual's merit. In these responses to Christina he launches those vividly physiological explanations that would undermine his dualistic theories for his more materialistic followers. Heat presses on the heart, animal spirits flood through the veins, the soul 'joins' matter, and the thoughts follow predetermined channels in the cortex; to account for individualized love, for example, Descartes sidesteps any discussion of the soul and proposes that childhood infatuations carve the brain into 'folds' that predispose the adult to feel 'la passion de l'amour' for someone who resembles that first love.[120]

This interactive discourse on erotic theory, 'essential to Descartes's whole work and to Christina's intellectual and spiritual development', took the form of a mediated courtship ritual in which the French ambassador Chanut served as go-between or 'metaphor', transmitting her questions, receiving letters destined for Christina's eye, and phrasing her responses;[121] the Queen herself, while professing personal ignorance of the passion in question, eagerly interrogated Chanut about his friend's person and achievements, responding like a romance hero to 'the painting you have made of him'. Descartes in turn, rehearsing in this correspondence ideas that would soon be developed into his treatise *The Passions of the Soul*, draws his examples of real love from the 'reciprocal' feelings of the two friends and from Chanut's own adoration of Christina. Pondering the extremity of love and hate, he reveals a heroic, even sublime conception of Eros as 'infinite dynamism', building

---

[119] Summarized in Iiro Kajanto, *Christina Heroina: Mythological and Historical Exemplification in the Latin Panegyrics on Christina Queen of Sweden* (Helsinki, 1993), 92–3; for widespread sexual slanders against Christina, see Ch. 4 n. 37 below.

[120] Letters to Chanut, 1 Feb. and 6 June 1647, *Œuvres et lettres*, ed. André Bridoux, Bibliothèque de la Pléiade (Paris, 1953), 1257, 1264–7, 1277–8. Descartes illustrates his theory of early brain-folding by citing his own weakness for cross-eyed girls (1277); like later theories of the unconscious trace left by childhood experiences (dispelled by talking it into consciousness), Descartes's explanation pre-dates the phenomenon without actually explaining it.

[121] Raymond, *La Reine et le philosophe*, 68–9.

a bridge between Tullia d'Aragona's speculations on the Infinity of Love and his own remarkable conclusion in the *Passions de l'âme*, that in certain 'great' passions excess leads to the supreme good. For Descartes the physiological 'vigour' of love inevitably produces 'excess', which must be condemned when the object is insignificant (though even the most *déréglée* passion yields a certain 'pleasure' or 'spice'). When combined with 'generosity' and directed towards a genuine good, however, erotic love—the desire to fuse with the person or object that seems to be the other half of one's being—enjoys a special status. Other fundamental passions are only beneficial in moderation, but Eros 'cannot be bad'; even in its 'most excessive' form *elle nous perfectionne*, it 'makes us perfect'—exactly the word that Diderot would later use for the young man's erotic education while reading *Aloysia*.[122]

The eroticized figure of the absolutist philosopher-queen exemplifies this heroic excess. Chanut experiences not merely respect, veneration, astonishment but 'une très ardente affection' generating 'heat' as well as 'light', as Descartes can sense from the 'flow' or rush of his prose style ('car votre style coule si bien, quand vous parlez d'elle');[123] deducing amorous passion from discursive energy and conforming both to his theories of the hydraulic body, he prepares the way for the exchange of idea and arousal explored at length in *L'Escole des filles*. (Even the bloodless Pascal adopted an amorous vocabulary when addressing Christina, explaining the 'ardour' he feels for both his calculating machine and her royal approval of it, which would be 'le couronnement et le dernier bonheur de son aventure'.[124]) Christina herself prolonged this eroto-philosophical dialectic after Descartes's death and her own abdication, posing to her Roman Academy similar questions about love's definition, physiological hermeneutics, universal presence, and ultimate significance; even her metaphysical speculations on infinity and eternity revolve around the soul's capacity to 'satisfy the immensity of our desire'.[125]

The royalist philosopher Margaret Cavendish, Marchioness and later Duchess of Newcastle, emulated Queen Christina in the realm of imagination, establishing fictive universities and absolute monarchies[126] while criticizing gendered assumptions about women's access to those institutions. Like Christina (to whom she was often compared) she articulates contradictory opinions on the question of women's educability, veering from wildly misogynist dismissal of their 'natural' weakness to

---

[122] *Œuvres et lettres*, 1264–8; *Les Passions de l'âme* (1648), ed. Geneviève Rodis-Lewis (Paris, 1966), arts. 79, 101, 111, 119, 139 ('Je dis que cette Amour est extremement bonne, pource que joignant à nous de vrays biens, elle nous perfectionne d'autant. Je dis aussi qu'elle ne sçauroit estre trop grande; car tout ce que la plus excessive peut faire, c'est de nous joindre . . . parfaitement à ces biens'), 141, 145. The idea of valorized and eroticized 'excess' was common to pornography (*RP*, Ch. 2, sect. 1 below) and religious mysticism, e.g. St Teresa of Ávila, *Vida*, ch. 39 ('tan excesiva la suavidad' of seraphic penetration).

[123] *Œuvres et lettres*, 1264.

[124] *Œuvres complètes*, ed. Jacques Chevalier, Bibliothèque de la Pléiade (Paris, 1954), 502–4.

[125] Transcript of Academy proceedings, 1656, and autograph MSS, cited in Åkerman, *Christina*, 256–7; cf. her marginalia in BL C 60.e.1, Stefano Pignatelli, *Quanto più alletti la bellezza dell'animo, che la bellezza del corpo* (Rome, 1680), 2–89.

[126] See *The Blazing World and Other Writings*, ed. Kate Lilley (1994), 134, 138–53.

fiercely feminist demands for equal education.[127] Her favourite form, the women's academy or debating group, allows her to dramatize these contradictions by assigning unreconcilable views to a spectrum of 'female orators'. Some of her speakers argue for a fixed female essence or nature (either inferior or complementary to the male) and like Jonson condemn the self-transforming impulse as 'Hermaphroditical', while others argue for nurture over nature: 'Strength is Increased by Exercise, and Wit is Lost for Want of Conversation; but to shew Men we are not so Weak and Foolish, as the former Oratress doth Express us to be, let us Hawk, Hunt, Race, and do the like Exercises as Men have, and let us Converse in Camps, Courts, and Cities, in Schools, Colleges, and Courts of Judicature, in Taverns, Brothels, and Gaming Houses, all which will make our Strength and Wit known.'[128] By including 'Brothels'—a surprisingly libertine detail, suggesting the aristocratic disdain for decorum that shocked Christina's visitors—Cavendish reminds us that, despite all their jokes about the School of Venus and the University of Courtesans, it is men who link education to the institution of illicit sexuality.

In addition to these feats of rhetorical ventriloquism, Cavendish also speaks directly to the public in prefaces and letters signed with her own name. From this vantage she issues withering condemnations that seem to endorse the male prejudice against women's schooling: 'the Education and libertie of Conversation which Men have is both unfit and dangerous to our Sex, knowing that we may bear and bring forth Branches of another Stock, by which every man would come to lose the property of their own Children.' Learning breeds bastards, and training girls in superficial 'female' accomplishments 'makes their Body a Baud, and their Mind a Courtesan'.[129] It is clear, however, that Cavendish only criticizes the trivializing, eroticizing approach to women's education, contrasting it to an ideal that derives from the *femmes fortes* of Europe and the revolutionary political interventions of Englishwomen.[130] Like other reformists in the opposite camp, she addresses herself 'To the Two Universities', but on this occasion she unequivocally ascribes women's political exclusion to coercive masculine 'opinion' rather than 'natural' deficiency: 'we are shut out of all power and Authority, . . . our counsels are despised and laught at, the best of our actions are trodden down with scorn, by the over-weaning conceit men have of themselves.'[131] A year later she extends this critique from 'publick Imployments' to 'eloquent Pleadings'.[132]

---

[127] Cavendish's anti-feminism is largely confined to *The World's Olio* (1656), product of a brief period in which she believed that women were permanently disabled by soft brain tissue; her physiology changed to keep pace with her developing feminism, as John Rogers shows in *The Matter of Revolution: Science, Poetry, and Politics in the Age of Milton* (1996), ch. 6, esp. 202. For Christina and Cavendish, see Pepys, 11 Apr. 1667, and Sophie Tomlinson, ' "My Brain the Stage": Margaret Cavendish and the Fantasy of Female Performance', in Brant and Purkiss (eds.), *Women, Texts and Histories*, 158.

[128] *Orations of Divers Sorts* (1662), 228, 229 (summarized in Londa Schiebinger, *The Mind Has No Sex? Women in the Origins of Modern Science* (Cambridge, Mass., 1989), 55–7).

[129] *The Worlds Olio*, fo. A5–ᵛ; *CCXI Sociable Letters* (1664), 50.

[130] e.g. Mary Cary Rande, *Twelve Humble Proposals to the Supreme Governours of the Three Nations* (1653), 7 ('That the Universities be new modelled').

[131] *The Philosophical and Physical Opinions* (1655), fo. B2ᵛ (omitted in the 2nd edn. of 1663).

[132] *Natures Pictures* (1656), fo. c1 (a reference I owe to Amy Greenstadt).

The operation of male 'conceit', the reactive and defensive impulse behind male fantasies of female schooling, emerges most clearly in Cavendish's *Female Academy*. In this oratorical comedy, the ladies' institution occupies centre stage, flanked by two grates behind which the two excluded groups—men and non-élite women—gather to observe and comment. The set speeches of the Academicians, Matrons, and 'Lady Speaker' (educational and parliamentary terms being interchangeable) alternate with brief, colloquial scenes of response from the margins. Thus Cavendish can present the Female Academy as the given, the pre-existent establishment endowed with discursive authority and central presence. The men then improvise their own 'academy' in the wings, 'very angry that the women should speak so much, and they so little'. Their motive is defined explicitly as 'mockery', their arguments hinge on the 'sin against Nature for Women to be Incloystered, Retired, or restrained', and their frame of reference is relentlessly sexual. One gentleman, for example, reacts to his exclusion by boasting that if men *were* admitted, 'there would be work enough for the Great Matrons, were it but to act the Midwife'. The presiding figure at a female college must be a midwife, and by the same analogy their deliberations must amount to nothing but *caquet*, gabbling or 'clucking'. (Cavendish's jealous, intruding men repeatedly use the imagery of hen house and beehive.) Jonson had similarly associated the Ladies' College with the jury of matrons and midwives, identifying their main business as secret sexual debauchery (sect. 3 above), and Cavendish's contemporary Richard Flecknoe elaborates the conceit when describing a 'School of young Gentlewomen': 'As for their work (which they most glory in) you have frequent *exemplars* of it, how some one or other (ordinarily) makes such *work* with them, as the stitches can never be pickt out again without the *Mid-wives* help.' Cavendish now separates this attitude from the authorial voice and reassigns it, quite literally, to the margins.[133]

The more Cavendish's male characters argue against the women's restrictions, the more they reveal their own. The Female Orations cover a wide range of topics and ideological positions—theatre, friendship, literary criticism, discourse theory, the set disputations recommended in contemporary conduct manuals like François Colletet's *L'Académie familière des Filles*,[134] elaborate prescriptions for courtship that could come from the pages of Scudéry's *Le Grand Cyrus*.[135] Some of the speakers in Cavendish's *Female Academy* endorse a misogynistic view of women's abilities and reduce their 'Wit' to 'wantonness' (656); others assert, against the libertine equation of intellectual development with sexual penetration, that young virgins can be 'as confident and knowing as a Married Wife' without compromising their virtue (676). In contrast to this diversity, the male academy is founded on the narrowest premiss:

---

[133] Cavendish, *The Female Academy*, in *Playes* (1662), 651–79, esp. 656–9, 672, 674, 678; Flecknoe, *Enigmaticall Characters* (1658), 45.

[134] Cf. Maurice Magendie, *La Politesse mondaine* (Paris, 1925), 687 n. 5 (he has only seen a 1665 edn., allegedly appended to *La Muse coquette* (though not to the BL copy that I saw), but the *privilège* dates from 1659 and an edn. might have appeared then, which Cavendish could have seen).

[135] In *The Female Academy* as in *Le Grand Cyrus* women excluded from the group, either because of low class or fear of being 'damned' by men try to identify with male attitudes in order to regain admittance (659, 662), though later the Academy becomes modish and everyone wants to join (673).

our minds are so full of thoughts of the Female Sex, [that] we have no room for any other
Subject or Object; wherefore let the Theam be what it will, our discourses will soon run on
them: but if we could bring women as easily into our arms as into our brains, and had we as
many Mistresses in our possessions as we have in our imaginations, we should be much more
happy than we are. (659)

In more decorous terms, Cavendish makes an observation shared by contemporary
pornography: like the obsessive brothel-goers in *The Practical Part of Love*, these
spokesmen for their gender 'blind themselves in poring on their two-leaved Book'.
Her Gentleman Speaker admits two principles that male-authored texts normally
suppress—that men are the true prisoners of sex, locked into their monomania or
compulsion to spy, and that the discourse of erotic liberation compensates for their
inadequacy. Cavendish's boys describe their own minds as creating an internal
space or 'room' rather like the dressing room in Jonson's *Epicoene*, where se-
questered males pursue their boundless yet infinitesimal fantasies of 'Venus'
School'.

Clearly it is the discursive institution of the *académie des dames*, and not the particular content of their speeches, that 'whets' the anger of the male spectators,
prompting increasingly hostile diatribes and noisy raids to 'unroost' the female
gathering. (The play and the rowdy bravado end when Matron actually visits their
room, and with abashed respect they entreat her to act as marriage-broker—a conventional ending to which she assents because this is 'not a Cloyster, but a
School'.[136]) Masculine complaints focus on both the range and the self-sufficiency of
'the women's Lectural discourse'. One less prejudiced observer finds that 'the men's
discourses are simple, childish, and foolish, in comparison of the women', only to be
answered that 'the subject of the discourse is of women, which *are* simple, foolish,
and childish' (my emphasis). Here and elsewhere in Cavendish's plays, the male
commentator takes on the sex of the subject observed: in *Youths Glory and Deaths
Banquet* one Gentleman declares 'I wish I were a Woman', after realizing the natural
abilities of the philosopher Lady Sanspareille; here in *The Female Academy*, conversely, masculine representations take on the supposed nature of the 'subject', naive
and sensual like Fanchon in *L'Escole des filles*, articulate only in 'thoughts of sex'.[137]
As the objector points out, these qualities are nowhere evident in the speeches they
have heard, and must be deduced from otherwise invisible 'Actions'. This absence of
confirming signs only exacerbates the spectators' problem, however. Even more
frustrating than the ladies' confidence and sophistication is their calm refusal to acknowledge, reflect, or ratify the men's vision of 'the Female Sex'—and consequently
of themselves. The Female Academicians do notice the male company at the grate,
gazing 'through the Hanging', and they listen politely to the gentlemen's orations,
'but they take no notice of them in their literal Discourses, [and] they neither

---

[136] 667, 674, 679; Schiebinger suggests that the use of trumpets to dislodge the female swarm alludes
ironically to John Knox's *First Blast of the Trumpet against the Monstrous Regiment of Women* (*No Sex?*,
34).
   [137] *Playes*, 145, 669 (among the markers of libertinism denounced by Garasse (703–4) was the desire to
change into a woman).

mention the men, nor their Discoursings, or Arguments, or Academy, as if there were no such men' (672). Rather than talking 'men' into existence, 'they go on their own serious way, and edifying discourses' (671).

Libertine expropriation of the women's school hopes to penetrate that 'hanging' and demolish the 'edifice' of discursive autonomy. Cavendish's *mise en scène* thus provides a hermeneutic model for my study. The 'grate' or transparent grid that demarcates the Female Academy, the perforated screen that fixes men's gaze and places them literally in the wings, permits vision in both directions. My readings of the core erotic-didactic texts—*La retorica delle puttane, L'Alcibiade fanciullo a scola, L'Escole des filles, The School of Venus, L'Academie des dames*—will emulate Cavendish's critical reversal of the perspective, framing the male desire to constitute the 'female academy' in exclusively sexual terms, to 'have all bred up in Venus' School'.

Pallavicino's *Retorica delle puttane* and Rocco's *Alcibiade fanciullo a scola*

The Aesthetics of Transgression

> These books . . . open, not fond and common ways to vice, but such subtle, cunning, new, and diverse shifts to carry young wills to vanity and young wits to mischief, to teach old bawds new school points, as the simple head of an Englishman is not able to invent. . . . Commonly they come home common contemners of marriage, being free in Italy to go whithersoever lust will carry them.
> (Roger Ascham, *The Schoolmaster*)

> Sarà di mestieri mutar il piatto nella coppa per presentargli da bere, nel qual caso fingasi Ganimede coppiere di Giove . . . occorrendo talvolta il mutar sesso per incontrare la varietà, madre de' gusti.

> A real professional will transform the serving-dish into the cup, presenting it for him to drink, and on this occasion she should feign herself Ganymede the cup-bearer of Jove; she is sometimes obliged to mutate her sex to find variety, mother of pleasures.
> (*La retorica delle puttane*)

'PORNODIDASCALIAN' discourse repeatedly dwells on the conjunction of illicit sexuality, formative public language, and the power of women, and the 'University of Love' trope usually involves some attempt to imagine Eros as rhetoric.[1] Even Margaret Cavendish, Duchess of Newcastle—who mocks and marginalizes the male sex–speech association in *The Female Academy*, as we have just seen in Chapter 1—expresses her fascination with the 'Attractive Power' of the courtesan-philosopher Aspasia, who taught all the great men of Athens 'to speak Eloquently' and who gave oratory lessons to their wives, even though they 'might learn her Vice with her Rhetorick'; this 'Power lay in her Tongue, which was a Bawd for the other end'.[2] We might expect this sexualization of public speech in England, where the gravest political conflicts pitched parliament against absolutism. (In English Civil War pamphlets women preachers aspire to 'Rhetorick' and parlia-

---

[1] 'Antolinez de Piedrabuena', *Universidad de amor* (Zaragoza, 1642), fos. 9ᵛ–10ᵛ ('Rethorique Interessée' in Le Petit's translation, 57); *The Practical Part of Love* (1660), 34.

[2] *CCXI Sociable Letters* (1664), 63.

ments are formed by commonwealthswomen 'whose *rhetorick* is *Ribaldry*.'[3]) But in fact the seventeenth-century *libertini*, the last Italian authors to exploit the tradition of genital dialogue stemming from Aretino and the private academies, had already given erotic rhetoric a characteristically baroque complexity and extremity.

Both the major discourses of 'anti-natural' sexuality discussed in this chapter— the artifice-obsessed *Retorica delle puttane* and the pederastic *Alcibiade fanciullo a scola*—emanated from the same free-thinking Venetian academy, the Incogniti. *La retorica* models a simulated heterosexual passion on the public art of rhetoric from which women were largely excluded (as Moderata Fonte and Margaret Cavendish protest). *L'Alcibiade fanciullo* (ascribed on its 1652 title page to 'P[ietro] A[retino]' but actually written before 1630 by the priest, philosopher, and rhetoric professor Antonio Rocco) removes the didactic-formative power from women completely, by concentrating exclusively on the seduction of Alcibiades by his schoolmaster. Rocco splits the *didascalia* from the *porno*, and heterosexual representation follows suit.

These two discourses of 'academic' extremity might be less well known than the texts cited so far—Aretino and Montaigne, *L'Escole des filles* and the *Satyra Sotadica*—but they play an essential heuristic role in this study. (Rocco's homoerotic version of the didactic narrative seems to have escaped imitation, except for the striking dissertation on sodomy in Chorier, discussed in Chapter 4 below, but Pallavicino's treatise inspired the 1683 *Whores Rhetorick*, dedicated 'To the most famous University of *London-Courtezans*'.) Together these scurrilous contemporaries of Milton and Descartes embody the counter-didactic feared (and sought) by visitors to Italy, defining new possibilities of wandering 'whithersoever lust will carry them', as Ascham put it in his *Schoolmaster* (the first epigraph to this chapter).[4] But they unsettle as much as they define. By naturalizing perversity and alienating conventional heterosexuality, they collapse Montaigne's dichotomy of male 'learning' versus female 'engendering', bookish study versus 'discipline born in the blood'. By devoting the utmost erudition to sodomy and whoredom, they break down the hierarchy of mental *ingegno* and physical lust, or what Aretino called the 'doctoral' discourse of the intellect and the 'honeyed' flattery of the body (Ch. 1, sect. 1 above).

Pallavicino reveals passion as an 'apparatus' or construction, the product of 'art' both in the sense of fraud and in the sense of aesthetic achievement; whatever his intention, in effect he affirms the sensuality of rhetoric and the inseparability of high culture and low pornography. As my second epigraph suggests, *La retorica* emphasizes the performative mutability of gender and the centrality of 'Ganymede' as a figure of universal desire. Rocco promotes this Ganymedism with arguments that disturb precisely because they are so 'natural', domestic, moderate, and well supported (by gathering authorities from all the respectable disciplines). *Alcibiade fanciullo* 'queers' the easy distinction between the perverse and the normal, throwing

---

[3] *A Discoverie of Six Women Preachers* (1641), fo. A3; *Newes from the New Exchange* (1650), 16–17.
[4] (1570), ed. Lawrence V. Ryan (Ithaca, NY, 1967), 73.

into relief the ubiquity of homoeroticism and 'epicene' boy-love in less partisan texts.

1. FERRANTE PALLAVICINO: 'WHORE'S RHETORIC', DOMESTIC FICTION, AND THE LIBERTINE SUBLIME

Pallavicino's *Retorica delle puttane* ('Dedicata alla Università delle Cortegiane più Celebri') is the most elaborate example of the sexualizing tradition that Cavendish roasts on the 'grate' of her Female Academy. By presenting the education of the courtesan as a course in rhetoric, Pallavicino turns a minor theme in Aretino (the equivalent of ornate diction and advanced perversion) into the organizing conceit of an entire book; however satirical or moralistic his intention, he endows his narrow subject with something like the *larghezza* that Tullia d'Aragona found even in 'vulgar lust' or the imaginary 'room' that Cavendish found so lacking in male spectators of the women's academy (Ch. 1, sect. 1, sect. 4 above). His bawd-preceptor claims to provide a complete body of 'theory' for her pupil to put into practice (97, *la teorica*), proposing the same epistemic totality and the same relation of book to life that Casanova discovers in Chorier. Pallavicino gestured towards moralism by claiming to expose rather than condone prostitution, but this failed to convince the papal Nuncio in Venice, who denounced the *Retorica*'s trickeries or 'furberie' and fuelled the persecution that soon led to his arrest and execution (137). Alongside these brief concessions to anti-erotic didacticism, the renegade canon and aristocrat declares himself an 'adherent', even an adorer of the hated courtesan, a self-conscious adept in the 'art' he pretends to expose; echoing Aretino and Montaigne, he eulogizes the 'whore's rhetoric' by disparaging comparison to the arts of war, dedicated to destruction rather than procreation and pleasure (116, 7–8).

Pallavicino's choice of Rhetoric as the discipline most analogous to sexuality was appropriate in several ways. Rhetoric was jealously guarded as the cornerstone of élite male education in part because *female* oratory evoked the chaotic image of the 'public' woman. The two goals of the 'porno-rhetorical' trope—to discredit the cultural aspirations of courtesans by bawdy travesty of the disciplines from which they were excluded, to discredit the intellectual aspirations of élite women by equating them with incontinence and public shame—had been joined at least since the fifteenth century: Chancellor Leonardo Bruni amused himself by composing the Latin oration that Emperor Heliogabalus might have made to the whores of Rome, and at the same time counselled his humanist friend Battista Malatesta to master every discipline *except* rhetoric, which would destroy her reputation utterly.[5]

But misogynist exclusionism alone cannot explain the strange achievement of Pallavicino's *Retorica*. All satirical applications of the 'University' curriculum to advanced sexual practice generate a shadowy endorsement of the conceit they intend

---

[5] Margaret Ferguson, Maureen Quilligan, and Nancy Vickers (eds.), *Rewriting the Renaissance: The Discourses of Sexual Difference in Early Modern Europe* (1986), p. xvi; for his oration *ad meretrices*, see Ch. 1 n. 85 above.

to render unthinkable—the idea of bringing sexuality from the mute realm of 'Nature' into the domain of discursive construction, under female supervision. Just as Cavendish creates male characters who imagine women talking men into existence (or leaving them in limbo by pursuing their own academic interests), so Pallavicino ascribes a kind of ontogenic power to female representation. Rhetoric did not merely add ornament to language, but empowered it with *enargia*, inducing in the listener a 'faith' in the virtual presence of the referent, 'as if before the eyes'.[6] Consequently Pallavicino gives the courtesan the skill of an artist, able to fabricate sexual identities, even sexual experiences, while remaining coolly aware that they are 'chimeras', fictions, *furberie*. By an even deeper irony, this 'female' art creates a kind of artificial boy, a transsexual 'Ganymede' for the bisexual aristocrat—perhaps echoing Quintilian's comparison of florid rhetoric, not merely to woman, but to the manufactured effeminacy of the eunuch.[7] As we shall see, the literary artifice of the author merges with the fictive skill of the accomplished 'mistress', constructing a discursive-erotic 'edifice' as intricate and devious as the rhetorical manual that it travesties.

By pursuing the parallel of erotic and rhetorical 'theory' in such relentless detail, Pallavicino brings out the covert similarity between the two arts of persuasion—both of which confound the distinctions between public and private, emotion and intellect, effect and truth, controlled exterior and passionate interior. The crafty politician Lord Burghley summed this up in a riddle: 'Qu. What strumpet of all other is the most common prostitute in the World? A. *Lingua*, that common-Whore, for she lies with all men.'[8] (For hostile critics, of course, rhetoric *was* a harlot, dangerously seductive and excessively ornamented.) Rhetoric was at the same time an 'exemplary art', the model to which other forms of expression adhere,[9] and (as Milton's *Of Education* reminds us) a technology of emotion, 'sensuous and passionate' like poetry itself. Its central concern with emotional persuasion persists even in those new intellectual movements that reject ornamental eloquence. Cartesian linguistics analysed the moving powers of the orator in purely corporeal terms—a project that Pallavicino cleverly anticipates.[10] Philosophical sensationalism, in Locke as in Comenius,[11] based abstract reasoning in concrete physical feeling and freely used the vocabulary of 'excitement' for the communication as well as the formation of intelligible ideas.

Rhetoric enjoyed the highest cultural status, and yet its persuasive goal made it unashamedly 'promotional', instrumental, and stimulative—precisely the criteria

---

[6] Cf. Jean-Pierre Dubost, 'Libertinage and Rationality', in Catherine Cusset (ed.), *Libertinage and Modernity*, special issue, *Yale French Studies*, 94 (1998), 63, and Joel B. Altman, *The Tudor Play of Mind: Rhetorical Enquiry and the Development of Elizabethan Drama* (1978), 45 (Apthonius' *Progymnasmata* says *fabulae* are effective because they Fidem faciunt, quia verum veluti ponunt ante oculos').

[7] v. xii. 17–18 (a ref. I owe to Lorna Hutson).

[8] William Cecil, Lord Burghley, *Precepts* (1637), cited in Patricia Meyer Spacks, *Gossip* (1986), 123.

[9] E. H. Gombrich, 'The Edge of Delusion', *New York Review of Books*, 15 Feb. 1990, 8.

[10] Géraud de Cordemoy, *Discours physique de la parole* (1677), 147–73.

[11] A point I owe to Jayne Lewis; cf. *Essay Concerning Human Understanding*, e.g. II. viii. 7, III. i. 5, ii. 6, 8, and Ch. 1 n. 52 above for Comenius.

that are now used to distinguish art from pornography. Most recent condemnations of pornography (with the exception of the radical feminist critique, which allows no mitigation by artistic quality) depend on a Romantic ideology of art removed from 'interest' and 'arousal', free from goal-oriented persuasion and palpable designs upon the reader. But rhetoric—and arguably all art in the early modern period—was *supposed* to arouse. It placed narrative at the service of public causes in public places, even while recognizing that the act of persuasion itself was intensely private.

According to a typical manual such as Cypriano Soarez's *De Arte Rhetorica* (the explicit target of Pallavicino's parody),[12] the inner core of the listener must respond to the dynamism of an orator skilled in disposing language and bodily gesture for 'maximum force' to be 'in affectibus potentissimus', most powerful in its effect on the emotions. As Soarez insists, every 'movement' excited in the listener—and passionate physical 'motus' is the source and goal of the rhetor's art—must also be felt by the speaker; Soarez here combines the double authority of the orator and the poet, Cicero and Horace: 'if you want to make me weep, you first must grieve yourself.' The rhetorician unpacks his heart with words (as Hamlet said of whores), in a direct transfer of homogeneous feeling equally distant from aesthetic impassivity and from the homoeopathic purging of emotion by catharsis. Paradoxically, rhetoric uses the most intricate verbal artifice to create a natural bond of integrity between speaker and hearer, a sense that the text emanates from a heart devoid of 'simulation and falsehoods'. Once this representative bond is established, the orator can bend or 'flex' the listener's soul, captivate and sustain emotion 'without satiety'.[13] Other theorists of rhetoric assume that it provides access to 'the privie thoughts and secret conceites', defining *inventio* as 'the power which investigates hidden secrets'.[14] When Pallavicino's bawd-professor defines 'bodily eloquence' in terms heavy with sexual implication, then, she need hardly alter the already-eroticized language of the rhetorical trainer: the voice 'moves the affections by making its forces penetrate through the ears'; gesture 'ravishes' by 'insinuating itself through the eyes' (88).

Pallavicino's porno-rhetorical treatise follows the subdivisions of Soarez's school textbook, recast into fifteen lessons that supposedly represent the fifteen-day cycle of the waxing moon—a suitable structure for the 'female' appropriation of public discourse. The seriocomic equation of the didactic *corpus* and the gynaecological body is thus manifested already in the form, which culminates when the moon be-

---

[12] *RP* title page, 10, 32, 86 (1673, 81, an excruciating pun, obscured by Coci's modernization, which turns 'Priscian' the grammarian into 'P. Cipriano'); see Abbreviations above for details of the texts cited.

[13] *De Arte Rhetorica Libri Tres, ex Aristotele, Cicerone, et Quinctiliano Praecipue Deprompti* (Cologne, 1591), fo. A3ᵛ, 35, 83 (referring to Cicero, *De Oratore*, II. xliv–xlv, Quintilian, VI. ii, and Horace, *Ars Poetica*, lines 102–3, 'si vis me flere, dolendum est primum ipsi tibi'), 87; for a general study of Soarez, see Bernard Crampé, '*De Arte Rhetorica*: The Gestation of French Classicism in Renaissance Rhetoric', in Philippe Desan (ed.), *Humanism in Crisis: The Decline of the French Renaissance* (Ann Arbor, 1991), 259–77.

[14] Henry Peacham, cited in Brian Vickers, '"The Power of Persuasion": Images of the Orator, Elyot to Shakespeare', in James J. Murphy (ed.), *Renaissance Eloquence: Studies in the Theory and Practice of Renaissance Rhetoric* (1983), 422; Cicero, *Tusc.* I. xxv. 61, cited in Altman, *Tudor Play of Mind*, 51.

comes a full *tondo*.[15] The bawd-preceptor works systematically through each category; every aspect of the courtesan's art and life finds its counterpart in this sexual *Institutio Oratoris*, which simultaneously satirizes the methodization of Eros and the prostitution of rhetoric. *Inventio*, for example, allows her to capture any customer, and to prompt extra gifts on any occasion, by 'folding herself into all the forms, and adjusting herself to all the steps' (or 'degrees') that might increase her profit (25); the pun on *gradi* (which could also mean 'pleasures') combines two recurrent ideas, the graduated stages of the sexual curriculum and the social 'degree' of the client. Pallavicino's key term for fabrication is *chimerizare*, a word that might recall the readers of *Rare Verities* 'commiting adultery with their own Chimeras' (1658, fo. B7)—except that here the subject of fantasy controls the consumer's perception. In Pallavicino's eroto-didactic manual the goal of 'Inventione'—subdivided into Nature, Art, Exercise, and 'Mutation' (where the original textbook has only 'Imitatio')—is to 'chimerize all the forms suitable for giving pleasure', and at the same time to make a chimera of *herself*, creating the impression that her caresses spring from love alone.[16]

This methodical self-production requires the mastery, not only of *Inventio*, but of every step in the art of rhetoric. *Dispositio* allows her to shape her performance as four sequential stages: the Exordium, in which she snares lovers by demure glances in public, 'turning herself into a display apparatus or projection screen', the Narration, in which she creates an intriguing and affecting home life to involve the client more deeply and render her yielding more plausible, the Confirmation, when the lovers actually go to bed, and the Epilogue, the 'quintessence of the art of love', when the lover is sent off with promises of an infinite multiplication of pleasures.[17] *Elocutio* or Ornament applies equally to the verbal and the physical: the courtesan's dress and lodgings must be as aristocratic as possible, avoiding the least suspicion of plebeian poverty or whorish vulgarity; her linen, skin, and orifices must be scrupulously clean (astringents may be used 'to mortify nature, but not to confound it'); the skills of her tongue—synonyms, *doubles entendres*, songs, and comic repartees, as well as the art of the kiss—must generate variety by 'mutation', 'conduplicate' the bodily delights of intercourse, and revive the 'desire to enjoy' after it is over.[18] (Like Fanny Hill later, Pallavicino's elderly speaker assumes that sex is fundamentally monotonous, and that sexual discourse must constantly strive to avoid repeating 'the same terms'.[19]) The cognitive infrastructure, or what Pallavicino calls 'the interior of

---

[15] 87. Pallavicino's use of the lecture form rather than dialogue prompts Peter Cryle to call *RP* 'traditional', 'rigid', and 'inelegant'; *Geometry in the Boudoir: Configurations of French Erotic Narrative* (1994), 22, 33–6.

[16] 23, 29. Coci emends to 'imitazione' (23) but 1642, fo. B1, and 1673, 22, both read 'mutazione', either a corruption in the text or a deliberate mutation of the original 'Imitatio'; cf. Soarez, *De Arte Rhetorica*, 18–19 (also listed in Coci's appendix I, *RP* 153), and *RP* 69, 'mutazione delli amanti'.

[17] 36, 44 ('formasi un'apparato e s'estende quasi uno strato'), 46–51, 66, and cf. 76, where *strato* is used literally for smooth skin.

[18] 51–3, 65, 76–80; the text clearly says that art must be used 'al mortificare la natura, non a confonderla'—we would expect a milder word like *modificar*, but 'mortify' is the reading in both 1642 (fo. D10ᵛ) and 1673 (75).

[19] *RP* 65; John Cleland, *Memoirs of a Woman of Pleasure* (1748–9), ed. Peter Sabor (Oxford, 1999), 91.

the soul', must be 'adjusted' as carefully as the body and the voice: the *Art of Memory*, with its system of Places and Images, enables the sexual 'orator' to keep track of multiple lovers (stowed simultaneously in a warren of small bedrooms), while Images, in the form of painted nudes and Aretinesque postures, also help her to simulate rapture for those dull or repulsive clients who 'think every woman melts for them'. Corporeal *Gesture* then becomes, paradoxically, the 'soul' of rhetoric, the semiotic component that allows the courtesan to 'authenticate' her wholly inauthentic verbal presentations of desire.[20]

Pallavicino's eroto-didactic treatise does expose the mechanisms of fraud, but at the same time it documents—or constitutes—a major shift in the discourse of illicit sexuality: behind the scenes the courtesan is shown up as the avaricious trickster of the Aretino tradition, but *what* she represents has already been transformed by the domestic turn. (In language, too, the Pallavicinian preceptor distances herself from her foul-mouthed, plain-speaking ancestry in Aretino, adopting a clean, periphrastic vocabulary as well as a complex sentence structure.[21]) No longer the earthy whore or the grand Renaissance courtesan, the seductress must simulate a respectable woman swayed by genuine passion.

The 'whore's rhetoric' must therefore conceal its artifice behind a veil of domestic fiction. Her *narrazione* invents an intriguing and affecting home life to involve the client more deeply and render her yielding more plausible. She evolves from a coarse trickster into a proto-novelist, 'sweetening her narrative by weaving in fascinating incidents figured in her own person', by 'distinct induction of particular accidents of her own life': these 'interwoven' representations of private life include adopting a Petrarchan disdain, displaying signs of religious devotion, transforming rival customers into kinsfolk, and pretending to be an orphan or the abandoned victim of a treacherous and cruel lover.[22] Pallavicino in effect *rehearses* novelistic realism by showing how to construct a new form of subjectivity, a consistent and close-woven character 'unfolded' (*piegata*) in all its particularizing 'details'. Gesture, voice, motion, interior decoration, and reading matter should form an 'authentic' model of affective individualism that the gullible client takes as a real person feeling 'all the effects of a profound and sincere love', for him and him alone (62–3). The courtesan should 'manage' her persona (*maneggiare*, 89), should 'finga di singolarizare' (74), use fiction to create the illusion of a 'singular' desire—the individualized, ineffable, constant passion that Queen Christina would pose to Descartes as a central issue in the philosophy of love, the *grande passion* that would drive contemporary novels like those of Scudéry and Lafayette.

The English adaptation, *The Whores Rhetorick*, spells out this link to *préciosité* and emotive fiction even more clearly. When the courtesan needs to construct af-

---

[20] 22, 83–5, 88; for 'authentication' see n. 32 below.

[21] Apart from *puttana* the bawd (though not the author) avoids the gutter words that Aretino's Nanna prefers to genteel periphrasis (*Ragionamenti*, I. i. 38 [43–4]), and warns her pupil that 'licentious' and 'unbridled' language 'nauseates' the client (58).

[22] 42–4 esp. 44, 48; for a fuller treatment of this 'protonovelistic' element, see my '*The Whores Rhetorick*: Narrative, Pornography and the Origins of the Novel', *Studies in Eighteenth-Century Culture*, 24 (1995), 297–306.

fective subjectivity in the throes of what she wants to be taken as an overwhelming and constant love, she naturally draws on the resources of 'Romance'. The ultimate goal is to marry the customer (a possibility only briefly entertained in the original *Retorica*, 34), and this requires combining the trickery of Shamela with the reclaimed sensuality of Fanny Hill. The courtesan must simulate, not just intense passion, but moral crisis. Several long and emotional speeches (in the English version) rehearse the outpouring of a lover pleading for a more legitimate relationship, 'torn in pieces' by the conflict of love, shame, and religious guilt, and these high-flown effusions are inevitably linked to 'the old Romantick Heathens', to 'Romantick Ladies', or to '*Cleopatra, Cassandra, Pharamond*, and others of that nature' (*WR* 65–6, 106). One of the most central and enduring narrative devices of the novel—the particularized character who develops through a wrenching crisis in the course of a 'profound and sincere' emotional relationship—appears first as a whore's trick.

If rhetoric is the conjunction of art and persuasion, then one might say that in *La retorica delle puttane* 'art' corresponds to trickery (albeit highly sophisticated) and 'persuasion' to sexual arousal (however tarted up to resemble Romance). Some of Pallavicino's parallels between rhetoric and erotics assume this simple model and serve the same repetitive point; the prostitute must use words and gestures to create the 'narrative' of true passion, in order to conceal her real mercenary motives. Occasionally, however, Pallavicino's involvement with the idea of sexuality-as-art takes him beyond this dichotomy of erotic surface and financial reality. With an impassioned ingenuity far in excess of what his moralistic exposée requires, he tries to imagine a 'corporeal eloquence', a sexual equivalent to the figures and tropes of rhetoric (*RP* 88, *WR* 193). Shakespeare's notion that Cressida's seductive body constitutes a 'language' (p. 54 above) is now played out in minute detail. Following the rules of good sentence structure, the courtesan should 'gratify her lover in the position of her members, to place them in that part of the period which may create the best effect' (76, *WR* 108). The figure called *Conversio* involves those 'turning' positions where the lovers couple side by side or the woman climbs on top (65). 'Metaphor' or *translatio* (the transposition of meaning from tenor to vehicle) is created by 'translating, not the words, but the member from the proper place to the other improper one—improper with regard to natural laws but not with regard to pleasing the appetite'; as in *L'Alcibiade fanciullo*, sodomy is declared the pinnacle of the erotic art, 'the most delightful metaphor' (57). 'Cataeresis', or shifting the meaning of a word to one near it, likewise means anal intercourse (the two *erari* or treasuries of love being so close together), and 'ironia' allows her to deny this perversion verbally while admitting it physically.[23] When John Evelyn objects to his children making 'unnatural figures and usages of yourselves',[24] he surely means not only the pictorial 'postures' of Aretino and Chorier, but rhetorical figures such as these.

---

[23] 61–2 (Coci silently corrects to 'cataeresis' but the pun on 'erari' suggests that the reading 'cataeresis' in the early editions (1642, fo. C9ᵛ; 1673, 58) is what Pallavicino intended); cf. 196–7 for the Latin definitions of *translatio* and other figures by Soarez.

[24] Letter cited Introd. n. 52 above.

As the older woman explains these sexual tropes to her acolyte, Pallavicino restores something of the higher meaning of 'art' that he describes elsewhere in a letter on the courtesans of Venice: not merely deceit, but the aesthetic heightening of reality, the crafting or 'fabrication' of pleasure, the production of the self-as-work-of-art, 'transmuted into a picture'.[25] Fashioning the erotic self in *La retorica* involves all the arts, musical and plastic as well as verbal. Like a Renaissance sculptor she must transform physical matter to 'conform to the idea of Cupid' (93). The 'figures' of her rhetoric are 'the chief ornaments of the theatre of eloquence', the means by which 'the representation of your persuasive powers becomes alive' (55). The most perverted of these tropes constitute a 'sublime' art which generates the maximum pleasure from precisely those tastes and orifices that nature has made most disgusting (57). Anal intercourse is associated with fictive and performative metamorphosis, with the ability to 'transform the serving-dish into the cup', and 'feign oneself Ganymede the cup-bearer of Jove'.[26] The most complicated visual device in this rhetorical guide to Images—'the figures of Aretino gathered into a single picture'— serves as a 'theatre', a repertoire of erotic roles, a musical score for the sexual *virtuosa* to play 'a toccata on the organ of the senses', running through all the different images and 'registers', *accelerando* and *crescendo* (85). Thus she creates 'diversity, sole seasoning of earthly delight', and 'matches the genius' of the client by 'exquisite' performance. This association of music, perverse performance, and 'mutation of sex to find variety, mother of pleasures' (89), recurs throughout *La retorica delle puttane*.

The rhetorical 'art' of the sexual professor thus challenges not only the official narrative of tender, private romance but the libertine-naturalistic philosophy that Pallavicino himself adopts to defend his own treatise. In the 'Author's Confession' that concludes the book he cites the most advanced reinterpretations of Aristotle to argue that all sexual desire is 'natural' and that artificially retaining semen leads to death by poison. But where his scientific source defines reproduction as the central point of 'natural' sexuality, Pallavicino narrows his working definition to an essentially excremental model, asserting that ejaculation is as natural and necessary as urination. (In his dismissive closing remarks he even describes the courtesan as a *cacatoio*, a chamber-pot or toilet.) At the same time he twists the naturalist argument in a different direction: since the least salacious animals (such as the mule or the basilisk) are considered sordid or noxious, therefore the greater the sexual urge the more excellent the individual. Abandoning the usual Aristotelian preference for the *medium*, Pallavicino argues that 'even the excesses of lasciviousness are signs of glory'; it is 'natural' to find the most outrageous appetite in 'the most noble and best organized constitutions', the 'persons of greater esteem' for their military, intellec-

---

[25] Cf. *Continuazione del Corriere Svaligiato* (1644; 'Villafranca', 1671), 149–50; for further similarities with the *Corriere*, see Coci, *RP* pp. lxxvi–viii.

[26] 81, cited as epigraph above; for 'Ganymedes' as a familiar term for sexually available youths, cf. 40 and Joseph Cady, 'The "Masculine Love" of the "Princes of Sodom": "Practising the Art of Ganymede" at Henri III's Court', in Jacqueline Murray and Konrad Eisenbichler (eds.), *Desire and Discipline: Sex and Sexuality in the Premodern West* (Toronto, 1996), 139–40.

tual, or literary gifts.[27] Descartes's pornographic contemporary thus proposes a
theory of Eros which anticipates the valorization of 'excess' that the philosopher invented for Queen Christina (Ch. 1, sect. 4 above). Descartes even seems to adopt
Pallavicino's conception of the great man, arguing that the mighty flow of hot
animal spirits in heroic constitutions explains why 'Herculeses and Rolands love
more ardently than other men'.[28]

With a flair for paradox typical of the Accademia degli Incogniti, these naturalist justifications bring to a climax a treatise that consistently values art over nature
and intellectualized 'method' over emotion. Like Tullia in *L'infinità d'amore*,
Pallavicino's old courtesan uses her expertise in 'unnatural' variations to pose test
cases that confirm her analysis of Eros, but in *La retorica* these transgressions are
strongly endorsed. By creating postures like the 'grazing sheep', borrowing from the
animals without descending into animality, 'the perfection of art has supplemented
the simple crudity of mere nature' (*la semplice rozzezza della natura*, 95). Like Tullia,
the bawd seems quite familiar with the bisexuality of the illicit realm and the
ubiquity of 'Ganymedes' and 'bardassi' (or *Socratici* in Tullia's terms), who provide
a conceptual and performative model for heterosexuality. Her constant recommendation of sodomy reveals that the laws of Eros are quite different from the laws of
Nature: sexual 'metaphor' involves translating the penis to a place 'improper' according to nature but quite appropriate for the pursuit of pleasure (*improprio in
riguardo de' naturali decreti, benché non in compiacimento dell'appetito*). The 'art' of
sex 'becomes sublime (*rendesi sublime*) principally by means of this trope of translation, when to obtain greater pleasure the soul derives its tastes from the very place
where Nature has collected signs of abominable disgrace' (57).

The case against Nature deepens when Pallavicino suggests that the most refined
clients—those 'persons of greater esteem' whose 'excesses' should be most valued—
really prefer their boys, and so the fictile courtesan can only achieve 'variety' and
'spiciness' by emulating male homosexuality. Once again he expands on a hint in
Aretino's *Ragionamenti* (II. i. 179 [136]), which advised the young courtesan to dress
in boy's clothes for her aristocratic clients, as well as alluding to the actual practice
of Venetian prostitution.[29] She turns herself *into* Ganymede to please the man
whose fundamental taste is pederastic, offering her anus as a 'cup' of divine nectar;
he secretly desires the boy but covers himself by pursuing the female simulacrum. In
the English version she 'makes herself Ganymede' in a different sense, enjoying an
interiorized 'Picture' of her own contrivance—a beautiful youth identified as her
'*Ganymede*'—while fashioning herself on the outside as a figure of 'natural', submissive, spontaneously responsive, 'female' sexuality (*WR* 166, 168).

The courtesan's association with musical virtuosity likewise reinforces the primacy or priority of pederasty. She must always be prepared to 'mutate' or 'change

[27] 117–22, 129 (contrast 120, where he *attacks* excess); Coci links Pallavicino's naturalism to Rocco and
to the Paduan-Aristotelian Giacomo Zabarella (pp. xcii–xcvii, 118).

[28] Letter to Chanut, 1 Feb. 1647, in *Œuvres et lettres*, ed. André Bridoux (Paris, 1953), 1267.

[29] Cf. Guido Ruggiero, *The Boundaries of Eros: Sex Crime and Sexuality in Renaissance Venice* (New
York, 1985), 119.

sex to find variety, mother of pleasures', and music provides both the vehicle and the tenor for this transformation: she should not only cultivate her own musical skills but also become expert in sodomy, play a toccata on every part of her body, because the most valued members of the élite 'often take musicians and castrati for their lovers' (their *bardassi* or boy-prostitutes).[30] This *Epicoene*-like equation of the cultured public woman with the singing catamite may reflect controversy within Pallavicino's academy, the musical branch of which was dominated by the singer and composer Barbara Strozzi; one satirist blames her because, despite having been 'well educated' in the ways of 'amore', she 'lavishes all her affection on a castrato'.[31] As Margaret Cavendish prompts us to expect, Pallavicino's image of the anti-natural, instrumentalized, self-mutating product of the 'Courtesans' University' might parody the actual ascendency of the *virtuosa* in the Venetian academy.

Unnatural too—according to the Aristotelian paradigm that Pallavicino claims to be upholding—is the active role that the courtesan-artist must assume. Her traditional deference to the tastes and 'genius' of the customer is soon revealed as another simulacrum. The bawd-preceptor explains that the man should ordinarily choose the positions 'to be imitated', but it is the woman who tests them or puts them into practice ('approvare') in such a way that 'they accelerate and increase to the maximum the much-vaunted happiness of star-struck lovers'. Though the man believes himself 'the Author and Instructer in this piece of obscene gallantry', the courtesan retains controlling power over the script, ownership of the means of seduction: her verbal and pictorial 'figures' are the primary reality, her sighs and facial expressions 'authenticate the words', and the figures of Aretino—by 'insinuating' desire into the male through the eyes—'authenticate' her self-representation, 'authenticate the force of her persuasion'.[32] He becomes the material rather than the patron of her Art, the instrument on which she plays her toccata. To help her achieve this advanced degree of dominance, *La retorica delle puttane* provides the necessary cognitive control and the philosophy that underpins it. 'The whole thing is simply opinion', the bawd theorizes, and we can only extract satisfaction from what we can fabricate or 'chimerize' in our own minds (*chimerizar tra noi stessi ne' propri pensieri*); the *Whores Rhetorick* makes the even broader and more Hobbesian claim that 'the whole series of carnal satisfaction does purely consist in fancy' (*RP* 84, *WR* 167). The erotic 'University' transmits this philosophy of controlled mutation by a kind of perverse parentage: the scandalous didactic authority of the bawd, who creates the next generation of courtesans and replaces the moral authority of the natural mother, paradoxically generates 'variety, mother of pleasures'.

---

[30] 88–9; for real-life English aristocrats taking boy-servants as lovers because of their musical ability, see Ch. 6 n. 50 below (Rochester) and Alan Nelson, *Monstrous Adversary: A Documentary Biography of Edward de Vere, Seventeenth Earl of Oxford (1550–1604)* (Liverpool, forthcoming).

[31] MS satire cited in David Rosand and Ellen Rosand, ' "Barbara di Santa Sofia" and "Il Prete Genovese": On the Identity of a Portrait by Bernardo Strozzi', *Art Bulletin*, 43 (1981), 253; cf. Juvenal's juxtaposition of musical passion and sexual experiments with eunuchs (VI. 366–84).

[32] *WR* 175; *RP* 65, 84–5, 91–2, 96 (the word in each case is *auttenticare*); for repeated instructions to match the *genio* of the client, see 27, 45, 85, and 90–1.

Rhetorical theory, as we have seen, contained within itself the paradox that Pallavicino adopts for sexual discourse: Art produces Nature, Intellect produces Passion, verbal manipulation produces emotional sincerity. Rhetoric was an art of the person as well as the text. In Soarez's terms, its 'maximum force' and 'most powerful affect' was generated by the combination of word, voice, gesture, and bodily energy (p. 76 above). As a rhetor, the trainee seductress must follow the lead of Demosthenes, who rehearsed every detail of gesture and deportment in front of a full-length mirror. (Here Pallavicino borrows yet again from Aretino, whose uneducated bawd likewise insists on studying gestures in the mirror, but the learned parallel with ancient Greece is entirely new.[33]) The seventeenth-century *cortegiana* inherits and acts out the central paradox in Castiglione's *Cortegiano*—that the courtier can only achieve the spontaneous inbred grace of *sprezzatura* by practising furiously in private (II. xxxviii).

Pallavicino and the English adaptor both insist on this Demosthenean self-fashioning as a perfect guide to the whore's 'new modelled Fabrick', a complete and methodical reconstruction of her 'face' that goes far beyond the self-adornment conventionally associated with 'women'. Like Castiglione's courtier, she must scrutinize every detail, from the façade of her house to her movements and exclamations in bed, and transform it into the appropriate sign of upper-class refinement and delicate sensibility; she must particularly eliminate the sort of violent movements 'proprio di facchini', suitable for porters (93). Like Aretino's Pippa, she must apply herself to her mirror in private, to be ready for the aristocratic client who will pose her in front of another, larger mirror that displays her in multiple postures. This preoccupation with literal and metaphorical mirroring, in rhetoric and courtly theory, might suggest the lack of an authentic 'central self'.[34] But the rhetorical manuals insist (as we have seen) that the orator's self-transformation should not just deal with the outside; virtually every treatise emphasizes the speaker's need for genuine feeling and 'privy thoughts', even when they drop the claim that the speaker must be ethically good in order to speak well.[35] Soarez in particular, an official handbook of Jesuit education for over a hundred years, is thoroughly imbued with Counter-Reformation interiority.

When raised to 'disciplinary' status, then, the scandalous arts of sexual arousal seem quite compatible with the prestigious arts of persuasion: rhetoric, only slightly less 'sensuous and passionate' than poetry, allowed no theoretical basis for distinguishing what we now call 'art' and 'pornography'. But Pallavicino adds a new twist—exploiting the potential contradiction, in official rhetoric, between artifice and integrity. For the whore's 'heart' is entirely fictitious. She 'folds herself', turns

---

[33] *RP* 94; *WR* 216–17, 221; *Ragionamenti*, II. i. 224 [233], and contrast II. ii. 274 [285].

[34] Cf. Richard Lanham, *The Motives of Eloquence: Literary Rhetoric in the Renaissance* (1976), 112.

[35] Cf. Joachim Dyck, 'The First German Treatise on Homiletics: Erasmus Sarcer's *Pastorale* and Classical Rhetoric', in Murphy (ed.), *Renaissance Eloquence*, 234–5, Vickers, 'Power of Persuasion', 419–22, and Judith Rice Henderson, 'Must a Good Orator Be a Good Man? Ramus in the Ciceronian Controversy', in Peter L. Oesterreich and Thomas O. Sloane (eds.), *Rhetorica Movet: Studies in Historical and Modern Rhetoric in Honour of Heinrich F. Plett* (Leiden, 1999), 43–56.

herself into a fictitious monster (*chimerizarsi*), 'stretches herself' into a surface or screen (*strato*), builds herself as an *apparato*, a controlled simulacrum of the passionate self-abandon that male customers like to think they inspire in 'women'. She precisely reverses the *libertin* formula 'inside according to pleasure, outside according to social convention' (*intus ut placet, foris ut moris*):[36] her exterior is all 'pleasure', whereas inside she must be 'dead to the world' like a nun entering the cloister (87), devoid of any response or feeling except the pleasures of control, security, and profit. All the meanings of *discipline* come together in this insistence on rigorous, ascetic self-denial. 'This rhetoric', the old professor demands, must become the substitute 'soul' of a mechanistic microcosm: 'let her recognize no other principle of life or motive force in all her operations; let her regulate her every act in conformity to it; may it maintain her in a tranquil state of imperturbable happiness' (87). (The English adaptation, aware of the political and scientific revolutions of the time, expands Pallavicino's 'soul' into 'a moving intelligence to regulate the new modelled Fabrick of your Heavens' (*WR* 221–2).) Like a more respectable author of conduct manuals—designed to produce precisely the opposite kind of 'woman', chaste and silent—Pallavicino attends to the least detail of bodily deportment: so for example *maneggiare la lingua* or 'the management of the tongue', a term normally used in manuals of verbal discretion, turns out to mean the precise physical use of the tongue in kissing (*RP* 89–90, *WR* 200).

Pallavicino is not entirely consistent in his denial of interior emotionality: at one point erotic pictures enable the whore to 'figure to herself' a beautiful youth or Ganymede, and so feel the appropriate 'gusto' in the arms of a hideous client. For the most part, however, she is told to 'subjugate the two greatest natural passions, love and disdain', and eliminate every possibility of arousal by a severe act of will. The greatest danger for the professional courtesan, as for the eighteenth-century libertine typified by Valmont, is to fall in love—Pallavicino's speaker having been reduced to beggary because of such a mistake.[37] By assuming that 'natural' gender identity can be wholly replaced by 'method', Pallavicino thus deepens a paradox formulated by Aretino: the courtesan, an assemblage or mirror-image of everything men expected from female sexuality, should 'not think of herself as being a woman', should strip off all 'concetto feminile' as if she is entering the convent, should 'retain nothing of the sex except the facility of weaving frauds' (87). To drive this message home, the English adaptation plagiarizes the blunter version of this paradox articulated by the old bawd in Aretino's *Ragionamenti*: 'Le Puttane non son donne, ma sono puttane' (I. iii. 127 [135]). Centuries of misogynistic satire had insisted that *all* women were whores, but in this libertine twist the old identity is disconnected, replaced by pure tautology: 'A Whore is a Whore, but a Whore is not a Woman.'[38]

And men, by the same logic of construction, are not men. The prostitute presents them with a calculated replica of their own fantasies of natural desire: she creates the

---

[36] Cremonini cited in Claude Reichler, *L'Âge libertin* (Paris, 1987), 22.

[37] 86–7 (and for repeated warnings against love 16, 82).

[38] *WR* 144 (and cf. 221–2); for the statement that 'Toutes estes, seirez e fustes | De fait ou de volenté putes', see Jean de Meung, cited in Coci, *RP* pp. liv–lv.

illusion of deliquescent passion, 'si dà a credere'—literally, gives herself to believe—
'liquefatta, dileguata e totalmente consumata', while actually feeling like wood or
marble (91), a sort of Pygmalion twice reversed. This 'female' liquefaction-effect is
pure theatre, pure posture, but (like her Aretinan picture) it serves to 'authenticate'
male illusion. She pretends to be *sviscerata*, disembowelled, turned inside out by
desire (84), while in fact retaining strict control over the inside/outside boundary;
instead, it is the deluded customer who spills over. As rhetorical theory recommended, *her* simulations create the 'faith' that *he* is feeling what he feels. 'The foolish man, believing *his* soul liquefied into delicious drops' (84, my emphasis), will
then 'put into practice' or 'experience' his own 'ardours'. (Pallavicino's term *approvare* contains both meanings.) Her carefully designed interior provides, literally,
the 'model' for him to 'imitate', the *apparatus* for producing the self as Man of
Pleasure; the mirror where she practises her spontaneous gestures becomes a device
for customers to 'multiply pleasures by multiplying themselves in the images the
mirror reflects, wanting to enjoy the representation of those delights they also feel
in the actual coupling' (94–5).

What, then, is the author's role in this conspiracy of fabrication? Does Pallavicino
claim the same power of arousal granted within the text to mirrors and pictures, or
to those conversations, songs, and games that drive out post-coital *nausea* and
restore 'il desiderio di gioire'? (The English adaptation significantly adds the
'facetious Novel' to this list of aphrodisiac representations.[39]) Certainly the mock-
deferential dedication pretends to equate the courtesan's achievement with the author's aspiration: 'I protest that I cannot write as well as you can perform, nor can I
invent (*chimerizare*) as many fictions and fourberies as you practise in an ordinary
day, your talent being greatly superior to the weakness of my mind; remember this,
that he who now gives you this book has already dedicated his heart to you' (4). It
would be easy to dismiss this as an uncomplicated irony, since the preface 'To the
Reader' claims a straightforward moral purpose, warning young men by exposing
and so destroying the prostitute's secret agenda, her 'finzioni e furberie'. Art has the
power to create as well as dispel the 'nausea of Venus'; the reader is invited to 'abhor',
to feel 'nausea' for the whole profession [40]
    The association of prostitutes with 'art', here as in Pallavicino's epistolary fiction,
claims to inspire moral indignation at their falsehood; their habit of 'painting themselves' (*dipingersi*), for example, shows them to be whited sepulchres, 'delusive
Appearances' who 'willingly transform themselves into Pictures'.[41] But his stance is
actually more Protean, and his relation to the arts of seduction more complicit. His
account of 'true art' in the Venetian letter conveys admiration as well as monition,

---

[39] *RP* 65, 89; *WR* 44, 197–8.
[40] 8–9, and cf. 105 and 126, where he explicitly claims to be writing against certain prostitutes ('Chi mi
conosce sa contro di quali puttane io scrivo'); here he seems to narrow his target to one hated individual,
leaving open the possibility that he accepts other kinds of courtesan.
[41] *Continuazione del Corriere*, 150, here cited in Charles Gildon's translation (*The Post-Boy Rob'd of his
Mail, or The Pacquet Broke Open* (2nd edn., 1706) 1st pagination, 185).

and in dedicating *La retorica* to the university of courtesans he begs to be given free entry on account of his brilliant writing.[42] If he exposes fraud, he also communicates a furtive erotic satisfaction, the pleasure of revealing secrets, sharing female space behind the scenes, stealing language that belongs to someone else, burying one's face in her most private things; it is no accident that Pallavicino also invents an important device for epistolary fiction in his *Corriere svaligiato*—the transgressive meta-narrative of 'the Post-boy robbed of his mail, or the packet broke open'. If he alerts the young man to danger, he also encourages the courtesan's self-improvement, praises the wisdom of tolerating prostitution, defends the naturalness of 'excessive' sexuality, and argues that these artful pleasures have their own 'honestà', 'nobiltà', 'grand manners', and 'elevated spirit'—more, in fact, than any other recreation (22). The papal authorities certainly did not accept his claim to expose evil, condemning his book in exactly the language that its author uses to condemn the prostitutes: in decisive terms, they issued orders to stamp out such *furberie* (p. 74 above).

When Pallavicino defends his own authorial art, moreover, his terms inevitably reveal its affinity with the 'fictions' and 'colours' of the prostitute. He speaks proudly of the 'tessitura' or weaving of his discourse—'this small contexture', as the English version puts it—in the same breath that he denounces the 'artificial tessitura' of female fraud; indeed, he speaks quite affectionately of the courtesan's ability to 'sweeten her narrative by weaving in' novelistic details, creating a 'ben intessuto discorso' (8, and cf. 64, 87). Pallavicino's self-reference in the preface shares many of the key 'disciplinary' terms that he later puts in the mouth of the bawd, justifying his scandalous topic according to 'la compositione regolata al methodo conforme al titolo' (1673, 9). When he encourages the 'curious' reader 'to penetrate the true fundaments' of this subject, he anticipates the bawd's instruction in how to 'penetrate' the client through the ears and eyes (7). If 'colours' denote deceit, they also stand for the *colorite tele* of his own composition (3). (Fanny Hill will fall into the same trap when she asks the sensitive reader to 'give life to the colours where they are dull, or worn with too frequent handling', a *double entendre* that ironically collapses the distinction between body and language that it purports to maintain.[43]) *The Whores Rhetorick* adds a public dimension to this parallel of sex and art: the prostitute tries 'to satisfie all men according to their several exigences'; the author 'would pretend with his Pen, to gratifie all Mankind' (*WR* 62, fo. A8ᵛ). The English preface then elaborates the parallels between pen and penis, prostitutional and authorial 'colours', into a surreal fantasy on green quills, tinted sheets, and venereal ink flowing with all the hues of the rainbow.

Even the most mocking passages of *La retorica delle puttane* admit that the courtesan-artist can be assessed in the same terms as the literary artist (*talento*,

---

[42] 4; Coci cites a striking anticipation in the equally scurrilous 16th-century writer Niccolò Franco (*RP* p. lxxv); in the 'Confessione d'autore' Pallavicino admits that he himself is an 'adherent' of the evil he purports to expose (116).

[43] Cleland, *Memoirs*, 91. Amy Greenstadt points out that the brilliantly executed 'colouring' of the rhetorician's art poses serious questions about how the reader can distinguish true from false; 'Engendering the Will: Rape and Authorship in Early Modern England', Ph.D. dissertation (Berkeley, 2000), 96–7.

ingegno, gloria), and in the final 'Confessione dell'autore' Pallavicino lays aside the vigilante pose and speaks directly of 'il mio lascivo genio' (117). He inherits from the courtesan culture the belief that 'lascivious' desire, however 'vulgar', can serve as a step towards a higher, cognitive Eros; as we have seen in Chapter 1, Tullia d'Aragona had already drawn this argument from the conjunction of erotic 'experience' and Platonic theory. Pallavicino clearly wants to enrol himself among those 'persons of greater esteem' who wield the pen so brilliantly because they handle the weapons of love so expertly, proving by their transgression that 'the excesses of lasciviousness are signs of glory' (122–3). In his justificatory preface, in fact, he explicitly claims the same 'glory' that painters achieve when they create a splendid image of something conventionally ugly—precisely his justification of sodomy, that trope of tropes, which manifests the 'sublime art' of producing the highest pleasure from the most abject practice (57). Just as 'translation' from vagina to anus leaves behind the 'laws of nature' and inscribes itself under the rubric of pure pleasure, so in the erotic-aesthetic realm 'ugliness is a fault in the original but not in the effigy'. Pallavicino envisages a proto-Flaubertian role for the artist, whose responsibility is not to discriminate against abject and scandalous materials but to render them with supreme aesthetic power, 'perfect execution'.[44]

And his moral stance, which seems at first to be based on Stoic or Aristotelian moderation, mutates into an almost Nietzschean superiority to moral norms. The guiding principle '*in medio sita est virtus*' ('Virtue is located in the middle') comes to mean that the virtuous man is 'indifferent', equally distanced from both good and evil, able to apply himself with equal spirit to both 'as the designs in hand may seem to require'.[45] *Disegno* and *virtuoso* clearly imply aesthetic rather than moral criteria. Here again the writer forges a link with the courtesan, whom he instructs to disregard 'right and wrong' and to transform the most bestial body functions into the highest art—manifesting her own amoral greatness, 'con spirito elevato'. She is repeatedly encouraged to apply herself with 'sublime' audacity to what is conventionally dishonourable, to ignore '*fas* and *nefas*' in her pursuit of higher goals, just as the Machiavellian statesman ignores them in the interests of 'ragione di stato'. As the bawd puts it in her closing summary, these 'lectures' teach not only 'the art of making simulation natural' but also the art of 'making *fas* and *nefas* equally allowable'.[46] The author likewise distances himself from 'li estremi del bene e del male', and delegates moral discrimination to the reader: the courtesan may read to improve her rhetorical and performative skill, the young man may either 'read to praise' or 'read to abhor' (9). Pallavicino remains 'indifferent', wrapped up in his own 'lascivious genius'.

---

[44] 6 ('Sono gloriosi que' pittori che co piscono nell'ammirabile dipingendo oggetti diformi; la bruttezza è colpa dell'originale non della effigie. Così non toglie il vanto ad operazione eseguita l'esser questa mala, e però biasimevole'); cf. WR fo. A8-ᵛ. Coci cites this passage to illustrate Pallavicino's naturalism (*RP* p. xciii, but it surely shows the opposite, a perverse violation of the 'natural' in the interests of an alternative aesthetic. For 'Glory' as a trademark word of the Incogniti see n. 47 below, and for further developments of this aesthetic theory in WR and contemporary critics, Ch. 8, sect. 2 below.

[45] 1673, 5 (Coci, *RP* 5, reads 'in media sita virtus est').   [46] 21 (and cf. 27), 57, 98.

2. *AMOUR PHILOSOPHIQUE*, OR THE SCHOOL OF SODOM:
   ANTONIO ROCCO'S NATURAL PERVERSION

Pallavicino's *Retorica delle puttane* exemplifies the double turn that will occupy
much of this book: the replacement of the trickster-whore by the domestic-affective
mistress (created in effigy by the well-trained courtesan), and the modulation
towards what I will be calling the libertine sublime—the cultivation of 'extreme'
sexuality as *summum bonum* and aesthetic masterpiece. Pallavicino's invention
flourished in the cynical and adventurous atmosphere of the Venetian Accademia
degli Incogniti—which pronounced him posthumously one of its 'Glories'[47]—and
it was especially fostered by the most 'unnatural' of all seventeenth-century libertine texts, Father Antonio Rocco's graphic account of how the revered Athenian
schoolmaster Philotime seduces his pupil Alcibiades, the most perfect example of
the *fanciullo* or sexually available youth. In this section I will interrogate Rocco's
Alcibiade fanciullo a scola more closely, particularly bringing out what this 'queer'
fiction shares with other discourses of intellectual libertinage: the ingenious redefinition of 'Nature' to support a philosophy of hedonism and Epicurism that borders
on the cannibalistic. Varying Montaigne's tribute to the 'engendered' consciousness
of women, Rocco impersonates the 'schoolmaster Nature' infusing knowledge into
the bloodstream, but reclaims this 'Socratic coupling' of mind and body for an exclusively masculine education. I will then conclude the chapter by glancing at the
idea of 'Sodomy' in the girls' school and the convent, building a bridge between
these Italian discourses of prostitution or pederasty and the subject of Chapter 3,
L'Escole des filles, ou La Philosophie des dames.

   We have already seen that many writers, pornographic and moralistic, perceive a
close affinity between illicit heterosexuality and the homoerotic enjoyment of boys:
Aretino and Pallavicino advise the courtesan to imitate the boy in dress and in bed;
Jonson's Clerimont lives with his 'engle' or catamite while using him to communicate with his mistress. For Foucauldians this interchangeability confirms the view
that homosexual 'persons' did not yet exist, that early modern sexuality offered
a range of 'sodomitical' acts or pleasures that carry no implication of fixed identity
or orientation.[48] Rocco begins with this assumption, showing the androgynous
Alcibiade desired by men and women alike, but soon moves on to argue for homosexual desire—in its Athenian form, felt by an older philosopher for his most beautiful pupil—as distinct, exclusive, and 'natural'. Rather than succeeding one another

---

[47] *Le glorie degli Incogniti* (Venice, 1647), 136–9, eulogizes Pallavicino without concealing his scandalous publications (though his rudest title has been toned down to *La rettorica delle meretrici*); Rocco's
Alcibiade remained in MS in 1647, and was therefore not listed in the highly laudatory chapter on him
(58–61).

[48] For the debate within Queer Studies prompted by Foucauldian linguistic constructionism (which
replicates the scholastic debate between nominalists and realists), see Joseph Cady, ' "Masculine Love,"
Renaissance Writing, and the "New Invention" of Homosexuality', in Claude J. Summers (ed.), *Homosexuality in Renaissance and Enlightenment England: Literary Representations in Historical Context* (1992),
10–11, 29–35, 37–8, and (from the opposite camp) Mario DiGangi, *The Homoerotics of Early Modern
Drama* (Cambridge, 1997), 1–23.

in a neat historical sequence, the act-definition and the person-definition coexist. Marsilio Ficino thought it 'natural' for philosophers to sodomize their male companions, and Giordano Bruno had already used the phrase 'natural inclinatione' for Socrates' attraction to 'the filthy love of boys', praising him for having resisted it.[49]

Rocco's Filotime expands on this assumption while reversing Bruno's moral theory, showering Socrates' most famous love-object with arguments for the 'philosophical' superiority of paedophilia; he even asserts that by following that 'inclination' we serve the will of God. *L'Alcibiade fanciullo* spells out in its fullest form the assumption that flourished throughout the period between Tullia d'Aragona's discussion of the 'Socratics' and Montesquieu's remarks on *amour philosophique*: that élite homosexuality provides the only way of reconciling Nature and Art, combining Eros and intellect into the elusive Platonic ideal.

L'Alcibiade circulated in manuscript for some twenty years before it appeared in print in 1651, sponsored by the leader of the Incogniti—who promoted it as a playful 'libretto da Carnevale', in the humanist tradition of 'festive little books'.[50] The first surviving edition (preserved in several collections and recopied in manuscript for the aristocratic connoisseur) bears the date 1652, a French imprint, and the mysterious initials D.P.A., which led some bibliophiles to ascribe it to Pietro Aretino (27, 96–7). The forematter invents a reformative purpose for this publication, deriding the sodomitical schoolmaster (in a colloquial sonnet apparently from the sixteenth century), warning readers against entrusting their children to such masters, and promising an uplifting sequel, *The Triumph of Alcibiades*.[51] This framing device thus recapitulates the hostile or comic treatment of the pedantic pederast typical of the previous century, familiar from Aretino's *Marescalco*, Bruno's *Candelaio*, or (most similar of all) the sarcastic sonnets that praised Benedetto Varchi as a 'new Socrates' who will only 'stick his deep knowledge' into pupils as young and beautiful as Alcibiades (Ch. 1, sect. 1 above). Within the text itself, however, the author's voice wholeheartedly shares the erotic experience and perspective of the philosophical schoolmaster, and his final line, anticipating the never-realized sequel, promises a narrative of 'enjoyments' and 'amorous embraces' even more 'lascivious' than the first (87). As in Pallavicino's 'lascivious genius', the once-pejorative word *lasciva* now conveys aesthetic approval rather than moral condemnation; both Incogniti support the idea of achieving 'glory' or 'sublimity' through transgressive excess.

Like Pallavicino but with far less ambiguity, Rocco reveals himself an 'adherent' rather than an opponent of the amorous speciality he depicts. At the first kiss, for example—when the pupil's breath reverses the passive–active hierarchy by

---

[49] As Giovanni dall'Orto points out in 'Socratic Love as a Disguise for Same-Sex Love in the Renaissance', in Kent Gerard and Gert Hekma (eds.), *The Pursuit of Sodomy* (New York, 1989), 49.

[50] Coci's edn. of *Alcibiade* (Abbreviations above), 95, and see her edn. of *RP*, pp. lxxxvi, xciv, for links between Rocco and Pallavicino; for *festivus* applied to books like Lucian and *Utopia*, see Carlo Ginzburg, *No Island Is an Island: Four Glances at English Literature in a World Perspective* (New York, 2000), 14–17.

[51] *Alcibiade*, 37–8; the appended poems of M.V. ('unidentified' by Coci, 95), which include four pro-sodomitical sonnets at the end of the book, certainly evoke an earlier tradition, and might be the work of a member of the Venier family (I am grateful to Margaret Rosenthal for sharing her impressions of these sonnets).

penetrating into his teacher's 'viscere'—the narrator himself bursts through the veil of third-person anonymity:

Filotime remained, truly pale and swooning. Mind and language cannot convey the precise details of what he felt. So, as his pen collapses under its burden, he puts another, living pen in charge of these high mysteries—my own; self-impregnated with the conception propagated by the mind, while desire softly breathes into it and writhes into a thousand postures, my pen reconfigures the deed and paints a natural portrait, without words, of our fortunate schoolmaster's happiness. (44)

Framed by narrative demonstrations of affect and descriptive blasons of the young man's beauty, the dialogue between Filotime and Alcibiade enacts a programme of seduction-as-education. The pupil marshals his objections to anal consummation; the teacher overcomes them and edges closer to that goal, gradually eliminating the space between theory and practice.

The eroticization of *persuasio* now moves into the narrative itself: *La retorica delle puttane* explains it, but *L'Alcibiade* performs it. (Rocco was himself a lecturer in rhetoric as well as philosophy, we should recall.) Gesture and exposition mingle thoroughly, despite Alcibiade's initial rejection of his teacher's advances. Wave after wave of reason-objection-refutation are punctuated by caresses that also serve as object-lessons: to define the perfect penis, for example—neither 'unripe' like a boy's nor 'sordid and stinking' like a grown man's—Filotime easily finds an example to hand in 'yours' (67). At the climax Alcibiade declares himself convinced by his master's final argument (or at least won over by his humour), strips off his clothes, and presents himself 'ready' for insertion: 'the desire for true knowledge bends me to your pleasures' (*ai vostri piaceri mi piega*, 85). He 'folds himself' like the Pallavicinan courtesan, but for a diametrically opposite motive—the free-willed voluptuous surrender that she merely simulates.

Rocco's *didascalia* unfolds through all the stages of the graduated curriculum, bringing into the prosodomitic argument the disciplines of natural philosophy, comparative ethnography, gastronomy, and theology. His goal is to recorporealize the Platonic doctrine of educational pederasty, exemplified by Socrates in the arms of Alcibiades himself (as memorably dramatized in the *Symposium*). *Orthōs paiderastein* or 'straight' homosexual love of a pupil, according to Plato, must be purified by physical abstention and thereby converted into a vehicle for higher knowledge, leading the acolyte step by step towards transcendence; Rocco cunningly retains the upward cognitive drive but literalizes the Socratic imagery of mental intercourse, pregnancy, and 'birth in beauty'.[52] He thus intensifies the corporealizing process begun by Leone Ebreo (for marriage) and Tullia d'Aragona (for illicit love with courtesans or *Socratici*). The 'steps' of this ascent are the formal debates that constitute the centre of the book—for example, an elaborate *paragone* of homo-

---

[52] Plato, *Symposium*, 206, 209, 210, 211b; for English readers, the most visible praise of Socratic 'correct pederasty' (as opposed to the wicked version allegedly advocated by Aretino and Lucian) is E.K. 's 'Glosse' on *January*, line 59, in Spenser's *Shepheardes Calender*.

and heterosexual intercourse in which Alcibiade's gallant pro-female arguments are swamped by counter-demonstration. The end result is to confirm Lucian's equation of exclusive homosexuality, the 'philosophic spirit', and the aesthetic life removed from mere biological 'necessity' (Introd. n. 33 above). And the keystone of the entire structure is its most outrageous paradox: Filotime's demonstration that the 'vice against nature' in fact fulfils Nature's dearest wishes for humanity.

One might have thought that sodomy—whether heterosexual or homosexual, performed by men or women—constituted the defining instance of the unnatural, the benchmark or stable point of reference that would establish firm criteria for identifying Nature. Surprisingly, however, many writers were prepared to argue that sodomy was indeed natural, or to imagine still more heinous sexual sins—thus undermining the unique position of sodomy as the *ne plus ultra* of transgression and the fixed pole that stabilized the significance of its opposite. Francis Bacon's *New Atlantis*, for example, denounces all the 'libertine' impurities of the West equally: 'lust against nature' and 'Masculine Love' (*amores masculorum*) are equivalent to— and no worse than—reducing marriage to an economic 'Bargaine', or 'the depraved Custome of change', or 'the Delight in Meretricious Embracements (where sinne is turned into Art)'.[53]
  Ficino repeatedly assumes it 'natural' for men absorbed in the pursuit of higher beauty to assuage their lower, genital urges with younger men (Ch. 1 n. 33 above). More conventional (or less Florentine) thinkers replace the dichotomy of 'contrary' orifices with something more like the dichotomy of Nature and Art: the profoundest sin is to visualize what should remain in darkness, to manufacture the ideal sexobject rather than accepting the body as found, to cerebralize what should remain humiliatingly 'brutal', to dissolve biologically fixed identity in favour of performativity—in short, to make nature your art. To add to the conceptual problem, this libertine artefactuality could itself be defined as natural, either because hedonistic excess stems directly from our postlapsarian 'nature', or because aesthetic activity is endemic to humans and distinguishes us from the other animals. A delicious confusion prevailed, shared by the pornographic defenders of sodomy and its moralistic assailants. The 'unnatural' status of the act was enshrined in everyday language and in the formulae of legal definition; indeed, unless the words 'contra naturae ordinem' were ritually included in the indictment, prosecution for sodomy could be legally invalid. And yet moralists both Protestant and Catholic insisted that sodomy stems directly from 'man's natural corruption', from 'our corrupt natures'.[54] Evelyn's letter to his son warns that 'unnatural figures' are all too natural; Montesquieu,

---

[53] *Nova Atlantis, Opus Imperfectum* (Amsterdam, 1661), 50–1 (appended to the Elzevier edn. of *Sylva Sylvarum, sive Historia Naturalis*); *New Atlantis*, ed. William Rawley (1627; 1635), 27.
[54] Cited in Alan Bray, *Homosexuality in Renaissance England* (1982), 26 (Edward Coke), 17 (John Rainolds, William Bradford); as Richard Godbeer points out in '"The Cry of Sodom": Discourse, Intercourse, and Desire in Colonial New England', *William and Mary Quarterly*, 3rd ser. 52 (1995), 265, Bradford derives all sins from fallen 'nature' and does not promote sodomy above the rest.

amused by visitors to Italy consumed by *amour philosophique* for the cross-dressed castrato, explains it as the work of 'Nature' too, expelled at one entrance and rushing back through another.[55]

The most systematic conflation of the 'natural' and the 'sodomitic'—among its attackers rather than its defenders—occurs in Father Garasse's furious assault on the naturalistic philosophy that supposedly underlies libertinism, an exposition that unravels the more he pursues it. The entire sixth book of *La Doctrine curieuse* (methodized into nineteen sections) is devoted to demolishing the libertine worship of Nature, supposedly substituted for God. According to this reconstruction of a philosophy never spelled out by the authors he accuses, 'our good mistress ... sweet Nature' justifies following every appetite without external restraint, 'refusing nothing to our body or our senses' provided we 'exercise their natural powers and faculties'. Thus the libertines allegedly claim the right to ignore the mechanical regulation of clocks (an idea that Garasse obtained by reading Rabelais's Abbey of Thélème as a literal manifesto), eating and sleeping whenever they want, and 'going about their immodest pleasures whenever brutality drives them to it'. Despite this insistence on 'Nature' as the key to the libertines' belief-system, however, Garasse reserves his greatest indignation for their anti-natural extremity, for their restless desire to change or violate nature, to become either beasts or angels—an observation that Pascal would later shape into a memorable *pensée*.[56]

For Garasse as for Rocco sublime perversity, not 'natural' ease, is the true goal of advancement in the curriculum of *libertinage*. In Garasse's imagination the libertines' 'immodest pleasures' involve not simple *brutalité* but the transvestite urge to become a woman or the 'Sodomite' desire for the anus. He returns relentlessly to the first poem in the *Parnasse satyrique* (uncritically ascribed to Théophile, who denied authorship at his trial), an exercise in anti-decorum that begins with the exclamation 'Phylis, tout est foutu'; the syphilitic speaker describes his imminent death, pretends to repent, and assures God in a solemn vow that henceforth he will renounce vaginal copulation and restrict himself to buggery. Garasse's mountain of naturalistic maxims, propositions, and counter-texts appears to deliver only this mousy 'Sonnet Sodomite', though he soon generalizes and detextualizes this short poem into evidence for Théophile's personal 'Sodomies'. At the climax of his argument, as if to fulfil the prophecy of the opening line ('everything is fucked'), Garasse discovers in this sonnet the sins of an entire city, calling down the 'flames of Sodom' on Paris for publishing such a book. The quintessential act of these Nature-worshipping libertines, then, turns out to be a monstrous affront to Nature—outdone only by the deliberate grotesquerie of Garasse's own text. The ingenious Jesuit draws attention to his own anti-decorum, explaining that to convey the true horror of libertinism he has fabricated a monster with the 'Frons meretricis' (the

[55] Loc. cit. Introd. n. 35 above, citing Horace's Epistle I. x. 24.

[56] 675–792, esp. 677, 726, 687 ('vaquer à ses plaisirs impudiques quand la brutalité y pousse', and cf. 712, 'vaquer à la propagation de leur sexe'), 703–6; for connections between Garasse, Pascal, and Rochester, see Ch. 6, sect. 1 below). The trial of Théophile, and Garasse's attack, must surely have been known in the academic circles of Venice and Padua where Rocco moved.

forehead of a whore) and the 'Lingua cinaedi', the tongue of a passive sodomite. In the preface to the entire book, in fact, he accuses the reader of forcing him to father a headless 'avorton' or misbirth, making the monster his own kin.[57]

Promoters of sodomy deftly penetrate these chinks in the concept of nature wielded by their enemies. The sixteenth-century dialogue *La cazzaria* (written by the founder of the Sienese Accademia degli Intronati, Antonio Vignali) argues that sodomy is only called 'contra natura' because the anus is situated on the opposite side from the vulva.[58] A poem with a similar title, *La cazzaria del C.M.*, asserts that the *cazzo* desires the *culo* because 'la natura' has made them both round; if Nature *had* forbidden sodomy she would have made the penis according to 'a different measure'. Alongside this argument from form or design comes a specifically human redefinition of nature: heterosexual-vaginal intercourse is fit only for animals (and Germans), but 'I want to do it as *persons* do it'; Nature has created us to 'fuck and refuck', which makes it quite natural to seek new ways and abandon the old ones for ever.[59] Another poet in the sixteenth-century tradition of ritual abuse (whose sonnets are appended to the early editions of *L'Alcibiade*) praises buggery as an 'art' invented by 'learned Greece'—perfected by 'Plato and Socrates with their boys'— while at the same time claiming to recognize *buggeroni* by their 'physiognomy' or natural constitution; homoerotic pederasty thus belongs both to Art and Nature. Whether innate or acquired, however, it remains the defining mark of the intellectual élite, *i più saputi*, who thereby fuse the cognitive and the erotic, distancing themselves as far as possible from cattle, dogs, and the 'lower classes' who 'fuck without knowledge' and confine themselves to the vagina.[60]

These arguments are rounded up and polished in *L'Alcibiade fanciullo a scola*. When Alcibiade first objects to the 'Vice against nature', for example, his tutor explains the phrase in anatomical terms without moral valence, repeating almost verbatim the argument in Vignali's *Cazzaria*: the anus is simply on the opposite side to the *natura* or vulva. 'Nature' in this case means 'birth-canal', according to its etymology, and has nothing to do with pleasures or passions; on the contrary, the real laws of nature dictate that 'those acts are natural to which Nature inclines us' (*sono naturali quelle opere a cui la natura ci inclina*, 51). Father Rocco himself maintained the identical naturalist interpretation of 'our tastes and delights', according to

---

[57] fo. a2 (comparing his book to an aborted 'monstre . . . sans teste' is tactless since his title-page emblem shows the Holofernes of libertinism freshly decapitated by Judith), pp. 703–4, 774, 778–9, 782–3; for the poem in which (pseudo)Théophile 'fait vœu à Dieu d'estre SODOMITE tout le reste de ces jours', see Frédéric Lachèvre, *Le Libertinage devant le Parlement de Paris: Le Procès du poète Théophile de Viau* (Paris, 1909), ii. 393–4. Garasse was himself accused of obscenity, as Pierre Bayle records in his *Dictionnaire* ('Garasse', a ref. I owe to Lise Leibacher-Ouvrard).

[58] ed. Pasquale Stoppelli, introd. Nino Borsellino (Rome, 1984), 67.

[59] BnF Enfer 562 (no place or date), fos. A2ᵛ, A4ʳ (fo. A4–ᵛ is a separate poem entitled 'Persuasiva efficace, per coloro, che schifano la delicatezza del tondo').

[60] Coci, *Alcibiade*, 89–91 (by the 'M.V.' who also supplied the prefatory poem, n. 85 below); libels against the *mignons* of Henri III also assumed that 'les bougres et les bougerons' could be recognized by their 'faces' (Cady, ' "Princes of Sodom" ', 137–39, 152 nn. 58, 67). The notion that (heterosexual) anal intercourse is a 'morsel fit for prelates' was commonplace, e.g. in Aretino's *Modi* sonnet 10 ('Io'l voglio in cul . . . un cibo da prelato').

reports filed with the Venetian Inquisition: from his sickbed he allegedly encouraged his friends to feel proud of having sexual experiences 'naturally and against nature', since the 'instrument' that conveys those pleasures 'was made by Nature'.[61]

In both *La retorica delle puttane* and *L'Alcibiade fanciullo*, the production of desire is triply unnatural according to the conventional categories understood by 'nature'. In libertine discourse as in contemporary theology, *Sodomia* or the 'crime against nature' did not simply mean male same-sex desire, but applied to various illicit penetrations, including what we might call *heteropaedophilia* or woman–boy love. In Pallavicino (and his English follower) the representation actively generates and 'imprints' the desire, the 'shadow' outperforms the 'real', and the woman lusts after the beautiful youth, the 'Ganymede'. *La retorica* promotes the artistic appeal of sodomy and encourages the courtesan to model herself on the more accomplished *bardassi* (sect. 1 above); she should 'feign herself Ganymede' and offer her 'cup' to the godlike customer, who is assumed to need what *L'Alcibiade* calls the 'spice' or *condimento* of simulated pederasty. (In Jonson's *Epicoene*, likewise, both the gentleman-hero and the Collegiate Lady enjoy the 'smooth cheek' of the catamite.) Ganymede thus defines the secret desires of both men and women, though both pretend to uphold the 'adult' form of heterosexuality.

From his opening page, Rocco exploits this polymorphous perversity and defends it as natural, marshalling increasingly ingenious arguments to prove his paradox. Nature's first act in *L'Alcibiade* is to fashion the young hero as an object of universal desire—broadening the appeal to readers beyond the narrow circle of committed pederasts. 'Industrious Nature', delighting in her own playfulness, 'confounds the feminine sex' by mingling the features of a young lady (*donzella*) with those of 'Ganymede, when he had the power to draw Jove from heaven to earth' (39). This portrait of youthful lability would have seemed more plausible, even natural, in an age that thought the gender of the seed and the child could be altered by diet, temperature, and timing.[62]

Ambiguous beauty places Alcibiade between active and passive, powerful and weak, heaven and earth, male and female; he is appropriately compared to the goddesses Diana and Ceres (40). Like the 'Boy' in Jonson who passes easily between master and mistress, he forms 'the erotic aim of two perspectives' (*bersaglio amoroso di due prospetti*), since all the girls 'pant after him' and all the male intellectuals 'idolize' him. At this labile stage, 'nature' has turned him into 'an inexhaustible Treasure Archive, where one finds whatever delights of love one most desires' (39); he does not need the courtesan's training in fictive and performative metamorphosis, since he conforms 'naturally' to the desire of *anyone* who comes to his 'Treasury' or seeks knowledge in his Thesaurus. The theologian and canon lawyer Lodovico Maria Sinistrari illustrates this plasticity of sexual identity with a case of 'true Sodomy' taken directly from the lips of a confessor: a noblewoman, tired of her husband after

---

[61] 31–2 (confession of Henricus Palladius of Udine, 23 Nov. 1648).
[62] Cf. Rudolph M. Bell, *How to Do It: Guides to Good Living for Renaissance Italians* (1999), 20–7.

bearing him three children, took as her lover 'a certain ephebe of twelve years old' whom she would 'know backwards' (*praepostere cognoscebat*), penetrating him anally with her erect clitoris.[63] She sounds very much like the courtesan enjoying her Ganymede or the young women 'panting after' Alcibiade.

Sinistrari's Greek borrowing *ephebus*—more precise than the Latin *puer* or the Italian *fanciullo*, and quite different from the modern English *boy*—can also be applied to the brief stage of Alcibiade's development when he is already nubile but still smooth and androgynous in appearance, the moment when élite ladies select their amorous playthings (according to Juvenal and Jonson). The theme is an ancient one, endlessly elaborated in the 'Boy-Muse' book of the *Greek Anthology* that Rocco seems to have known in manuscript, but it also fascinated the Renaissance. Vast numbers of Italian and English plays (whether or not the female parts were actually played by youths) turn on the plausibility of grown women passing as active young men, and vice versa; Jonson's Epicœne and Shakespeare's Rosalind (who chooses the alias 'Ganymede') are only the best-known examples. In the 'Treasury' offered at the threshold of Rocco's *Alcibiade*, gender appears still more malleable: active–passive roles switch at will; the young pupil penetrates the venerable teacher; men and women, seducers and readers, all 'pant' alike for this Ganymede. He descends from a lyric tradition of transsexual beauty, from the boy in Horace whose long curls and 'ambiguous face' make him indistinguishable from a girl, and from Renaissance attempts to imagine women imagining their ideal love-object—a pliable youth with the eyes of Venus and the tool of Priapus.[64]

In keeping with his conception of the ephebe as 'Tesoro', Rocco's lingering description of Alcibiade (40–1) presents him as an object for connoisseurship and consumption. Subject to mutation according to the kind of pleasure his suitor is seeking, Alcibiade has become a fictile artefact: a still-life of milk and flowers, a courtly toy made of pearls and rubies, a temple of 'Doric architecture', a Renaissance system of proportion that allows the viewer to infer the penis from the nose and the 'giardinetto' from the mouth. Reversing the dynamics of the Pygmalion legend, 'inanimate statues' want to kiss him. This opening blason, which clearly celebrates the author's own virtuosity as well as the artefactuality of youthful beauty, returns at the climax of the book when Alcibiade finally flings off his robe. In the expansive mode of enjoyment rather than anticipation, Rocco sculpts a figurine fit for the most excessive *Wunderkammer*. Alcibiade's 'vivacious spheres' are 'sprinkled with privet and narcissus flowers', an echo of Ovid's *Metamorphoses* reminding us of

---

[63] *De Delictis et Poenis, Tractatus Absolutissimus* (1700; Rome, 1754), 234, 235, 240; anonymous tr. of the 'De Sodomia' chapter as *Peccatum Mutum: The Secret Sin*, introd. [stolen from] Montague Summers (Paris, 1958), 40–1, 45, 66–8; for a discussion related to lesbianism but not hetero-pederasty, see Judith C. Brown, *Immodest Acts: The Life of a Lesbian Nun in Renaissance Italy* (New York, 1986), 17–19. Sinistrari's case rests on two crucial texts, Thomas Bartholin's anatomy of the distended clitoris (Ch. 3 n. 146 below) and Seneca, *Epistles*, XCV. 21, which he reads quite literally: women, 'born to take the passive role' (*pati natae*), have found a way 'to enter men' (*perversum commentae genus impudicitiae viros ineunt*, 234/40–1).

[64] Horace, *Odes*, II. v (and for women as the active partners in affairs with a Ganymede-like 'boy', cf. I. v and III. xx); Jonson, 'A Celebration of Charis' (her ideal 'man' must have '*Venus* and *Minerva*'s eyes' (VIII. 141)).

other beautiful youths. His ruby-milky-cinnabar hand brings to mind flowering gardens, celestial arches, and starlight. His 'majestic' anus, 'like a budding rose', combines the pigments of 'living snow' and 'shell-pink dye'. His graceful movement (as he 'folds himself' into the submissive posture) 'would have given an erection to statues of bronze and marble' (85).

Establishing Alcibiade as Nature's work of art prepares us for the central scene of argument, Filotime's anatomical-philosophical demonstration that 'every act is natural if Nature inclines us to it'. Since looking at beautiful boys satisfies a 'natural inclinazione', and since Nature makes nothing in vain, then that beauty must serve the 'ultimate end' of accomplishing pleasure (51). Nature generates the strongest love between 'those who most resemble each other', and the *fanciullo* is far closer to the man (though retaining some female features that sanction the interchangeable 'use' of boys and women). The noblest parts of the body are those (like the hand) adaptable to many functions; sodomy dignifies the arse by appropriating it to higher ends, thereby realizing Nature's intentions. To encourage this honorific treatment, the Heavens conferred upon it their own spherical form, the *tondo* of the sun and moon (51–2): Nature designed this convex 'ritondetto', in fact, to form a 'perfect union' with the concave of the older man's belly during sodomitical penetration (66–7). In short, whoever fails to appreciate the 'flavours' and 'delights' imparted by Nature demeans her and 'si disnatura', *denatures* himself (52).

Alcibiade's attempt to counter-argue from analogies with the animals is easily parried by evoking that tenet central to libertinism and humanism alike—the superiority of humans and the wisdom of nature in creating us radically different from the beasts. The strictest moralists would agree that the proper construction of sexuality minimizes what humans have in common with 'brutes', and in this they would be seconded by the Archangel Raphael in *Paradise Lost*.[65] Rocco develops this principle into a paean to the goddess Natura herself, chief patroness of pederasty. For once, libertine discourse resembles (or imitates) Father Garasse's seductive parody ('la Nature nostre bonne maistresse . . . la douce Nature', 677). That 'alma madre' conferred on us the gift of cognitive enjoyment and the capacity to satisfy a multiplicity of appetites; we should no more settle for one form of sex than we would eat only a single kind of food. Sounding a theme that will echo throughout *L'Escole des filles* and Chorier's *Satyra*, Rocco contrasts the common instincts of animals with the 'diletto dalla conoscenza' that distinguishes at least the better sort of humans. (For good measure, he also describes at great length those nobler species that actually *do* enjoy homosexual love, including cockerels, dogs, lions, and dolphins.[66]) Human copulation, of which pederasty is the highest form because furthest from animal necessity, should always involve pleasurable *conoscenza*, which in this high-art context signifies connoisseurship as well as knowledge.

---

[65] Cf. Evelyn cited Ch. 7 n. 81 below, and *PL* VIII. 581–2.

[66] 54–5; for animal homosexuality (still common on sheep farms) cf. Bernadette J. Brooten, *Love between Women: Early Christian Responses to Female Homoeroticism* (Chicago, 1996), 155, 273, and Brantôme, *Les Dames galantes*, ed. Maurice Rat (Paris, 1947), 124 (lesbian weasels kept as pets).

Filotime takes care—when Alcibiade presses him on the ancient question, whether boys or women give the greater pleasure—to define this 'diletto dalla conoscenza' as a *mutual* awareness, a cognitive and scopophilic *interchange*. Rocco takes his cue from the classical arguments on this issue, even-handedly debated in Plutarch's *Erōtikon*, the pseudo-Lucian *Erōtes* (then thought to be a genuine work), and Achilles Tatius' *Clitophon and Leucippe*, whose contrast between the natural beauty and odour of boys and the artificial make-up and perfume of women seems particularly influential on *L'Alcibiade*.[67] But in stressing mutuality he departs from the Hellenistic model, which—while certainly more tolerant than the Christian dichotomy of natural and unnatural—could still be criticized for reducing one sexual partner to the passive object of male pleasure. Ancient bisexuality constituted an isosceles triangle, with women and boys (interchangeably) forming the base and the mature, active male at the top. The choice between hetero- and homo-might have been determined by 'taste' rather than fixed identity or 'orientation',[68] but the apex of the triangle was maintained by power. The lyrical *Greek Anthology* may praise 'buggery' as an invention of human *logos* that exalts us above the animals— 'unreasoning creatures' bound to a 'single mode' of copulation—but it then adds a misogynistic twist, that men 'ruled by women' are no better than dumb beasts themselves.[69] The subordinate male was normally *discouraged* from responding sexually, as some seventeenth-century reconstructions of antiquity realized: in a historical drama by the Earl of Rochester, 'deare Boyes' are valued above women precisely because they experience no pleasure and their love is therefore 'disinterested'.[70]

Rocco's comparison of the two pleasures, in contrast, seems to emphasize the transformative experiences shared by *all* lovers—while pushing the claims of epheberasty, at first subtly and then violently. He concedes that in both hetero- and homosexual intercourse the physical manifestations (touch, heat-transfer, mingling fluids) serve as 'symbols and linkages for the lovers' souls', gathering individual sense-impressions into a 'compendium' and allowing them to be 'shared interchangeably'. Whatever the sex of the individuals the 'virtú unitiva d'amore' works through them, inspiring a 'most ardent wish for transformation' that can only be satisfied by trying to 'fill every hole with hand or tongue' (65). Rocco here expropriates for homoerotic and genital propaganda the central doctrine of Renaissance Platonism. Tullia d'Aragona defined the 'higher' love as the desire to transform oneself into the love-object, and tried to reinvent an acceptable form of consummation

---

[67] 17th-century versions tended to censor this part of the novel, chs. II. 35–8 (as noted in the Loeb edn., which even in the 20th century translated it into Latin rather than English), so use of it by Rocco and by Chorier (Ch. 4, sect. 3 below) would have seemed bold.

[68] Cf. David Halperin, 'Historicizing the Sexual Body: Sexual Preferences and Erotic Identities in the Pseudo-Lucianic *Erôtes*', in Domna C. Stanton (ed.), *Discourses of Sexuality from Aristotle to AIDS* (Ann Arbor, 1992), 236–61, esp. 255; on p. 247 Halperin points out that ancient pederasty cannot be equated with the modern category 'homosexual', but I use this term in its narrow meaning to identify modes of genital combination.

[69] XII. ccxlv, a eulogy of 'buttocking' (*pugizein*) found only in the Palatine MS recently discovered by Salmasius and moved to Rome in 1623; the *libertin erudit* Rocco may well have known about it.

[70] 161, a passage added when he adapted Fletcher's *Valentinian*.

that would bring about this reciprocal transmutation; but the return of physicality undermines her separation of higher 'reason' from low 'desire' and forces her to conclude, with Lucretius, that the merging of bodies is impossible (Ch. 1, sect. 1 above). Rocco exploits this fissure or shortfall in heterosexual materiality by claiming that only in the coupling of men with *fanciulli* can true blending be achieved.

Desire wreathes bodies into the 'internal amorous symbol' of 'perfect union', the convex fitting into the concave, and mobilizes every organ to 'suck in the beloved images' (*le lingue baciatrici si suggono le amate imagini*). The lovers 'breathe in one another', drawing 'paradisal air' into their hearts, while their 'spirits gaze on one another' (66). The philosopher-mentor has grasped Lucretius' diagnosis of sex itself as a *simulacrum*, a vain attempt to ingest and incorporate the image of the other; but Rocco has turned Lucretius' complaint into a celebration. Unlike the contemporary *Escole des filles*, which simultaneously intellectualizes the enjoyment of the postures and laughs at those who 'fuck their ideas' (Ch. 3, sect. 3 below), *L'Alcibiade*'s School for Boys teaches that iconophilia and cerebral intensification are the supreme fulfilment of Nature's plan.

Rocco never endorses complete mutuality on the physical plane, as described in the prose *Puttana errante* when the heroine's male cousin and a friend of the same age take turns buggering each other.[71] Filotime recognizes that some men like to 'change the proper function' or *mutar l'officio dovuto*, implying that the boy is advanced enough in puberty to take the active role too, but he himself has no wish to 'turn the world upside-down' (67); the vertical separation of older-active and younger-passive subsists even when imagining its opposite. Nevertheless, Rocco departs from his strict Athenian model in two important respects: he emphasizes affective mutuality, and he insists that the passive recipient too must become palpably aroused, even 'weeping' the same 'juicy substance' that active lovers 'distill'.[72] He draws from the lyric *Greek Anthology*, which celebrates the lively, mobile 'lizard' of the older youth,[73] and perhaps from contemporary practice. In the most explicit account of an Italian boy-prostitute's life, the protagonist at his most seductive is clearly old enough to ejaculate, since one client drinks his sperm 'as if it were leek syrup'.[74] The ideal of mutuality, awkwardly coexisting with the pupil–teacher hierarchy, demands what Bruno called 'a scholar of white ink as well as black'.[75]

This ostensibly attractive doctrine of mutuality (complete in the homosexual, compromised in the hetero-) turns out to form the thin end of a misogynist wedge that Filotime drives between Alcibiade and his 'natural' defence of women, as if in

[71] 63–4/9; see Abbreviations above for details of this 16th-century text.

[72] 67, but contrast 81 ('Nei fanciulli, per difetto dell'età, non vi è questo seme' and therefore they do not desire to penetrate).

[73] XI. xxi, XII. iii, ccxlii, poems only in the Palatine text (cf. XII. vii, disparaging heterosexual sodomy).

[74] Vatican MS Capponiano 140, *Dialogo intitolato la Cazzaria* (Vignali's dialogue, to which is added the continuation unique to this late-16th-century MS), 'Parte Seconda', fo. 86 (he only becomes too hairy for his line of work at the age of 20, fo. 93ᵛ).

[75] *Il candelaio*, ed. Giovanni Aquilecchia and Giorgio Bárberi Squarotti, tr. Yves Hersant (Paris, 1993), 43.

preparation for another kind of thrust. Rocco gradually abandons his polymorphous acceptance of all comers for a masculinist disparagement of women that recalls passages in his rhetorical writings.[76] Filotime loads women with abuse for their distended genitalia, depraved desires, and imperiously destructive characters (71–2). He describes heterosexual intercourse as awkward and ill-fitting, the mingling of seeds as 'enervating and revolting', marriage as nauseatingly monotonous, and the female body as a 'horrifying labyrinth' (66, 73). In this highly interested description the breasts remain as inert as 'bladders filled with air', in contrast to the ideally responsive boy—whose penis 'stands firm, grows proud and angry, takes various shapes . . . jousts, beckons, weeps, laughs sweetly, applauds, concurs', as if it were itself a little person (67, 69).

Every objection that Alcibiade raises to this performance gives the professor the chance to strengthen his case for pederasty as an art of refinement and reciprocity, equally opposed to the 'nausea' of heterosexuality and the 'butchery' of commercial or coercive sodomy (63–5, 73, 81–2). He admits the filthiness of anal intercourse, but only in working-class boys ignorant of proper behaviour and hygiene; the emphasis on cleanliness and fine manners in the prostitution manual now serves to distinguish the 'civil and well-born' *fanciullo* from the street' hustler or *bardasso*. When the pupil points out that the buggering schoolmaster is everywhere condemned, Filotime extols the pedagogic value of true 'love' and 'voluntary enjoyment', in contrast to those brutal teachers who force and injure their boys (and thus deserve that reputation). When Alcibiade quizzes him further on the issue of reciprocity, asking what pleasure the boy can receive, the teacher responds both physically and intellectually: suddenly erect ('incazzito', or literally endowed with a *cazzo* or phallus), he lectures Alcibiade about those 'liveliest' boys endowed with more exquisite sensitivity, either because their 'fucking spirits' are more abundant and their nerves as densely clustered as the strings of a musical instrument, or because they were sodomized in the womb. Needless to say, only the 'discipline' of a gifted teacher can let them realize this anatomically determined capacity for pleasure (70, 77–83).

Rocco thus transforms the crude facts of sodomy into a visual and cognitive 'philosophical' system, acting out his flattering idea that Nature herself has made the pederastic élite 'speculativi' (72). Evelyn and other moralists warn against what they call 'speculative Lusts' (Introd. above), but for Rocco's philosopher-seducer the speculation of eye and mind frees him from biological necessity and lets him devote himself entirely to beautiful boys like Alcibiade. In Rocco the pun on *speculativi* and *culo* bobs just below the surface, but in Renaissance sodomitic poetry the link is quite explicit: 'Il cul possi chiamar specchio del cazzo'; the arse can be called the mirror of the prick.[77] In the hard-core homosexual literature that Rocco summarizes and refines, the *culo*—the focus of men's gaze—is conceived not only as a luminous convex mirror but as a eye with its own power of enhanced vision: 'just as

---

[76] Cf. 'Amore è un puro interesse' and 'E alla brutezza', cited in Coci, *Alcibiade*, pp. xci, xcix; Rocco also denounces the capriciousness and selfishness of the *fanciullo*.

[77] *Cazzaria del C.M.*, fo. A2, and cf. Aretino, *Modi* sonnets 11 and 14.

only the Eagle, Queen of Birds, is permitted to fix her gaze on the Sun, so the Arse, the similitude of that Planet, is permitted to fix its gaze on Princes.'[78]

Filotime's 'speculative' reconstruction of the ideal body merges with his systematic *apologia pro sodomia*, in effect working through every 'discipline' in the curriculum. He speaks as an art connoisseur when he evaluates the relative beauty of male and female, as an anatomist when he identifies erotic sensibility with the organization of nerves and the internal linkage of anus and genitalia, as an anthropologist when he records the numerous cultures that accept homosexuality, incest, or bestiality (57–60). It is a legal and cultural historian who explains the Athenian laws against sodomy ('ragione di stato' opposing the dictates of reason and nature) and the biblical story of Sodom: with a revisionist ingenuity worthy of Voltaire, Rocco asserts that Moses made up this frightening fable for purely material and pragmatic reasons, to protect the bituminous lake (a valuable source of minerals) and to keep up the birthrate during the desert crossing, when Israelite soldiers transferred their affections to *putti*.[79] Rocco adds biblical scholarship to his credentials when he points out—quite plausibly, though shocking to orthodox interpretation—that Sodom was punished for violent rather than sexual crimes, that no classical author ever mentions the place, that Solomon built a temple to boy-love (60–1), and that the prophet Isaiah condemns only relationships with 'foreign boys' (*pueris alienis adhaeserunt*), implying approval of one's own.[80]

Rocco's interpretations of bodily form constitute a version of the religious argument from design, and on this 'natural' basis he develops a wicked blend of Greek and Judaeo-Christian theology. 'Our Gods' themselves enjoyed Ganymede and Hyacinthus, and Love himself is a beautiful boy (57–8, 84). Citing the homoerotic adventures of the Olympian gods was a standard ploy in Renaissance celebrations of sodomy, and may echo poems in the Palatine *Greek Anthology* that evoke the 'nectareous' lovemaking of Zeus and Ganymede (xii. lxviii, cxxxiii); one version of the *Cazzaria* also anticipates Rocco by reinterpreting biblical and classical history (Cain and Abel were lovers, 'Plato loved Alcibiades so wholeheartedly that he fucked him day and night').[81] According to the Inquisition, Rocco himself equated Divine Grace with the pleasure of orgasm (31), and his Athenian characters mingle their Olympian speculations with renegade Christian ideas. Man cannot be blamed for God-given 'frailties', and we must 'love our neighbour as ourselves' erotically as well as charitably (62–3). It is absurd to assume that God would punish sodomy in some cases and not others; he would then 'change his mind', show fear, destroy the world

---

[78] *Cazzaria*, 'Parte Seconda', fo. 109ᵛ (numbered in MS '110'), and cf. 108ᵛ (Argus was 'fucked' by Jove and rewarded with 'cento culi, non cento occhi'); Michael Rocke, *Forbidden Friendships: Homosexuality and Male Culture in Renaissance Florence* (New York, 1996), 136, mistranslates 'Augelli' as 'angels'.

[79] 56, 59–60; by leaving a blank in the text (58) the printer avoids actually naming Moses as the cunning legislator (as the notorious *Treatise of the Three Impostors* would do), but the reference is unmistakable.

[80] Vulgate text of Isaiah 2: 6; King James's 'please themselves in the children of strangers' comes closer to Rocco's interpretation (62) than the more recent 'ally with the children of foreigners'.

[81] 'Parte Seconda', fos. 106ᵛ–107ᵛ, 108ᵛ–109.

2]   *2. Pallavicino and Rocco*   101

he has made—a great clock powered by the 'inclinations' he planted in us and wants us to follow (59). At the climactic consummation Filotime goes one step further into deism and declares the Gods superfluous: Heaven and Paradise are now incarnated in Alcibiade's embrace, 'more perfect' and 'more glorious' than any happiness the soul or body could receive apart.[82]

If all these academic discourses serve a single master-discipline, it is gastronomy. Epicurean transformation of the senses into *diletti dalla conoscenza* makes the pederastic philosopher literally a man of taste. The pleasure he takes from his boys, even when they turn away in disdain, provides the *condimento* or 'seasoning' of his existence (45, 67). Filotime constantly uses meat metaphors to demarcate the exquisite from the revolting: copulating with women (even anally) resembles coarse cowbeef, love between full-grown men evokes the foul taste of goat's flesh, whereas the 'accurate' senses of the gourmet seek out veal and kid, redolent of milk and ambrosia. Rocco's rhetoric of mutuality is severely challenged by these images of consumption, and finally shattered when Filotime reveals that his favourite kid would be 'a little insipid' before the age of 9, though the plumpest boys excite desire 'even in the cradle'.[83]

Figurative gourmandise becomes literal when he describes the 'condiment' (52) that Nature has placed in the rectum and the 'odoretti' that anoint the penis after consummation. Just as melons, bread, or wine exude their own natural bouquet, so 'the beautiful peach' has its own 'perfume of amber and civet'. One particularly 'wise and experienced' lover, who took pleasure in 'softly licking' the anus, withdrew in horror when his *fanciullo* added rose-water to the 'natural' aroma of his own 'flower'. The 'discreet lover' will 'research' his love-object carefully (since most boys still resemble 'bladders' or 'latrines'), recognizing that the most delicious food—pigeon, melon—tastes all the more disgusting when it is unripe or spoiled (70–1). To judge from the final consummation-scene Filotime indulges in self-portraiture here, since the first 'tribute' he pays to the naked Alcibiade is with his 'tongue'. Resembling 'a hungry baby sucking milk from the breast' but with a more furious appetite, he 'licked, sucked, drank, relished that most ambrosial liquor' (86–7). As well as maternal nourishment, the tongue also seeks *albergo* or 'shelter', completing the association with helpless infancy. Once again, the 'natural' mother of anatomical destiny is replaced by a mother of invention, with the paedophile as her nursing child.

Rocco expands this relish for sexual juices into a general theory of desire as an appetite for seminal 'nectar'—irrespective of 'whether the vessel be round or square' (56). Ironically, given his 'speculative' rejection of heterosexuality, he expresses a sperm-fixation that was shared by contemporary scientists and theologians of

---

[82] 86 (cf. Ch. 1, sect. 1 above for Tullia d'Aragona's affirmation that the ensouled body is nobler than the soul alone).

[83] 67, 69, 75–6. The connoisseur's account of the delights offered by boys of different ages is a motif that Rocco could find both in Italian sources (like the Vatican MS *Cazzaria*, 'Parte Seconda') and in the Palatine version of the *Greek Anthology*, notably xii. iv (where each line is devoted to a different year from 12 to 17, after which the youth becomes unsuitable because he wants to reciprocate). Rocco's cut-off age of 18 for pederasty, when 'kids' turn into 'goats' (76), is confirmed by Sinistrari (Ch. 4 n. 117 below).

procreation. Deriving by nature from the best part of the blood and the most concentrated 'animal spirits', only the sperm can 'pluck' the instrument of clustered
nerves (81) and convey knowledge directly to the brain. Rocco wrote a notorious
treatise on the mortality of the soul (28) and shared with other Incogniti like
Pallavicino a materialist conception of cognition as heat and 'spirit'. (Milton had
likewise come to see the soul as mortal and the sperm as 'the best substance' of body
and soul combined.[84]) It is Filotime's physico-theological lecture on seed that finally
prompts Alcibiade to declare 'the desire for true knowledge bends me to your pleasures'. The human brain being naturally cold and moist requires 'tempering' and
purging, and the seed of a scholar performs this service with unique and miraculous
efficacy 'by virtue of its native warmth'; when 'transmitted via the lower part of the
giardinetto' it shoots into the brain a stream of 'well-disposed spirits' that then 'actively dispose the pupil to receive qualities similar to those of the operator' (84–5).
Filotime exaggerates for comic effect here (Alcibiade surrenders to his *scherzi* as
much as to his arguments), but the humour is seductive rather than dismissive, and
the physiology corresponds to what he argues in earnest. Rocco's erotic materialism
rehabilitates the hostile caricature of the schoolmaster who addresses his beloved
boy as 'receptacle of my doctrinal seed', who 'sticks' learning into his brain or 'hunts
for Knowledge up the arsehole'.[85]

L'Alcibiade brings out most clearly a paradox that *L'Escole des filles* will soon
borrow to explain heterosexual pleasure: that hedonists and libertines, utterly opposed to ecclesiastic teaching on sexuality, still worship the sperm and evaluate
sexual options according to whether that 'best substance' is properly deployed. Filotime even condemns masturbation, in terms that would satisfy both Counter-Reformation theology and high-Victorian medicine: it creates addiction, fetishizes the
'image' rather than 'the real object', makes the face pale and the penis lanky, hastens
death by sucking out brain-matter and *sangue vivo* (or what Milton would call the
'precious life-blood of a master spirit'). Precisely because 'Nature puts all her energies into preparing matter for generation', from the purest part of the blood, it must
not be wasted.[86]

The scandal of Rocco's *Alcibiade*, then, consists not merely in its shameless eulogy
of forbidden pleasures like anilinctus, but in its expropriation of the mainstream
language of pedagogy and cognitive science. Filotime shares with his contemporaries metaphors of educational promise—to 'infuse solid and deep doctrine', to
'insert seeds of fertile and delightful doctrine into your retentive faculty', to 'open
your mind'—that become literal in the act of penetration, just as they will in the
heterosexual version, *L'Escole des filles* (39, 42, 50). The seed-image comes directly
from Plato's *Phaedrus*,[87] and we recall from Chapter 1 that Milton's pedagogy 'stirs

---

[84] Columbia edn. xv. 228–50, 48 (*CPW* vi. 400–14, 321–2), and see Ch. 3 n. 118 below.
[85] Bruno, *Candelaio* (Ch. 1 n. 90 above); 'Il Lasca' to Varchi (Ch. 1 n. 31); prefatory poem 'Di M.V. ai
maestri di scola', *Alcibiade* 38 ('la scienza per lo cul cacciate', a similar phrase being used in the publisher's
preface, 37).
[86] 74 (but he had relieved himself by masturbation earlier, 49).
[87] 276 (the seeds or *spermata* of true rhetoric planted in the beloved pupil, closely analogous to the
stream of visual particles that flows between lovers and stirs the 'germs' of their soul (251)).

seeds' and 'inflames infinite desire'; Milton's account of his own education in erotic philosophy ('having had the doctrine of [Chastity] with timeliest care infus'd') even replicates the passivity that makes the seed-model unacceptable to modern educators, and his choice of liquid 'infusion' rather than agrarian implantation reinforces the pederastic analogy.[88] Rocco's explanatory-seductive paradigm—an influx of hot spirits, fashioning the brain to receive cognitive impressions that inspire love for the individual who sends them—anticipates the psychology and physiology of Eros that Descartes invented for Queen Christina in the 1640s. As we shall see at greater length in *L'Escole* (Chapter 3 below), Cartesian erotics could provide a new scientific basis for the phallocentrism, or more precisely spermatocentrism, that Donne had flaunted as a metaphysical conceit: 'I planted knowledge and Life's Tree in thee.'

'True Sodomy', if not an 'utterly confused category' as Foucauldians maintain,[89] was nevertheless capacious enough to loosen firm distinctions between men and women, active and passive, Nature and Art. It always involved non-procreative genital penetration, but Sinistrari and countless other authorities applied it to women as well as men, to heterosexual pederasty as well as homosexual coupling.[90] Aquinas may have placed sodomy among those sins 'by which human beings lost their reason while engaged in venereal acts',[91] but for the neoclassical or proto-Enlightenment libertine those 'acts' stimulated 'reason' to the utmost degree. In ancient Greece and again in this period epheberasty was the 'philosophical' sin, the form of desire most intimately associated with the *diletti dalla conoscenza* where connoisseurship and cognition meet. 'Socratic love' for its adherents signifies discursive authority, Gnosis, education; we have seen in Chapter 1 that Milton adopts Socrates and Alcibiades as the normative model for his own bond with his beloved tutor Thomas Young, and Montaigne proposes the 'Socratic exchange' of sex for

---

[88] *CPW* I. 892 (and see Ch. 1, sect. 2 above); Cryle (using a 19th-century French translation) observes that Filotime's planting metaphor eliminates 'show and tell' and defines teaching as 'something done to the pupil by the master' (*Geometry*, 72).

[89] Cf. G. S. Rousseau, 'The Pursuit of Homosexuality in the Eighteenth Century: "Utterly Confused Category" and/or Rich Repository?', in Robert Purks Maccubbin (ed.), *'Tis Nature's Fault: Unauthorized Sexuality during the Enlightenment* (Cambridge, 1988), 132–68.

[90] For 'sodomy' (sometimes qualified as 'true' or *vera sodomia*) applied to European women before Sinistrari, see e.g. Thomas Maria Sanchez, *De Sancto Matrimonii Sacramentum Disputationum Tomi Tres* (1602; Viterbo and Venice, 1737), book X, disputation iv, number 5; Loraine Daston and Katharine Park, 'The Hermaphrodite and the Orders of Nature', in Louise Fradenburg and Carla Freccero with Kathy Lavezzo (eds.), *Premodern Sexualities* (1996), 129; Leibacher-Ouvrard, 'Tribades et gynanthropes (1612–1614)', *Papers on French Seventeenth-Century Literature*, 24 (1997), 529; Elizabeth Susan Wahl, *Invisible Relations: Representations of Female Intimacy in the Age of Enlightenment* (Stanford, Calif., 1999), 22–3, 274 ('sodomitesse' in a marginal gloss to the King James Bible); Godbeer, 'Cry of Sodom', 266, 267–8, 269. Cf. also Dympna Callaghan, 'The Terms of Gender: "Gay" and "Feminist" *Edward II*', in Callaghan et al. (eds.), *Feminist Readings of Early Modern Culture: Emerging Subjects* (Cambridge, 1996), 296, and Karma Lochrie, 'Presumptive Sodomy and its Exclusions', *Textual Practice*, 13 (1999), 295–310 (though only one of her medieval citations actually uses the word *sodomia*, 309 n. 16).

[91] Cited in Brown, *Immodest Acts*, 16. Though Brown assimilates female 'sodomy' to lesbianism (16–20, 133–4), my category *epheberasty* fits the case she studies better; the deponents all agreed (whether or not they ascribe a sexual motive) that the Abbess Benedetta was transformed into the angel Splenditello and took the form of 'a beautiful young boy of fifteen or sixteen' (122).

wisdom as the basis for a new, improved heterosexuality. Why, then, should openly pederastic texts like Rocco's *Alcibiade* be so rare? Why should the libertine imagination focus so relentlessly on the Female Academy, the *école des filles*, the *académie des dames*, the School of Venus?

I suggest that Roccoesque or 'queer' eroticism underlies the ostensibly heterosexual tradition studied in the following chapters, that *L'Escole des filles* and its successors pursue the same goal as *L'Alcibiade*: an aestheticized, voluntary, Epicurean sexuality, an *amour philosophique* removed as far as possible from mammalian 'necessity'. In the terms of Margaret Cavendish's *Female Academy*, the slippery premodern concept of *female* sodomy created a 'room' to pursue this vision without unduly threatening the masculinity of author or reader. The sins of women alone together in schools and convents—what Sinistrari and others called the 'mute sin', the *peccatum mutum* that dare not speak its name, that must be silenced even at the execution of its perpetrators—provoked infinite fascination and endless chatter among male observers stationed in the wings. Sinistrari himself, author of the most detailed account of lesbian and epheberastic 'Sodomia' among women, warns that this unmentionable yet highly representable crime is particularly rife 'in Colleges of women'.[92] The English poet and traveller courtier Thomas Killigrew—an expert in cloistered sexuality since he studied the possessed nuns of Loudun at first hand—conjured up such a college in his comedy *Thomaso, or The Wanderer*:

> if I would breed a *Thais* or another *Lais*, or put *Ovid* again to School to learn a new art of love, I would send him to study at the grate of the Convertites, where *Aretine* should be made an ass, and blush the publishing his dull postures, compar'd to the ingenious lust that's practis'd in their cells.

We will see the same fantasy of unbridled woman-to-woman lust, a collective erotic self-figuration that recapitulates and goes 'beyond' Aretino, in the 'female' initiation-dialogues reconstructed in Chorier's *Satyra Sotadica* and in *Vénus dans le cloître* (Ch. 4, Ch. 7 below). Killigrew's mouthpiece-character defines convent sex as the supreme instance of 'ingenious lust', the ultimate experiment that sets new standards of depravity and leaves benchmark figures like Ovid and Aretino far behind. Far from the Convertites or Magdalenes repenting their past excesses, 'with double sin they act them o're again, while the spirit of lust plays two parts alone'; bodily and mental desire 'act' on the inner stage, doubling the transgression by combining 'two parts' into one, the passive and the active, 'the lover and the loved, till what was fornication in their house becomes Sodomy in their Cell'.[93]

The domestic-heterosexual tradition of *L'Escole des filles* and its followers, to which I will now turn, grows out of that 'Cell', that overheated 'room' in which—to revive Montaigne's term—women 'engender' a sexual knowledge more advanced

---

[92] *De Delictis*, 236 ('in Collegiis foeminarum', mistranslated in *Peccatum Mutum*, 51); for the 'muting' of specifically female sex crimes, see also Brown, *Immodest Acts*, 19–20.

[93] *Thomaso*, part II, in *Comedies and Tragedies* (1664), 458; for Loudun, see Ch. 3 n. 22 below. Perhaps because of its anti-Catholic slur, Behn seems to have ignored this episode in both the plays she recycled from Killigrew's text, *The Rover*, parts I and II.

(yet somehow more primitive) that anything dull male authors can contrive. The 'Cell' can be interpreted as a place of 'discipline' and punishment, a protective enclosure, a breeding ground, a secret orifice, a unit of signification. Libertine reconstructions of this imaginary recess—variously titled school of 'Nature', School of Venus, College of Ladies, prison-house of sex, 'discipline born in the blood'—pay tribute to women's formative power, while at the same time putting them in their place, 'reducing' them to 'rules of practice'. But as always we must pose the question: who is being sent to school? By reintegrating the 'pornographic' tradition with Rocco's *Alcibiade* and the various permutations of 'straight pederasty' in Platonic erotics, I mean to redefine the subject of eroto-didactic discourse. The category of 'woman' in these transvestite 'schooling' texts certainly performs its routine misogynistic task, but it also stands for the 'other' sex, for *amour philosophique* of whatever gender, free to pursue 'speculative' or 'ingenious lust'.

3

Sex(ed) Education for the Age of Descartes

L'Escole des filles, ou La Philosophie des dames (1655)

Up, and at my chamber all the morning and the office, doing business and also reading a little of *L'escolle des Filles*, which is a mighty lewd book, but yet not amiss for a sober man once to read over to inform himself in the villainy of the world.   (Samuel Pepys, diary for Sunday, 9 February 1668)

Or, en ceste posture où la femme est dessus et l'homme dessoubs, il y a une ressemblance de ceste métamorphose, par la mutation des devoirs qui est réciproque; au moyen de quoy l'homme se revest entièrement des passions de la femme, et ceste posture luy figure qu'il a changé de sexe, et la femme réciproquement s'imagine d'estre devenue homme parfaict dans la situation qu'elle luy faict garder.

So, in this posture where the woman is on top and the man underneath, we find a resemblance to this metamorphosis [of each into the other], by reciprocal mutation of obligations; by this means the man clothes himself wholly in the passions of the woman, and this posture gives him the impression that he has changed sex, and the woman reciprocally imagines herself transformed into a complete man in the position that she makes him keep.

(*L'Escole des filles*, II. 142–3)

THE shift from Italy to France, as the principal source of libertine discourse and ideology, pivots around the dialogue *L'Escole des filles* (with its second part *La Philosophie des dames*), published, prosecuted, and burnt by the public hangman in 1655. This anonymous account of a young woman's sexual initiation—ascribed inconclusively to various authors including Aretino, Claude Le Petit, Paul Scarron, and the marquise de Maintenon[1]—wholeheartedly endorses the 'domestic turn' that the Aretine tradition, culminating in Pallavicino's *Retorica delle puttane*, envisaged only as a courtesan's trick. Though it adopts the dialogue form and plagiarizes certain episodes from Aretino, this French text changes the characters and the motivation dramatically, effectively turning Aretino inside out: descriptions of

---

[1] See Pia (Abbreviations above), p. XIV ('tiré de l'Aretin') and nn. 14, 44 below; the authorities conveniently pinned responsibility on the co-publishers Michel Millot and Jean L'Ange, whose careers otherwise give little reason for ascribing a full-length erotic fiction to them.

delirous coupling, rare in the *Ragionamenti*, become the principal subject, and social satire moves into the forematter (a Mystic Table of Contents which parodies the methodical self-improvement treatise) and into incidental comments on *précieuses* and Platonists. What Pepys soberly calls 'the villainy of the world' now means frank, unembarrassed sexuality rather than street crime and extortion. 'Love', or at least erotic pleasure valued for its own sake, has replaced 'Money' as the supreme goal.[2] The protagonists are no longer butts of satire or figures of extremity but didactic models, embodiments of normative lust, 'bonnes bourgeoises' (p. XLIX) rather than brilliant but sinister prostitutes.

L'Escole des filles retains the premiss of a philosophy tutorial in sexual technique, but the character of the teacher, and therefore the proposed relation between *ars erotica* and personal experience, have changed crucially. Pallavicino injected high intellectual seriousness into the genre, methodically analysing the minutiae of erotic gesture and its 'authentication', but his mouthpiece remains the grotesque old bawd of Aretino. Now the preceptor becomes a seductive confidante, a cousin only a few years older than her pupil. In this respect *L'Escole* provides the model for Tullia in Chorier's *Satyra Sotadica*, who educates and seduces her younger cousin, for the two nuns in *Vénus dans le cloître*, and for countless later libertine instructresses. Desire must still be *taught*, but no longer as an art or 'rhetoric' for constructing a false impression of passionate abandon. The 'philosophie des dames' escapes from mere parody and evolves in two directions that (as we shall see) frequently contradict— towards Enlightenment naturalism, and towards the kind of voluptuary phenomenology glimpsed in my second epigraph, where the 'postures' previously consigned to courtesans are analysed as 'figure' and cognitive interchange.

Compared to its Italian predecessors *L'Escole des filles* is not radically new, but it recombines elements to make what can be taken for a fresh start. The pseudo-Aretine prose dialogue known as *La puttana errante* begins in the same vein— cheerful domestic 'fucking' among family members and social equals, rudimentary changes of posture—but then goes on to turn the heroine into a full-blown prostitute. Piccolomini's *Rafaella* ends the same way as *L'Escole*, training the younger woman for discreet adultery, but lacks the sexually explicit details.[3] Ironically, in view of its campaign for 'natural' pleasure and unbridled heterosexual coupling, the closest Italian model for the French *School for Girls* is Rocco's exclusively 'unnatural' and homoerotic *Alcibiade fanciullo a scola* (Ch. 2, sect. 2 above), where the process of dialogic initiation—the premise of higher knowledge injected through the phallus—similarly brings about the young student's voluptuous 'opening' of mind and body.

For all its apparent simplicity, *L'Escole des filles* has produced a bewildering range

[2] Peter Naumann, *Keyhole und Candle: John Clelands 'Memoirs of a Woman of Pleasure' und der Entstehung des pornographisches Romans in England* (Heidelberg, 1976), 36; Ruth Larson, 'Sex and Civility in a 17th-Century Dialogue: *L'Escole des filles*', *Papers on Seventeenth-Century French Literature*, 24 (1997), 496–511, claims to find Aretinesque sexual satire under a veil of domesticity and educational parody, but does not cite specific borrowings.

[3] Already in the 18th century the marquis de Paulmy noted this source in his library catalogue (Pia, p. XLIV).

of interpretations. Recent male critics claim that it utterly fails to describe the female genitals, indeed that it demonstrates the 'impossibility' of knowing them.[4] Joan DeJean, in contrast, finds that it pays unprecedented homage to the vulva, thereby initiating a more absolute form of heterosexuality and a more modern erotic discourse that 'give[s] censors nowhere to look but at sexuality'.[5] Historians of the Enlightenment see *L'Escole* as a strong predecessor, criticizing Church and State; DeJean—at least initially—found it lacking in 'corruptive complexity', 'blasphemy', and 'violence', and therefore on the side of 'political orthodoxy'.[6] Revising this first impression she gives more credit to what I call the domestic turn, to the ordinariness of the protagonists and the modernity of voicing women's right to pleasure and the means to achieve it. But she still sees it as a pure, univocal text, largely un-complicated by multiple transgressions, alternative forms of desire, and 'libertine philosophizing'.[7]

Compared with the marquis de Sade—or with Nicholas Chorier, discussed in Chapter 4 below—*L'Escole* does offer a muted alternative, perhaps 'monotonous and explicative'.[8] But the authorities considered it profoundly subversive at the time, and ordered it severely punished. DeJean remarks on the lack of 'any trace of sexuality other than hetero'.[9] I will argue that traces of perverse or philosophical complexity can indeed be spied here, faintly in the case of lesbianism, strongly in the case of *iconophilia* and Rocco-style epheberasty. These speculations begin to queer heterosexism itself, even while the narrative remains fixed on the affairs of man and woman. Conventional boundaries of male and female, person and artefact, agent and patient are not dissolved entirely by *La Philosophie des dames*, but they come to seem increasingly fluid.

1. THE LADIES' DELIGHT REDUCED INTO RULES OF PRACTICE? *L'ESCOLE DES FILLES* DEPLOYED

Pepys's celebrated reaction to *L'Escole des filles*, prurient and horrified, begins by placing it at the intersection of Italian and French clandestine discourse. In his shock at discovering that this 'Girls' School' was not the educative text he had ex-pected—a gallant and sophisticated French novel to share with his wife—Pepys pronounced it 'the most bawdy, lewd book that I ever saw, rather worse than *putana errante*—so that I was ashamed of reading in it' (13 January 1668). It is hard to see by

---

[4] Mitchell Greenberg, *Baroque Bodies: Psychoanalysis and the Culture of French Absolutism* (2001), 83, 88, 99, 100–1 (following Jean Mainil).

[5] *The Reinvention of Obscenity: Sex, Lies, and Tabloids in Early Modern France* (2002), ch. 2 *passim*, esp. 72–4, 83.

[6] 'The Politics of Pornography: *L'École des Filles*', in Lynn Hunt (ed.), *The Invention of Pornography: Obscenity and the Origins of Modernity, 1500–1800* (New York, 1993), 116.

[7] *Reinvention of Obscenity*, 74–7, 83.

[8] Jean-Pierre Dubost, *Eros und Vernunft: Literatur und Libertinage* (Frankfurt, 1988), 51 (making it allegedly an example of Foucault's *scientia sexualis*).

[9] 'Politics of Pornography', 116.

what criterion *L'Escole* could be considered 'worse' than the pseudo-Aretine *La puttana errante*; in Pepys's terms it is more genteel, more philosophical, and less perverse, all its sexual numbers taking place between one man and one woman, in the genital rather than the anal channel. But he still found the French text more disturbing, partly because of the contrast between the demure title page and the erotic scenes within, and partly because its scenes of varied coupling do indeed take place in an ordinary *bourgeois* family like his own, rather than in a clearly demarcated red-light zone, convent, or brothel. *L'Escole* does incorporate some elements from the prose *Puttana errante*: the ingénue's discovery of the genitals, the identification of the postures as they arise in the narrative. But the horizon has been transformed by the turn away from prostitution; the formal 'pornographic' account is at once more restricted (to a single boy–girl affair) and more open, since the lovers anticipate 'over a hundred postures' and experience 'a hundred thousand delights' rather than enacting a prescribed numerical schema (I. 25, 49, II. 78).

How then does this new 'educational' text relate to the misogynistic tradition of mocking the 'academy' of female sexuality by reducing it to a brothel? Do the French text and its English translation—*The School of Venus or The Ladies Delight Reduced into Rules of Practice*—reassert the old canard, that intellectual advancement creates 'public women'? Margaret Cavendish had turned the tables by revealing the narrow focus of this sexualization drive; traumatized by the autonomous '*Female Academy*', her male characters admit that 'our minds are so full of thoughts of the Female Sex, that we have no room for any other Subject or Object' (Ch. 1, sect. 4 above). Does the new domestic fiction provide more 'room', or less?

The English translator certainly forges a link between the forbidden text and the forbidden places of illicit sexuality, naming the book in a way that revives dormant associations with the 'puttana errante'. Openly prostitutional works like *The Wandring Whore* and *The London Bawd* define the brothel as 'the School of Venus', and this phrase is in turn adopted as the English title of *L'Escole*, enhancing the ambiguity of the French 'filles'. Even in the original French text the innocuous-seeming title *L'Escole des filles* gives way in the second half to *La Philosophie des dames*, which invokes not only the satirical attack on *les femmes savantes* but also the kind of pornographic triumphalism that we have studied in Chapters 1 and 2. Women were barred from higher education, so Pallavicino dedicates his *Retorica* to the 'University of Famous Courtesans', Claude Le Petit translates the *Université d'amour* with added sexual details, and the English *Practical Part of Love* invents an entire 'University of Love' with bawdy equivalents for every item on the syllabus, its library featuring the female sex as a 'two-leaved book'. In an era of striking advances in women's intellectual and cultural presence—the age of the *salons* and Saint-Cyr, Madeleine de Scudéry and Françoise de Maintenon, Anna Maria van Schurman and Bathsua Makin, Christina of Sweden and Lady Anne Conway—this pornotropism seems like a hysterical counter-reaction.

L'Escole des filles decriminalizes this didactic trope, to be sure. The entire book becomes the 'school', and the learning process, no longer a set of tricks requiring technological mastery and suppression of feeling, becomes a personal discovery, an awakening-and-surrender to the 'truth' of sexual pleasure. But the French text is no less ideological, despite having suppressed the kind of references to *puttanismo* openly flaunted by Aretino and Pallavicino. Women's teaching orders were rapidly expanding in France, and in both countries a new generation of rational feminists were centring their demands on the thesis that proper education would release their intellect from the restraints of biology; *L'Escole des filles* (the school for daughters? maidservants? prostitutes?) teaches that the sole purpose of women's life on earth is 'fucking'. (The ingénue in the French version discovers that 'il semble que l'on ne soit garçon et fille que pour cela', which the English translator elaborates into a full-blown ontology: 'we were created for Fucking, and when we begin to fuck we begin to live, and all young People's Actions and Words ought to tend thereto'.[10]) The female voice is expropriated, obviously enough, to drive home the message that sexual education constitutes the only true liberation for women. As that English title suggests, the main ideological task of libertine representation is to equate 'the School of Venus' with 'the Ladies' Delight', reducing both to neoclassical 'Rules of Practice'.[11] In Sarah Fyge's words, 'They would have all bred up in Venus' School.'[12]

We should be careful, however, not to assume the same reductiveness in the act of exposing it. Trick or not, interiorization (novelization, domestication, characterization) creates 'room' for play beyond the confines of ideological intention. The *mise en discours* may produce secrets less reassuring to phallocentrism, lessons that undermine the master discipline. *The School of Venus*, we should recall, is also the title of a broadside ballad (*c.*1680) in which a young woman learns the disappointing truth about male detumescence. *Garçons* as well as *filles* are inscribed into this universal school, reduced to an epiphenomenon of a sexuality constructed by the 'rules of practice'. And the *institutrice*, brought to life by the exigencies of representation, may take on the autonomy that satire seeks to deny: simulated voicing, fabricated authorship, congeals into authority.

The publication, dissemination, and suppression of *L'Escole des filles*—which have attracted more attention than the text itself—reveal a powerful will to believe. Aficionados and prosecutors alike confer on the 'mighty lewd book' an almost magical ability to collapse the distinction between representation and practice, to shake the foundations of 'good morals and Christian discipline', to corrupt the subjects of Charles II, to destroy 'all those Fundamental Principles and notions of Modesty, decency and Virtue', or to 'debauch, poison and infect the minds of all the youth of this Kingdom'.[13] (Similar assumptions about the efficacy and applicability of the text

---

[10] *Escole*, II. 61; lost English translation, *The School of Venus*, cited from the King's Bench trial records of 1745 (hereafter 'KB'), p. '48', partly transcribed in Thomas, 23; see Abbreviations above for details of these versions.

[11] Ian Hunter, David Saunders, and Dugald Williamson, *On Pornography: Literature, Sexuality and Obscenity Law* (New York, 1993), relate these 'rules' to their Foucauldian reading of *L'Escole* (5, 33).

[12] Introd. n. 19 above.

[13] Legal records of 1655 cited in Pia, 177 ('contre l'honneur de Dieu, de l'Eglise et fort contraire aux bonnes moeurs et dissipline chrestienne'); 1680 indictment of *The School of Venus* ('a most wicked, scandalous, vicious and illicit book'), Greater London Record Office, Middlesex Session Roll MJ/SR 1582

underlie twentieth-century campaigns against pornography.) As my Pepys epigraph suggests, *L'Escole des filles* was certainly read for furtive pleasure masquerading as 'information', 'corrupting' his mind and body in the privacy of his chamber. But numerous exhibitions of this notorious title give it a wider circulation and a more public recognition: the Paris hangman acknowledges the work in the very act of suppressing it, burning it into the memory of the assembled crowd; Dutch pirates redesign it for a transnational market, using a punning imprint ('Fribourg, Chez Roger Bon Temps') that could only appeal to English readers like Pepys; London playwrights like William Wycherley cite it to produce a *frisson* on the public stage, as when the libertine Horner lists the fashionably shocking imports that he might bring back from France—'Bawdy Pictures', 'new Postures', and 'the second Part of the *Escole de Filles*' (Ch. 5 below).

The original publishers evidently planned a covert infiltration of the élite as well as the popular reading public, commissioning a respectable-looking frontispiece from the eminent book illustrator François Chauveau (fresh from engraving the famous Carte de Tendre for Mlle de Scudéry's *Clélie*), arranging for fifty copies to be printed on quality paper and properly bound: 'eight or nine' of these were sent to Scarron and presumably circulated among his acquaintance—including his young wife, the future Mme de Maintenon, royal mistress and founder of Saint-Cyr.[14] Though the authorship of *L'Escole* has never been proved conclusively, its publishers attempted to father it on several renegade aristocrats of the previous generation (pp. XXII–XXIII, 182, 186), just as English pornographers would claim the posthumous parentage of 'Rochester'. Writing the sex life of an ordinary *bourgeoise* evidently still required an aristocratic cachet. Within the book itself, in fact, one preface insists that young girls must read it because it comes from the pen of a modern author greatly in favour at Court for his 'wit and high birth' (p. XLVIII); this advance puffing of a writer *tout à fait spirituel*—'totally brilliant' rather than 'wholly spiritual'—anticipates the materialization of *esprit* that runs throughout the dialogue itself.

In France—despite the burning of nearly 300 copies with the effigy of the publisher—this 'filthy, impudent, infamous book' became part of the seductive equipment of courtiers and ministers. Apart from Pepys, the best-documented case of ownership involves no less a figure than the Finance Minister Nicholas Fouquet, the friend of Mlle de Scudéry, the patron of Molière's *École des maris*, and the collector of literary-erotic trophies.[15] According to the confiscators who discovered and

---

(hereafter cited as 'Middx.'); KB prosecution. The French prosecution of 1655 was not the last; DeJean (*Reinvention of Obscenity*, 65) cites the brutal punishment of yet another alleged author as late as 1669.

[14] Pia, 178, 182, 183–4, 184–5; Foxon, 33, Pia, pp. XXX–XXXII, and DeJean, 'Politics of Pornography', 122, speculate on Scarron's authorship.

[15] Among his confiscated manuscripts was a letter of sexual bargaining supposedly written by Scarron's widow before she became marquise de Maintenon. Pia (pp. XXXI–XXXII) denies its authenticity, but Jean-Michel Pelous, *Amour précieux amour galant (1654–1675)* (Paris, 1980), 221, finds conclusive a transcription in Martin Lister's journal; this MS, published in John Lough, 'Comment travaillait le grand Corneille', *Revue d'histoire du théâtre*, 2 (1950), 454, only proves that such trophies were circulated *as* authentic in Maintenon's lifetime.

burned the book after his arrest in 1661, Fouquet had installed it in the 'secret cabinet' of a *petite maison* furnished for his mistress, the sexual 'school' meticulously
implanted in a custom-designed space with an 'entrée mysterieuse' like the female
body itself.[16] He evidently intended a kind of Valmontian education, moulding his
own ingénue according to the 'rules of practice' already prescribed in the secret
book. Even closer to Court, the correspondence of Bussy-Rabutin and Mme de
Sévigné recounts the scandal precipitated by finding a copy of *L'Escole* behind the
bed of one of the maids of honour. Rather than showing autonomous female consumption of this text (as scholars often assume) the episode actually provides
another case of masculine implantation, since 'Monsieur le Duc' gave it to her—
presumably so that she could carry out the command of the printed preface,
'reciting it to your friends and sending them all to School'.[17] In earlier anecdotes
where maids of honour are confronted with an explicitly obscene or 'Aretine' text,
the intention is to give them 'a pitiful fright';[18] in the age of the 'feminocentric'
Escole, gossip implies their voluntary participation in the reading—even though
the result was more punitive, the entire group losing their position at Court.

Louis XIV himself intervened to purge the Dauphine's female entourage of this
contagion, just as he had intervened to suppress the evidence of libertine literacy in
another scandal, twenty years earlier: the complaint of the nuns of St Catherine
against sexual harassment by their Franciscan supervisors, cast into words on their
behalf by Alexandre Louis Varet. Like the author of *L'Escole*, these irregular monks
infuse women's 'education' with 'a *spirit of Wantonness and Libertinism*'. Among
other sins of mismanagement, Varet identifies two that are specifically textual: the
cordeliers write down the nuns' confessions and circulate them amongst themselves,
'to *favour their design* upon those whom they had a mind to *seduce*'; and they lavish
them with corrupting literature (novels, comedies, amorous 'catechisms') in order
'insensibly to ingage them in vitious inclinations'. Particularly effective for making
the nuns 'susceptible of the Affections which they endeavoured to cherish in them'
was that work of demonic excess, 'L'Ecole des filles'; in Varet's own words—closer to
the 'motions' of mechanical philosophy and the *motus* of rhetorical persuasion—by
recommending *L'Escole* these libertine teachers sought to 'les rendre susceptibles
des mouvements qu'ils taschoient de leur inspirer'.[19]

Phantasms of the girls' school as erotic-textual theatre—like Killigrew's vision of
the convent outperforming 'Aretino's Postures' (Ch. 2, sect. 2 above)—are updated
in this real-life example, and in turn provoke fictional emulation: in *Vénus dans le*

---

[16] Le Petit, *Œuvres*, ed. Lachèvre, pp. xix, xx; for Scudéry and Fouquet, cf. DeJean, *Tender Geographies*
(New York, 1991), 61–2.

[17] Sévigné, *Correspondance*, ed. Roger Duchêne, Bibliothèque de la Pléiade (Paris, 1972), iii. 335, 1308;
Escole, p. XLVIII. Pia recounts the anecdote without including the crucial detail of the donor (p. XLI).

[18] *Gossip from a Muniment Room, Being Passages in the Lives of Anne and Mary Fytton, 1574 to 1618*, ed.
Lady Newdigate-Newdegate (1897), 32 (an Elizabethan courtier lectures the noisy maids 'with a payre of
spectacles on his nose and Aretine in his hand'), a ref. I owe to Raymond Waddington.

[19] Varet, *Factum pour les religieuses de Sainte Catherine lés-Provins contre les Peres Cordeliers* ([Paris?],
1668), 60, and cf. 57, 59, 74, *The Nunns Complaint against the Fryars* (1676), 46, 54–5, 101, and Roger
Thompson, *Unfit for Modest Ears* (1979), 144–7.

cloître the nuns describe and criticize the two books given them by their libertine 'spiritual' directors, *L'Academie des dames* (Jean Nicolas's adaptation of Chorier) and the inevitable *Escole des filles* (Ch. 7, sect. 4 below). In each case—the policing report on a corrupt ministry or the fictional episode of canon-formation—the lewd book functions as what Peter Cryle calls 'a gift bestowed compellingly on the pupil'.[20] Indeed, the distinction between fact and fiction, text and body, breaks down in commentary on these scandals. Alexandre Varet happens to have written educational theory and anti-novel polemic as well as reporting on the corruption of the nuns, and the three themes mesh together seamlessly: when he warns young ladies about the effects of fiction (the genre dominated by women authors like Scudéry), he denounces exactly the process that *L'Escole des filles* hopes to achieve, the creation of a pleasure-driven and male-oriented female subject through textual-sexual agency. Novels 'redouble the ardours of their passions', and translate the 'movements of fictitious heroines' directly into the soul, the gestures, and the actions. Such books are 'dangerous' because they provoke in their female readers 'the desire to raise in men who look at them' the same passions 'expressed so agreeably' on the page. The female-voiced text for Varet produces, not a passive sensualist, but an active *metteuse-en-scène* who can master 'disguises' and 'finesses', extend the representation into real action, control the inmost feelings and perceptions of her spectators.[21]

Interiority in the seventeenth century, recent research suggests, was conceived in images that vividly evoke the physical realm even when repudiating it in favour of mind or spirit. In devotional writing as in Varet's polemics against lewd fiction, the distinction between verbal representation and bodily 'movement' becomes hazy. During the celebrated exorcisms of Loudun, according to Killigrew's eyewitness report, demonic possession was explicitly located in the nun's vagina.[22] The principal demonologist at that convent, Jean-Joseph Surin, had earlier described the dramatic moment when one of his flock suddenly experienced herself as 'banished and confined to her interior, as if in a profound solitude that offered vast spaces to hide from the eyes of men; . . . she dwelled there, where Love kept her fully occupied'. In a letter given paradigmatic status by Nicholas Paige, Surin argues that rather than feeling alienated by this inward exile, 'the very word *intérieur* ravishes her' and inspires her to become a vocal teacher of others, urging them 'to enlarge and dilate their interior incessantly'.[23] Spatial, textual, and anatomical interiors, rhetorical, physical, and spiritual dilation, seem interchangeable in this state of rapture, as they do when another moralist advises young women to 'leaf through their inner book' in search of the word made flesh, *feuilleter votre livre intérieur où on apprend la*

[20] *Geometry in the Boudoir: Configurations of French Erotic Narrative* (1994), 21.

[21] *De l'éducation chrestienne des enfans* (Brussels, 1669), 184–5; 1678 English tr. cited by J. Paul Hunter in 'The Loneliness of the Long-Distance Reader', *Genre*, 10 (1977), 466, 471.

[22] J. Lough and D. E. L. Crane, 'Thomas Killigrew and the Possessed Nuns of Loudun: The Text of a Letter of 1635', *Durham University Journal*, 79 [NS 48] (1986), 259–68, esp. 265: 'being asked where the Devill was, the Frier and she Confest in her Thinge:)' (punctuation *sic*).

[23] Cited in Paige, *Being Interior: Autobiography and the Contradiction of Modernity in Seventeenth-Century France* (Philadelphia, 2000), 1.

parolle incarnée (Ch. 1 n. 46 above). Exploiting this fluid area between intimate text and visceral anatomy, *L'Escole* tries to provide an explicitly sexual two-leaved book that still delivers some of the 'ravishment' and 'dilation' promised by contemporary devotion.

2. 'LEAF THROUGH YOUR INNER BOOK':
FOREMATTER AS FOREPLAY

The early editions of *L'Escole des filles* clearly cultivated the effect that captivated and disturbed Pepys, the shocking contrast between demure title page and lascivious 'interior book'. (The 1655 edition has indeed vanished as its prosecutors hoped, but we can reconstruct it from Dutch copies and from the trial documents themselves.) Neither of its title pages, the engraving by Chauveau or the printed one that follows, signals the erotic contents of the dialogue; only retrospective knowledge invests Chauveau's domestic interior with illicit significance, as the dialogue turns the bed, the mirror, and the abandoned sewing-basket into props for the erotic *mise en scène*. The sober title itself anticipates textbooks of social advancement like François Colletet's *Académie familière des filles* and comedies of enlightenment like Molière's *École des femmes*. While brazen Italian texts like *La puttana errante* or *La retorica delle puttane* declare their obscenity in the very title, *L'Escole* presents itself quietly and respectably. The title *L'Escole des filles* proved bland enough, in fact, to be used for a contemporary comedy and for at least three works of proper conduct and female accomplishment, which follow the pornographic work in time and cash in on its allure.

The meta-didactic engraved frontispiece displays the transmission of knowledge from woman to woman through the medium of the book. (No example has survived, and Chauveau himself had given the plate away before his interrogation; the 'Fribourg' edition contains a crude but apparently accurate copy, however (Fig. 4).[24]) As Ruth Larson observes, this image of instruction refers more to the *idea* of book-learning than to any passage in *L'Escole* itself: there is in fact no episode in which the older Susanne points to a book called 'l'École des filles', and Chauveau's book-within-the-book likewise shows a scene unrepresented in the text though common in traditional manuals of instruction—the preceptor sitting under the branch of a tree addressing a pupil who stands.[25] Chauveau's frontispiece can be interpreted as pointing to the discrepancies between oral interaction and printed codification, especially when compared to his better-known frontispiece for Molière's *École des femmes*. Uncannily, the 'interior book' in the *Escole* seems to be a miniature copy of the Molière frontispiece, even though it was done eight years earlier; the sexes are reversed, however, with the female seated and the male standing.

---

[24]   Pia, pp. XIII–XIV, 184.
[25]   'The Iconography of Feminine Sexual Education in the 17th Century: Molière, Scarron, Chauveau', *Papers on French Seventeenth-Century Literature*, 20 (1993), 499–516, esp. 500–3 (502 shows the two *Escole des filles* title pages side by side, whereas in fact they follow one another in an unfolding sequence); see also my 'Visual Realism of Comenius', *History of Education*, 1 (1972), 122–3.

Oral authority in this latter image (Fig. 5) represents a singularly useless precaution, since Molière's Arnolphe (like Dom-Pèdre in Scarron's *Précaution inutile* and Pinchwife in Wycherley's *Country-Wife*) constitutes the forbidden knowledge of sexuality in the very act of forbidding it.[26] One English adaptation, in fact, closed this gap between frontispiece and text by introducing an illustrated book into the dialogue itself: '*Katy*. It seems this pleasure hath many postures. *Fanny*. . . . above a hundred; have you but a Little patience and I will describe them by the help of a Little Book I have here which will shew you Every different posture as I go on in my description.'[27] Like the obedient scholar in *La puttana errante*, the young acolyte identifies these images as she recounts her experience, and thereby draws attention to the additional plates ('after the Manner of Aratine') that adorn this edition.

The printed title page reinforces its key words (*école-philosophie-dames*) with the Latin motto, *Agere et pati*; the older woman will train her pupil in the appropriate occasions 'to act and suffer'—or rather, as we retrospectively realize, to take the active and passive role in bed.[28] The Aristotelian identification of woman with *patient* and man with *agent* had been so deeply infused into medicine and law that one expert could argue against the very existence of hermaphrodites 'because the internal and fundamental principal . . . of man is opposed to that of woman, because one consists in activity and the other in passivity, one in giving and the other in receiving'.[29] But libertine 'schooling' undermines this model of biologically fixed identity by creating an oxymoronic *female agent*, acting with what Ben Jonson called 'hermaphroditical authority' (Ch. 1, sect. 3 above).

Later versions of the title page tease the reader with further variations on intellectual discipline and gender propriety. The 1668 'Fribourg' edition draws attention to, yet crucially conceals, the added materials that 'augment' it: violently obscene poems like 'The Combat of Prick and Cunt'[30] are presented with coy ellipses, suggesting some improving theme such as the combat of soul and body, while the equally rude Table of Contents is made to sound like a Cartesian exercise in 'methode' or a Comenian textbook, where each 'Curiosity' can be found by tracing its 'marked number' (Fig. 6).[31] In another edition, the title page announces that the

---

[26] See Ch. 5, sect. 3 below (both Arnolphe and Pinchwife are anticipated in Scarron's *Précaution inutile*).

[27] KB '21–2' (Foxon, 36); in these extracts from the illustrated English version Fanny (or perhaps the prosecutor) has inserted into an account of her husband's caresses phrases like 'as in Plate 2', 'as in Plate 3', etc. (KB '32', '33'), not in the original (where named 'postures' are in fact quite few, e.g. pp. LIV–LV, II. 71 and 80).

[28] This motto *was* used in the original MS (Pia 187) as well as in the 'Paris', 1667 edn. (BnF Enfer 112); Chorier (*Satyra*, V. 146) identifies it as Livy's definition of the true Roman spirit and applies it to sado-masochistic flagellation.

[29] Speech to the Bureau d'Adresse, Paris, 1636, cited in Lorraine Daston and Katharine Park, 'The Hermaphrodite and the Orders of Nature: Sexual Ambiguity in Early Modern France', in Louise Fradenburg and Carla Freccero with Kathy Lavezzo (eds.), *Premodern Sexualities* (1996), 129–7.

[30] Not mentioned in the trial records, but Canon Maucroix seems to ascribe it to the indicted publisher Jean L'Ange ('Un Ange enregistre, dit-on, | Les combats du V. et du C.'), in Louis Perceau (ed.), *Le Cabinet secret du Parnasse: Théophile de Viau et les libertins* (Paris, 1935), 189.

[31] BL PC 29.a.16 (the Table Mystique, but not the numbering-system, was already in the 1667 edn.); in his edition (p. XL) and in his *Les Livres de l'Enfer du XVIe siècle à nos jours* (Paris, 1978), col. 419, Pia transcribes this title page (from a 19th-century reprint) as if the rude words existed there, misrepresenting the effect of concealment.

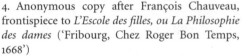

4. Anonymous copy after François Chauveau, frontispiece to *L'Escole des filles, ou La Philosophie des dames* ('Fribourg, Chez Roger Bon Temps, 1668')

5. François Chauveau, frontispiece to Molière, *L'École des femmes* (Paris, 1663)

book is already essential reading in convent libraries, and promises thirty-seven engraved 'belles figures' (a number that to the cognoscenti would suggest the posture-series of *La puttana errante*).[32] The English translation replaces the original motto with a riskier and more erudite Latin epigraph, the distich from Secundus that Casanova expounded for his prurient English visitor (Introd. above). (One newspaper advertisement draws attention to this provocative quotation by citing it in full.[33]) Secundus' question to the grammarians—why is cunt masculine and prick

---

[32] Undated 'Liège' edn., apparently seen at auction and described in [Jules Gay], *Bibliographie des ouvrages relatifs à l'amour, aux femmes et au mariage*, 4th edn, ed. J. Lemonnyer, ii (Lille, 1897), col. 61; the '37 plates' announced on the printed title page were already missing when it reached the saleroom.

[33] Foxon, 35, confirmed by KB.

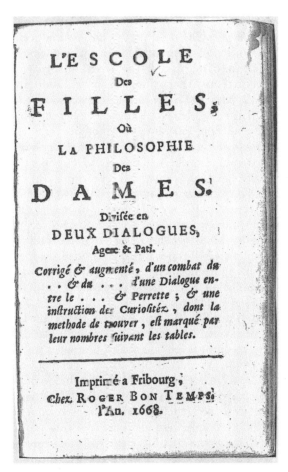

L'ESCOLE

Des

FILLES,

Où

LA PHILOSOPHIE

Des

DAMES.

Divisée en

DEUX DIALOGUES,

Agenc & Pati.

Corrigé & augmenté, d'un combat du
. . & du . . . d'une Dialogue entre le . . . & Perrette ; & une
instruction des Curiositéz , dont la
methode de trouver , est marqué par
leur nombres suivent les tables.

Imprimé a Fribourg,
Chez ROGER BON TEMPS.
l'An. 1668.

6. *L'Escole des filles*, title page

feminine?—spells out the paradox implied in the cryptic *Agere et pati* and unsettles
the very idea of an 'internal and fundamental principal'; agency cannot be simply
aligned with gender, as long as the *cunnus* is dominant and the phallus passive.

Taken together, then, frontispiece and title page suggest the authority of the book,
the discipline of 'method', the desire for self-improvement through the conduct
manual or educational treatise. Are we dealing here with a merely destructive
parody? Comparison with other contemporary 'École des filles' titles suggests, instead, the ironic reversibility of 'moral' and 'libertine' pedagogy. One Dutch compilation on the 'Art of Being a Woman'—a pious mother–daughter dialogue followed
by a collection of moralizing poems—tries to catch the reader's eye by calling itself
L'Ecole des Filles or The School for Young Daughters and pretending to be translated

from French.[34] A more worldly but equally virtuous French dialogue, originally called *L'Escole morale des filles*, altered its title to *L'Escole des filles, en dialogues* as if to exploit the notoriety of the libertine version. This dialogue between a beautiful young woman on the brink of marriage and her recently married female mentor defines the 'Fille' entirely in terms of her feminine allure and amorous destiny, skirting many subjects that preoccupy the erotic *Escole*. As promised in the opening advertisement, the two 'Maistresses de cette escole des Filles' or 'enlightened female Directors' teach the emergent 'Fille' how to negotiate multiple suitors, how to 'manage' one's charms with 'adresse' (while still remaining 'innocente'), how to steer between the extremes of intellectual pretension and *galanterie*, how to avoid those 'dangerous' books that 'put vanity and love into a Girl's mind and heart' (Scudéry is permitted but Montaigne contains too many 'choses libres'). She must learn to differentiate herself from the *esprits forts* (women who speak Latin and despise feminine triviality) and from those loose women who learn Italian to 'express their amorous passion' and who turn the conversation to 'choses un peu trop libres'. Already worried about seeming 'trop sçavante pour une Fille', the younger speaker asserts that 'some Women' join the men in initiating this compromising 'freedom' of discourse—surely an allusion to the salacious conversations of Susanne and Fanchon that make up the original *Escole*.[35]

Another book of the same title and format as the lewd original exploits the similarity quite deliberately; evidently meant to circulate in the literary underground, it turns into a plea for traditional religion after a few pages of explicit obscenity. Shameless references to the 'Vit' and 'Con' or the 'Art foutatique' show how far this pious fraud is prepared to go in ensnaring readers for the 'Seconde Partie, ou sont contenus les vrays et solides enseignments d'une Fille'.[36] (If Wycherley knew of this work, Horner's reference to the 'second part' might be even more ironic.) This ingenious triple dissimulation complicates and reverses the strategy of *L'Escole* itself: the dissolute treatise, with its *libertin* doctrine of external conformity and secret hedonism, pretends to hide behind a solemn didactic and exegetical structure, enticing the reader with its numbered index and its methodized 'Table Mistique et Allégorique selon le Sens Moral et Littéral'; the devotional text, on the other hand, pretends to be the sort of lewd book that advertises itself from behind an educational façade.

Far more thoroughly than the other French and Dutch *Écoles* [*morales*] *des filles*, this faux pseudo-*Escole* exploits the symbiosis of libertinage and traditional morality rather than denying it. Poised between two didactic procedures, the Socratic

---

[34] D.V.W. (tr.), *L'Ecole des Filles ofte Schoole voor de Jonge Dochters* (Amsterdam, 1685), BnF Z-37862; the internal titles of the text use only the Dutch words and the subtitle *De Kunst der Vryery*.

[35] Paris, Bibliothèque de L'Arsénal, 8° S.3757, *L'Escole des filles, en dialogues* (Paris and Avignon, 1672), fo. a2 ('deux Directrices éclairées'), pp. 16–18, 22, 49, 51, 59, 61, 118–19; the publisher Antoine du Périer, who also provides the preface and a commendatory poem praising girls for their Beauty, Empire over our Hearts, 'inevitable charms', etc. (fo. a6), refers to the work as *L'Escole morale des filles* (fo. a3), as in the drop-heads to both parts (1, 139). See also Linda Timmermans, *L'Accès des femmes à la culture* (1598–1715): *Un débat d'idées de saint François de Sales à la marquise de Lambert* (Paris, 1993), 117–19.

[36] R.D.V., *L'Escole des filles* (n.p., 1658), i. 6, 12; cf. Foxon, 33–4 and plate VII.

person-to-person dialogue and the more abstract printed manual, both of these 'foutatique' *Escoles* exploit the secrecy of one medium and the physicality of the other.[37] They aim to produce an interior state of arousal and receptivity, whether it leads to educational self-improvement, to libertine desire, or to devotional submission.

Turning from the innocent-seeming frontispiece and title page to the forematter of his 'mighty lewd book', Pepys's horrified fascination would have been first provoked by the verbal obscenity that rapidly invades the initial 'girls' school' tone. The 'Epistre invitatoire aux filles' might pretend, with silky arrogance, to prepare 'belles et curieuses damoiselles' for marriage, euphemistically promising them what devotional manuals and conduct books also promise: just like the *Escole* [*morale*] *des filles* this book will provide a handy list of wifely '*devoirs*' and '*préceptes*', 'infallible secrets' for capturing men, tips on how to reconcile 'honour' with 'industry and address' in the pursuit of pleasure.[38] But the 'Argument' and the 'Table Mistique' speak more and more transgressively, reintroducing gutter names for the genitalia and whorish titles for the 'postures'. (By the time we reach the second dialogue, of course, the pretence has long been shattered and the unctuous politeness of the 'Advertissement aux dames', urging them to avoid 'dishonour' by performing the most advanced postures, becomes openly offensive.[39]) Moving from indecency to blasphemy, a papal 'Bulle Orthodoxe' pronounces anathema against any able-bodied reader, *male or female*, who fails to 'spermatiser ou estre stimulés de quelque émotion spirituelle ou corporelle'.[40] Pepys obediently carries out this injunction, like a true convert recording his interior motions in the diary: we recall that *L'Escole* 'did hazer my prick para stand all the while, and una vez to decharger'.

The self-conscious staging of 'mighty lewdness' culminates in a commendatory poem to the 'Autheur foutu d'un foutu livre', written by that complex, Rochesterian figure Claude Le Petit.[41] (Le Petit is not mentioned in the trial papers and could have written his violent anti-*précieuse* 'madrigal' in the later 1650s, at the same time that he was adding bawdy details to *L'Université d'amour* and turning 'the most beauti-

---

[37] Cf. Larson, 'Women, Books, Sex and Education in 17th-Century French Literature', Ph.D. dissertation (Yale, 1991), 50–86 (on the erotic *Escole des filles* but not the other works with this title).

[38] pp. XLVII–XLVIII. As Lise Leibacher-Ouvrard implies, the buried anti-*précieuse* pun in the second syllable of *invitatoire* is presumably deliberate; 'Femmes d'esprit ou substance étendue? *L'École des filles ou la Philosophie des dames (1655)*', in François Lagarde (ed.), *L'Esprit en France au XVIIᵉ siècle*, Actes du 28ᵉ congrès annuel de la North American Society for Seventeenth-Century French Studies (Paris, 1997), 191.

[39] II. 57–8; this epistle does sound like a parody of L'Ange's sugary dedications to great ladies (cf. Pia, pp. XXXVIII–XXXIX).

[40] p. LXI (the 1667 edn., fo. *12, had an ellipse where 1668 reads 'spermatiser'); DeJean, *Reinvention of Obscenity*, 64, ingeniously suggests that the 'Bulle' parodies the *privilège* officially required to publish, though in fact it appears in a less conspicuous place, 'inserted at the end in some copies' of the 1st edn. (Pia, 196, 199) and placed between the Table and the Madrigal in 1667.

[41] p. LXIII; entitled 'Sur l'Escole des filles, madrigal' in the contents-list of his *Bordel des Muses, ou les neuf pucelles putains. Caprices satyriques de Théophile le jeune* (Leiden, 1663), of which only a fragment survives (*Œuvres*, 105), but extant texts of *Escole* (Dutch piracies) add a garbled version of Millot's name, the co-publisher indicted *post facto* as the author ('A Monsieur Mililot').

ful thoughts of St Augustine' into intensely erotic devotional verse.) In this short poem, which takes every opportunity to play on the literal and metaphorical meanings of *foutre*, Le Petit revives the deliberate anti-decorum of his *libertin* predecessors in the school of Théophile de Viau ('Phyllis, tout est foutu . . .').[42] In a poem by the sieur de La Porte in the 1622 *Quintessence satyrique*, 'la belle et docte Alizon' reviews the various schools of philosophy and concludes on the basis of 'expérience' that 'le souverain bien | Ne se trouve qu'à foutre bien', the only *summum bonum* is a good fuck.[43] Echoing this *femme savante libertine*, Le Petit represents the central philosophical and practical goal of the dialogues that follow as a crudely Epicurean 'art of living': the author of *L'Escole* 'dans tous [s]es foutus écrits | Fai[t] voir que bien foutre est bien vivre'. He *makes us see*, somewhat violently, that 'to fuck well is to live well', and to this end provides 'Cent arguments foutus . . . pour faire foutre en cent façons'. The reader is led to expect an advanced posture manual, codifying the 'hundred ways' where the Italians had listed a mere thirty-six; later illustrated versions were perhaps suggested by the need to gratify this expectation, as well as by the original frontispiece.

Le Petit's equivocal commendation confers a kind of inverse glamour on this author 'fucked' in all his works, extracting a kind of offensive sublimity from abjection—precisely the art that *La retorica delle puttane* recommended for the courtesan. Just as Pallavicino's artist achieves 'gloria' from disgust (Ch. 2, sect. 1 above), so this 'foutu livre . . . te rendra pour jamais glorieux'. Moreover, the real 'glory' of *L'Escole* lies not in its expertise but in its linguistic gesture or stylistic impact: in a resolutely modern way ('par une nouvelle coutume') its 'prose' knocks us out, blows us away, or 'nous fout par les yeux'—literally, 'fucks us in the eyes' (p. LXII). The material text, rather than serving as a transparent vehicle, becomes the direct source and object of arousal. Despite its simulation of female experience, the 'School for Girls' embodies a crude phallic power, forcing the reader into the passive role. If the adolescent Le Petit had a hand in writing *L'Escole* itself, as many suspect, this celebrative-abusive definition of libertine authorship would be doubly appropriate.[44]

In the main body of the text, this aggressive libertine project unfolds only gradually; the opening pages establish the domestic setting and the naive character of the *fille* who is to be schooled. As the 'Argument' explains, the two dialogues progress like a language tutorial from the most rudimentary to the more complex. In the first part

---

[42] Ch. 2 n. 57 above.

[43] Perceau, *Théophile*, 80. Leibacher-Ouvrard links it to a later recycling of the poem in *L'Academie des dames* (Ch. 7 n. 45 below); see 'Pseudo-féminocentrisme et ordre (dis)simulé: La *Satyra sotadica* (1658–1678) et l'*Académie des dames* (1680)', in Roger Duchêne and Pierre Ronzeaud (eds.), *Ordre et contestation au temps des classiques* (Paris, 1992), i. 193–202 n. 20.

[44] Frédéric Lachèvre, *Mélanges* (Paris, 1920), 91, infers from the poem that Le Petit 'dut également revoir le texte et y mettre probablement du sien' (though he does not explain why Millot and L'Ange never mention him); H.-J. Martin assumes that Le Petit is the 'probable' author, in Martin et al., *Livres et lecteurs à Grenoble: Les Registres du libraire Nicolas (1645–1668)* (Geneva, 1977), 93, 682, while Leibacher-Ouvrard notes that he 'perhaps committed' the dialogue itself ('Femmes d'esprit?', 193). Le Petit's knowing treatment of 'the author' is matched in the commentary-like 'Table Mistique', which at one point remarks that a certain passage was slipped in 'without the author's knowledge' (p. LV).

(*L'Escole des filles* proper) Susanne instructs her younger cousin Fanchon in the mechanics of sex and the legitimacy of pleasure; in the second part Fanchon recounts her physical initiation with her neighbour Robinet—novelistically situated as a Paris merchant's son so wealthy that he has chosen to leave the business and pursue genteel leisure—and then (like a heterosexual copy of Rocco's Alcibiade) showers her mentor with increasingly recondite questions. Both women thereby construct a 'Ladies' Philosophy', and the second part uses that phrase as its title. The text thus enacts the graduated curriculum, moving from the simplest catechism to an elaborate analysis and defence of the life of copulation, raised to a higher plane by 'connoissance' and intensified by what would then be considered wildly transgressive perversions (gazing at the naked body, touching the genitals, reversing the missionary position still ordained by the Church). Susanne is characterized as 'sçavante et spirituelle en amour' but apparently not in any other sphere, and her 16-year-old cousin begins as a *tabula rasa*, with an inarticulate 'itch' but no vocabulary for sex and no sense of what the organs might be for (pp. XLIX, I. 26). Fanchon exemplifies the type defined by La Rochefoucauld, who cannot experience love unless they have 'heard it spoken'.[45]

Susanne's erotic-didactic task is quite literally to 'mettre l'amour en la teste de sa Cousine', defining her pupil in Comenian (or Gradgrindian) terms as a receptacle for concrete facts. As the 'Argument' explains, she does this 'par les discours comme de fil en esguille', with discourse as fine as thread through the eye of a needle, moving from plainwork to fine embroidery. (Note the irony of using the sewing metaphor for an instructional programme that destroys the willingness to sew.) Susanne matches her cousin's *naïveté* by inventing 'naivités' in the aesthetic sense, fresh and vivid descriptions 'so pleasing that they make her mouth water'. She 'represents the sweets of love' so skilfully that she can instruct and excite Fanchon with almost mechanical precision, bringing her 'à point nommé' at the moment when (by clever pre-arrangement) Robinet the prospective lover arrives, and action takes over from discourse.[46]

The first dialogue thus corresponds to Comenius' 'mother-school' or 'Exciting-Place of the Senses', where education consists of pointing to objects and inculcating links between simple words and sense-impressions, planting the 'roots' of later disciplines.[47] (The childlike aspect of Fanchon is maintained throughout by Susanne's addressing her with *tu*, while the younger cousin always uses *vous* to her senior tutor.) Taking her cue from Fanchon's account of seeing a dangling thing like a *boudin blanc*, Susannne creates a language of farmyard and kitchen more suitable for a peasant than a merchant's daughter: the genitals become 'a Hogs Pudding', 'the slit of our Cunt', the 'Cherry', 'a Cows Teat' (an oddly female and nutritious metaphor for the phallus).[48] Like Valmont corrupting Cécile in Laclos's *Liaisons*

---

[45] *Maximes*, 136, cited in Introd. above.
[46] pp. XLIX–L, text emended according to the 1667 edn., BnF Enfer 112, fos. *4ᵛ–5.
[47] Ch. 1, sect. 2 above.
[48] I. 9, 12–16; English phrases from Middx. and KB ('12' is identical in both, proving that the 1680 tr. was recycled in 1745).

dangereuses, she teaches her the crudest words (*con, cul, vit*) as if they were the correct ones.[49] This element of homeliness recurs even after the cultural level has supposedly risen: ejaculate is 'like boiled sauce'; the vagina sounds like dough being kneaded; the penis excited by the hand 'looks like someone who is trying to vomit but can't'—an image actually plagiarized from Aretino, so regressing to an earlier stage of libertine discourse.[50] In the ostensibly sophisticated second dialogue, the mock-heroic and periphrastic presentation of the genitals likewise reverts at times to crude physicality, with an undertone of violence obviously intended to be comic ('what a brave sight is it to see the workman of Nature sprout out at the bottom of a Mans Belly, standing stiffly, and shewing his fine scarlet Head with a thwacking pair of Stones to attend its motion, expecting every minute the word of Command to fall on'). The English translation takes this military imagery still further: 'Be not afraid of having thy Quarters beaten up, though the Prick be never so big, indeed it may scare a tender young Virgin.'[51]

Rather than 'beating up' or breaking down the tender young virgin, Susanne's catechistic style elicits and embroiders Fanchon's own naive questions, so that her activation as sex-object seems to be a voluntary discovery, a dialogic self-constitution as libertine subject. Needless to say, this 'catechism' yields results directly opposed to the principles that upheld 'good morals and Christian discipline' (as the prosecutor realized in 1655). Fanchon asks 'will bad things happen? . . . isn't it forbidden?' and Susanne replies with a cascade of specious reasoning: honour is merely reputation, and since Robinet is 'discreet' nobody need know; if Robinet tells, Fanchon will dismiss him and no one in town will respect him any more; God will know, but he will tell nobody; in any case, sexual pleasure is no more than a 'peccadillo'. The entire edifice of moral condemnation is (too casually) revealed as the political construction of masculine power: 'I cannot think leachery a sin; I am sure if Women govern'd the World and the Church as men do, you would soon find they would account Fucking so lawful as it should not be accounted a Misdemeanor.'[52] This passage in the English translation seemed scandalous enough for the prosecution to transcribe it into both the 1680 and the 1745 indictment.

Susanne aims to produce the absolute opposite of the little book wielded by Arnolphe in Molière's *École des femmes*, 'Les Maximes du mariage ou les devoirs de la femme'.[53] As critics note, Arnolphe's 'maxims' contain inscribed within them the scandalous alternative he is trying to blot out; I would argue that the same is true of the libertine converse. The clear-cut opposition of 'mighty lewd book' and

---

[49] Cf. DeJean, 'Politics of Pornography', 114.

[50] I. 21, 44, 24 (cf. Aretino, *Ragionamenti*, II. i. 167 [173]). Jean Mainil, *Dans les règles du plaisir: Théorie de la différence dans le discours obscène romanesque et médical de l'Ancien Régime* (Paris, 1996), 62–3, argues that, while the penis is concretely represented, the vulva is not only an absence but 'impossible' to describe.

[51] Middx. tr., augmenting II. 161–2; for the military phrase that replaces the French 'saccager', cf. Rochester's 'Disabled Debauchee', 45 ('Bawds Quarters beaten up').

[52] I. 28–9; Middx. tr. Carolin Fischer, *Éducation érotique: Pietro Aretinos 'Ragionamenti' im libertinen Roman Frankreichs* (Stuttgart, 1994), 235, cites this passage as a genuine 'critique of society and Church', rare in the 17th century.

[53] Cf. Larson, 'Molière, Scarron, Chauveau', 512–14.

'Christian discipline' is compromised in two respects. First, libertine liberation is quite compatible with 'bourgeois' self-improvement and marriage. When Fanchon agonizes that she will be struck off the marriageable list and driven out of society, Susanne assures her that this secret initiation into pleasure will give her precisely the inner poise that men desire in a wife; her 'connoissance intérieure' will render her 'self-sufficient', 'better at speaking' (in respectable conversations about 'choses bonnes et honnestes'), and thus more eligible in the market. (The translation adds a note of cultural inferiority: 'by thy private fucking thou wilt attain to a kind of Confidence which is much wanting to most of our English Ladies.'[54]) And secondly the life of hedonistic freedom turns out to be just as rule-bound as marriage. As we shall see, subservience to pleasure generates a list of *devoirs* just as long as that proposed by Church and State, promulgated by the traditional husbands treated satirically in Molière's *École des femmes* but sympathetically in *Les Femmes savantes*. Disciplinary language dominates even in the earliest scenes, for example when Susanne insists on the proper technique for handling the penis, 'comme il faut que tout se fasse par ordre et dans les règles du plaisir' (I. 23). This striking insistence on the 'rules of pleasure' suggested the reductive 'Rules of Practice' prominently displayed in the title of *The School of Venus*, and continues to echo in academic studies of *L'Escole des filles*.[55]

In the second part, Fanchon's body has been penetrated and her tongue set free; the two-part structure provides a cleft or breach, imitating the change of mind before and after 'dépucellage', and the dialogue can thereby graduate from 'l'école des filles' to 'la philosophie des dames'. The 'bold accustoming' that Milton rather wistfully admired in male libertines (Ch. 1, sect. 2 above) has now been installed in the female sexual subject. Following Susanne's instructions in the first part, which constantly prompted her to ignore her mother and listen to 'the words of men' (I. 5), Fanchon now rejects maternal tutelege and the traditional roles of her gender: before, 'I was only good for sewing and keeping silent', but now she is voluble and intelligent, her mind 'opened' by sex.[56] (The 'Table Mistique' remarks at this point 'comment l'esprit s'ouvre en chevauchant' (p. IV), echoing Rocco's pun on 'opening the mind' of Alcibiade and anticipating La Fontaine's notorious *conte* 'Comment l'esprit vient aux filles', where the heroine likewise 'could only sew and spin' before she goes to 'school' with the local priest.[57]) This sexualization of enlightenment clearly seeks to demolish the cornerstone of the feminist education campaign, the thesis (argued for example in Margaret Cavendish's *Female Academy*) that the educated woman

---

[54] I. 32; KB '27' (Foxon, 36).

[55] e.g. Herbert DeLay, ' "Dans les reigles du plaisir . . .": Transformation of Sexual Knowledge in Seventeenth-Century France', in Wolfgang Leiner (ed.), *Onze Nouvelles Études sur l'image de la femme* (Paris, 1984), 10–20.

[56] II. 61, and contrast 63, where Fanchon 'pretends to be at my work sewing' (*mon ouvrage*) as she waits for Robinet.

[57] *Contes*, IV. 1 (published in 1674 and banned for corrupting morals and 'inspirer le libertinage', as Anne L. Birberick shows in *Reading Undercover: Audience and Authority in Jean de La Fontaine* (1998), 106).

can become 'as confident and knowing as a Married Wife' *without* losing her virginity (Ch. 1, sect. 4 above). As in *L'Alcibiade fanciullo a scola* we are asked to believe in what we might call the phallepistemic theory: the penis becomes the supreme instrument of truth, inducer or creator of mind, even though the dialogue supposedly shows women transmitting *their own* 'inward knowledge' or connoisseurship.

Genital infusion has already made Fanchon 'mieux disante' or 'better at speaking', as Susanne promised, but that verbal confidence seems narrowly channelled into hostility against her 'bigot of a mother' (II. 59), darkening the rosy picture of female solidarity in sexual enlightenment. Early in the first dialogue, Susanne had already undermined Fanchon's mother's authority by declaring that she too has secret lovers (I. 11)—which should, according to Susanne's own logic, make her *more* intelligent and authoritative. Fanchon now boasts herself 'bonne à tout ce que l'on voudra', but she is only substituting the external authority of worldliness (*on*) for that of the mother. And her newly 'opened' discourse further suggests (perhaps unwittingly) that sexualization has unsettled rather than confirmed her own identity. Rather than discovering 'suffisance de toy-mesme' as she banters and contradicts her mother, she reports that 'now I am talking as if it was another person' ('je discours comme si c'estoit une autre'). Fanchon now declares herself 'founded in reason', situating herself in a tradition of equating consummation and cognition that stretches back to Tullia d'Aragona and forward to *Paradise Lost*, where marital sexuality is likewise 'founded in reason'.[58] But her 'reasoning' consists largely in rationalization of her pleasure-giving role and ingenuity in concealment. At times the new domestic sex-heroine resembles the old courtesan-trickster expert in the 'art of *puttanismo*'—especially in the English translation, which coarsens Susanne's praise of this new mental alertness: Fanny will soon become, not 'fine et rusée à ce jeu', but 'as cunning and deep a Whore as any in the Nation'.[59]

But does the relation between representation and practice really resolve itself into a simple, phallocentric empiricism? Though now in theory words have turned into things and 'experience is more valuable than discourse', the actual discussion reverts over and over again to the topic of language: what lovers say to each other and why, what the different gestures, cries, and postures signify when their meaning is spelled out, what is the precise difference between *enfiler, enconner, besoigner, foutre, chevaucher*. As Fanchon takes over the narrative role, Susanne's responses collapse the distance between description and copulation ('You make it last so long! . . . I seem to be there!' (II. 67–8)). Throughout the long second dialogue, speculation is interrupted by the 'action' only to resume with renewed vigour. Indeed, the blunt declaration that 'l'expérience vaut mieux que le discours'—or 'the Practique Part was better than the Theorique'—is put into the mouth of Robinet immediately after he confesses ignorance on the philosophical questions Fanchon asks him.[60] As a

---

[58] II. 61–2 (and cf. *PL* IV. 755); Robert Darnton interprets Fanchon's sexual-mental awakening in wholly positive terms, as 'the first step toward the acquisition of intellectual independence' ('Sex for Thought', *New York Review of Books*, 22 Dec. 1994, 69), an Enlightenment-Whiggish reading shared by Fischer, *Éducation érotique*, 236–7.

[59] II. 60; KB '47' (Thomas, 22).

[60] II. 80; 'Roger' cited from the KB tr., '64' (Thomas, 30).

relatively mindless stud he is at once central to, and excluded from, the 'grand raisonnement sur le plaisir d'amour' (p. LV).

The author's summary makes it clear that the emotional core of the book, the 'thread' that draws us through it, is the linguistic seduction of the reader, for which the Susanne–Fanchon interchange serves as pretext or foreplay. These 'mouth-watering' discussions will explore the totality of love ('tout ce qui apartient à l'amour') in a manner so 'rare, stimulating, playful, novel, subtle and convincing' that 'they inspire love in the readers', and even the most fastidious ladies—or perhaps 'the most disgusted'—will find something to satisfy them.[61] Fanchon's responses within the text act as a model for this verbal seduction: 'je sens une émotion toute pareille dans la description que vous m'en faites' (I. 48). Following the logic of the 'Papal Bull', and thereby prescribing the reaction of future readers like Pepys, Fan-chon testifies to her cousin's descriptive powers by exclaiming 'je descharge!', a verbal and physical ejaculation in the present tense of the dialogue (II. 141). Intratextual arousal recurs at other climactic passages, for example the military scene of 'sacking' or 'beating up quarters' ('Quelle douce cruauté! J'enrage'), confirming the worst fears of the twentieth-century anti-pornography movement.[62] The goal of La retorica delle puttane—indeed of all rhetoric—has now been recreated in the domestic school of girl-talk: the unmediated fusion of discursive and orgasmic 'motion', not filtered through a novelistic narrative but directly voiced by the subject herself.

3. *LA PHILOSOPHIE DES DAMES*, OR THE COGNITIVE POSTURE

L'Escole's 'philosophical' credentials depend on its 'methodical' arrangement and its attempt to raise eroticism to the level of 'theory', as well as on its direct borrowings from Plato, Lucretius, and Descartes. Its self-conscious attention to language, and to the cognitive dynamics of the lovers' interaction, transforms the basic sexual act into what Evelyn called 'speculative Lust'. At moments—however fleeting—this produces an ideal of awareness and mutuality that transcends the narrow interests of masculinism and its reductive definition of female 'reason'. These 'hauts raisonnements, tirés de la plus subtile doctrine de l'amour', constitute an élite female reader, a 'past mistress' distinguished from those ignorant and unresponsive lovers who 'have not had the theory before the practice' (II. 58). Without this libertine con-noisseurship, sex is a mere mechanical tickling or discharge; with it, 'an inexhaustible well-spring of thoughts'. As in Plato's hierarchy of lower and higher Eros, the unenlightened find only physical pleasures in copulation, 'without knowing

---

[61] p. L ('Argument'), and cf. II. 119 ('vous en feriez bien venir l'eau à la bouche'); Larson, 'Women, Books, Sex', 77, notes that 'Susanne has caused Fanchon's mouth to water—and other things as well.'

[62] II. 162 (cf. 'violences douces' I. 53). Mainil's interpretation (*Règles du plaisir*, 71–5, 77) depends on giving the maximum emphasis to the violence of this 'saccager' passage, which supposedly obliterates the earlier unheroic treatment of the phallus and the feminist implications of episodes like the 'woman on top', restoring the traditional doctrine of woman as 'silent' and subordinate, and sending the whole pedagogic process into the 'abyss' (78); this means ignoring large segments of the second dialogue (discussed in sect. 3 and 4 below) and downplaying the discursive activity of the two dialogists.

where they come from', whereas the connoisseur enjoys 'the sweet imaginations which the mind conceives as it receives' the body's messages (II. 146). As the English translator put it, 'we do not Fuck like Beasts who are only prompted thereto for generation's sake by Nature, but with knowledge, and for Love's sake'—in the original, 'par amour et par connoissance de cause'.[63] *L'Escole* here borrows for heterosexual pleasure Rocco's equation of superior love with the 'diletto dalla conoscenza'.[64] No wonder the 'Table Mistique' singles this passage out as an 'Instruction méthodique et plus spirituelle que les autres' (p. LVI).

By insisting on 'knowing the cause', Susanne embodies and literalizes the Renaissance personification of Philosophia, a stately woman flanked by boys who carry the motto 'CAUSARUM COGNITIO' (Fig. 2 above). Fanchon gives clear signs of candidacy for this academy when she exclaims, in response to Susanne's lecture on the 'hundred thousand *douceurs*' that delay orgasm, that 'there would be many more things to say if one were to ask the particular reason for each one' (I. 53). In this context Robinet seems 'undertheorized'—as graduate students would say—when he fails to answer Fanchon's newly urgent question about the origin of the postures that he teaches her.[65] By clinging to 'the Practique Part' and rejecting 'the Theorique', he consigns himself to the role of journeyman or laboratory assistant, even though the entire episode is supposedly staged for his benefit. Indeed, as a walking phallus he matches perfectly Susanne's description of the 'workman of Nature'. Despite fitful attempts to make him a dashing 'honnête homme' and an educational leader explaining his 'reasons', Robinet's principal role is to confirm the association of his name with plumbing.[66]

To explain the 'cause' of erotic pleasure, the philosophical Susanne adapts the Aristophanic theory of Eros in Plato's *Symposium*, which interprets desire as a striving to reunite with the sliced-off part of the original self. (Humans were created double-headed, eight-limbed, and in some cases androgynous, until Zeus punished them with separation.) This mythology of primal unity had already been expropriated by Rabelais,[67] and even in *La puttana errante* couples struggle to 'fuse two bodies into one' (107/36). But the libertine dialogue expands these casual references into an explanatory paradigm, evidently drawing straight from Descartes's abstract and methodical reworking of the myth in *Les Passions de l'âme*.[68] *L'Escole*'s version of the Platonic androgyne is more ambiguous and more genital-centred, however. Copulation signifies both the futile striving of inadequate halves and the narcissistic desire of 'two perfect wholes' to be 'transformed one into the other' (II. 142), the 'most ardent wish for transformation' that Rocco had discovered at the core of desire (Ch. 2, sect. 2 above). *L'Escole* shows the influence not only of Rocco and Descartes but of Renaissance Platonism, perhaps transmitted through dialogues

---

[63] II. 96–7; KB '77' (Thomas, 32).   [64] *Alcibiade*, 54 (Ch. 2, sect. 2 above).

[65] II. 80 ('il n'estoit pas assez sçavant').

[66] I. 33, II. 78, and cf. Larson, 'Women, Books, Sex', 76.

[67] See my *One Flesh: Paradisal Marriage and Sexual Relations in the Age of Milton* (Oxford, 1987, 1993), 68.

[68] Arts. 80 and 90.

like Tullia d'Aragona's *Infinità d'amore* (Ch. 1, sect. 1 above). But the sixteenth-century courtesan never claimed, as *L'Escole* does, that primal unity meant the perpetual interlocking of the 'two members' (II. 136). In Plato's original fable the whole body was fused—seed being squirted from external organs onto the ground—and penetration was only invented after the fall, a feeble compensation for a union forever lost; in the libertine fantasy, the *Urmensch* is locked forever in copulation.

Despite the strategic 'naivetés' of its opening pages, then, I am not convinced that the 'sexual explicitness' of *L'Escole des filles* is 'completely without philosophical implications', as DeJean once asserted.[69] To 'authenticate' its *femme–femme* dialogue, *L'Escole* collages together numerous details from earlier philosophers of love and gender, including *cinquecento* women writers like Tullia d'Aragona and Moderata Fonte. (Fonte's *Merito delle donne* provides a plausible source for Susanne's feminist critique of male lawmaking and her revisionist treatment of Platonic myth.[70]) Among contemporaries—as Lise Leibacher-Ouvrard has shown—*L'Escole* engages with the physiology and erotology of Descartes in many places and at many levels.[71] This can only partly be explained as a satire against those mid-seventeenth-century feminist intellectuals who passionately espoused that philosopher.

Cartesianism rapidly branched into opposing tendencies, splitting along unresolved contradictions in Descartes's own theory of the mind–body relation.[72] By eliminating the vegetative and sensitive faculties of the soul, which Aristotelian materialists like Pallavicino retained as a convenient way to valorize sexual desire, Descartes was forced to assign the body a far greater role in the passions and the appetites. Though he famously insisted that the mind has no sex, in effect he redefined 'the sphere of the intermingling of mind and body' as a sensuous realm gendered feminine.[73] The supreme dualist thus lent his support to a mechanistic form of materialism; despite its title, *Les Passions de l'âme* is largely concerned with the physiology of hot, pumping fluids and interwreathing pipes. And Descartes's physiological explanations for what his theory rendered impossible—the direct interaction of mind and body—created unintended comic possibilities by attaching inordinate importance to a small nub of flesh called the pineal gland. This double inheritance is nicely encapsulated in Molière's *Femmes savantes*: when Bélise explains how she admits 'thinking substance' in her lover but not 'la substance étendue' (v. iii. 1685–6), *she* thinks that Cartesianism endorses her anti-corporeal purity, while the *audience* responds to 'extended substance' as a comic euphemism for the phallus.

I would argue, in fact, that in many respects the narrative of sexual education confirms and exemplifies Cartesian 'method'. The explicitness of the libertine dialogue satisfies the Cartesian demand for clear and distinct ideas, and its exclusive

---

[69] 'Politics of Pornography', 116.

[70] (1600), ed. Adriana Chemello (Venice, 1988), 53, 70; *The Worth of Women*, ed. and tr. Virginia Cox (1997), 90, 115.

[71] 'Femmes d'esprit?', *passim*.

[72] See Aram Vartanian, *Diderot and Descartes: A Study of Scientific Naturalism in the Enlightenment* (Princeton, 1953), *passim*, and Susan James cited in Preface n. 8 above.

[73] As Genevieve Lloyd argues in *The Man of Reason: 'Male' and 'Female' in Western Philosophy* (1984), 50.

focus on sexuality reflects the analytic search for first principles; Descartes himself sometimes included love and hate, as well as the *cogito*, among the irreducible constituents of his being.[74] *L'Escole des filles* should be read as half parody and half application, not just in its tubular physiology but in its 'discourse on method' and the process of discovery it unfolds: isolation in a heated room, elimination of customary prejudices and external authorities, introspection and lucidly ordered exposition of the fundamentals derived from it. 'Private fucking' becomes at once the object and the space of knowledge, the insulated 'stove' where (im)pure thought can flourish undisturbed. Fanchon's newly 'opened' reason and her genitalized ontology ('we were created for fucking, and when we begin to fuck we begin to live') is not so much a failure of the *cogito* as a corollary of it. As Yves Citton remarks of contemporary impotence anxieties, in the age of Descartes 'the *Cogito ergo sum* has as its inverse and shadow a *Coeo ut sim*, I fuck in order to be'.[75]

Susanne's *connoissance de cause*, like Rocco's 'diletto dalla conoscenza', derives from a close analysis of the various 'postures' and perversions that distinguish the expert lover from the 'beast'. Sexuality is constructed as a cognitive system made up of gestures, glances, and the particularly intense forms of language uttered during copulation. Under the pressure of desire (or more precisely 'la contemplation de leur jouissance') lovers' speech turns into 'hieroglyphics', a remarkable analytic-descriptive concept that anticipates by three centuries the 'pornogrammes' that Roland Barthes discovered in de Sade.[76] In the brief and often obscene phrases of the bedroom whole sentences are packed into a monosyllable, and Susanne like a good anatomist reveals their inner structure: if the man exclaims 'mon cœur!', for example, it means that 'he would like to slip in his member all the way to her heart'. (Unfortunately she does not explicate the woman's cry 'mon fils!', which she mentions only to show the security risk posed by noisy lovers.) Susanne confirms the *précieuse* critique of obscenity parodied by Molière, by taking individual syllables as the vehicles of illicit sexual meaning. Language becomes more authentic and more transparent in these 'hieroglyphic' pictograms, 'in which are seen the vivid painting of the beloved object in the mind's eye, while the soul rejoices in this knowledge (*se réjoui[t] dans ceste connoissance*)' (II. 117).

In libertine as in Comenian education, perception becomes *la vive peinture* that excites pleasurable knowledge; Susanne's key phrase condenses two of Comenius' favourite concepts, *viva autopsia* or living eyewitness, and *orbis pictus*, the 'painted' beauty of the tangible world that generates ideas in the mind. The resultant erotic 'hieroglyphs' might resemble the 'figures' of *La retorica delle puttane*, except that they are involuntary, spontaneous, and emotionally driven. The process of 'authen-

[74] Cf. Jean-Maurice Monnoyer, 'La Pathéthique cartésienne', in his edn. of Descartes's *Les Passions de l'âme* (Paris, 1988), 19, and Leibacher-Ouvrard, 'Femmes d'esprit?', 188.

[75] *Impuissances: Défaillances masculines et pouvoir politique de Montaigne à Stendhal* (Paris, 1994), 67, developing Georges Falconnet and Nadine Lefaucheur's reformulation *je bande donc je suis*.

[76] *Sade, Fourier, Loyola* (Paris, 1971), 162. Part of the following analysis has appeared in my 'Divulgence, "Autopsy", and the Erotic Text: *L'Escole des filles* and Chorier's *Satyra Sotadica*', *Papers on French Seventeenth-Century Literature*, 29 (2002), 465–73.

ticating' desire by looks and gestures, for Pallavicino the supreme achievement of the fraudulent courtesan, here denotes sincerity and participation.

Susanne's concept of the 'hieroglyph'—an entire scene compressed into a moment that is simultaneously a hyper-significant sentence and a 'vivid painting'— explains many of the unorthodox techniques and postures adopted by the 'educated' mistress and passed on to her pupil. Grasping and stroking the penis (to take a recurrent example) is the equivalent of saying ' "I take pleasure in touching that with my hand because it is all my good and my happiness" '; for men this gesture 'est suffisant pour expliquer tous les mouvemens du cœur de leur dame' (II. 131). Like *L'Escole* itself, the errant hand 'makes explicit' those mysterious inner 'movements' of female pleasure whose invisibility continues to fascinate and frustrate the hardcore pornographer.[77] Quite early on, Susanne instructs Fanchon in the 'virtues of the girl's hand' and its 'power to give pleasure' (I. 21)—when applied according to strict 'orders' and 'rules' (23)—and in the *Philosophie* this power to arouse is further reinterpreted as the capacity to draw out a discourse of mutuality: manual 'designation' of the favoured organ proves that love 'wants to share all its goods equally' (II. 130–1).

No less than six pages are then devoted to what a more reductive age would call the hand-job, temporarily subsuming the philosophical dialogue into the instruction manual. This gesture—lusciously described to bring out the painterly contrast between the 'main blanche et délicate' and the 'shameful' red penis 'spitting' its seed against the fingers—actually 'penetrates to the depths' of the man and produces greater pleasure than copulation itself. Italian pro-sodomite literature had already converted the argument from design into a justification of forbidden practices (Ch. 2, sect. 2 above). According to Susanne, male anatomy is specifically 'designed' by Nature to receive the female hand, which serves simultaneously as an organ of pleasure and knowledge: 'everything has its reason, if one is willing to pluck it.' This 'penetrating' action seems to reverse agency and subservience even when performed as a service to the male—a reversal given another twist in the English translation, when Katy describes Roger 'making me lay my powerful hand upon his prick'.[78]

This lingering fascination with the hand can be interpreted in two ways. As Susanne herself explains, it is the 'symbol of friendship' (II. 132), emblematizing those higher cultural values that elevate the base sexual act above animality; Rocco, as we saw in Chapter 2, used the nobility of the hand to transfer glamour to the anus by analogy. For Marin de Mersenne, 'the art or the science and industry of the hand is so great that several have called it one of the principal instruments of wisdom and of reason'.[79] The elegant white hand epitomizes not only the refinement of the lady but her creativity, an idea parodied when Susanne dwells on its ability to *cause*

---

[77] The main thesis of Linda Williams, *Hard Core: Power, Pleasure, and the 'Frenzy of the Visible'* (Berkeley and Los Angeles, 1989; expanded edn., 1999).

[78] II. 130–5 (in the 1668 edn., 160–6); KB '62' (amplifying the phrasing of II. 77), my emphasis.

[79] Tr. in Elisabeth Le Guin, ' "As my Works Show Me to Be": Physicality as Compositional Technique in the Instrumental Music of Luigi Boccherini', Ph.D. dissertation (Berkeley, 1997), 1.

7. Pierre Dumonstier Le Neveu, *Artemisia Gentileschi's Hand*

rather than merely enhance erection (II. 134, 152). Women artists would frequently emphasize the hand in their self-portraits, and male critics invariably praised the 'little, white, tender hands' of the *virtuosa*.[80] One fellow-painter commemorated (and isolated) her hand in a life-sized drawing (Fig. 7); calligraphic inscriptions on this drawing equate the *sçavante* artist with the 'sçavoir faire' of her 'worthy hand', whose miraculous products 'ravish the most judicious eyes'.[81] In an age when ladies wore gloves, the hand was already an intimate sight obtained by undressing, and these associations of artistic 'ravishment' only increase its erotic charge.

Pepys's encounter with *L'Escole des filles* provides a cruder explanation, however. Surviving copies are small enough to fit into one hand, the classic definition of the erotic text recorded by Rousseau.[82] Despite its heterosexual and feminocentric pretence, the fundamental erotic act for the book's probable readers was solitary male

---

[80] Fredrika H. Jacobs, *Defining the Renaissance Virtuosa: Women Artists and the Language of Art History and Criticism* (Cambridge, 1997), 65, 86, 103–4, 121, 122, 128, 135, 169, 174, 182.

[81] Mary D. Garrard, *Artemisia Gentileschi: The Image of the Female Hero in Italian Baroque Art* (Princeton, 1989), 63–4, 503 nn. 102–3, fig. 49.

[82] This often-cited phrase (e.g. DeJean, 'Politics of Pornography', 110) supposedly records the words of a *female* reader.

masturbation, and this description (with female stand-in) provides the 'money shot' they require.[83] The author seems to adopt the position in which Fanchon once glimpses Robinet, holding his own 'engine' and gazing at it fixedly (II. 77).

Susanne's emblematic or 'hieroglyphic' interpretation of sexual techniques extends from the hand to the whole repertoire of performances hitherto expected only of the 'Protean' courtesan, but now recommended for the couple. The kiss (analysed into all its different subdivisions) becomes a sign of 'amorous fantasy without limits' and an 'image et représentation' of other kinds of conjunction (I. 49–50, II. 140). Rubbing the genitals across the face and body likewise reveals the deep Platonist–Cartesian desire to unite with the separated half of our own being, since any 'resemblance' of union is as exciting as the thing itself; it declares, with some ambiguity, that the woman's thighs, breasts, and face are 'aussi bien partie de l'homme que les autres' (II. 139–40). Does this mean they are human, deriving from the original unity, or that they 'belong to the man'?

The most densely significant of these sexual hieroglyphs—and the one most frequently condemned in confession manuals and how-to books for married couples—is the inverse posture, or what would later be called 'The World Turned Upside Down'.[84] When the woman climbs on top, Susanne explains, this 'mutual exchange of duties and wills' suggests the possibility of being 'transformed one into the other'; from a distance, it even becomes hard for a voyeur to tell which sex is which. This is the 'métamorphose d'amour' that stirs us most intensely—a diagnosis apparently shared by modern psychoanalysis and by the seventeenth-century reader, since here Fanchon 'discharges' for the first time.[85] Aretino's Nanna had told Pippa how to stimulate a client and take him from above, so that 'when he sees himself being mounted by the woman he was going to ride, he dissolves with delight like a man who is coming', and in Susanne's first lecture-dialogue this passage is plagiarized and amplified; the boy is now 'fucked by the woman he should have been fucking'—the verb has changed to *devoir*—and in exchange he experiences a continuous orgasm ('comme s'il deschargeoit continuellement').[86] During her encounter with Robinet Fanchon obediently combines two of the passages that her professor borrowed from Aretino, continuing the chain of apprenticeship to an older master or 'past mistress': she guides Robinet's penis with her hand, climbs into the 'riding' position, and then tells him 'que je besognais'—in the translator's words, ' "I Fuck thee my Dear." '[87]

The woman-on-top position recurs throughout *L'Escole des filles* as a paradigm of

---

[83] Williams, *Hard Core*, 83–4 and ch. 4 passim.

[84] In an 18th-century French text cited in Mainil, *Règles du plaisir*, 67; cf. Rudolph M. Bell, *How to Do It: Guides to Good Living for Renaissance Italians* (1999), 33, 38.

[85] pp. LIX, II. 142–3, 147; cf. Lawrence S. Kubie, 'The Drive to Become Both Sexes', cited in Tassie Gwilliam, *Samuel Richardson's Fictions of Gender* (Stanford, Calif., 1993), 57–8.

[86] I. 24, translating *Ragionamenti*, II. i. 167 [173] (the same passage contains the image of the vomiting penis cited p. 122 above); Mainil, *Règles du plaisir*, 67–9, 78, cites what are in fact Aretino's words to prove the originality of *L'Escole*.

[87] II. 79, KB '63–4' (Thomas omits); cf. Aretino's *Modi* sonnets 4, 7, 14.

heightened eroticism and mutual cognitive interchange; the metatextual 'Table Mistique' goes out of its way to remark on the author's special fondness for this position, 'repeated so many times' (p. LIX). It prompts the first of Fanchon's many 'why' questions and the first of Susanne's statements of gender-levelling: 'the boy gets more pleasure from being ridden than from riding' (*chevaucher*) because from below 'he can better judge her good will'; his body-language 'says that he wants to submit himself to her in all humility, that he is not worthy to take the upper position' (I. 25). In *La Philosophie des dames* the hieroglyph is fully expounded, reclaiming for heterosexuality the 'interchangeable sharing' and mutual 'transformation' that Rocco had eulogized in pederasty (*Alcibiade*, 65). As Susanne explains, in the philosophical but ambiguous passage that forms the second epigraph to this chapter, the man is 'reborn' (according to one edition) or 'clothes himself wholly in the passions of the woman, and this posture gives him the impression that he has changed sex, and the woman reciprocally imagines herself transformed into a complete man in the position that she makes him keep'; literally, the posture *luy figure* or 'figures forth to him' the sense of gender fluidity.[88] The hierarchical significance of top and bottom remains the same, but the active woman can 'make' the man keep the 'situation' that genders him female. Or perhaps she imagines herself as a man kept under? Or else the posture *per se* is the grammatically dominant 'elle' that keeps both sexes in order?

The posture itself thus has the power to 'figure forth' each partner into a 'reciprocal mutation' of mind and body, a 'resemblance' of the primal androgynous union or exchange of identities (II. 143). The male oscillates between the roles of spectator and participant in this metamorphic theatre, 'better judging the woman's good will' because she assumes an active, performative part. (The title page motto, *Agere et pati*, clearly alludes to this titillating role reversal.) He 'sees and feels' her movements, 'admires' her cooperation, interprets the signs of orgasm in her eyes while 'comparing' these 'pure rays from the true mirrors of the soul' with the messages sent by her limbs and organs, and 'believes' that her body, though it cannot see, is feeling a comparable pleasure. This interaction of sight, touch, and interpretation serves to 'assure him that he is really loved', to 'assure him of his happiness'—which at times he 'seems to doubt' (147–8). At such moments of close analysis, the obscene little book almost seems to extend the Carte de Tendre rather than to reverse it.[89]

This repeated need for reassurance locates *L'Escole des filles* on the cusp between whorish past and materialist future. Versed in previous libertine literature, the male might well be afraid of encountering a Pallavicinan trickster-heroine, brilliantly trained to fake the most spontaneous passion. *L'Escole* certainly shifts attention from the social setting to the underlying mental processes, and this discussion of

---

[88] II. 143 (cf. the earlier reading 'renait' for 'revest', 1667 edn., 132); Greenberg, presumably advancing his psychoanalytic paradigm, describes this wish for transformation as an 'underlying drive', 'unconscious' and 'probably unknown to the text [it]self' (*Baroque Bodies*, 105, 96), even though it is spelled out with Cartesian clarity.

[89] Cf. DeJean, *Reinvention of Obscenity*, 66–7 (noting the ironic fact that Chauveau engraved both Scudéry's map and *L'Escole*'s frontispiece).

inverse postures forms the high point of Cartesian reasoning: when Fanchon grasps the 'rapport' between Susanne's two 'ways of conceiving'—the two-halves theory and the mutual transformation of man and woman 'considered as two perfect wholes'—the teacher exults in this confirmation of her method, which proves that 'raisons de la cause' have been properly deduced from 'effects' (II. 143). But the new philosophy brings a new concern, that bodies and minds might never meet. Lovers in Donne aspire to be so 'inter-assured of the mind' that they need not be concerned about the body;[90] here, in a Cartesian universe where the other could be a mere automaton, they long for the reverse.

The erotic bond is conceived as a kind of mutual voyeurism or self-mirroring: 'there is nothing which excites more than seeing and being seen', a pleasure 'that no human tongue can worthily express ; to see one's partner take an active role is to experience 'a happiness which has no equal' (I. 51, II. 147). Chiming with Claude Le Petit's vulgar praise of the author, 'fucking' seems to take place mainly 'in the eyes'. To excite Fanchon in preparation, Susanne describes herself and her lover gazing at each other's bodies, posing each other for candlelight inspection, and coupling in many different postures; synaesthetically, this visual interchange shows the lover 'taking as much pleasure in being touched by me as he had in touching me'. Prefiguring and literalizing Evelyn's concern with 'speculative lust', she wishes that they could have a real mirror, 'to contemplate our postures better'. Once again, the equipment of the Italian brothel migrates into the French discourse of sincere desire. Susanne's pupil is supposed to take this longing-to-see as a normal effect of companionate desire—a far cry from the trickery and posturing rehearsed in *La retorica delle puttane*.[91] In the English version, published only a few years before Evelyn warned about speculative perversion in the marriage-bed, domesticity is further enhanced by making Susanne's lover her 'Husband'.

The mutual gaze was highly valued, of course, in Platonist theories of ideal love and in traditional commendations of matrimony. As medical writers insisted, God was supposed to have devised the face-to-face position in order to distinguish us from the animals, adding to the genital urge a cognitive and aesthetic desire to generate fresh images that will match the beauty of what we see in the other's regard; children are 'vivid and fresh representations' of ourselves—*vive* and *naive* in the aesthetic sense, like Susanne's first 'representations' of sex.[92] Now *L'Escole* expropriates this model for non-reproductive, libertine sexuality. Pleasure derives from discursive offspring, literal 'representations' with the same vividness and freshness. In orthodox theories of sex and marriage, biological reproduction is the principal locus for the formation of normative identity, which sexual deviance and deformity

[90] 'A Valediction Forbidding Mourning', lines 19–20.

[91] I. 47; for mirrors in Aretino and Pallavicino see Ch. 2 n. 33 above, and for actual ownership of mirrors see Annik Pardailhé-Galabrun, *The Birth of Intimacy: Privacy and Domestic Life in Early Modern Paris*, tr. Jocelyn Phelps (Oxford, 1991), 164–7.

[92] Jacques Duval, *Des hermaphrodits, accouchemens des femmes, et traitement qui est requis pour les relever en santé* (Rouen, 1612), 9 ('vif, et naivement representé'), partly cited in Stephen Greenblatt, *Shakespearean Negotiations: The Circulation of Social Energy in Renaissance England* (Berkeley and Los Angeles, 1988), 84; for 'naiveté' denoting skill in erotic representation, cf. *Escole*, p. L.

help to define by contrast. Libertinism now claims the monstrous as the norm. But it still draws upon a paradigm of 'reproduction'; its postures and perversions attempt to achieve that Cartesian–Platonic union in which 'man and woman formed one single body joined together by those two members, which were enclosed one within the other in such a way that man never died, and *se reproduisoit continuellement*' (II. 136). Libertines 'reproduce themselves' in the image rather than the flesh.

Here, then, is one of the fundamental contradictions of speculative or intellectual libertinism: conceptual figuration and 'metamorphosis' become the *primary* source of desire, even in a text ostensibly devoted to the primacy and stability of physical fruition. 'Le comble du plaisir amoureux' (II. 133), the summit of erotic pleasure, is discovered not in mutual orgasm but in tactile or visual 'hieroglyphics', in *interpreting* the feel of the hand or *watching* the partners exchange positions. The sense of touch is analysed at great length—culminating, as we have seen, in an appropriately luxurious description of masturbation—but even these manual pleasures are mediated through the mental picture, the aesthetic and symbolic contrast between the ugly organ and the cultivated white hand, emblem of lofty friendship and artistic accomplishment. In theory, of course, all these ideas and representations are mere simulacra, deviations from the full intercourse which, in pornography as in conventional marriage doctrine, constitutes the be-all and end-all of sexuality. But these 'tromperies de l'amour' often surpass the real thing. The kiss, for example, 'is an image and representation of the prick entering the cunt to unite with its other half', and since love 'looks for conjunction in everything and in every way', the 'two halves' meet in the act of 'knowing this symbol'; as a result, 'the imagination enjoys this empty figure almost as much as if the real pleasure were attached to it' (II. 140–1).

Susanne is careful here to maintain the superiority of penetration, without which sex could take place entirely 'à la teste': representation is *almost* as exciting, but the 'figure' is still 'vaine'. Fanchon's response, however, suggests that 'knowing' the simulacrum—the mental image, the 'figure', the *symbole*, the present narration—lacks nothing in immediacy. For it is at this precise point that she confirms Susanne's narrative effectiveness by releasing her own seed, staging her own 'money shot': 'Ma cousine, je descharge!' (II. 141). Like Pepys she 'discharges' in direct response to linguistic provocation, without needing a mediating body or 'real thing'. The orgasm is represented as happening without masturbation, as in a wet dream or an actual coupling.

The carefully simulated 'philosophy' of *L'Escole des filles* comes under threat from its somewhat crude masculine ideology, however. Its most inventive doctrines—the immediacy of discourse, the self-governance of the enlightened woman, the erotic power of mental images—struggle on almost every page with an aggressive and reductive phallocentrism. In theory at least, the vivid, 'autopsic' analysis of sexual performances as 'hieroglyphics' of mutual reassurance and cognitive interchange applies equally to both participants, who are conceived as autonomous perceiving subjects irrespective of genital anatomy. But in practice the phallus takes over everything. No sooner is young Fanchon's mind 'opened' than she is plunged into confusion, since she can think of nothing but the genitalia of her lover (II. 150). Susanne's explanation preserves the illusion of mental autonomy: Fanchon is still 'making' this 'representation'; 'her desire' is still working like an artist or educational illustrator, 'placing things before the eyes as vividly as if they were present'. But the result is 'that the whole idea of Beauty discovered in the object loved—the beauty of the face and the composition of the limbs, which are incomparably more beautiful than the two genital organs of man and woman—is nevertheless effaced and as if subjected to this other idea' (151). This political language ('effacée et comme soubmise') suggests the clash rather than the happy conjunction of 'idées' and 'représentations'. Mind becomes a kind of reflex, subjected to the all-consuming 'figure' of the genitalia. When the pupil starts to experience an educated form of desire that reproduces the didactic force of the teacher, all she comes up with is an ugly, domineering prick.

Given the liberationist and anti-conventional polemic of *L'Escole des filles*, it is surprising how often the language of mutuality slides into the language of obligation, duty, *devoir*. Fanchon slips from description to prescription in her first postcoital statement; since boys and girls are 'born to fuck', then all their thoughts and actions '*ought* to lead' to sex (II. 61, my emphasis). The inverted position arouses because of the 'mutation des devoirs qui est réciproque', the 'eschange mutuel des devoirs et des voluntez' (II. 143, 147). Spontaneous desire hardens into rule-bound duty, for the 'boy' as well as the 'girl'. In many episodes, however, this reciprocity lapses into a patriarchal gender assymetry, in which the man wishes and the woman obeys. Love 'wants to share all its goods equally, so that one never has more than the other'—but the best way to express this is to 'designate' the penis as the sole source of 'happiness' (II. 130–1). The lover 'wants love to transform him into the beloved object', and therefore the woman *should* climb on top, a lesson hammered home by repeating 'elle le doibt' (142). Partners must always render due benevolence when the other person wants it—but Robinet already needs 'reminding' of this (75).

Susanne's interjections often reduce her to the spokeswoman of phallocracy. The postures are 'the flavours that take men, and we must let them do it' (II. 86); she uses the word *ragousts* or tasty stews, as if this were just another cookbook, recalling the gourmet treatment of sodomy in Rocco's *Alcibiade* and Descartes's account of the pleasures of disorderly love, in his correspondence with Queen Christina.[93] Despite her lively portraits of the woman on top, Susanne also maintains that even in ideal conditions the woman's body 'does not belong to her, and she cannot refuse anything that he demands' (165). She finally admits that men value *les filles* for their 'obedience in how they dispose themselves' (the verb is *s'agencer*), and lends her voice to the doctrine that women should be 'supple' and 'obedient to the desires of the boy, and *s'agence[r] en toutes les postures*' (168, 164–5). Ironically, then, the book denounced by Alexandre Varet for subverting 'discipline' and turning nuns away from their 'devoirs' turns out really to *be* the conduct manual it mocks.[94] We see once

[93]   *Œuvres et lettres*, ed. André Bridoux (Paris, 1953), 1268 (the letter to Chanut cited n. 112 below).
[94]   *Factum pour les religieuses*, 59 (*Nun's Complaint*, 54).

again that libertinism has its own 'discipline', not always distinguishable from the rigid conformity imposed by would-be absolutist husbands; Arnolphe in *L'École des femmes* and Susanne in *L'Escole des filles* both wield a Little Book subtitled 'les Devoirs de la femme'.

The ambiguity of the verb *agencer* reminds us how slippery is the designation of agency in this work ostensibly devoted to the 'mistress' as discursive subject. Is the 'agent' a self-activating individual or an employee made to do the bidding of others, often in secret? In its reflexive form *s'agencer* implies autonomy, but Fanchon's usage suggests the opposite: Robinet 'me fait agencer' in embarrassing postures, 'made me activate myself' (II. 85). (The impersonal 'Table Mistique' drops the re-flexive altogether when summarizing this passage, which simply shows 'why men *agencent* women in so many different postures' (p. LV).) Two definitions of educa-tion clash here as they do in Molière's *École des femmes*—joyous self-discovery and authoritarian transfer of 'duties'—but the libertine initiation-narrative leans to-wards the latter. Whatever the theory of gender transcendence by mutual metamor-phosis, in practice the male characters often take the initiative and assume the instructor's position.[95] Susanne's lover, for example, 'showed me all his splendid limbs, and wanted me to fondle them, taking as much pleasure in being touched by me as he had in touching me', but the point of the exercise is to 'teach me to do things that *he* found agreeable' (I. 47, my emphasis). Fanchon obediently 'learns' from the doltish Robinet—an effect amplified by the English translator, who calls his in-structions 'Love Lectures' and Katy an 'Apt Scholar'—and endorses his project of turning her into 'one of the girls most skilled at giving contentment to men'.[96] Women must be trained to simulate the active role, but it is the man who orders the performance, dictates the postures, arranges his partner as an object of contempla-tion. Optatives become imperatives. *S'agençant en toutes les postures*, she must submit out of voluntary love—or at least 'par bienséance' (II. 164)—to what the clear-eyed prostitute does for hard cash.

Even the subjective description of pleasure seems subjected to masculine inter-ests. The female-persona voice wears quite thin, and we hear the tone of the boys' club: 'the firm, plump breast fills the hand agreeably . . . after the breast one comes to the thighs, and one tastes a different kind of pleasure feeling those two columns of alabaster . . . a beautiful thigh pleases our senses and excites our appetites mar-vellously . . . it's always more pleasant for the cunt to be too narrow than too wide' (I. 50–2, II. 152). Male desire is rendered in lingering, masturbatory detail, with the female perspective added as a perfunctory supplement ('The woman, who is on top, also considers things from her point of view and makes her own reflections upon each posture' (II. 148)). At times, even the *pretence* of mutual benevolence drops away, when the crude words shouted in bed—supposedly 'hieroglyphics' of trans-

---

[95] Leibacher-Ouvrard, 'Femmes d'esprit?', 192, underlines the fact that the man '*makes* the woman take' certain positions; Cryle, *Geometry*, 25, highlights the originary role of Robinet and Susanne's lover.

[96] II. 60, 78–9; KB '63' (Katy declares herself 'desirous to be Instructed in these Mysteries', where the original merely uses *apprendre*).

formative desire—are described as 'injuries' and insults; men 'enjoy using the words that provoke the most shame in us, to render their victories more celebrated'.[97]

The balance of the sexes shifts constantly, nevertheless. The return of speculative philosophizing crowds out those scenes of initiation where male preceptors dominate. They remain shadowy figures, consigned to the realm of 'practice' rather than 'theory', kept back from the immediate present of the dialogue itself. Corporeal *praxis* gains its significance when, as Larson puts it, it is 'sublimated into language in the form of stories and becomes a pleasure currency which the two women exchange. . . . Erotic pleasure not only opens Fanchon's mind, it offers her access to the narrator's position,' and therefore to the verbal seduction-by-description (of the interlocutor, of the reader) that '*is its own practice*'.[98] The authority of Robinet is further limited by his mechanical anatomy, his ignorance and incuriosity about the *cause* of desire, and his need to be 'instructed' by Susanne (p. XLIX), 'told his duty' even on that crucial afternoon that splits the dialogues in two ('je lui conteray comment il se doibt comporter', I. 55). When he establishes his own school it seems quite artisanal in comparison to Susanne's academy: perhaps recalling his own apprenticeship to the rag trade, he sets samples of cotton, wool, and felt under Fanchon's bottom, calling out the name of each to 'teach her how movement ought to be done'.[99] Elsewhere we glimpse the lovers in a more gentrified setting, discovering secret sexual opportunities in the midst of leisure-class domesticity—singing, paying social visits, sitting out a dance at her mother's birthday ball (II. 77, 101–4, 106). But the initiative in these scenes belongs as much to Fanchon as to Robinet, and he never regains the instructor's role.

Susanne's lectures certainly include blatantly ideological messages from the sponsor, conduct-book prescriptions of subservience and obedience. But obedience to what? To the code, not the man. Susanne insists upon 'les convenances', which dictate that the woman should agree to everything with a display of titillating bashfulness, while the male (after an initial period of attentiveness) should be bold and violent; once inside, in fact, he should *not* hold back out of conventional decency or 'bienséance'. It might seem that rules and *convenences* have yielded to animal masculinity, prevailing over an abjected, silenced woman. But this too is part of the rule-bound dialogic game, prompting a new script: she should complain about his hurting her 'par bienséance' or 'par forme' (II. 162–4).

The lonely pleasure of the woman-on-top certainly seems flat in comparison to the lushly described ecstasy of the man 'reassured that he is loved', but it displays an intellectual component that his lacks: she 'makes her own reflections upon each posture, recounting them in sequence one by one, each with its proper name and its different flavour' ('en suite à les conter toutes une par une, qui a son nom propre

---

[97] II. 118; cf. II. 79 (Robinet calls her 'ma fouteuse, et austres injures à quoy il prenoit plaisir'), 111 ('des injures et des villaines paroles' explained as 'par amour').

[98] 'Women, Books, Sex', 76 (citing II. 63, 77).

[99] II. 88–9 (changed by the English translator into the patriotic 'Red, White and Blue Cloth', KB '71'); the 'Table Mistique' advertises this episode as a 'Méthode curieuse et excellente à une fille pour apprendre à chevaucher juste en un quart d'heure' (p. LV).

aussi bien que ses ragousts différents', II. 148). In this research triangle, he gazes at
her and she consults the invisible encyclopedia—consults and 'augments' it too,
since *conter* signifies not merely enumeration but recounting, narrating, *telling* in
every sense. She is Art to his Nature, mind to his body, book to his act. She owes
primary allegiance to the 'vivid painting in the mind's eye', the hypostatized *idea* of
libertine education and the discursive opportunities it affords. Hence it proves
quite difficult to determine who is the 'mistress' and who the apprentice. From the
start, Susanne enforces the strictest discipline on Fanchon: masturbating the boy
must be carried out 'comme il faut'; the 'well-instructed girl' must perform everything 'according to order and within the rules of pleasure'. Acting out Secundus'
paradox, this submission to the notorious *règles du plaisir [masculin]* actually renders her dominant, gives her the 'power' to 'penetrate'. Putty in her hands, 'the boy
cannot prevent himself from having an erection', and thereafter 'obéit à tout ce
qu'elle veut', obeys her wishes entirely (I. 23–4).

4. CARTESIAN EROTICS: 'NATURAL' GENERATION AND THE MECHANICAL BODY OF PLEASURE

L'Escole's attempts to construct an erotic 'Natural Philosophy' prove as contradictory as the politics of education. Seventeenth-century libertine polemic sought to
reinstate the physical in the heartiest possible way, insisting (in Susanne's terms)
that no pleasure and no love can exist without the 'huge truncheon of flesh' and
large helpings of 'boiling' sperm, served up by the 'workman of Nature' with his
'thwacking' stones.[100] (The use of 'Nature' in such phrases endorses a pseudo-
feminocentric phallus-worship apparently untroubled by the discrepancy between
that implement and the anatomical penis.) But libertinism also promoted an absolute polarization of value between the gross and ignorant sensualist and the true
voluptuary, for whom the 'Idea' is paramount. We do these things 'non pas comme
les bestes, par brutalité et par necessité, mais par amour et par connoissance de
cause' (II. 96–7). What distinguishes humans from animals, who are driven by
'brutality and necessity', is precisely their reflective and aesthetic 'cognizance'. Desire
is prompted, *not* 'for generation's sake by Nature' (as the English translator put it)
but by heightened cerebral 'knowledge', by 'sweet imaginations', 'high reasonings',
'images and representations'. Abstraction drives and controls the body, and assumes
the subject-position in language: as Susanne explains, 'perverse' modes of intercourse are invented and assumed 'because the idea wants it so' (*parce que l'idée le
veut ainsi*), because of 'some resemblence between that conjunction and the true,
natural one' (140).

In some respects, of course, the ideology of the 'natural' drives proto-
Enlightenment eroticism and fuels its protest against the artificial restrictions

---

[100] II. 113–14 ('un baston de chair, gros, long et estendu'); cf. I. 21 ('bouillie') and Middx. tr., cited p. 122
above.

imposed by Church and State. Father Garasse, who practically created French libertinism in the course of his attacks on Théophile de Viau, accused the *libertins* of substituting Nature for God and justifying their excesses as natural (Ch. 2 n. 56 above);
a second-generation text like *L'Escole des filles* finds that a wise and prevenient
'nature' deliberately designed the testicles and anus so that women could fondle
them during penetration (II. 133). We know from homoerotic apologia like Rocco's
Alcibiade that Nature could be invoked as the supreme instigator of pleasures conventionally branded 'unnatural'. In *La cazzaria del C.M.* Nature urges us to seek
novelty in copulation, to distinguish us from the animals, while Rocco argues that
we fulfil Nature's plan by abandoning animal instinct and pursuing the 'diletto dalla
conoscenza';[101] this is precisely the voluptuary-cognitive humanism that *L'Escole des
filles* uses to promote an advanced form of heterosexuality, 'naturelle' and yet
somehow against nature. The argument will resurface again in the English
burlesque drama *Sodom*: Nature has given the animals merely 'one poore rule', one
mode of copulation, 'But man delights in various ways to swive.'[102]

L'Escole's ambiguous treatment of 'Nature' derives from its double purpose—as a
satire against the 'Platonic' *précieuses*, and as an alternative philosophy of eroticism.
Each of these projects assigns a different status to the animal drives, not necessarily
compatible. Though she repudiates the 'brute beasts' and reinstates Platonic concepts like the primeval hermaphrodite and the supreme Idea, Susanne must punc-
ture Fanchon's romantic distinction between true Love and 'amours brutales'.
Erotic desire prompts girls to 'chimerize a thousand delicious thoughts' without
knowing where they come from, and so creates the *illusion* that love can subsist
without consummation—apparently the opposite effect from the absolute genitalization of the mind that Fanchon reports. But in fact *all* varieties of love are animalistic: Madeleine de Scudéry might call for a love purged of everything 'brutale', but
Susanne assures her cousin that 'elles sont toutes brutales, m'amie'.[103] The 'Table
Mistique' amplifies this anti-Platonic scorn by satirizing those who 'chevauchent
leur idée', who 'fuck their Idea' (p. LVII). This contemptuous phrase entered the
libertine repertoire, at the risk of destroying its own intellectual premisses; by the
eighteenth century, 'foutre en idée' had been inserted into the catalogue of 'postures'—a man masturbated by an elderly woman while gazing at the representation
of an absent mistress.[104] Libertinism at once exalts and despises the body, embraces
and repudiates the 'natural', fetishizes and satirizes the 'Idea'.

The slippery concept of 'nature' is constantly evoked as a code word in *L'Escole*'s
campaign to 'trample all shame underfoot', as Fanchon puts it (II. 60). Fanchon and
Susanne both refer to her vagina as her *nature*, following the Italian usage of Vignali
and Rocco; this synonym alternates freely with the vulgar *con* and the mechanistic
engin, as if fulfilling the author's suggestion that Nature and Art cooperate to
'invent' new forms of desire (I. 26, II. 57, 69, 150, 151, 164). Early prosecutions of

---

[101] See Ch. 2 above, nn. 59, 66 (*Alcibiade*, 54).   [102] 323; cf. Lyons, 143 ('one poore way').

[103] II. 111–12, 114; cf. *Clélie*, cited in Leibacher-Ouvrard, 'Femmes d'esprit?', 192.

[104] Posture 20 in BL PC 30.b.19, *Histoire et vie de l'Arretin, ou Entretiens de Magdelon et de Julie* (n.p.,
1783), 56 (not in earlier versions of the prose *Puttana errante*).

the book recognize this coding of 'Nature': the co-publisher Jean L'Ange excused it as 'rien que le naturel mais un peu libre', but the interrogator insisted that it offended against 'les bonnes mœurs et la discipline cretienne'; one indictment of the English translation singles out the passages of naturalistic propaganda placed in the mouths of the female speakers ('Fucking is so natural, that one way or another Leachery will have its vent in all sorts and conditions of People'), and interrupts the transcription to gloss 'the first motion of nature' as 'the crime of fornication'.[105] *L'Escole des filles* theoretically relies on the 'natural' as the epistemic touchstone that validates the mental 'figure', but in narrative practice reverses this priority. When the 'Idea' inspires acts that contemporaries like Evelyn would undoubtedly denounce as *un*natural, such as forcing the genitals against the breasts or the face, Susanne explains it by the 'resemblence between that conjunction and *la véritable naturelle*' (II. 140). But this 'veritable' stratum or 'natural' mode is just what the book rejects as *brutale*, limited, and merely animalistic. Nature is valued only as the idea of its own transgression.

Indeed, total immersion in the physical, the ostensible goal of desire, would extinguish the condition that enables it. Training in *l'école des filles* and *la philosophie des dames* produces an anti-natural 'past mistress', valued for having transformed mere 'fucking' into an 'art', willing to violate taboos which were far more deepseated then than now, bold in discussing forbidden topics, and eager to perform in the exhibitionist theatre of postures.[106] Moreover, her agency *creates* male desire rather than merely responding to it. Only with such an advanced lover will the man be sufficiently aroused to 'invent caresses to perform on you' (II. 97), 'inventions' which aim to make direct contact with the mind. In a passage outrageous enough to have been recorded in the 1680 prosecution, Susanne proves that 'the mind can love as much as the body' by citing the effect of her *salon* conversation:

I have heard my Friend say sometimes, when he hath heard me maintain an argument smartly (*discourir sur des matières relevées et honestes*), he was mad to be Fucking me on the spot, the cleverness of my wit so tickled him, that he could not rule his stiff standing Tarse, but desired to thrust it in my body to reach the soul of me, whose ingenuity pleased him so much.[107]

This play with the sexual parallel of mind and body anticipates La Fontaine, whose *conte* 'Comment l'esprit vient aux filles' hinges on the naive girl's belief that 'esprit' is a synonym for penis (p. 123 above). Here, however, the man seems the greater ingénu, furiously searching for the place where he might 'fuck the soul' or fuse the penis with the pineal gland; still further removed from the 'natural' order, *he*

[105] Pia, 181 (interrogation of Jean L'Ange); 1680 Middx. prosecution, translating 'le foutre estant naturel comme le manger et le boire' (II. 125) and adding an echo of the Anglican liturgy. Cf. La Fontaine's 1665 defence of the *Contes* as 'un peu libre', cited in Birberick, *Reading Undercover*, 87.

[106] Cf. II. 96 ('l'art d'aymer'), 81, where Fanchon, like the reader addressed in the 'Advertisement' (58), is declared 'passée maistresse en ce mestier'; in English this became 'arrived to such a perfection in the art of fucking' (KB '66'; Thomas, 30).

[107] Middx. prosecution; *Escole*, II. 119, 120 (cf. *Les Caquets de l'accouchée* (Paris, c.1890), 196, sexualizing the 'haut et relevé discours' of philosophical feminism.

fucks *her* ideas rather than his own. The most intense form of this cerebral prurience, in *L'Escole des filles* as in the sonnets attributed to Aretino, is the metamorphic
'wish to be all prick, to slip entirely inside you'.[108] Nevertheless, if this wish were
granted the lover would be shut off from the 'summit' of libertine pleasure, that of
contemplating and visualizing one's own posture, 'seeing and being seen'.

In answer to her pupil's questioning, Susanne does create an ingenious 'philosophy' to patch this gaping contradiction between body and idea. As we have seen, she
is heavily indebted to Descartes, drawing attention to her 'Method' and lifting the
theory of primal unity directly from *Les Passions de l'âme*. But Descartes's Platonic
fable cannot satisfy Cartesian standards of demonstration. Susanne knows that it is
only a 'correspondance de l'amour', an emblematic analogy like the *tromperies* that
excite the lover, or what her pupil aptly calls a 'façon de concevoir' (II. 143). Like
Descartes himself, she therefore tries to ground erotic myth in a detailed physiology
of arousal. Pallavicino's Italian courtesan created the *illusion* of being 'liquefatta' by
desire (Ch. 2, sect. 1 above), but the Cartesian libertine sincerely believes in the new
science of fluid mechanics, and explains all arousal as a hydraulic system. As the 1680
translation puts it,

Corporal desire or the first motion of nature . . . by degrees ascends unto Reason, where it is
perfected into a spiritual Idea; so that this Reason finds an absolute necessity of uniting one
half to the other half. When nature hath what she requires, that Idea or Spiritual vapor by
little and little dissolves itself into a white liquid substance like milk, which trickling softly
down through our Backbone into other Vessels, at last becomes the pleasure of which before
'twas only the Idea.[109]

Saint-Evremond criticized Scudéry's 'falsely delicate' ideal of love because it 'converts movements into ideas'.[110] Here the conversion-process is laid bare, but in the
interests of domestic science rather than satire; the 'Idea' and the 'mouvement de la
nature' coalesce in a cyclic system of fungible fluids.

This hydrostatic model of sexual excitement was becoming common in erotic
discourse. Milton's nephew John Phillips, for example, versifies it in the 1656
Sportive Wit—perhaps drawing on his uncle's research into Sinibaldi's
Geneanthropeia:

> Oh it comes, it comes amain
> Up this lane to my brain,
> And distilleth down again.[111]

But *L'Escole* gives it a distinctively Cartesian twist, attempting to define the precise
interaction and priority of the material and the mental, with a 'clear and distinct'

[108] II. 97; cf. *Sonetti lussuriosi di M Pietro Aretino* ('Venice, 1556', but in fact an 18th-century reprint),
Vienna, Österreichische Nationalbibliothek, BE 5 X 69, sonnet 5, where the female speaker wishes that the
man could become 'tutto cazzo'.

[109] Middx. prosecution, translating and modifying *Escole*, II. 137; the 'Table Mistique' draws attention
to this passage as 'Autre définition de l'amour par idée' (p. LVIII).

[110] Cited in Leibacher-Ouvrard, 'Femmes d'esprit?', 192, and Elizabeth Susan Wahl, *Invisible Relations:
Representations of Female Intimacy in the Age of Enlightenment* (Stanford, Calif., 1999), 202.

[111] First part, fo. C5ᵛ (for Milton see Ch. 1 n. 49 above).

concreteness that emphasizes the physiological. Descartes's own accounts of arousal were hardly less corporeal. Love arises, he explains to Queen Christina, because 'the matter of our body flows ceaselessly like a river', the heart feeds upon this nutritive stream, 'the soul joins itself willingly to this new matter', and abundant animal spirits then flood into the brain.[112] In the published *Passions de l'âme* Descartes comes even closer to Susanne's explanation: unusually 'gross and agitated' spirits congest the brain and, 'fortifying the impression made by the first thought of the love-object, oblige the soul to fixate on that thought'.[113]

But how *can* the two substances of thought and matter act upon each other? In *L'Escole des filles* Physiology appears to obey Reason: in the English version Reason 'finds an absolute necessity of uniting one half to the other half'; in the more complicated French original, the 'idea or vapour' causes Reason to 'examine with greater awareness the fine advantages that would accrue if this half were to be united to its other half' (II. 137). Yet this *cognoissance* derives from corporeal motion and dissolves back into it, quite literally, as 'a white liquid substance like milk'. *L'Escole's* Cartesian cycle of vapour-spirit-idea-reason-fluid-pleasure brings up to date the physical climax of Rocco's *Alcibiade* (Ch. 2, sect. 2 above), when metaphors of 'planting the seed of knowledge' become literal, and the philosopher's sperm shoots directly into the pupil's brain to generate new ideas—a paradigmatic instance of that phenomenon impossible to observe or theorize, the direct interaction of mind and body.

Susanne's trickle-down model is obviously meant to reconcile the mind–body polarity inherited from Descartes with the luscious physicality beloved of the *libertins érudits* and neo-Epicureans. But embracing materialism also brought its problems. Physiological reductionism runs the risk of making the heroic lovers seem like idiots: 'The soul by the violence of this great pleasure descends and thinks noe more of it self, but leaves the functions of reason empty and unprovided'; pleasure lives 'not in the head but in the arse, *entre con et coüillons*' (II. 138). Comic and philosophical motives evidently clash here, but the contradiction is not only one of genre. Materialists inevitably had to confront the legacy of Lucretius, and Lucretian erotology (despite Rocco's rapturous account of 'sucking in the image') emphasizes the futility rather than the supreme pleasure of copulation: 'all is in vain', since lovers 'can rub nothing off, nor penetrate, nor pass with their whole body into another'. We see the power of this canonical account in writers far more idealistic than *L'Escole*. When Tullia d'Aragona tries to include corporeal sexual union in her modified Platonism, for example, she runs aground on Lucretius: though full consummation helps us homogenize with the love-object 'as much as possible', bodies cannot ever really penetrate one another, and desire must remain unfulfilled (Ch. 1, sect. 1 above). The Lucretian inheritance, then, defined sexuality as a shadowy 'simulacrum' by its very nature, the dream-image and the act of love being equally vain at-

---

[112] Letter to Chanut, 1 Feb. 1647, in *Œuvres et lettres*, 1260, 1267.
[113] Art. 102, and cf. 107; for links between *L'Escole's* theory of orgasm and other phenomena in Descartes, see Fischer, *Éducation érotique*, 239 (tears) and Leibacher-Ouvrard, 'Femmes d'esprit?', 189 (laughter).

tempts to achieve an impossible immediacy; the only solution, Lucretius insists, is to destroy the phantom of love by scattering the seed at random. To adapt Susanne's terms, lovers can only ever couple with 'vaines figures' or 'chevaucher ses idées', with no 'véritable naturelle' or Real Thing against which to measure the representation.

Despite heroic assertions to the contrary, *L'Escole des filles* cannot escape this Lucretian blankness. Lovers may be striving to fuse into a single primal union, but after intercourse, Susanne admits, the separated halves always 'withdraw in sadness, seeing that it does not happen' (II. 137). The narrative illustrates this withdrawal, for we hear hints that after only a few weeks the stout young Robinet has already lost interest; Fanchon remarks that 'he doesn't come to see me as often as I would like', and that she will need to remind him of his duty as a pornographic hero, coupling on demand (II. 62, 75). (In her demystifying anti-Platonic lecture Susanne had already drawn upon Lucretius' theory of depletion: 'those who love the most are those who fuck the least' (II. 114).) In the event, the two women content themselves with constructing an ideal couple, compensating for the limits of the body by fabricating their own simulacrum; as Susanne recognizes early in the dialogue, 'la fantaisie amoureuse . . . n'a point de bornes (I. 50). In this imagined pornotopia the male is unflaggingly virile and infinitely inventive, the female endowed with 'so many beauties that the gallant will already be lost in delight and transport before he reaches the target' (II. 158). The vocabulary of loss and darkness intrudes even into the ideal, however. Susanne's phrase for the goal or centre of genital love—*arrivé jusques au noir*—refers to the bull's-eye in archery but literally means the blackness, the dark place. Fanchon's interruption draws attention to this eerily resonant image, which the 'Table Mistique' calls an 'appelation figurée et philosophique du con' (p. LIX). Libertine 'figuration' and erotic 'philosophy' empty into the void.

The most striking contradictions in *L'Escole des filles'* natural philosophy involve the physiology of procreation. Ironically, the cerebral 'façon de concevoir' gets most of the attention while bodily conception is treated with flippant disregard. Susanne teaches the heretical doctrine of voluntary, voluptuary eroticism, freed from 'brutality and necessity'—the inescapable, mammalian facts of biology; the English translation spells out what this means by inverting the familiar words of the marriage service, insisting that lovers do *not* come together 'for generation's sake'. Despite their celebration of the lusty animal body, the *libertins* share Father Garasse's contempt for *brutalité*, and despite their deterministic science of arousal ('an absolute necessity of uniting one half to the other half') they repudiate *nécessité* for the delights of *connoissance*.

However scandalous to 'Christian discipline', this sexual liberationism shares certain underlying assumptions with traditional theology: a desire to transcend the prison-house of flesh without losing the resurrected body, a definition of salvation as release from a 'necessity' epitomized by procreation and childbirth, the locus of original sin. St Augustine's conception of Edenic happiness—and resurrected bliss—depends on rescuing the pleasurable aspects of the body from involuntary 'necessity'; before the fall (Augustine explains) the genitalia were as flexible and controllable as the hand, obeying the will entirely, so that copulation resembled putting on a glove.[114] *L'Escole* evokes this vision of lapsed voluntarism when it juxtaposes the hand and the penis, as does Rocco's argument that the best forms of sexuality are those furthest removed from *bisogna* or necessity[115] and Rochester's lyric 'The Fall', which laments in Augustinian terms the separation of volition, desire, and performance (26). Claude Le Petit, who praised the obscenity of *L'Escole* and perhaps wrote it himself, likewise emphasizes amorous freedom when he versifies 'the most beautiful thoughts of St Augustine'. Le Petit contrasts the misery of a life 'enslaved to vice' and 'filled with despair by necessity' to the 'charming pleasures' of an erotic relationship with God; the Incarnate Word who 'loves the flesh' and seduces the soul with 'sweet impostures' of resemblance to himself strongly recalls the mutual narcissism of *L'Escole*, the 'tromperies d'amour' and the 'images de conjonction'.[116] And Le Petit's image of celestial influence 'flowing from a breast so fecund in sweetness' (101) recalls both the specific physiology of arousal (the 'white rain like milk' flowing into pleasure) and the general paradox of sexual naturalism: libertinism celebrates a secular version of 'fecundity in *douceur*' and 'reproduction' in love, even though it repudiates physical reproduction entirely.

In the fallen state, of course, procreation was not only a 'necessity' but an obligation, and 'Christian discipline' used the procreative criterion to determine the exact moral valence of every sexual act, according to whether the semen was ejected into the proper vessel. Medical science reinforced this fixation by ascribing astonishing properties to the sperm, even though the old Aristotelian one-seed theory (which gives generative power to the male alone) had largely yielded to a more egalitarian model of conception, requiring the simultaneous spurt of male and female seeds: Descartes thought of it as a yeasty ferment, Sinibaldi as an 'electric force', Harvey as a 'plastic art' or 'immaterial Idea' that brings forth children exactly as the painter's brain procreates images.[117] Milton rather resentfully defined the semen as 'the best substance of [a man]'s body, and of his soul too as some think', while the early microscopists populated it with fully formed homunculi.[118] One might assume that the extramarital and hedonistic school would escape from this reductive impulse, which subjugates the entire experience of sexuality to its biological and spermatic function. Nevertheless, Rocco's homosexual philosopher denounces masturbation because it diverts the precious seed from its true goal (the brain of Alcibiade), and Susanne in *L'Escole des filles* hammers home an equally normative definition of what constitutes a 'veritable' sex act. She demands not only the physical reality of

---

[114] See my *One Flesh*, 44–6.

[115] *Alcibiade*, 55 ('Un uomo sopra gl'altri s'innalza per aver più virtù e manco bisogno', like God himself), and cf. pseudo-Lucian in Introd. n. 33 above.

[116] *Les Plus Belles Pensées de saint Augustin* (Paris, 1666), 17, 30, 43, 50, 58.

[117] Descartes, *Les Traitez de l'homme et de la formation du foetus* (Amsterdam, 1680), 92 (and *passim*); Sinibaldi, *Geneanthropeia* (Rome, 1642), col. 614; William Harvey, *Exercitationes de Generatione Animalium* (Amsterdam, 1651), 557–8 (tr. Martin Lluellin, *Anatomical Exercitations Concerning the Generation of Living Creatures* (1653), 543–6).

[118] See my *One Flesh*, 200 (citing Milton, *CPW* ii. 271), and Clara Pinto-Correia, *The Ovary of Eve: Egg and Sperm and Preformation* (1997), ch. 6.

penetration but the ejaculation of seed, proposing a ludicrously mechanical equation between the volume of sperm injected and the amount of pleasure experienced by the woman: 'it is the semen that *causes* the pleasure', in fact (II. 135, my emphasis). Logically this is quite untenable. Libertinism distinguished itself from official Christian morality by separating sexuality from procreation and replacing 'brutal' physicality with refined techniques and mental configurations. In theory, this applies equally to women and to men, but in *L'Escole* women are forced back into a mirror-image of the narrowest possible orthodoxy, their sexuality entirely dependent on the disposition of the masculine seed.

This bizarre recuperation of the mechanics of reproduction evidently required further support, since it is repeated and intensified in the verse 'Dialogue entre le fouteur et Perette' that flanks the prose in the 'Fribourg, 1668' edition. This crude poem, virtually the only libertine dialogue between speakers of the opposite sex, rails against those women who regard sperm as 'poison' and insist that 'the dry prick is good'—that is, who want men to give them pleasure without making them pregnant. The argument given to the female mouthpiece grows increasingly aggressive and contemptuous: such women may as well sleep with *castrati*, they eat the ham without the sauce, they must be 'punished' and forbidden to make love at all.[119] In the main text of *L'Escole* the same themes are delivered by Susanne as bland statements of what women 'really' like and dislike; the violent hostility of the verse-dialogue allows us to hear what the prose suppresses—the anger and fear inspired by the idea of an autonomous female libertine, insisting that sexual freedom must be linked to contraception and procuring her own pleasures when she cannot trust male responsibility.

The cavalier treatment of pregnancy in *L'Escole des filles* epitomizes the coercive, ideological undertow of a work sometimes described as 'innocent' and idyllic.[120] From the start Fanchon shows that, ignorant as she is of sexual anatomy, she knows perfectly well the dangers of exposure and disgrace (I. 28–32), and when Susanne finally explains that sperm causes conception—weeks after Fanchon has begun full intercourse at her instigation—the acolyte's reaction is likewise one of panic: 'I could well be pregnant' already (II. 128). Her mentor proceeds to demolish this fear, dismissed in advance as 'frivolous' (p. LVII), with an avalanche of arguments even more contradictory than those used to dispel the fear of gossip and exposure. Pregnancy almost never happens, or only after several years, and even then it is statistically negligible: 'You only conceive once in nine months, and you make love many times; . . . for every hundred girls who fuck in secret, hardly two get pregnant' (II. 121, 127). Science reassures her that a couple can only conceive if they ejaculate at the same time—which they *must*, according to the spermatocentric model of pleasure; Susanne's seductive descriptions of orgasm repeatedly emphasize the

[119] Pia, 175–6 (not in the 1667 edn.); the whore 'Perette' already features in the *Cabinet satyrique*, so this poem might hark back to an earlier and cruder stage of French *libertinage*.

[120] Foxon, 31; Thomas, 57, 59, 60. Thomas's transcription of KB supports his Edenic reading by silently omitting phrases like 'He Tortured me so as I cryed out' ('54–5', translating 'Voyant que je ne voulois pas', II. 70).

irreplaceable excitement of this double 'discharge' (I. 48, II. 135). Then she claims that conception only happens if the buttocks are clenched and the cervix moved forward. But that is exactly what Fanchon has been doing; indeed, at the crucial moment (according to her own account) she 'cannot prevent herself' from performing this movement, just as she cannot avoid 'discharging' in response to the erotic narration of her mentor-*menteuse* (II. 128–9).

As she persuades Fanchon to ignore the problem of conception Susanne thus plays card after card, blithely unaware that they do not form a coherent hand. She assures Fanchon that lascivious movements scatter the seed and prevent conception (an idea borrowed from Lucretius, who dictates immobility for wives because pleasure is irrelevant to marriage). She promises an infallible formula for safe abortion ('remedies which never fail to work'), but then recommends a change of dress to hide the swelling abdomen:

> How many pregnant wenches are there, that dayly walk up and down, and by the help of Busques and loose garbs hide their great Bellies till within a month or two of their times, when by the help of a faithful Friend they slip into the Country, and rid themselves of their Burthen, and shortly after return into the City as pure Virgins as ever.[121]

As a general rule, the higher the social scale of the female participants in libertine discourse, the more thoroughly it conceals the vital link between pleasure and contraception: the aristocratic ladies in Chorier's *Satyra* pay scarcely any heed to the issue, whereas the frankest whore- and rogue-biographies assume the ubiquity of contraception, abortion, and infanticide.[122] *L'Escole des filles* has cleaned up this tradition, but conspicuous traces remain; its middling, *bourgeois* realism means that the problem of pregnancy, and the techniques for avoiding it, are mentioned but not thoroughly addressed. Susanne lists a number of devices that more 'timid' women use—an impressive array of masturbatory toys, techniques for deflecting the sperm, 'a little piece of linen' to 'put on the head of the prick' (II. 126)—but discourages Fanchon from pursuing them and never incorporates them into her normative descriptions. Lodovico Maria Sinistrari encountered in the confessional a man who always used 'a pig's membrane pulled over the prick . . . so as not to make his Beloved pregnant'—a relatively minor sin for Catholics because it should not be considered real intercourse—but no such consideration appears in *L'Escole des filles*.[123]

Bearing a bastard—in reality a source of ignominy and mortal danger at every level of society—is presented as a lark among friends, with the man always paying for the child's upbringing. French legal history shows, however, that all pregnancies outside marriage had to be declared publicly, while failure to do so would confirm the capital crime of presumptive infanticide if the child died. One defendant

[121] Middx. tr. of *Escole*, II. 129, 121; the English version had, more realistically, inserted a passing reference to 'fear of Great Bellies' much earlier (KB '26'). Fischer (*Éducation érotique*, 240–3) and DeJean (*Reinvention of Obscenity*, 76–7) take a more positive view of *Escole*'s treatment of contraception.

[122] e.g. *Puttana errante*, 90/27, *The Practical Part of Love* (1660), 22, Francis Kirkman, *The English Rogue and Other Extravagants*, part 3 (1671), 84.

[123] *De Delictis et Poenis* (1700; Rome, 1754), 234; unlike later dogmatists Sinistrari relegates condom use to the less serious category *mollities* or 'softness'.

believed that her mother had died of grief and shame because of her pregnancy. Another gave birth alone in the lavatory of a Paris tenement—where she had relocated in what the judge assumed was an attempt to conceal her pregnancy, just as Susanne advises—and was forced to confront the battered corpse of a new-born recovered from the septic tank. (Her Fanchon-like naïveté in insisting that she never knew she was pregnant might have earned her the lenient sentence of whipping, branding, banishment, and confiscation of all personal goods.[124]) In contrast, Susanne declares the fear of pregnancy so trivial that the well-schooled mistress should never mention such concerns in the man's presence, but instead should consider her ruin the supreme happiness: 'abandon yourself entirely to someone you love, just as he wills it' (II. 127).

Susanne's promise of abortifacients and obstetric advice links her to that dark figure of the male imagination, the bawd-midwife or Mother Midnight (a perverse reflection on the gentlewoman's traditional expertise in home health-care and herbal remedies). As in faux-feminist satires like the *Caquets de l'accouchée*, women's discursive autonomy and 'philosophical' self-assertion must be sullied by association with the secret arts of clandestine sexuality. Susanne recommends Fanchon to find 'a midwife whose conscience obliges her to keep the delivery secret' (II. 122)—*une sage-femme* in French—and she herself becomes a 'sage femme' in another sense, a lecturer in the undercover *philosophie des dames*. The 'Collegiate Ladies' in Jonson's *Epicoene* had also flaunted their knowledge of contraception and abortion, and the introduction to *Rare Verities* jokes that popular sex manuals make 'every Lady a Peripatetick, and sworn Philosopher' (Ch. 1, sect. 2 above). Renaissance gynaecologies still incorporated the supposedly genuine writings of Cleopatra on 'how to prevent a woman from conceiving' and 'how to produce an abortion'.[125] Louise Bourgeois, midwife to Queen Marie des Médicis, advised her daughter (in a text reprinted in France and England throughout the seventeenth century) never to be persuaded or bribed into teaching the technique of abortion, and never to let another woman into her house for a clandestine lying-in, a practice tantamount to 'maquerellage' or 'Panderism'. (She may attend the birth 'in an honest place', and keep the matter secret, if she gently urges the errant mother to repent in future.) Bourgeois learned from her own mistakes, and her account makes sobering reading after Susanne's light-hearted advice; she once took in two women pregnant outside wedlock (one of them a person 'of quality') and watched them 'in such fits of despair, that I could hardly bring them out of them again'.[126] Contemporary legal evidence also allows us to grasp the 'remedy' of abortion offered to Fanchon:

[124] Alfred Soman, 'Anatomy of an Infanticide Trial: The Case of Marie-Jeanne Bartonnet (1742)', in Michael Wolfe (ed.), *Changing Identities in Early Modern France* (1997), 248–72 (a reference I owe to Matthew Gerber); the standardized legal interrogation resembles Susanne's list of remedies quite closely, and includes the (trick?) question 'Why, when you knew that you were pregnant, did you not stay in your part of the country and confide in one of your relatives, who would have helped you in your travail without creating any scandal, and taken charge of your child?' (256).

[125] Caspar Wolf (ed.), *Gynaecio-um, hoc est, De Mulierum . . . Affectibus et Morbis* (Basle, 1566), cols. 22, 28–30; Susanne also claims the 'secret' art of concealing lost virginity (I. 28).

[126] 'Instructions à ma Fille', in *Observations diverses sur la sterilité, perte de fruict, foecondité, accouchements, et maladies des femmes* (Rouen, 1626), ii. 208–10; 'T.C., I.D., M.S., T.B., Practitioners', *The Compleat Midwifes Practice* (1656), 120–2.

women were searched with an 'iron instrument' like a skewer, or died with their foe-tus after swallowing 'ratsbane'.[127]

Susanne's didactic strategy—training Fanchon in the utmost skills of the 'mis-tress' but withholding crucial biological facts—lays the groundwork for Valmont's treatment of Cécile, another voluptuous ingénue fresh from girls' school; Valmont exults in the prospect of giving another man a bride not only gutter-mouthed and whorish in bed, but actually pregnant without knowing it. *L'Escole des filles* repli-cates the insulation or sequestration from the world on which convent education supposedly depends. In particular, it assumes the ease of maintaining secrecy in a society that ruthlessly exposes 'female' secrets. From the start Susanne urges Fan-chon to repudiate the teaching of her mother and 'listen to the words of men' (I. 5), yet at the same time discovers in male discourse a merciless impulse to show and tell.

In its faux-feminist moments the dialogue articulates, then conveniently forgets, the iniquities of the double standard: men are never punished for boasting about the 'bad things' they do; men continually describe their sexual conquests without the slightest loss to their reputation, violating women's honour and de-stroying their social position even when there is no truth in their slanders; women can do nothing whatsoever about this calumny, so they may as well make sure that the gossip is true (I. 29–31). Just as men's domination of Church and State bends morality to enforce their interests, so masculine slander-mongering conspires to keep women 'in continual fear'. This blatantly contradicts the assurance, only a page or two later, that Fanchon runs no risk of dishonour because no one will tell, or that Robinet's indiscreet boasting will cause *him* to be ostracized, or that a clandestine sex life will give Fanchon the self-assurance desired in a wife (sect. 2 above). It turns out, in fact, that her secret joy and inner confidence will come from 'mocking' the sexual activity of other women (32). The theme of *les paroles des hommes* returns with unusual force in the discussion of linguistic decorum: young men love to gather on street corners and comment, in the foulest language, on female passers-by they claim to have 'fucked'—but they only do this to 'women about whom there is a rumour', and somehow this does not include 'you and me'.[128] Needless to say, *L'Escole* itself constitutes precisely such an act of telling.

This farrago of accurate observations and preposterous arguments tears the fabric of the fantasy, and allows us to see the real consequences of the liberationist programme. The fragments of feminist analysis, divorced from any context in Su-sanne's thoughts or actions, serve as ragged peepholes onto a world structured by masculine power, not mutual desire. The invitation to secret pleasure, begun in the oily mock-courteous tones of the opening 'Epistle' and then continued in the exhor-tations of Susanne, seems particularly menacing when we return to pure hedonism after these glimpses of ruin. Most of the second dialogue upholds the 'pornotopian' vision of pleasure isolated from worldly concerns. When the repressed problem of

---

[127] John Keown, *Abortion, Doctors and the Law* (Cambridge, 1988), 6, 7, 8–9.
[128] II. 84–5 (and cf. KB '68', which adds even more details to Susanne's specimens of obscene boasting); Fonte, *Merito delle donne*, 51, 53 (*Worth*, 87, 90) had already linked men's sexual defamation of women with the fact that they made the laws.

conception does return, in a cheerfully cynical summary of 'how the world goes' at the very end of the work (II. 166), it unravels the whole notion of an easy progression from *école des filles* to *philosophie des dames*: men avoid *les filles*, and confine their pursuits to married 'ladies', because of the 'danger' of unwanted pregnancy, the 'peine' of keeping it hidden, the 'ressentiment' of her parents, and the 'money to pay the Justice when everything becomes known' (169). *L'Escole* shows a certain worldly realism here, recognizing some advantages for women in the relative security that followed an arranged marriage; Christina of Sweden observed that 'Men marry because they know not what they are doing, and girls marry to set themselves at liberty, under the shelter of a husband.'[129] Even here, however, the problems of premarital sex—the family's revenge, the burdens of childbirth, the cost of lawsuits, nursing, and housing—are assessed entirely from the male point of view. Susanne brokers a marriage for Fanchon, finally, because adultery is cheap and convenient for Robinet. The old aristocratic idea of the husband as a safety-device or 'cover' for adultery now migrates into the *bourgeoisie*: 'le mary sert de couverture à tout.'[130]

L'Escole des filles works hard to impose a traditional phallocratic model on the new philosophy of sexual freedom, but in that process it raises the ghost of a different kind of libertinage under female control, generating alternative forms of pleasure and refashioning 'nature' into a more serviceable simulacrum. The mentor-mouthpiece constitutes this free female activity by castigating it, ridiculing such 'timid' resources as dildos, effigies, and infertile males in sufficient detail to make them sound viable. In the blunt verse 'Dialogue' the spokeswoman for normative heterosexual coupling delivers what is supposed to be an unanswerable objection: if sperm were not the sole source of women's pleasure, 'the prick of a *castrato* would be just as dear to us' (176). In the more circumstantial prose dialogue, this rhetorical conditional expands into a distinct possibility.

The *chastré* or eunuch is in fact the first and most suggestive of the fabricated sex-objects cited by Susanne. *L'Escole* brings to light a long tradition of enjoying this form of man-in-effigy. 'Greek and Roman ladies' would couple with *castrati* 'to give themselves pleasure from the friction of the stiff member, and also because it bore some resemblance to the truth'. To this day, Turkish women enjoy this delight 'whenever they can find it', prompting further preventive surgery; stiff-membered *chastrés* (without testicles but otherwise well equipped and capable of erection) have 'all three pieces cut clean off, making them into full eunuchs' ('de les faire pour eunuques, de leur couper les trois pièces *rasibus*').[131] The *castrato*-lover thus brings

---

[129] *Ouvrage de loisir, ou Maximes et sentences*. Maxim VII. 64, in Johann Arckenholtz (ed.), *Memoires concernant Christine, reine de Suede*, ii (Amsterdam, 1751), 28; *Works* (1753), 67.

[130] II. 169; cf. Marguerite de Navarre, *Heptaméron*, I. x (now that Floride is married 'vostre honneur peult estre couvert'), Jonson, *Epicoene*, III. iii. 204, and Chorier, *Satyra*, II. 37. Though Susanne obviously prepares Fanchon for a life of discreet but unlimited adultery, Mainil believes that these closing pages recommend marital 'missionary' sex as the best (*Règles du plaisir*, 72–4, 77).

[131] II. 94–5; the English translator specifies that full penectomy was introduced 'of late' by 'a Turkish Emperor' shocked at 'seeing a Gelding cover a Mare' (KB '75'). For the slang word *rasibus* cf. the French translation of Secundus (Ch. 7, sect. 2 and Fig. 15 below).

together two exotic and prestigious locales, Imperial Rome—whose satirists defined (or invented) the excesses of the ancient aristocracy—and the Turkish harem, the locus of all modern perversions: credulous travellers report that in the seraglio men couple with men, women 'imitate' them by developing passionate lesbian attachments, and cucumbers must never be served whole.[132]

Concern with the anomalous potency of the castrated was not confined to Orientalist fantasy. Sixtus V wrote a Papal Brief banning the 'sterile and voluptuous' practice of marrying eunuchs, common enough for Erasmus to joke about it in his *Senatulus* or 'Parliament of Women'.[133] A century later, the popular sexologist Nicholas Venette devotes an entire chapter, and Charles Ancillon an entire treatise, to 'whether Eunuchs are capable of marrying and making Children'.[134] We have seen that, even before the passion for male operatic sopranos swept through France and England, before Montesquieu reports that the eunuchs in the Roman theatre inspire *amour philosophique* in even the most normal viewer, the eminent composer Barbara Strozzi was accused of lavishing all her love on a *castrato*.[135] Medical authorities like Sinibaldi (evidently the source of Susanne's description) confirm that eunuchs 'certainly copulate', and that those who 'guard women in Asia', if caught in the act of adultery, are punished with 'total amputation of their virility'.[136]

In *L'Escole des filles*—as in Wycherley's *Country-Wife*, whose hero claims to have undergone the same *totius virilitatis amputatione*—the eunuch is greeted with vigorous expressions of disgust: Lady Fidget's 'foh, foh! . . . stinking mortify'd rotten French Wether!' amplifies Fanchon's 'Fi, fi, de ces gens là!'[137] Horner decodes these exclamations as tokens of secret desire, marking Lady Fidget's disappointment rather than her affronted modesty, and Fanchon's outburst is equally disingenuous in its own way. Only the spermatic obsession prevents her from seeing that these Roman and Turkish ladies already have the perfect 'cover' for a life of hedonistic security, for what the Church condemned as 'voluptez steriles et criminelles'. The potent *castrato*, capable of erection without ejaculation, literally embodies the libertine ideal: sexuality divorced from the dangers and responsibilities of repro-

---

[132] Cf. David Michael Robinson, 'To Boldly Go Where No Man Has Gone Before: The Representation of Lesbianism in Mid-Seventeenth- to Early Eighteenth-Century British and French Literature', Ph.D. dissertation (Berkeley, 1998), 15, 53–4, 125, 268, 314–15.

[133] Papal Brief of 27 June 1587, summarized in Jean Gerbais, *Traité du pouvoir de l'Eglise et des princes sur les empeschemens du mariage*, 2nd edn. (Paris, 1696), 441; Erasmus, *Opera Omnia*, part I, vol. iii, *Colloquia*, ed. L.-E. Halkin et al. (Amsterdam, 1972), 631. Cf. also *Les Privilèges et fidelitez des chastrez* (1619), 4, reprinted in [Charles Brunet (ed.),] *Recueil de pièces rares et facétieuses*, ii (Paris, 1873), perhaps a source of *Escole*, II. 169–70, on the costs of illicit pregnancy.

[134] Venette, *Tableau de l'amour consideré dans l'estat du mariage* ('Parma', 1688), 542–52, Ancillon, *Traité des eunuches* ([Berlin], 1707), and cf. Leibacher-Ouvrard, 'L'Eunuque anathème et prétexte: Économie libidinale et construction de l'hétérosexualité', in Olga B. Cragg and Rosena Davison (eds.), *Sexualité, mariage et famille au XVIIIᵉ siècle* (Sainte-Foy, Québec, 1988), 11–26, esp. 19–20 (Ancillon's eunuchs 'par catachrèse' and 'par figure' (16) suggest the influence of Pallavicino's sexual applications of rhetoric).

[135] Introd. n. 35, Ch. 2 n. 31 above. The situation in Rome resulted directly from Sixtus V's reform of stage and choir; see Yvonne Noble, 'Castrati, Balzac, and BartheS/Z', *Comparative Drama*, 31 (1997–8), 28–41, esp. nn. 9 and 24.

[136] *Geneanthropeia*, cols. 415–16.   [137] *CW* I. i. 253, II. i. 279; *Escole*, II. 95.

ductive biology. In Augustinian terms, he experiences resurrection freed from the necessity of 'disobedient' orgasm and detumescence.

Susanne's ancient Roman source, the breathless catalogue of feminine evil in Juvenal's sixth satire, explains in detail how the priapic eunuch is 'made by the lady' (*a domina factus spado*). Juvenal is attacking the excesses of connoisseurship. Alongside those ladies who cultivate an adulterous passion for singers he places those who 'delight in the soft kisses of eunuchs, to avoid the need for abortion'. They select 'a youth already warm and ripe in the groin'—indeed, already flaunting a member like that of Priapus 'the guardian of gardens'—and then have him cut to their specifications; empowered by the right to mutilate slaves, they go one step further than the 'noblewoman' in Sinistrari who kept an *ephebus* and moulded him to her own sexual invention. Just as the opera star is castrated to preserve his voice at its otherwise precarious peak, so the ephebe is selected for his unusual combination of beardless smoothness and spectacular genitalia—the ambiguous moment that Rocco defines as yielding 'Treasure' to any lover that applies—and surgically altered to maintain him at that stage. His 'two-pounder' testicles are removed in order to guarantee that he 'possesses the phallus' forever, or more accurately (since his *domina* or patroness has ordered this intervention for her own pleasure) to keep him perpetually *possessible-as-phallus*. He becomes both property and artefact, 'carved for his Lady's use' as Dryden put it in his translation—a specially commissioned sculpture that expresses her cultural power as well as her need for 'sterile pleasures'.[138]

The theme of the disposable phallus—always 'plastic', as Judith Butler would say[139]—returns with more urgency after Susanne's belated explanation of where babies come from. In response to the universal fear of pregnancy and exposure, 'all sorts and conditions' of women invent devices to serve their pleasure more reliably:

Wenches that are not rich enough to buy statues must content themselves with Dildoes made of Velvet, or blown in glass, Prick-fashion, which they fill with lukewarm Milk, and tickle themselves therewith as with a true Prick, squirting the Milk up their bodies when they are ready to spend. Some mechanick Jades frig themselves with Candles of about four in the pound; others, as most Nuns do, make use of their Fingers.[140]

The ubiquity of these 'engines'—statues, dildos or *godemiches*, candles, sausages, fingers—makes them sound less like an aberration than the norm, less a surrogate than the Real Thing for which the anatomical appendage stands in. (This universality is amplified in English by the liturgical phrase 'all sorts and conditions'.) And if they must be understood as a 'representation' or supplement, to what organ do they 'really' relate? The French term *godemiche* (spelled *gaudemichi* in *L'Escole* and

---

[138] Lines 366–78, in Dryden, iv. 176–9 (modern edns. of Juvenal include lines discovered more recently, so I cite from the text published *en face* with Dryden's 'Juvenal: Satyr VI'); E. Courtney, *A Commentary on the Satires of Juvenal* (1980), 309–10, cites studies that show, ironically, the ability to copulate fading eighteen months after the operation.

[139] Cf. *Bodies That Matter: On the Discursive Limits of 'Sex'* (1993), 61 ('defined by its very *plasticity, transferability*, and *expropriability*'), 62–3 ('the phallus as transferable or plastic property').

[140] Middx. tr. of *Escole*, II. 124–5; cf. Lucian, *True History*, I. 22, where the Moon-people sport 'prosthetic genitals of ivory, or (among the poor) of wood'.

supposedly derived from *gaude mihi* or 'rejoice in myself') could evoke the clitoris as well as the dildo; medical writers record that 'professionally impudent women' would call their clitoris '*gaude mihi*' or 'Contempt-for-Men' ('le mépris des hommes').[141]

The most elaborate artefact in Susanne's list of representations, and the one most resembling the *castrato* 'carved' for his lady's use, is 'a bronze statue of a man, painted in flesh colour and furnished with a powerful engine of softer material, straight and hollow'; the princess who designed and commissioned it gives herself a liquid injection at the appropriate moment, by pressing 'a certain spring' concealed at the back (II. 123). In a single act of patronage, ironically, this fictitious princess encapsulates the erotology of advanced libertinism: she replaces 'brute necessity' with connoisseurship; she creates a 'reproduction' in flesh-toned image rather than flesh itself, manufactured and hand-operated; she confounds the conventions of *agere et pati* by simultaneously submitting to this 'male' object and controlling it; and she confirms the Cartesian mechanistic physiology, insisting (like the master himself) that 'man' can best be understood 'as a statue'.[142] *L'Escole*'s intention, of course, is quite different. Susanne never ceases to ridicule these invented 'engines' for their lack of reality, their mediated 'resemblence to the truth'. But that 'truth' has already been mediated by the connoisseurship of images and the 'artificial' separation of pleasure from procreation. Susanne worships sperm as the essence of reality itself, an indisputable criterion for distinguishing the eunuch or statue from the ideal lover. But 'invention' fills that gap too: Susanne defines the pleasure-fluid as 'a thick white liquid like boiled sauce' (*une liqueur blanche et espaisse comme bouillie*) and 'a white rain like milk'; identically, the glass dildo emits 'warm milk' and the princess fills her statue with 'une certaine liqueur chaude et espaisse, blanche comme bouillie' (I. 21, II. 124, 137).

Susanne's efforts to subordinate these simulacra to the 'true Prick' enforce an epistemological hierarchy with serious consequences in contemporary law and medicine. Judges repeatedly condemned women to death for wielding the 'fraudulent' dildo and passing as husbands.[143] Science and law—acting together to prosecute sexual transgression and to determine cases of annulment for impotence—did not merely condemn artificial devices, but discovered artefactuality in the transgressive body itself, female as well as male. Even without the benefits of surgery, the impotent husband could find himself denounced in court as a 'faux mari', as 'the image of a husband destitute of all reality'. The simulacrum must never enter the marriage-bed, the realm of the *véritable naturelle*. As if in response to the virile

[141] Duval, *Hermaphrodits*, 68, cited by many scholars including Leibacher-Ouvrard, 'Tribades et gynanthropes (1612–1614): Fictions et fonctions de l'anatomie travestie', *Papers on French Seventeenth-Century Literature*, 24 (1997), 523; cf. Bartholin's Latin version ('Contemptus virorum'), n. 146 below.

[142] Leibacher-Ouvrard ('Femmes d'esprit?', 188) cites 'le *Traité de l'homme* cartésien', the opening paragraphs of which hypothesize man as statue.

[143] Cf. Wahl, *Invisible Relations*, 20–5; Judith C. Brown, *Immodest Acts: The Life of a Lesbian Nun in Renaissance Italy* (New York, 1986), 14; Lynne Friedli, '"Passing Women": A Study of Gender Boundaries in the Eighteenth Century', in G. S. Rousseau and Roy Porter (eds.), *Sexual Underworlds of the Enlightenment* (Chapel Hill, NC, 1988), 235, 239, 252 n. 7.

eunuch, the conditions for proving manhood by physical examination became stricter; erection alone could no longer be considered proof of marital competence, unless ejaculation or 'true coitus' could be produced.[144]

Meanwhile, women were accused not merely of *wielding* the 'fraudulent' phallus, but of growing their own. According to contemporary science, the clitoris belongs simultaneously to Nature and to Art. Sinibaldi describes it varying with the seasons, swelling and subsiding like vegetation, and yet he still calls it a 'pseudovirga' or 'false penis', as if deliberately fabricated to deceive.[145] Thomas Bartholin, agreeing with many other anatomists, asserted that (unlike the penis) the clitoris can be enlarged by handling, that regular masturbation makes it swell even larger than the phallus, attaining the dimensions of 'a goose's neck'; this self-made artefact allows women to choose lovers of their own sex, justifying its synonym *Contemptus virorum* or contempt for men (a detail borrowed from a French colleague).[146] In this alarming and enviable confirmation of Secundus' grammatical paradox, the *cunnus* does indeed become the more masculine organ, which presumably makes the phallus a pseudo-clitoris. When Sinistrari's 'Christian discipline' ordains the death penalty for acts of female 'sodomy'—with other women and with male *ephebi*—the entire case rests on Bartholin's anatomy of the clitoris and its hand-crafted hypertrophy; the ecclesiastical lawyer repeats every detail, including the neck of the goose.[147]

Underlying *L'Escole*'s prattle about statues, eunuchs, dildos, and fingers is a sense that the *gaude mihi* may indeed translate into the *mépris des hommes*, that women could combine the forces of nature and art to configure themselves differently, and that as a corollary 'real men' might constitute artefacts of pleasure ontologically indistinguishable from the princess's statue. The Académie des Dames teaches women the possibility of crafting almost-men whom they can 'carve' or control at will, their command over attractive slaves or youths guaranteed by a kind of sculpting power over their own bodies. The statue-sequence in *L'Escole* evokes, even as it belittles, the idea of autonomous sexuality without 'real' men—an idea that contemporary science linked to lesbianism and *contemptus virorum*. This alternative scenario is sketched, however briefly, when Susanne admits having 'seen and touched' Fanchon's 'white, plump, dainty thighs' (II. 65), and cannot be dismissed as unthinkable. Even the assertive heterosexuality of the 'Girls' School' reveals affinities with Killigrew's vision of 'Sodomy' in the convent (Ch. 2 n. 93 above) or the lesbian initiation-scenes of Chorier's *Aloisia Sigea*, to which I will turn in the next chapter.

---

[144] Pierre Darmon, *Le Tribunal de l'impuissance: Virilité et défaillances conjugales dans l'Ancienne France* (Paris, 1979), 78, 193, 194.

[145] *Geneanthropeia*, col. 536.

[146] *Anatomia Reformata, ex Caspari Bartholini* . . . (Amsterdam, 1651), 186–7; the goose's neck, perhaps a rare case of what Vernon Rosario identifies as 'so-called female pseudohermaphroditism' (private communication), was observed by Felix Platter and reiterated e.g. in Jean Riolan the Younger, *Anthropographia* (Paris, 1626), 295 (Riolan also goes on to bring in tribadism in Sappho, Martial, and the Epistle to the Romans). Unacknowledged English recyclings of these anatomists are cited in Emma Donoghue, *Passions between Women: British Lesbian Culture 1668–1801* (1993), 34–53.

[147] *De Delictis*, 234, 235 (*Peccatum Mutum*, 41–3 49).

L'Escole's propaganda for 'reality' dissolves as, *malgré elles*, the protagonists praise women's allegedly surrogate inventions, matching them to their own erotic theory and discursive practice. These unreal and unnatural artefacts perfectly epitomize the natural philosophy taught in Susanne's school. Like Hobbes, who reduced love and lust to the same 'indefinite desire of different Sex, as natural as Hunger', Susanne must prove that 'fucking is as natural as eating and drinking' (II. 125)—but her prime evidence is the ubiquity of artificial dildos. And when Fanchon discovers the ultimate proof that sex and mind sustain one another, she finds it in the princess's hominoid statue: 'de quelle invention l'amour n'est-il pas capable?' (II. 124). The aggressive naturalism that caught the eye of the magistrate ('Fucking is so natural, that one way or another Leachery will have its vent . . .') turns out to conceal a preference for 'invention' and figuration.

The dialogue itself confirms this priority when Fanchon asks Susanne to define the perfect couple, a priapic, fully sexed version of those blazons of ideal beauty compiled by Firenzuola and his contemporaries. Though *L'Escole* does its best to promote real, heterosexual, penetrative experience over shadowy 'ideas', we have seen that the phallic young man who embodies this ideology has already shown signs of flagging; the verbal image pointedly fills that blank, making 'un assemblé parfaict de ces deux moitiés accouplées' whose 'coupling' takes place only in the text (II. 159). This 'perfect assembly' is a triumph of art over nature, part Renaissance courtier and part Cartesian automaton: well-fashioned bodies combine with polished manners and fluent discourse, but (as with Susanne and Fanchon themselves) 'tous ses discours' lead towards sex as if preprogrammed (II. 155).

Susanne's description of this ideal couple brings out precisely the artefactuality she condemns in other iconophiliacs. Like a patroness commissioning a statue, she 'wishes' or 'demands' a list of features whose perfection consists in resembling the *objet d'art*: the buttocks are ordered 'hard, swelling and separate, as in marble statues'; the genitalia must be placed according to a system of proportion ('six fingers below the navel'); the connoisseur's hand should 'glide between pillars of marble'; the entire surface should be 'taut, homogeneous and polished under the hand'— *lissée* like oil paint, *unie* like a statue carved from a single stone, and *bandée* like the phallus itself.[148] The 'Table Mistique' makes the high-art language even more explicit by calling this description, the crowning passage of the entire *Escole des filles*, a 'tableau' and the comparison of male and female beauty a 'Parergon' (pp. LIX–LX). The man must have the Herculean build to lift the woman and fling her into various prescribed postures 'like a puppet that you work at pleasure' (*comme une marionnette que l'on agence à son plaisir*, II. 160), but meanwhile the narrator pulls *his* strings, 'agencing' him the same way. As they weave their increasingly idealized dialogue, Susanne and Fanchon fabricate their own princely statue or full-sized working toy—the subject of pornotopia, his *engin* always at the ready and 'warm milk' perpetually gushing at the turn of a little tap. In short, a *Robinet*.

---

[148] II. 157 (cf. 161, where the 'little red head' of the penis must protrude 'two fingers' from the foreskin); one detail in this ecphrasis, the pubis 'cotonée d'un poil brun', suggests a humbler craft more compatible with Robinet's interest in textiles.

5. POSTSCRIPT: THE PRISON-HOUSE OF SEX

'Little Books' like *L'Escole des filles* must evidently be interpreted both as material objects and as would-be institutions, 'assemblies' of erotic-didactic fantasy organized around the fiction of the female speaking agent. They do their work, in fact, at the boundary of these two zones: the physical meeting of book, hand, and body serves as the vehicle for 'schooling' or 'disciplining' the reader into a libertine subject (all of whose thoughts and actions *ought to* lead exclusively to sex). This is what the fictional Fanchon shares with the quotidian Pepys. The diarist's surrender to the mistress-text causes him not only to *décharger* but to write it down in French. His moralistic excuse (to 'inform himself' in worldly wickedness) conveys an ironic truth, since he is indeed formed by the encounter, making *L'Escole des filles* a School of Men as much as a representation of what women really do behind the scenes.

The subject should therefore be educable, supple, and plastic—but to what does he or she conform? Susanne occasionally preaches simple subservience to male desire, insisting that the female member of her ideal couple be '*souple* and obedient to his will' (II. 164). Her more detailed account, however, establishes the primacy of the simulacrum: the accomplished product of modern education should not only dance, sing, and copulate expertly, but *love reading* books of amorous instruction and erotic fiction ('aymer la lecture des livres d'amour, soubs prétexte de s'instruire à parler proprement sa langue naturelle'). Under the 'pretext' of polishing her language, creating the famous 'natural' conversational style that upper-class French-women exported to the entire civilized world,[149] she must *bend herself to the erotic depiction*, making 'son esprit souple aux belles passions d'amour qui y sont représentées'. Pallavicino's courtesan captures her clients by fabricating novelistic 'incidents', but the new domestic-libertine subject 'lets *herself* be captivated by the incidents of the novel as if they were her own' (II. 156). This is exactly the self-captivity experienced by Fanchon within the text and by future readers and pupils in scenes of imagined reception.

Once again, the ubiquitous Claude Le Petit provides a vividly reductive example, forcing the text upon us both as institution and as object. When he gathers together a collection of his scurrilous short verse—including the commendatory poem on the *auteur foutu* published in *L'Escole des filles*—he calls it *The Brothel of the Muses*, as if the publication itself constituted the room or building of public sexuality. As Herbert did with his *Temple*, Le Petit provides a liminary poem or prefatory invitation, calling in the 'Prétieuses' as readers. He belabours them with an offensive gift, insulting them as 'Courtisanes d'honneur, putains spirituelles' while pretending to offer the 'spiritual' ecstasy they crave. In this *Bordel des Muses* (Le Petit promises) the dualism of mind and body mutates into a parallelism, confounding Descartes's insistence that the mind has no sex: if 'the mind has its prick as well as the body' (*l'esprit a son vit aussi bien que le corps*), then the reader's soul will feel 'transports | A

---

[149] Cf. Benedetta Craveri, 'The Lost Idea', *New York Review of Books*, 2 Dec. 1993, 40–3, and *La civiltà della conversazione* (Milan, 2001).

faire descharger la femme la plus froide'—an exact equivalent to the spermatic 'émotion spirituelle ou corporelle' demanded by the Papal Bull at the head of *L'Escole* (p. LXI). (Susanne's lover subscribes to the same philosophy when he plunges into her vagina in search of her *esprit*, as does Susanne herself when she explains how the 'idea' turns into 'white rain'.) And if the body should be aroused during this 'spiritual' copulation,

> Ce livre en long roulé, bien égal et bien roide,
> Vaudra bien un godemichi.[150]

'This book rolled lengthwise, nicely smooth and stiff, | Would be as good as a dildo.'

Le Petit's sonnet strongly resembles the texts that surround *L'Escole*, not only the *auteur foutu* poem but the 'Epistle' that invites the reader and the pseudo-papal Bulle Orthodoxe that prescribes 'spermatizer' as the only proper response to this arousing text. The mock-courteous 'Venez dans ce bordel vous divertir, mes belles,' recalls the lubricious familiarity of *L'Escole* ('Je vous invite, donc, mes belles . . .'), as well as older poems urging the fair to read and learn from pornography.[151] The lewd reference to the *vit* unfolds, and literalizes, the pun embedded in the title 'Epistre invitatoire'. The promise of 'transports to make even the coldest woman discharge' echoes *L'Escole*'s claim to 'satisfy even the most fastidious of ladies' (p. L), and confirms the 'spermatic' model of reader response ordained in the Papal Bull and enacted in the dialogue when Fanchon 'discharges' for Susanne. Le Petit's *Bordel* sonnet shares with his *Escole* madrigal the ruinous obscenity that makes him an *auteur foutu*, unable to separate the different meanings of *foutre* and thus unable to seduce his reader into the illusion that 'to fuck well is to live well' (sect. 2 above). But though his aggression takes a crudely masculine form, it is not quite true that he 'force[s] these women to confront the materiality of the body and its desires'.[152] There is no body in either poem; agency has been transferred from the author to the material text.

L'Escole des filles 'fucks' the reader's eyes like an ithyphallic demon, and *Le Bordel des Muses* gets rolled up and inserted as a *gaude mihi*—the slim, unbound pamphlet-as-phallus meeting the vulva as 'two-leaved book'. In the Music School of his *Université d'amour* Le Petit discovers a singing Muse who holds 'an instrument of ivory in her hand, whose name I can't properly tell you since I didn't see its figure distinctly';[153] now, like the hard-core filmmakers analysed by Linda Williams, he forges his own art into a 'distinct figure' for the unperceivable interiority of female pleasure. The original publishers of *L'Escole* were concerned with physical quality (delivering 'good paper' copies for insertion into the luxurious inner cabinet of the *petite*

---

[150] 'Aux Prétieuses', *Œuvres* 108; except for the truncated final line, this sonnet closely matches Le Petit's parallel invitation to male readers ('Courtisans de Priape', also 108), who are likewise assured that 'L'esprit qui prend plaisir aux discours satyriques | Deschargera sans doute, entendant ces accords.'

[151] A 16th-century MS of the prose *Puttana errante*, now in Chantilly, begins with a sonnet that orders the 'belles voyantes ce livre' to learn its contents and put them into practice; see Claudio Galderisi (ed.), *Il piacevol ragionamento de l'Aretino: Dialogo di Giulia e di Madalena* (Rome, 1987), 113.

[152] As argued by Wahl, *Invisible Relations*, 203.

[153] *L'Escole de l'interest et l'Université d'amour* (Paris, 1662), 116.

maison), and Le Petit plays off this already literalized conceit. Masculine presence gives way to the despised simulacrum, to a Word not so much Incarnate as Incartate. In a further irony, the form of the sonnet belies even this boast, since the final 'go-demichi' line contains only seven syllables; the poem falls short in reverse imitation of the message it delivers—that the text itself, reliable in shape and length, can serve as a surrogate penis. 'Descharger' remains the supreme touchstone of textual effi-cacy, but the *belles* must use their own invention (supplementing Le Petit's 'impos-ture') if they want to achieve that climax in which text and body fuse together.

This moment of textual-sexual yielding or mutual collapse, projected within the original text when Fanchon 'discharges' in response to Susanne's description, is recapitulated in the book's imaginary reception-history. In the 1684 *Parliament of Women*, for example, a vivid speech describing the 'melting' effect of *L'Escole des filles* inspires its adoption as an official course-book in the new national curriculum for women. As one of the newly enfranchised speakers recounts her days in board-ing school, the properties of French ('what a pretty melting Language!') combine with the dissolute 'Subject' of *L'Escole*, which likewise 'melted me even into a gelly of Extasie'; gifts of confectionery persuade the French mistress to share this 'pretty lit-tle neat Book (if I had it here I could kiss it) called *Eschole defilles*', and the kissable book then turns its reader into a dessert. She confesses—in a flurry of dashes and exclamations that break the thread of her oration—that arousal destroyed her abil-ity to concentrate on the traditional 'Work' of her needle. In the same infinite re-gression that Susanne invents for the female novel-reader, the schoolgirl devours 'The Girls' School' only to find herself replicating the heroine Fanchon, 'discharg-ing' within the text and abandoning traditional female accomplishments for new kinds of improvement, cultivating the 'strange Passions it wrought in me', the 'Ex-pressions' that 'made my blood daunce' modish new dances. The satirist clearly in-tends a conventional gibe at women's lustfulness and irresponsibility, but his scene of reading unwittingly raises a more complex issue: *L'Escole des filles* may try to im-pose masculinism and heterosexism, but within the Female Academy it provides a pleasure independent of male presence, and inspires a community of self-pleasing women. The parliamentary speaker tells how, following suggestions by the French teacher and commissioning other women to make translations for her, she pro-gresses from *L'Escole* first to Aretino and then to the more advanced dialogues of Chorier's *Aloisia Sigea*—'a Book so ravishing——I lost my Virginity with only hearing it read'. The new libertine canon 'would certainly increase our contempt and hatred of Men, when we could have our Business done by hearing only'.[154] As in Le Petit, the book takes over from the penis, though here the medium is the shared reading itself rather than the rolled-up paper. The representation 'vaudra bien un godemichi'—but the *gaude mihi*, the source of autonomous female pleasure, resembles not the phallus but the *mépris des hommes*, the 'pretty little neat' organ that encourages 'our contempt and hatred of Men'.

---

[154] 30–2, 80, 102, 136; this book-length satire incorporates several passages from Erasmus' 'senate of women', including the jest about virgin wives who marry eunuchs (33, cf. n. 133 above).

Regarding *L'Escole des filles* as a school of Venus, a formative textbook or 'institution' rather than a merely titillating parody, means locating it at the confluence of two furious debates: the philosophical question of embodiment—whether the mind is sexed—and the political question of women's education. *L'Escole* is not merely a mockery of education but a distorted vision of its efficacy: Fanchon provides the model pupil, miraculously improved in inner poise and *connoissance* as her mind is 'opened', and Susanne the controlling *institutrice*, the sexual equivalent of the *salonnière* or the director of schools. Alexandre Varet, we recall from section 1, finds fiction 'dangerous' because it prompts the female reader to elicit and control the desires of men. The increasingly active role of women in their own education triggers this sense of danger—what Cartesian feminists would call a 'panic terror' in male critics, a fear of women's influence that merges sexual and discursive agency.

L'Escole belongs among the critiques of women's intellect, and debates over formative reading and sexed education, that raged throughout France and England at all levels of print culture. Its early date—contemporary with Michel de Pure's *La Prétieuse* and years before Molière's *École des femmes* and *Femmes savantes*—prevents us from dismissing it as a 'low' derivative of canonical satires. *L'Escole* foregrounds the irreducible physical referent that politer texts could encode. A kind of explosive origin, it leaves traces or splinters in later 'disciplining' texts that would certainly repudiate such a 'depraved' ancestor. The feminist militant in Samuel Chappuzeau's 1661 *Académie des femmes*, for example, calls on women to 'tame their masters' and 'for once, rule them and get on top' (*prendre le dessus*); for the reader whose eyes have been 'opened' by *L'Escole des filles*, it is difficult not to see female bodies 'riding' their men.[155]

L'Escole des filles and its successors (*L'Academie des dames, Vénus dans le cloître*) mirror not only the debates over female education but the new women's teaching orders—a pedagogic movement already 'swelling' by the mid-seventeenth century, which according to one historian produced 'an education more varied, more practical, more developed for girls than for boys'.[156] They founded schools for 'all sorts and conditions', including 'seminaries for mistresses' or Académies des Dames, and their goal was not just to spread Counter-Reformation Catholicism and needle-work throughout France, but to create families more 'policées' run by mothers more 'civilized', more fluent in correct French, and more 'precocious'.[157] The emulous libertine counter-text provides a new catechism, class-plan, training manual, and pedagogic 'theory' for a new Order of Venus. Even the odd detail of the Papal Bull can be matched in the history of the teaching orders, since some of them were in fact founded by such a document, charging them to combat heresy and to train future generations in 'the arts suitable for a free woman'.[158]

[155] *Le Cercle des femmes (1656) and L'Académie des femmes (1661)*, ed. Joan Crow (Exeter, 1983), 93.

[156] Jean Perrel, 'Les Écoles de filles dans la France d'Ancien Régime', in Donald N. Baker and Patrick J. Harrigan (eds.), *The Making of Frenchmen: Current Directions in the History of Education in France, 1679–1979* (Waterloo, Ontario, 1980), 75.

[157] Roger Chartier and Dominique Julia, 'L'Éducation des filles', in Chartier, Julia, and Marie-Madeleine Compère, *L'Éducation en France du XVIe au XVIIIe siècle* (Paris, 1976), 231–47, esp. 244; Perrel, 'Les Écoles de filles', 75–83, esp. 82–3.

[158] Chartier and Julia, 'L'Éducation des filles', 236.

The new campaign for women's intellectual education raged on two fronts, taking on both the traditional domestic ideal and the scandalous alternative definition of 'free women' offered by libertine texts like *L'Escole*. Conduct books insisted that women of all classes should devote themselves to good works and textile handicrafts, literally enmeshing them in the material world; seventeenth-century feminists oppose the traditional arts of 'sewing and keeping silent' to the new skills of scholarship and conversation—an uncanny parallel to Fanchon's sexual 'enlightenment'. Cartesian dualism encouraged them to separate mentality from embodiment, and so to escape the argument that female physiology 'naturally' rendered them incapable and inferior.[159] Anti-sexual feminism and hypersexual fiction both oppose 'brute necessity' in favour of the Idea. One female-voiced poem, for example, criticizes (and impersonates) the masculine doctrine that women's 'sex' precludes all possibility of mental development:

> Your Sex, that prison of your Souls,
> Your rational unbounded Mind controuls.[160]

L'Escole articulates precisely this doctrine, but the ventriloquism of dialogue allows the stricture to appear as a liberating self-discovery. Critics may have attacked *The School of Venus* for teaching 'Diversity of Lewdness',[161] but its 'Diversity' seems crucially limited to forms of pleasure which reaffirm the doctrine that 'Sex' imprisons women's souls and 'controls' their freedom. Hard-core libertinism does at least regard men and women as equally products of their sexual plumbing, whereas 'polite' attacks on women's education propose a kind of gendered materialism: women but not men are prisoners of their sex.

In many ways the erotic dialogue, ostensibly liberating and anti-traditional, takes up the conservative position in contemporary arguments over women's education. *L'Escole*'s promotion of hedonistic abandon mimics, and implicitly destroys, Anna Maria van Schurman's thesis that women should pursue intellectual pleasure as an end in itself, or, as Bathsua Makin puts it, 'there is in all an innate desire of knowing, and the satisfying of this is the greatest pleasure'.[162] Guez de Balzac denounced women's learning on the grounds that 'women should be all woman' (*il faut que les femmes soient tout à fait femmes*), an argument only one step removed from the libertine insistence that sex constitutes the whole essence of woman. (Balzac's attack on what he called mental 'cross-dressing' singles out women who discuss the philosophy of 'metamorphosis', precisely the term that Susanne uses to explain the appeal of strange postures.[163]) Juan Luis Vives argued that even high-born ladies should work with their hands rather than conversing with men or reading amorous

---

[159] See Anna Maria van Schurman, *Whether a Christian Woman Should Be Educated, and Other Writings from her Intellectual Circle*, ed. and tr. Joyce L. Irwin (1998), 43, and Erica Harth, *Cartesian Women: Versions and Subversions of Rational Discourse in the Old Regime* (1992), ch. 2.

[160] *Triumphs of Female Wit . . . or, The Emulation* (1683), 10.

[161] John Dunton, *Athenianism* (1710), 2nd pagination, 230.

[162] Joyce Irwin, 'Anna Maria van Schurman: From Feminism to Pietism', *Church History*, 46 (1977), 53; Schurman, *Whether a Christian Woman Should Be Educated*, 32; Makin, *An Essay to Revive the Ancient Education of Gentlewomen* (1673), 25.

[163] See Ian Maclean, *Woman Triumphant: Feminism in French Literature, 1610–1652* (Oxford, 1977), 138 (cf. 142), and DeJean, *Tender Geographies*, 47–8.

fiction (strictly forbidden because it excites the erotic imagination);[164] *L'Escole* repeatedly urges 'les dames' to pride themselves on their skill at giving men pleasure with the hand.

How far, then, does *L'Escole* share the conservatism later expressed in Molière's *Femmes savantes*, where the down-to-earth *bon bourgeois* mocks the intellectual *précieuses* and confines woman's 'philosophy' to 'forming the morals of her children, supervising her household staff, and regulating her expenses' (II. vii. 573–6)? We have already seen the ironic relation of *L'École des femmes* to its scurrilous predecessor: Molière's Horace and *L'Escole*'s Fanchon both see Eros as a natural force that stimulates 'invention' and 'sharpens the wits', but Susanne's rule-bound instruction, and her assumption that *l'amour* is something that needs to be 'put into the head', make her more like the repressive guardian.[165] *L'Escole*'s meaty assertion of the physical clearly foreshadows Molière's satire against those *précieuses* like Bélise (and Mlle de Scudéry) who delude themselves that they have repudiated corporeal desire and 'extended substance', while its bristling obscenity makes a stand for plain-speaking against the euphemisms of the *salon*. Nevertheless, by a dramatic irony only surprising on the surface, *L'Escole* brings out some affinity between *libertines* and *précieuses*. Like Philaminte in *Les Femmes savantes* (IV. i. 1127–30), the libertines are quite happy to promote 'reason' over 'matter' and mind over body if this lets them redistribute power within the household. Like Armande in the same play, they repudiate humdrum marriage in search of 'elevated desires' and 'nobler pleasures' that will lift them above the common lot of humanity (I. i. 33–45)—though they seek this transcendence in sex intensified rather than sex denied.

Molière's anti-corporeal *femmes savantes* are prefigured in their scandalous opposites, even down to their linguistic theory. They share an underlying faith in the sexed concreteness of language, the power of the monosyllable to convey an entire 'hieroglyphic' of desire: if Molière's female academy tries to expunge words containing *con* and *cul* from the dictionary, Susanne has already confirmed their sense of danger by making those same language fragments the supreme expressions of 'injury' and 'love', writing them out as fully obscene sentences. *L'Escole*'s initial pun on *invitatoire* perfectly exemplifies Philaminte's point that 'dirty syllables' are used to 'insult women's modesty'.[166] In the literary-critical scene, Philaminte herself receives the insult thrust upon the 'Précieuses' by Claude Le Petit: as she responds to the most banal phrase in Trissotin's poem, 'running all the way to the bottom of the

---

[164] *The Education of a Christian Woman: A Sixteenth-Century Manual*, ed. and tr. Charles Fantazzi (2000), 59–61, 78.

[165] III. ii. 747–51 (Maxime I, which dictates that the good wife should 'se mettre dans la tête' the interesting fact that she 'gets into bed with another man' to serve him alone, contrary to 'the usual behaviour of wives nowadays'), III. iv. 920 (Horace exclaims 'L'amour sait-il pas l'art d'aiguiser les esprits?'); for further parallels between Molière and *L'Escole des filles*, see Ch. 5, sect. 3 below.

[166] *Femmes savantes*, III. ii. 909–18; for a real-life parallel, see Françoise d'Aubigné, marquise de Maintenon, *Lettres sur l'éducation des filles*, ed. Théophile Lavallée (Paris, 1854), 126 (she protests vigorously when she hears that the girls of Saint-Cyr are prudishly objecting to words like 'culotte', 'curé', and 'curieux'), and Lise Leibacher-Ouvrard, 'Le Conforme et l'incongru: *L'Éclaircissement* de Pierre Bayle *sur les obscénités* (1701)', *Papers on French Seventeenth-Century Literature*, 29 (2002), 451–63.

soul, one feels a trickling *je ne sais quoi* that makes one swoon'.[167] Molière comes per-
ilously close to Le Petit's eroticization of reading and to *L'Escole's* account of the
Idea, *coulant* or trickling through the channels of concupiscence; the *je ne sais quoi*
behaves exactly like the *gaude mihi*.

The upward trajectory of *L'Escole des filles*, from basic 'schooling' to 'la philosophie
des dames', reminds us that the feminocentric movement extended to higher learning, to the realm of the university and the academy. Queen Christina founded her
own academies both before and after leaving the Swedish throne, and formulated
questions that placed love and passion at the centre of philosophical discourse;
L'Escole borrows directly from Descartes's *Passions de l'âme*, the late work most
influenced by this 'feminized' agenda. The libertine dialogue's preoccupation with
the language of sex challenges the linguistic purity demanded by the *précieuses*
and the new sense that women create the best form of the vernacular, but it also
mocks the contributions of polyglots like Aloisia Sigea in the sixteenth century or
Schurman in the seventeenth. Makin conceives her reform as 'An Essay to Revive the
Ancient Education of Gentlewomen'; in protest against a trivial modern pedagogy
exclusively focused on social accomplishments, she longs for the age of Renaissance
humanism that produced erudite women like Lady Jane Grey and Queen Elizabeth
I. (Makin herself lived out this dream in the pre-Revolution decade, corresponding
with Schurman in Greek.[168]) The difficulty of reconciling 'ancient' erudition with
'modern' sociability was cruelly exploited in the most significant libertine dialogue
of the century, to which I turn in Chapter 4. Nicholas Chorier replaces the
bourgeoises Susanne and Fanchon with learned Renaissance women, sexually and
intellectually liberated, and ascribes the authorship of his 'depraved' work to their
contemporary Aloisia Sigea.

In France, the tide ran against strenuous intellectual work and favoured a feminized programme of worldly conversation devoid of pedantry, an endless discussion of amorous passion, stylistically 'polite' but drenched in seductive nuance.
Despite all the satire against *précieuses* and *femmes savantes*, French intellectual life
was largely redefined to emphasize qualities in which women supposedly excelled
men: taste, discernment, wit, *agrément, finesse, délicatesse*.[169] They were assumed to
provide the 'polish' in *politesse*, a service that Du Bellay in the sixteenth century had
given to the 'Old Courtesan' (Ch. 1 n. 13 above). Gallant discourse assigns the ladies
an almost infinite power to 'form', fashion, and shape the *honnête homme*, which
irresistibly recalls the princess's statue in *L'Escole des filles*: Colletet's *Académie familière des filles* insisted that men must learn 'conversation' from women if they wish to

---

[167] III. ii. 778–9 ('On se sent à ces vers, jusques au fond de l'âme, | Couler je ne sais quoi qui fait que l'on
se pâme').

[168] See Schurman, *Opuscula, Hebraea, Graeca, Latina, Gallica*, ed. Friedrich Spanheim (Leiden, 1648),
164–6 (*Whether a Christian Woman Should Be Educated*, 67–8).

[169] Jacqueline Lichtenstein, *La Couleur éloquente: Rhétorique et peinture à l'âge classique* (Paris, 1989),
20–1 (*The Eloquence of Color: Rhetoric and Painting in the French Classical Age*, tr. Emily McVarish
(Berkeley and Los Angeles, 1993), 12), and cf. 18, 20–22, 35.

become (or appear) 'du monde';[170] Marie de Miramion, herself the founder of one of the teaching orders, declared that 'c'est parmy les femmes que l'on apprend veritablement la langue françoise'—exactly Susanne's 'pretext' for learning erotic *souplesse* from romantic novels.[171]

'Most writers of the Grand Siècle', Jacqueline Lichtenstein discovers, 'pay inexhaustible homage to the superiority of feminine reason.'[172] In 'modern' circles philosophy became in effect *la philosophie des dames*, ironizing the irony of the pornographer's title. This ostensible triumph produces the dangerous corollary— dangerous in an era when women were pointedly excluded from the academies, however much credit was given to the *salons*[173]—that 'ladies' philosophy' could be praised-and-belittled as an adjunct of their sexiness and charm. In retrospect, Susanne's lover becomes a paradigm for all these *galant* worshippers of female hegemony. As she 'discourses on elevated and respectable matters' he is 'mad to be Fucking', or more precisely 'it seemed that he was fucking my mind as he tickled my body, so much pleasure did he take in searching for my soul inside' (II. 120). The aggression that underlies this tribute to Susanne's 'honneste conversation' may be gauged from the previous anecdote, when the same lover goes to 'some prostitute or other' (*quelque fille*, 116) to satisfy a 'love' supposedly felt for her. His aphrodisiac response inverts rather than exalting the *matières relevées* that caused it.

This contradiction can be felt even in the most fervent and outspoken Cartesian feminist, François Poullain de La Barre. His 1673 *De l'égalité des deux sexes* asserts (two decades after Susanne) that laws are set up merely to enforce male hegemony, that arguments from existing social custom are worthless, that girls are artificially conditioned to define themselves as sex-objects, and that women must therefore be granted the right to true education, whose goal is to 'regulate our passions and to moderate our desires'. It is only the 'terreur Panique', the 'panic terror' of ignorant men, that prevents women from leading academies and universities; only the 'bizarre imagination of the vulgar' believes 'that study makes women more wicked'.[174]

Poullain claims to separate his own 'philosophical' discourse from sexually tainted and trivial *galanterie*, and yet his arguments for female superiority include the gallant, Gallic assumption that women excel at 'polishing' men emotionally and culturally: 'if men want to enter the *beau monde* and play their part there, they are obliged to go to the Ladies' School (*l'école des Dames*) to learn politeness, complaisance, and all the appearances now considered essential for the *honnête homme*'.[175] Poullain grounds his argument for equal educational opportunity on the Cartesian principle that 'the Mind has no Sex' (84), and he insists that mingling thought and passion is the fatal flaw in male thinking that generates misogynistic prejudice (70,

---

[170] See Maurice Magendie, *La Politesse mondaine* (Paris, 1925), 714 n. 5.
[171] Maclean, *Woman Triumphant*, 150; cf. Chartier and Julia, 'Éducation des filles', 238.
[172] *Couleur éloquente*, 20.   [173] See Harth, *Cartesian Women*, 17–18 and *passim*.
[174] *The Equality of the Two Sexes*, ed. A. Daniel Frankforter and Paul J. Morman (Lewiston, NY, 1989), 18, 154, 114, 110 (translations mine).
[175] Ibid. 6–8, 36.

158). And yet his feminist counter-argument showcases women's beauty (specifically related to their sexual difference), their seductive rhetoric, and their innate affinity with the passions. Women's 'natural' eloquence is principally manifested in writings about the passions, and 'all the beauty and all the secret art of eloquence' consists in 'touching the spring of the passions' (44). For Poullain, women's discursive power is inseparable from their attractiveness; their pleading in court gives 'pleasure', and their intellectual speeches 'touch' the listener with that well-known euphemism for erotic excitement, 'je ne sçay quel agrément' (46). Poullain comes to resemble the misogynist opponent he conjured up earlier, who sarcastically comments that it would be 'plaisante' to see a woman lecturing as a professor (16). Woman's superiority depends on their 'natural' beauty, and its power to 'excite' and 'agitate' the passions—suddenly an estimable rather than a lamentable capacity—makes them our 'Mistresses'.[176] In contrast Marie de Gournay, Montaigne's adopted daughter and Poullain's ancestor as author of the 1622 *Égalité des hommes et des femmes*, dismisses this courtly feminization of thought and language with robust contempt.[177]

We might conclude (first) that the travestic, sexually rampant 'teaching text' accompanies the debate over women's education like a ribald doppelgänger, and (secondly) that the fictive reception-history of the 'School of Venus' brings out the doubleness at the core of those debates. The English entrepreneurial journalist John Dunton, who circulated several titillating anecdotes about *The School of Venus* and the 'Diversity of Lewdness' it teaches,[178] expresses this duplicity quite clearly in his newspaper advice column. In addition to peddling stories about the demand for *L'Escole des filles*, Dunton launched the *Athenian Mercury*, a kind of English *Mercure galant* that answered readers' queries about the most ticklish issues in their lives. When a correspondent asks whether women can be educated at all, Dunton argues the modern case for women's improvement, cutting through decades of controversy on both sides of the Channel by bluntly asserting (like Susanne in *L'Escole* and Poullain in *L'Égalité*) the injustice of male-dominated laws depriving them of equal education. The original letter-writer links female education to illicit sexuality, masculine 'power', and the 'natural' weakness of the sex: he asks whether he should tutor 'a particular Friend amongst the Fair Sex, over whom I have some Power', even though he believes it 'impossible their natural Impertinencies shou'd ever be converted into a solid Reasoning'. Most probably both voices, the erotic-didactic correspondent and the Cartesian-idealist editor, are fabricated by Dunton himself—and their common ground is soon apparent.[179]

The *Mercury*'s reply concedes nothing to women's own demands—the right to be considered disembodied—and in effect rebuilds the prison-house of sex with some

---

[176] Ibid. 146–8 (cf. 132, where he warns *against* the danger of 'stirring the passions' by thinking about sexual anatomy).

[177] Cf. Cathleen M. Bauschatz, 'Marie de Gournay and the Crisis of Humanism', in Philippe Desan (ed.), *Humanism in Crisis: The Decline of the French Renaissance* (Ann Arbor, 1991), 285–90, and for women's philosophy in her *Égalité*, Ch. 1 n. 67 above.

[178] See n. 161 above and Ch. 5 n. 6 below.

[179] *The Athenian Oracle*, 2nd edn. (1704), i. 382–3.

added gilding. The argument for women's mental superiority derives just as much from gendered physiology ('the softness of their Flesh, which is a sign of goodness of Wit . . . the moist Constitution of their Brain'). Though Dunton asserts that women's cooperation would speed up scientific discovery, he still sees their intellectual potential as a by-product and safeguard of 'their Purity and Chastity. . . . For 'tis a thing hitherto unheard of, that a Woman was learn'd, and not Chaste and Continent.'[180] Dunton's self-annulling, gallant exaggeration pretends to ignore the flood of misogynist rhetoric that identified women's learning with sexual transgression, making *la philosophie des dames* synonymous with the most advanced erotic knowledge. He claims exemption from the 'bizarre imagination' that his source Poullain denounces as a 'panic terror' of the vulgar, who (like Susanne) equate the 'opening' of mind and vulva. This topos is expanded to incredible length (as we shall see in Chapter 4) by Nicholas Chorier, in his pseudo-feminine and genuinely erudite 'Dialogues of Aloisia Sigea'.

---

[180] Ibid. 383; if this issue was written by Dunton's co-editor Samuel Wesley then it is even more disingenuous, since Wesley was perfectly aware of Chorier's pornographic impersonation of the erudite lady (Ch. 6 n. 3 below). The *Mercury* may be citing directly from Vives (cf. *Education of a Christian Woman*, 65) and from A.L.'s tr. of Poullain, *The Woman as Good as the Man, or The Equality of Both Sexes* (1677), ed. Gerald M. MacLean (Detroit, 1988), 114 ('the lovely Sex, being of a Temperature more Fine and Delicate than ours, would not fail (at least) to match ours, if it applyed it self to Study').

4

Erudita libido

Nicholas Chorier, Aloisia Sigea, and the
Secrets of Love and Venus

Then she told me of another Book, call'd *Aloysia sigea*, which was in Latin . . .
and I can assure ye, Mrs Speaker, that it is not for nothing that Latin is call'd the
Language of the *Whore*. For certainly never did any Book in this World give such
an absolute and perfect accompt of *Cupids* Tacticks as that Book: 'tis a Book so
ravishing——I lost my Virginity with only hearing it read.

(The Parliament of Women (1684), 31–2)

Mutari amat Proteus Amor.

(Chorier)

THE two memoirs of reading that introduce this book—Pepys's furtive consumption of *L'Escole des filles*, Casanova's precocious deployment of the 'theory' he derived from Chorier—define the two texts universally recognized as the pillars of
seventeenth-century libertine discourse. The Parliament of Women decrees 'that
Aloysia Sigea, L'Eschole de fils, and *Peter Aretines* discourses be translated, and fairly
Printed for the Particular good of the Female Common-weal', while banning all
other books and closing down both universities (136–7). Reception-fantasies of
L'Escole always replicate some of its claustrophobic domesticity; encounters with
'Aloisia Sigea', the presumed author of Chorier's dialogues, open up a playful, élite
realm of 'erudite' libido, 'unnatural' experiment, and 'Protean' perversity. The formative power of this single text is attested by expert witnesses as diverse as Diderot,
Casanova, and Samuel Wesley, the co-editor of the *Athenian Mercury* and the
grandfather of Methodism. By 1680 it had penetrated so far into English society
that schoolboys were reading it in a London dissenting academy, as we shall see in
Chapter 6 below.

Even facetious allusions recognize the multiple appeal of *Aloisia Sigea*. Uncoding
the Latin 'secrets' or '*arcana of* Love and Venus' promised in the title—according to
the women's parliament cited in my first epigraph—will yield the totality of truth
about sex, the 'absolute and perfect account'. If Amor equals Proteus and the essence
of desire is metamorphosis, then the prison-house of gender can crumble; the book
itself can 'mutate' into a primary agent, take the reader's virginity, empower the
'female commonwealth', and inspire 'contempt and hatred of Men'. As we shall

see, Chorier's fiction does create powerful and articulate female speakers who un-settle the foundations of heterosexuality and quash the convictions of misogynist satire. But it remains severely divided between 'contempt' and 'celebration'. And it raises a further question endemic to pseudo-feminocentric fiction: whether it is a textbook or a satire, which sex is the primary subject? Does this 'Academy' discipline women or men?

This chapter will pursue the various ramifications and contradictions of this most advanced simulation of the female *libertine érudite*. Aretino polarized female sexuality and intellect, defining an ideal sex-object whose tongue is 'honeyed' but not 'learned' (Ch. 1, sect. 1 above); Chorier's blazon of ideal beauty gives double value to the 'flexible' and 'wanton' tongue, for its agility in kissing and its volubility in expressing thoughts that would otherwise never be properly formed, both its functions producing 'honeyed delights' (VII. 228). In Chorier's complicated dia-logue, the two cousins Tullia and Octavia perform as well as describe the educa-tional encounter of sensible bodies and expansive ideas, evoking an entire universe of modern science and classical allusion. I will particularly emphasize the issues of Latinity and aristocratic voluptuarism, Cartesian erotics and mind–body priority, the 'Sapphic' independence of the female narrators, and the place of figuration and visualization in philosophical Eros. The concluding section focuses on the role of erotic education in the formation of males for polite society.

1. 'SO SALTY, SO CHARMING': CHORIER'S LATINITY AND THE FICTION OF FEMALE AUTHORSHIP

The neo-Latin prose dialogue *Satyra Sotadica de Arcanis Amoris et Veneris*, published in the 1660s as the work of Aloisia Sigea but in truth written by the Dauphinois attorney and historian Nicolas Chorier, has probably done more to constitute the *discours de la sexualité* than any other early modern text. Like the erotic poetry of Johannes Secundus, it circulated (and survived) under the re-spectable cover of Latinity, though by 1800 there had been at least fourteen versions in three modern languages, as well as some thirteen Latin editions; in the Private Case of the British Library, for example, versions of this single work outnumber every copy of every work by de Sade. (Recalling the Council of Trent's allowance of 'lascivious' classics that display *sermonis elegantiam* (Ch. 1 n. 84 above), some ver-sions used the neutral textbook title *Joanni Meursii Elegantiae Latini Sermonis*.) One of Chorier's seven dialogues had been translated into English by 1676, and four years later a much-altered translation of the whole text appeared in France under the mock-educational title *L'Academie des dames*; the abridgement of this vernacu-lar version continued to be reissued for over a hundred years.

We shall see in Chapter 8 that the Latin *Satyra* rapidly became a touchstone in de-bates over eroticism and obscenity in literature: the poems of Rochester, in particu-lar, were coupled with 'Meursius' as examples of how 'the Beauty of the Expression, and the Strength of the Spirit and Fancy, have given a Sort of Merit to Lewdness', and half a century later the *Memoirs of* Fanny Hill were excused in identical terms. Chorier's *Satyra Sotadica* includes virtually every topos that we now recognize as 'the invention of pornography', and indeed Lynn Hunt, introducing a collection of essays on this very theme, produces as her earliest example of the French word *pornographique*—in the modern sense—a reference to books 'which one calls *sotadique* or pornographic'.[1] Nevertheless, though Hunt traces the term *sotadic* to the Greek sodomite-poet Sotades, she does not recognize this central allusion to Chorier's title. Modern sexuality could be understood as a footnote to Chorier, but his faux-female, faux-classical text and its influence have been very little studied until now.[2]

Whereas *L'Escole des filles* appeared anonymously, the *Satyra Sotadica* could be called hypernomymous. As the twin code names *Aloisia* and *Meursius* indicate, Chorier published it under a double pseudonym (Fig. 8). Like its exact contemporary *Les Lettres portugaises*, it was supposedly written by an Iberian woman and later translated. But in Chorier's case he chose verifiable, historical authors. The alleged Latin translator (Jan van Meurs or Meursius, 1579–1639) really did write indecent poems and treatises on ancient festivities, including phallic and Aphroditic rituals.[3] And the alleged author of the Spanish original—Aloisia Sigea or Louise Sigée, a French expatriate living in Toledo—really did achieve international recognition as a linguist and poet before her early death in 1560. She even composed a Latin dialogue between two young women, comparing the pleasures and dangers of Court life with those of retirement.[4] Sigea flourished in the educational revival of the high Renaissance, a contemporary of erudites like Margaret Roper, poets like Louise Labé—famous in Chorier's own region for her erotic poetry and her campaign for women's education—and great courtesan-authors like Veronica Franco or Tullia d'Aragona, who wrote her own treatise on love and sustained a kind of 'Academy' (as we saw in Chapter 1 above). Chorier reinforces his historical claim by surrounding his text with a learned apparatus. Prefaces and extracts from chronicles summarize Sigea's achievements and praise her refusal to accept 'abject and stupid' domesticity. She also appears in a commendatory poem 'In Praise of the Erudite Virgin Who Wrote a Satire against Turpitude'—a poem that Chorier acknowledged as his own work even though he denied writing the *Satyra* itself—and again in an epistle appended to the second edition, written in her own persona 'from the Elysian Fields'.[5]

---

[1] *The Invention of Pornography* (New York, 1993), 14 and n.

[2] Foxon, 38, provides an accurate summary, but most recent statements about Chorier (with exceptions noted below) use an abridgement of the French *Academie des dames* (a loose adaptation) or a second-hand summary of the original; the only comprehensive critical studies are those of Lise Leibacher-Ouvrard, cited *passim* below.

[3] e.g. *De Puerperio Syntagma*, in *De Funere* (The Hague, 1604), and *Graecia Feriata* (Leiden, 1619), esp. 53; for his erotic verse, see n. 30 below.

[4] *Duarum Virginum Colloquium de Vita Aulica et Privata* (1552), ed. and tr. Odette Sauvage as *Dialogue de deux jeunes filles sur la vie de cour et la vie de retraite* (Paris, 1970), with biographical introduction; Chorier himself, according to his *Adversaria* (see Abbreviations above), iii. 31, wrote a comparison of the active and contemplative life.

[5] *Satyra* (see Abbreviations above), 1 5–22, 313–19; cf. 'De Laude eruditae virginis, quae contra turpia Satyram scripsit', in Chorier's own *Carminum Liber Unus* (Grenoble, 1680), 84–7.

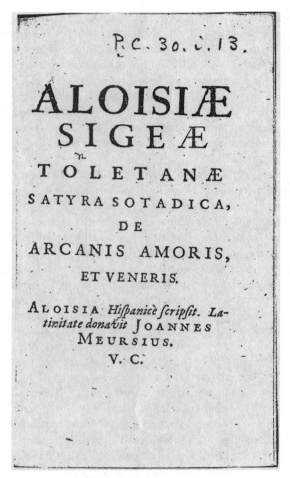

8. 'Aloisia Sigea' [Nicholas Chorier], *Satyra Sotadica de Arcanis Amoris et Veneris* (Lyons?, *c*.1665?), title page (British Library, PC 30.i.13)

This paratextual fabrication of a sexually emancipated female author, collapsing together the Renaissance-humanist and courtesan-poet traditions, is reduplicated *within* the text. Female impersonation had become the norm in male-authored sexual discourse since Aretino's *Ragionamenti*, and *L'Escole des filles* had begun to develop girl-talk into a 'philosophie des dames' (as we saw in Chapter 3). But no one reading Aretino could imagine that the dialogue was actually written by someone like its speakers, and Aretino asserts his strong authorial personality in his prefaces as well as in the burlesque characterization of his street-wise prostitutes. The preface to *L'Escole* asserts that a renegade courtier really wrote it, and clearly condescends to its *bonnes bourgeoises* interlocutors. Chorier, however, shrouds his own presence in pseudonymity and promotes his characters to the authorial classes. The speakers of his dialogues, Tullia and Octavia, are themselves versions of the fictitious Aloisia, a combination of pornographic fantasy and self-conscious intellectual. We shall see that they continually quote and imitate other writers, authorize themselves by claiming literary genealogies, and insert narratives, letters, and learned essays into the dialogue, with intertextual commentary. Tullia may refer to erotic discourses as 'trifles', dismissing her own expertise with aristocratic *sprezzatura*, but they are still '*erudite* little books about trifles' (*his de nugis eruditas libellis*) and they promote a fantasy of erotic-intellectual power: 'everything yields to educated desire', to *erudita libido*.

In both *L'Escole des filles* and the *Satyra Sotadica*, the instructional format—an innocent but intensely motivated girl in the position of the young Casanova, initiated by a more experienced woman—forces us to be aware of the linguistic and cognitive dimension of sexuality. Nevertheless Susanne's 'philosophy' in *L'Escole* remains quotidian and vernacular; Fanchon's education consists largely of basic physiology, posturology, and deception-technique, while the links to Plato and Descartes remain hidden. In Chorier, on the other hand, the erudite Tullia—whose name suggests Tullia d'Aragona as well as the degenerate aristocrat whom Juvenal attacks for nocturnal rambling (VI. 306–8)—fiercely defends the intellectual life, attacking the 'arrogant and stupid malignity' of those envious men who oppose women's education and who hint that the learned woman is inevitably unchaste.[6] But though Chorier vastly expands the possibilities of sexual education, and though he creates brilliant and uninhibited characters, he actually confirms the misogynist position attacked by these 'female' educators, since their intellectual activity turns out to be wholly enclosed and defined by sex. Whereas the real Aloisia Sigea was famous for learning some dozen languages—a feat emulated by Chorier's contemporary Anna Maria van Schurman—Tullia retails thirteen Latin synonyms and Greek etymons for the female genitalia, and forty-six for the male (III. 42–4, 48–9). *Savante* as she was, Susanne could only muster six apiece (I. 12, 16).

Chorier's double fiction of authorship allowed him to exploit two discursive effects at once: the emotional expertise associated with female authorship, and the classical authority of Latinity. Latin might have been considered the 'Language of the Whore'—as *The Parliament of Women* puts it—not merely because of its liturgical use in the Roman Church, but because it granted the freedom to discuss sexual subjects and to mingle the serious and the jocular. Latin created channels of international and transhistorical exchange between classical Rome, Renaissance humanism, and seventeenth-century science: in Chorier's seamless fiction, Tullia emulates the Empress Messalina in the villa of a Renaissance duke, and the sixteenth-century educator Juan Luis Vives explains the Cartesian theory of the pineal gland

---

[6] I. 24–5 ('homines, per malignitatem quandam arrogantam et stultam, eas opes invidunt'); cf. Ch. 3 n. 180 above for defences of learned women's chastity in Dunton and Vives.

(VI. 213, VII. 292); in Thomas Bartholin's anatomical treatise, an influential account of the clitoris is embroidered with speculations about Sappho and the history of lesbianism.[7] When Chorier has Tullia tease Octavia about her little slit or *rimula* (V. 81), he echoes a famous line in Théodore de Bèze's erotic verse, notorious because de Bèze became one of the founders of Calvinism.[8] These freedoms were largely but not exclusively male. The Latin culture shared by Secundus and Chorier enabled the homosocial bonding of Casanova and the English milord, passing over the mother even while joking about the 'masculine' power of the *cunnus* and its enslavement of the *mentula*. Poullain de La Barre, the ostensible champion of female education, notes that women instinctively mistrust even their own children if they speak Latin in their presence, assuming that it must conceal some 'impertinence'.[9] On the other hand, enough women had gained fame as Latinists to make their participation in Chorier's erotic text a tantalizing, even titillating possibility.

Classical practice encouraged a form of wit—*sales* or 'salty things'—that combined mental brilliance with sauciness and salacity. Civic authorities would organize comic debates on concubines and prostitutes, 'full of urbane humour and salty wit',[10] and the puritanical Milton draws attention to the *sales* in his aggressively bawdy Latin oratory.[11] Even the austere Aloisia Sigea—the sixteenth-century humanist herself, not Chorier's fabrication—recognized that the attraction of Court life lay in the 'audacities' of its conversation between the sexes, its language 'seasoned with salt and charm', *lepidis et sale conditis*.[12] Chorier, as we shall see, invited readers into 'Sigea's' dialogue in exactly the same terms.

In this neo-Latin medium classical allusion becomes naturalized. Ancient Greece and Rome provide Chorier with a dense web of quotation (often indirect or parodic) and a cast of characters who serve as benchmarks of sexual transgression: Messalina for multiple coition, Sappho for 'honourable' lesbianism and literary prowess, Byblis and Iphis for bewildering youthful desire, Philaenis and Elephantis for the invention of 'postures'.[13] The title *Satyra Sotadica* aligns him with Petronius' *Satyricon*—a loose, dialogic, non-judgemental kind of satire rather than the formal diatribes of Juvenal—and with the scurrilous writings of Sotades, Martial's byword for the intersection of sexual and literary perversion. The Greek poet's preference for the passive-receptive position in sodomy exactly matches the reversible form of

---

[7] *Anatomia Reformata, ex Caspari Bartholini* . . . (Amsterdam, 1651), 186 (and see n. 74 below).

[8] Ch. 1 n. 86 above.

[9] *The Equality of the Two Sexes*, ed. A. Daniel Frankforter and Paul J. Morman (Lewiston, NY, 1989), 42.

[10] *De Fide Concubinarum in suos Pfaffos, Jocus et Urbanitate et Sale Plenissimus*, in *Quodlibeto Heidelburgensi* (n.d., n.p., but Heidelberg, c.1501).

[11] Prolusion VI and *Pro Se Defensio* (Columbia edn. xii. 244, ix. 94).

[12] *Duarum Virginum Colloquium*, 77, 79, and cf. 151–5 for Blesilla's moralizing rebuttal (men's *sales* are nothing but *lenocinii* or bawds' tricks, and when you think you are *lepidas* men merely find you *garrulas* and therefore promiscuous), which incidentally does *not* convince the younger woman.

[13] For Chorier's classical citations, see Leibacher-Ouvrard, 'Transtextualité et construction de la sexualité: La *Satyra Sotadica* de Chorier', *L'Esprit créateur*, 35/2 (Summer 1995), 51–66; for the homoerotic Iphis story, cited by Tullia in *Satyra*, II. 36–7, see Isaac de Benserade, *Iphis et Iante*, ed. Anne Verdier with Christian Biet and Lise Leibacher-Ouvrard (Metz, 2000).

his lyrics, according to Martial's epigram 11. lxxxvi; the 'upside-down song' and 'the bugger Sotades' himself (*carmine supino . . . Sotaden cinaedum*) can each be read both backwards and forwards. (When Milton threatens to give an opponent 'a rough *Sotadic*', he intends a kind of literary rape.[14]) Chorier's form derives from Lucian's *Dialogues of the Hetairai* and, more distantly, from the Socratic dialogues of initiation into Eros. Antiquity provides him with philosophical code names for contemporary positions ('Epicurean' for libertine, 'Stoic' for Christian) and aetiological myths that explain and thereby vindicate sexual variations; to justify fellatio, for example, Tullia adapts Phaedrus' version of the Prometheus story, itself a travesty of the original (n. 68 below).

Both the historical Sigea and Chorier's libertine simulacrum evoke Socrates as the supreme touchstone of wisdom. In the *Satyra*, however, Socrates is not the otherworldly ascetic cited by the real Sigea, but the convivial hedonist and lover of young men like Alcibiades—Lucian's Socrates rather than Plato's.[15] Chorier participates in the Greek revival most spectacularly expressed in Antonio Rocco's *Alcibiade*, and one of his male characters attributes to Socrates the concept that Rocco had applied to the labile, intersexual stage of Alcibiade's beauty (Ch. 2, sect. 2 above); not the ephebe, but women-in-general now constitute a *vivum libidinum thesaurum*, a living treasury (or dictionary) of lust, at the service of man's pleasure (VII. 243). The philosophy of 'Socratic' playfulness is particularly evoked in the last and most complex section of Chorier's work, called *Fescennini* after the phallic harvest- and wedding-songs of ancient Rome.[16] The Socratic link and the general idea of a 'Satyra Sotadica' were probably suggested by a passage in the letters of the younger Pliny that epitomized urbane participation in the carnival of erotica: 'Yes, I sometimes write lewd little verses, and I also listen to comedies, watch mimes, read lyrics and understand Socratics. Sometimes moreover I laugh, I joke, I play; to sum up all these innocent recreations in one word, I am human (*homo sum*)' (v. iii). Renaissance scholars had produced three different readings of this influential letter: some followed the manuscripts and so placed *Socraticos* (dialogue-philosophies of 'unnatural' Eros) among the pleasures of a gentleman, some accepted the variant reading *Satyricos*, but most assumed that what Pliny really intended was *Sotadicos*.[17] These variants nicely encapsulate Chorier's text, which manages to be all three at once.

Chorier's intense classical retrospection should not conceal his links to the most up-to-date speculation in natural philosophy, however. Like gravity and the circulation of the blood, modern 'pornography' appeared first in the ancient medium of Latin. As I suggested in Chapter 1, the boundary of play and earnest was as unfixed in the scientific discourse of sexuality as in Chorier's erotica. Tullia's 'salt' erudition

---

[14] *Colasterion, CPW* ii. 757.

[15] Lucian, *True History*, II. 17, 19, pseudo-Lucian, *Erōtes* (Introd. n. 33 above), 54, and cf. Ch. 1 n. 29 above; contrast Sigea, *Duarum Virginum Colloquium*, 175–7, 213, and *passim*.

[16] Cf. *Adversaria*, iii. 51, where Chorier refers to the mock-legal 'fescennini' he wrote for Mardi Gras, and Leibacher-Ouvrard, 'Transtextualité', 63, for his interest in 'antique carnival'. *Oxford Latin Dictionary*, s.v. 'Fescenninus' 2, shows that the word was linked to the *fascinum* or phallus.

[17] See *Epistolarum Libri X*, ed. Johan Veenhusius (Leiden and Rotterdam, 1669), 279.

belongs in the same discursive world as Giovanni Benedetto Sinibaldi's *Genean-thropeia*, which dwells at length on aphrodisiacs, perverse *figurae*, Priapic rituals, and the 'arts of aphroditic love', weaving in numerous examples of sexual transgression in antiquity: the exploits of Messalina, the courtesan 'dodecamechanus' who invented the posture-series, the man who infiltrated the all-female religious ceremony.[18] Sinibaldi announces on his title page that he will convey not just the mechanism but the 'affectiones' and 'Voluptas' of generation—in a manner 'jucunde' as well as 'methodice'—and follows this up with a spirited assault on a prudish and illiterate enemy, gathering classical authorities to support (not the medical usefulness) but the pleasure of sexual explicitness: Horace's recommendation to delight as well as instruct (combining the *utile* and the *dulce*), Petronius' carefree Epicurean defence of sexual pleasure against the frown of Cato, Martial's demonstration that such texts 'cannot please unless they have a prick', *nisi pruriant*, unless they feel arousal and in turn arouse the reader.[19] The same ideas and the same authors reappear in Chorier's *Satyra*, which likewise weaves anatomical instruction and classical erudition into an eroto-didactic manifesto.

The medical writer and the *pornographe* share the goal of *embodying* language, generating a rhetorical equivalent to the phenomena they teach. Thus Sinibaldi's stylistic practice matches his theory, amplifying his genital descriptions with the same abundant landscape vocabulary that Tullia uses to elaborate the newly aroused body of Octavia. His chapter on reducing the over-large penis, for example, replicates the distended organ with its 'jocund' amplification of epithets and images; the engorged prose confirms Martial's point that writings about sexuality must themselves have the *mentula*.[20] Tullia and Octavia might seem lacking in one part of this requirement: they *pruriant*, but how can they be *mentulatae*? Partly, of course, by possessing the discursive power conventionally associated with the phallus, the 'grammatical' masculinity located (as Secundus puts it) in the 'cunt'. But Sinibaldi provides a literal equivalent, a female form of engorged or priapic language. His term is *nymphomania*—not (as some scholars argue) an invention of eighteenth-century *sensibilité*, but produced in this baroque synthesis of sex and language. *Nymphomania* for Sinibaldi presents itself as a fervent amplification of discourse: it causes women not only to 'choose well-hung men to skirmish better in Venus' arena' (*in Venerea palestra velitentur*, a reminder that Chorier's first dialogue is entitled *Velitatio* or 'Skirmish'), but to 'burst out in a talkative, lascivious, provocative, shameless way', speaking of nothing but *voluptate aphrodisia* in the most obscene style.[21] *Lascivae, procaces, impudentes* . . . these are precisely the terms that Chorier's female characters use to celebrate, not to denigrate, their own seductive loquacity.

[18] (Rome, 1642), cols. 36–9, 457–90, 154–6, 20–1, 241, 237–8.

[19] Title page, fos. †4–5, citing Horace, *Ars Poetica*, 343, Petronius, xxx, Martial, i. iv and xxxv ('non possunt sine mentula placere').

[20] *Geneanthropeia*, col. 328 ('De penis vasta mole diminuenda').

[21] Ibid., col. 190 ('furor ille uterinus, a Graecis nymphomania dictus'), pre-dating the alleged first use of the term (1769) announced in G. S. Rousseau, 'Nymphomania, Bienville, and the Rise of Erotic Sensibility', in Paul-Gabriel Boucé (ed.), *Sexuality in Eighteenth-Century Britain* (Manchester, 1982), 96.

Tullia's Latinate erudition, 'salty' wit, and literary allusiveness (classical, Renaissance, modern) all serve to establish her 'prurience' as a conscious achievement. She displays the symptoms of *nymphomania* not as a disease but as a controlled programme of education-through-arousal and mastery of multifarious discourses. 'Nymphomaniac' language is not merely discursive but performative and gestural, calling into play the body it recounts. This is most evident in the scenes that Tullia and Octavia act out together, like the early lesbian seduction and anatomy lesson (in a dialogue named *Fabrica* after Vesalius's famous treatise). We should of course recognize the Rabelaisian *mock*-didacticism of Chorier's work. It is certainly preposterous and comic when Tullia presents her learned etymology of 'cunt' and 'prick', her professorial manner conspicuously belying the raw simplicity of the subject matter. When she derives genital words from intellectual words, making *cunnus* and *mentula* cognate with conciousness and mentality, then we suspect a kind of satirical, 'uncrowning' reductionism: the seat of the mind is always in the genitals, *entre con et coüillons* as Susanne would say. But this comic fusion of mind and sex also works the other way. *Fabrica* produces the kind of anatomical knowledge that served Casanova as his 'theory'.

In *L'Escole des filles* it was Fanchon's own desire, acting independently of her will, that 'met aussi vivement les choses devant les yeux que si elles estoient en effect présentes' (II. 151), but now Tullia herself exercises this power, associated with Comenian education and with the successful rhetorician.[22] Her description of the vagina first endows it with vigorous agency (squeezing, sucking) and then exalts it as the tube or telescope that brings humanity from dark nothingness into the light of life; immediately, the pupil articulates the same movement. In Tullia's anatomy theatre, Octavia feels that when her teacher touches and describes her vulva she can 'see everything hidden in the depths of my viscera, as if it were placed before my eyes', *quasi ob ocula posita*.[23] Previous libertine discourse certainly brings the viscera into play: in the homoerotic bond explicated by Rocco, the pupil's breath penetrates into the teacher's *viscere*, and he returns the compliment with an injection of seed; Pallavicino's courtesan can simulate a 'sviscerato affetto', literally a gut-spilling emotion, but the reader knows it is just a fake.[24] Octavia's quasi-ocular experience is an illusion too, but one willingly sustained by both partners. It is important to remember that the two cousins are making love as they speak, showing as well as telling; rather than adopting the maxim of Molière's Dom Juan that *il faut faire et non pas dire*,[25] they are breaking down that distinction. Like an orator, Tullia not only places the unseeable 'as if before the eyes' by vivid words, but accompanies them with gestures that—in this special case—do not so much illustrate as constitute the object. Arousal plus knowledge creates a kind of speculum, literally

---

[22]   See Ch. 1, sect. 2 above (Comenius) and Ch. 2 n. 6 (the rhetorician Apthonius). Part of the following analysis has appeared in my 'Divulgence, "Autopsy", and the Erotic Text: *L'Escole des filles* and Chorier's *Satyra Sotadica*', *Papers on French Seventeenth-Century Literature*, 29 (2002), 465–73.

[23]   III. 45; Mitchell Greenberg, *Baroque Bodies: Psychoanalysis and the Culture of French Absolutism* (2001), 84, emphasizes the 'seeming' in this passage, using only a 1910 translation ('il me semble') and missing the strong meaning of the Latin *videri*.

[24]   *Alcibiade*, 44; *RP* 84.   [25]   Introd. n. 23 above.

educating Octavia by drawing out her own hidden interior until it is as palpable as Comenius required, sensed *ad vivam autopsian.*

Rather than by a metal instrument, Octavia 'dilates' by the natural process of erection and lubrication, in response to the expansive combination of touch and speech. Rather than submitting to the eye of a doctor, she leafs through her own interior book, like countless imagined readers of the libertine text. It may be objected that Octavia resists and feels pain, or that the vagina does not literally extrude. But character and organ both warm to the subject: first in Tullia's description, then in Octavia's own body, the female sex 'opens' of its own accord and 'shoots' ejaculate as a counterpart to the stream of speech (*dehiscit* III. 43, *projecit* II. 36, *ejecit* V. 87–8). Tullia's natural-philosophical demonstrations continue the scientific discourse of Charles Estienne, who asserts—in the essay accompanying Fig. 3 above, where the speculum and the erotic body combine—that the womb 'dilates itself', 'sucks out' and 'throws together' the sperm (*exsugit, conjicit*).[26]

In Chorier, the interplay of knowledge and sensation does not stop at the moment of 'vivid self-witnessing', but develops its own momentum. From the start, the teacher's hand, eye, and voice moved in close coordination, fondling, piercing, and 'washing over' her pupil.[27] Now Tullia demonstrates the pleasures of introspection by fixing her gaze and spreading Octavia's thighs, while Octavia in turn interrogates the visual beam: 'what are you doing to me with those prying eyes of yours? . . . what do you see inside?' (III. 45). Each leading question leads from ocular emission to digital '*intro*mission', back to discursive incitement, and so to new embraces. While this exchange could take place in any language, it is particularly sustainable in Latin, hinging on the parallels of *vita, videor, videre,* and *visceri, emissiciis, introspicere,* and *intromittere.* It is significant that the French adaptation of 1680 omits almost all these interactive details.[28]

Tullia's 'salty' response to her pupil's exclamations, inviting Octavia to explore her vagina in return, continues to weave together the literary and the scientific. Since teacher and pupil have already become lovers, this show-and-tell session will perfectly fulfil the Horatian requisite; it will be 'Utile tibi, et mihi dulce', 'useful for you and sweet for me' (III. 47). The entire dialogue celebrates the freedom of generic exchange made possible by Latinity, and Chorier (or his publisher) confirms this in the arrangement of his text, appending two triumphant examples of neo-Latin sexology. One volume ends with the brilliantly forged correspondence between the medical researcher Soranus and Queen Cleopatra, discussing her sexual excesses and providing aphrodisiac prescriptions (Ch. 1 n. 88 above). And this is followed by a colophon from Johannes Secundus, the celebrated distich on gender—'Why is the cunt masculine and the prick feminine?'—that Casanova combined so wittily with the body of Chorier's text (Fig. 9).

[26] *De Dissectione Partium Corporis Humani* (Paris, 1545), 289–90; in *La Dissection des parties du corps humain* (Paris, 1546), 314, the Latin 'opus ad dilatationem' becomes *se dilater.*

[27] Cf. II. 32–3 ('oculorum aciem', 'oculis lustras?').

[28] *Academie,* i. 25; a later lesbian passage, however, adds 'vos expressions sont si vives et si naturelles, que vous representés les objects comme si on les voyoit, comme si en les sentoit' (66).

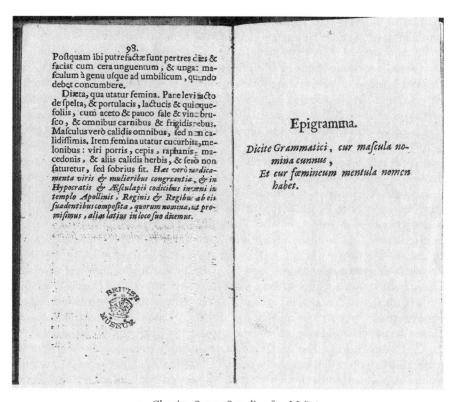

9. Chorier, *Satyra Sotadica*, fos. M7ᵛ–8

Chorier's authorial fiction—a vernacular, Mediterranean dialogue telling the inside story of upper-class *nymphomania*, translated with expansive commentary by a sensuous northern Latinist—turns out to be surprisingly plausible. Scandalous texts did come down this way: Caspar von Barth's *Pornodidascalia* (Frankfurt, 1623), a section from Aretino's *Ragionamenti*, was translated into Latin from a Spanish version just as Meursius was supposed to have translated Sigea. (As if to confirm this affinity, *Pornodidascalia* would later be combined in one volume with Chorier.[29]) Meursius' own poems include an elegy 'Ad Venerem et Cupidinem', a heroic epistle from Byblis—whose incestuous desire, recreated in Ovid's *Metamorphosis* IX, Tullia cites to explain Octavia's nascent feelings (I. 28)—epigrams on (Catullus') Lesbia and (Secundus') Neaera, and a luscious epithalamium which describes sex as 'tender combats and sweet battles' (*teneros lusus et dulcia proelia*); in this wedding-poem, another reminder of the extraordinary licence permitted neo-Latin writers, Meursius invites young girls to sing 'lasciva carmine molli | Fescennina'.[30] (Chorier's longest and most outrageous dialogue is entitled *Fescennini*, and we shall see that

---

[29] BL PC 29.b.21.   [30] *Poemata* (Leiden, 1602), 127 ff., 155–66, 198, 199, 214–20.

the playful military-genital parallel runs throughout the *Satyra*.) Meursius—an expert in festivals and priapic rites—has already made the link between 'Fescennine Songs' and *Fescennini* as a synonym for the sex act itself: Milton would similarly jest about 'Fescennina' performed in the woodshed with the maid,[31] and Chorier creates a scene where nuns gather round the bed of their freshly deflowered Mother Superior and 'sing Fescennine songs' (VII. 249). To confirm this literary-historical genealogy of 'lascivious' celebration, a few pages later Octavia cites Claudian's *Fescennina de Nuptiis Honorii Augusti*, one of the 'saltiest' marriage-poems of antiquity (302–3).

Chorier reinforces the historical plausibility of his author-effect (not to mention his speaker-effect) by constant evocations of Renaissance culture, vernacular as well as Latinate. The orgy in the Roman Villa Orsini, for example, includes Ercole Rangoni, mentioned by name in Aretino's *Modi* sonnet 12, appended to the celebrated 'postures' of Giulio Romano. The female speakers legitimize their own expertise in this field by referring to the erotic images of Titian and the Carracci, tracing them in turn to ancient medals—struck to establish the authority of Sappho herself, their ancestress and patroness—seen in the Orsini collection (sect. 4 below). The *Satyra*'s supposed Spanish-Dutch-Latin authorship recalls Johannes Secundus himself, the most celebrated of the Dutch-Latin erotic poets, whose mistress Neaera was reputed to have been a courtesan of Toledo, the home town of the historical Sigea. Chorier's last and longest dialogue, the seventh, is indeed set in sixteenth-century Spain, and features historical characters like Vives, the scholarly theorist of female education and the implacable enemy of erotic reading for women; since the real Vives paid such obsessive attention to the sexual implication of every glance, word, and gesture that might distinguish the chaste virgin from the prostitute, it seems wickedly appropriate to cast him as a salacious instructor who trains his pupils to simulate chastity in public and whorishness in bed with him.[32] In her survey of male homosexuality Tullia reviews Giovanni della Casa's 'pretty little book' in praise of pederasty, the still-notorious *Capitolo del forno* (VII. 280). Sigea herself, looking back from the Elysian Fields, lists among her companions in the literary Pantheon not only classical wits (Ovid, Petronius, Martial, Pliny the Younger) but Boccaccio, Aretino, Rabelais, Berni, and Machiavelli. Her *female* peers, in contrast, come only from antiquity: Sappho, Philaenis, Elephantis, and Sulpicia the satirist.[33]

In her letter from Elysium, Aloisia Sigea further claims a topical interest by identifying her characters as 'Duchesses, Marchionesses, and Countesses' whom she knew intimately during her lifetime (2, 20); here Chorier clearly emulates the scandal chronicles of Pierre de Brantôme (written in the sixteenth century and known in manuscript before they were printed in the 1660s), which provide much of the

---

[31] *Pro Se Defensio*, Columbia edn. ix. 95 (and cf. *Lycidas*, 69, where he struggles with the temptation of 'the tangles of Neaera's hair', i.e. the pleasures of emulating Secundus and Meursius); Milton's erotic education, like Octavia's, starts with Ovid (Ch. 1, sect. 1 above).

[32] *The Education of a Christian Woman: A Sixteenth-Century Manual*, ed. and tr. Charles Fantazzi (2000), 74–8, 117, 127, 130–1, 153–4; for the fictional Vives's training of Margarita (*Satyra*, VII. 297) see sect. 5 below.

[33] 'Summo Viro Aloisia ex Elysiis Hortis' (6–21).

classical erudition as well as infinite examples of lubricious *grandes dames* who 'hide
the secrets of their schools' but 'give lessons' to other women. (Brantôme even included the story of 'two beautiful girl cousins from an aristocratic family' who conduct a lesbian affair for three years and then become 'excellent whores'—a capsule
biography of Tullia and Octavia from the gossip-monger's point of view.[34]) These
hints of topicality form a bridge between Sigea's own period and the time of publication *circa* 1660. Chorier admits in his memoirs that all his life he has composed
unflattering *Anecdota* about his contemporaries, and these fragments could well
make the *Satyra* into a kind of *roman à clef*; 'Le Sieur Chorier', a papal count and
senior member of the provincial *noblesse de robe*, here revenges himself on the *noblesse d'épée* or hereditary aristocracy, whose weapons seem securely in the hands of
their 'Duchesses and Countesses'.[35]

By promising in his preface to deliver *narratiunculae* or 'little stories' Chorier
aligns himself with the secret histories of his own day, morsels of salacious gossip
about identifiable great ladies—the *Historiettes* of Tallemant des Réaux, assaults on
the comtesse d'Olonne in *La Comédie galante*[36] and Bussy-Rabutin's *Histoire
amoureuse des Gaules*, or the scandalous accounts of Queen Christina. Chorier's
Tullia recapitulates many features of the Swedish Queen, reported or invented: the
intellectually ambitious patron of Cartesian philosophy, founder of academies and
art collections, is represented as 'more like a brothel-madame than a monarch',
promiscuous with men but most intensely involved with another woman (and thus
'of the humour of Sappho'); anti-*précieuse* and shockingly salacious in conversation, given to quoting the lewdest passages in Martial and Petronius from memory
(and especially keen to talk about 'Sodomy'); sceptical in religion, friendly with *libertins érudits* in Chorier's own circle, and always ready to mock the sexuality of the
clergy. On her travels through Europe the real Christina made a point of visiting
both the linguist van Schurman and the courtesan Ninon de Lenclos, apparently
unwilling to separate learning from sex. The prince de Condé found her prepared to
'authorize the vice of every nation and every sex', and much the same could be said
of Chorier's 'nymphomaniac' heroines.[37]

2. SEX, COGNITION, NARRATIVE

The driving force of Chorier's dialogue, then, is the 'fusion of mind and sex'—a
spectacular reversal of the Cartesian-feminist assertion that 'the Mind has no Sex'.

---

[34]   *Les Dames galantes*, ed. Maurice Rat (Paris, 1947), 328–9, 123 (and *passim*); Chorier several times
cites Brantôme's MS memoirs in his *Histoire generale de Dauphiné*.

[35]   *Adversaria*, iv. 167, iv. 155, iii. 13; for the title of nobility in earlier publications, see *Les Recherches du
Sieur Chorier sur les antiquitez de la ville de Vienne* (Lyons, 1659) and n. 99 below.

[36]   Discussed Ch. 7, sect. 1 below

[37]   Susanna Åkerman, *Queen Christina of Sweden and her Circle: The Transformation of a Seventeenth-
Century Philosophical Libertine* (Leider, 1991), 1, 39–41, 77, 103, 124, 301–4, 313–15. For Chorier's friendship
with courtiers and enemies of Christina, see *Adversaria*, iii. 55 (Nicholas Heinsius), 65 (Gabriel Naudé),
iv. 165, 207–9 (Gregorio Leti).

This vastly dilated and wholly libidinous parody of women's educational aspirations, where everything is 'placed before the eye', carries the idea of carnal knowledge to its furthest extent: the bedroom becomes the classroom, erudition becomes passion, 'salty' wit becomes salacious excitement, insight 'flows spontaneously' like sperm, and vice versa. This interfusion is concisely stated—and wittily exemplified—in Tullia's initial explanation of her didactic task. On the eve of her wedding, Octavia seethes with desire but knows nothing about its anatomy; like Molière's Agnès on a similar occasion, she feels something that she can only express as a *je ne sais quoi*, a *nescio quis aestus* (I. 26). Tullia has been instructed by Octavia's mother to instruct the younger woman—the transmission of knowledge being matrilinear in this heavily male-oriented text. Significantly, she must convey not just the *Fabrica* but the 'more recondite secrets' of the marriage-bed (I. 30), the 'Arcana of Love and Venus' promised in the title. And the eroticization of learning itself seems to be among these 'secrets': as Tullia puts it, the more she 'pricks up her ears' during her lessons now, the easier and more frequent will be her husband Caviceus' erections ('arrige aures: tam sane arrexerit Caviceus facile et frequenter, ut tu aures ad hunc sermonem arriges', II. 34).

This erotic-intellectual drive never remains simple or mechanical, but moves restlessly on to more 'recondite' forms and expressions. As the bashful Octavia passes each stage of her initiation, she is introduced to more perverse and multiplex activities, and her role in the narration grows correspondingly fuller. We pass from lesbian embraces to straightforward (if wildly exaggerated) marital intercourse, and then to a variety of illicit affairs and forbidden practices. Anal intercourse, for example, dominates one section, both as an actual experience and as the subject of a long lecture-series (sect. 3 below); though she does condemn such experiments, the effect of Tullia's explanation is to condone sexual variation, to evolve a kind of relativistic anthropology *à la* Rocco, rooted in the sexual history of the ancient world. Like Christina, she 'authorizes the vice of every nation and every sex'.

The floods of erudition released at each new stage of Octavia's enlightenment undermine, not only the traditional taboos, but the supremacy of the heterosexual and genital model. The naive Octavia will assert that male penetration gives a more 'solid' and 'true' pleasure than lesbian sex, or that fellatio and sodomy are unnatural; Tullia will concur, but her illustrations suggest the contrary. (The dissertation on Lesbian history that concludes the second dialogue, for example, also suggests that it was natural for the Greek heroes to take lovers of their own sex—an observation that pre-empts her later condemnation of male homosexuality.) And as the erotic perversity grows, so does the narrative complexity. Octavia is bashful and tongue-tied at the beginning, but by the end she finds herself recounting how her mother Sempronia swallows the sperm of her lover, the monk Chrysogonus, and how he in turn had persuaded her by describing another couple who practise this delight. This narrative-within-a-narrative-within-a-dialogue is itself framed visually and discursively; Octavia sees her mother's genitals through a peephole described as a *rima* or genital slit, and her narrative then prompts still further anecdotes about other friends' oral-genital activities. As Tullia remarks, this is a *salsa res* or 'salty matter', meaning both the man's seed and the utterance in Octavia's mouth (VII. 240–5, 254).

With this proliferation of sexual topics comes a shift in vocabulary. New practices are increasingly described in cognitive and aesthetic terms, as 'the crown of multifarious erudition', as the 'indulgence of one's genius', as 'genres' of pleasure, as 'stories', as 'figures' and 'images' of Venus. In the grand orgy scene of Colloquium VI, '*Mutata figura* excites the drooping libido'; in the 'Fescennine Games', ejaculating between the breasts becomes a '*Veneris imago*', fellatio 'a new *voluptatis genus*'.[38] Far more than in *L'Escole des filles*, sexual instruction gives way to sexual connoisseurship.

The structure of the *Satyra Sotadica* expresses the same 'nymphomaniac' movement towards erotic and discursive excess. The two-dialogue, before-and-after form of *L'Escole des filles* mutates into an escalating series. Part 1, first published independently, consists of five 'Colloquia' or dialogues, themselves containing embedded narratives of the speakers' earlier experience: the first four and a half stay within the pale of marriage (except for the lesbian interludes), piously concentrating on genital anatomy and the pains of defloration, but the massively enlarged fifth Colloquium (entitled *Libidines* in the plural) ends by revealing the secret practices behind the façade of marriage.[39] Part 2 (Colloquium VI, *Veneres*) combines erotic philosophy with a series of orgiastic 'postures' explicitly modelled on these of Elephantis and Aretino. Part 3 (Colloquium VII, *Fescennini*), imperfectly related to the *Veneres* but unquestionably part of Chorier's original conception, interweaves theoretical speculation, anticlerical satire, descriptive anecdotes like the 'salty' fellatio-scenes, and portraits of contemporaries.[40] In this Menippean farrago of narrative modes—including, as we shall see, elements of *préciosité* and sentimental novel—the discursive framework literally splits apart; since it purports to be transcribed from an old manuscript, it is printed with gaping lacunae. This seven-dialogue, three-volume structure is further marked by prefatoria and appendices: the extracts from 'Cleopatra' and Secundus, the 'Elysian Fields' epistle, the poem in praise of Sigea's morality (which is in fact a further debate between Venus and Minerva over whether the *Satyra* reproves or inflames desire). The length as well as the outrageousness of Chorier's *colloquia* grows exponentially, an effect muted in later

[38] e.g. VI. 179, 181, VII. 231, 234, 242, 245, 286, 297.

[39] The 'Parts' are indicated in the first surviving edition (BL PC 30.i.13 (my Fig. 8), BnF Enfer 257), recognizable by its three separate paginations and reduced-size font at the end of 'Pars Altera' (84). Foxon, 38–9, gathers records of three earlier editions with only six dialogues, but no copy is known to have survived; the first preface ('Monitum Lectori' refers to an even earlier *five*-dialogue version, though it describes VI and VII accurately as coming attractions.

[40] The scene changes to Spain, and Octavia's opening claim that no man other than her husband has seen her naked seems implausible after the orgies of Colloquium VI, but this dialogue is unmistakably described in the earliest preface and included in the earliest surviving edn., prior to the inaccurate 'Amsterdam, 1678' edn. that *claims* to publish it for the first time. For scholars who ignore this important final dialogue (never translated into English), see Ch. 7 n. 61 below. Anne M. Menke refers to the whole *Satyra* as 'a curious little work' in 'Authorizing the Illicit, or How to Create Works of Lasting Insignificance', *L'Esprit créateur*, 35/2 (Summer 1995), 84; as in her dissertation (Harvard, 1990), Menke reads only a 1910 translation (by 'B. Villeneuve') that silently omits large portions of the text.

French abridgements[41] and entirely suppressed in the English adaptation of 1684–1740, which (as we shall see in Chapter 7) prunes Chorier's deliberately excessive text back to three marital dialogues.

Chorier's earlier preface, written as the publisher's 'Warning to the Reader', emphasizes and re-enacts this cultivated enormity (1–3). He begins by pretending that Aloisia Sigea wrote a strictly moral work, exposing the whoredoms of the aristocracy. (This vision of Sigea as a crusader against lewdness resurfaces intermittently, in the commendatory poem and in parts of the Elysian Epistle.) The moral smoke-screen rapidly clears, however; introducing the first five dialogues only (for a projected first edition that has not survived), he whets the reader's appetite for the forthcoming sixth and seventh, recommending not Sigea's probity but her linguistic freedom and erudite sensuality. These last dialogues, evidently drafted if not yet published, will outstrip the others 'in artistry and brilliant impudence' (*arte et procacitate ingeniosa*), terms that give an aesthetic cachet to Sinibaldi's diagnosis of 'nymphomaniacs' as *lascivae, procaces, impudentes* (sect. 1 above). The sixth will not merely describe, but 'project figures before your very eyes', while the *fabellae* and *narratiunculae* of the seventh will 'feed the soul with an Attic banquet, properly salted, by which one is never satiated' (3). The invitation appeals to an unmitigated *plaisir du texte*, the equivalent of erotic passion itself. The 'publisher' even claims that Sigea writes so well about these orgies because she includes 'her own story' (2).

In Aloisia Sigea's letter from the Elysian Fields, written later as the preface for a six-dialogue version, the identical language of salt and charm appears in the mouth of the pseudo-author herself, applied not merely to the coming attractions but to the entire work. The specific word *lepor* or charm (often combined with the equally erotic *sal*) expressed a high literary, personal, and cultural ideal for antiquity and for the Renaissance: Johannes Secundus calls his sister and fellow-poet *lepida* as well as *mellea, venusta, docta,* and *polita*;[42] Elizabeth Weston, a writer of such propriety that she calls her work *Parthenica* or *Virgin Matters* even after she marries, can still celebrate *melleus lepor* in her mildly erotic complimentary verse.[43] The historical Sigea had praised language *lepidis et sale conditis* (sect. 1 above), and now her libertine persona invites us to enjoy what have already been identified as her own experiences, improved by Meursius' 'happy genius' and 'Attico sale condita . . . tam salsa, tam lepida' (21), 'seasoned with Attic salt . . . so saucy, so charming'. If she adds to her *salsa* the promise of 'useful precepts for living well', *utilia bene vivendi praecepta* (3, 21), the criterion is no longer moral-ascetic but Epicurean and *bonne vivante*. Chorier's authorial ventriloquism thus creates a more urbane, 'seasoned' version of Le Petit's poem on the author of *L'Escole*, persuading us that *bien foutre est bien vivre.*

---

[41] Jean-Pierre Dubost, mistakenly citing a late, abridged *Académie des dames* as if it were the original (cf. Ch. 7, sect. 2 below), still notices the 'spiral' or 'Progression der textuellen Ökonomie' (*Eros und Vernunft: Literatur und Libertinage* (Frankfurt, 1988), 59).

[42] *Johannes Secundus: The Latin Love Elegy in the Renaissance*, ed. and tr. Clifford Endres (Hamden, Conn., 1981), 20–1; cf. Lucretius, I. 15, 28 (Introd. above) and William Fitzgerald, *Catullan Provocations: Lyric Poetry and the Drama of Position* (Berkeley, 1995), 36–8 (esp. Catullus, XVI. 17), 52, 90–5, 110–11.

[43] *Collected Writings*, ed. Donald Cheney and Brenda M. Hosington (2000), 26, 42.

Characters and social relations within the text, likewise, grow more expansive and dissolute from one dialogue to the next, as they devote more and more 'artistry' to their 'ingenious impudence' or *procacitas*. As David Foxon puts it, 'the plot continually provides new shocks as apparently stable background figures like mothers and husbands are disclosed as having highly irregular relationships; it is as though a series of gauzes were lifted showing each time more complex groupings' (38). In the earlier dialogues Tullia drops some hints about the *Escole-des-filles*-style sexual freedom of women behind the 'veil' of marriage, which Octavia either ignores (II. 37) or repudiates with traditional scorn (IV. 54). Octavia's mother Sempronia is presented as a severe moralist in the opening conversation (I. 29), and up to the fifth dialogue, although she takes a suspiciously active part in her daughter's wedding night, she recommends virginity and wifely obedience. Then the 'veil' is lifted. The flagellation to which she submits herself and her daughter, ostensibly to purify them from the pollution of intercourse, turns out to be a masochistic sport (V. 119–23, 143–7). In anecdote after anecdote, the formidable mother is revealed as a past mistress of perversity. Living up to the bad reputation of the historical Sempronia, she features as the original seducer of Tullia, a connoisseur of ephebes and 9-year-old girls, dissolving in hot embraces with her own daughter.[44]

The husband-and-wife sections of the book, taken as normative by some critics, thus occupy less than a quarter of the *Satyra Sotadica*, in effect serving as a false front. Once Octavia is safely within the fold of marriage she enters a wildly inventive Realm of the Senses, controlled by the female characters and particularly by Sempronia, who is both the ruler of appearances and the *magistra ludorum*, the supreme comic inventor. Tullia is at first a friendly cousin to Octavia and a supporter of traditional morality, then a physical lover (sometimes called 'sister' or 'spouse' in the warmth of passion),[45] and then a procuress who installs her between two men, hoping to have her receive twenty ejaculations in a single night; this takes place in the 'second part' or sixth dialogue, where the two men also become interlocutors. Nor do these stages succeed one another in a neat, developmental succession, for Tullia and Octavia return to their Sapphic embraces as they recount these heterosexual adventures. The cast-list grows still more multifarious in the final seventh dialogue, to match the looser structure and the scene-shift from Italy to Spain; though only Tullia and Octavia speak, their anecdotes and reported conversations bring in dozens of named sixteenth-century figures, including not only Vives but François I of France. Chorier's 'complex groupings' become a series of violent contrasts—sodomites versus heterosexuals, Stoics versus hedonists, brutal priapists versus tender adolescents. Colloquium VII is a complete representation of the *vita sexualis*, with an increasing emphasis on the outer limits of experience; characters are polarized into bringers of divine ecstasy or agents of mortification and death.

---

[44] V. 90–1, 103–4, 113; for her affair with the servant boy Jocondus and her gift of the *ephebe* Robertus, see sect. 5 below. Vives mentions Sempronia and Sappho together as counter-examples to his praise of chaste learned women (*Education of a Christian Woman*, 65), and Spanheim pointedly contrasted Queen Christina to them (Ch. 1 n. 119 above).

[45] e.g. IV. 54, 56, 76.

This attempt to grasp (or construct) the total phenomenon of sexuality distinguishes Chorier's *Satyra Sotadica* from its predecessors—and evidently encouraged later readers like Casanova to believe that the subject could be learnt entirely from one book. The pseudo-Aretine *Puttana errante* may create characters who call themselves '*scienzata*' (100/33) and claim to know all the 'postures', but its mechanical listing conveys no Protean inventiveness, no sense that the mind can outstrip the body, no self-consciousness of language or literary allusion; since the younger speaker is an experienced prostitute rather than an ingénue, the narrative offers no initiation, no gradual discovery of perversity or dissolution of taboos heightened by resistance. *L'Escole des filles* develops a phenomenology of 'metamorphosis' and 'hieroglyphics', and gestures grandly towards the 'hundred' postures and the 'infinite' capacities of invention (II. 78, I. 46), but these promises remain largely soft-focused and unrealized. '*Aloysia Sigea*', on the other hand, provides what the Parliament of Women calls 'an absolute and perfect account of Cupid's *Tactics*'. It is not only an encyclopedia of sex but a sexual universe, a 'pornotopia' constructed from a single point of view, where everything is subordinated to the erotic.

Chorier tells us in his memoirs that he had once written 'two satires, one Menippean and one Sotadic',[46] and this pairing of genres allows us to see the 'Sotadic' *Satyra* as a priapic variant of the Menippean satire, an 'Anatomy' in the discursive as well as the physiological sense, sharing what Julia Kristeva identifies as the qualities of the *ménipée*—'carnivalesque, supple and variable as Proteus'.[47] It exemplifies, as well as thematizes, the Protean element that makes lust 'fabricate all things' (Introd. n. 27 above). Chorier's libertine text fits Northrop Frye's description of the Menippean genre in many ways: it 'relies on the free play of intellectual fancy' rather than social observation, its characters are constructed around a single occupation or idea, its form is dialogic and expansive, tending towards the exuberant *symposium* or 'encyclopaedic farrago', but it still creates 'a vision of the world in terms of a single intellectual pattern'.[48] Like his pornographic predecessors, the distinguished historian and antiquarian Chorier can only attempt this unitary perspective by simulating an all-female discourse.

In the interests of this 'absolutizing of sex', as one critic calls it, all the processes that generate the text are themselves eroticized.[49] The idea of a 'Sotadic' correspondence of sexual perversion and textual form derives from Martial's brief epigram on the buggery-poetry of Sotades (sect. 1 above), but in Chorier this conceit sustains an enormous narrative. The act of listening—for the pupil and for the reader, her surrogate—becomes an aural erection; we recall that Tullia instructs Octavia to

---

[46] *Adversaria*, iii. 31; when confronted in 1680 he denied writing the extant *Satyra Sotadica*, but praised its literary excellence (iv. 201).

[47] *Semeiotikè* (Paris, 1969), 165, applied to Chorier in Leibacher-Ouvrard, 'Sexe, simulacre et "libertinage honnête": La *Satyre Sotadique* (1658/1678) de Nicolas Chorier', *Romanic Review*, 83 (1992), 276.

[48] *Anatomy of Criticism* (Princeton, 1957), 309–12; in *Satyra*, 6–8, Varro appears in the Elysian Fields and Rapin boasts of the success of 'Satyra Mennipea mea'.

[49] Peter Naumann, *Keyhole und Candle: John Clelands 'Memoirs of a Woman of Pleasure' und der Entstehung des pornographisches Romans in England* (Heidelberg, 1976), 51 ('Lust tritt an die Stelle von Geld, was eine Verabsolutierung des Sexus unter gleichzeitiger Lösung von der Komödie anzeigt').

arrige her ears so that her husband might *arrigere* his penis. The pupil in turn, once she has been deflowered, promises ɔ 'distil into your soul through the ears, with my arousing description, the pleasures which the god of marriage has just rained into my body' (V. 82). Sperm and *pruriginosa descriptio* combine into a fluid exchange of *voluptates*, circulating like rain between Hymen, Octavia, and Tullia; it was aural-seductive passages like these, presumably, that 'ravished' the speaker of the Parliament of Women and gave her the idea that reading *'Aloysia'* would 'increase our contempt and hatred of Men', since 'we could have our Business done by hearing only' (first epigraph, above).

Throughout the dialogue, literary and erotic performances are appraised in terms that promote their convergence. Octavia's initiation takes the form of successive 'institutionis conjugalis capita' (V. 113), the 'heads' of an argument in rhetoric or the 'chapters' of a book—which then becomes the founding text of a new order, like Calvin's *Institutiones* of Geneva or Vives's *De Institutione Foeminae Christianae*. Copulation evolves into a *fabula* in four scenes (VI. 163, 173). Literary and erotic expertise develop in tandem: as Octavia warms to the subject that initially embarrasses her, she shows her increased brilliance by bringing in erudite jokes and poetic fragments, including an erotic distich that Tullia herself had 'transmuted' from Virgil (IV. 68).

Just as Milton gave the 'simple, sensuous, and passionate' art of poetics a climactic position in *Of Education*, so Tullia's curriculum gives a major role to eroticized literary criticism. As in the contemporary novels of Mlle de Scudéry, the narrative contrives to introduce poems or letters which are then analysed by the protagonists to bring out the amorous sensibility of the writer.[50] Reading one such intertext—a plaintive, *portugaise*-style letter from their friend Laura to her lover Rangoni—Tullia discovers in the acumen, strength, and expertise of her writing an equivalent capacity in bed: such *acumine et vi ingenii* makes Laura, not an 'artless' romantic victim (as Octavia first thinks), but a literary-erotic heroine. If she reveals herself so 'knowing' and *ingeniosa* as an author, then 'many forms of Venus will be invented' when she puts her genius into practice (VI. 195). This scene of libertine reading must have struck or tickled many nerves. Male critics seemed particularly bothered about *femmes savantes* becoming critics, thereby undermining their femininity: Jonson's Collegiate Ladies become hermaphrodites by asserting their right to review plays; Guez de Balzac fears that literary criticism and 'metamorphic' philosophy will ruin women's chances of pleasing him by showing themselves 'all woman', *tout à fait femmes* (Ch. 1, sect. 3, Ch. 3, sect. 5 above). Chorier pretends to assume the opposite. Women's appreciation (and display) of literary invention manifests precisely their gendered sexuality: as 'Aloisia Sigea' herself claims in the Elysian Fields epistle, an originary tradition reaching back to Sappho and Elephantis proves that *aptiores*

[50] See Patricia Hannon, 'Desire and Writing in Scudéry's "Histoire de Sapho"', *L'Esprit créateur*, 35/2 (Summer 1995), 37–50, and Elizabeth Susan Wahl, *Invisible Relations: Representations of Female Intimacy in the Age of Enlightenment* (Stanford, Calif., 1999), 189–91. In her own correspondence Scudéry remarks about a poem sent to her by Catherine Descartes, 'En m'apprenant, Iris, que vous saver rimer | Vous m' apprenez aussi que vous savez aimer' (cited Wahl, *Invisible Relations*, 111).

sunt feminae his rebus depingendis, 'women are more capable of depicting these matters' (21).

The erudition that gives Tullia and Laura their discursive authority—an exclusively 'female' and sexual erudition, of course, valued only as an extension of the *ars amatoria*—once again encourages the convergence of the physical and the mental. Octavia will be 'more learned' or 'doctior' in bed with her husband, and after Tullia's etymology course she will be able to 'lie with him in Greek'; Juvenal's (and Jonson's) satire against pretentious Hellenists who *concumbunt graecè* has been triumphantly turned into a compliment.[51] Tullia defines herself as an 'Oedipus' for Octavia, which means that she explains her inchoate longings by matching them to canonical literary representations like Ovid's description of Byblis's passion for her brother or Iphis's desire for another woman (I. 28, II. 36–7). Tullia continues to act as Octavia's 'Oedipus' by explaining every part of her body as she brings it to life with her caresses, and by interpreting her erotic dreams. These dream-interpretations (a motif borrowed from Aretino) play a pivotal role in the text, reinforcing the universal focus on sexuality and anticipating the later proliferation of perverse enjoyment: when Octavia dreams of a spear-wielding satyr in Colloquium IV, for example, this is made to signify not only the brutality of the impending penetration but the multiple joys of cuckolding her husband thereafter (IV. 53–5). By first stimulating and then lecturing upon all Octavia's impulses, sensations, and parts, Tullia effectively refashions her as a 'Socratic' or Roccoesque *vivum libidinum thesaurum*, an encyclopedic treasure-house or Comenian reference book 'where men compile and look up their pleasures, extracting their desires in hot torrents' (VII. 243).

The dialogue form itself contributes to the mingling of erotic and linguistic play, allowing Tullia and Octavia to slip back and forth between action and discourse like the characters in drama. The 'interior book' becomes palpable and the 'word' is 'made flesh' in startling ways. The physicality of their interchange solves the contradiction that Maurice Roelens finds at the heart of the philosophical dialogue, between 'the pure transitivity of philosophical discourse' and 'the use of language as a connoting, revealing, *incarnating* system'.[52] Even the simpler French version strikes one critic as 'completely disturbing the link between showing and telling', or 'sweep[ing] away the traditional ambivalence between erotic matters and their rhetorical evocation', collapsing the erotological into the erotographic.[53] In fact, the cognitive, the discursive, and the corporeal often conflict in Chorier's dialogue, particularly in the long sequences of exhaustive heterosexual coupling. But these Sapphic scenes constitute a kind of idyll, where narration and copulation are not only interfused but interchangable.

---

[51] II. 34, IV. 55; see Leibacher-Ouvrard, 'Transtextualité', 54, for a more negative interpretation, and Ch. 1 n. 108 above for Jonson's use of Juvenal, VI. 191.

[52] 'Le Dialogue philosophique, genre impossible? L'Opinion des siècles classiques', *Cahiers de l' Association Internationale des Études Françaises*, 29 (May 1972), 47 (my emphasis).

[53] Dubost, 'Libertinage and Rationality: From the "Will to Knowledge" to Libertine Textuality', in Catherine Cusset (ed.), *Libertinage and Modernity*, special issue, *Yale French Studies*, 94 (1998), 61–5, esp. 62, 63.

In *L'Escole des filles* too, Fanchon and Susanne respond physically to each other's descriptions ('ma cousine, je descharge!'), but the opportunities for action are rarely developed; the primary lesson in sexual anatomy consists in verbal explanations almost devoid of show-and-tell, and we only learn in passing that Susanne has once touched Fanchon's thighs, 'blanches, grosses et douillettes' (II. 65). In Chorier, by contrast, discussion constantly boils over into demonstration—first in the *Tribadicon* or lesbian initiation of Colloquium II, and then in later scenes where they come together once again to recount ostensibly heterosexual experiences. When the initiative shifts to Octavia after her wedding night, she still hails her cousin as the one who can satisfy 'all her senses and thoughts', and promises to infuse her with a narrative that will bring Tullia's joys to a climax without diminishing her own. She then 'depicts the thing so vividly' that Tullia cannot control herself, and they collapse into bed once again. The pupil now seduces the teacher by rendering sex *ad vivum*, once again recalling the *viva autopsia* that excites the senses in Comenian pedagogy. In the height of description-induced passion Octavia exclaims 'what is the shadow compared with the body?', but it is not clear whether she is thinking of the narrated body of her husband or the real finger that she is thrusting into her cousin—who had asked her to serve her 'as a husband'. Octavia's rhythmic cries force us to see the symmetrical bodies of the two cousins, 'cunt to cunt' and 'breast to breast' (V. 88). With each gasp she alters the usual masculinist assignment of reality and shadow, and begins to see both her heterosexual experience and her narration as 'shadows' compared to the present excitement.

The interchange of word and sex does not subside with consummation, but drives on towards greater revelation, placing everything before the ear and eye. As in a successful Comenian education, juices and words 'flow spontaneously' together. In her orgasmic frenzy Tullia too cries out something that changes everything—calling out the name, not of Octavia or her husband, but of her hitherto concealed lover Lampridius. In this moment Tullia engenders a whole new subject of anecdote, which will later turn again from discourse to action: she will 'share' all her secrets in Colloquium V, and in Colloquium VI she will share Lampridius too, simultaneously as a lover and a dialogist. Octavia seizes upon this implication of the word 'share' (*dividere*), and congratulates her mentor for endowing 'the word' with its 'most salacious sense'. The sudden introduction of an illicit male paradoxically strengthens their Sapphic bond, as they stage a version of Eve Sedgwick's triangle-game 'between women', putting Lampridius into play as word and thing. Tullia's lesson in material semantics—her 'philosophy', as Octavia calls it—draws them back to the conversation, 'ad sermonem', and the erotic-discursive cycle moves onward (V. 88–9).

Just as narration and description become sexual acts, so their underlying mental phenomena are thoroughly identified with the physiology of sexual arousal. *L'Escole's* rather crude equation of 'opening' the mind and the vagina now receives the grammatical sanction of etymology. In Tullia's elaboration, *cunnus* and *mentula* derive from Greek *konnein*, to understand, and Latin *mens*, the mind (III. 42, V. 92). Renaissance theories of ideal female beauty are revised according to the principle that the *mentula*, and not the eye, is the only true judge of beauty; blind men may call it blind, but in fact it is *lusca* or one-eyed (an appropriate image since Chorier himself had lost one eye in a sports accident).[54] The grammatically feminine penis acquires precisely those intellectual qualities most valued in the female protagonists (*erudita, ingeniosa*), when seeking out new openings like the mouth or the anus. In the older *satyrique* tradition the scarlet phallus defies all philosophy and 'fucks Socrates and Plato', but now that organ herself becomes 'philosophical'.[55] Neverthe-less, parity is not achieved: whereas male arousal always involves some separation between two alternative centres of consciousness, female arousal involves the trans-fer of the entire being, a sexed equivalent to the state of interiority induced by reli-gious devotion.

In a conversation reported in *Fescennini*, the author's namesake and compatriot Aloisia Fonseca vividly describes this envagination of mind:

'When Rodericus's dagger first plunged into my body up to its hilt', Aloisia said, 'all my sensa-tions and all the faculties of my soul rushed into that part of me. A good number of my rela-tives were gathered in the next room, talking noisily; to my amazement, I heard them from that part of me. Candles were burning all the time; I saw them from that part of me. When Rodericus came—this is marvellous—I was all in my cunt, or rather, I was all cunt (*in cunno tota eram, aut tota cunnus*). Any intelligence that I had—and people say I have quite a bit—was pulled down into that seat of pleasure by intelligent desire (*quid in me ingenii . . . per-pulerat ingeniosa libido*).' (VII. 221)

'Soul' and 'body', normally distinct entities, seem to coalesce in the sexual climax, while *ingeniosa libido* assumes the subject position. Grammar collapses into Secundus' paradox, the feminine *tota* governed by the masculine *cunnus*. Aloisia has found a way of being *tout à fait femme* that would presumably horrify rather than gratify Guez de Balzac. Exiled into her 'dilated' interior like the religious disciple de-scribed by Nicholas Paige, 'c'était là où elle habitait et où l'amour la tenait occupée'.[56] Aloisia hears, thinks, and *exists* in her vagina, a living embodiment of the libertine alternative to Descartes's principle: *coeo ergo cogito*.

As in *L'Escole des filles*, Cartesian physiology provides an up-to-date vehicle for this very un-Cartesian collapse of mind and body. The *tota cunnus* phenomenon is a liquefaction-effect, not faked (as in *La retorica delle puttane*) but sincerely felt (as in Susanne's descriptions of the 'white rain' or her lover's efforts to 'fuck her soul', dis-cussed in Chapter 3). Even after her first orgasm, Octavia describes the trickling fluid as her 'soul escaping' (V. 87). This effect is typically elaborated in the orgiastic Colloquium VI, and extended from the female speaker to the male. Octavia

---

[54] VII. 222, 228, and cf. *Adversaria*, iii. 21.

[55] VI. 199, VII. 244, 265 (Eleanor's 'wise cunt' is greeted by 'philosophicis duabus mentulis'); cf. François de Maynard in Louis Perceau (ed.), *Le Cabinet secret du Parnasse: François de Malherbe et ses escholiers* (Paris, 1932), 119–20 ('Treve de cet amour honeste | Dont Platon traite en ses discours. | Pour moi, de quoi le V. lubrique | Est toûjours droit comme un baton | Et rouge come un rubrique, | Je fous et Socrate et Platon' [variant, 'Ne demande rien que practique [donc] | Je foutrois et vous et Platon']).

[56] Ch. 3 nn. 23, 163 above.

exclaims that Rangoni is turning her into a 'Venerei salis gurgitem', a whirlpool of Venereal brine, a salty version of the vortex or *tourbillon* central to Cartesian cosmology. Correspondingly, the Frenchman La Tour turns himself into a pumping-station according to Descartes's physiological theory, attempting to thrust back Tullia's 'escaping soul' with movements that suggest that 'though he could not put in his whole body, at least he could pour into me all his longings, needs, desires, thoughts and loving soul'.[57] *Ingeniosa libido* pulls the woman's mind into her 'seat of pleasure', but equally the man desires to turn his body into a phallus and his soul into sperm. *Mens* aspires to be *mentula*, however impossible this may be. Speakers in 'Aretino's sonnets' want men to *diventar tutto cazzo* or 'turn entirely into prick' (Ch. 3 n. 108 above); in Chorier this blunt urge becomes the desire to convert concentrated mental phenomena—*desideria, libidines, cogitationes*—into hydraulic impulses.

Chorier's encyclopedic, pornotopian, 'nymphomaniac' display of erotic erudition is thus bound with links of parody and emulation to the central concerns of seventeenth-century philosophy. The entire structure exemplifies Descartes's *Discours de la méthode*, proceeding from simple to complex (part 2). Even though the *Satyra* is set in the sixteenth century, Chorier's characters are preoccupied with Cartesian erotics: Tullia and Octavia explore the parallelism of body and soul in the moment of ecstasy, the point where the *passiones animae* combine with the hydraulic economy of bodily fluids while no less a figure than Juan Luis Vives explains the working of the pineal gland as part of his erotic-intellectual initiation of a young pupil (VII. 292). Chorier could be seen as a 'left' or materialist Cartesian in the line that culminates in La Mettrie, whose *École de la volupté* grapples with the same issues and reproduces the same contradictions.

Chorier's striking use of the word *conatus*, the striving of primary desire that defines humanity,[58] invites comparison with Spinoza—who built his *Ethics* around the same central term, interchangeable with *libido*. From Spinoza's point of view, of course, Chorier makes this ontogenic urge narrowly sexual and its goal a mere local 'titillation', a form of bondage to the body at its most shameful, a 'passion' in the sense of being acted upon, and diminished, by external causes and 'indistinct ideas'. (Adultery is especially revolting because it forces us to contemplate the excretory organs of a stranger.) But Spinoza's dual-aspect philosophy refuses to separate God, Nature, and Mind, insisting that affect and desire (in their active rather than passive form) can lead to the highest good the philosopher, like the libertine, defines his goal as a supreme intellectual love that involves 'all the modifications of the body', and believes that 'desire arising from reason cannot be excessive'.[59] Spinoza understood that sexuality could be taken for the *summum bonum* by its devotees, and

---

[57] VI. 177 (cited Ch. 6 n. 43 below), 211; compare *Escole*, II. 97 ('Il . . . souhaitera d'estre tout vit pour se couler tout en toy').

[58] e.g. I. 26, III. 44, IV. 65 (*ultimo conatu* for the final thrust that completes defloration), VI. 199, VII. 234.

[59] *Ethica*, IIIP6–9, IIIP35S, VP16, IVP61; Stuart Hampshire, *Spinoza* (1951; Harmondsworth, 1965), esp. 122–3, 127, 133, 142.

insists that libido can be a *means* to that supreme good, defined as enjoyment (*fruatur*) of the knowledge that the mind is at one with the whole of Nature.[60] Chorier may use *summum bonum* as a synonym for the vulva itself (VI. 188), but he intellectualizes sex so much that the physical becomes a mere vehicle for the play of mental configurations; in Chorier as in Spinoza, the *conatus* strives to transform the body into 'clear and distinct ideas' and thereby to attain freedom through power of mind. Furthermore (as we shall see in the next section), in Chorier's *Satyra* as in Descartes's *Passions de l'âme* explorations of the intensest moments of desire— where one might expect a materialist fusion of mind and body—lead paradoxically to a renewed sense of dualistic separation, a renewed assertion of the supremacy of the mental.

3. SAPPHIC AUTHORITY AND THE EROTICS OF MIND

In the most obviously didactic parts of the *Satyra*, when mothers speak to daughters on their wedding night, a straightforward hierarchy and priority is established: body dominates mind, men dominate women, and 'natural' libido dominates everything. It is not simply that sexuality creates mind—Virgil's *mentem Venus ipsa dedit*, already a commonplace in Montaigne—but that the male sex, the *mentula*, has sole responsibility for creating *mens* in woman. Sempronia explains to Octavia, as she congratulates her on becoming 'a woman', that husbands pour joys into the body and 'bona mens' into the soul through the same tube. Octavia volunteers in addition that 'whoever opens our vulva with his manly pole also opens the mind that is hiding there', and Tullia piles it on even thicker: the organ that 'knocks out virginity and knocks in mind' is called *mentula* precisely because of 'its natural faculty of creating mind in us' (V. 91–2). Chorier seems here to share Rocco's phallepistemic certainty—more plausible in a homosexual schoolteacher than in a matriarch like Sempronia—that the penis is the only tool for infusing true knowledge (Ch. 2, sect. 2 above). Since Tullia's main evidence is Octavia's livelier role in the dialogue, the expansive structure of the book seems designed to confirm this combination of radical materialism and traditional masculine ideology. As in *L'Escole des filles*, women become ingenious, and their discourse proliferates, once they have been 'opened' and infused with male potency. The general principle is reiterated in the orgy scene: 'quam perspicax fututrices ingenium'; 'how perceptive is the mind of women who fuck!' (VI. 188).

These phallocentric pieties are not always securely maintained, however. We have already caught the hint that the husband's erections might somehow *depend* on the wife's erect attention, that the *amour philosophique* of two women might outlast the joys of the marriage-bed, that the *umbra* or 'shadow' of representation might compete with a reality that depends on mere physicality. Motherly lectures on phallic

---

[60] *De Intellectus Emendatione, Opera*, ed. Carl Gebhardt (Heidelberg, 1925), ii. 5–6, 8 (and cf. *Ethica*, IIIP39S); Edwin Curley (ed.), *A Spinoza Reader: The Ethics and Other Works* (Princeton, 1994), 3, 5.

epistemology follow scenes in which they press burning kisses on their daughters' mouths, aroused to the utmost by their narration. In Colloquium VI the two female speakers 'prolong Venus until dawn, in free and libidinous conversation', after their male lovers have left exhausted, unable to reach the goal of twenty penetrations (VI. 194). As Octavia falls asleep on the eve of her wedding, with Tullia sprawled between her thighs, she remarks that 'listening to you, no satiety will ever seize me' (III. 50); in the same words Chorier himself recommends the last and most discursive of his dialogues, the salty banquet 'cujus nulla unquam capit satietas' (3).

The implied primacy of female-generated and female-shared discourse over masculine coition is reinforced at several points in this final banquet-dialogue or libertine *Symposium*. Aloisia Fonseca may declare her absolute 'concentration' in the genitals—as Fanny Hill does a century later—but her pleasures are evidently centred in the witty dialogue, the freedom of her tongue, the badinage with Octavia about her 'ingenious fucking' and her 'brilliant part' (VII. 221). Octavia makes this primacy explicit in the seductive speech that persuades Aloisia to reveal her secrets: 'the best part of enjoyment is playful, salty wit' (*melior gaudii pars in jocis, in salibus*, 220). It is this ability to 'speak' pleasure, Octavia insists, that transforms sex into an art form and raises us above the animals. The pupil exclaims at the beginning of the *Satyra* that she would rather be *docta* like Tullia than satiated with physical pleasure (II. 34), and by the very end nothing has changed her mind; the delights of heterosexuality can in no way equal the delights of *fabulae*, and she 'would rather spend all day talking thus, than all night thrashing around with the god of Love himself' (VII. 311). Tullia's lesbian instruction has not only 'modelled' Octavia's ethical viewpoint or crafted it as fiction ('mores meos ipsa finxisti'), but has actually created her: 'I *am* Tullia; . . . I received my life from my parents, but my mind from you' (VII. 225, 233, 312). It is Tullia's tongue, and not the penis of any man, which has given her *ingenium*, and 'without *ingenium* woman is nothing but mud' (VII. 312).

Chorier's entire work ends poised between extreme misogynistic disgust and a triumphant mentalism that denies the basis of traditional misogyny, the equation of women with their 'natural' bodies. Tullia ask rhetorically, 'if she does not rise up from her own humble condition by a fervent effort of the soul, what is more abject, miserable, and polluted than a woman?' The mindless and 'abjectly' domestic woman is nothing but 'a chamber-pot to piss in'—an insult that Pallavicino had reserved for the common prostitute.[61] But she can transform herself and escape the excremental by a self-generated exertion of the mind, a 'fervido animi conatu' of which Spinoza could be proud.

It must obviously be recognized that these visions of female autonomy are concocted by a male author for a readership versed in Latin and therefore largely masculine, with tantalizing exceptions. As in Casanova's triangular conversation with the English visitor and his tutor, text and reader form a bond across the bodies of women evoked by, but excluded from, the discourse. Celebrating female intellect is

---

[61] *Satyra*, 1, VII. 312, Pallavicino, *RP* 121, 129; cf. Leibacher-Ouvrard, 'Transtextualité', 60, 66 n. 29, for a source in Seneca.

dubious when gender fantasy has created the 'female' who proclaims it, and representing the erotic union of women is notoriously subject to expropriation. In Chorier as in other authors, lesbianism can be framed as a titillating 'number', an attempt to reassure and arouse men rather than assert female self-sufficiency. (Even Margaret Cavendish recognized that 'it is a temptation to an Husband, to see two She-friends Imbrace, and Kiss, and Sport, and Play, which makes the Husband to desire to do the like, not with his Wife, but his Wives Friend'.[62]) Both 'women' may effectively submit to the male gaze, stand in for male phantasms of arousal without detumescence, or reproduce a heterosexual paradigm: Tullia claims the role of a 'man' with Octavia, and pictures herself as Mars swooning over her 'soft, honey-gold Venus'; Fernandus Portius, discovering his sister Enemonda 'indulging her genius' in bed with another woman, assumes a teasing, simulated anger and turns the situation into a heterosexual opportunity, 'flinging himself' into the scene as the male reader does vicariously.[63]

Chorier's Tullia, Octavia, and Aloisia are certainly 'Is in Drag', thinly veiled female impersonations. It does not follow, however, that male-authored male characters (and female-authored females) somehow come closer to an authentic reality unmediated by representational codes; Chorier's fictional persons can legitimately be analysed as provisional theses or speculations, embodiments of his *theory* of female desire, even if they cannot be accepted as 'real' women. And it would be naive to assume that such characters—or any aspect of the text, for that matter—can be wholly determined by the author's controlling intention. To show his invention, to indulge his 'salty' genius, Chorier creates figures who exceed his ideological purpose and who hold their 'unnatural' positions with unseemly persistence. We shall see that, even after the fullest possible experience of 'nymphomaniac' heterosexuality, Tullia still declares that she loves Octavia more intensely, and desires her more fiercely, than she desires any male.

We might expect the idealist promotion of expression over action to fade when Chorier describes heterosexual rather than lesbian experience. But in fact Tullia's depictions of men bring into question both the privileged role of the phallus in creating mind, and the superiority of physical reality to mental shadow. The equation of *mens* and *mentula* subsides soon after it is established: the penis has only a limited and self-serving understanding, rebelling as in Plato against 'the empire of the mind which is seated in the head' (Introd. n. 28 above); masculine sexuality benefits '*not* the mind *but* the mentula' (III. 42). Octavia soon brings out the ludic potential of the 'two-headed' man, and Tullia imagines the lower organ humbly 'submitting himself bare-headed at the court of his *domina*' (50). This comic scenario clearly inspired Casanova's solution to Secundus' riddle—the *mentula* is feminine because she is always the 'servus' or slave—and recalls the more sinister *domina* in Juvenal (Ch. 3 n. 138 above) who likewise exerted her authority over the

[62] *CCXI Sociable Letters* (1664), 43.
[63] II. 36, 39 (Octavia asks, 'if you are a *tribade*, a *fricatrix* and a *subagitatrix*, what am I?' and to solve this terminology problem Tullia declares her 'Cypridem meam mollem, mellitum, auream'), VII. 286; for *indulgere genio* see Persius, V. 151.

detachable parts of well-hung slaves, 'carved for her use'. The phallus becomes a distinct creature, female in gender as in Secundus, who can rise and go about her business even when her owner is asleep. In one scene a row of *mentulae* listen intently to a philosophy lecture; in another they politely greet their professor, the 'sapiens et liberalis cunnus' (VII. 274, 265) or wise and liberal Master Cunt. Earlier, when Octavia appreciates her sleeping husband's body as if it were a sculpture, his penis wakes up before he does because it/she is aware of the gaze of its/her 'domina'.[64]

Chorier's staged contests of Sapphism and heterosexuality, representation and corporeality, lead inexorably to the philosophical ambiguity of 'Nature'. Nature in libertine doctrine signifies both the supreme sanction of desire, the Enlightenment goddess of pleasure, and the abject, the bestial, the excretory 'mud' from which women must fashion themselves by 'a fervid *conatus* of the mind'. Like the openly homosexual Rocco, Chorier conceives sexuality both as a 'natural' physical inclination and as a play of cerebral and discursive *figurae*, to be cultivated and recombined in the spirit of aristocratic connoisseurship. This dichotomy can never wholly be resolved, since libertine discourse must reintroduce *some* explicit physicality to distinguish itself from the respectable text; nevertheless, the preference in Chorier is increasingly given to élite voluptuarism, to whatever opinions and pleasures are furthest removed from 'the grovelling malignity and stupidity of the vulgar herd' (VII. 220). Consequently the dialogue is riven with conflict whenever *ingeniosa libido* takes a recherché and 'unnatural' form, and particularly when that form is homoerotic.

Despite her worship of sexual 'fiction' and 'invention', the philosophical Tullia does attack certain variations as 'against Nature'. The long section on anal intercourse, for example, closes with an ultra-orthodox condemnation that limits 'Nature' strictly to biological procreation (VI. 208–9). This diatribe against the 'unnatural' rings quite hollow, however, since it follows too abruptly an impressive Roccoesque gathering of arguments *for* the ubiquity, historical prestige, and natural origins of homosexual desire. Like her namesake Tullia d'Aragona, she inserts a brief, summary denunciation into a much longer (and friendlier) philosophical-historical speculation.[65] Her condemnation occurs in a context that entirely subverts the biological-procreative argument, the orgy in Colloquium VI during which Tullia finds anal penetration disturbingly enjoyable: she feels 'filled with a *je ne sais quoi* of furious arousal (which I didn't think possible), and I wouldn't doubt that I could get used to it if I wished' (VI. 175), especially since she is naturally drawn to the pleasure of the unfamiliar ('inassuetis gaudemus', 216). The bottom may give her only a *titillationis umbra* or 'shadow of arousal' (208), but we know that the shadow

---

[64] V. 102, anticipating La Fontaine's *conte* 'Le Cas de conscience'; cf. Anne L. Birberick, *Reading Undercover: Audience and Authority in Jean de La Fontaine* (1998), 107, 109.

[65] Ch. 1, sect. 1 above; cf. Chorier's own technique in *Recherches sur les antiquités de la ville de Vienne*, where (to explain the street name 'Rue du Bordel public') he denounces the wickedness of prostitution and then gathers abundant evidence for its acceptance in antiquity ('nouvelle édition', Lyons, 1828, 470–3).

potentially rivals the real thing. We also learn that Tullia's and Octavia's husbands have already attempted to penetrate them anally, though without success (198–9)—further domesticating the impulse to explore new orifices, and preparing for the breast-ejaculation and mouth-penetration of the final dialogue. Like Pallavicino's bawd-preceptor Tullia and Octavia seem entirely familiar with the male taste for 'girls who mutate themselves into boys', both in the classical literature and in their own experience; the older cousin even declares herself an *experta* in these matters, and describes in improbable detail the mentula's delight in being 'compressed' and 'sucked' by the rectum.[66]

Tullia's relativistic, proto-Enlightenment dissertation on the history and morality of sodomy (VI. 197–208) glistens with naturalist arguments from Renaissance Italy (warningly labelled 'false' (202)) and with normative *exempla* from the ancient world. The Celts, she informs us, reviled heterosexuals and excluded them from public office. Sodomy has always appealed to the wisest philosophers and the most refined tastes, to the *delicatiores* or those whom Milton called 'of a more delicious and airie spirit' (*Of Education*, Ch. 1 n. 57 above), whereas the vaginal French are 'stupid' and 'dense' in regard to anal pleasure. Roman literature never once condemns the love of young men; Lucian and Achilles Tatius debate the virtues of pederasty and heterosexuality evenhandedly, without taking a moral position. (As we saw in Chapter 2, the ancient 'comparison of the two loves' also forms the core of *Alcibiade fanciullo*.) Octavia's interruptions reinforce the authority of these classical models; she remarks how convincing Tullia sounds when marshalling evidence *for* the practice, or how she too has omitted to mention whether she approves or condemns it. This dialogic revelation of Tullia's ambiguity prompts her sudden switch to a condemnatory vocabulary, tonally and conceptually at odds with the prevailing cool neoclassicism. Moreover, the 'false' arguments themselves unravel the Nature–custom dichotomy that supposedly underlies Tullia's uncharacteristic conclusion—that the only acceptable sexual acts are those that lead directly to procreation.

Articulating the common ground between 'Christian discipline' and the pederastic-hedonist Rocco, Tullia insists that all manifestations of *libido* proceed equally from the 'materials' of which we are formed, the 'corrupt flesh' common to the entire species (VI. 200, 204, citing Genesis 6: 12). She explains the Italian and Spanish taste for sodomy in gross anatomical terms—vaginas having been stretched by the hot climate and overuse (VI. 206). Here and elsewhere, she cites Petronius and Lucretius to reinforce the thesis that all creatures are driven by fundamentally the same 'affections' deriving from the same 'combination of members' (*pari membrorum compage*, 200). Most spectacularly, Tullia begins the entire discussion of sodomy with an explicitly naturalistic explanation, reinforced with the authority of Socrates and Plato, for the pederastic love enjoyed by so many ancient leaders and philosophers. In an argument strongly reminiscent of Rocco's *Alcibiade*,

---

[66] VI. 173, 206, and cf. 204 (the passage that caught the eye of Baudelaire, discussed in the Epilogue below); cf. Pallavicino, *RP* 89.

Tullia points out that Nature designed only a small proportion of the seed for pro-creation; once that modicum has done its reproductive work the vast surplus of sex-ual energies and juices should be devoted to pleasure—just as most grain and fruit serves to feed and delight other creatures rather than propagating the plant itself. Indeed, 'Queen Nature' would not have granted the capacity to ejaculate anywhere, and thus to derive pleasure from any orifice, if the seed were exclusively destined for generation. To prevent this hedonistic-spermatic theory seeming too male-oriented, Tullia specifically cites the anatomical channel that lets women too eject their surplus seed—a feat we have seen her perform often, particularly in her Sapphic seduction of Octavia.[67]

Naturalizing arguments for unnatural acts reverberate throughout the final 'Fescennine' dialogue, too. To overrde Octavia's objections, Tullia makes up a ver-sion of the Prometheus myth proving the 'natural affinity' between the phallus and the female mouth: the first woman drank the clay-stained water that Prometheus had used to wash after he 'penis finxit', fashioned the penis (from a purer grade of clay, but still from the same *lutum* or 'mud' that represents base matter untrans-formed by the 'fictive' drive).[68] When the subject turns again to sodomy, Tullia pro-duces another erudite-humanistic interpretation of anatomy: echoing the 'Socratic' definition of the female body as a *thesaurus* of interchangeable pleasures, she asserts that 'just as you can go to Heaven from anywhere on Earth'—Sir Thomas More's favourite maxim—'so from all parts and inflections of a woman's body one can ar-rive at the supreme pleasure, the Heaven of Venus' (VII. 279). Tullia here endorses a theory that would abolish the distinction between perversion and normality, sodomy and legitimacy. Treasure can be coined *ex omnibus muliebris corporis part-ibus et inflexionibus*, and from every corner of boys' bodies too—as the following episode makes clear, when Vives makes an impassioned speech to the buttocks of his most beautiful pupil.[69] Tullia flips once more into a fierce denunciation of sodomy in response to Octavia's distaste, but after hearing about Vives's devotion to *posticae Venus* she softens her tone completely. Whatever direction it takes, Love is still iden-tical to Nature; remove one and you remove the other. To confirm this comprehen-sive naturalism she cites the words of Justina Gomez, a Mother Superior ardently in love with her nuns. Though Gomez reintroduces Pallavicino's crude excremental definition of the natural—everyone needs to 'piss', and without a 'chamber-pot' they will do it anywhere—she still inscribes homoeroticism within the category 'Nature'. Whether closed off by the convent walls or by a (presumably innate) distaste for the opposite sex, women will naturally turn to their own kind (VII. 281–2).

---

[67] VI. 200–1; Tullia's later refutation of this naturalistic argument (209) falls back on the unconvinc-ing notion of superfoetation, insisting that women can conceive again at any time during pregnancy.

[68] VII. 245 ('Hinc penis cum feminae bucca *nata* affinitas', my emphasis), and cf. Leibacher-Ouvrard, 'Transtextualité' 56; Tullia's myth 'mutates' *Phaedrus' Fables*, IV. vx and vxi (sometimes numbered IV. xiii in 17th-century edns.), which likewise revolve around Prometheus moulding the genitals.

[69] VII. 281; making Vives a pederast is particularly ironic because he interpreted the homosexuality of Virgil's second Eclogue as an allegory of lofty literary friendship, in *P. Vergilii Maronis Opera, Quae Quidem Extant, Omnia* (Basle, 1561), 26–7

Lesbianism plays an even more central role than male pederasty in Chorier's narrative rehabilitation of the 'unnatural'. It is the second dialogue or *Tribadicon*, in fact, that establishes the pattern of naive objection and erudite, relativistic lecture—a pattern that explains and thereby condones even those sexual 'mutations' singled out for condemnation. In this early dialogue, for example, Tullia assures Octavia 'it is hardly surprising that a virgin should be loved by a virgin, considering that the greatest Heroes once found objects of desire in their own sex (*suo in sexu incentiva libidinis suae*)' (II. 38). Throughout the *Tribadicon* Tullia and Octavia make new figures in both the corporeal and the rhetorical sense, repeating the same word with different inflexion to bring out the symmetry of coupling female bodies.[70] Octavia exclaims that her teacher-lover 'presses mouth to mouth, breast to breast, womb to womb' (*os ore premis, pectus pectore, uterum utero*). Tullia fills the role of *domina* by repeating this figure in the imperative mode and then immediately exulting in her power to fabricate the erotic other: 'Artifex tibi sum ego Veneris novae, quae nova es'; like an artist she crafts or fashions a 'new Venus' for her new lover (II. 35). The same dance of paired body parts, and the same tribute to her power as *artifex*, recur whenever their passion flares up again; in the 'Fescennine' seventh dialogue, for example, they shower each other with passionate expressions of mutual love, and Octavia continues to declare herself 'crafted' or 'ficted' by her mentor (pp. 185, 189 above).

Throughout the *Tribadicon* Tullia locates same-sex desire within the natural order, as a manifestation of the 'Venereal force that drives all living beings'—a concept given scientific and literary credence by pointed quotation from Lucretius' *De Rerum Natura* (II. 38). As in *L'Escole des filles*'s discussion of dildos, the unnatural becomes the supreme instance of the natural. But it is the creative and aesthetic aspect of lesbianism that Chorier emphasizes in this literary drag act; Tullia as *artifex* stands in for the authorial function itself, inventing new 'figures' and new 'metamorphoses'. Octavia's role might seem reduced to the passive material of Tullia-Chorier's 'art', but the dialogic exchange shows that she is really playing the *fausse naïve* to encourage the older woman, exerting her own control over the visual-corporeal dynamics. At the moment of vivid *autopsia* cited in section 1 above, Octavia provokes further probing by asking Tullia what is shooting forth from her eyes and what she is seeing 'inside' the labia she opens (III. 45). When she smilingly pretends not to understand the 'fruits' of that 'garden' where Tullia has fixed her fingers and her eyes, her mentor calls out 'Percipio nequitias tuas: hortum certe tuum, quae de meo objicis, tam nosti quam ego meum' (II. 33) ('I see how wicked you are: for sure you know your own garden as well as I do my own, since you are flinging it against mine'). Octavia is not merely 'rubbing' vulvas, as a *tribade* or *fricatrice* should do, but 'projecting' or 'throwing' hers against her cousin's—literally 'objecting' the sexual centre that has already captured her lover's visual attention. It was precisely this verb (*objicio, objectum*) that Chorier himself used in his preface, to

---

[70] Technically, *traductio* combined with *epizeuxis*; cf. the earlier representation of lesbian mirroring in Donne(?), *Sappho to Philaenis*, lines 49–50 ('Hand to strange hand, lippe to lippe none denies; | Why then should they brest to brest, or thighs to thighs?').

convey the intended effect of his most libertine dialogue—which 'flings figures against the eyes', *figuras objicit ob oculos*.

This mutual seduction occurs at an early stage in the work, and Chorier perhaps intended the heroines' bond to be passed off as a prelude, rehearsal, or developmental stage. (Some critics have jumped to this conclusion, without tracing the recurrent lesbian theme through the later, perverse, postmarital dialogues.[71]) Certainly Tullia uses Octavia's imminent wedding as a pretext, and so explains everything by translating it into heterosexual terms. To initiate the seduction she declares 'I am in love with you the way you are in love with your fiancé' (*Ut tu Caviceum, sic te ego*). She intends to 'act the role of Caviceus', but draws attention to her lack of the proper tool. After filling her cousin's 'little boat' with ejaculate, however, she boasts that 'I have been a man to you, my spouse, my wife! . . . I have completed the work' (*tibi ego vir fui, mea sponsa, mea conjux . . . perfeci opus*). When Octavia innocently asserts that only a man could give her 'solid' pleasure, Tullia humours her by modifying her earlier claim that *all* ladies lust after brilliant young women; now she limits lesbianism to an 'alia via' or alternative for unmarried virgins who need to avoid pregnancy and scandal (II. 36, 37). Most of the episodes recounted in the following dialogues are relentlessly heterosexual, or anticipate the conventions of later pornography by presenting women's copulation as a scene to be viewed and interrupted by a male, who literally projects or 'flings himself' into the active role—as in the episode of Enemonea caught in the act by her brother, cited above.

Nevertheless, it would oversimplify this Protean dialogue to say that lesbianism remains permanently fixed in the hierarchy of values below heterosexual consummation. Just as Tullia alternates between 'disciplinary' condemnations of sodomy and 'enlightening' justifications—always in response to shocked interjections by Octavia—so she oscillates between two modes of understanding lesbianism. Though she never denounces Sapphic desire, and always keeps it under the banner of Nature, she sometimes underrepresents it as a mere substitute for men and sometimes overrepresents it as the *sine qua non* and *ne plus ultra* of educated eroticism.[72] We might call these the phallocentric and the philosapphic modes. Even while expounding the substitute model Tullia slips in some universalizing claims: *all* ladies of any taste, all but the most 'stolid' and 'stony', want to seduce 'shining and polished girls' like Octavia (worshipped in the same words that Secundus showered on his

---

[71] e.g. Peter Cryle, *Geometry in the Boudoir: Configurations of French Erotic Narrative* (1994), 24 ('the supposed threat of lesbian autonomy melts away to nothing'); for less cursory readings of Chorier's problematic relation to Sapphism, see Leibacher-Ouvrard, 'Transtextualité', 55, Ros Ballaster, ' "The Vices of Old Rome Revived": Representations of Female Same-Sex Desire in Seventeenth and Eighteenth Century England', in Suzanne Raitt (ed.), *Volcanoes and Pearl Divers: Essays in Lesbian Feminist Studies* (1995), 19–21, and Wahl, *Invisible Relations*, 218–36 (though I disagree that Chorier 'ultimately' endorses the insufficiency of lesbianism (219)).

[72] Before Chorier these models can be found separately: in Aretino's *Ragionamenti* (1. i. 27–8 [33]) and the pseudo-Aretine *Puttana errante* (65/10) the heroine's lesbian initiation is immediately declared unsatisfying and never recurs; in the 16c. *Premier Acte du synode nocturne des tribades* attributed to Guillaume de Reboul, BnF Enfer 489, 'tribades' are permanently fixed in their own institution and maintain its separate historical and pictorial traditions, including a set of heroic tapestries in which Philenis 'handles the external orifice of her cousin's womb' (20), as Tullia will do.

beautiful and accomplished sister); *all* French, Italian, and Spanish women would rush into it if shame did not hold them back. The lustier they are by nature, the more lesbian their passion (II. 36–8).

Tullia's own past and present confirm this vision of intensity and durability. Once initiated by her friend Pomponia (an experience she now reduplicates for Octavia) she has never been able to relinquish this pleasure, and now it exceeds even the joys of marriage. Significantly, this 'absolute' Sapphism recurs in the narrative rather than fading away at the threshold. Tributes to Pomponia's beauty and brilliance (*venustas, lepores, ingenium*) keep rising to Tullia's lips (IV. 56–7, 68, 76), and her jocular presence during the wedding night throws an ironic light on that supreme ritual of heterosexuality. Tullia and Octavia resume their affair in the very act of re-counting those first marital experiences, 'showering' discourse and seed at once. (After the first encounter Octavia exclaims that her cousin has 'rained' an unknown liquid into her, *depluisti in me*, but soon she will 'distil' into Tullia what her husband *depluit* or 'rained' (II. 36, V. 82).) Tullia's preference for Octavia is echoed by Francesca in the final dialogue, who declares that she could have 'all the noblest and most salacious pricks' and yet still prefers to 'indulge her genius' with Enemonda (VII. 286). It is her Sapphic love that synthesizes erotic desire and mental 'genius', whereas men are mere pricks; it is the male intruder, not her 'blind desire' for another woman, that constitutes the *pis aller* forced on her by circumstance.

Even the notorious claim to play the 'man' (assumed when Octavia has no idea of what a lover could be) dissolves with the first orgasm. Tullia may not own a crude labourer's 'sledgehammer and crowbar' to break in (II. 35), but she still ejaculates '*into* the little boat'—*in cymbam*, using the accusative of motion and direction— and thereby *perfecit opus* or 'completed the work perfectly' with the seed-throwing equipment she already has (without recourse to a dildo, as she proudly reminds Octavia (39)). As in *L'Alcibiade* and *L'Escole*, seed is the essential substance; the injection of sperm defines the *opus*, and according to the two-seed theory both sexes ejaculate and both possess organs instrumental to that end.[73] Does this mean, then, that Tullia sports the freakishly enlarged clitoris described by anatomists like Bartholin and jurists like Sinistrari (Ch. 3 n. 147 above), the member essential to convict a woman on the capital charge of 'sodomy'? Chorier toys with the sources for this idea; when Tullia claims an affinity with Sappho or Philaenis, the reader probably recalls that both women were cited in medical discourse as an example of clitoral hypertrophy and 'Contemptus virorum', or that Martial's Philaenis sodom-izes boys and girls with reckless abandon.[74] But Chorier never mentions such an enlargement, even when Tullia explains the *fabrica* of the clitoris and describes her husband playing with it (III. 44). For Callias that appendage is a *robinet*, causing handfuls of warm fluid to gush forth and prompting further exchanges of witty talk,

---

[73] Cf. *Alcibiade*, 81–5 (Ch. 2, sect. 2 above), *Escole*, II. 135 (Ch. 3, sect. 4); Jean Riolan the Younger, *Anthropographia* (Paris, 1626), 293, derives *clitoris* from a Greek word meaning 'lascivè semen effundere', and then goes on to associate that organ with lesbianism.

[74] Bartholin, *Anatomia*, 186; Martial, VII. lxvii ('Pedicat pueros tribas Philaenis') and cf. Ch. 2 n. 63 above.

but it is evidently not a rival phallus. Whenever Tullia and Octavia come together, Chorier forces us to contemplate normal or 'natural' women locked in an embrace.[75]

Clear distinctions between kinds of libido blur, in any case, because in the foreground of the text discursive pleasure mingles so thoroughly with corporeal. Tullia represents what Montesquieu would call 'philosophical love', the passion that heterosexuals naturally feel for artificially crafted beauties of their own sex, and she invests her erotic energy in the Pygmalionesque power of the *artifex*, the conceptual mastery and cultural authority of the erudite. Heterosexual or otherwise, Chorier's inset narratives and tableaux remain framed within the dialogic present: two women in bed together, exciting one another with their fluent tongues as much as with their 'adulterous fingers'. (Male homosexuality, in contrast, is discussed but never shown in action.[76]) Same-sex narrative exchange becomes not only the equivalent of copulation but the preferred form.

We have already seen the inexhaustibility of 'storytelling' and the interchangeability of ears and vulvas, 'prurient description' and genital 'rain'. As late as the 'Fescennine' seventh dialogue, Octavia prepares for her most important narrative, her seduction of Vives's beautiful boy-pupil, by spelling out the parallel between sexual enjoyment and 'pouring the most secret thoughts of the soul' into Tullia, who replies 'I have drawn you into the intimate fibres of my breast' (VII. 261–2). This destabilizing of two interdependent hierarchies—hetero-over homosexual, natural reality over aesthetic 'shadow'—begins in the *Tribadicon* itself. Since feeling the arrows of Octavia, Tullia 'despises' even her hyperphallic husband and seeks 'the totality of pleasure' (*voluptatem omnem*) only in her sister-cousin's arms. When Octavia presses her for an explanation she queers her own argument, abandoning her earlier phallocentric theories (lesbianism as an *alia via*, outlet, or rehearsal for the real thing). Instead she glorifies the 'Heroines' of antiquity and expounds the Lesbian literary and artistic heritage, the historical tradition of Sappho and Philaenis which 'ennobles' tribadism and gives women their special authority over the depiction of Eros (II. 38–9).

In her panegyric genealogy of lesbianism—and in her account of the origins of sexual art and literature, we shall see in section 4—Tullia lays claim to the same discursive and historical authority that Madeleine de Scudéry claimed by naming her autobiographical character 'Sapho'. But now the erotic basis of Sappho's art— expunged or at most hinted in Scudéry—has been fully reinstated. In simulating a scholarly female libertine of the High Renaissance, Chorier has actually anticipated the scholarly editor Tanneguy Le Fèvre, praised in Joan DeJean's *Fictions of Sappho 1546–1937*. Le Fèvre's 1664 biographical note emphasizes Sappho's high-cultural status, characterizes her sexuality quite openly, and makes no reference whatever to

---

[75] Cf. Leibacher-Ouvrard, 'Transtextualité', 55 (linking Philaenis also to Martial, I. xc, more explicit about Bassa's overgrown organ); Wahl, *Invisible Relations*, 231–2 (and ch. 1 *passim*).

[76] As Leibacher-Ouvrard notes ('Transtextualité', 59), contrasting Rocco's *Alcibiade*. Lesbian activities are also restricted in one area: Tullia and Octavia never apply their mouths to the vulva, unlke Theodorus (VII. 240) and Gonzalva (245).

alleged relationships with males, a position DeJean finds both sympathetic and 'startling';[77] Tullia does all this, and in addition endows her with 'nobility' and foundational authority for her own *erudita libido*.

4. THE PRIMACY OF FIGURATION

Masquerading as Aloisia Sigea, Chorier invents a salty 'female' wit that reshapes both homoerotic and heterosexual encounters in terms that undermine heroic masculinism. Likewise, the 'female' dialogists transform sex from a simple phallic urge, diametrically opposed to reason, into a sophisticated play of images and tableaux, a *catalogue raisonné* of delights like the 'Postures' and pleasure palaces of Aretino and Giulio Romano. After this philosophical and artistic elaboration, the standard 'missionary' position can be reintroduced—indeed freshly appreciated—not as an orthodox or procreational norm but as one in a gallery of *figurae Veneris*, all of which the speaker has experienced and evaluated according to a hedonistic calculus. The straight embrace is valued for its mutual exchange of glances and its efficacy as a mental picture: 'what sweeter thing can be fashioned by thinking?' (VI. 216). *Quid dulcius cogitando fingi potest?* The supposedly 'natural' mode becomes an instance of *cogitation* and *fiction*, the Promethean or Pygmalionic powers that 'fashioned' Octavia in the first place.

It may be objected that Tullia and Octavia merely shift from one masculine code to another, from simple phallocratic naturalism to a philosophic-humanist erotology dominated by 'the divine Aretino', scourge of women as well as of princes. But Tullia explicitly establishes a female origin for this way of 'mutating' sex into figures. Her learned accounts of pictorial figuration, in the last two dialogues, in fact mesh tightly with her genealogy of Sapphic desire. A common historical source authorizes both the lesbian bond of the two cousins (which melts the partitions between representation and action) and the classical art of the *figurae Veneris* inherited from Sappho by way of Aretino.

In the advanced sixth dialogue, when Octavia praises her encyclopedic knowledge and creative deployment of the postures or 'Veneris modi', Tullia once again inserts herself into an ancient gynaecocentric tradition. After she describes a particularly elaborate orgy in which she copulates with four men at once, Octavia exclaims 'How many figures you mutated yourself into, to give pleasure!' (*Quot te in figuras mutasti, ut placeres!*, VI. 214). The arts that Tullia has embodied so fully are then traced to two Greek women, the courtesan Cyrene (called 'Dodecamechanos' because she invented the twelve best techniques of copulation) and the artist Elephantis, who transformed the practices of her day into pictures which then became the model for future voluptuaries striving ' "pictas opus edere ad tabellas" '—to perform the 'work' according to the painted tableaux, to bring action up to the level of representation (VI. 214). (Tullia here quotes *Priapeia*, 4, though the poem in

[77] (1989), 55–6.

fact refers to paintings derived from the *books* of Elephantis.) Elephantis is thus the source both of Tullia's self-mutations and of Chorier's entire project; we recall that Elephantis and Aloisia Sigea appear together in the preface as archetypes of female privilege in the depiction of Eros, the proof that 'women are more capable of depicting these matters'. (In the Elysian Fields epistle they are joined by a third ancient authority-figure, Philaenis—variously identified as the Greek author of postures, the inventor of lesbian sex, and the reputed lover of Sappho.) The verbal descriptions of 'the divine Pietro Aretino' (full of 'satyric salt' like Chorier's own dialogues), and the pictures of 'those supreme painters Titian and Carracci', stem from the same Graeco-Roman female-authored heritage.[78]

This performative-representational history, ancient and modern, collectively illustrates the principle that Tullia herself now fulfils in person and in discourse: 'quot inflexiones, quot corporis conversiones, tot sunt Veneris figurae' (VI. 214) ('the number of Venus' figures is equivalent to the inflexions and conversions of the body'). Pallavicino had included *conversiones* among the 'figures' of sexual rhetoric, but Chorier now frees them from the stigma of prostitution and the closed system of numbered 'postures'. The *Veneris figurae* are as numerous as the 'inflexions' and 'turnings' of the body. Indeed, mere numeration is inadequate to grasp and teach the full range of 'pleasures'; the individual tastes and preferences of a *docta* like Tullia produce in effect an infinite series of *figurae*, a generative grammar of 'inflections'. Reversing the line from Virgil's *Georgics* that justified reducing all forms of sexuality to the same discipline, Tullia pointedly insists that '*non* idem omnibus amor', love is *not* the same for all (214, my emphasis).

Once again, Octavia primly responds that only one way is legitimate and that all other variations are evil and shameful. Once again, Tullia endorses her cousin's naive conservatism in terms that demolish its premiss: the one position *ex naturae praescripto* is in fact the bestial quadruped position recommended for breeding purposes by Lucretius, to be used by married couples to whom pleasure is irrelevant. After thus denaturing Nature, Tullia then joins Octavia in commending the conventional face-to-face 'figura'. Her rhetoric subsumes heterosexuality into the Sapphic tradition, reconstituting the 'common usage' as a further instance of the rhythmical symmetry already enjoyed by our heroines in person. In earlier dialogues Tullia and Octavia generated cries of 'Ut admoves pubem pubi! Ut committis cunnum cunno! Ut haeris pectus pectori!' (V. 88), continuing the rhetorical-grammatical pairing of body parts begun in the 'tribadic' Colloquium II (II. 35, n. 70 above). Now the missionary position 'pectus pectore, ventrem ventre comprimat, pubes pubi colludat' (VI. 215). This is the context for Octavia's remark 'what sweeter thing can be fashioned by thinking?' (216).

In the seventh and final dialogue this chain of representative authority is completed. Amidst other *fabellae* and *narratiunculae* Tullia wages a campaign against those 'Catos' who would censor nudity in art and genital explicitness in discourse;

---

[78] VI. 214; Aretino 'bene multas [figuras] in colloquiis suis expressit satyrico sale', and thus matches the praise of 'saltiness' initiated in the preface (sect. 1 above).

more precisely, Chorier targets those Counter-Reformation forces who sought to regulate the marriage-bed by strengthening the Church's prohibitions against over-frequent repetition, unseemly movements, and experiments with 'new figures'. Tullia contrasts this futile attempt at repressive legislation with the liberal procla-mations of the ancient Roman *senatulus* or ladies' parliament, which allowed up to seven copulations per night, encouraged the mutual enjoyment of vigorous move-ment, and declared the posture or *figura* a matter of individual taste.[79] (She endorses their numerical limit because, in her twenty-five-orgasm Roman orgy, she started to lose interest after 'six or seven'.) Bolstered by classical authority, Tullia takes the in-dividualizing principle even deeper than she did in the sixth dialogue; paradoxi-cally, everyone is free to abandon regulation and discover their own principle of excess, to invent and perform more postures than can possibly be captured in dis-course or painting, because the all-female 'senate' has established it as a rule.

The further Tullia goes back in history, the higher the level of state endorsement and the broader the range of permitted transgressions. The fountainhead of the Chorier-Sigea-Aretino-Elephantis tradition is Sappho herself, 'the tenth Muse'—already invoked in the *Tribadicon* as the woman who 'commended' and 'ennobled' the Lesbian name and the lesbian practices first invented by the aristocratic Philaenis (II. 38–9). The rulers of Lesbos, 'the most brilliant of the Greeks', issued coins in honour of Venus 'sculpted with the various figures, including unusual ones'. Tullia has actually seen two of these Lesbian coins in the collections of the Roman Villa Orsini, the setting for the four-man orgy recounted in Colloquium VI, and she describes them as follows: 'In one, the naked Sappho struggled in a tribadic duel with a naked girl; in the other a naked man, steadying himself on his right knee, lifted up a naked girl and drove his spear into her, while she encouraged him by spreading wide her thighs' (VII. 278–9). The two cousins discuss these coins with playful erudition—Octavia jokes about genuflexion, and Tullia invents an oath ('per nummum oblongum venereum tuum') that turns Octavia's vulva itself into 'a slot-shaped coin' or medal of Venus—but underlying this badinage is real antiquar-ian knowledge and a serious point about the cultural construction of sexualities.[80] Tullia interprets these objects as the official commemorative coinage of the philoso-pher-kings of Lesbos, who thereby endorse the even-handed respect for sexual variation that Plato ascribes to Aristophanes in the *Symposium*: male and female homosexuals, like heterosexuals, all derive by the same splitting process from the various kinds of primal person. In the 1680 French version, traceable to Chorier's milieu if not to Chorier himself, Octavia adds that she has seen 'a Medal in Florence' showing the homosexual union of Jove and Ganymede under the motto 'Amori Vera Lux'.[81]

---

[79] VII. 276–7. Leibacher-Ouvrard, 'Transtextualité', 60, 66 n. 26, notes resemblances to Erasmus' *Senatulus* (Ch. 3 n. 133 above), but I can find no direct source; contrast Tullia's accurate citation of Roman anti-sodomy laws (280, 335).

[80] Chorier probably knew the ancient posture-bearing tokens called *spintriae* (though they are Roman not Greek), and his 'Orsini' connection may allude to Fulvio Orsini, who published a medal of Sappho in his *Imagines et Elogia Virorum Illustrium et Eruditorum, ex Antiquis Lapidibus et Nomismatibus* (Rome, 1570), 38.

[81] *Academie*, ii. 75 (cut from the abbreviated version and therefore from modern reprints).

This mintage of official *figurae* defines the originary moment of 'ennoblement' that launched the twin traditions in which Tullia places herself, élite lesbianism and encyclopedic publication of the 'arcana of Venus'. She calls it in fact a 'publicum auctoramentum' (VII. 278), both an 'authorization' and a coming-to-authorship— something quite different from the private and deceitful 'authentication' of passion recommended in *La retorica delle puttane* (Ch. 2, sect. 1 above). From these medals flowed all subsequent representations of 'the figures', just as all medical knowledge derived from the tablets hung up in the temples of Aesculapius and Apollo. By this means Philaenis (now understood as a transmitter of the heritage rather than its inventor) and Elephantis (now correctly identified as an author) derive their images from Sappho; because they 'had them before their eyes and in their hands' they were able to write 'his de nugis eruditas libellis', these 'erudite little books about trifles'.[82]

The context for Tullia's genealogies of figuration definitively separates the *figura* from the 'natural' sexuality it supposedly represents, revealing the limits of the physical and the hollowness of the 'pornotopian' insistence on endless priapic vigour. Ostensibly the sixth dialogue *is* a fantasy of phallic power, cross-cutting as it does between two orgies populated by improbably virile 'athletes' and 'Heroes'. But the possibility of 'being satiated even to loathing' is written into the scenario from the start (VI. 169), and Octavia expresses relief that her two lovers failed to achieve their goal of twenty ejaculations: 'That which fatigues pleasure is not itself a pleasure' (194). She is glad to turn from action to 'free speech' at this moment, to share with Tullia the stylistic-erotic pleasure of analysing Laura's letter (sect. 2 above).

A similar turn occurs after Tullia exhausts four men as lovers and as topics of conversation. Though she remains the heroic victor after the full twenty-five assaults, she describes herself as disgusted and benumbed. Unlike Juvenal's Messalina— whose target of twenty-four copulations per night she has just surpassed—Tullia is 'satiata' as well as 'lassata', and this *taedium Veneris* lasts for three months (VI. 213). But while physical sex drives itself literally and explicitly *ad nauseam*, the manipulation of mental images continues afresh: after 'the nausea of Venus grew dull in our collapsing loins', she and La Tour (her French favourite among the four athletes at the Villa Orsini orgy) 'served each other as a vehicle to call back and repeat the games that seemed so far from us' (VI. 214). Tullia does not specify what this 'revocation' consisted of, only hinting that it will provide another year's worth of narrative, and end in her lover's murder. But her discussion of the mutating 'figures of Venus', which follows immediately (as Octavia forces the conversation away from this tragic ending), reaffirms the superiority of sex as artefact and mental idea. Her prime examples and predecessors are chosen according to aesthetic rank: Elephantis in the ancient world, who shaped the libido of the Emperor Tiberius; among the moderns 'divini vir ingenii, *Petrus Aretinus*', and '*Titianus* et *Carracius*,

---

[82] VII. 279; Octavia almost derails this discussion by suggesting that Elephantis was really a respectable matron maligned by a hostile writer who composed a scandalous text in her name (exactly what Chorier did to the historical Aloisia Sigea), but Tullia turns this into a tribute to the power of writing (and to Aretino). For *nugae* (trifles), cf. VII. 226, 270, Catullus, I. iv, Martial, IX. i, XII. ii, and Leibacher-Ouvrard, 'Transtextualité', 53, 65 n 11.

summi pictores'. And their achievement cannot be interpreted as simple fidelity to a pre-existent physical phenomenon: many of these *figurae*—here conceived not merely as 'positions' but as pictorial configurations—cannot actually be performed in the body, 'even by lovers whose joints and limbs are more flexible than any we can conceive' (VI. 214–15).

For the *libertin érudit* Chorier—ventriloquizing the voice of the sixteenth-century female intellectual—'Idea' mediates between High Renaissance art theory and the mental image as defined by Descartes and Locke. Mind and speech are thus given a heroic role in the process of figuration: it is 'meditating and commenting', rather than mere physical desire, that creates the full range of erotic *figurae*. Just as 'nothing is impervious to the impetuous desires of the soul', so 'nothing is difficult to an exultant and disordering intellect' (*nihil cogitationi exsultabandae et intemperanti difficile*); the 'soul' and its 'cogitation' can refashion everything to its image, 'finding the smooth path in the precipice' (VI. 214–15). As Octavia later proclaims to Aloisia Fonseca, 'Eruditae libidini prospere omnia cedunt'; everything happily yields to educated desire (VII. 220). Indeed, the most recondite 'figures' can take place *only* in the realm of the imagination. Meditation produces 'more things than can really be done'; 'the body cannot easily do all that the mind persuades' (VI. 215). Tullia's phrasing (*impotentis animi desideriis*) brings out the curious instability of the body–mind relation; desire is *impotens* in the classical sense (impetuous, unbridled, powerless to restrain itself), but also in the modern sense, already established in Chorier's native French. The same word is applied to the phallus itself— 'partem tam virilem, . . . tam impotentem' (III. 47–8)—with similarly ironic effect. In the earlier marital dialogues Tullia might have persuaded her naive pupil that the *mentula* possesses a 'natural faculty of creating *mens* in us' (sect. 3 above), but in these hypererotic later dialogues neither *mens* nor *mentula* can reach their goal of complete fusion, and of the two the mind is the more trustworthy. Now the restless yearning for ever more baroque copulation, the pouring of all one's desires and cogitations into fresh configurations, is revealed as the mind's compensation for *Veneris nausea*.

It seems, then, that the decoy title attached to Chorier's work after 1680— *Elegantiae Latini Sermonis*, elegances of the Latin language—might offer a better description than the original 'Secrets of Love and Venus'. Certainly the seventh dialogue promotes the discursive and the cognitive to new heights. Posture-making is now understood to be, not a taxonomic device or transcription of reality, but a theoretical construction, and the voluptuary ideal develops into a mastery of these images, a capacity to 'invent Venuses' as Laura did.

We have seen that, in the verbal seduction of Aloisia that launches this dialogue, Octavia proclaims 'salty wit' to be the best part of pleasure. Venus is most fully manifested, most 'pure and unmixed', in these *sales et fabellae* (VII. 220–1). Octavia offers a profane version of Socrates' initiation into the mysteries of Love by the prophetess Diotima, showing Aloisia the *gradus* or steps that lead to the *summum bonum* of erotic delight, steps which lead beyond the 'vulgar' and the physical: 'As it is sweet to enjoy these pleasures, so it is delicious to remember the enjoyment. There are people who find the supreme pleasure in hoping for or recording pleasure, who feel Venus more in telling than in enjoying.' This clearly parallels de Rochefoucauld's maxim about those who would never experience love unless they had heard it spoken of, and anticipates the widespread mockery of those who enjoy sex only in the mind, 'fucking their ideas' (as L'Escole des filles puts it). But Octavia endorses the position rather than belittling it: 'by remembering (recordando), they make permanent those pleasures that slip away in the flow of the moment; pleasures even increase as they are repeated in the memory' (VII. 220). In her narrative it is the uneducated nurse Manilia who urges the lovers not to waste time in fabelli, who agrees with Dom Juan that 'il faut faire et non pas dire'.[83] The high-born and finally enlightened Octavia, in contrast, promotes the power of the eroticized imagination, the 'erudite libido' to which 'everything happily yields'. This does not mean that physical collapse and Veneris nausea will vanish, as they do in the shallower forms of pornography, but that, armed with high-libertine philosophy, 'you may find true pleasure even in the shadow of pleasure', the voluptatis umbra.[84] This principle is repeated throughout the final dialogue. Octavia cites two male friends—mirror-images of the author and his reader?—who recount all their experiences to each other, and thereby make whole days and nights of happiness out of 'pleasures that slip and fall away in a moment', fluxas et uno caducas momento voluptates (VII. 241). Tullia contrasts the abject sex-addict, who undergoes endless orgasms without feeling any of the 'fiery sparks' that moderation preserves, with the true philosophical voluptuary, for whom 'libido can survive itself' and pleasure can rise up 'from its own death' (277).

At the heart of libertine discourse—adumbrated by L'Escole des filles and now relentlessly developed by Chorier—we find this paradox: the cult of unbridled physical enjoyment, of total immersion in the forbidden delights of the body, leads to a fetishization of the mental idea and the shadowy representation. At one point in the final dialogue, however—the point where the mutation principle is most clearly articulated—idea and picture themselves come into conflict. Even as she defines the ars et ratio of erotic movement, and describes the images of Sappho that authorize her own narrative, Tullia suggests that imaginative abundance and individual inventiveness go beyond the limits of representation, breaking apart the encyclopedic project of codification associated with Elephantis and Aretino: 'Nemo narrando dixerit figuras omnes, nec posuerit ob oculos pingendo. Mutari amat Proteus Amor.'[85] ('No one can describe all the figurae in narrative, nor place them against the eyes in painting. Love is a Proteus who loves metamorphosis.') Mutari amat Proteus Amor. La retorica delle puttane had advised the courtesan to 'mutate' into Ganymede, and L'Escole des filles had found titillation in the 'métamorphoses de l'amour' (Ch. 2, sect. 1, Ch. 3, sect. 3 above). But Tullia's Protean maxim—so concise

---

[83] VII. 268, 284 ('facto opus est, non dicto'), though cf. 285 when she applauds the 'acta fabula'.

[84] VII. 220; cf. the 'titillationis umbra' of buggery (VI. 208).

[85] VII. 278, a 'mutation' of Ovid, Ars Amatoria, I. 761? Despite this continual insistence on 'infinite' mutation, Cryle believes that 'Chorier's characters are content to recognize an acceptable range of pleasurable positions' (Geometry, 23).

and lapidary that the French adaptation *L'Academie des dames* left it in the original Latin (ii. 74)—places the metamorphic capacity at the constitutive centre of sexuality. Figuration seems to slip out from any paradigm that Tullia proposes: the enumerated systems of 'Cyrene' or 'Aretino' are left behind by the flexible, aroused body; the body is left behind by the mind's inventiveness; even the resources of 'narration' and pictorial 'ob-jection' are left behind by the unrepresentable, hyper-individual *nescio quid*, the supplement of libidinous excess.

5. THE SCHOOL OF MEN: GENDERED POWER AND THE FORMATION OF THE *HONNESTE HOMME*

The philosophy of Chorier's *Satyra Sotadica*, spelled out with increasing clarity by his 'female' protagonists, expresses a kind of Manichaean conflict of opposites. It is a philosophy of life over death, light over dark, delight over repulsion, energy over inertia, 'fictive' power over mere 'nature', 'infinite' mutation over constraint and circumscription, festive play over rigid solemnity. Its models are the Epicurean Petronius, the Pliny who feels most human when reading 'Sotadics' or 'Socratics' (sect. 1 above), and the naturalistic Montaigne; Tullia's diatribe against those who glorify images of warfare but censure any depiction of nudity and sexual pleasure is translated directly from that source.[86] And the supreme philosophical hero is Socrates—not the strict idealist celebrated by Plato or Sigea, but the *pruriens Socrates* (VII. 262), the Roccoesque philosopher swept away by desire, 'doing delicious things with Phaedo or Alcibiades', who lends his authority to a kind of hedonistic humanism:

Qui sunt sapientissimi, non ideo hominem exuerunt, et ingenitos abjecerunt humanitatis affectus; nec possent, ut maxime vellent. Sed sensus est humanitatis nullus in homine, sine voluptatis gustu, nisi hebes et corruptus. Is vere est sapiens, qui norit dulce esse desipere in loco.[87]

The wisest thinkers have never stripped off the human, nor despised the innate emotions of humanity—nor could they, however much they wished. But there is no sense of humanity in mankind without the taste of voluptuous delight, and those who lack it are dull and corrupt. He is truly wise, who knows how sweet it is to play the fool on the right occasion.

Chorier weaves his text around two classical principles, the jocoserious art of *erudite nugari* or learned trifling, and the Horatian injunction to 'desipere in loco', the carnivalesque or Fescennine capacity for wise foolery at the appropriate time. Octavia inscribes her teacher into this philosophical hall of fame, and defines the goal of 'this erudite little book of trifles', when she declares 'you are learned yourself, and you always trifle learnedly' (*erudita es, Tullia, [et] soles erudite nugari*, VII. 226).

---

[86] VII. 278; Montaigne, *Essais*, III. v. 856–7/669–70 (and cf. Pallavicino, *RP* 7–8).

[87] VII. 232, citing Horace, *Odes*, IV. xii. 28; after 'corruptus' some editions quote from Petronius xxx here (Lavagnini, 333), the same lines in praise of Epicurus and erotic pleasure that Sinibaldi cites (sect. 1 above).

At the rhetorical high point of the work, when Octavia invites Aloisia Fonseca to share her sexual experiences in words, erotic pleasure becomes the light that transforms life into a work of art, 'sculpting or painting' the visible world (VII. 220). In Tullia's expansion of 'Socratic' philosophy, the 'lux voluptatis' becomes the sun that sustains 'man, the sum and pinnacle of all natural things'—and she uses the species-word *homo* or human rather than the gender-word *vir*, the male. Those who abstain from pleasure 'will become their own sepulchre, alive and yet not alive, dead and yet not dead' (232). The reduction of woman to the sexual realm, typical of later pornography, can thus be presented as an expansion of the principle of life: 'we live to love and to be loved; she who will not be loved or love is already entombed, already rotten with the stench of disease' (222). But this celebration of the life-force in no way commits Chorier to animalism or naturalism. Desire must be *erudita* before 'everything yields' to it. Sex must be intellectualized and intellect sexualized. We have seen that 'salty' wit and 'prurient' imagination come to be the primary reality, while the physical comes to be associated with *nausea* as much as with pleasure. The body and the self have no fixed essences, being subject to plasticity and metamorphosis: *Mutari amat Proteus Amor.*

In the sexual arena, however, play is rarely innocent. Philosophies of 'man' easily degenerate into patriarchal ideologies, promoting the interests of *vir* rather than *homo*. Tullia may be *erudita* in the feminine, but true wisdom, even on her lips, is masculine. In theory both male and female can share in this transformation of sexuality into a pure flame of erotic cognition, rising above all problems of ageing, impotence, 'nausea', pregnancy, rejection, disapproval, exposure, and economic necessity. But a realistic female reader could not set aside these darker considerations and could not, like Casanova, read Chorier as a practical guide to sexuality: as Mary Wortley Montagu would later say of her fiancé's sexual propositions, ''tis play to you, but 'tis death to us'.[88]

Chorier's mentalism adds a new complication to the politics of sexuality; precisely *because* the 'figura' has taken over from the normative reality of the body, control over configuration becomes of paramount importance. Partners are no longer yielding to a natural urge that subsumes them, or fulfilling a higher purpose by propagating children, but manoeuvring for the director's chair in a dramatic production. Who will impose their image on whom?

Despite their philosophy of sweetness and light, Tullia and Octavia often depict gender relations as a vicious assertion of power. The pain of flogging metamorphizes into arousal under the supervision of the priest-Stoic Theodorus. The anus is transformed into a site of painful 'titillation' by Aloisius and Fabricius. Husbands turn the wedding night into a blood-soaked ritual more like rape or female circumcision than consensual union. Rangoni, Caviceus, and Chrysogonus insist on ejaculating into the hand, cleavage, and mouth because men have a 'right' to define any part as an 'image of Venus' at his disposal, a 'part by which she is woman' (V. 100, VII.

---

[88] Cited in Patricia Meyer Spacks, ' "Ev'ry Woman is at Heart a Rake" ', *Eighteenth-Century Studies*, 8 (1974–75), 28.

231–2). It is these imperious males, in fact, who propose the doctrine that 'the entire body of a beautiful woman is one cunt' (VI. 182), or 'a *thesaurus* of pleasure' to be scripted according to man's desires. This last doctrine is used to justify not only the extension of genital status to the whole body ('tota cunnus'), but the misogynistic rejection of the vagina itself; Chrysogonus—the most brutal of the 'Stoics' and the one who claims the *libidinum thesaurus* line for Socrates—interprets the principle of metamorphosis to mean that all of a woman's parts must become sexual organs at his command, that the mouth is the pure and true vagina, unpolluted by stench and infection.[89] This violent refashioning of the female according to a masculine sign-system is carried to a telling extreme by Alphonsus Gusman, who selects his 13-year-old wife according to the principle that a small mouth betokens a small vagina. When he finds this is not true he rapes her anally—not as a voluptuary whim, but in order to produce shrieks of pain and thus to confirm the expected image of powerful defloration; he must keep up his reputation for his male friends, who are listening in the next room (VII. 224).

Even in 'normal' marital relations the discourse of lovers is shot through with the language of power, with language *as* power. Husbands and mothers deliver homilies of obedience in the very act of copulation. Callias breaks down Tullia's resistance by insisting that her vagina is his by law: 'Why do you stop me from freely enjoying my own goods? Is that fitting in someone with such a literary education?' (IV. 63, *decet bonis instructam litteris, ut tu es?*). Caviceus *orders* his wife Octavia, in both senses of the word, during another protracted defloration-scene; he commands her to submit to pain ('this is how the thing is done: endure without moving') and he disposes her in the position he requires: 'This is what I want. First spread and open your thighs as well as you can. Present to the penis the vulva which is to be split; and in that position, without changing, allow me to carry through my pleasure to the end' (V. 86). As if instructed by Gilles Deleuze, he adopts the crude imperative mode characteristic of 'pornography' as opposed to the higher genre of 'pornology', which invokes 'pure reason' and 'relates language to its own limitation'.[90]

Perhaps the most disturbing aspect of pornography is its creation of female characters who eroticize their own submission. When we see men striving to *impose* their view that women should be totally identified with their sex, *tout à fait femmes*, we can at least see it as a contested ideology; but when Aloisia Fonseca declares happily that 'in cunno tota eram, aut tota cunnus', the opinion has been naturalized. Female spontaneity is expropriated in the interests of male fantasy. The newly-wed Octavia seems willing to accept the role of inventory assistant, told to 'count the number of times I strike' and to 'see that you don't lose count'; Tullia piously intones that 'the husband is the legislator of the wife'.[91] In yet another wedding-night scene,

[89] VII. 243; Susan Griffin, *Pornography and Silence: Culture's Revenge against Nature* (New York, 1981), 38–9, cites this passage (from Phyllis and Eberhard Kronhausen and therefore out of context) as typical of all pornography and all male conceptions of women.

[90] *Présentation de Sacher-Masoch: Le Froid et le cruel* (Paris, 1967), 17–18, 22.

[91] V. 99 (Caviceus' imperiousness is slightly mitigated by addressing his wife as 'mea hera' and using the second person subjective rather than the imperative to convey his orders).

Catharina Herrera calls on her son-in-law to show no mercy to her daughter ('Remember you are the husband; let her feel she is the wife'), and only after an intensely bloody defloration does she 'recognize' her own child (VII. 301–2). A would-be lover urges Octavia to realize 'the true Octavia' by yielding to his desires (VII. 238), but here again identity depends on submission to a man. Husbands and lovers endorse the same system of enclosure, both conceptually and literally: when Tullia's husband fits her with a jewelled chastity belt her lover rejoices, since he has a duplicate key.[92]

The fellatio-scenes of Colloquium VII show this most blatantly. Chorier's 'females' promise to obey the man's pleasure 'in ipsa nausea', and joke about giving a flute recital or not being able to object because their mouths are full; Tullia's Prometheus myth claims a 'natural affinity' between the penis and the female mouth, and her lyrical recreation of Socratic philosophy likewise serves to justify cock-sucking (VII. 232, 243–5). Mancia Marino declares that 'we please our husbands only because we are women'—'uno nomine', 'under a single name' or 'noun'—and consequently it hardly matters where men choose to prove this 'title' as long as it gives pleasure (VII. 244). Octavia does express her opposition to fellatio, but praises Tullia's philosophical justification in terms that suggest another kind of oral play ('Belle ludis in vocabulo', you play so prettily on the word). And her analysis of the kiss produces in metaphor precisely the mingling and inversion of upper and lower body sought by the *erudita mentula* in the more lurid oral scenes: the mouth is 'the labia of the upper vulva', kissing is 'the coition of souls in the upper mouth while the bodies join in the lower mouth', the penis is 'the food of the vulva', sperm is the 'saliva of pleasure' (VII. 228–9).

But the politics of representation cannot be considered straightforward, exempt from the principle of mutation. These bids for masculine authority are often undermined by their context or weakened by ironic juxtaposition; their significance is thrown into play, pulled in different directions by the competing needs of genital arousal, philosophic scepticism, and narrative realism. Aloisia's self-definition as 'tota cunnus', as we have seen, is put into question by a context that shows discourse to be a rival rather than a secondary pleasure. The fellatio-scenes that seem to glorify masculine power are subverted by Tullia's learned commentary, which associates oral pleasure with old and feeble men, with the Emperor Tiberius and other butts of Roman satire (VII. 241–2). (The most rabid urges and the most blatant attempts to dominate are in any case given to the most despised characters, the bullying monk and the scrawny Stoic.) The mother who 'recognizes' her daughter Margarita by her virgin blood is a dupe, since Margarita has already been initiated by her tutor Vives. Tullia may sometimes mouth the doctrine of submission, and her husband may gloat over his 'possessions', but even on the wedding night she gives him a surprisingly liberal manifesto: 'mancipium, si volueris ad obsequium, liberam, si volueris ad honorem'; 'if you would like obsequiousness, keep me in slavery,

---

[92] V. 138–41; Leibacher-Ouvrard, 'Sexe, simulacre', 273, suggests further symbolic resonances of the chastity belt, which also 'binds' the male libertine to a repertoire of roles.

if you want honour, set me free' (IV. 66). And her subsequent adventures prove him ludicrously incapable of 'enjoying his goods' exclusively.

Phallic supremacy in Chorier largely depends on a heroic metaphorics of conquest, which again proves surprisingly labile. The imagery of military triumph and military assault (stabbing with spears, thrusting with clubs, breaking down gates, discharging catapults) is constantly expropriated by the female protagonists, just as it was expropriated by the authentic courtesan-poets on whom Tullia and Octavia are modelled; Veronica Franco challenges her slanderer first to a real duel and then to a 'skirmish' in bed, promising to enforce her victory by climbing on top, and Tullia likewise emerges from her orgy with 'four champions' as an Amazonian 'victrix' who 'fought and won the day', crowned with the laurel of Venus.[93] Men may wield the 'club of Hercules', but it is observed by Omphale, the most famous dominatrix in antiquity (VII. 241, 301). Readers familiar with the 'Love's War' topos would hardly read martial vocabulary as an unmitigated expression of violence, the point being the lack of fit between tenor and vehicle, the fact that (in Donne's words) love's pikes and bullets *do not hurt*.[94] In the *Skirmish* of the first dialogue or the *Duellum* of the fourth, both combatants emerge victorious; in Claudian's bloodthirsty Fescennine poem, cited in Colloquium VII, both bride and groom look forward to being wounded (302–3). Certainly the boundary between the literal and the metaphoric can grow faint, especially in the early scenes that grossly exaggerate the trauma of penetration. In the later dialogues, however, the 'female' characters police that border. On Octavia's wedding night, for example, Sempronia interrupts the bridegroom as he starts to grow violent, admonishing him that 'this should be a game, not a battle'; the mother is here no longer the passive butt of exclusive humour (as in Casanova) or a remote prude (as in *L'Escole des filles*), but a powerful intervening voice that makes the son-in-law immediately 'dissolve into venereal sweat'.[95]

Political imagery is likewise transferred from one gender to the other. The phallus might be termed a 'sceptre', but a sceptre wielded by Venus. More often she becomes a *serva*, a *fugitiva*, a prisoner, or else—still true to her gender in Latin—a powerful female warrior, 'queen of members', 'heroine', *diva*, and 'empress': 'superbam illam imperatricem mentularum!'[96] Could Fanny Hill have used these terms? This juggling of agency and 'playing with vocabulary' creates an infinitely regressive contest between the sexes. When Margarita Herrera orders the 'proud mentula' of her tutor Vives to 'come to prison, you wretched slave' (VII. 298), she is following *his* script and acknowledging *his* didactic authority. He had instructed her to 'speak freely, like a prostitute' with him, but to act chastely with her husband on

[93] VI. 169–70, 213 (and cf. III. 41, 46); Margaret F. Rosenthal, *The Honest Courtesan: Veronica Franco, Citizen and Writer in Sixteenth-Century Venice* (1992), 190–3 (and cf. 222, 'amorous war'). Leibacher-Ouvrard argues that (however playful) Chorier's phallic-military imagery lacks the 'abjection' that pervades his vaginal metaphorics ('Transtextualité', 57).

[94] Elegy XX, 'Loves Warre', line 38.

[95] V. 87 (and cf. VI. 170, where Tullia asks Lady Orsini to make the orgy 'a duel, not a battle (*duellum sit, non pugna*)').

[96] VI. 191 ('flammascenti Veneris sceptro'), VII. 240, 253, 256, 297, 298, 303; the French *Academie des dames*, ii. 51, turns the 'empress' (256) into the 'Roy des Vits'.

her wedding night (297). Nevertheless, in doing so she assumes the sado-masochistic language of fierce *domina* and cowering *serva*. Who is on top here?

'Female' author-surrogates come to control the scenography as well as the vocab-ulary of the sexual encounter, moreover. It is Tullia, and not the male heroes of the Villa Orsini orgy, who emerges as the 'legislator' of Colloquium VI; her role within the copulation-drama now resembles her role as narrator and instructor, which al-ready allows her to produce, dispose, and evaluate the *figurae Veneris*. Earlier in the dialogue, when Tullia first admits the four men, language and orgasm compete in a furious race for completion: Fabricius barks out his laconic orders and Tullia attempts a verbal response, but the flood of 'venereal foam' quenches at once the feeling and the phrase.[97] But in later scenes Tullia gains full control of sexual config-uration, arranging Octavia, Lampridius, and Rangoni in complex tableaux. What Susanne did in dialogue and retrospect, Tullia does during the act itself, naming the postures, commenting on the sensations they arouse, and directing the traffic of penetration—correcting the Aretinesque Rangoni, for example, when he suggests entering Octavia by 'a new way' (VI. 189). (He passes off his transgression as a 'slip of the tongue'; he meant a *nova figura* and not a new orifice.) In this hypersexual realm she starts to resemble the patriarch's wife commended in Molière's *Femmes savantes*, who devotes her philosophy to managing her servants and regulating the flow of 'expenses'. In the spirit of the *artifex*-pedagogue and the biological re-searcher, she works her material with her hands as well as with her tongue. Tullia effectively creates the scene in language, as much for the reader as for the participants: 'Stretch out on your back! . . . What is that salacious tail you are offer-ing and brandishing so proudly? . . . Turn around and put Rangoni down between your thighs! . . . The greedy cunt has eaten your prick raw!' (189–90). In this re-presentation the female organ, elsewhere celebrated as the *vagina victrix et fulmina-trix* or *victrix et laureata concha*,[98] does indeed resume the active and dominant role that it had been granted in Secundus' epigram. It seems appropriate that Secundus' poem, or more precisely the two lines uttered at the Casanova dinner party, were placed as the tail-ornament to this dialogue (Fig. 9).

One consequence of Chorier's cult of the 'erudita', then, is that his 'female' char-acters, however much they are intended as embodiments of male fantasy, must be presented as thinking subjects rather than as genital mechanisms, as 'Oedipus' rather than 'cunnus'. The *Satyra* may be intended as a 'school of love', but its faculty do not remain woodenly didactic lay-figures. Their inventive wit gives them a con-siderable presence, independence, and authority, while the male characters—apart from the bisexual schoolmaster Vives—are conspicuously less well endowed. Tullia, Octavia, and Sempronia inhabit a fictitiously circumscribed sexual realm, as limited as pastoral or epic, but within the confines of that *boutique fantasque* they gain more and more control over the realities of phrase, perception, and event.

---

[97] VI. 172; note that Tullia adopts her initial submissiveness because another female authority-figure orders it (VI. 169).

[98] III. 46 ('victorious vagina sending out lightning bolts'), V. 80 ('victorious conch-shell crowned with laurel').

Chorier's book of sex embodies the same range of attitudes as his earlier writings, now lost but described in his memoirs: in the 1630s, in addition to the 'Sotadic' and 'Menippean' satires, he wrote an explicitly misogynistic treatise simply entitled *Woman*, whereas in the 1640s he published a *Philosophia honesti viri*, recommended by Sorel as *La Philosophie de l'honneste homme du Sieur Charier*.[99] On the misogynist side, the *Satyra* certainly functions as a *thesaurus* of all the features that render pornography disgusting—the mingling of prurience and disapproval, the fetishization of pain in delirious scenes of flagellation, the preposterous exaggeration of male potency. (Rangoni, whose sperm supposedly runs in a continuous stream, creates a more truthful picture when he protests that Tullia has eaten his entire penis: 'Give me back the one I lent you, you bad girl! The one you've given me isn't mine! I don't recognize it!' (VI. 183).) The grotesque defloration- and fellatio-scenes, with their disgust at the natural female anatomy, clearly express the theme of the earlier satire, 'the hatred that one should have towards women'.[100] But if this work is 'fundamentally anti-feminist',[101] as some critics have argued, it is not *securely* anti-feminist. On the contrary, odious statements are given to antagonistic speakers, revealing sexual politics as a contested area rather than an immutable condition, and framed by increasingly eloquent counter-arguments for *libertinage honnête*.

As the dialogues develop beyond the marital stage, the pursuit of *philosophia* and *honestas* leads to a higher evaluation of female sexuality, and generates an amused, free-floating, non-judgemental voice, delighted by the torrent of desire and the odd varieties of its expression—the voice of Petronius rather than Juvenal. As a *libertin honnête* Chorier enjoys and promotes the élite sexual freedom that 'Aloisia Sigea' allegedly exposes. His philosophy of dissimulation, his elaboration of a secret world behind a screen of respectability, likewise expresses a principle central both to the cult of *honnêteté* and to sophisticated libertinism: *intus ut placet, foris ut moris*; on the inside act according to pleasure, on the outside follow the conventions of society.[102] Tullia expresses her philosophy in a dictum so epigrammatic that the *Academie des dames*, which expands this section considerably, keeps it in the Latin ('Palam vive omnibus, clam et in tuto tibi'; live publicly for everyone, live secretly and safely for yourself).[103] 'Common usage' and 'civil life' are best maintained by keeping the veil in place, and cultivating pleasure in private.

Chorier's 'female' protagonists develop an urbane and ironic counter-ideology, a strategy of dissimulation and subversion that turns a world bound by the rules of sexual politics into a world of free play, where the political exists only as a trace that increases the piquancy of pleasure: 'imagine that everything is permitted and prohibited at the same time' (V. 111). Wifely obedience is now set in context. If 'the wife's

[99] *Adversaria*, iii. 31, 43, 63; Sorel cited in Leibacher-Ouvrard, 'Sexe, simulacre', 271 (the best study of Chorier's relation to *honnêteté*).

[100] *Adversaria*, iii. 31 ('Sermonem de odio habendis mulieribus, cui *Mulier* titulus fuit').

[101] Roger Thompson, *Unfit for Modest Ears* (1979), 33.

[102] The connection to Cremonini's motto (Ch. 2 n. 36 above) is made by Leibacher-Ouvrard, 'Transtextualité', 58, and Claude Reichler, *L'Âge libertin* (Paris, 1987), 22–3 (incorrectly ascribing the speech to the supposed author Aloisia Sigea).

[103] V. 113, and cf. *Academie*, i. 127.

supreme happiness depends on the judgement of her husband', if female virtue depends entirely on a reputation for chastity, if everyone in this Cartesian world goes 'larvata' or masked on the stage of society,[104] then she simply has to maintain a simulacrum of slavish marital devotion, reserving her freedom for the private sphere. At this point Tullia unveils the true maternal philosophy of Sempronia, the mother whom Octavia must obey in every respect: 'Every woman with a judicious mind should hold for certain that she was born for her husband's pleasures—and that all other men were born for hers.' Control of representation, control of metamorphosis, is the essential tactic not only in the bedroom but in society at large: 'Turn yourself into all the figures like Proteus, as your husband shall command'; thereby all other men can be your tools, and the wife can become 'the *artifex* of her own happiness'.[105] The principle of obedience, in which the sexual descriptions are fitted into a didactic and conventionally male-suprematist framework, turns into a principle of excess, as Sempronia and Tullia arrange all kinds of erotic theatre for their own pleasure, to the astonishment and then the delight of the newly initiated Octavia.

The mother-figure Sempronia controls not only the mechanics of sex, the 'invariable geometry' of what goes where with whom,[106] but also the definition of sexuality and the distribution of its various functions. Like Tullia and Vives after her she adopts the role of erotic preceptor, at a very early age recruiting the 14-year-old servant Jocondus as a performer in her sexual theatre (V. 104–16). At her prompting the precocious ephebe then penetrates the younger girls in her circle, including Tullia—a preparation that throws doubt on the painful defloration-scenes that we have already read. (The cycle of initiation continues when Jocondus applies his didactic skills to Tullia, using her for an anatomy lecture as Tullia would later use Octavia.) Jocondus is what Fanny Hill calls the servant-lad Will, 'a pretty piece of woman's meat';[107] for Fanny this is only a fleeting episode to be obliterated by the normative relationship with Charles, whereas for Sempronia Will is the Norm.

Chorier's libertine matriarch thus takes upon herself the sexual authority elsewhere assigned to the male seducer or to female anti-heroines like Pallavicino's bawd, *L'Escole*'s Susanne, or Laclos's Merteuil. In a later episode (V. 123–9) she marries Jocondus to a suitably naive wife, locking her into a chastity belt and forbidding him to sleep with her except as a strict husbandly duty, to beget offspring; he must keep all his fire for the mistress. She holds the key, literally and metaphorically, to the distinction between wifely-procreative-official sex and illicit-pleasurable-inventive sex—a distinction crucial to conventional morality, of course, and then firmly controlled by men. Vives attempts to regain control of this distinction in his lengthy initiation of Margarita, teaching her to alternate on command between outraged virtue and whorish invitation (VII. 296–9). In Sempronia's case, she enforces her

---

[104] V. 112–13, echoing Descartes's motto *larvatus prodere*.

[105] V. 113, 103; it is difficult to accept Cryle's conclusion that in Chorier 'Ars erotica is exercised submissively, within the space of the marriage bed' (*Geometry*, 24).

[106] Boucé, *Sexuality in Eighteenth-Century Britain*, p. x; for Sempronia's opposition to the 'geometrical' approach, see VII. 260.

[107] John Cleland, *Memoirs of a Woman of Pleasure*, ed. Peter Sabor (Oxford, 1999), 80.

instructions by an extra piece of trickery that multiplies the ironic reversals at a dizzying rate: as Valmont would later do with Cécile in *Les Liaisons dangereuses* (at Mme de Merteuil's request), she initiates the young fiancée into the joys of vigorous sex and teaches her all kinds of gestures and specialities, confident that this evidence of whorish expertise will so horrify the husband that he will be permanently repelled—and thus free to concentrate on precisely the same delights at the hands of his imperious mistress.

Chorier's Sempronia, part resentful parody and part tribute to the formative power of female authority, reminds us that mothers, governesses, and other figures *in loco matris* still wielded great influence over the social and sexual development of young men. (Chorier idealized his own 'brilliant and beautiful' mother, a gifted violinist who died at the age of 33.[108]) Aristocratic mothers indulged their sons' 'lascivious' side—Isabella d'Este signs off a letter to her son in the name of two women friends or servants who 'kiss and touch your thighs and that other part that gives us more pleasure'[109]—and provide opportunities for illicit or homosexual affairs, 'doing everything to make their boys attractive and giving them apartments with separate entrances'.[110] Mme de Sévigné counselled her son on the most intimate sexual matters—his treatment by Ninon de Lenclos, his impotence with a young actress—and ordered her son-in-law to regulate marital sex and plan future pregnancies to minimize the danger to her daughter.[111] In the French *congrès* or public impotence trials that Chorier undoubtedly knew, matrons gather round the bed during the attempted coupling, check on its progress, and handle the genitals of both sexes to determine what happened. Commentaries on these trials—attended by Sévigné in a spirit of unrestrained hilarity, as if she were watching a comedy—constantly evoke the figure of the mother-in-law, who violates decency by making sex public, renders her daughter 'incontinent', administers abortifacients, fabricates virginity, and intrudes into the sanctum of the marriage-bed, 'desirous of witnessing the conjugal act in her presence'.[112] Sempronia strongly resembles these intrusive, sexually expert mothers.

Even when the adolescent moved away from the maternal home, he could serve under a different female authority, a cultural rather than a biological matriarchy. The 14-year-old Wycherley, for example, was sent to be polished in Angoulême, where Julie de Montausier continued the tradition of the *salon* designed and directed by her mother Mme de Rambouillet; even in old age he recalls being 'often admitted to the Conversation of that most accomplish'd Lady', leaving him 'equally

---

[108] *Adversaria*, iii. 35 (shortly after he writes his misogynistic work *Woman*).

[109] Cited in Lionello Puppi, 'Immaginazione e immagini erotiche in Giulio Romano', *Eidos*, 9 (1991), 53.

[110] John M. Najemy, *Between Friends: Discourses of Power and Desire in the Machiavelli–Vettori Letters of 1513–1515* (Princeton, 1993), 319, paraphrasing Francesco Vettori.

[111] *Correspondance*, ed. Roger Duchêne (Paris, 1972), i. 210–11, 214–15, 227–8 (letters to Mme de Grignan, 8, 22 Apr. 1671).

[112] Pierre Darmon, *Le Tribunal de l'impuissance: Virilité et défaillances conjugales dans l'Ancienne France* (Paris, 1979), 104, 125–8, 176, 211, 214, 215–16, 218; Chorier's intimate enemy 'Tubero' was a son of Président Lamoignon, who campaigned to abolish the *congrès*.

pleased with the Beauty of her Mind, as with the Graces of her Person'—an indelible fusion of the erotic and the intellectual.[113] French women were assigned a crucial role in 'forming' the élite male, defining correct usage and inculcating taste, urbanity, charm, gallant fluency in conversation, sensitivity to the finer points of *amour*—everything that was ridiculed in rearguard attacks on the *précieuse*. *Honnêteté* and the 'honneste homme' were widely regarded as women's inventions, just as women were credited with transforming philosophy (Ch. 3, sect. 5 above): in 'modern' intellectual conversation, as in Chorier's dialogues, the austerely idealistic Socrates of Plato is replaced by a worldly, feminized 'Socratine', 'pedantic' abstraction by a 'seductive image' of truth and 'un esprit perspicace dans la recherche des plaisirs'.[114]

The unresolved question, which divided Mlle de Scudéry from Ninon de Lenclos and prompted anti-*précieux* satire was how far erotic, corporeal love entered into this requisite *galanterie* and *politesse*. Officially, an ostensibly feminist thinker like Poullain de La Barre insists that 'the Mind has no Sex', and yet he assumes that true civility can only be learned in the highly sexed 'Ecole des Dames' (Ch. 3, sect. 5 above); unofficially, a discreet affair with an experienced women was considered obligatory for 'entering the world', an essential stage to complete the 'self-perfecting' started by early reading in '*Aloysia*' (as Diderot assumes in his character of Sélim). This division mirrors the split in Chorier's earlier work, between 'Sotadic' sexuality (with a misogynistic subtext) and the 'philosophy of the *honnête homme*'. The *Satyra* itself, however, gradually brings these divergent tracks together.

We can trace this convergence in Chorier's evolving definition of *honestas* (honour, decency, respectability). At the outset of the *Satyra* Tullia merely brushes shame aside and sets convention on its head. In the mid-section, laying out the theory of dissimulation and the practice of covert adultery, *honestas* loses all intrinsic meaning and simply becomes the ability to be perceived as virtuous. But towards the end a less cynical counter-morality emerges, linking honour to freedom rather than chastity, stressing the legitimacy of pleasure, and finding 'true *honestas*' in sexual enlightenment. At one point in the Roman orgy, for example, the aristocrat La Tour proclaims that he and his three friends are *lascivi* but still *honesti*, that the brothel 'ought to be made honourable' and libido 'adorned' (*honestandi lupanaris, ornandae libidinis invenimus rationem*). Octavia suggests the oxymoron 'honourable brothel' (*honesta lupanar*) to define the pleasure-house where Tullia enjoys her encounter with these four noblemen, echoing La Tour's own claim to 'bring honour to the *lupanar*', but Tullia accepts only the first word—'inhonesti vocabuli maligne detorques significationem', for *lupanar* is associated with the vulgar crowd and with economic necessity.[115] By repudiating even this oxymoron she distances herself from Pallavicino's praise of the 'Puttana honorata' who gives in to pleasure without asking for money, from Le Petit's glowering address to 'Courtisanes d'honneur', and

---

[113] B. Eugene McCarthy, *William Wycherley: A Biography* (Athens, Oh., 1979), 24–5.

[114] Ian Maclean, *Woman Triumphant: Feminism in French Literature, 1610–1652* (Oxford, 1977), 146 (and cf. ch. 5 *passim*); Jacqueline Lichtenstein, *La Couleur éloquente* (Paris, 1989), 17–18, 20, 22, 33–6.

[115] VI. 196, and cf. V. 113, VI. 171, VII. 259, 272, 309 (Tullia calls herself 'honesta pellex' (i.e. *paelex*, concubine), but ironically).

from the entire tradition typified in Du Bellay's old courtesan, who recalls the era when her house was 'quasi comme une escolle ouverte | D'honnesteté'. Pallavicino's *Retorica* and *L'Escole des filles* had toyed with the idea that sexual pleasure might have its own 'honestà', or that mothers who grant their daughters freedom will 'make their *honesteté* shine forth with even greater *éclat*', but in a context of withering sarcasm.[116] Tullia and Octavia—if not their sly puppet-master Chorier—take these ideas seriously enough to rescue them from prostitution. In the most important initiation-narrative of Colloquium VII the erotic education of the future *honnête homme* is given full narrative weight.

Sempronia's sexual 'formation' of the pubescent Jocondus, awakening his *mens* and his *mentula* in a way that was supposedly the privilege of the male, is re-enacted in her daughter's seduction of Vives's favourite schoolboy Robertus, the modern Alcibiades. (Both boys encounter the *femme savante* at the threshold age of 14, like Sélim in Diderot's fiction and Wycherley in real life.[117]) Robertus provokes the longest single episode in Chorier's book—indeed the master-episode, since Octavia keeps returning to him in an otherwise fragmented dialogue—and the one that most resembles the respectable discourse of *honnêteté*.[118] The sexual details flow as profusely as ever, with an added pederastic emphasis on Robertus' ephebic youth and marmoreal buttocks, which Vives declares finer than those of Ganymede, Hylas, and Antinous, more satisfying to *erudita libido* than the breasts of Hebe (VII. 281). But the narrative mode has become self-consciously novelistic. Octavia establishes the tone with a detailed descriptive tableau in which she sits quietly sewing a silk bedspread, working on some figures that her mother has asked her to complete because she is 'an outstanding *artifex*', and Robertus materializes as if embroidered into her handiwork or conjured up by her half-sleeping thoughts.[119] The seduction is slow-moving, psychologically detailed, elevated by poetic and mythological ornament, enriched by lengthy dialogue, in marked contrast to the rapid-fire insertion and ejaculation that elsewhere represents successful copulation. The lovers are correspondingly tentative, deferential, introspective, and seemingly overtaken by their own emotions—not at all the jaded priapians of the orgy-scenes. These Robertus-scenes confirm Deleuze's intuition that higher-order 'pornology' transcends 'erotic language reduced to the elementary functions of command and description', but entirely refute his Sade-derived notion that it must also become abstractly violent and impersonal.[120]

---

[116] Pallavicino, *RP* 106, 22 (discussed in Ch. 2, sect. 1 above); Le Petit, cited Ch. 3, sect. 5 above; Du Bellay, cited Ch. 1 n. 13; *L'Escole*, 'Epistre invitatoire aux filles', p. XLVII.

[117] Cf. *Parliament of Women*, 31, and Sinistrari, *De Delictis et Poenis* (1700; Rome, 1754), 240–1: boys under 14 are exempt from punishment for sodomy (torture and death at the stake), unless they are especially cunning, while the 14–18 age group get a mitigated sentence.

[118] VII. 260–73, 280, 282–5; contrast Leibacher-Ouvrard's thesis that in Colloquium VII, 'mis à part un épisode exceptionnel où une femme initie un enfant à un amour tendre qui a la rareté de l'utopie, l'abjection domine dans ces micro-récits' ('Transtextualité, dissimulations et fonctions de l'obscène: La *Satyra Sotadica* de Chorier', 1992 MLA paper, 8).

[119] VII. 268 (dated 20 May); contrast the treatment of needlework (and mothers) in *Escole*, II. 61 and *Parliament of Women*, 31, Ch. 3, sect. 5 above.

[120] *Présentation de Sacher-Masoch*, 18, 22.

Robertus exemplifies the configuring power of his female preceptors. Sempronia selects and grooms him, awakens Octavia's interest in him by means of a letter, creates a script for him, designs his costumes, and sends him to Octavia as a present;[121] she then sets strict limits to his time and behaviour so as to preserve the boy's strength and heighten the pleasure of both partners. His mother Manilia (the sister of Octavia's nurse) delivers him in a ceremony of manumission, undresses him, advises the lovers, and guides them with her hands in the act itself. Octavia takes him through the steps that lead to the *summum bonum*, sometimes playing with the command-language that her husband had used on her, sometimes assuming the tone of the primary-school teacher questioning each gesture ('What are you looking for under there?' 'What are you hoping to do with that charming thing?') and so defining and inciting each new stage of arousal. It is now the women who sing the song of triumph from the *Ars Amatoria*, and the boy who is 'wounded' or painfully deflowered as his foreskin tears away.[122] Like the beautiful but potent youths selected and 'carved' by Juvenal's Roman matrons, or the statue fashioned for the princess in *L'Escole des filles*, Robertus performs 'active' penetration but in every other respect obeys his mistress's commands passively. Like Pallavicino's courtesan, but for quite different purposes, he 'conforms to the idea of Cupid' (*RP* 93). Like the 'Boy' in Jonson's *Epicoene* he passes easily into female space, there to be fondled and dressed in clothes of either sex.

Robertus enters like a masquer or an erotic-mythological figure brought to life by a female Pygmalion, a living embodiment of the primacy of figuration. As Lise Leibacher-Ouvrard puts it, in these scenes reality and representation, word and action, 'fantasm' and 'sensation', adsorb each other in a slow waltz, dissolving any 'principle of priority'.[123] On his first visit he is dressed as Diana and indistinguishable from a woman, while for the consummation-scene he becomes Amor himself, complete with wings and a quiver. The Diana costume would recall Jove's seduction of Callisto in that guise, vividly rendered by the School of Fontainebleau (Fig. 10)—a *femme* conception of the transformed deity that made it easier to imagine a couple like Tullia and Octavia in the first place.[124] Robertus' entry as the winged Cupid, while Octavia is lost in her own thoughts unaware of what is about to happen—gains an added *frisson* from its parody of the Annunciation.[125] The Amor-and-Psyche scenario again evokes graphic images produced and circulated in Chorier's France: Fig. 11, by Claude Mellan after Simon Vouet, shares Octavia's frank enjoyment of the juvenile body with its minuscule penis, and like Chorier himself reinterprets antique and Renaissance eroticism through modern expressive means, experimental foreshortening and chiaroscuro.

---

[121] As Rochester, in real life, sent his French page with a commendatory cover-letter (Ch. 6 n. 50 below).

[122] VII. 268–70 (cf. V. 86), 272; the painful breaking of the *frenulum* or ligament holding the prepuce, a feature strangely absent from male-authored sexology, is vividly represented in Jane Sharp, *The Midwives Book, or The Whole Art of Midwifry Discovered*, ed. Elaine Hobby (New York, 1999), 23–4, 28.

[123] 'Sexe, simulacre', 274–5.

[124] When Queen Christina appeared as Diana in one of her own masques it provoked off-colour jokes punning on 'Cephal[l]us' (according to Åkerman, *Christina*, 145, 299).

[125] I am grateful to Martha Pollak for suggesting this interpretation.

10. Pierre Milan after Primaticcio, *Jove Seduces Callisto in the Guise of Diana*

Surrounded by darkness, Vouet's and Chorier's heroines both expect a monster and find an ephebe.

These conceits are sustained both in the lovers' dialogue and in Octavia's narrative recreation. Robertus is 'a work fashioned by Venus and the Graces', and to imagine their embraces Tullia should 'think of Psyche's night with Cupid; such was mine with Robertus. I am the Soul to him, he is Love to me' (VII. 261, 271). He forms himself into *figurae Veneris*, but he has also been formed by them. Though he is a virgin, he explains that he knows about lovemaking from having seen 'paintings of the play-acting of Venus'. Now *he* is ready to play his part in the 'fabula' prepared by his mentors (264), literally assuming the costumes and the postures they dictate. Like the lovers envisaged in the *Priapeia*, who faithfully perform the images created by Elephantis, he will 'bring forth actions to match the pictures' (270). On the brink of his initiation, then, he finds himself in exactly the same position as Casanova: each has been instructed by an earlier depiction, Robertus by his paintings and masque rehearsals, Casanova by his own source of 'theory'—this very text.

Chorier's Robertus embodies all the ambiguity and allure of the ephebe, the 'Epicoene', the pleasure-thesaurus, the 'Ganymede' of unfixed gender and 'ambiguous face'. Octavia explicitly introduces him as an '*ephebus* whose form you would prefer even to Apollo's' (VII. 261). Like Rocco's Alcibiade (Ch. 2, sect. 2 above) Robertus is equally adored by 'girls' and 'scholars', and like Alcibiade he is equated with Diana as well as Ganymede. He represents the desirable side of the *adolescens*—a term that in Chorier denotes both the callowness of youth, ignorant and fearful of female anatomy, and the *jeunesse dorée*: Joannes Meursius, for example, created his

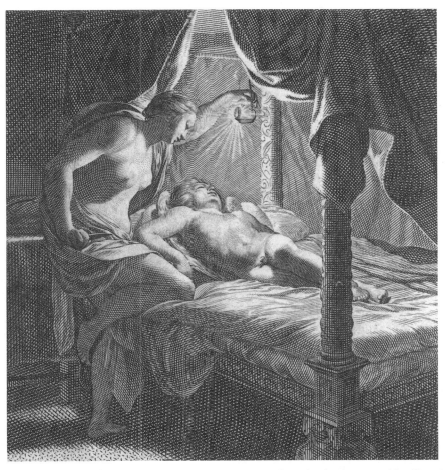

11. Claude Mellan after Simon Vouet, *Psyche Contemplates the Sleeping Amor* (detail)

brilliant translation when he was 'an adolescent, scarcely beyond the ephebe stage' (*adolescens et vix ex ephebo egressus*, 2). Like Shakespeare's Ganymede-Rosalind or Viola, he passes as an active young man and a physically convincing woman, provoking homo- and heterosexual desire in noblemen and ladies alike. Metamorphosed into Diana he provides an alibi for Octavia, who describes the affair to her female friends as lesbian rather than heterosexual; spurred to creative deception, she invents new words ('her' vulva is a *cunniculum*) and new myths, 'Sappho wrestling with Andromeda'.[126] Robertus' appeal lies precisely in his plasticity. Vives worships him as a 'Ganymede' from Renaissance sculpture (281), and Octavia as an artistic *opus* 'modelled' by Venus herself—which prompts us to recall earlier scenes

[125] 285–6 (selecting 'Andromeda' from her list of Sappho's girlfriends, II. 38).

in which the same artefactual qualities were brought to the fore, for example when she dwells on the passive beauty of her sleeping husband, like 'a marble statue' (V. 102). If Robertus' attempted seduction by Vives echoes *L'Alcibiade fanciullo a scola*, then his adoption as Octavia's plaything recalls Sinistrari's case history of the noblewoman who kept her own *ephebus* as a sex toy (Ch. 2 n. 63 above)—but with one significant exception. As we have seen in the lesbian episodes, Chorier never hints at physical hypertrophy: it is Octavia's great spirit, not her giant clitoris, that achieves what Vives attempts in vain.

The amours of Robertus and Octavia make a pointed contrast to the hyper-masculinism that largely dominated the marital dialogues and that recurs intermittently throughout the later parts. Chorier certainly invests in the devices that would later come to dominate pornography and obscene satire—savage penetrations repeated nine times a day, ever larger *mentulae* (up to 14″ × 7″), neurotic descriptions of the yawning chasms of women.[127] But a thread of scepticism always runs through Tullia's and Octavia's discussion of these prodigies. The over-large penis is reported to be uncomfortable rather than exciting (V. 110). Abject representations of female genitalia are given to absurd figures like Chrysogonus the Stoic or Prince John of Portugal, known as 'the prince of masturbators'—who maintains that the best possible vagina is the one made by his own hand (VII. 259). Tullia's hands-on instruction, we recall, inspired Octavia to feel with Comenian vividness that she can 'see everything hidden in the depths of my viscera, as if it were placed before my eyes' (sect. 1 above). In pointed opposition, misogynist complaints about women and their organs are ascribed to *inadequate* visualization. Male accounts of vast vaginas and insatiable 'learned' women are satirized as the misconception of 'ridiculous adolescents' who guess at women's interiors from glimpses of the exterior (III. 43). These ignorant boys—the word is in fact the comparative *adolescentiores*, meaning more immature or more callow than average—infer the invisible truths of female sexuality from what they never manage to witness vividly, and fill in the blanks with their own fears and prejudices. No *viva autopsia* for them, no erotic-didactic speculum, no fusion of flesh and affect—only the absurdity of empty speculation.

Tullia even confronts the obsessive focus on genital size, and dismisses the search for physical rules and proportions as fit only for 'Geometers of Love'. She insists that the genitals are perfectly adaptable to each other (or more accurately, that *women's* can stretch to accommodate any size), while Octavia assures her (and the male reader) that size is irrelevant to the individualizing experience of love: 'The penis that pleases the lover and the beloved is long and thick enough; . . . I would rather have a little pin pushed into my vessel by a friend, than a beam-like club by anyone else.'[128] It is to corroborate this principle, in fact, that Octavia first narrates her experiences with Robertus (6″ × 1″)—a narrative that Tullia finds exceptionally arousing because it extracts the maximum pleasure from a trifling object: *Mira es*

---

[127] Parodied in III. 47, where Octavia assumes an exaggerated horror at Tullia's chasm, wide enough to swallow Quintus Curtius *and* his horse, greatly to Tullia's amusement.

[128] VII. 260–1; cf. *Escole*, II. 110–11 ('quand un homme que l'on ayme bien n'en auroit pas plus gros que le petit doigt, on le trouveroit meilleur que le plus grand d'un autre qu'on n'aimeroit pas tant').

nugarum artifex; 'you are a wonderful creator of trifles' (VII. 261, 270). In the fluid, polymorphous configuration made possible by epheberasty, Secundus' paradox is further complicated because each sex is simultaneously 'slave' and 'queen'—as Robertus and Octavia declare they are to each other (267, 284).

In what must be a deliberate contrast, before their own long-drawn-out consummation Robertus and Octavia watch a very different copulation-scene featuring the flagellating monk and Stoic Theodorus:

> He pushes his huge phallus into her secret insides. 'You're killing me, you torturer', shouts Eleanor. He was offering eager jerking movements; soon his catapult exploded. 'That isn't making love (*Venerem exercere*)', she says, 'but the most wretched laceration. You put death into my body.' (VII. 265)

At times it seems that Chorier has upheld one half of Comenius' motto ('let everything flow spontaneously') but forgotten the part about banishing violence; here both principles fall into place. In this contrast of episodes libertine fiction faces a clear choice: the minimal brutal mode of later pornography—associated with the hypocrisy and repression attacked everywhere in Colloquium VII—or the elaborate and refined eroticism of pornologic romance, the forming-ground of *honnêteté* and the precursor of the 'novel of worldliness'. One is clearly associated with 'the light of life', the other 'puts death into the body'.

The brilliant discussion of postures and mental images in Colloquium VI is inspired, quite explicitly, by the desire to banish the thought of death—one of Tullia's Italian lovers has assassinated her favourite La Tour—and throughout the final dialogue episodes of mortification and vivification are suspended together in formal symmetry. Two sisters emerge from their wedding night simultaneously, one bursting with enthusiasm, the other nauseated and 'near death'.[129] In an episode almost worthy of Marguerite de Navarre or Mme de Lafayette, Clementia goes through the kind of agonizing crisis that *The Whores Rhetorick* merely fakes; by refusing her former lover in disgust and holding true to what she considers her 'true self', she causes both of them to die miserably (305–8). (Tullia declares her a 'heroine', but Octavia condemns her as a 'Stoic'.) In another historical narrative that darkens the closing pages, the furious duc de Châteaubriand murders his wife to punish her affair with King François I, prompting further gloomy reflections on adultery and suicide (309–11). Though Chorier's text as a whole remains fragmented and inconclusive, the preference in these contrasting narratives of life and death clearly goes to the sunlit eroticism of the salty conversations, the lesbian episodes, and the seduction of Robertus, played out in a private sensuous world where woman is the controlling power: in erototopia rather than pornotopia.

Libertine discourse thus speaks with contradictory voices when it tries to encompass the 'philosophy of the *honnête homme*'. The central movement of Chorier's book seems to be the expansion and dissolution of its own premises, the shift towards the cerebral and the figural, the principle of metamorphosis and

---

[129] VII. 233–5 (perhaps parodying the gruesome symptoms of lost virginity in medical writers like Duval, cited in Darmon, *Tribunal de l'impuissance*, 169–70).

excess. Reaching for whatever will elude the 'grovelling' multitude and the 'malignity' of those who despise education, he creates an improbable combination of refined *sensibilité* and 'absolute' sexual extremity, *préciosité* and *libertinage*. The *Satyra* certainly remains divided in its treatment of gender relations. For much of the text woman remains an adjunct of masculine desire, abject matter or 'mud' to be modelled into a *cunnus* by the hands of the Promethean author. Even the pseudo-female and pseudo-philosophical heroine defines woman as a physically disgusting 'chamber-pot' who can only be redeemed by a 'mind' inculcated by the male author, a 'mind' devoted to confirming the claustrophobic enclosure of woman within the private realm of sex.

On the other hand, woman is the deflator of phallic pretension, the ruler of representation, the source of *honnêteté*, and the fashioner of identity. Sempronia, Tullia, and Octavia function as did their contemporaries in the French *beau monde*, to 'form' their young initiates under the erotic authority of a female mentor; in this respect Chorier is closer to Diderot or Crébillon than to Aretino. And from these scenes of mingled ecstasy and socialization he derives the moral, apparently without irony, that here 'women lead and Nature makes men follow', that a love affair with a beautiful woman teaches more than Plato ever could, that here the young man learns not only pleasure but *veram honestatem* (VII. 282–3). This model of initiation-into-*honnêteté*, where women take the lead, fashions male identity just as fully as the gross priapic masculinism that flourishes in the earlier dialogues. Robertus exclaims after the first embrace that 'I have entered life', and Sempronia confirms that 'you have been made a man' (VII. 272).

PART II

Libertine Canonization:
Reception-History and the Erotics of Literary Response

Early Responses to
L'Escole des filles

Pepys, Wycherley, and Traces of Molière

After dinner, we into our dining-room and there to singing all the afternoon
(by the way, I must remember that Pegg Pen was brought to bed yesterday
of a girl; and among other things, if I have not already set it down, that hardly
ever was remembered such a season as this for the smallpox as these last
two months have been, people being seen all up and down the streets,
newly come out after the smallpox; but though they sang fine things, yet I
must confess that I did take no pleasure in it. . . . We sang till almost night,
and drank my good store of wine; and then they parted and I to my chamber,
where I did read through *L'eschole des Filles*; a lewd book, but what doth me
no wrong to read for information sake (but it did hazer my primick para
stand all the while, and una vez to decharger); and after I had done it, I
burned it, that it might not be among my books to my shame; and so at night to
supper and then to bed.

(Samuel Pepys, diary for Sunday, 9 February 1668)

MRS DAINTY. Who, by his breeding, wou'd think he had ever been in *France*?
LADY FIDGET. Foh, he's but too much a French fellow . . . pray, let's be gone.
HORNER. You do well, Madam, for I have nothing that you came for: I have brought over
    not so much as a Bawdy Picture, new Postures, nor the second Part of the *Escole de Filles*;
    Nor——
QUACK [apart to Horner]. Hold for shame, Sir; what d'ye mean? you'l ruine your self for
    ever with the Sex——
SIR JASPAR. Hah, hah, hah, he hates Women perfectly I find.

(William Wycherley, *The Country-Wife*, I. i. 251)

PART I established the parameters of the erotic-education trope—a 'discipline
born in the blood' or imported from books? an 'Academy for Ladies' or a covert self-
fashioning device for men?—and then explored the core Italian, French, and Latin
texts of what would later be classified as 'libertine literature' or 'the invention of
pornography'. Part II will go further into the reception, dissemination, translation,
and canonization of this hard-core curriculum. I will concentrate more on the
richly documented English readership, but I also analyse successive versions of

L'Academie des dames and *Vénus dans le cloître*, influential in France as well as England. In these case studies of dramatic impersonation, aestheticized transgression, and erotic poetics, and again in my final look at the afterlife of seventeenth-century libertine discourse, I will briefly implicate more canonical figures of French literature: Molière, Pascal, even Baudelaire.

In Chapter 5, building on the two well-known cases that supply my double epigraph, I will examine not only how the libertine canon was received but how citing the 'womanizing' text constructs a kind of man. Ostensibly, the subject is female. *L'Escole* shows the 'opening' of Fanchon's mind and vulva; Chorier represents the didactic transformation of the young Octavia into a *femme savante libertine* like the mentor Tullia or the author Aloisia Sigea. But the text arouses the male reader to 'inform' or 'perfect' *himself*. This mirroring becomes explicit in the crowning episode of Chorier's last dialogue, as we have just seen in Chapter 4: the academically gifted and exquisitely sensitive adolescent 'becomes a man' in Octavia's bed, and thereby becomes a model for the schoolboy reader and a double of the translator/co-author Meursius, the brilliant Latinist who expanded upon Aloisia while still himself an *ephebe*.

Reading between the lines of my selected authors, I contextualize and unpack their libertine allusions to show what sort of man they represent to their audiences. Pepys becomes the 'sober man' and ideal householder who nevertheless forges his most intense sexual bond with *L'Escole des filles*, who 'informs himself' in that domestic-libertine fantasy while informing on his private desires. The dramatist Wycherley creates the artificial man Horner, the self-proclaimed 'Machiavelli' who pursues pleasure with the same assiduity that his cuckold-rivals apply to 'business'. Horner fancies himself a representative of that 'quicksighted philosophical age' when whoring becomes a science, and his opening attack on those who 'force Nature' aligns him with Comenian education.[1] But his nature is equally forced by the libertine texts and conventions he embodies. Wycherley uses Horner's brazen mention of *L'Escole* to fabricate an 'effigy' of the eunuch lost in mere sterile representation, 'ruining him self' in public as a cover for future conquests (almost equally sterile, as I will argue). Since the playwright was himself 'formed' in the French *salon*, and since Horner plays so heavily on his 'filthy' French experiences, I read his libertine 'imports' as an episode in Anglo-French literary relations, ending by placing him between the clandestine *Escole des filles* and Molière's two comedies of a similar name, *L'École des maris* and *L'École des femmes*.

We have seen throughout this study that the fascination with women's sexual education diverts attention from the constructedness of masculinity, the open secret that Montaigne articulates and mystifies when he separates male book-learning from female instinct. Only in Chorier's final dialogue can the pederastic-formative scenario be fully reclaimed for heterosexuality ('you have been made a man') and then only in fragmented episodes. Men fashion or (in Pepys's word) 'inform' their

---

[1] Introd. n. 66, Ch. 1, sect. 2 above.

own identities as they fabricate unsettling images of women teaching women. The didactic pretext embodied in the title *L'Escole des filles* and continued in successive translations—*The School of Venus, L'Academie des dames, The School of Love*—conceals a dialectic of emulation and rejection that runs throughout the new canon and its critical reception-history. Certainly these representations intend to discipline what Montaigne called the 'discipline born in the bloodstream', the allegedly natural sexual knowledge that women 'engender' (though it seems to require a library of artificial books). We shall see in Chapter 6 that aggression as well as admiration increases when the critic swallows Chorier's fiction of female authorship and promotes Aloisia Sigea to the position of Professor Emerita. But the real subject taught in the Girls' School is male dependency on instruction. Given the all-pervasive desire to turn the libertine text into a voluptuary 'school', and given the underlying need to represent the 'making of a man' in female disguise, we might expect to find links between the eroto-didactic topos and the institutions of boy's education. How appropriate, then, that the first mention of the English *School of Venus*, the earliest English records of Chorier, and the clearest evidence for belief in the authenticity of Sigea's authorship should come quite literally from boys' schools.[2]

Moving from Pepys in 1668 to Wycherley in 1675 allows us to glimpse, not only the personal processes of 'becoming a man' and 'ruining the self', but the cultural context in which the trope of erotic 'schooling' could be received. Before my close reading of Pepys, then, I will briefly reconstruct the English reception-history of *L'Escole des filles* and its translation *The School of Venus*, significantly subtitled 'the Ladies' Delight Reduced into Rules of Practice'. As I have argued throughout this book, pornography could not be marketed as conduct literature unless the institutions of women's education were already eroticized. Pepys's successive reactions to *L'Escole* ('the French book which I did think to have had for my wife to translate') will be read against libertine (per)versions of the boarding school and the reading lesson, amplifying the paradigmatic scene of curriculum-building that I have already cited from *The Parliament of Women*. Feminists of the period recognized the ideological effect of these fabrications, confining women in a space that leaves 'no room for any other Subject or Object' (Margaret Cavendish), or 'breeding them up in *Venus* School' (Sarah Fyge). The poet and novelist Jane Barker complains that salacious literature has created 'an Inlet to that Deluge of Libertinism which has overflow'd the Age', anticipating that her own attempt to revive the romance of 'Heroick Love' will be attacked 'for confining the Subject to such strict Rules of Virtue and Honour';[3] *L'Escole des filles* and *The School of Venus* prove, however, that libertinism itself proposes 'rules' just as 'confining'. Cavendish teaches in her Female Academy that these 'Rules of Practice' define the male rather than the female mind, that the 'Subject' they confine should more accurately be enrolled in The School of Men.

---

[2] For details, see Ch. 6 n. 3 below.

[3] Introduction to *Exilius, or The Ban'sh'd Roman* (1725), fo. A2-ᵛ, probably written by 1688 (n. 7 below).

1. PEPYS'S SCHOOL OF VENUS

Pepys's autoerotic encounter with *L'Escole des filles* furnishes the starting point for studying the dissemination of libertine literature, not only because of its early date and transparent-seeming diary form, but also because it embodies the dual focus typical of the eroto-didactic project. Which sex is in question here? Does the schooling text confine 'girls' to the rules of masculine pleasure, or vice versa? Pepys devours a book called 'the School for Girls' in the midst of a life story obsessed with *filles* of every kind, heterosexual in the sense that he is constantly handling the different 'things' of maids, actresses, and married women; and yet his account of reading *L'Escole* concentrates entirely on himself, on the condition of his *primick* and the goal of 'informing himself'. Whether in the diary or in prose fiction, does writing sex refer to a closed realm of fantasy or to potential 'Rules of Practice'? Does it take place in pornotopia or 'in the wickedness of the world'? The *Escole* passage seems to belong in both locations, expressing a solitary, insular privacy and yet famously enmeshed in quotidian reality; Pepys's hard-core moment is juxtaposed by association and parenthetical memory to the material substratum of the body (Peg Penn's childbirth, an epidemic of smallpox) and to the cultural activities of the Restoration *bon bourgeois* family, where the host makes music all afternoon but 'confesses' to feel no pleasure, the 'sober man' drinks his good store of wine, and the bedroom fire illuminates, then destroys, this new candidate for inclusion in the Pepys Library. As we shall see, the associations of this 'idle roguish book . . . worse than *putana errante*' reach out into every part of Pepys's existence: his anxieties about affairs of state, his inability to 'school' his own wife and servants, his obsession with young female subordinates whom he could classify as *filles*.

The English reception-history of *L'Escole des filles* (as Pepys and Wycherley suggest) brings into focus another duplicity of this lubricious book—its capacity to slip between the extremes of public and private, even to confound their polarity. *L'Escole* was simultaneously prosecuted to extinction and flaunted in the most public places. Though Pepys consumed his copy in intense seclusion (and tossed it into the fire after a single reading), he bought it in a conspicuous and crowded bookshop, in the Strand near the New Exchange. Not a single copy of any translation has survived— we have only the fragments considered scandalous enough to transcribe into indictments—and yet we can trace *L'Escole*'s passage through English culture by copious allusions on stage, in books, and even in newspaper advertisements. (We learn, for example, that as late as 1744 Grub Street recycled the 1680 translation of *L'Escole des filles* with engravings 'after the Manner of Aratine'.[4]) Even the prosecution documents reveal the book's ubiquity; the Stationers' secret agent was able to buy *The School of Venus* in Tower Hill, 'Leaster feilds', Pall Mall, The Temple, and Westminster Hall (Foxon, plate I). John Hoyle, the bisexual friend of Aphra Behn, felt no Pepysian inhibitions about including *L'Escole* 'among his books'; in Hoyle's library, meticulously listed in a printed auction catalogue, one could find virtually

---

[4] Advertisement reproduced in Foxon, 3.

the entire libertine canon that now must be read in the 'Private Case'—Aretino's *Ragionamenti* and Chorier's *Satyra Sotadica*, *L'Escole des filles* and *Vénus dans le cloître*, alongside the *satyrique* poets, memoirists, and medical writers who form their context.[5]

On both sides of the English Channel, the concrete evidence shows only *men* buying and deploying this ostensibly female-voiced book, enjoying it in autoerotic solitude (as in the instance of Pepys) or inserting it into women's houses to transform them into 'The School of Venus or the Ladies Delight'. (In Chapter 3 I discussed cases involving the disgraced minister Fouquet, the maids-in-waiting at the French Court, and a provincial nunnery infiltrated by libertine monks.) Literary allusions to *L'Escole*, in contrast, try to persuade us that women are the principal consumers, that it is women who turn text into *praxis* or (in John Dunton's words) 'leave the *School of Vertue* for the *School of Venus*'.[6] These imaginary reception-scenes stage a public exposure of women's secret desires and covert activities, evidently sexualizing their increased participation in education and literary culture. In a single year (1688) one publisher of *The School of Venus*, Benjamin Crayle, also brought out Jane Barker's *Poetical Recreations* and prepared her romance for publication, as if responding to a new appetite for 'authentic' women's writing; ignoring, or rather confirming, her complaint about the 'Deluge of Libertinism', he mixes Barker's genuine poems with an anthology of indecent and at times quasi-pornographic verse.[7]

In the 1684 *Parliament of Women* the new (mock)assembly of autonomous women enshrine '*L'Eschole de fils*' in their national curriculum alongside Aretino and Chorier. In *Erotopolis, or A New Description of Bettyland* (also 1684), the 'shepherdesses' develop a reading-list of canonical 'classics' that equates the lewd book with fashionable female-authored novels as well as with lower-class romances: '*Ibrahim Bassa*' and '*Grand Cyrus*'—by the prestigious Madeleine de Scudéry—mingle with '*Amadis de Gaulle*, *Hero and Leander*, *The School of Venus*, and the rest of those classick Authors, by which they are mightily improv'd both in Practice and Discourse' (59–60). This satire on female 'improvement' ('reduced into Rules of Practice' as the *School of Venus* itself promises) picks up a theme already sounded in the theatre. In John Learnerd's *Rambling Justice* the gullible country squire, left alone in a lady's 'Chamber', discovers '*Lescholle de Files*', a pretty French book' and other hard-core texts in her 'Study'—falling into a trap laid by the witty heroine, who reverses the strategy of *La retorica delle puttane* by posing as a courtesan; though she remains technically virtuous, the dramatist still assumes that she knows

---

[5] BL SC 1036 (10), *Bibliotheca Hoyleane, sive Catalogus . . . Librorum* (1692), esp. pp. 4 and 7; Roger Thompson's table in *Unfit for Modest Ears* (1979), 203–5, shows another five acknowledged copies of *L'Escole* in library catalogues.

[6] *Letters Written from New-England, A.D. 1686*, ed. W. H. Whitmore (Boston, 1867), 113.

[7] Foxon, 11; Barker, *Poetical Recreations* (1688), ii. 32 (cited Ch. 8 n. 39 below), 95–7, 142 ff., 219 ff. (explicitly sexual passages translated from Ovid, Lucretius, and Cornelius Gallus). For Crayle's plan to publish Barker's romance *Scipina* (probably the text I cite in n. 3 above), see Carol Barash, *English Women's Poetry, 1649–1714: Politics, Community, and Linguistic Authority* (Oxford, 1996), 196; Kathryn R. King, *The Poems of Jane Barker: The Magdalen Manuscript* (Oxford, 1998), 20, speculates about 'amorous' and pharmaceutical relations with Crayle.

the book and can procure it as her bait.[8] Wycherley's Horner initiates this allusion-game when he taunts the pseudo-respectable City ladies by naming 'the second Part of the *Escole de Filles*': *their* expertise in the forbidden text—their knowing enough to be shocked—reveals the secret concupiscence that the rest of the play will prove, but *his* expertise suggests the impotence and misogyny underlying his expropriation of female sexuality. The would-be libertine might *wish* to find *L'Escole des filles* and *Annotations upon Aretines Postures* in the intimate space of a willing woman's study, but the man who mentions such texts in mixed company actually shatters decorum and proves that 'he hates Women perfectly'.

Pepys's response to *L'Escole des filles*, in the context of the events and concerns recorded in the diary that year, epitomizes the tendency to convert historic initiatives in women's education into 'pornographic' fantasies of absolute sexual abandon. As Margaret Cavendish realized, the male imagination hollows out the Female Academy and replaces it with a space entirely filled by (its own) thoughts of sex, leaving 'no room for any other Subject'. The desire to define all female education as 'Venus' School' spread far beyond the confines of the French erotic dialogue. As we saw in Chapter 3, the scenes of reading and curriculum-planning in *The Parliament of Women* project the pornotropic vision into the English boarding school, the native equivalent of the Continental convent that generations of writers had imagined as a pressure-cooker of 'ingenious lust' and female 'Sodomy'. The London girls' school represented the height of the 'educational revolution'[9] achieved by English-women, but hostile critics never tired of citing it as living proof of their failure. For Richard Flecknoe the 'School of young Gentlewomen' can only create work for the midwife (Ch. 1 n. 113 above). For the *Tatler* generations later, the quickest way to demolish Mary Astell's plan for a secular-intellectual convent is to jeer at the sensual and materialist stamp that ladies receive in 'boarding school' (Number 32), a place where girls read *Aristotle's Problems* instead of true morality (Number 68, perhaps by Swift).

    Though none was as grand as Mme de Maintenon's Saint-Cyr, the girls' schools around London constituted important centres of cultural formation: in Tottenham Bathsua Makin revived the intellectual education of the Renaissance humanist; in Chelsea pupils and staff mounted performances of Purcell's *Dido* and Blow's *Venus and Adonis*, a meta-didactic event since that opera interrupts its tragic business to show the schoolmistress Venus giving a spelling lesson to a class of Cupids.[10] On a less heroic plane, schools in Bow and Hackney offered the middling classes 'accomplishments' that would improve their chances in the labour- and marriage-markets, though they could also generate problematic liaisons outside parental

---

[8] Cited Introd. n. 82 above.

[9] Peter Earle, 'The Female Labour Market in London in the Late Seventeenth and Early Eighteenth Centuries', *Economic History Review*, 2nd ser. 42 (1989), 334 (summarizing David Cressy).

[10] Tercentenary Edition, ed. Anthony Lewis (Monaco, 1949), 57–65. For other operas produced in girl's boarding schools see James Anderson Winn, *'When Beauty Fires the Blood': Love and the Arts in the Age of Dryden* (Ann Arbor, 1992), 224.

control.[11] Pepys, in contrast, focuses his most intense sexual infatuation on a school-girl from Bow, and regards Chelsea and Hackney as venues for erotic spectacle; the genteel village of Hackney became his favourite destination, and 'that which we went chiefly to see was the young ladies of the schools, whereof there is great store, very pretty'.[12]

The libertine and bawdy discourse of Pepys's England levels the high-cultural as-pirations of the girls' school by subjecting it, literally, to *pornographia*; associations with prostitution mean that 'sexing' the establishment also declasses it. The 'English Rogue' in Richard Head's picaresque novel goes straight from the bawdy house to the girls' school (disguised as a *fille de chambre*), and this infiltration provokes his most explicit and effusive eroticism.[13] (Like Chorier's Colloquium VII and the attack on Astellian education in *Tatler* 32, *The English Rogue* revives the Boccaccian fantasy of the young priapist who gains free run of the convent, broaching the quin-tessential women's space.) The 'London Jilt' began her career at boarding school, where her ambitious parents sent her to learn refinements rather than useful skills, thereby ensuring that she would be 'brought up in some sort of Libertinism'.[14] The 'Exchange-Wench' is supposedly 'educated at 11 or 12 in Hackney'—a pun that links the respectable girls' school, the horse for hire, and the whore.[15] Girls' schools are ex-plicitly presented as training-grounds for prostitution in *Erotopolis* (the same text that defines the classics of female 'improvement' as Scudéry and *The School of Venus*); since they fail to teach young women the traditional women's arts of house-hold management, the libertine-conservative narrator explains, 'as soon as they come out of these places, they presently travel into *Betty-land*, and never more return into their own Country' (151–2). The generic name 'Bettyland' signifies at once the nation of serving maids and the land of whores, as if *filles de chambre* and *filles de joie* were interchangable. Entering the subculture of illicit sexuality via the 'école des filles' involves a kind of exile, a total loss of social identity—a cruelly real-istic version of what Fanchon celebrates with naive glee, declaring that she feels like 'another person' after losing her virginity (*Escole*, II. 62). Even the most rudimentary opportunities for professional training—apprenticeship to a luxury trade, pupil-lage with a midwife, Lady Davenant's Nursery for young actresses—must be stuck with the label 'Bawd' or 'Punk', and conversely the brothel becomes a 'School of Venus' and Billingsgate a 'Seminary'.[16] Whoring, schooling, and fishwife obscenity merge into one vast *double entendre* that can only mean one thing.

A symmetry thus develops between the travesty of education, tainted by reduc-ing it to prostitution, and the mock-heroic whore-biography, which presents her initiation as an elaborate education. A mock-epitaph from the 1650s calls the dedicated whore 'the sucking School-mistresse of Love', strangely combining the

---

[11] Earle, *The Making of the English Middle Class: Business, Society and Family Life in London, 1660–1730* (1989), 186–7.

[12] 21 Apr. 1667, and cf. 22 Mar. 1663; see Abbreviations above for edn. cited.

[13] *The English Rogue Described* (1565), 1st pagination, pp. 95–9 (fos. G8–H2).

[14] *The London Jilt* (1683), 2.   [15] *The Character of an Exchange-Wench* (1675), 3.

[16] Ibid., *passim*; Dryden, *Mac Flecknoe*, lines 70–8 (*Works*, ii. 56); Edward Ward, *The Rambling Rakes, or London Libertines* (1700), 4. For the phrase 'school of Venus', see Introd. n. 19 above.

attributes of milky infancy and magisterial authority.[17] In *The Practical Part of Love* (1660), the pornodidactic theme begun in the 'University of Love' (Ch. 1, sect. 3 above) continues when the bawd-teacher Ventricia brings back the latest technology from London and sets up a school of illicit pleasure ('they call it a Dildo, and I must shew you what kind of Physick it is, and how to use it', 60). Following this, Helena takes a kind of contemplative retirement to complete her studies, like Milton's years at Horton; 'considering onely what her Mother and her Tutresse (not bountiful Nature) had designed her,' she 'applied herself wholly to the *Cyprian* Language and Customes' (63). The same words ('Tutoress', 'Doctress') are used for the genuine accomplishments of women intellectuals[18] and for the secret arts of the bawd or 'Mother Midnight'.

In pornotopia, the 'room' where men learn to imagine women learning sex, 'improvement' is both evoked and parodied. Boarding-school pupils organize tutorials on *L'Escole des filles* with their French mistresses and commission translations of 'Aloisia Sigea'. Helena transforms herself according to the anti-natural 'design' of her mother and her tutoress, epitomizing in miniature the self-fashioning cultural agency promoted in *L'Escole* and Chorier. Maids of Honour teach one another special techniques of masturbation—a common theme of Restoration lampoons.[19] These scenes of 'unnatural' instruction express a fear, or hope, shared by the libertine dialogue and the conservative conduct book: gender identity, far from being immutably determined by 'Sex', becomes alarmingly plastic, constructed by a web of cultural artefacts such as 'conversation', 'motion and gesture of the body', and (most importantly) written texts; women's education mutates into 'des sciences qui portent à la dissolution', or what we might call dissolute disciplines.[20] This fear of the agency women might gain through expropriating the instructive text, common throughout conduct literature, is summed up in Tom Brown's brief but malignant 'Essay on Women'. The fashionable Miss is created by libertine discourse, formed by a 'Tutoress' armed with 'rare Histories of Lust, of Fornications, and Adulteries', with '*Ovid's Art of Love*, and perhaps with some of a worse stamp'; like any good teacher, she brings these canonical texts to life by 'illustrating the difficult Passages with her own Annotations and Observations'.[21] Such imaginings confirm the central point that we have gathered in our readings of Continental libertine literature: that the representation of sexual education focuses a larger concern with cultural power and autonomy, as they are realized through literacy and authorship.

One episode in Head's 1665 *English Rogue* shows this inverse linkage of literacy and sexual 'education' in full force. When the picaro-hero seduces and abandons a

---

[17] 'An Epitaph on a Whore', in *Wit and Drollery* (1656), 20.

[18] Cf. *OED*, s.v. 'doctoress' (Evelyn tells Pepys that Helena Cornaro 'received the degree of Doctoresse at Padua').

[19] Cf. John Harold Wilson, *Court Satires of the Restoration* (Columbus, Oh., 1976), 33, 35, 65, 67 ('the Tartar', who teaches women 'to frig with [their] toes', may be either one of the ladies-in-waiting or John Coxe, publisher of *The School of Venus*), and 'A Littany for the Lady Mary Ratcliff', Bodleian MS Firth c. 16, p. 245: 'From learning to Fr-g before she coud sp—d . . . kind Heaven deliver us'.

[20] Cf. Ian Maclean, *Woman Triumphant: Feminism in French Literature, 1610–1652* (Oxford, 1977), 139.

[21] *Works* ('4th edn.', 1715), iv. 40–1.

farmer's daughter, he leaves her with a jaunty and provocative poem—written explicitly for his own 'satisfaction' in the full knowledge that she cannot read—which explains how grateful she should be for her training in erotic sophistication. Far from being 'undone', the poet declares to the reader while pretending to address the victim, she has been created anew by his curriculum, schooled in all the movements and touches that allow her to fulfil her destiny; these rarefied techniques

> will render thee belov'd unto
> Experienc'd men, for very well they know
> Woman was made for recreation,
> For mans delight and procreation.

(The same conservative doctrine of women's ancillary purpose is driven home in *L'Escole des filles*, when Fanchon reports that her lover wants to make her 'one of the girls most skilled at giving contentment to men' (Ch. 3 n. 96 above).) As in *L'Université d'amour* and *The Practical Part of Love*, the rogue finds comic-didactic equivalents for the most advanced courses in the academy—the drama of the bedroom, division and multiplication through pregnancy, the prosody of copulation ('Did I not teach thee Poetry that right?'); like more serious educators, he equates poetry with the most 'sensuous and passionate' moment of the curriculum. This is all summed up as 'Learning far above thy Sexes reach'.[22]

Head reproduces exactly the ideological double-take of *L'Escole des filles*, simultaneously reducing woman to a sexual object and exalting sexuality by promoting the hierarchic opposition of crude rustic sex and 'refin'd' eroticism. As in *L'Escole* and *Aloisia Sigea*, he disparages mere animality ('Man loves not like a beast the act of kind') and promotes self-conscious, aestheticized performance; 'the *feat* | Of *acting* well upon *Loves Theater*' is compared at length to the '*art* of *acting*' itself, in a simile that makes him the 'Poet' of her 'Lines' (100–1). Thus *he* has performed the anti-natural self-fashioning that reactionary moralists denounce in women themselves:

> I took thee and refin'd thee, made thee new,
> Alter'd thy nature, chang'd thy former hue . . .
> Where hadst thou all thy *breeding* but from me
> Who *bound* thee first, and now have made thee free? (99–100)

Combining the educational theory of Rocco's *L'Alcibiade* (higher knowledge injected through the phallus) with the grand air of a monarch ennobling his mistress, he claims that his sexual infusions have given her '*Gentility*'—though in fact he is leaving her pregnant, disgraced, and '*common*' (101–2). The practice of the vagabond seducer, common in every village when a verbal promise was thought to constitute a formal betrothal, is here exalted by the theory of high libertinism, enveloping sexuality in an aesthetic distance that corresponds all too precisely to the

---

[22] 2nd pagination, pp. 97–100 (fos. Gg–2ᵛ); cf. Donne's elegy 'Natures lay Ideot, I taught thee to love' (Ch. 1 n. 37 above).

physical distance left by his departure. Unlike *L'Escole*, however, Head's artful-picaresque narrative makes no attempt to disguise this mockery as a *philosophie des dames*, created by and for women themselves.

The prospect of encountering something called *L'Escole des filles* incites in Pepys a similar response: in his pursuit and consumption of the 'idle roguish book', as in all his interactions with female 'schooling', he splits himself into a 'sober man informing himself' and an English rogue bent on sexual tomfoolery. Pepys's erotic imagination tends to focus around a single compelling figure; after the King's mistress Lady Castlemaine, his second great obsession was the young maid-companion Deborah Willett, hired as a way of giving his wife greater mobility and freedom to participate in the entertainments of London while he attended to 'business'. The rash visit to the bookseller in search of pornography—indeed, the whole embroilment of his sexual life with texts and images—is clearly associated with the installation of Willett in the upwardly mobile household. The very title *L'Escole des filles* must have evoked her. He mentions several times, when first announcing her appointment, that she came to them from 'the school at Bow' after seven or eight years of formal education (24 and 27 Sept. 1667). For her, the growth in women's education would mean social advancement and cultural proficiency; for Pepys, the 'school of maids' meant the supply of 'very pretty' sex-objects, the intensification of desire, the confirmation of the 'philosophical' doctrine that the true vocation of *les filles*—servants, prostitutes, daughters—can be summed up as 'Fucking'. For weeks he admits he cannot get the 'little girl' out of his mind, and he prepares for the evening of her arrival with a series of sexual encounters that include a visit to the Swan Tavern, where 'I did fling down the *fille* there upon the chair' (30 Sept. 1667, my emphasis; he had also been 'tumbling la little fille' there on 20 May). 'Flinging down the *fille*' is what Pepys shares with the aggressive-priapic English rogue, mingling excitement and abjection into a single faux-didactic impulse. Both the priapist and the sober man write scripts of desire over the head of the girl pupil; both 'hate women perfectly' if they aspire to an education above their station.

The famous passage in which Pepys describes his experience with *L'Escole* might seem, at first sight, isolated from the larger concerns of eroto-didactic ideology. He does not mention women's desire, the ostensible subject of the dialogue, but instead concentrates on his own arousal, produced entirely by this encounter between the solitary male and the 'mighty lewd book, but yet not amiss for a sober man once to read over to inform himself in the villainy of the world'. Pepys constructs for himself a double space ('Up, and at my chamber all the morning and the office, doing business and also reading a little of *L'escolle des Filles*') and a double identity, as priapic adventurer and disciplined man of business. He makes love to the book more fervently than to his human partners, his 'primick' (as he encodes it) remaining erect for the duration and even 'discharging'; he seems already to mirror the lonely figure described in the book he reads, *chevauchant son idée* or 'fucking his Idea' (*Escole*, p. LVII). Frank as this autoerotic self-portrait is, however, Pepys must still frame it as a story about education, about the 'information' of 'a sober man'—an impassive third-person figure distinct from this underworld of furious arousal and unlimited pleasure. As I pointed out in the Introduction, to regard this simply as denial or repression is to ignore the performative, extrovert effect of his Mediterranean lingua franca; private experience flows into a language that reveals the social formation of Pepys's consciousness and implies the scrutiny, even the applause, of an audience.[23] Chains of association bind the 'mighty lewd book' *L'Escole des filles* to the larger world of career, city, and family, to schooling-as-discipline and education-as-cultural-advancement, to Pepys's relation with *filles* in every sense of the word.

The explicit eroticism of *L'Escole des filles* must have evoked a powerfully divided response in Pepys, part comforting identification, part confirmation of his worst fears about female sexual freedom and the collapse of 'Christian discipline'. The scene of reading created for the diary replicates the situation of the young 'female' protagonists, as he 'discharges' in response to linguistic provocation and then writes it out in French. *L'Escole's* preoccupation with visual pleasure and hand-to-genital contact matches his own predilections, too: of the innumerable sexual encounters recorded in the diary, a large proportion are manual or voyeuristic. In *L'Escole* itself (as we saw in Chapter 3) Susanne declares 'seeing and being seen' the supreme pleasure; for Pepys, unable to 'command himself in the pleasures of his eye' according to his own confession (25 April 1666) the libertine text allows erotic enjoyment of the visual and mental 'idea' in isolation from mutual relationship or responsibility, 'seeing' *without* 'being seen'.

Full sexual intercourse occurs quite rarely in Pepys's diary, and fluctuates according to the political and domestic climate. In the marriage-bed, sex flourishes during the fierce argument over his infatuation with Deborah Willett, but ceases completely during the 'half-year' that the British navy reached its lowest point in recorded history, when the Dutch entered the Medway and fired the ill-equipped fleet. Pepys's 'private' experience, like his private language, re-enacts public affairs of state, which in turn could not be separated from the all-too-visible sexuality of the monarch and his mistresses.[24] If 'the King's greatest pleasure hath been with his fingers, being able to do no more' during this Dutch crisis, then Pepys might feel solidarity in 'discharging' himself over this masturbatory text or failing to make love to his wife (30 July, 2 Aug. 1667). Mere escapism cannot explain the complex response to *L'Escole*, however. The darting, free-associative writing of the diary reveals unresolved tensions and incomplete exclusions: Pepys dissociates himself by using the third person ('a sober man') but then relocates himself '*in* the villainy of the world'; his description of a musical gathering, which separates the morning and evening pornography sessions, hints at an erotic subtext (the energetic singing of 'Mr

---

[23]   Cf. Harry Berger, Jr., 'The Pepys Show: Ghost-Writing and Documentary Desire in *The Diary*', *ELH* 65 (1998), 557–91, esp. 565.

[24]   See my 'Pepys and the Private Parts of Monarchy', in Gerald MacLean (ed.), *Culture and Society in the Stuart Restoration: Literature, Drama, History* (Cambridge, 1995), 95–110, and *Libertines and Radicals in Early Modern London: Sexuality, Politics and Literary Culture, 1630–1685* (Cambridge, 2001), 19–20, 167–73.

Tempest' who 'understands everything at first sight' suggests seductive power and sexual vigour); and Pepys's parenthetical mention of childbirth and smallpox shows his mind still running on the troublesome associations of sex.[25] As in *L'Escole* itself, the social and physical realities of procreation return unbidden into a text ostensibly devoted to free-floating pleasure. The liberationist 'school of women' exacerbates the anxieties that propel him to seek it out.

Pepys's desire to consume the erotic text clearly stems from professional and national troubles. The Great Plague a few years earlier generated intense dream-images of performing the 'postures' with the King's mistress (15 Aug. 1665), and so forged deep associations between sexuality and epidemic that now intrude into the '*escholle des Filles*' entry ('hardly ever was remembered such a season as this for the smallpox as these last two months'). The disastrous performance of the navy, which undermined the sexual bond with his wife and complicated his identification with the sovereign, now threatened to destroy his career. In early 1668 Pepys was under investigation for his handling of prize money, and his fling with *L'Escole* is surrounded by entries that reveal his profound fear of 'miscarriage' and his need to 'perfect my Narrative' before the hearing; safe sex, or sex in the form of narrative, would provide an alternative representation of these pressures—not a simple 'escape' but a transposition or parallel reality. In the diary entries preceding the 'Lord's Day' when he read the book in full, temporal and spatial juxtapositions reveal sexuality as the means of splitting the same moment into 'business' and 'pleasure'. On 6 February, for example, he goes 'to the office, where a while busy; my head not being free of my trouble about my prize business, I home to bed. This evening coming home I did put my hand under the coats of Mercer, and did touch her thigh.' On the 8th, he goes for an urgent consultation with his co-defendant Captain Cocke—the handsome and musical friend in whose bedroom he had recalled the dream of Lady Castlemaine eighteen months earlier—who had likewise been called to account for prize money. Immediately after this meeting he rushes to buy *L'Escole*, and we can speculate that to 'decharger' over a wicked text guarded against the possibility of being discharged for keeping bad books.

Entangled with these fears of professional 'miscarriage' were the long-standing problems of Pepys's childless and culturally mixed marriage. *L'Escole des filles* had brought marital concerns into focus even before Pepys first mentions it in the diary. Evidently he had seen the book on one of his increasingly frequent visits to the bookseller to build up his library and thereby his cultural capital. Before actually reading it he conceived of *L'Escole* as 'the French book which I did think to have had for my wife to translate' (13 Jan. 1668)—a bridge between the half-French wife and the English husband, a construction project that might fill the conspicuous absence of children. Pepys oscillated between hope and resignation as Elizabeth's 'terms' continued, marking out the time of the diary,[26] and as late as 26 July 1664 he consulted a gossiping-feast of women to get advice on fertility techniques. It seems

---

[25] Cf. Francis Barker's reading of the bowdlerized text (Introd. n. 6 above).
[26] Stuart Sherman, *Telling Time: Clocks, Diaries, and English Diurnal Form, 1660–1785* (1996), 70.

clear, however, that his surgical operation for bladder-stone had ruptured his semi-nal vesicles and left him in an ironic situation resembling the 'carved' eunuchs of an-tiquity, constantly available for priapic pleasure but unable to procreate. (*L'Escole* itself describes these creatures vividly, we recall.) The midwife-author Jane Sharp gives a typically blunt 'warning' to men who survive that operation: 'they so rend and tear the seed vessels, that such persons are never able to beget Children, they may hatch the Cuckows Eggs, and keep other mens if they please, but they shall never get any themselves.'[27] Pepys's fervid combination of jealousy and infidelity can be explained not only by his social position—as a City husband, traditional can-didate for cuckolding—but by his medical condition; zoologists report that the cas-trated chimpanzee 'copulates much more frequently than normal animals', and the same may be true of other primates.[28]

Pepys once consulted a 'school of women' on his failure to become a father, and now he imagines that *L'Escole des filles* will solve the problem of occupying a child-less spouse understandably discontented by a husband so devoted to 'business' and adultery. To translate a sophisticated but subtly didactic French text—the 'School' for young women like herself—would provide her with intellectual stimulus, pro-ductivity, and self-esteem without the danger his jealous mind most feared: a pri-apic intruder, idle, roguish, yet irresistible, exerting a sovereign power to seduce. How shocking to discover that this improving book *is* such an intruder, 'worse than *putana errante*', bursting with instructions for the young French wife and her younger confidante, able to dismiss fears of pregnancy and enjoy new-found free-dom under the 'cover' of a husband. By a triple mirroring, Pepys could see himself in *L'Escole* as Robinet, the expert man of pleasure 'schooling' the young maid in all the postures, as the cuckolded husband unable to control Susanne-Elizabeth and Fanchon-Deborah as they construct their own world of secret pleasure, and as the princess's statue—the simulacrum of a man who pumps out hot fluid whenever the mistress's hand commands, offering no danger of pregnancy.

By hiring a young *fille* fresh from a London girls' school, to give Elizabeth the free-dom to move around town without him, Pepys unwittingly shifted his own world closer to the institution depicted in libertine discourse—the *dissolute family* in which perverse and anti-procreative sexual pleasure replaces kinship and defer-ence.[29] This counter-family, powerfully represented in legal prosecutions of sexual disorder as well as in pornography itself, parodies and inverts the godly image of the family evoked in Milton's *Paradise Lost*, where 'wedded Love' (explicitly sexual even in Paradise) is hailed as the epistemological foundation for all other bonds:

---

[27] *The Midwives Book, or The Whole Art of Midwifry Discovered* (1671), 18; cf. Dympna Callaghan, 'The Castrator's Song: Female Impersonation on the Early Modern Stage', *Journal of Medieval and Early Modern Studies*, 26 (1996), 321–53, esp. 332.

[28] Clellan S. Ford and Frank A. Beach, *Patterns of Sexual Behavior* (1951; New York, 1972), 231.

[29] The most lurid example might be the Earl of Castlehaven's household, accused of multiple sex crimes so heinous that the grandmother of an 11-year-old rape victim refused to give her shelter, 'feare-full least there should be some sparkes of [her] misbehaviour remaining which might give ill Example to the young ones which are with me'; see Barbara Breasted, '*Comus* and the Castlehaven Scandal', *Milton Studies*, 3 (1971), 216.

by thee
Founded in Reason, Loyal, just, and Pure,
Relations dear, and all the Charities
Of Father, Son, and Brother first were known. (IV. 750–7)

In *La puttana errante*, in *L'Escole des filles*, and in Chorier's *Aloisia Sigea*, 'Reason' works instead to replace wedded love with libertine desire: aunts and cousins become tutors and lovers, husbands become 'couvertures', fathers disappear, mothers become figures of contempt or progenitors of secret pleasure, spiritual counsellors and junior manservants become priapic playthings to be disposed of at will. Prosecutors were right to fear these books' effect on 'Christian discipline', even though to the analytic eye they reproduce much of the structure they purport to destroy. Looking at its demure title page (Fig. 4 above) Pepys imagined *L'Escole* as a conduct book, shaping his Anglo-French household into the kind of family that a worldly but 'sober' man might command—one of those 'familles plus policées' and 'civilisées' that the educational revolution and the improvement of women hoped to achieve (Ch. 3 n. 157 above). Behind that façade he found a 'dialogue between a married woman and a maid' alarmingly close to what he, and many contemporaries, feared in the autonomous pairing of two free women.[30] Like the voyeur-reader implied (and sometimes depicted) in the libertine dialogue, he must regain control by interjecting himself, by conquering the maid or 'flinging down the *fille*'.

The (pseudo)feminocentric libertine texts of Europe evidently translate into categories for organizing experience even before they are literally translated into English. When Pepys declares *L'Escole des filles* 'worse than *putana errante*', he asserts his preference for the Italian whore-tradition despite his obvious fascination with the 'domestic turn' embodied in the French dialogue (and soon to be intensified in *The School of Venus*, where Fanny's lover in the French becomes her husband in English). Many features of the prose *Puttana errante*—the bawdy satire against Catholic clerics, the cheerfully precise accountancy of the list of postures, the casual picaresque of the 'wandering whore' herself, the clear demarcation between the *puttana* and the rest of the world—would have been easier for Pepys to accept than the steamy household fornication of *L'Escole des filles*, explicitly set among 'bonnes bourgeoises' like his wife and Deborah Willett. As the commander of the household, he could expect to give Willett the sort of 'schooling' he gave to an earlier maid who had mimicked their next-door neighbour (5 Nov. 1662), and his erotic obsession with the new maid develops in situations associated with literacy and didacticism. To translate *L'Escole* into his own life might feed his fantasy of 'schooling' the *fille* Deborah, but it might also generate disturbing images of what went on during office hours with the dancing master and the music teacher, with Mr Tempest or

---

[30] For a legal case involving a Tullia-like female mentor, see Thomas Ivie, *Alimony Arraign'd* (1654). Mirabell in Congreve's *Way of the World*, IV. i, stipulates only half-jokingly that his future wife 'admit no sworn Confident, or Intimate of your own Sex' to enable her affairs.

Captain Cocke; singing lessons, for example, are precisely the decoy that Robinet and Fanchon use to conceal their secret copulation (II. 77).

Pepys's obsession with Deborah Willett uncomfortably straddles the two genres of sex-writing represented by *L'Escole* and *La puttana*. At first, what Pepys enacts with her resembles a scene from *L'Escole*, where sexual opportunities are grabbed amidst the ordinary round of middle-class domestic and social life—while Fanchon is drying a petticoat on the stove, or sitting out a dance; Pepys's most intimate contact involves slipping his hand into her 'cunny' while she combs his hair after supper.[31] What Pepys calls his 'bad amour' smoulders throughout the weeks of anxious 'miscarriage' and convulsive bouts with *L'Escole*, his embrace of the literary *fille* temporarily suppressing his desire to throw himself on the flesh-and-blood version. On 31 March 1668, apparently provoked by the sight of her handling writing materials and weeping, Pepys 'did take her, the first time in my life, sobra mi genu and did poner mi mano sub her jupes and toca su thigh'; images of authorship and sensibility revive at once the master's sexual assertiveness and the diarist's polyglot garrulity. (Like Chorier, he might have nurtured the fantasy that women's writing translates into sexual inventiveness.) His wife's discovery of this deep-petting scene shatters the domestic-erotic paradigm, however, and forces the affair (though technically unconsummated) into the 'puttana errante' mode. In a conflict that takes place as much in the realm of discourse as in the physical realm, Elizabeth insists on defining the scene in terms of (Samuel's) errancy and (Deborah's) whoredom. Pepys, in his turn, tries to unravel his attempt to realize the domestic-pornographic *Escole des filles* by looking for the book he thought it was, 'the French book which I did think to have had for my wife to translate'. Fashioning their own Anglo-French culture, the childless couple had been studying *Le Grand Cyrus* together (in translation); to conclude and assuage the furious argument provoked by his infatuation with 'Deb', Pepys bought the same author's *Ibrahim* (in French), apparently the most 'escapist' and least feminist of Scudéry's novels.[32] Unwittingly, he prefigures the 'classick' canon of female reading satirized in *Erotopolis, or A New Description of Bettyland*, where *Cyrus* and *Ibrahim* mingle with *The School of Venus*.

The imaginary *Escole des filles* was supposed to adsorb his wife's discursive energies—she was not merely to read but to 'translate' it—and deflect an aspiration to authorship that might otherwise take a critical turn. In the early 1660s Elizabeth St Michel Pepys had herself written a poignant narrative of her married life, complaining of her enforced idleness and isolation; her husband ranted, tore up the manuscript, and flung it into the fire, the ultimate and most provocative sanction against the discursive 'child'.[33] (The same fireplace probably received *L'Escole* five years later.) Behind his furious bravado Pepys was cut to the quick by her complaint,

---

[31] 25 Oct. 1668; cf. *Escole*, II. 104–8 (the hole burned in Fanchon's *cotillon* on the former occasion proves useful to the seated lovers on the latter).

[32] 21 May 1667, 24 Feb. 1668, and cf. 21 June 1668. For the conventionality of *Ibrahim, ou L'Illustre Bassa* compared to Scudéry's other novels, see Joan DeJean, *Tender Geographies* (New York, 1991), 80–1.

[33] 13 Nov. 1662, and cf. 9 Jan. 1663. When Archbishop Laud burned one of Lady Eleanor Davies's works before her eyes she accused him of having 'ravished her childe'; cf. Esther S. Cope, *Handmaid of the Holy Spirit: Dame Eleanor Davies, Never Soe Mad a Ladie* (Ann Arbor, 1992), 68.

and began to encourage her in creative pursuits like music, painting, and dancing lessons, suppressing the paroxysms of jealousy occasioned by this schooling. What he learned from sexual gossip and libertine reading evidently fed these fears of what she might become in other company. Immediately after hearing about Lady Castlemaine's expertise in 'all the tricks of Aretin that are to be practised to give pleasure', for example, Pepys's mind turned to other forms of intimate 'practice'; he grew frantically jealous of Elizabeth's dancing master, surreptitiously checking when a lesson was scheduled whether she 'did wear her drawers today as she used to do' (15 May 1663). Now, on 12 January 1668, Elizabeth again rages against her lack of 'money and liberty', and the next day Pepys rushes to the bookshop in search of that elusive *Escole des filles* that would allow her to be both the French mistress and the disciplined wife.

Elizabeth Pepys's response to domestic libertinism is to intervene in her husband's fantasies and take command of the scenario. On the night she discovers the 'cunny' scene she reveals that she has converted to Catholicism, and over the next weeks she not only watches Pepys's eyes constantly, but divulges that she has been propositioned by numerous superiors including 'my Lord' Sandwich, as if reconstituting herself as the desirable (and Continental) married woman of *La Philosophie des dames* (25 Oct., 3, 5, 10 Nov. 1668). When she forces *la fille* out of the house altogether, the covert association of illicit text and illicit sex once again breaks out in Pepys's mind. On the day after Deb's departure he roams London desperately looking for her, first trying the notorious prostitution-street Whetstones Park ('where I understand by my wife's discourse that Deb is gone'), and then going straight to the very bookseller that had supplied *L'Escole des filles*. But now Elizabeth's 'discourse' has won the day; instead of acquiring more male fantasies about erotic schoolgirls, he fortifies himself with a vast consignment of French novels 'for my wife's closet' (16 Nov. 1668).

In this war of scripts between husband and wife, it is she who 'by her discourse' sends him to the haunt of street-walkers, and she who *inscribes* her rival into the narrative of prostitution. Elizabeth twice threatens to slit her nose, the traditional punitive marking of the whore (19 and 20 Nov. 1668), and immediately invents the verbal equivalent of this gesture, enacting her anger on her ex-companion's social body rather than in the flesh: she forces the craven Pepys to write 'Deb' a letter in which he calls her 'whore'. He complies with this, even though he never actually took Willett's maidenhead, on the slippery grounds that 'I did fear she might too probably have been prevailed upon to have been a whore by her carriage to me.'[34] Even his private confession is evasive, for we would expect him to write '*my* carriage to *her*'. In subsequent scenes Pepys does his best to impose the whore-paradigm on the young woman whose livelihood he has destroyed, at the same time smugly approv-

---

[34] 20 Nov. 1668. Male control of representation, in this case, mitigated the insult; Pepys's clerk William Hewer winked at him while he wrote the 'whore' letter, literally conniving at a scheme to withhold this part of the letter from Deb herself (which he did, on 21 Nov.); the two men participate in a routine that anticipates the stage business of *CW* iii. ii, where two conspirators dupe a third party by deploying gestural language that contradicts the verbal script.

ing of her resistance to it and 'counsel[ling]' her to remain chaste (18 Nov. 1668). As when he reads *L'Escole*, Pepys splits himself into the man of pleasure and the man of business, piously gratified and relieved when his former *fille de chambre* responds so unwillingly to his violent attempts to rewrite her as a *puttana errante*.

The very close of the diary confirms that Pepys not only 'selectively lives a writable life', as Harry Berger puts it,[35] but 'in-forms himself' by forcing others into scripts derived from his libertine reading. Only the collapse of this eroto-autodidactic system can explain the sudden decision to stop writing and the intensely mournful tone of the announcement. Pepys relinquishes his favourite activity and resigns himself to 'that course which [is] almost as much as to see myself go into my grave'. He refers to his failing eyesight, of course, but his words seem to encompass a different calamity; he can still 'see' himself taking this desperate course, and he prays for strength to endure this seeming death '*and* all the discomforts that will accompany my being blind' (my emphasis). He is mourning the death of the diary itself. Strictly speaking, Pepys's crepuscular gloom is not justified: the renunciation of private writing will save him from the blindness he fears, and his staff can still keep a full record of daily events, as he recognizes when he 'resolve[s] from this time forward to have it kept by my people in long-hand'. What grieves him is having to renounce the secret sexual part of his writing, having to 'be contented to set down no more than is fit for all the world to know'. 'Or if there be anything', he continues in a moment of faint optimism, 'I must endeavour to keep a margin in my book open, to add here and there a note in short-hand with my own hand' (31 May 1669). What is this *something* that has now dropped out of his life completely, or may at best live on intermittently in the margins?

Blindness serves as a cover for Pepys's commanding passion, the desire to consume both *L'Escole des filles* and Deborah Willett, 'in-forming himself' at the point where they converge. Pepys's closure of the diary suggests that he fears becoming one of those obsessive figures inscribed in the whore-biography, whose vulvic researches run so deep that they 'blind themselves in poring on their two-leaved *Book*'.[36] Explaining how he could 'keep a margin in my book open', he makes explicit (if parenthetical) the mysterious 'thing' that has sustained the writing up to this point: the full phrase runs 'if there be anything (which cannot now be much, now my amours to Deb are past . . .)'. ('Deb', or more accurately '.Dveb', is the last word of the diary to be written in shorthand and 'premature garbling'.[37]) It is not his eyesight that kills the diary—he has felt for a long time that he may 'undo my eyes almost every time that I take a pen in hand, and he still plans to write and read his own marginal notes—but the collapse of a vision of himself organized around 'bad amours', protagonist of a libertine discourse in which the erotic occupies the centre of the page and not the margin, in which the sole purpose of earthly existence is not getting but spending. This vision and this experience may be intensely private, but Pepys's happiness still depends on its being 'set down' in writing. Looking back over

---

[35] 'Pepys Show', 584.   [36] *The Practical Part of Love* (1660), 35 (cf. Ch. 1 n. 76 above).
[37] 31 May 1669; Richard Luckett, Pepys Librarian, kindly described the shorthand in a private communication.

his text, in which the *cosas* and *mamelles* and *primicks* have actually occupied only a small proportion, Pepys equates the book of life with the book of sex. He has scripted his own version of *L'Escole des filles*, but the escape of Deborah Willett writes 'The End' to both volumes. Shockingly, Elizabeth Pepys herself died before the end of the year, and Pepys immediately settled into a long-standing relationship with a woman of the housekeeper class. Yet the personal diary does not resume, does not survive the necrology of desire inscribed into the utterance 'now my amours to Deb are past'. The *fille* could not exist without the *dame*.

2. 'THE SECOND PART OF *L'ESCOLE DES FILLES* . . .': WYCHERLEY'S FRENCH IMPORTS

As my second epigraph shows, Horner's attack on respectable women in the first scene of *The Country-Wife* involves the aggressive flaunting of his knowledge of *L'Escole des filles*, a work whose bare mention will 'ruine' him with the sex it ostensibly liberates. To confirm rumours of his recent surgical castration (and thereby to destroy his previous reputation as a dangerous ladies' man), he behaves with calculated rudeness to the wife of Sir Jaspar Fidget, the quintessential Pepysian man of business, and to other ladies in his citified circle whom he hopes to identify as sexually available. As in Terence's *Eunuchus*, the protagonist feigns sexual incapacity to gain access to the *gyneceum*; as in Jonson's *Epicoene*, this male simulation of a non-man (conflating elements of Jonson's boy and transvestite) opens up opportunities to expose the inner workings of a 'school of women', an exposé in which sexual and satirical motives can barely be separated. By confronting these rigidly virtuous characters with *La Philosophie des dames*—that is, the more advanced 'second part' of *L'Escole des filles*—Horner simultaneously establishes his eunuch alibi and sets up an epistemic test to deconstruct the respectable exterior of *les dames* and ratify the 'philosophy' of the libertine text he cites.

Naming *L'Escole des filles* in mixed company clearly places the speaker outside the pale and 'ruines' any chance of conversation between man and woman. Horner thereby adds conviction to his eunuch disguise, calculating (quite rightly) that his audience will assume an inverse relation between representation and action. His deployment of the book of sex is taken as prima facie evidence that he has no sex of his own: Sir Jaspar, the soon-to-be-cuckolded husband, deduces that 'he hates women perfectly'; the supposedly virtuous 'gang' of ladies, rather than expressing cool indifference, recoil with exaggerated exclamations of disgust directed at his 'filthy' genital pathology rather than his breach of decorum. According to Horner's experiment, this aversion reveals their inner libidinous natures, or (in his colloquial term) proves them 'right' for sexual exploitation.[38]

Reading *The Country-Wife* in the context of *L'Escole* and Chorier's *Satyra*, we can see that Wycherley derives this erotic-empiricist experiment not only from the

[38] On epistemic experimentation, see Peter Hynes, 'Against Theory? Knowledge and Action in Wycherley's Plays', *Modern Philology*, 94 (1996), 163–89; for the sexual use of 'right' (not in *OED*), see my *Libertines and Radicals*, 212, 317 n. 23.

scientific revolution of Restoration England, but from the French sources that Horner parades so scandalously. Sir Jaspar correctly surmises that Horner has turned 'pleasure' into a 'business',[39] and he clearly uses the libertine text as a training manual. Susanne's advice to Fanchon in *L'Escole* is expanded by Chorier into a general principle of absolute sexual abandon and total exterior respectability, which then provides the blueprint for Horner's research: *intus ut placet, foris ut moris*; on the inside act according to pleasure, on the outside follow the conventions of society (Ch. 4, sect. 5 above). Fanchon's disgusted reaction to Susanne's account of the eunuch—'Fi, fi, de ces gens là!'—is translated almost verbatim in the 'foh, foh!' that Wycherley repeatedly gives to his prude-characters, suggesting that the English playwright is himself subjected to the authority of the French original, enshrining *L'Escole* as a master-text or secret touchstone. Meanwhile the parallel plot— Horner's seduction of the naive 'country wife' of the title, unwittingly helped by her Moliéresque husband Pinchwife—confirms this dependency since it embodies the central theme of Fanchon's education in *L'Escole des filles*, the supposed 'opening' of the female mind by the onrush of sexual experience. Within the course of the action Margery Pinchwife evolves from ingénue to illicit lover, as Fanchon does between the first and second parts of *L'Escole*; reinforcing the similarity, Wycherley also provides Horner with an experienced married woman (like Susanne) and a young miss evading her mother's watchful eye (another variant of Fanchon).

Horner aggressively maintains the working fiction of the libertine dialogue, that women are its subjects and consumers (concealing the patent truth that it is men who 'inform themselves' there); what these *précieuses* really 'came for', he snarls, is the clandestine thrill of the libertine text. Wycherley of course intends this as part of Horner's eunuch-persona, a deliberately misleading front. Like all the other 'signs' in the play it must be decoded to show the opposite of what it proclaims, and in this case the knowing part of the audience is directed to reverse the point: Horner is really potent and therefore really loves women, and his understanding should be trusted in a world of false appearances. Lest we miss this principle of ironic reversal, Wycherley spells out his meaning in the last four lines, where Horner himself explains that for men to be truly 'prized' by women they must learn to be despised by other males. Most fellows simulate heterosexuality to 'pass for Women's men with one another', but he is the exception. The identical point is then made in an epilogue given to Elizabeth Knepp (Lady Fidget), identifying Horner as the true 'Womans Man'. Ventriloquizing the authentic female voice, this closing message to the audience (like the theory of true beauty in *Aloisia Sigea*) elevates the phallus into the supreme touchstone of truth; men can deceive each other by boasting of nonexistent sexual prowess, but in bed nothing can be faked—'we Women———— there's no cous'ning us.'[40]

---

[39] II. i. 282 (see Abbreviations above for edn. cited); Lady Fidget retorts that a husband who abandons his wife, even to Horner, will be sure to 'have her bus'ness done' (a phrase used in *The Parliament of Women*, Ch. 3 n. 154 above, for the orgasmic effect of *Aloisia Sigea*).

[40] v. iv. 352; 'Epilogue spoken by Mrs. Knep', 354. The homoerotic implications of womanizing and cuckolding in *CW* are spelled out in Eve Kosovsky Sedgwick, *Between Men: English Literature and Male Homosocial Desire* (New York, 1985), ch. 3.

But the ideological need to write 'Women' into the libertine scenario threatens to upset this neat strategy of reversal, since many of Horner's faux-hostile comments are subsequently endorsed by the action of the play. Rather than softening in the subsequent pursuit of pleasure, his harsh satyric attitude is intensified as the cuckolding plot moves on. By Act V the 'virtuous gang' have confirmed all the misogynistic theses barked out by Horner in Act I, coming to him precisely for the secret pleasures represented in *L'Escole des filles*, and so submitting themselves to the libertine script. Like Robinet and Fanchon, they improvise their brief encounters in the midst of the genteel social round, most famously during an afternoon visit (interrupted by Sir Jaspar) in which Lady Fidget and her allegedly castrated 'companion' pretend to be dealing in expensive imported china.

Horner's sexless condition derives supposedly from 'an *English-French* disaster, and an *English-French* Chirurgeon' (I. i. 249), and like many falsehoods in the play this points towards his true doubleness. Cultural translation is placed on the agenda by the question he himself provokes in his '*Escole de Filles*' outburst: what has he 'brought over from France', and what has he left there? Horner simulates those failing husbands who featured in French impotence trials, claiming to fit the legal category 'impuissance accidentelle'—resulting from surgery, venereal disease, or (in his case) both—even though a real court would accuse him of 'pretendüe impuissance supposée pour veritable'. During his formative years in France Wycherley might well have picked up the virulent discourse directed against normal-seeming men suddenly proved to be eunuchs ('abomination, . . . half-men, half-women'), including the much-publicized case of the handsome, confident marquis de Langey, treated with boisterous derision by aristocratic ladies like Mme de Sévigné (just as Horner is classed among 'Half Men' by a former friend and treated to 'the Womens contempt and the mens raillery' when he appears in the theatre after his supposed operation).[41] But in what sense can this social and surgical disaster be called 'English-French'? We have seen in *L'Escole* (and in the French adaptation of Secundus) a certain national fascination with the man who has undergone 'total amputation of his virility'—*rasibus* in the French idiom, 'all's gone' in the words of Horner's gallant friend Harcourt (I. i. 254, and cf. Ch. 3 n. 131 above). The English could imagine their own venereal surgeons collecting enough '*Nuts* of Priapus' to button a large cloak, but syphilis itself remained incurably 'French'.[42] For Wycherley as for Pepys, shuttling back and forth across the Channel brings the French disease and French gallantry, *L'Escole des filles* and the language to describe its solitary enjoyment, sexual incitement and sexual catastrophe.

With rather heavy-handed irony, Wycherley shows the significance of France

---

[41] *CW* I. i. 254–5 (and cf. v. iv. 342, 351, for the persistence of Horner's 'French Capon' alibi); Pierre Darmon, *Le Tribunal de l'impuissance: Virilité et défaillances conjugales dans l'Ancienne France* (Paris, 1979), 31, 36–7, 86–7; Lucien Soefve, *Nouveau Recüeil de plusieurs questions notables . . . jugées par arrests d'audiences du Parlement de Paris* (Paris, 1682), ii. 324; Yves Citton, *Impuissances* (Paris, 1994), 79.

[42] 'A Lady of Quality', *Fifteen Real Comforts of Matrimony* (1684), 101 (and cf. 35, 'more than Circumcis'd').

changing within seconds from the source of good 'breeding' to libertine contempt for virtuous wives ('too much a French fellow'), and then to repulsive sexual deficiency ('filthy French Beast, foh, foh!' 'stinking mortify'd rotten French Wether!').[43] Horner claims to have left everything in France, and *not* to have brought over any 'Bawdy Picture, new Postures, nor the second Part of the *Escole de Filles*, Nor——' Chorier's *Satyra Sotadica*, he might have said before Quack interrupts him, leaving open the possibility of an infinite series of French artefacts each worse than the one before. And yet he obviously *has* brought back an expertise in the secret literature of sex and in the secret workings of desire—particularly the desire of those 'right' but respectable married women depicted in *L'Escole* and Chorier, Brantôme and Bussy-Rabutin. His own Don-Juanesque ambition is likewise expressed in an 'English-French' concept; like a clandestine version of the mountebank or alchemist, he promotes himself as the universal solvent of social and sexual partitions, the '*Pas par tout* of the Town' (I. i. 254)—an Anglo-Gallic compound obviously supposed to mean passepartout rather than 'not everywhere'.

Though Horner's ostensible goal is to provoke the ladies by mocking their secret desire for erotic figuration, each of the items on his negative shopping list—the 'Bawdy Picture', the 'new Posture', and the libertine book—turns out to reflect upon his situation, define the limits of his sexuality, and illuminate some larger preoccupation of Wycherley himself. The erotic 'Picture', for example, reappears in *The Country-Wife* as an image of Horner's own sexuality, and recurs at several points in Wycherley's verse and drama as a self-conscious reflection of the act of writing. In his earliest poem, a comic travesty of *Hero and Leander*, Wycherley dwells on the graphic work of 'modest *Aretine*', who manages to reconcile art and 'Nature' by removing all fig-leaves and displaying the 'craveing chincke 'tween maiden thighs'—a prefiguration of the English author's 'plain-dealing' art of exposure.[44] But in *The Country-Wife* art signifies both incitement and substitution, both seductive skill and frigid artificiality. When Old Lady Squeamish offers Horner her granddaughter's picture, he declares 'I love a woman only in Effigie, and good Painting as much as I hate them' (IV. iii. 323). He says this to maintain his eunuch façade, of course, but by this point in the play—the famous 'China' scene—we suspect that the façade may correspond to his real desires. He 'loves women in Effigie' just as Pygmalion did, as controllable embodiments of an imagination fed by misogynistic disgust; he loves the image of a conquest, the projection of his own genius, a statue created by his gaze. As Pinchwife warns his country wife, such libertines do not love women but 'look upon [them] like Basilicks, but to destroy em' (II. i. 268). However grotesque his own treatment of women, Pinchwife's comments on other men normally turn out to be reliable.

'China' becomes an ironically appropriate vehicle for Horner's acquisitive urge, alongside these other images of applied art. Earlier in the scene his behaviour to

---

[43] I. i. 251–2, II. i. 279.

[44] Wycherley censored these lines when they were published in 1669, but inked them back into a presentation copy now in the library of the Victoria and Albert Museum, London, Dyce 17.P.55, pp. 28–9 (for the printed text cf. *Works*, iv. 84–5).

Lady Fidget in private, before the interruption of those they need to deceive, was indeed as hard and brittle as porcelain; rather than melting into gallantry, he retains his cold mixture of satiric contempt and aesthetic detachment, boasting about his Machiavellian strategy and generalizing about 'women' as if they were mere *objets de virtu*. When Lady Fidget later addresses Horner as 'thou representative of a Husband' (v. iii. 342), she encapsulates his un-lover-like coldness as well as his 'Effigy' status. The ironic relation of reality and appearance reverses itself, as buffoons like Sir Jaspar turn out to have stumbled on the truth: 'he hates women perfectly' unless they conform to his image.

'China' allows Lady Fidget to 'have what I came for' (iv. iii. 319), a phrase that significantly echoes Horner's original 'Bawdy Picture' outburst ('You do well [to exit], Madam, for I have nothing that you came for'). Wycherley himself is improvising on a hint in Jonson's *Epicoene*, where the Collegiate Ladies boast of conducting affairs in '*China* houses', and his onstage surrogates keep the game running.[45] China provides a 'cue' for theatrical action (as Horner explicitly recognizes), an alibi for Lady Fidget's exit into his bedroom under the very eyes of her husband, and an image of the sex-as-artefact that results. The two connoisseurs re-emerge from their lightning-fast coupling at a perfect comic moment, framed by yet another image of art. Squeamish has just returned wide-eyed from a search of Horner's rooms, where 'I have been staring on the prettyest Pictures': she has either discovered the secret cabinet where he keeps his new 'postures', or seen the lovers through a pornographic spy-hole. On the very phrase 'prettyest Pictures', Horner and Lady Fidget re-enter from the bedroom into the framed space of the stage, frozen (until the laughter subsides) in a tableau of post-coital exhaustion. The glamorous pair—Charles Hart, famous as a lover of Nell Gwyn and the Duchess of Cleveland, and Elizabeth Knepp, Pepys's favourite actress and occasional mistress—form a kind of Lely double portrait; to adopt Pope's famous account of Restoration portraiture, 'the sleepy Eye' must have revealed 'the melting Soul'.[46] Since both Horner and Sir Jaspar insist on his 'coming into her the back way', this scene provides two of the three items on the original list, both 'a Bawdy Picture' and 'new Postures'.

This play on 'Effigy', 'representative', and 'Picture' reminds us that Horner's stratagem involves a double semiotics. On the one hand, the sign gives access to a privileged reality and becomes the key to manipulating a society that, in Hobbes's phrase, respects only 'signs of power'. On the other hand, the sign is a mere two-dimensional substitute, the front for image-mongers and cheats, impressive in inverse proportion to the real quality of the goods. Virtually all the central issues in *The Country-Wife* involve some sort of semiotic conundrum provoked by the opacity of the sign: Horner resorts to his eunuch trick because *all* women, 'right' or not,

---

[45] Arthur Friedman cites several allusions to china-houses in *Epicoene* and other writings by Jonson (*CW* iv. iii. 318). Note other similarities: the women's group dropping their mask, boasting of their various social and sexual freedoms, and discussing men from a connoisseur's point of view; the young stud wooing three of them simultaneously and forcing them to remain silent on the subject; the man falsely claiming to be impotent, with horrified reaction from the ladies.

[46] *The First Epistle of the Second Book of Horace, Imitated*, lines 149–50.

have adopted a fashionable air of sexy complaisance—a problem more commonly faced by women trying to decide when male gallantry is sincere; Harcourt and Alithea, the only characters engaged in marital courtship, must decide whether to take marriage as a 'sign of interest' or a 'sign of love'.[47] The problem preoccupied Wycherley even late in life, when he compared the youthful-looking portrait in front of his collected poems to a shop-sign that palms off spoiled goods: 'So must sophisticated Wit, as Wine, | The worse it is, have but the better Sign' (*Works*, iii. 23). In *The Country-Wife* this kind of crude mockery comes from the dupe-character Sparkish, directed by Horner's plot to call him 'a sign of a Man, you know, since he came out of *France*, heh, hah, he' (L i. 258).

Adopting the eunuch as disguise brings out the fragile relation between these two theories of seeming. The problem is already encapsulated in Wycherley's Roman and French sources. Terence's faux-eunuch, thoroughly excited by a picture of Danaë receiving the golden shower (which he contemplates in company with the 'girl' he wants to seduce), worries that unless he pounces 'I would really be who I was simulating' (*is essem vero, qui simulabar, Eunuchus* 606). The eunuch is difficult to 'simulate' confidently, moreover, because he comes in different varieties and strengths of sexual ability, as *L'Escole* explains. For Lady Fidget and her friends, Horner provides something very like the artificial men they could have read about in that 'second part of *L'Escole des filles*' that he keeps from them—an effigy of a man 'carved for his lady's use' and deprived of his inconvenient attributes.

This mechanical body of pleasure, as I called him in Chapter 3, is exemplified by the princess's statue and by the partial eunuch enjoyed in ancient Rome and modern Turkey, still able to achieve erections and give pleasure to women without the risk of pregnancy. In *L'Escole des filles*, in Juvenal, and in medico-legal treatises, the reader could easily discover that 'eunuch' is not the all-or-nothing category that Horner requires for his deceit. Even Pepys, with his ruptured seminal vessels and constantly agitated primick, could be classified as an 'accidental eunuch'; like Horner he exhibits the accelerated frequency of genital presentation that scientists have induced in castrated apes, and the methodical determination to win that increases when wayward racehorses are gelded. Depending on how much was removed and when, the eunuch represents both sides of Horner's disguise, the absolute asexuality he presents to jealous husbands, and the heightened performativity he presents to potential lovers—artificially separated from procreation but necessarily as brief as adolescence, since the erectile capacity fades after a few years.[48] The idea of

---

[47] II. i. 272. The shifting significance of the sign has been remarked upon by (among others) David M. Vieth, 'The Country Wife: An Anatomy of Masculinity', *Papers on Language and Literature*, 2 (1966), 349–50; Deborah C. Payne, 'Reading the Signs in *The Country Wife'*, *Studies in English Literature*, 26 (1986), 403–19; Michael Neill, 'Horned Beasts and China Oranges: Reading the Signs in *The Country-Wife'*, *Eighteenth-Century Life*, 12/2 (May 1988), 3–17; my 'The Culture of Priapism', *Review*, 10 (1988), 19; Sedgwick, *Between Men*, 59.

[48] See Ch. 3 n. 138 above; the surgeon Jacques Guillemeau (cited in the context of French impotence trials by Darmon, *Tribunal de l'impuissance*, 36) asserted that removing both testicles need not bring sexual relations to an end.

Horner as a priapic castrato—to some extent 'really who he simulates'—is made more plausible by the fact that Wycherley nowhere mentions Horner's bastards or the danger of pregnancy by him, in contrast to other rake-heroes like Dryden's Celadon, Congreve's Valentine and Mirabell, or Gay's Macheath.

The multiple meanings of the eunuch can be reconstructed from within *The Country-Wife* itself, as well as from clandestine libertine writing. In the opening scene, Horner's medical co-conspirator compares him to a famous hermaphrodite, the street-vendor Aniseed Robin—as if removing the organs of one sex gave him the attributes of both, causing sexuality to proliferate rather than wither. (In a strangely beautiful song of the period, Aniseed Robin 'got a Child of a Maid, and yet is no man, | Was got with child by a man, and is no woman.'[49]) From the start, then, the associations of Horner's disguise confound the extremes of deficiency and abundance. Another chain of ambivalent association begins when Sir Jaspar, gloating over the prospect of placing Horner in charge of the females in his household, fancies himself the Grand Signior of Turkey employing Horner as 'my Eunuch' (III. ii. 303, IV. iii. 327). Since this ignorant businessman has not 'brought over' the second part of *Escole des filles*, he will not have read the description of Turkish women 'giving themselves pleasure from the friction of the stiff member' of their eunuch guards, who only have 'all three pieces cut clean off' when the master catches them in the act (Ch. 3, sect. 4 above). Samuel Butler makes a similar assumption to Sir Jaspar's in his character of 'A Squire of Dames', which closely resembles the effeminized existence that Horner's ex-friends and rivals imagine for him now that 'all's gone': 'he is an *Eunuch-Bashaw*, that has Charge of the Women, and governs all their public Affairs, because he is not able to do them any considerable private Services. . . . He is a Kind of Hermaphrodite, for his body is of one Sex and his mind of another.'[50] Like the quack doctor and the City husband, Butler associates castration with hermaphroditism (confusing sexual deficiency and sexual plethora) and with the Orientalist trope of the harem—except that he gives so much social power to the sexless guardian that he becomes a 'Eunuch-Bashaw', oxymoronically combining the castrated and the castrator, the master and the slave. Wycherley's Pinchwife might correspond to this paradoxical figure, a tyrannical and jealous patriarch, impotent to prevent his own cuckolding, who tries to regain command by wielding a preventive knife—though in his case he turns it on his spouse rather than on his palace guard.

For Butler and for Wycherley's discredited cuckold Sir Jaspar, the 'Turkish' trope encourages a conceptually innocent reading, which places Horner in a simple binary: he is *either* an absolute eunuch *or* a 'full' man. Importing *L'Escole des filles* into the hermeneutics of the play, on the other hand, provides a series of halfway sexualities that plunge Horner's disguise into dramatic irony. It is difficult to determine how far Wycherley intended this ambiguity, which is deepened rather than resolved by other allusions to 'Turkish' sexuality in his writings. In a satirical poem on

[49] 'Dainty Fine Aniseed Water', from John Hilton, *Catch as Catch Can*, 2nd edn. (1652), performed by The Baltimore Consort on CD *The Art of the Bawdy Song* (Dorian, 1992), track 16; cf. *CW* I. i. 249 (where Friedman cites Charles Cotton's poem on Aniseed Robin).

[50] *Characters*, ed. Charles W. Daves (Cleveland, 1970), 212–13.

Court pimps, for example, he refers to the Turkish tradition of selecting their military leaders from 'Schools of Venus' (*Works*, iii. 51). But does he mean brothels, a common meaning of this phrase and the title of *L'Escole des filles* in translation, or seraglios with eunuch guards, as the Orientalist context suggests?

Of the various kinds of 'Half Men' explicitly mentioned in Wycherley's play by characters who fail to realize the significance of what they are saying, the most resonant is the Italian singing castrato. Old Lady Squeamish sees in Horner 'as harmless a man as ever came out of *Italy* with a good voice', placing him in a long tradition of bawdy speculation on the male soprano, and raising the question of precisely what sort of eunuch he is: Harcourt assumes that 'all's gone', like the Turkish guard after the Bashaw has finished with him but Lady Squeamish's castrato analogy suggests a more alarming rival. In *La retorica delle puttane*—which Wycherley must have known, since he imitates its dedication in his next play *The Plain-Dealer*—the musical castrato is identified as the principal sexual interest of the élite client, so that the courtesan must 'mutate herself into Ganymede' to give pleasure; another Italian satire attacks the composer Barbara Strozzi for 'wasting all her love' on a castrato, proving that his appeal migrates across gender boundaries (Ch. 2 n. 31 above). By the early eighteenth century Lady Squeamish's assumption of 'harmlessness' would seem impossibly naive. Montesquieu observed Englishmen smitten with *amour philosophique* for castrati (Introd. n. 35 above), while satirists often depict society women's affairs with Italian singers like Farinelli—who could 'give uninterrupted Joys | Without the shameful Curse of Girls and Boys', having greater 'power to please' than conventional men because he can 'stand it to the end' without 'flagging'.[51] The castrato embodies the paradox of increase-through-depletion: 'Strange that the Loss of all our Store | Should make us able to do more.'[52] Successive English editions of Charles Ancillon's *Eunuchism Displayed*, the fullest treatment of eunuch sexuality, explain that it is 'Occasion'd by a young Lady's falling in Love with Nicolini, who sung in the Opera' (1718), or simply retitle it *Italian Love* (1740). 'Italian love' for a long time denoted homoeroticism or sodomy, thanks to Aretino's sonnets, the prose *Puttana errante*, and Rocco's *Alcibiade*; now this repertoire expands to include the castrato, appealing to either sex in either role—a sort of passepartout to all bedrooms. Hints scattered throughout *The Country-Wife* allow us to see Horner as 'a man come out of Italy' in more ways that Lady Squeamish dreams of.

Despite the 'French' nature of his supposed affliction, the 'real' Horner—not only the strangely convincing eunuch-misogynist he presents to the world, but the private self he reveals to his partner-victims—might well seem more 'Italian'. He proclaims himself the '*Machiavel*' of sex, and exploits the ambiguous position of the Italian *cicisbeo*, who could be either a Petrarchan/Platonic attendant or a sanctioned lover; Lady Fidget's play with the terms 'Mistress' and 'Gallant' exploits the same

---

[51] *The Happy Courtezan, or The Prude Demolish'd: An Epistle from the Celebrated Mrs C[onstantia] P[hillips], to the Angelick Signior Far[i]n[el]li* (1735), 6–7 (note that the unknown author fits eunuch-love into the model of *heteropaedophilia* by having Phillips call him 'delicious Boy!', 4).

[52] *The Rakes Progress, or The Humours of Drury-Lane, a Poem in Eight Cantos, in Hudibrastick Verse* (1735), 18.

ambiguity, defining him as a harmless 'Squire of Dames' to her husband's satisfaction, but retaining the hard-core meaning for herself (and the knowing audience).[53] Horner's interest in 'new Postures' and 'coming in the back way' allies him with Aretino and *La retorica delle puttane*—a hint reiterated (and presumably emphasized by audience laughter) when Pinchwife orders Margery to inscribe her letter 'on the back side, for Mr. *Horner*' (IV. ii. 314), or when Horner tries to get rid of her by 'letting her down the back way' (V. iv. 346). In the Pinchwife segment of the plot, where the eunuch pretence never comes into play and Horner acts as his priapic self, his sexual response to Margery confirms the 'Italian' implications of the 'back way': he is strangely cool and irritable when they are alone together without disguise, but he reacts positively when he receives a naively direct letter from her, and ecstatically when she puts on breeches to pass as the ephebic 'little Sir James'. The 'country wife' arouses him best as an artefact and as a Ganymede. We are struck by the rapidity with which Horner bundles Margery off after copulation, and by his 'Machiavellian' interest in the plot rather than the fruition; as in the case of the amorous castrato, his short-term availability is constantly threatened by the fading of desire. In the closing moments of the play he re-establishes his eunuch disguise by lamenting to the assembled company that he can never be a husband, while the music and the epilogue proclaim him still the virile maker of cuckolds.[54] Reading Horner as an 'Italian lover' undermines this certainty.

It may seem perverse to associate Horner with ambiguous or defective sexuality, since until recently critics have assumed that he represents healthy devotion to natural pleasure and the triumph of the 'life-force'.[55] Wycherley himself encourages us to read him as a true womanizer, as he insists in the pseudo-feminocentric Epilogue and in *The Plain-Dealer*: in a scene modelled on Molière's *Critique de L'École des femmes*, the discredited and prudish Olivia denounces (and therefore endorses-in-reverse) Horner's rampant 'Town-bull' priapism (II. i. 411). Even those readers who recognize that his ironic eunuch pose is in some way true after all, that he really 'can't be' a husband emotionally, still assume that his physical equipment works splendidly.[56] But how good *is* he in bed? Margery seems favourably impressed with him after a single bout, in comparison with her 49-year-old husband, but more expert witnesses express their doubts. Lady Fidget enjoys her pretty piece of china (even though *she* had to do the 'toiling and moiling' to get it), but feels quite certain that he has none left in his collection; Horner himself admits that 'she was too hard for

---

[53] IV. iii. 318; for the shifting meaning of 'gallant' see II. i. 278, 279, 280 and n., 282, V. iv. 345.

[54] V. iv. 352; I accept Gerald Weales's conjecture, in his edn. of *The Complete Plays of William Wycherley* (New York, 1967), 370–1, that the 'Dance of Cuckolds' specified at *CW* V. iv. 352 went to the well-known tune 'Cuckolds all a-row', which Pepys records being played at Charles II's request at a ball at Court (31 Dec. 1662).

[55] e.g. Virginia Ogden Birdsall, *Wild Civility: The English Comic Spirit on the Restoration Stage* (Bloomington, Ind., 1970), ch. 6, esp. 156; Harold M. Weber, *The Restoration Rake-Hero: Transformations in Sexual Understanding in Seventeenth-Century England* (Madison, 1986), 55.

[56] Cf. Katherine M. Rogers, *William Wycherley* (New York, 1972), 61, and Anthony Kaufman, 'Wycherley's *The Country Wife* and the Don Juan Character', *Eighteenth-Century Studies*, 9 (1975/6), 220; for an updating of this view that invokes 'discourse' rather than psychology, see Douglas Ford, '*The Country Wife*: Rake Hero as Artist', *Restoration*, 17 (1993), 83.

me, do what I cou'd', and Squeamish says explicitly 'I have known you deny your China before now'. When he later asks Lady Fidget to confirm his sexual prowess ('You have found me a true man I'm sure'), she answers 'Not every way—', and it is she who closes the Epilogue with the reminder that, when it comes to the truth of sex, 'there's no cozening us'.[57]

These hints of physical incapacity resonate with those points in the dialogue where impotence is explicitly invoked. For a man confident enough to risk being 'despised' by his male peers, Horner seems unduly aware of his erectile frailty (like Wycherley himself, who wrote numerous poems on the subject of impotence). At a critical moment in his verbal persuasion of Lady Fidget, he warns her that 'if you talk a word more of your Honour you'll make me incapable to wrong it'; like the name of God at a Satanist ceremony, he explains, the word Honour 'makes the charm impotent'.[58] Her shocked response ('Nay, fie, let us not be smooty'), like her earlier indignation when she encounters the 'filthy French Beast', again uses surface prudery to convey her aversion to sexual disappointment—but it also underlines how powerfully transgressive it is to utter the word 'impotent' in a context of seduction. As in Pepys's reading of *L'Escole des filles* or Horner's own response to Margery's letter, verbal representation is assumed to exert a direct force on the genitals, but that force may oppose as well as incite desire; Sex and the Word are so closely linked that one can produce or obliterate the other.

Horner's unwittingly self-referential list of imported pleasure-toys goes from the 'bawdy picture' to the 'new posture' and culminates in an imaginary library, beginning with the 'second Part of the *Escole de Filles*'. I have already suggested that the book plays a crucial role in establishing Horner's initial alibi, since to mention it at all is construed as a violently misogynistic act that confirms his total impotence. As with the 'Effigy' and the 'Half Man', however, the libertine book also provides a constitutive source for Horner, making him what he simulates. Despite his scorn for mere 'representative' words, in a sense Wycherley's rake-hero *is* that elusive 'second Part' or follow-up, an assemblage of supplementary representations 'brought over' from the French and Italian libertine canon. Ironically, *The Country-Wife* resounds with echoes and endorsements of the texts that Horner advertises by their absence.

Horner's 'Italian' genealogy supplements the French connection he flaunts in the face of those he wishes to shock and seduce. 'New postures' certainly evoke Aretino, subject of Wycherley's wit and emulation in *Hero and Leander*, and Horner's frolics with the androgynous 'little Sir James' might suggest Rocco's *Alcibiade*, since he clearly knows how to extract erotic 'treasure' from the ambiguous boy-girl. But the

---

[57] IV. iii. 321–2 (the scene in which Lady Fidget drinks a toast to 'thou representative of a Husband'), V. iv. 341, 354. Robert Markley, *Two-Edged Weapons: Style and Ideology in the Comedies of Etherege, Wycherley and Congreve* (Oxford, 1988), 175, emphasizes Horner's sexual exhaustion in the china-scene and the mechanical entrapment in his own plots that makes him 'becom[e], for a short while, what he pretends to be'.

[58] IV. iii. 317; cf. *PD* V. iii. 502 (Manly's indignation threatens to 'make Revenge itself impotent, hinder me from making [Olivia] yet more infamous'), and for the real-life linkage of special words, impotence, and anti-liturgic magic in France Darmon, *Tribunal de l'impuissance*, 41.

most obvious debt is to *La retorica delle puttane*. Pallavicino turns illicit sexuality into a *disegno*, Wycherley into a 'new design' (IV. iii. 316). Like Pallavicino's mistress of manipulation, Horner explicitly applies Machiavelli to the 'business' of amorous intrigue, and in many ways he constitutes himself according to her prescriptions for the courtesan: he subordinates everything to the stratagem, manipulates the rhetoric of appearances, cultivates an exterior that proclaims him 'dead to the world', derives the maximum Eros-effect from images while remaining fundamentally devoid of feeling, invents ingenious alibis like the china shop, and juggles multiple liaisons by stowing his lovers (or clients?) in different rooms of his lodgings—just as the old bawd recommended. Equating the (hyper)masculine Horner with the (pseudo)feminine courtesan might seem far-fetched, but the 'virtuous gang' of City ladies, once they have obtained the china they came for, explicitly call him a male prostitute, dubbing him 'Harry Common'.[59] Wycherley's own identification with *La retorica* becomes clear in *The Plain-Dealer*, whose heavily ironic dedication to an infamous brothel-keeper echoes many details from Pallavicino's preface to 'the University of Courtesans'.[60]

Horner's explicit mention of *L'Escole des filles* might seem more direct and 'plain-dealing', but it contains its own equivocation. Strictly speaking, he cites an effigy of a book rather than the work itself, since no separate publication called *The Second Part* actually existed. Wycherley presumably means *La Philosophie des dames*, the second of the two dialogues that make up *L'Escole* and the one more suitable to the philosophical town ladies (whereas the first dialogue applies more to the rural ingénue Margery Pinchwife). But Horner might be projecting a wholly fictitious sequel, or adding another level of trickery by alluding to one of the innocuous works that used the same title, like the premarital advice-dialogue reissued in 1672, or R.D.V.'s counterfeit *Ecole des filles* of 1658. The term 'Seconde Partie' itself appears not in the pornographic *Escole* but in R.D.V.'s pious fraud, the pseudo-libertine text that traps the reader by seeming to be wicked and then mutating into a 'harmless' treatise on Christian marriage.[61] Horner would clearly identify himself with the first *Escole*—on the cover an innocent devotee of female 'improvement' (suitable for Mrs Pepys to 'translate'), but fiercely priapic when opened. Nevertheless the moralistic 'Seconde Partie', where the phallic bravado and obscene vocabulary give way after a few pages, better represents his triple dissimulation: in Horner and in the faux-pornographic tract, flaunting the phallus is itself a front.

Many details of *The Country-Wife* do directly correspond to the libertine *Philosophie des dames*, however. The city ladies' rejection of the priapic but inadequate eunuch sounds very like Fanchon's reaction to the same figure in *L'Escole*, as we

---

[59] v. iv. 345 (for the name, cf. Doll Common in Jonson's *Alchemist*); the whorish implication of Horner's stratagem is anticipated in Wycherley's *Hero and Leander* ('he who is of Female good Name chary, | With the whole Sex is sure as't were to marry', *Works*, iv. 95).

[60] See my *Libertines and Radicals*, 205–6, 315 n. 12.

[61] R.D.V., *L'Ecole des filles* (n.p., 1658), ii. 1 (title page to second part); the work of the same title published by Antoine du Périer (Ch. 3 n. 35 above) explores the exact issues that constitute the Alithea plot in *CW* (how to evaluate competing suitors for marriage, how to combine strict virtue while enjoying the dangerous delights of the town).

have seen. Though the central device of the 'country' plot comes straight from Molière—the artificially protected ingénue suddenly inspired to heights of ingenuity by feelings of desire, using materials supplied by her tyrannical keeper in the very act of teaching her what not to know—Wycherley transposes it from courtship comedy to sex farce and thus into the illicit world of *L'Escole*, since the awakening takes place *after* marriage. The urban 'gang' represent those who have already graduated from this school, and the scene where they reveal the philosophy of pleasure behind the mask of married respectability (v. iv. 340–5) reads like an accelerated version of Fanchon's or Octavia's initiation into married life—total erotic freedom in the private world, total conformity on the outside (since *honestas* consists only in making people believe you have it). Even the 'genuine' characters subscribe at times to the *libertin* idea of marriage as a gateway to unlimited sexual adventure for upper-class wives: when Harcourt tries to persuade Alithea to break off her engagement to Sparkish, he insists that if she marries a fool she 'wou'd be thought in necessity for a cloak'.[62] His assumption matches the philosophy of *L'Escole des filles* precisely: unmarried girls live in constant fear of pregnancy and ruin, but a husband 'sert de couverture à tout' (II. 169).

Wycherley's heavy-handed play with the different meanings of 'honour', a major theme of the city-wife plot, is strikingly anticipated in the mock-polite introductions to both parts of *L'Escole des filles*. In the dizzying regressive logic of Horner's exchanges with Lady Fidget, diametrically opposed meanings of honour clash according to whether the word applies to men or women, to sexual prowess or social standing, to the attraction that initiates an affair or the trustworthiness that will keep it secret.[63] As we have seen, Lady Fidget talks so much about her honour-as-official-reputation (while praising Horner as a man willing to win honour in the sexual test-bed by sacrificing his honour among men) that he starts to lose the capacity to wrong it. Similarly, the 'Epistre invitatoire aux filles' exhorts mothers to grant their daughters 'complete licence' and thereby 'make your *honesteté* shine forth even more brightly'; honour is 'a fine thing', and this book will teach the sure way to achieve the *honneur du monde* since it encourages 'industry and address in hiding what one is not supposed to know'. The 'Advertissement aux dames' that prefaces the second dialogue shifts the paradox into the openly sexual realm exploited by Wycherley: ladies who decline to learn the postures and pleasure-techniques of *L'Escole des filles* actually 'font déshonneur à leur sexe' and deprive their lovers—'those who have the honour of possessing you'—of the chance to learn by sharing these 'ideas'.[64]

In one instance the English comedy even intensifies *L'Escole*'s effort to split apart verbal representation and corporeal reality, honour-in-the-world and

---

[62] *CW* II. i. 272; cf. the ending of Wycherley's first play, 'the Bondage of Matrimony, no—— | The end of Marriage, now is liberty, | And two are bound——to set each other free' (v. ii. 115).

[63] e.g. II. i. 281: Lady Fidget asks if Horner is 'so truly a Man of honour, as for the sakes of us Women of honour, to cause yourself to be reported no Man? No Man! and to suffer your self the greatest shame that cou'd fall upon a Man', and when he urges her to test his claim empirically replies 'Well, that's spoken again like a Man of honour.'

[64] *Escole*, pp. XLVII–XLVIII, II. 57–8.

honour-in-bed. Susanne dissuades Fanchon from her maternal morality by insisting that 'La virginité est une très-belle chose en paroles et très-laide en ses effects' (II. 167), virginity is a pretty thing in words but quite ugly in its effects. Wycherley weaves this dichotomy into one of his comic variations on the theme of honour, in a three-way interchange between Sir Jaspar, his wife, and Horner—

SR. JAS. Ay, my dear, dear of honour, thou hast still so much honour in thy mouth——
HOR.   That she has none elsewhere——.

This reworking actually brings the passage closer to the proverbial phrasing of *The School of Venus*, the translation of *L'Escole* that first circulated at almost the same time as *The Country-Wife*: 'Virginity is a fine word in the Mouth, but a foolish one in the Arse.'[65] (It is quite conceivable that in performance Charles Hart would have used the coarser version of the phrase, with 'elsewhere' substituted in the printed version.) In this case the French original is less incisive than the demotic English, and we witness in a single passage the hybridization of European *libertin* ideology and native bawdy discourse.

Other details suggest that the French-educated Wycherley had access to Chorier's *Satyra Sotadica* as well as to *La retorica delle puttane* and *L'Escole des filles*. When the 'virtuous gang' complain about men who neglect fine ladies and prefer the coarsest scraps at the ordinary (v. iv. 343), we hear Tullia's complaint that 'men neglect beautiful wives and run after cheap whores, preferring a coarse meal of brown bread and rough wine to the feasts they could have at home' (VI. 216)—a theme that he had already broached in *The Gentleman Dancing-Master*: 'our impatient am'rous Guest, | Unknown to us, away may steal, | And rather than stay for a Feast, | Take up with some coorse, ready meal' (II. i. 172). When the resourceful chambermaid Lucy compares marrying Sparkish to laying out a corpse, and blames her mistress Alithea for passing over 'love, the life of life' (IV. i. 304–5), we recall Tullia's philosophical assertion that 'we live to love and to be loved; she who will not be loved or love is already entombed, already rotten with the stench of disease' (VII. 222). The conclusion of *The Country-Wife*, when Margery is locked up and silenced by Horner just as she had been by her husband, confirms what we are told by the episode in Chorier where Tullia's husband fits her with a jewelled chastity belt, much to the delight of her lover (who has a duplicate key). In each case the husband and the seducer are equally keen to place a lock on a woman's sex, so that the 'Honour' conferred by libertine celebration amounts to little more than an ornamental version of the sex-as-prison topos. Once again Lady Fidget's pun on 'thou representative of a Husband' seems prophetic.

Chorier likewise provides a source or parallel for the phallic epistemology that runs throughout Wycherley's play—indeed through his entire œuvre, since the

---

[65] *CW* II. i. 277; Middx. translation (see Abbreviations above). In Molière's *Critique de L'École des femmes*, scene iii, Uranie records that the *laquais* taunted ladies who objected to the obscenity of the earlier comedy by shouting out 'qu'elles estoient plus chastes des oreilles que de tout le reste du corps'; see also Rochester's letter on the honour of royal mistresses, Ch. 6 n. 5 below.

early *Hero and Leander* calls the erect penis 'The sole unfeigned way Lass to com-
mend' (*Works*, iv. 89), and the late *Plain-Dealer* defines the bed as 'the proper Rack
for Lovers' where otherwise unknowable truths will be forced out.[66] In the seventh
colloquium of the *Satyra Sotadica* Renaissance theories of beauty are subjected to
the principle that the penis is the sole infallible judge and erection the only reliable
criterion (VII. 222); in *The Country-Wife* Horner 'scorns' mere verbal declarations
of potency and assures Lady Fidget that 'I desire to be try'd only', meaning that only
palpable erection and penetration can prove him true to his word. (Alternatively,
the sceptical reader might construe the phrase to mean that his 'desire' is confined to
such experimental moments, that 'trial' is the only thing that arouses him.) Lady
Fidget endorses this phallocentric proof-urge in the warmest possible terms ('all
Men of honour desire to come to the test'), and in the closing epilogue drives home
the idea of the erect penis as an epistemological touchstone: 'men may still believe
you Vigorous' on the basis of mere signage, 'But then we women'—with a suggestive
pause, marked in print by a long dash—'there's no cozening us.'[67]

3. *L'ÉCOLE DES FEMMES* OR *L'ESCOLE DES FILLES*?

Above all, the driving conceit of *The Country-Wife*—the sudden spurts of inventiveness that inspire women once desire has incited them to escape their confinement—had been central to both *L'Escole des filles* and Chorier's *Satyra*. *L'Escole* sets
out to show the simultaneous 'opening' of vulva and mind ('comment l'esprit
s'ouvre en chevauchant'), and the sexual variations and devices of the second part
prompt Fanchon to praise the wonderful 'invention' that love inspires—a comment
on the princess's statue, and therefore hard to assimilate into the Montaignean doctrine that women's mental ability derives solely from 'the school-master Nature'
(pp. LIV, II. 124). As we saw in Chapter 4, Chorier elaborates a whole phallocratic
theory of *mens* and *mentula*, *cunnus* and consciousness, reinforcing it with exclamations on the sex-inspired cleverness of his female characters: *quam perspicax fu-
tutricibus ingenium!* 'how perceptive is the mind of women who fuck!' (VI. 188). The
'schooling' of the sex, the exclusive identification of women's education with sexual
development, is crucial to the libertine project in England as well as France. All three
of *The Country-Wife*'s plots hinge on sudden female ingenuity in the interests of the
fututrix, and Pinchwife is quite right to underline this, however wrong his violent
attempts to prevent it: 'Love, 'twas he gave women first their craft, their art of de-
luding. . . . Why should Women have more invention in love than men? It can only
be, because they have more desires, more solliciting passions, more lust' (IV. ii. 311).

---

[66] IV. ii. 481 (the sentiment is given to the villainous Vernish, but is quite consistent with Wycherley's
own assumptions); cf. Hynes, 'Against Theory?', 165–71, and for a more general analysis of identity, act,
and 'proof' in phallic performance (based on French impotence literature), Citton, *Impuissances*, 64–7.

[67] II. i. 281, 354 (contrast I. i. 250, where Horner expresses the *fear* that his former mistresses might
come to his lodgings to test with their 'sense' whether his verbal report of impotence is in fact true).
Wycherley may also be recalling Brantôme's remark on the sexual adventurousness of great ladies, 'toute
personne d'esprit veut essayer tout', *Les Dames galantes*, ed. Maurice Rat (Paris, 1947), 29.

Pinchwife, like Montaigne, classes women with the 'school-master Nature' and the 'discipline born in the blood' (as opposed to the artificially constructed text that men need to counteract their intrinsic deficiency), but he draws the opposite conclusion; rather than accepting his sister Alithea's innocent freedom and his wife Margery's adolescent desire, he tries to inscribe his own repressive text onto them—almost literally, when he threatens to write in Margery's face with a penknife.

The source for these cognitive plot developments is normally located in another French 'school', Molière's *L'École des maris* and *L'École des femmes*—both comedies that hinge on the folly of shutting women up and the miracles of invention that Love can inspire in country girls. In the most famous speech of *L'École des femmes*, the eager suitor Horace rhapsodizes over the 'great school-master Love' who can 'sharpen the wits' and 'teach us to be what we never were'.[68] (Horace adds a new twist to Montaigne's theory of differently gendered sexual 'discipline', the starting point of Chapter 1 above: he himself proves the deficiency of young men left to their own devices, since he is telling all this to his arch-rival without realizing it, but unlike Montaigne he drives a wedge between 'nature' and the teaching faculty of desire when he declares that Love 'destroys the obstacles of Nature in us'.) Wycherley undoubtedly borrows much from Molière, making his work a kind of English-French palimpsest; this literary hybridization reenacts his own education in the circle of Julie de Montausier. But his French inheritance is more complex and multilayered, including not only the presentable *Écoles* for husbands and wives but their scandalous and contaminating precursor, *L'Escole des filles*. Pinchwife's version of the erotic-didactic topos—attributing the sexually awakened woman's invention to obscene 'lust' rather than gallant *amour*—steers far closer to the libertine dialogue than to the canonical comedies that echo its name.

We should in any case not separate the Molière inheritance too rigidly from the hard-core libertine line. Decorous enough in vocabulary for public performance, his plays still generated the kind of scandal that he milks to the full in the *Critique de L'École des femmes*. (For Joan DeJean, Molière's entire career as a print author derives from his canny exploitation of a vulva-fixated 'obscenity' learned from *L'Escole des filles*.[69]) Like Wycherley later, Molière creates a censorious *précieuse* character to complain about the author's obscene *double entendre*, thus denying and advertising it at the same time; when Climène complains in scene iii of the *Critique* that the 'dirty bits' in *L'École des femmes* 'put your eyes out' ('les saletés y crèvent les yeux') she sounds like Claude Le Petit commending *L'Escole des filles* for 'fucking us in the eyes' (Ch. 3, sect. 2 above). Chapter 3 has already traced other parallels between *Filles* and *Femmes*, similar in name and frontispiece. Shared circumstances and internal allusions link them still closer. The most illustrious owner of the libertine text, Nicolas Fouquet, commissioned a private performance of *L'École des maris* at Vaux;

---

[68] III. iv. 900–20 (see Abbreviations above for edn. cited): 'L'amour est un grand maître. | Ce qu'on ne fut jamais il nous enseigne à l'être; | Et souvent de nos mœurs l'absolu changement | Devient, par ces leçons, l'ouvrage d'un moment; | De la nature, en nous, il force les obstacles. . . . L'amour sait-il pas l'art d'aiguiser les esprits?'

[69] *The Reinvention of Obscenity: Sex, Lies, and Tabloids in Early Modern France* (2002), ch. 3 *passim*.

since that play concerns the folly of a man who believes that '*les filles* are what we make them', and ends with the maidservant inviting the audience to send such brutish husbands 'à l'Ecole chez nous', the whole text could be considered a subtle variant on the title in Fouquet's private collection.[70]

The titles and sometimes the content of these 'schooling' comedies gave off a pleasing aura of indecency. The notoriety of *L'Escole des filles* can hardly have been forgotten, and the phrase 'escholes de marys' could denote the scandalous transformation of the marriage-bed into a training-ground for 'Aretino's Postures'—as we saw in the gossip chronicles of Brantôme (Ch. 1, sect. 1 above). Chorier recalls his personal friendship with Molière during the comedian's sojourn in the south,[71] and Chrysalde's worldly, indulgent advice on cuckoldry in Act IV of *L'École des femmes* matches quite closely Tullia's explanation of Octavia's dream in the fourth Colloquium of the *Satyra* (expanded still further in the post-Molière translation *L'Academie des dames*). For a publicly acclaimed author Molière is unusually direct in his representation of sexual arousal: Agnès in *L'École des Femmes* testifies with Comenian vividness to the 'tickling sweetness' and the 'je ne sais quoi' that she feels 'moving inside her';[72] Philaminte's similar declaration in *Les Femmes savantes* (Ch. 3 n. 167 above) ostensibly describes literary rapture, but equally reveals the 'je ne sais quoi' that 'trickles' through her; Tartuffe barely conceals his salacity as he hovers over the heroine's nubile body. Chorier pushes these themes to the limit, of course, in Octavia's account of her sexual 'opening' and in the Sadean scenes of priestly flagellation in Colloquium V; despite the obvious difference in linguistic propriety, however, Chorier's translator emphasizes his continuity with Molière by referring to the lustful priest as 'ce Tartuffe'.[73]

In several ways the preoccupations of the central character in *L'École des femmes* expand upon the forbidden classic with a similar name, just as its frontispiece by François Chauveau enlarges the miniature book in the education-scene that the same engraver made for *L'Escole des filles* eight years earlier (Figs. 4 and 5 above).[74] Arnolphe is not merely a puritan or 'man of business' but a specialist in libertine literature, a quoter of Rabelais, and a collector of 'contes gaillards' which he combines into a twenty-year research programme on cuckoldry—a fate his entire intellectual and emotional life is devoted to avoiding (I. i. 118–20, I. iv. 306). When he describes his erotic-didactic experiment with Agnès as 'philosophizing' (III. v. 994), when he repeatedly taunts the 'raisonnement' that leads Agnès to prefer her young suitor and plot an elopement (v. iv. 1541–6), and above all when he exclaims

---

[70] II. iv. 511, III. viii. 1114. Numerous command performances of *Maris* were staged in 1661, so the text cannot have been prepared exclusively for Fouquet, but the allusion (capitalized *sic* in the old-spelling Imprimerie nationale edn.) is still striking.

[71] *Adversaria*, iv. 134 (in a posthumous tribute to Molière, he wishes he could renew the friendship established long ago in Vienne and Lyons).

[72] II. v. 563–4 ('La douceur me chatouille et la-dedans remue | Certain je ne sais quoi dont je suis toute émue').

[73] *Academie*, ii. 35.

[74] For a comparison of the educational methods in both *Escoles*, see Larson, 'The Iconography of Feminine Sexual Education in the 17th Century: Molière, Scarron, Chauveau', *Papers on French Seventeenth-Century Literature*, 20 (1993).

Il faut qu'on vous ait mise à quelque bonne école!
Qui diantre tout d'un coup vous en a tant appris?

Someone must have sent you to a good school!
Who the hell taught you so much about it all of a sudden? (v. iv. 1497–8)

we see fragments of *L'Escole des filles* working their way to the surface like shrapnel.
Arnolphe is haunted by the possibility that he might already be acting in some
'second part' of the libertine schooling text. When he rages against this 'idiot girl
who knows more about it than the cleverest man', *le plus habile homme*, he echoes
Montaigne's ironic reflection on men who study pornography to make themselves
habiles (Ch. 1, epigraph). But whereas Montaigne ascribed women's 'discipline' to
mere blood and nature, Arnolphe's fears have been heightened by generations of
articulate women and by a tradition of libertine writing that eroticizes reason. He
seems to contradict himself when he reviles Agnès as both *sotte* and *belle raison-
neuse*, when he sneers at her simple expressions of erotic need by comparing her to
the supposedly sexless and over-educated *précieuses*. We should recall, however, that
raison is a key word throughout *L'Escole des filles*, and that the preface to the *Philosophie des dames* promises 'hauts raisonnements, tirés de la plus subtile doctrine de
l'amour' (II. 58). Arnolphe's mind has been so stamped by the 'School for Girls' that
he cannot separate the voice, the reason, and the sex.

Arnolphe's strict campaign of sexual and pedagogic repression succeeds, therefore, in planting in the audience's mind a phantom image of Susanne's or Tullia's
educational project. As if secretly programmed by Michel Foucault, his prohibitions and interrogations turn into show-and-tell sessions that map out Agnès's sexual body almost as clearly as Octavia's, leading inexorably to that overdetermined
'autre chose' (II. v. 571) of which Agnès herself seems unaware. In his infamous definition of true innocence, he claims that he wants a bride who cannot even play the
word-game *corbillon* ('What Goes into my Basket?') where every answer must end
in -*on*; he wants her to imagine a real picnic-basket with a *tarte à la crème* rather than
thinking up a list of rhyme-words that might include *couillon* and *con* (I. i. 95–9). As
was obvious at the time,[75] the unintentionally suggestive 'cream tart' provides an
even more vivid representation of that organ that dare not speak its name, as if
Arnolphe (played by Molière himself) had to fill in the blanks he forbids his fantasy-
wife to know about.

The most notorious *double entendre* arises when Arnolphe quizzes Agnès on exactly where Horace took her and what he took, interrupting all her answers after 'the
——', in terror of what he might hear.[76] The interruption of 'il m'a pris le ——'
(which turns out to be only *le ruban*) became instantly notorious for raising
women's blushes and curiosity, which is obviously the intention despite the denials

[75] Georges Mongrédien (ed.), *La Querelle de L'École des femmes* (Paris, 1971), i: *Comédies de Jean Donneau de Visé, Edme Boursault, Charles Robinet*, 56–7, 146–7, mention the *tarte* as self-evidently scandalous
(like the Marquis in *Critique*), but explaining it was apparently unnecessary; the equally notorious soup
simile from II. iii. 432–4 (revealing the grossness of the author rather than his peasant character, according to Visé, 29) made the equation of rustic food and genitalia entirely explicit.

[76] II. v. 571–82 (the entire sequence begins and ends with questions about 'autre choses').

programmed into Molière's *Critique*: the effect of the 'two-letter word' is particularly well described in Donneau de Visé's *Zélinde, ou La Véritable Critique de L'École des femmes* and in Edme Boursault's *Portrait du peintre* (both 1663), where a certain Marquise rushes to 'see Agnès's *Le*' and the Count reports that 'when I saw the pose the Actress assumed I thought that the innocent girl was going to say something else'.[77] Even La Fontaine attacks the ribbon-scene, a surprising turn from the author of 'Comme l'Esprit vient aux filles' (Ch. 3 n. 57 above). This comic routine, reinforced by the actress's bodily posture, gave the masculine article *Le* the same bawdy valance as 'china' in Wycherley's *Lordon*; one critic, posing as a woman author outraged by Arnolphe's disparagement of them, discredits Molière by exposing such devices as borrowings from old bawdy songs and 'livres Satiriques', a genealogy that certainly includes *L'Escole des filles*.[78]

Arnolphe's hysterical response shows him trapped in his own game of *corbillon*: whatever the actual referent of 'he took me by the ——', he always supplies the dread monosyllable that ends in *on*. (This was clear to seventeenth-century readers, skilled like *L'Escole* in 'hieroglyphic' reading, but the deconstructionist critic finds that 'Agnès's *le* cannot designate any single organ as the graspable center of female sexuality'.[79]) In Molière's French as in Secundus' Latin, the masculine *con/cunnus* dominates the field of play—a paradox underlined by Agnès's first piece of trickery, when she obliquely refers to Horace as '*La*', the feminine article.[80] This much-debated *Le*-scene encapsulates the ironic similarity of two 'schools' united by opposite goals. Molière's Arnolphe wants a woman robotically programmed to 'pray to God, love me, sew, and spin' (1. i. 102), whereas *L'Escole des filles* orders her to reject that narrow list of four duties and replace it with one even narrower obligation, 'Fucking'. Before, Fanchon declares, 'I was only good for sewing and keeping silent', but now she dutifully believes 'we were created for Fucking, and when we begin to fuck we begin to live, and all young People's Actions and Words ought to tend thereto' (pp. 123, 110 above). Both strive to 'put something in the head' and so to prefabricate the *fille* according to an absolute theory of the total absence, or total presence, of sex.[81]

Molière can show the ingenuity of romantic love—represented in *The Country-Wife* by Alithea's willingness to lie on Harcourt's behalf as early as Act II—but French classical decorum prevents him from showing invention 'opened up' by the immediate prospect or aftermath of sex, *mens* stirred up by *mentula*, except through

[77] Mongrédien (ed.), *Querelle*, i. 126 ('Quand je vis que l'Actrice y faisoit une pose, | Je crûs qu l'innocente alloit dire autre chose'); in Charles Robinet's *Panegyrique de L'École des femmes* (also 1663) this 'Rebus' has become so familiar, and indefensible, that it can be referred to as 'l'Equivoque du Le, qui force le Sexe à perdre contenance, et le redüt à ne sçavoir qui luy est le plus seant, de rire ou de rougir' (208).

[78] Mongrédien (ed.), *Querelle*, i, pp. xii (La Fontaine), xxvii, 30–1, 41, 64 (Zélinde, who identifies herself in Arnolphe's sneer against 'femme qu compose').

[79] Barbara Johnson, *A World of Difference* (Baltimore, 1987), 85 (in her essay 'Teaching Ignorance: *L'École des femmes*').

[80] 11. v. 627 ('La' or 'là', which Arnolphe sarcastically repeats as 'Monsieur La' (630), can of course also be a warbling nonsense syllable or a distracing 'over there').

[81] Cf. *Femmes*, 111. ii. 749, Maxime 1 ('se mettre dans la tête') and *Escole*, p. XLIX ('mettre l'amour à la teste de sa cousine').

comic substitution-games with *le*, 'autre chose', 'tarte à la crème', or *je ne sais quoi*. Wycherley, in contrast, lets the *fututrix* perform during the course of the action and (in the china-scene) practically under the nose of the audience. Consequently, all his erotic-didactic borrowings from Molière are suffused with a more explicit sexual presence and thus brought closer to their common roots in clandestine discourse.

The mechanics of Margery Pinchwife's trickery depend heavily on Molière's *Écoles*: like Isabelle in *Maris* and Agnès in *Femmes*, she contrives to send first a love-letter, and then herself, in an ambiguous guise that appears to be hostile or contrary.[82] Since Arnolphe repeatedly attacks women authors and literary *précieuses*, and proposes a total ban on Agnès using pen and paper after marriage, we can assume that Molière means to equate female *écriture* and sexual liberation in a positive light. Her actual letter, however, is agonizingly correct in its grammar and its concern for impropriety, even though her (still more naive) suitor interprets it as a 'sweet' expression of unmediated 'nature'.[83] In Chorier and in Wycherley, on the other hand, epistolary authorship manifests the writer's sexuality directly. Laura's letter, though written 'without art', shows Tullia and Octavia how inventive she must be in bed (Ch. 4, sect. 2 above); Margery's letter, *naïve* in both senses since it gives a vivid picture of 'rubbing knees' with Horner as well as expressing her childlike defiance and fear, arouses Horner by its immediacy and absence of jaded conventionality, its lack of Flames, Darts, and Dissimulation (*CW* iv. ii. 314, iii. 327).

When Pinchwife laments the 'free education' that has led to Alithea's supposed ruin, he is echoing Molière's Sganarelle and Arnolphe, participating in a Moliéresque drama of social delusions and competing educational philosophies. When he repudiates Horner's offer to teach Margery 'breeding', however, he evokes something much more corporeal and direct: 'To be taught! no, Sir, . . . [*Aside*] I'll keep her from your instructions, I warrant you!' 'Love's school' is a recurrent theme in Wycherley's play, from the 'Catechisme' of Sparkish and Harcourt to the roll-call on the last page, where each man recites a sentence of the 'doctrine for all Husbands'—a virtual translation of Molière's title. Here, however, Pinchwife thinks only of the school of sex, the direct infusion of knowledge through the instrument praised for its pedagogic powers in Rocco's *Alcibiade*, in *L'Escole des filles*, and in the earlier dialogues of Chorier's *Satyra*. It is the word 'taught', more than the potentially bawdier 'breeding', that triggers his explosion.[84] Wycherley thus transcribes

---

[82] Though Margery's specific device, a veil that allows her to switch identities, had been used in Abraham Cowley's *Guardian* (1641), revised as *The Cutter of Coleman Street* (1663).

[83] iii. iv. 940–51 (for Arnolphe's slurs against women writing, see i. i. 87–96, i. iii. 244–8, iii. ii. 776–9 (Maxime VII), and for his attack on Agnès's emotional frankness as *précieuse*, v. iv. 1542); Johnson points out the 'acrobatics of subordination' and the 'self-censorship' of the letter, setting it against the almost-universal tendency of critics to agree with Horace's 'fatuous' naturalist interpretation ('Teaching Ignorance', 80, 82–3).

[84] i. i. 261 (accepting Friedman's suggestion that the stage-direction *Har*. 'would refer more appropriately to Horner'), iii. ii. 295–6, v. i. 334, v. iv. 351; for the pun on 'breeding', cf. Richard Head's *English Rogue*, p. 231 above.

the comedy of 'schooling' onto the physical plane of the philosophical libertine and the *perspicax fututrix*, thereby creating his own 'second Part' or extension of *L'Escole des filles*. He 'brings back from France' precisely what Horner pretends not to have and his auditors pretend not to want.

6

Rochester and Oldham

'Heroic' Pornography in the Shadow of Aloisia

> Such natural freedoms are but just,
> There's something generous in mere Lust.
> But to turn damned abandoned *Jade*,
> When neither *Head* nor *Tail* perswade,
> To be a *Whore* in understanding,
> A Passive *Pot* for *Fools* to spend in . . .
>
> > (Rochester)

> Hadst thou the Pow'r as well as bold Design
> To outdo Nero's Pimp and Aretine,
> Or that fam'd Spanish Whore—
> Who shews how far her Sex can Conquest boast
> Ore ours both acting and describing Lust;
> 'T had bin Heroick, and deserv'd our Praise,
> 'Tis something to be great in Wickedness.
>
> > (Oldham)

THE wholehearted female sensualist created by the libertine text—for whom reasoning and desiring come in the same moment—provided a mirror and object-lesson for the male reader seeking to perfect himself. She holds out the possibility of synthesizing 'lust' and 'invention' into what Chorier called *erudita libido*, and thus anticipates Elisabeth Rowe's account of the 'philosophick libertine', who 'pursues pleasure for the sake of demonstration, pausing, reasoning, and making critical reflections on every enjoyment'.[1] But in Chapter 5 we saw only fragmentary 'reflections' of this aspiration: the contemplative but internally divided consumer of erotic images, the 'designing' serial seducer who comes close to 'ruining himself' by revealing his affinity with the sexual deficiency he simulates, the seeker after epistemological certainty in a phallus seen to be hollow. The philosophical libertine character intermittently adopted by Pepys or dramatized by Wycherley—and by Molière in *Dom Juan*—seemed to contemporaries most fully embodied in the poet and wit John Wilmot, Earl of Rochester. As in the case of his French predecessors Théophile de Viau and Claude Le Petit, his own life was assimilated to the various

---

[1] Introd. n. 68 above.

extreme personae he created in daringly obscene verse, and like Le Petit's that life
burned out abruptly; Rochester was spared public execution, but died of syphilis
and alcoholism at the Christ-like age of 33, after a much-publicized conversion from
his earlier flamboyant atheism. Though (unlike Pepys and Wycherley) he does not
directly flaunt his knowledge of *L'Escole des filles* and Chorier, he does allude to the
originary figure of Aretino, and identified with that satiric priapist enough to commission a self-portrait in which he bestows a laureate wreath on a pet monkey (who
shows his critical acumen by tearing a leaf out of a scarlet book and sitting on a pile
of folios); this re-enacts the irreverent gesture of Aretino himself, who dedicates his
first *Ragionamenti* 'To his Monkey' and invites him to rip up his pages.[2]

The first section of this chapter uncovers the many traces of libertine study in
Rochester, the most notorious (and now the most canonical) English poet of sexual
transgression. His lyrics and dramatic monologues simulate various fractions of
homo libertinus and act out his central contradictions—between philosophical
'understanding' and sensuous 'enjoyment', between tributes to the 'generosity' of
lust and attacks on the sensuality of free women, between an extreme self-defeating
masculinity and an unfulfilled desire for the kind of 'liquid raptures' that Chorier
had represented in his female protagonists. Later sections explore the poet and
schoolteacher John Oldham—disciple and companion of Rochester, posthumously praised by Dryden. His poetic fragments and rough drafts, studied here for
the first time, articulate the earliest recorded response to 'Aloisia Sigea', understood
as a courtesan-author who outperforms men both in action and in discourse (as my
second epigraph shows). Oldham's conflicted representations of the libertine
woman author link him, I suggest to the first translation of Chorier and to *Sodom*,
the first sustained attempt at pornography in English. Section 3 reads the various
versions of this burlesque drama alongside Oldham's own obscene poetry, as
attempts to achieve the same 'heroic' transgression that he praises in Aloisia.

It was while working at Whitgift's School in Croydon that Oldham composed a
Latin poem 'In Aloisiae Sigeae Toletanae Satyram Sotadicam' and celebrated 'her'
exploits in several verse fragments still discernible among his unpublished foul
papers. (Oldham's connection with Chorier's erotic classic may have been even
closer: we shall see in section 3 that the English version of Colloquium IV, dated four
years earlier than the French *Academie des dames*, appears in a manuscript containing several works by Oldham and the earliest drafts of *Sodom*—the subject of his
longest and rudest commentary on libertine representation.) In several of his rough
drafts Oldham also flaunts allusions to Aretino, *L'Escole des filles*, *The School of
Venus*, *Sodom*, the lewd poems of Rochester, and the 'lectures' of bawds and midwives, mingling abhorrence and admiration; these fevered speculations on the

---

[2] Cf. 76 (Aretino's Postures in St James's Park, p. 268 below), 115 ('I have seen Physicians Bills as Bawdy
as *Aretines* Dialogues'), 400 n. 142; see Abbreviations above for the Rochester edn. cited. For an alternative view (uninformed by the Aretino echo) that has Rochester *removing* the laurel from a simian
Dryden, see Kirk Combe, *A Martyr for Sin: Rochester's Critique of Polity, Sexuality, and Society* (1998),
162 n. 18, 168 n. 39, and Keith Walker, 'Lord Rochester's Monkey (Again)', in Nicholas Fisher (ed.), *That
Second Bottle: Essays on John Wilmot, Earl of Rochester* (Manchester, 2000), 81–7.

forbidden curriculum were evidently written in the midst of grading, since some of them are composed on the backs of recycled Latin exercises by his pupils. Perhaps, like Casanova's tutor, the ex-Puritan teaching assistant alerted his boys to the scandalous text by forbidding them to read it. At almost exactly the same time Samuel Wesley, father of the founders of Methodism, recalls that his fellow-pupils at Newington Green Dissenters' Academy 'had Meu[r]sii Elegantiae. Aloysia Sigilla Terentia and octavia, and [sic] the most lewd abominable Bookes that ever blasted christian Ey'. (When this letter was published, in an attempt to discredit the dissenting academies, the editor multiplied the titles of iniquity by changing this to '*Meursii Elegantiae, Aloysia Sigaea Terentia,* and *Octavia*'.) In view of what Oldham was scribbling, Wesley probably should not have naively assumed that 'those [Bookes] you will believe our Tutors knew not of, nor did they direct us to the former'.[3] On both sides of the staffroom door, young men were savouring secret knowledge and schooling themselves in the *Arcana Amoris et Veneris*.

1. THE AESTHETICS OF TRANSGRESSION IN ROCHESTER AND CHORIER

Looking back from the eighteenth century, Samuel Johnson saw Rochester as a figure constituted by the libertine text as well as by the frenetic attempt to translate it into reality; for Johnson, his writing grew out of 'a course of drunken gaiety and gross sensuality, with intervals of study perhaps yet more criminal'.[4] That 'study' must have included the clandestine dialogues of his own generation as well as the sources he explicitly cites or translates (Lucretius, Petronius, Aretino, Ronsard, Hobbes, Boileau). In particular, Rochester and Chorier share individual images and phrases as well as larger concerns like the Protean refashioning of the body in the process of arousal, or the replacement of orthodox morality by a classicizing hedonism; both authors are preoccupied with the intellectual life of sexually active women, and both make a cult of erotic complexity and extremity. Disciples like Oldham and Robert Wolseley cite *L'Escole* and Chorier's supposedly female-authored *Satyra* in their critical writings, and associate them explicitly with 'our great witty bawdy Peer', as Oldham called him (section 2 below). As we shall see in Chapter 8, Wolseley defends the aesthetic integrity of Rochester's obscene verse by equating his achievement with the acknowledged classics of arousal, '*Aloisia Sigea*' and '*L'Escole des Filles*'.

The philosophical turn in Rochester takes two forms. Like Pepys, his quotidian discourse (letters, conversations recorded by others) is occasionally lit by flashes of

---

[3] Oxford, Bodleian Library, MS Rawlinson C.406, p. 109, copy of letter of Oct. 1698; *A Letter from a Country Divine* (1703), 14.

[4] 'Rochester', in *Lives of the Poets*. Ever since the posthumous publications of 1680 and 1691 his poems had been split into two canons, one respectable enough to be recycled in the multi-volume collection of British poets for which Johnson wrote the Lives, the other circulating in the clandestine market; the two were only combined in 1968, and the obscene part of the œuvre still has numerous disputed attributions.

self-conscious reflection, as if the 'sober man' were commenting on the inflamed priapist. As in Wycherley (another member of his witty inner circle), his lyrics and dramatic monologues display various facets of the rake-hero's erotic-ontological quest—motivated by the desire to find epistemic certainty in the phallus, yet always prepared to subordinate the pursuit of pleasure to a 'Machiavellian' stratagem of calculation. Wycherley and Rochester share so many motifs, so close in date, that it becomes impossible to tell who originated them. Rochester's comment in a letter on royal mistresses 'whose honour was ever soe extensive in theire heads that they suffered a want of it in every other part'[5] might be a source, or an echo, of Horner's similar quip about Lady Fidget, already derived from *L'Escole des filles* (Ch. 5, sect. 3 above). When Lady Fidget and Horner urge each other to 'come to the test' they re-enact (or inspire) Rochester's simulation of a fatuously confident Don Juan, boasting that

> Wee whose Hearts doe justly swell
> With noe vaineglorious pride,
> Knowing how Wee in Love excell,
> Long to bee often try'd. (34)

The Rochester-effect is marked, however, by a distinctive striving for extremity. In his most famous lyric he posits 'Love rais'd to an extream' as the only trustworthy phenomenon in a world of flux and deceit, and therefore torments himself and his lover with jealousy because this is 'the only Proof twixt her and me | We love and doe not Dream'; the 'Fantastick fancys' and 'fraile joys' of love can easily be faked, 'But pain can ne're deceive' (28). Here Rochester anticipates not only the villainous twist in Wycherley's *Plain-Dealer*—where the bed becomes a 'Rack' for men to extort the painful truth from women—but de Sade's assertion in *La Philosophie dans le boudoir* that pain is the most intense and therefore the most reliable sensation: 'les effets du plaisir sont toujours trompeurs dans les femmes; . . . il faut donc préférer la douleur, dont les effets *ne peuvent tromper*.'[6]

Like Horner, Rochester offers his audience an assemblage of textual representations, an Anglo-French synthesis with Italian overtones. One of his contributions to literary history is the 'imitation' or 'allusion' to a classical text, translating Horace (for example) into a racy, up-to-the-minute idiom that lets the reader glimpse unforeseen connections between ancient Rome and modern London. This palimpsestic form of 'imitation' also incorporates the clandestine canon of early modern Europe. Scholars have recognized the influence of French *libertin* and *satyrique* poetry on Rochester's ideas, linking the attack on abstract reason in his *Satyr against Mankind* to writers like Jacques Des Barreaux; both poets denounce the unnecessary miseries brought by excessive intellect, and propose to 'enjoy' the world rather than to 'know' it (though for Rochester the pain of consciousness should

---

[5] *Letters*, ed. Jeremy Treglown (Oxford, 1980), 75.
[6] *La Philosophie dans le boudoir*, in *Œuvres*, Bibliotheque de la Pléiade, iii, ed. Michel Delon and Jean Deprun (Paris, 1998), 67 (emphasis mine); and cf. Wycherley, *Plain-Dealer*, IV. ii. 481 (cited in Ch. 5, sect. 2 above).

logically give *greater* enjoyment).[7] We should add that Rochester's attitude and style, as well as his passing philosophical expressions, derive from the *satyrique* tradition of meticulously crafted verse and violently obscene diction. In one parody of a contemporary love-song, Rochester gives Phillis the extravagant urge to receive a 'Prick' in 'every pore' and every orifice, even 'to wish those eies Fuckt out' (102). He seems to compete directly with his French predecessors, here outtopping the commendatory poem by Claude Le Petit that had praised *L'Escole des filles* for 'nous foutre par les yeux'.

Rochester's desire to give the additional twist, which we might call literary (per)version, leads him to create chimeras or hybrids of the 'classic' and the 'pornographic'. When he rewrites Ronsard's imitation of Anacreon's ode to a drinking cup, for example, he overlays his French source with hints of Italianate pederasty: the goblet must show not wreathing vines but 'Two lovely Boyes . . . The Type of Future Joyes' (41)—a deliberately blasphemous recreation of Rocco's idea that the joys of heaven can only be found in a boy's embrace (Ch. 2, sect. 2 above). The homoerotic associations of this vessel recall Pallavicino's advice to the courtesan to 'fashion herself as Ganymede' and 'mutate the dish into the drinking cup'. Rocco's opening image of Alcibiade as Ganymede, his 'treasure' eagerly rifled by libertines of both sexes, is sharply refocused in Rochester's 'Disabled Debauchee', when the impotent syphilitic looks back over glorious moments in his earlier career:

> Nor shall our Love-fits *Cloris* be forgot,
> When each the well-look'd Linkboy strove t'enjoy,
> And the best Kiss was the deciding Lot,
> Whether the Boy Fuck'd you, or I the Boy.[8]

Again, classical imitation meets modern (per)version; Horace's graceful ode on the beautiful, long-haired youth as *arbiter pugnae*, referee of the mock-heroic battle between the man and the woman who want to possess him, becomes a convulsive 'fit' using the language and the characters of the London street.[9]

Even more serious philosophical verse like the *Satyr against Mankind*, verbally chaste enough to be printed in Rochester's lifetime, pushes 'imitation' in the direction of libertine extremism. Here he adapts Boileau's version of Juvenal's fifteenth satire, on the superiority of beasts to men and instinct to reason. Boileau himself updated his ancient source with topical references to sexual scandal (the female deer never drags her mate into court to demand public proof of his impotence, for ex-

---

[7] 58 (title of the first printed edn., 1679), and cf. 122 for a line of French *libertin* verse apparently by Rochester; Des Barreaux's influence is traced in Dustin H. Griffin, *Satires against Man: The Poems of Rochester* (Berkeley and Los Angeles, 1973), 176–9.

[8] 45; notwithstanding the reading of one Oxford MS (541, 'Whether the boy you fuck't, or you the boy'), Rochester does not seem aware of heteropederastic sodomy (Ch. 2 n. 63, Ch. 3 n. 138 above) and retains the conventional notion that the male will take the active role even with a woman as dominant as the 'tigress' rival in Horace's ode III. xx.

[9] For the context in upper-class riot, see my *Libertines and Radicals in Early Modern London* (Cambridge, 2001), chs. 4–6.

ample).[10] But Rochester alters Boileau by linking him back to the first-generation *libertin* revolt, specifically by importing the version of philosophic naturalism that Father Garasse had ascribed to Théophile and his wicked peers (Ch. 2, sect. 2 above). Rochester might well have taken Garasse's list of outrages as a personal bible. In conversation he defends the 'beauty' of obscene slander (compare Garasse's attack on 'Extravagances des Libertins touchant la beauté des Esprits'), asserts that religious belief is purely a matter of personal disposition and cannot be induced by external force (like the *libertins* who proclaim 'qu'il n'y a rien de plus libre que la creance, et qu'il ne faut forcer ou contraindre personne à croire cecy ou cela'), and refuses to accept that God would intervene in human affairs or restrict 'the use of Women'.[11] Rochester's personal beliefs, at least as he performs them in conversation with an ambitious clergyman, seem to mirror precisely what Garasse deplored.

Rochester's *Satyr* explores the recurrent theme of Garasse's sixth book, the sensuous self-sufficiency of the animals, the natural goodness of 'the body's pleasures', and the consequent obligation to enjoy them 'as much as one can'—indeed 'never to refuse the senses'. 'God and Nature put man in the world to enjoy its pleasures' even more thoroughly than the animals do, and 'God would have done man wrong' had he placed any restraint on enjoyment. Most strikingly, both in Garasse and in Rochester the (simulated) libertine attacks the very idea of subjecting the appetites to 'certain hours and seasons', to the external and mechanical regulation of the clock. Rochester's evidently sincere speaker attacks the religious enthusiast for 'false Reasoning', using hunger as his example: true Reason, according to his definition, bids him seek food when the body naturally needs it; the 'cheat' of conventional reason asks instead 'what's aclock?', 'perversly' mocking and even 'destroying' an appetite good in itself.[12] (As in Garasse, the analogy between hunger and sexual appetite is ubiquitous by implication.) This acrobatic reversal of normality and perversion has no counterpart in Boileau's more measured satire.

Rochester recognizes that his praise of animals is a 'Paradox' (63), that unreflective instinct cannot serve as a model for human desire. He adopts instead a high-libertine definition of 'right reason', a counter-philosophy that binds reason to serve the passions and raise them to a new intensity. Garasse had stumbled over the same contradiction when he denounces the libertines for simple 'brutality' and asserts that 'human pleasure' is 'more excellent and elevated' (713), leaving the door open for texts like *L'Alcibiade fanciullo* and *L'Escole des filles* to make exactly the same argument on behalf of heightened erotic connoisseurship. Tullia d'Aragona had already hinted at a rapprochement between reason and 'lascivious love', but in

---

[10] *Satires*, VIII, lines 143–6.

[11] Garasse, fo. e1[r–v] ('Table de toutes les Sections', headnotes to I. ii, III. v); Gilbert Burnet, *Some Passages of the Life and Death of John Earl of Rochester* in *FCH* (*Critical Heritage*, see Abbreviations above), 54, 65–6, 72.

[12] Garasse, fos. e3[v]–4 (headnotes to VI.vi, vii, ix, x–xi, xiii, xix), p. 726 ('c'est une honte de regler et attacher ses appetits à telle heure, et au son de cette cloche . . . car au lieu de regler l'heure par nostre appetit, nous captivons nostre appetit aux heures', an idea probably derived from Rabelais's idea that clocks are banned in the Abbey of Thélème); Rochester, 59–60 (all subsequent citations of this poem from pp. 57–63).

L'Alcibiade, in *L'Escole*, and especially in Chorier's *Satyra* cognition and reason are discovered in the very phenomena of arousal, and the entire resources of the mind are devoted to enhancing erotic pleasure (a synthesis that Molière's Arnolphe tries to destroy by attacking Agnès's *raisonnements*). Rochester likewise uses the august term 'right reason' for mind in the service of 'Sense', not merely accepting or defending the 'natural' urges but enhancing them by cerebral ingenuity 'to keep them more in vigour'. (Hostile readers read this proposal as a shocking misapplication of the intellect and a licence to revive the spectacular sexual perversions of Tiberius and Sardanapalus.[13]) Nevertheless this libertine-intellectual synthesis—a sybaritic version of Pascal's 'le cœur a ses raisons que la raison ne connoit point'—failed to escape the contradictions of libertine masculinism, to transcend sexual ideology in the interests of pure *diletto dalla conoscenza* (as Rocco put it).

Rochester's thinker and the rake-heroes of Restoration drama proclaim their allegiance to Wit and Sense, but they are unable to reconcile these two components of the libertine character, intellectual brilliance and passionate sensuality. They show their wit, and their freedom from conventional beliefs, by adopting a sensualist, materialist, and determinist philosophy that denies intellect and freedom altogether. Simultaneously, they submit all appearances and all behaviour to a cynical, penetrating, 'Machiavellian' rationalism that subordinates pleasure to calculation, and that reveals the hollowness of the 'life of sense' they ostensibly espouse. Abstract Reason and anti-sensual Philosophy, in Rochester's great *Satyr*, are condemned as an *ignis fatuus* that leads into a wilderness of abject despair ('Hudled in dirt the reasoning Engine lies'), whereas the new 'right reason', the intellect adapted to the service of the animal senses, must be the sole arbiter of the individual. And yet Rochester's poem deconstructs its own sensualism, since the physical is nothing but 'dirt', Wit nothing but a kind of whoredom, and the animal a metaphor for human aggression, corruption, and stupidity. His enemy still 'thinks like an Asse', and the poet's vision of sensuality heightened by cognition still belongs with earlier libertine attempts to lift us above the beasts.

We should not look for consistent themes and positions in Rochester, however. His chosen method is lyric indirection, and his beliefs are consigned to exaggerated personae or veiled in aristocratic irony; his positions are already abandoned, true only for 'this livelong Minute'[14] or realizable only as a yearning for the impossible. His drive towards performative excess and histrionic posing is neatly encapsulated in an autograph fragment on sexual bashfulness (11), where he exclaims 'Could I but make my wishes insolent, | And force some image of a false content!' Nevertheless,

---

[13] *An Answer to the Satyr against Mankind* (*c*.1679), attributed to Richard or Edward Pococke, 2; see Rochester, 56, for his rebuttal, and for earlier uses of 'raison' or 'dritta ragione' in scandalously sexual contexts, see *La cazzaria del C.M.* (Ch. 2 n. 59), fo. A3ᵛ ('la dritta raggion del cazzo in culo'), Ch. 3 n. 109 above, Ch. 7 n. 52 below. Rochester's project to discriminate false from 'right' reason (compatible with sexual pleasure) might also be compared to Horner's experimental search for 'right' women (Ch. 5, sect. 2 above).

[14] 26 (from Rochester's most philosophical lyric, 'Love and Life', where he turns Hobbes's demonstration of the insubstantiality of past and future into a plea that he only be expected to remain faithful for 'the present moment' (25)).

one preoccupation remains central both in Rochester's poetry and in the libertine dialogue: the complex relationship between cognition and sexual arousal, the extreme moment where 'Reason lies dissolved in Love'. In the remainder of this section, I would like to trace this Chorieresque inheritance in Rochester's two most aggressively priapic and obscene narrative poems, *A Ramble in St James's Park* and *The Imperfect Enjoyment*.

Rochester's poetry acts out in a particularly 'insolent' way the contradictions that tear apart all the libertine texts we have studied so far: a philosophy that aims to release sexuality from guilt-ridden prejudice, to rethink it as natural pleasure or rational art, clashes with a renewed desire to control women and abuse them for the freedoms that libertinism itself makes possible. The *Satyr against Mankind* attacks false metaphysics in favour of a proto-Enlightenment 'right reason' wholly integrated with the passions. Erotic love, which Rochester's most sympathetic female character calls 'That Cordiall drop Heav'n in our Cup has throwne, | To make the nauseous draught of Life goe downe', provided the chief opportunity for such an integration of sense and thought: as Chorier's Tullia puts it, *cunnus* here merges with consciousness, *mens* with *mentula*, and the result is an antidote to *nausea*.[15] In *A Ramble in St James's Park*, however, Rochester showers vitriol on a woman who seems to have achieved precisely this fusion of passion, cognition, and expression.

After sauntering through the park and regaling us with the promiscuous scene, the speaker glimpses his mistress Corinna chatting with a group of rival wits, and this vision of sexually driven discourse ignites a fit of jealousy that dominates the rest of the poem. Rochester frequently praises fellow-authors who match external behaviour to internal drives, converting language and creativity into an instrument of sexuality: his friend Sedley excels in seductive, 'mannerly Obscene' poetry that can 'dissolve' virgins and 'impart | The loosest wishes to the chastest heart' (72); another alter ego 'never Rhym'd but for my Pintles sake' (259), subordinating his literary career entirely to his penis. Even Artemiza, his female philosopher of love and nausea, gleefully accepts the equation of 'Whore' and 'Poetesse' because it spurs her literary invention. Creating the persona of this Tullia-like 'Arrant Woman' helps Rochester articulate his own itch to write, drawn to it precisely because ''tis the worst thing that [he] can doe', evidently 'Pleas'd with the Contradiction and the Sin' because transgression provides the vital 'force' needed to produce 'insolent' images.[16] In Rochester's libertine theory as in Chorier's, sense and reason cooperate to produce sexual 'vigour'. But in *A Ramble* the woman who speaks her sex becomes a monster.

When Corinna accepts the advances of her foppish seducers, Rochester stages a freakish variant of the *bijoux indiscrets* scenario, the fantasy of the speaking vagina. In his convulsive anger, the rambler grotesquely reconfigures her thinking features

---

[15] 64 (*A Letter from Artemiza in the Towne to Chloe in the Countrey*); for sex–mind theories in Chorier see Ch. 4, sect. 2 above.

[16] 64; for these and other links between 'Witts' and 'Whores' (58), see my *Libertines and Radicals*, 40, 239–44.

and inverts her organs, so that 'at her *Mouth* her C—says yes'. He clearly responds
to the discursive 'Power' that Margaret Cavendish celebrates in the courtesan-
philosopher, a power that 'lay in her Tongue, which was a Bawd for the other end'
(p. 72 above). In Rochester's poem, however, this equation of mouth and vulva takes
an increasingly disturbing form as the rambler imagines Corinna—or more accurately her 'lewd *Cunt*' personified—'spewing', 'devouring', and 'full gorged' with the
emissions of half the Town.[17] Once the sexual-intellectual contract breaks down,
Love *is* the nauseous draught.

Throughout the *Ramble* these diatribes alternate with more positive evocations
of sex as public art, first in the eroticized landscape of St James's Park itself, then in
the ideal libertine life that Corinna has allegedly betrayed. Waller's heroic poem on
the newly improved park had equated the 'amorous shade' of the trees with the gallant love of the courtiers and urbanites who frequent them; in Rochester's burlesque
version, correspondingly, the trees themselves exemplify the kind of 'love' made
under their shade (*'Bugg'ries, Rapes,* and *Incests'*), by contorting themselves into the
infamous Postures that bore the name of Aretino. Rochester could not resist lam-
pooning Waller's description of Charles II's 'manly posture' as he plays the ball-
game pell-mell; now the monarch's tastes are genuinely reflected in the landscape he
has commissioned, since 'Each imitative Branch does twine | In some lov'd fold of
Aretine.' Dubious characters from every level of society—lords, whores, car-men,
pimps, divines, rag-pickers, heiresses—all gather under this grove transmuted into
the sign of Aretino, and 'here promiscuously they swive'.[18] Human interwreathing
thus replicates the tableaux formed by the landscape architecture, imitating the
vegetation that is itself 'imitative' of that twice-removed yet ever-present original, Aretino's postures.

The rude vocabulary and outrageous rhymes of *A Ramble* identify it as a travesty
of that late Renaissance genre, the erotic Elysium. Tasso laid its foundations by
defining the Golden Age as an idyll of sexual freedom destroyed by the iron constraints of artificial Honour, and Thomas Carew elaborated it in 'A Rapture', where
former devotees of chastity 'study' Aretino and carve his postures on the bark of the
trees; in Rochester, the trees themselves naturally 'twine' into those unnatural figures. Aphra Behn similarly anthropomorphizes and eroticizes the landscape when
she imitates Tasso's famous chorus, transforming it into an emblem of untram-
melled female Eros: in the Golden Age, before 'Tyrant Honour' placed its constraints so heavily on women, the very branches of the trees formed 'Mystick
Twines', 'Exchang'd their Sweets, and mix'd with thousand Kisses'—an exact

---

[17] 78–9 (orthography restored from Textual Notes, p. 592); further citations of this 166-line poem
come from 76–80. *A Ramble* has been widely discussed by critics: see esp. Barbara Everett, 'The Sense of
Nothing', in Jeremy Treglown (ed.), *Spirit of Wit* (Oxford, 1982), 25–7; Warren Chernaik, *Sexual Freedom
in Restoration Literature* (Cambridge, 1995), 74–8; Stephen Clark, ' "Something Genrous in Meer Lust"?
Rochester and Misogyny', in Edward Burns (ed.), *Reading Rochester* (New York, 1995), 27–30; my
Libertines and Radicals, 120, 202, 221–2, 227.

[18] 76–7; cf. Edmund Waller, 'On St. *James's* Park as lately improved by his Majesty', *Poems, &c.* (1664),
159, 162, expanded upon in Mark McDayter, ' "Some Lov'd Fold of Aretine": Genre, Intertextuality, and St
James's Park in the Late Seventeenth Century', *Seventeenth Century*, 11 (1996), 229–58.

counterpart to the freely flowing hair, and unambiguous expressions of desire, that they could then enjoy.[19] Rochester's more convulsive version of the topos at once endorses and destroys this vision, torn between travestic violence and nostalgic rapture, naturalistic celebration and offensive denunciation of female desire.

St James's Park thus becomes the quintessential libertine space, an 'All-sin-sheltring Grove . . . consecrate to *Prick* and *Cunt*', populated by adventurously promiscuous aristocrats in the mould of Tullia and Octavia, and hedged round by 'imitative' branches that 'twine | In some loved fold of Aretine'. Transgression becomes the norm and aestheticized pleasure the goal, bodies and trees equally striving to emulate the canonical figurations of Aretino. (At least since Montaigne, we saw in Chapter 1, Aretino had provided the classic 'registers' of masculine self-formation.) Why then should this scene fill the Rochesterian rambler with such a precarious mixture of approval and loathing? Since he refuses to endorse conventional morality and (in theory) grants women the same 'natural freedoms' as men, his motive cannot be the simple jealousy of a Pinchwife or an Arnolphe. What *is* it about Corinna and her lovers that irritates him so much, and what counter-ideal does he accuse them of betraying?

While contemporary moralists like John Evelyn fret about misapplying reason and turning copulation into speculative and artful 'postures',[20] Rochester articulates the equal but opposite anxiety, the fear of *insufficient* artistic prowess. As Judith Butler reminds us, performativity brings its own constraints.[21] One consequence of the aestheticization of sexuality is to add new rivalries to the warlock's brew of phallic pride and possessive jealousy: the rambler and Corinna fight over which of them exhibits true intellect and authorial originality, true *auctoramentum* as Tullia put it. In the climactic passage that I use as the first epigraph to this chapter, Rochester takes pains to insist that her crime is not sexual promiscuity *per se*; had she maintained her commitment to true libertinism, total and principled abandonment to pleasure for its own sake, she would still have been heroic:

> Such nat'rall freedoms are but just,
> There's something gen'rous in meer Lust. (78)

Absolute commitment to the sexual would be 'generous'—a word that denotes ethical altruism, of course, but which primarily referred to the physical signs of breeding, the vibrancy, grace, and energy of the thoroughbred. Like the trees, she would have been both 'natural' and transcendent. Instead she has become 'a *Whore* in understanding', yielding to the 'Noise and Colours' of the superficial fop. His rivals are not real men but flimsy simulacra who 'look, and live, and love by Rote', products of 'Abortive imitation' rather than authentic or 'generous' appetite. In

---

[19] *The Golden Age, A Paraphrase on a Translation out of French*, i. 30–3; both Carew (Introd. n. 82 above) and Behn rework the 'O bell'età di orc' chorus in Tasso's *Aminta*, which also features in the French adaptation of Chorier's *Satyra* (Ch. 7, sect. 2 below).

[20] Introd. n. 52 above.

[21] *Bodies that Matter: On the Discursive Limits of 'Sex'* (1993), 94–5.

consequence she herself becomes an inauthentic automaton driven by neither her mind or her vagina, 'a Passive *Pot* for *Fools* to spend in' rather than a fellow-activist.

It is good policy (as another poet of the period put it) to talk with men of wit and lie with fools,[22] but in this case Corinna has chosen the wrong kind of fool, the artificial rather than the natural:

> Had she pickt out to rub her Arse on
> Some stiff-Prick'd *Clown*, or well hung *Parson*, . . .
> I the proceeding shou'd have prais'd
> In hope she had quencht a Fire I rais'd. (78)

The rambler's fury is not based on a simple hatred of female sexuality or a traditional denial of mind to women, then. Conduct literature dictated 'a passive understanding' for women, but Corinna is attacked for *neglecting* her active intelligence, for consorting with pretentious idiots who talk and make love 'by Rote'. Official morality imposed a strict modesty on women that allowed them no initiative in the choice of partners, and Rochester's fellow-wits supported exactly the same distribution of active and passive roles: as the Earl of Dorset put it, 'Nature's turned when women woo; | We hate in them what we should do.'[23] This speaker, on the other hand, encourages Corinna to choose the best physical specimens for her bed without prostituting her 'understanding'. He would have praised her had she conformed to the libertine ideal that Tullia articulates at the very end of Chorier's dialogue: a woman should follow her pleasures to the utmost, and exert her 'fervid mind' to the fullest extent, otherwise she will be 'nothing but a chamber-pot to piss in' (*Sua si non surgat ab humilitate, fervido animi conatu, . . . Matula est immeienti concubino*).[24] In her stupid adventures in the park 'neither *Head* nor *Tail* perswade'. Susanne in *L'Escole des filles* had placed erotic reason 'not in the head but between cunt and balls' (II. 138), but Corinna falls somewhere in between, since she will be neither *bien amusée* nor *bien baisée*. She becomes precisely what Tullia warns against, 'A passive pot for fools to spend in'.

In the imaginary space of sexual freedom, then, lovers fight about intellectual passivity and shallow taste. The rambler accuses Corinna of compromising the *ingenium* and *fervidus animi conatus* that (for Rochester as for Chorier's Tullia) lifts sexuality out of the realm of nausea and excretion. Like Valmont and Merteuil, they battle over which of them has upheld or betrayed the goal of turning 'mere lust' into a valid art of extremity. The 'imitation' performed by the living branches stands for the right kind of sexual-aesthetic mimesis, as opposed to the 'abortive imitation' of the affected courtier whose success with Corinna occasions the poem's anger. To be productive rather than 'abortive' (generating fresh images of transgression rather than actual children), sexuality must emulate the supernatural vegetation rather than the subhuman fop.

[22] William Walsh, 'Epigram upon Caelia', in Phyllis Freeman, 'Two Fragments of Walsh Manuscripts', *Review of English Studies*, NS 8 (1957), 400.

[23] *Poems*, ed. Brice Harris (New York, 1979), 34.

[24] *Satyra*, VII. 312; in the 1684 *Parliament of Women*, a satire that explicitly cites Chorier (Ch. 4 above), one member complains that women are used by men as mere 'Bed-pans and Close-stools' (6).

The 'loved fold' of the branches concisely suggests three components of libertine desire: autoerotic celebration of one's own *souplesse*, extraction of pleasure from what Tullia called the *inflexiones* and *conversiones* of the other's body, and affectionate familiarity with the Aretine corpus. The phrasing of these startlingly sensuous lines recalls another ecphrastic moment in Rochester's poetry, the Anacreontic description of a drinking vessel ('*Vulcan* contrive me such a Cupp'). Ronsard's version asks the craftsman-god to adorn the cup with the 'folding' or *repli* of the fruit-laden vine,[25] but Rochester (as we have seen) chooses 'two lovely boys' as his decorative motif and wants to see 'Their Limbs in amorous folds entwine' (41). The grammatical ambiguity of 'entwine' encapsulates the overlapping patterns of agency in this 'contrivance' of visible pleasure: is it imperative or descriptive? do the two bodies entwine themselves, forming their own sodomitic 'Cell' (as Killigrew might have called it)?[26] or are they braided together by the master-hand of Vulcan, at the behest of the princely commissioner? Nubile 'boys' are chosen, not merely to give the requisite *frisson* of Greek love, but because of their pliability; like Rocco's Alcibiade, they constitute a resource or 'treasure' to be laid out according to the designer's genius. By emphasizing their homogeneity (*two* lovely boys rather than a master-and-pupil scenario) Rochester allows their 'limbs' to be subsumed into the decorative vocabulary, repeating like acanthus leaves or tendrils. But if the 'loved folds of Aretine' convey the characteristic *pli* of baroque decoration, they also evoke the opening and closing of a page, the gutter of a book, or the crease of a map—'lovingly' consulted in the autoerotic privacy of the study. The 'fold of Aretine' might even suggest a newly discovered body part named after some erudite explorer, like the tubes of Fallopius.

These textual and corporeal meanings all refer to clandestine artistry in the bedroom, theatrical deployment of the most intimate 'folds'. But folding and wrapping connote protective enclosure as well as erotic display. The 'Aretine' phrase thus introduces the curious blend of perverse pleasure and comfort that wells up later in the poem where we might least expect it, in the jealous diatribes. Just as Chorier switches disconcertingly from frenetic priapism to the tender voluptuarism of Octavia and her adolescent boy-lover Robertus, in the final dialogue of his *Satyra*, so Rochester performs a domestic turn in the midst of travesty and abuse, voicing a surprisingly lyrical lament for the rambler's remembered 'home'. As he rages against Corinna the speaker recalls the former 'tender hours' that she has now 'betrayed',

> When leaning on your Faithless Breast
> Wrapt in security, and rest,
> Soft kindness all my pow'rs did move,
> And Reason lay dissolv'd in Love. (79)

That Audenesque 'faithless breast'—a real 'image of content' however 'false'—still gave him the 'security' of engulfment and liquefaction, even though (like the

---

[25] Cited in Rochester's *Poems*, ed. Keith Walker (Oxford, 1984), 246; cf. Marianne Thormählen, *Rochester: The Poems in Context* (Cambridge, 1993), 22.

[26] Ch. 2 n. 93.

'teeming Earth' that generates the display of Aretine postures) Corinna was just as promiscuous then as now.

In this dream of libertine-domestic bliss, the dissolute life really does culminate in the lover 'believing that his soul is liquefied into delicious drops'—the crowning illusion that Pallavicino's courtesan was taught to induce—and the active male seems to adopt the position of Rocco's homoerotic philosopher submitting to his pupil, 'relishing his most ambrosial liquor like a hungry baby sucking milk from the breast' (pp. 85, 101 above). Another lyric of Rochester's brings out yet more clearly this nexus of sexual extremity, liquefaction, and maternal care; in 'Absent from thee I languish still' Rochester excuses his own infidelity as a compulsive self-alienation from the '*safe* bosome . . . Where love and peace and truth doe *flow*'.[27] In the *Ramble* this milky 'flow' extends to the orgasmic fusion of mind and body, when 'Reason lay dissolv'd in Love'. When he is '(w)rapt' inside the disposing power of the sexual master-mistress, the 'Boy' can metamorphose still further, from a pattern of 'folds' and 'branches' into a sentient fluid. The paradigm of enjoyment becomes a 'soft kindness' more like the female orgasm than the male, 'a dissolving of our whole Person' (as Chorier's English translator puts it).[28] The 'dissolving' power praised in Sedley's verse refers specifically to female deliquescence and surrender, but here Rochester's male persona records a yearning to be the one dissolved: arousal makes him, not the hyper-masculine walking phallus imagined in Aretino's sonnets and in lampoons like 'Signior Dildo', but the gender-bending 'all cunt' or *tota cunnus* of Chorier's seventh dialogue.[29]

Unfortunately this state of quasi-infantile peaceful fluidity, of benign rather than revolting sexual liquefaction, cannot easily be reconciled with consciousness. In 'Absent from Thee', Rochester conjures up his vision of the 'safe bosom' precisely in order to justify abandoning that partner and pursuing casual affairs; in syntax as ambiguous as his tone, the inconstant husband explains that his 'fantastick mind' must experience 'The torments it deservs to try, | That Tears my fixt heart from my love' (29). In this post-coital section of the *Ramble* the dichotomy is expressed more succinctly: 'Reason lay dissolved in Love'.

The masculine extremism of the *Ramble* alternates, then, with a transgressive longing for precisely those 'female' gender positions that masculinism debars. In his list of the past freedoms he pretends to condone in Corinna, 'Rochester' assumes the role of the perfect wife as defined by Halifax, ruefully accepting her husband's de-baucheries,[30] politely waiting up for his rambling and promiscuous partner, offer-ing her a little cordial to finish the evening ('My Dram of Sperme was supt up after, | For the digestive Surfeit Water'); as in Secundus' oft-quoted epigram on the gender of the genitals, the *mentula* becomes the little woman and the 'lewd Cunt' the swag-

---

[27] 29 (my emphasis); cf. Thormählen, 'Dissolver of Reason: Rochester and the Nature of Love', in Fisher (ed.), *That Second Bottle*, 30.

[28] *A Dialogue between a Married Lady and a Maid* (1740), 13.

[29] *Satyra*, VII. 221; see Ch. 3 n. 108 above for the Aretinoid sonnet, and Rochester, 248–57, for the court burlesque poem 'Signior Dildo' (probably not by him).

[30] *Advice to his Daughter*, in *Works*, ed. Mark N. Brown (Oxford, 1989), esp. ii. 372–4.

gering master, prime subject of the household as well as the sentence. The rambler denounces Corinna for a kind of scandalous publication, for 'betray[ing] | The Secrets of my tender houres' to the riff-raff she meets in the Park. But what *is* this secret, exactly? In whose 'Love' did he lie dissolved?

The imagery of liquefaction that runs throughout this poem—a powerful cultural operator which we see also in Evelyn's warning against relaxed and insatiable 'seminal vessels'[31]—reveals a certain congruence between the idealized domestic past and the 'loathsome dalliances' that now 'prophane' it (80). When the rambler gives his blessing to 'generous' lust, he presents it in hydraulic terms that recall the Cartesian explanations of erotic plumbing in *L'Escole des filles*: the 'Spermatick Sluce' of the well-hung yokel or vicar would have 'fill'd her *Cunt* with wholesome Juice', 'quenching' the fiery thirst that he himself had raised. This nutritional endorsement of 'natural' promiscuity gives way to memories of actual evenings when Corinna's vagina would come 'home' overflowing with other men's sperm, a walking reservoir of encyclopedic sexual experience. He claims to have participated quite gladly in her polymorphous adventures, relieved of his responsibility to 'quench a fire I raised' and evidently deriving a homoerotic pleasure from the situation into which he 'dissolves'. The alien sperm revolts him at times—as he indulges in the misogynistic fantasy of 'a vast *Meal* of Nasty Slime', literally extracted by Corinna's 'devouring *Cunt*' from the 'Brawn' of porters and footmen—but within moments it becomes a convivial cup, a 'wholesome Juice', a digestive liqueur. Past happiness, like the 'future joys' imagined on the drinking cup, involves 'twining' with a mass of boys' limbs or crowning in a flood of male emission; those moments of 'tender' security, when his reason lay 'dissolv'd in Love', occurred after Corinna returned home 'Drencht with the Seed of half the *Town*'. (This taste, then and now, goes by the name 'buttered bun'; satirists diagnosed a similar predilection in Charles II.[32]) The narrator imagines himself consumed and subsumed into what he elsewhere calls the 'juice of Lusty Men', refashioning the 'Cunt' as a secure or 'enfolded' version of the Aretine landscape he discovers in the Park.[33] To adapt Behn's rosy euphemism, he and Corinna's other lovers 'exchanged their sweets, and mixed with thousand kisses'. Those 'secret' and 'tender' dealings resemble in miniature the orgiastic, public sexuality of the space where he now rambles: 'Buggeries, Rapes, and Incests' are rolled into one; categorization itself lies dissolved in love.

In that other poem of tenderness and vituperation against 'Corinna', *The Imperfect Enjoyment*, the protagonist is no longer the feeble man who doubts his ability to quench the fire he raises, but the priapist hero suddenly struck impotent. In Rochester's version of this ancient topos, the man suffers not from total

---

[31] Letter cited Introd. n. 52 above.

[32] Gordon Williams, *A Dictionary of Sexual Language and Imagery in Shakespearean and Stuart Literature* (1994), i. 181–2.

[33] 23 (and cf. 526, 'The Lusty juice of men'); for a perceptive study of homosociality in Rochester, including the *Ramble*, see Duane Coltharp, 'Rivall Fopps, Rambling Rakes, Wild Women: Homosocial Desire and Courtly Crisis in Rochester's Poetry', *Eighteenth Century*, 38 (1997), 23–42.

non-erection, as in Ovid or Petronius, nor from *ejaculatio praecox*—the problem in such predecessors as Thomas Nashe's *Dildo* and Benech de Cantenac's *L'Occasion perdue recouverte*, where the scene of temporary spillage gives way to a more successful penetration, resuming the heroic vocabulary of conquest and siege-breaking. The impotence-monologue flourished throughout the seventeenth century, especially among the French contemporaries of Théophile and the poets of Restoration England: Wycherley returned to the subject endlessly, and Aphra Behn herself produced a memorable 'imitation' of Cantenac's poem, stressing the nymph's disappointment and lopping off the recovery-scene. Rochester draws on a common stock of motifs—the diagnosis of excessive 'love' as the cause, the exaggerated rhetoric of despair, the boast of 'ten thousand' earlier conquests, the curse on the cowardly member. But his version involves a more complex interaction of arousal, utterance, and cognition, paralleled only (as far as I know) by one episode in Chorier: the bridegroom 'dissolves into venereal sweat' when the commanding voice of his mother-in-law tells him to change the metaphor that controls his performance, making sex a 'game' and not a 'battle' (*Satyra*, V. 87; Ch. 4, sect. 5 above).

Floating in a pre-coital ecstasy that already resembles the 'soft kindness' of female orgasm, Rochester's speaker interprets Corinna's intensified kissing as just such a command. The poem begins with a state rarely represented in libertine discourse, though it is recommended for married couples in popular manuals like *Aristotle's Masterpiece*—a state of intense and *mutual* arousal before the action begins, 'Both equally inspir'd with Equall fire, | Melting through kindness, flameing in desire.'[34] In this condition physical and mental attributes mingle (Corinna lies naked in 'my longing Armes'), and abstractions serve to heighten the sensuality, exemplifying Rochester's doctrine of 'right Reason'.

The male speaker is already 'melting through kindness', then, when Corinna's

> nimble tongue (love's lesser lightning) plaied
> Within my Mouth; and to my thoughts conveyd
> Swift Orders, that I should prepare to throw
> The all-dissolving Thunderbolt below.

As in *L'Escole des filles*, the inarticulate but expressive gesture at the peak of arousal is interpreted as a 'hieroglyphic' or compressed sentence (Ch. 3, sect. 3 above), but in this instance the woman's 'Orders' change everything. He must now pull himself together and concentrate his efforts, serving her pleasure by becoming more Jove-like, more priapic, less polymorphous and diffuse. Once again, *dissolve* is the key term. In the new order 'dissolving' should become a transitive rather than an intransitive verb: *he* must dissolve *her* with his thunderbolt, just as Sedley's masculine poetry dissolves the 'vanquished maid'.

What follows is exactly the reverse. The Rochester-figure experiences not a sexual

---

[34] 13 ('eager fire'), with MSS variant from 517 ('Equall fire'); subsequent citations of this 72-line poem come from pp. 13–15. For the idea of 'equal' arousal see Roy Porter and Lesley Hall, *The Facts of Life: The Creation of Sexual Knowledge in Britain, 1650–1950* (1995), 44, and Yves Citton, *Impuissances* (Paris, 1994), 29 n. 2 (Régnier).

ejaculation but a panicky cold sweat, interpreted (by combining Cartesian hydraulics and face-saving metaphorics) as an ebullition of semen from the entire body: 'In liquid raptures I dissolve all o're, | Melt into sperm and spend at every pore.' Though critics often assume that he experiences premature ejaculation,[35] the figurative nature of this orgasm becomes clear when he later berates his penis for having '*Refused* to spend' (15, my emphasis); Corinna wipes cold 'clammy Joyes' from her entire 'body'. The impotence trial of the marquis de Langey witnessed a comparable reaction to an official 'order' to copulate: 'he had not the least emotion where he should, but sweated so much that he had to change two shirts.'[36] The immediate cause of this whole-body liquefaction is the guiding touch of Corinna's 'busy hand', a gesture given extraordinary power in *L'Escole des filles* and in Rochester's own 'Song of a Young Lady to her Ancient Lover'. But *The Imperfect Enjoyment* reverses the effect of that female-voiced poem, where the 'nobler parts' regain 'warmth and Vigour' from her 'reviveing hand' while remaining somehow distinct from the 'person'.[37] Though the impotent speaker will soon turn to language to compensate for the missing member, reconstituting it by his curse as an object separate from himself, at present it is 'I' and not some detachable 'whore-pipe' that 'dissolves all o're' and then lies 'Trembling, Confus'd, Dispairing, limber, dry'.[38]

The biomorphic wish articulated by libertine discourse from Aretino to Chorier, to convert oneself entirely into sperm, has ironically been granted. Rochester's priapist has achieved what his previous Don Juanism aspired towards, the infinite multiplication of sexual sites, the fantastic sexualization of 'every pore', elsewhere ascribed to female desire. Chorier's Alcisia reports from the Elysian Fields that true pleasures rush upon her 'everywhere and from whatever side' (*undique et undequaque*), limited only by 'the vertiginous rapture of a restless mind' (*Satyra*, 5–6). Rochester's Phillis, transported by 'amorous Rage and extasie', imagines

> all my Body larded o're
> With darts of Love so thick
> That you might find in every pore
> A well stuck standing Prick.[39]

In *The Imperfect Enjoyment* the male passes through the same Protean transformation, but with a crucial loss of control. All agency (and blame) has been transferred

---

[35] e.g. Leo Braudy, 'Remembering Masculinity: Premature Ejaculation Poetry of the Seventeenth Century', *Michigan Quarterly Review*, 33 (1994), 177–201.

[36] Cited in Pierre Darmon, *Le Tribunal de l'impuissance: Virilité et défaillances conjugales dans l'Ancienne France* (Paris, 1979), 218.

[37] 30; cf. a poem by Saint-Pavin cited in Kathleen Collins, 'Pleasure's Artful Garb: Poetic Strategies of Denis Sanguin de Saint-Pavin (1595–1670)', in David Lee Rubin (ed.), *Continuum: Problems in French Literature from the Late Renaissance to the Early Enlightenment*, iii: *Poetics of Exposition* and *Libertinage and the Art of Writing*, 1 (New York, 1991), 131 (the poet happily sodomizes Alison, but when she asks for vaginal insertion, and takes his penis in hand, he ejaculates and 'ruins her dress').

[38] 14; cf. 'Rochester to his Whore-Pipe', *The Works of the Earls of Rochester, Roscomon, Dorset, Etc.* (1721), ii. 187–97.

[39] 102 (also called 'Mock Song' since it travesties a love-song by Sir Carr Scrope); for a less parodic version of whole-body arousal see 36 ('She found a pulse in ev'ry part | And love in ev'ry Vein').

to the already-aroused female body. Not only her hand but 'any part' could have reduced him to liquid raptures, since 'Her hand, her foot, her very look's a C—t' (14, 517, 353). Rochester's sly parody of Dryden's *Conquest of Granada* ('Her tears, her smiles, her every look's a Net') transforms the Petrarchan-heroic mistress into something more like Shakespeare's Cressida: 'There's language in her eye, her cheek, her lip, | Nay, her foot speaks' (*Troilus and Cressida*, IV. v. 55–7). Cressida's 'wanton spirits *look* out | At every joint and motive of her body' (my emphasis), and Corinna's 'very look' is not merely a 'C—t' but a hyperactive organ that can gaze, reach out, persuade, suffuse, and transform. As in Phillis's song the woman's eyes are defined as sexual organs, but in this case they will not be 'fucked out': quite the reverse. The male has become the object rather than the director of the 'all-dissolving' process, totally sexualized and yet totally deliquescent, controlled by a force outside himself—precisely the condition to which he aspired to bring the 'Ten Thousand' victims of his previous sexual conquests. In short, *he* is the 'Cunt'. More fully than in *A Ramble in St James's Park*, Rochester's 'image of a false content' is identified with what he would identify as female arousal.

As in many earlier impotence-monologues, the speaker tries to bluster his way out of this 'withered' state by describing the phallic vigour he claims as his normal condition. Susanne in *L'Escole des filles* had proved that, when the man exclaims 'mon cœur!', he really means that 'he would like to slip in his member all the way to her heart' (p. 128 above); Rochester ascribes a similar goal to the member itself, which 'shou'd convey my soul up to her heart' and which did so in the past. With comic and blasphemous hyperbole he objectifies it as

> This Dart of love whose piercing point oft Try'd
> With Virgin blood Ten Thowsand Maids have dy'd,
> Which Nature still Directed with such Art
> That it through every Cunt reacht ev'ry heart.
> Stiffly Resolv'd t'would Carelesly invade
> Woman or Boy, nor ought its fury staid;
> Where ere it pierc'd a Cunt it found or made.[40]

Here Rochester assumes the voice of the cocksman who 'longs to be often tried', who boasts of 'swiving more whores more ways than Sodom's walls | E're knew', of buggering pages and link-boys or discarding mistresses like linen.[41] His mighty javelin would hitherto 'invade' woman and boy alike, while a few manuscripts even read 'Man', obliterating the essential difference between what Rocco called the 'veal' of youth and the 'goat's flesh' of the adult male (Ch. 2, sect. 2 above); his dart can be airily indifferent to gender, age, and orifice because 'Where'er it pierced a Cunt it found or made.' The key word here is 'made'. The phallus is imagined as both a

---

[40] 14–15 with variants from 518 (Love, 15, 353–4, prefers the 'heterosexual' reading 'invade | Woman, nor Man, nor ought its fury stayd', even though this renders meaningless the climactic idea of 'making' a vulva where none existed). The priapist's claim perhaps echoes the 11,000 martyred virgins of Cologne and 'Saul hath slain his thousands, David his ten thousands' (1 Samuel 18: 7).

[41] 34, 43, 38, 274, 45. These performances of the Rochester-figure need not all be ascribed to him; see my *Libertines and Radicals*, 321 n. 59, for the authorship of 'To the Post Boy'.

weapon and an inscribing tool, creating or redefining the non-genital parts as
'Cunt'. Because Corinna has already reached the state he ostensibly desires ('Her
hand, her foot, her very look's a Cunt'), she leaves him no work to do, no material to
exercise his power upon. His desire collapses.

Once again, it is Chorier who provides the closest analogy by showing us what is
involved in 'making' the *cunnus*. At one point this happens quite literally, when
Tullia invents an episode in which Prometheus models the genitals out of clay, apart
from the rest of the body (Ch. 4 n. 68 above). Empowered by this myth, which proves
the 'natural' affinity of penis and female mouth, Chorier's imperious males demand
to use every fold and orifice, spelling out the ideology behind their appetite: both in
the early wedding-night sequences and in the later orgies and fellatio-scenes, they
insist that male pleasure can define any feature as 'the part by which she is woman',
that 'the entire body of a beautiful woman is one cunt' (*aiunt totum pulchrae
mulieris corpus cunnum esse unum*). Chorier's female mouthpieces obligingly repeat
these homilies, accepting male penetration-as-definition 'wherever it is sought',
assigning themselves the ungrammatical label *tota cunnus*, and describing their
arousal in terms that flatter the improbable male dream of a controllable penis.[42]
(Poet and pornographer share a common source in St Augustine, whose vision of
prelapsarian genital control Rochester transcribes in the wistful lyric 'The Fall'.) As
de Sade would later do, Chorier invents a man whose sperm runs in a continuous
stream like urine, and then invents a woman who finds this delightful: 'How
smoothly you are pissing in! You'll fill me with this fervent seed, I think, and out of
a girl you'll make a whirlpool of Venereal brine.'[43] Corinna performs just the same
metamorphosis on 'Rochester', turning *him* into 'liquid raptures all over'.

Both Rochester and Chorier seem at times to support a grossly polarized sexual
politics: man is the active force who 'makes' the woman a passive receptacle or fluid
vortex; the phallus is a spear or battering ram, a vast pump or beam engine, a 'Dart
of Love', 'stiffly resolved', stained with the blood of ten thousand virgins and an
unspecified number of men and boys. But Chorier undermines this polarity, as
we have seen, by contrast with the gentler Robertus scenes. Nor do his female protagonists simply submit to male commands: Octavia's praise of Rangoni's power to
turn her into a 'whirlpool' is a challenge as much as a description—one that the
soon-to-be-exhausted male does not actually meet. Rochester may well have derived his sense of female expectations from such passages, believing (like his friend
Oldham) that the *Satyra* was an authentic work by Aloisia Sigea.

Chorier's model of female erotic agency thus presents Rochester with a dilemma
in the representation of masculinity too: is the appropriate response 'adolescent'
ephebic softness or barbaric priapism? Instead of creating a phallic automaton to

---

[42] *Satyra*, V. 100, VI. 182, VII. 243–4; Octavia's remark at VII. 231–2 that men 'will seek alternative lodgings for their penises everywhere in our bodies, and find them too' (*diversoria et stabula quaesierunt in
corporibus nostris, et invenerunt*), seems particularly close to Rochester's boast that the phallus 'found or
made' a vulva wherever it pierced.

[43] *Satyra*, VI. 177 (Octavia to Rangoni, 'Quam immingis suaviter! Me implebis, puto, semine hoc
fervido, et, e puella, Venerei salis gurgitem facies'); cf. Blangis in Sade's *120 Journées de Sodome* and
Minski in *Juliette*.

na's 'Swift Orders', Rochester invents a male subject who *prefers* the
...assionate liquefaction, but who achieves only an abortive imitation
...nds 'at every pore'. The man whose private letters bewail 'soe great
...portion twixt our desires and what [Fate] has ordained to content them'[44]
could not remain a loyal phallocrat for long; priapic bravado grows increasingly
absurd as the poem proceeds, the Homeric 'Dart' becoming a cowardly street bully
and then 'a Common Fucking Post' for whores to rub against (15), a passive and un-
feeling wooden shaft now devoid of heroic or mock-heroic association. An earlier
poet of the 'machismo of impotence'[45] contrasted the chivalric lance of his erect
state, able to 'enter the lists' ten or twelve times a night, with the 'wooden trunk' of
the fallen organ.[46] For Rochester, *both* images apply equally to the erection. As in
Chorier's Latin, the phallus is *impotens* even when it is working; as in *La Parnasse
satyrique du Sieur Théophile*, the 'Coward Prick' has *'never* given satisfaction'.[47]
Phallic success, and therefore true manhood, betrays the mutual self-enhancement
of sensation and thought that Rochester calls 'right reason'. Inverting the ideal
expressed in the *Satyr against Mankind*, both his models of masculine 'Vigour' lack
'Sense'. The irony of the poem, then, is that both forms of sexual response—uncontrollable amorphous dissolving and insensate automatic priapism—deserve the
title 'Imperfect Enjoyment'.

What then constitutes a *perfect* enjoyment, and what are the obstacles that prevent it? Libertine literature offers various explanations for impotence. In the prose
Puttana errante, for example, a man loses his erection at the thought of 'having to
put it where twenty-five louts had been', but recovers when Giulia offers him her
anus (92/28), while in Antonio Beccadelli's *Hermaphroditus* the problem of the man
whose 'penis grows stiff with women he does not like', but who 'cannot get an erection with the woman he enjoys', is solved even more simply: Quintius should 'put his
own fingers up his anus', as men have done ever since Paris made love to Helen.[48] If
impotence does stem from a neurotic inability to combine arousal and liking—the
explanation favoured by Beccadelli and Rochester as well as Freud—the early
modern solution is to break out of conventional channels, penetrating wherever
and whomever in a 'careless' polymorphic rapture. Thus the neo-Latin poet Pacifico
Massimi celebrates his recovery from genital malfunction with the brag that, now
his *mentula* has risen again, 'any boy whatever, any girl whatever who meets it will
certainly have this beam to shit out again!'[49]

Rochester's protagonists often imitate this pose of heroic bisexual sodomy—
competing with Cloris for the handsome link-boy, declaring conventional intercourse a drudgery fit only for 'the Porter and the Groom' while one's page 'Can doe
the Trick worth Forty wenches' (38)—and the correspondence shows that this was

---

[44] *Letters*, 241–2.   [45] Claude Rawson, 'Systems of Excess', *TLS* 29 Mar. 1985, 335–6.

[46] Mathurin Régnier, Elegy IV ('L'Impuissance, Imitation d'Ovide'), *Œuvres complètes*, ed. Gabriel
Raibaud (Paris, 1958), 229; according to Susan Faludi, *Stiffed: The Betrayal of the American Man* (New
York, 1999), ch. 10, 'wood' is now the preferred term for erection in the pornographic film industry.

[47] (1660), 37 ('Poltron V. que tu as fait bien le vaillant . . . Jamais à mon desir tu n'as pu satisfaire').

[48] *L'Œuvre priapique des anciens et des modernes* (Paris, 1914), 104 (cf. Aretino, *Ragionamenti* I. i. 26
[32], where a sexual jouster charges with his finger up his own rectum).

[49] *Les Cent Élégies: Hecatelegium, Florence, 1489*, ed. Juliette Desjardins (Grenoble, 1986), 122.

more than a literary pose: Rochester passed on a French page to his friend Henry
Savile with a cover-letter recommending his musical and sexual talents, much as
Chorier's fictional Sempronia had sent a letter to her daughter with the adolescent
Robertus. Rochester describes himself (in French) as *un bougre lasse* and might have
known the French Court circle that dabbled in 'Italian' sexuality; his more reckless
personae hint that epheberasty is a higher and more philosophical form of Eros (as
in *L'Alcibiade fanciullo*), that 'two lovely boys' constitute 'the type of future joys' as
well as forming a convenient rhyme.[50] In *The Imperfect Enjoyment*, however,
the careless invasion of men and boys belongs on the lowest rung of the libertine
hierarchy of values; his recreant organ may have held up in such encounters, but
this only shows its 'brutall vallour', its allegiance to 'Lewdness' as opposed to 'Love'.

If 'Love' is the desiderium, however, it must be 'Love raised to an extreme', and this
heightening may itself prevent fulfilment. As another, anonymous, 'Imperfect
Enjoyment' poem warns, 'Love turns impotent when strain'd too high.'[51] The mild
'security and rest' of quasi-feminine deliquescence does not satisfy Rochester's fantastic mind, filling him with contempt and distrust as well as longing: he wants liquid raptures, but he gets only clammy joys. If such 'content' must be declared 'false',
he resorts to more 'insolent' methods to 'force' a strong image. Deprived of the high
Elysian pleasure he desires—an intense mingling, strangely reminiscent of Milton's
angels, without the impediment of particular organs—he falls back on the opposite
extreme, the crude priapism whose inadequacy sent him on the search for alternatives in the first place. In the final couplet of *The Imperfect Enjoyment*, the impotent's
previous self-denunciation is transferred to Corinna with a vindictive threat of
gang-rape, a subtext from Aretino or the *Puttana errante* masquerading as concern
for her right-to-pleasure; still addressing his errant member in the second person,
he concludes

> may Ten Thousand abler Pricks agree
> To doe the wrong'd *Corinna* Right for Thee.[52]

As in the 'Mock Song' where Phillis longs to be larded like butcher's meat and *foutue
dans les yeux*, female desire is here travestied and punished by grotesque images of
multiple assault. Under the guise of 'doing right', Rochester takes refuge in the
pornographic fantasy he has already shown to be hollow, the infinitely 'able' phallus.

'Forcing an image of a false content' necessarily turns sexuality into an artefact, and
the literature of impotence sometimes explains it as the result of a misfit between
nature and art. Rochester's ex-priapist recalls the time when 'Nature still Directed'

---

[50] *Letters*, 160, 230 (for other 'boy' allusions see pp. 264 and 274 above); Paul Hammond, 'Rochester's
Homoeroticism', in Fisher (ed.), *That Second Bottle*, 51–2, 55, emphasizes the detachment and lack of
interest in these occasional pederastic poses. Rochester evidently knew Grammont, one of the alleged
founders of the 'Italian Order' (n. 87 below).

[51] Opportunistically attributed to Rochester, and therefore included in Love's edn., Appendix
Roffensis, 269.

[52] 15. The pseudo-concern for what the disappointed woman 'deserves' may derive from Florent
Chrestien's impotence-poem (Ch. 1 n. 14 above), analysed in Citton, *Impuissances*, 59, as concealing a
cruel tendency to subject her to the Tout-Puissant.

his fucking-post 'with such Art | That it through every Cunt reach't every heart'; but apart from the convenience of the rhyme this happy synthesis had little to hold it together. Father Garasse clearly hounded the French *libertins* for extremely artificial transgressions—transvestism, sodomy, shameless literary virtuosity—even though he purports to blame their worship of Nature (Ch. 2, sect. 2 above). To praise 'Art' in sexual matters could be a back-handed compliment: in libertine literature, conspicuous artifice in the boudoir often denotes a diseased or inadequate sexual drive. The dextrous Young Lady in Rochester's lyric promises to give 'All that Art can add to Love' while loving 'without art'—but however delightful this promise may sound, it is still made to an Ancient Person with 'frozen' members.[53]

The highest goal of *libertinage honnête* is to transform mere animal copulation into a conscious work of art, certainly. In Chorier's final dialogue, Robertus's masque-like disguises and emulation of erotic tableaux signify, not the exhaustion of sexuality, but its proper 'management' (Ch. 4, sect. 5 above). On the other hand, a similar anecdote in Roger de Bussy-Rabutin's scandal chronicle of the comtesse d'Olonne reveals that the dress really does make the man, that natural desire can be generated or annulled by artificial representation, that masculinity depends on assuming control of the production: a young lover of that imperious aristocrat, dressed as a girl just as Octavia dresses Robertus as 'Diana' to give him a safe disguise for his visits, finds himself totally unable to achieve an erection, 'split between imagination and reality' and stripped of the 'courage' conferred by male accessories.[54] As early as the 1535 *Tariffa delle puttane di Venegia*, the free artistic expression of the courtesan is assumed to inhibit desire, as when elaborately plaited pubic hair causes a customer to lose his erection;[55] as late as Aphra Behn's *Love-Letters*, the hero is stricken with comic impotence when obliged to disguise himself as the chambermaid, an episode presumably modelled on Bussy's (ii. 56–61). Art can thus enhance 'perfect enjoyment' or else destroy it, according to whether the artist's perspective coincides with the active sexual role.

In Cantenac's *Occasion perdue recouverte*, for example, Lysander dissolves in *ejaculatio praecox* when the woman yields without preamble, but recovers his full vigour when he can impose a controlling aesthetic distance on the situation, gazing at her sex from a concealed viewing-hole; like the unwilling transvestite in Bussy-Rabutin, he can enter her once she adopts a sleeping position. The more he finds himself in a situation from libertine fiction, the stiffer his penis. Lest this seem another study in febrile perversion, the author underlines the success of the 'enjoyment' and its congruence with the male reader's desires: he himself begins to feel '*Loves dart*' gliding into his heart 'with slippery sweetness'—exactly the experience

---

[53] 30; cf. Helen Wilcox, 'Gender and Artfulness in Rochester's "Song of a Young Lady to her Ancient Lover"', in Burns (ed.), *Reading Rochester*, 6–20. For an earlier compilation of French writings on the paradoxes of self-as-art, see Domna C. Stanton, *The Aristocrat as Art: A Study of the Honnête Homme and the Dandy in Seventeenth- and Nineteenth-Century France* (New York, 1980).

[54] *Histoire amoureuse des Gaules*, ed. Antoine Adam (Paris, 1967), 84–9 (narrated by the sufferer himself, the duc de Guiche, one of the alleged founders of the sodomitic order mentioned in n. 87 below); Citton, *Impuissances*, 36–7.

[55] ed. Guillaume Apollinaire (Paris, 1911), 48–50.

that 'Rochester' claims to have induced in ten thousand girls and boys—and this arousal inspires him to believe that 'I am *Lysander*, and enjoy his Fate'. Cantenac is 'forc'd to yield' his pen to the strength of his imaginary desire, which fills his fancy with 'strange *Chimaeras*'; in contrast, the female author who translates this poem into English endorses no such 'female' sensibility and briskly cuts off the author's coda with the entire recovery-episode, the return of what she punningly calls 'that fabulous *Priapus*'.[56]

The art of sexual extremity mandated by Chorier—mustering the forces of 'right reason' to achieve what Rochester calls 'Love raised to an extreme' or 'pleasure raised to the top' (23)—thus confirms the contemporary sense that 'straining too high' produces impotence. We saw in Chapter 5 that for Wycherley this heightening took the form of excessive verbal performance (in *The Country-Wife*) or excessive anger (in *The Plain-Dealer*). But when he imitates Rochester directly—writing his own 'satire against reason and mankind' on the thesis that the Senses should govern Reason and that natural animal sexuality should become our ideal—Wycherley attributes the collapse of desire to the contradictions within libertine hedonism itself: humans have replaced natural appetite with 'forc'd Rules', not to clamp down but to 'stimulate Desire', to turn it into 'Art' and thereby to create an illusion of infinite erotic pleasure (*Works*, iii. 153–4). Rochester's own dramatic impersonations of the man 'curst with constant Sensuality' (as his friend Wycherley puts it) strain constantly against the limits of corporeality and mortality, like those *libertins* discovered (or invented) by Garasse who violate their own nature by turning themselves into a woman, an angel, or an animal (703–6). In the most up-to-date version of this biomorphic fantasy, the protagonist turns herself into a masculine-feminine *tota cunnus*, and Rochester's character follows suit.

If *The Imperfect Enjoyment* dramatizes the results of this conflict between Nature and Art, Rochester's lyric 'The Fall' spells out the underlying nostalgia for an effortlessly controllable plastic body, versifying St Augustine's lament for the 'disobedience' that entered the genitals after the fall of Adam. (Rochester, like Claude Le Petit, draws libertine effects from *Les Plus Belles Pensées de Saint Augustin* (Ch. 3 n. 116 above).) In the words of 'The Fall'—published in the seventeenth century as the authentic voice of a woman poet—impotence exemplifies this alienation of 'enjoyment' and 'desire', 'will' and 'pleasure', 'wish' and bodily performance; the 'part' that women love is intrinsically 'frail'.[57] As Pascal observes of Rochester's forebear Des Barreaux, the struggle to escape this fallen condition might take a libertine or an ascetic form, but both attempts at transcendence are essentially the same: 'man is neither angel nor beast, and . . . anyone trying to act the angel acts the beast.'[58] Thus

---

[56] *Wit and Drollery: Jovial Poems*, 'Corrected and Amended, with New Additions' (1682), 16, text checked against 'Pierre Corneille' (more probably Benech de Cantenac), *L'Occasion perdue recouverte*, 'Nouvelle édition' (Paris, 1862). For Behn's much-studied version of the first third of Cantenac's poem, entitled 'The Disappointment' (and published in Rochester's clandestine *Poems* of 1680), see her *Works*, i. 65–9.

[57] 26, included in the 2nd edn. of *Female Poems* by the (probably fictitious) poet 'Ephelia' (1682), 164.

[58] *Pensées*, number 317, 329, in *Œuvres complètes*, ed. Jacques Chevalier, Bibliothèque de la Pléiade (Paris, 1954).

we can situate Rochester's defiance midway between the transformational fantasies of Aretino, the *satyriques*, and Chorier (the desire to become *tutto cazzo* or 'all sperm', the impulse to defeat death by 'fucking Adam and Eve' or masturbating in the face of the Gods[59]) and the despairing outbursts that Milton gives to characters who protest against the ignominy of embodiment. Adam blames God for designing sexual intercourse, Samson blames him for confining eyesight to a single vulnerable organ rather than diffusing it throughout the body so that we 'might look at will through every pore' (*PL* X. 888–95, *SA* 93–7). Rochester—applying Milton's phrase to his own mix of 'amorous rage and ecstacy'—imagines arousal in uncannily similar terms: an active female body covered with vaginal eyes, an imperfectly passive male who ejaculates from 'every pore'.

2. LIBERTINE CANONIZATION: JOHN OLDHAM, *SODOM*, AND THE CHALLENGE OF ALOISIA SIGEA

Behind Oldham's critique and emulation of libertine discourse—apparently the first response to Chorier's *Aloisia Sigea* in any language—we can always detect the dazzling figure of Rochester, whom he impersonated in several mock-heroic Pindaric odes, and who responded with enthusiastic applause and a personal visit. The connection between the two poets hinged on a specific incident that critics have related to Rochester's 'ontological insecurity', when he and his gang smashed a valuable royal sundial because it presumed to 'fuck Time'.[60] Oldham's ode entitled 'Satyr against Virtue', or 'Suppos'd to be spoken by a Court-Hector at Breaking of the Dial in Privy-Garden', had been proposed to him by the Court Wits as a dare, to 'vindicate his reputation' as a poet; though this wild eulogy of transgression obviously parodies Rochester it was interpreted as an entry-ticket rather than a diatribe.[61] To be snatched up into the most exclusive and scandalous social circles must have turned the Croydon schoolteacher's head, already bursting with moralistic indignation and envious identification. Oldham declared (in a funeral elegy) that he owed his entire poetic gift to Rochester's 'all-teaching tongue' working inside him, while he frequently adopts the same subjects and 'imitates' the same poems (like Boileau's eighth satire or Anacreon's ode on the drinking cup, which he converts to heterosexuality). Making the most of his own college education, Oldham used both English and Latin as bridges into that realm of patronage. Rochester is probably the intended reader of a Latin letter drafted among his poems, a Plinyesque simulation of sophisticated hedonism in which Oldham describes himself drink-

---

[59] See Aretino, *Modi* sonnet 1 ('Let's fuck so much we die, so that over there we can fuck Adam and Eve, the ones who discovered so shameful a thing as death'), (pseudo)Théophile (n. 86 below), and (pseudo)Bussy (Ch. 7 n. 17 below).

[60] Chernaik, *Sexual Freedom*, 79.

[61] See Raman Selden, 'Rochester and Oldham: "High Rants in Profaness"', *Seventeenth Century*, 6 (1991), 89–103. Oldham's holograph (Bodleian Rawl. Poet. 123, hereafter 'MS') dates the poem 'Croydon July 1676' and names the speaker as 'a Court Hector' (i.e. a generic type) but later impersonations like the 'Dithyrambique' name Rochester explicitly.

ing wine, enjoying the present moment, and (like Tullia) inventing *sales* or 'salty' amusements.[62]

The abandoned drafts in Oldham's verse manuscript often try to link Rochester to Chorier as exemplars of 'Heroick' obscenity. Phrases like 'glorious Infamy . . . Our witty bawdy Peer . . . great performers of the Kind . . .' hover in the margins of 'Upon the Author of the Play call'd *Sodom*', and 'our great witty bawdy Peer' appears alongside Aretino and Chorier in another poetic fragment related to *Sodom*, describing the typical reading of a libertine. Rochesterian phrases and attitudes echo throughout Oldham's verse, published and unpublished. 'Upon *Sodom*' several times borrows the excruciating *done't/cunt* rhyme from *The Imperfect Enjoyment*, and Rochester's final attack in *A Ramble* on anyone who 'dares prophane the Cunt I swive' becomes an unwillingness to 'profane my Fundament' with the pages of that execrable play. In another panegyric-satyric ode, Sardanapalus on his funeral pyre achieves the state of passionate liquefaction that eluded 'Rochester' in bed with Corinna, 'At every Pore dripping out Scalding Lust'.[63]

Oldham felt the need to protest that 'I envy not our witty bawdy Peer', still claiming him as 'ours' even while repudiating 'the loth'd wretched Fame he dos acquire | Which Hell, Debauches, Claps and Lust inspire' (*Poems*, 545). His yearnings to be accepted by the Court Wits, to achieve the 'greatness in wickedness' that he finds in Aloisia Sigea, conflict with his middle-class Nonconformist revulsion at aristocratic decadence and its profane sexualization of art. In his recanting 'Apologie' or 'Epilogue' to the Rochesteroid Pindaric which retroactively defines that performance as emulation rather than parody, Oldham again attacks 'damn'd *Placket* Rhymes | Such as our *Nobles* write'. Rochester had casually pretended to compose verse 'for his Pintle's sake', but Oldham asserts that the entire aristocracy writes for the placket, the flap in the clothing that covers (and defines) the genitals. All their poetry is sexually inspired—

> So lewd they spend at Quill; you'd justly think
> They wrote with something nastier than Ink—

and all of it, not merely the impotent specimens, is 'nauseous'. The young moralist on the other hand, if his poetic '*Genius*' could only match the greatness of the age's sin, would 'shoot his Quills, just like a *Porcupine*' (69). Turning his sex to anger, he would spend at every pore.

In the *Sodom* poem, which follows the 'Apologie' immediately in the clandestine 1680 edition of Rochester, Oldham creates his most pathological version of this fusion of erotics and poetics, though now the object of his satire is not a bawdy peer but an impotent Witwould, caught between high-libertine aspirations and plebeian talent. To express his contempt for obscene discourse, Oldham 'out-Sodoms

---

[62] Oldham, MS p. 107 ('fabulis, salibus, facetii '); Selden, 'Rochester and Oldham', 89, 90, 94, 101–2 (for Oldham's funeral elegy, see also Ch. 8, sect. 3 below).

[63] Rochester, 14, 80; Oldham, *Poems* 344, 350 (and cf. 347), MS pp. 90, 220. See Abbreviations above for the Oldham edn. cited.

Sodom'[64] by inventing obscene combinations of discursive and genital functions. We shall see that, even in this unambiguously grotesque and hostile mode, Oldham still borrows his imagery from Rochester. But if we pursue the manuscript drafts of this poem rather than the printed version, we discover a third person in bed with Rochester and Oldham. Mediating between the extremes of the 'great' and the 'bawdy', Oldham summons up the figure of Aloisia Sigea as a touchstone for the aesthetics of transgression, the point of reference for judging Rochester, *Sodom*, and himself. In the 'Apologie' he explains that his Muse felt obliged to impersonate 'a lewd Punk o'the Town', the female equivalent of the rake-voice (68); in the supposedly real Aloisia Sigea, Oldham encounters a 'heroic' version of this libertine-poetic accomplishment.

Oldham gathers much of his libertine expertise into a verse character of a lecherous connoisseur, a free-standing fragment that he attempted to integrate into the longer poem on *Sodom*. (Oldham may originally have planned a satire with interlocutors, in the manner of Horace and Boileau, on the general subject of obscenity in action, discourse, and literature.) At some point in this unrealized verse conversation

> Another strait did in the talk succeed
> So lewd, his very mouth did guelding need:
> Slav'ring with lust as if his Tongue had came
> From whence his prick did, and had done the same.[65]

Oldham's grotesque image of male erotic discourse emulates his contemporary Samuel Butler, who declares that the ribald 'talks nothing but *Aretine*'s Pictures' and 'plays an After-game of Letchery with his Tongue much worse than that which the *Cunnilingi* used among the old *Romans*'.[66] Both 'characters' display a similar double allegiance, which renders them complicit with the cultivated obscenity they attack; by an interpretation of decorum that would have seemed quite intelligible to Martial or Catullus, their pseudo-moralistic diatribes are more obscene than what they denounce, and just as expert in recondite perversion. Language and sex concur here, the upper organs of intellection and discourse thoroughly interchangeable with the lower organs of generation—as Chorier had envisaged when he made the 'one-eyed' penis the best judge of ideal beauty (Ch. 4 n. 54 above), and as Rochester had projected onto the female libertine Corinna, whose 'Cunt' speaks directly from her mouth.

Oldham's sketch of the libertine emphasizes his misapplication of education: he

---

[64] J. W. Johnson, 'Did Lord Rochester Write *Sodom?*', *Papers of the Bibliographical Society of America*, 81 (1987), 145.

[65] MS p. 220; see my article ' "Aloisia Sigea" in France and England: Female Authorship and the Reception of Chorier's Erotica', in Kathleen Clark (ed.), special issue, *Œuvres et critiques: Revue internationale d'étude de la réception critique des œuvres littéraires de langue française*, 20 (1995), 281–94, for an earlier version of this Oldham material, and for a full transcription, see my 'John Oldham on Obscenity and Libertine Discourse: Unpublished Verses from Bodleian MS Rawlinson Poet. 123', *Notes and Queries*, 247 (2002), 346–51.

[66] 'A Ribald', in *Characters*, ed. Charles W. Daves (Cleveland, 1970), 246–7.

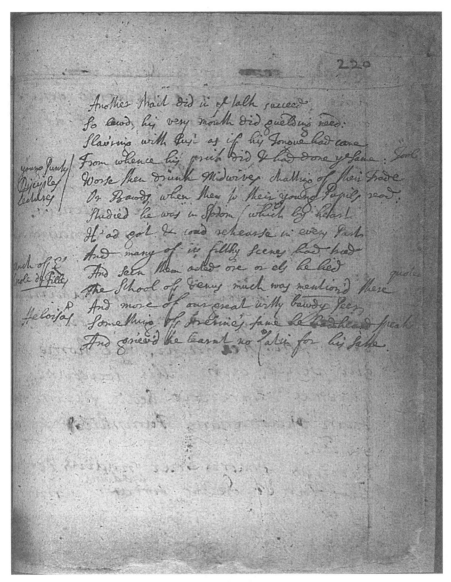

12. John Oldham, draft related to 'Upon the Author of the Play call'd *Sodom*'? (Bodleian Library, MS Rawlinson Poet. 123, p. 220)

is erudite or 'Studied' in *Sodom*, and this scandalous learning makes him worse than 'Bawds' reading to their 'young Pupils' (In the margin, visible in Fig. 12, the usher-poet toys with other eroto-didactic phrases like 'young Punks', 'Disciples', and 'lectures'.) A distinct programme of reading has induced the speaker's anamorphic condition, in which the mouth needs castrating and the tongue drips genital fluid—and Chorier is tentatively placed among the authors that contribute to this squalid abuse of language. The man's conversation chiefly consists of memorial reconstruction and performance of 'filthy Scenes' from *Sodom*, 'which by heart | H'ad got and cou'd rehearse in every Part'. In addition to the English burlesque, Oldham specifies *L'Escole des filles*, the *School of Venus* translation, and the poems of 'our great witty bawdy Peer'—an obvious reference to the wicked Earl whose embrace made him 'ours'. (In an earlier draft the French title of *L'Escole* appears alone, whereas in this copy 'Escole de Filles' haunts the margin but the main text reads 'The School of Venus much was mention'd there', apparently the earliest allusion to that English version.) Aretino remains out of reach because the would-be libertine had 'learnt no Latin', a blunder which can either be attributed to the author or to the character; a real expert would know that Aretino wrote in Italian, though the classics tutor might have been more familiar with Barth's translation *Pornodidascalus*. Chorier joins this company as the ghost of an idea, appearing in the margin (appropriately suspended between Rochester and Aretino) as 'Heloisas', the poet's conflation of two names that he obviously associates with female authority on love, Héloïse and Aloisia.

In this character of the dirty talker Oldham seems unsure how to evaluate his roll-call of clandestine texts; they confuse the boundaries of decorum and the hierarchies of class and gender, being at once ignominious and glamorous, associated with the aristocratic excesses of Rochester as well as the low discourse of bawds and 'drunk Midwives chatting of their Trade'. The unnamed author of *Sodom* is likewise 'Bawdier than bawds turn'd Midwifes' (MS p. 90). In these unpublished verse fragments—as in responses to 'Aloisia Sigea' by other writers of the English Restoration—sexual discourse can be identified not with masculine solidarity but with the female proletarian activities of midwives, the only group (outside the closed circle of the physicians) licensed to speak and publish on sexual topics. When Tom Brown wanted to condemn Dryden for translating the sexual parts of Lucretius' *De Rerum Natura*—the very passages that Lucy Hutchinson had refused to handle because this would be fit work for the midwife—he could think of no greater insult than to say they belonged with *Culpepper's Midwife* and the dialogues of 'Aloisia Sigea'.[67] Midwives, as we have seen, evoked at the same time ribald humour (associated with their handling of private parts, their lewd-talking 'gossip', and secret sexual arts) and a certain respect for their privileged relation to the word: having taken an oath to speak the truth when they obtained their licences, midwives pronounced in court on virginity, pregnancy, and potency were believed to control the linguistic and sexual development of the child by the way they dealt with the umbilicus, and in concert with the mother had responsibility for declaring the true paternity of the child. At one point the entire political system of Britain hinged on this link between 'gossiping' and verbal truth: when satirists wanted to discredit the female birth-

[67] Cited in Foxon, 6.

witnesses who swore to the delivery of a son and heir to King James II, they wheeled out the now-familiar libertine canon, equating these female authorities with 'L'Eschole de Filles' and with 'Fam'd Sigea'.[58]

In other poetic fragments Oldham tries to re-establish some hierarchy by isolating and raising the 'famed' figure of Aloisia Sigea to a status like that of the aristocrat Rochester, at once 'bawdy' and 'great'. In the second epigraph to this chapter, Sigea is the [in]famous 'Spanish Whore' who takes her place alongside Pietro Aretino and 'Nero's Pimp' Petronius. (Oldham seems to have accepted her as the actual author of Chorier's dialogue, and in this he is not alone: when the Latin text was placed on the Index, an honour given to Aretino but not to Chorier's French-language contemporaries, the author was still listed as 'Aloysia Sigia'.[69]) 'Heloisas' might hover in limbo as a supplementary example of the lecher's bad reading, but in closely related drafts of the poem 'Upon Sodom' we shall see that Sigea emerges as the positive ideal against which to measure the miserable failure of the English travesty. In his fitful scribbles if not in his published work, Oldham claims for libertine writing that 'greatness' of passion that fascinated contemporaries like Descartes and Queen Christina.

In Oldham's Latin poem on Sigea's Satyra Sotadica—a few scraps of which survive in drafts of the parallel work on Sodom—she is apparently praised for her capacity to soar ultra infames, 'beyond' the infamous'; in contrast, the English would-be libertine author has 'Sunk quite below the reach of Infamy' (MS pp. 84, 88, my emphases). As far as we can tell from the surviving Latin lines, Oldham's vision of Sigea echoes Rochester's oxymoronic attack on Corinna for 'bring[ing] a blot on infamy' (A Ramble, 79), but directly imitates Chorier's poem in ostensible praise of Sigea's virtue, which presents her soaring to the 'sublime arch' of heaven, overreaching the limits of 'Nature', and changing sex from a heroine to a 'hero'.[70] One fragmentary line defining male responses to the scandalous text—'Turgent indomiti gliscente libidine nervi' ('Uncontrolled penises swell with mounting lust')—shows the apprentice schoolteacher emulating Chorier's explicitly sexual Latin in the midst of his English poetic drafts and the scraps of Latin attempted by his pupils (MS p. 86). Another fragment plays with the parallelism of tongue and penis, speech and sexuality (MS p. 83)—a theme broached in the character of a libertine and disgustingly elaborated in the lines on Sodom.

In the unfinished drafts of the English Sodom poem, though not in the more compact version published in Rochester's Poems of 1680, the intention is distinguished from the execution. In the throes of composition Oldham creates two

---

[68] 'The Deponents', Nottingham University Library, Portland MS PwV 42, fo. 423 ('Not that I wou'd (for I am very Jealous) | Wrong Fam'd Sigea, or L'Eschole de Filles [rhyme sic], | By making room for these to put them out, | For these were Maids of Honour without doubt'). For midwives' supposed influence over the tongue, genitals, and even gender of the infant, see Louise Bourgeois, Observations diverses sur la sterilité (Rouen, 1626), 157–8, and Jane Sharp, The Midwives Book (1671), 22–3.

[69] Index Librorum Prohibitorum . . . [including] Appendix usque ad Mensam Junii 1704 (Rome, 1704), 305 (using the wording of the 1st edn. title page my Fig. 8).

[70] In the Satyra (314) presented as the work of Daniel Heinsius (Chorier's authorship was not avowed until 1680 (Ch. 4 n. 5 above) whereas Oldham's poem dates from May 1677).

parallel versions of the poem, driven by diametrically opposite theories of the relation between moral and aesthetic criteria: in one, Aloisia Sigea rules; in the other she
has been wholly expunged. His confusion is expressed in one unplaced line by the
rhetorical question 'What Honour is't how well soe're thou write?' (MS p. 91). Sigea
embodies the possibility of achieving a perverse *honestas* by writing 'well' on a bad
subject, whereas in the 1680 tidied-up version that option has vanished completely:
Oldham resolves the contradiction by excising every reference to glorious obscenity
or sublime libertinism. In those drafts that are still dazzled by the sophisticated
Latin of the *Satyra*, however, the foul-mouthed *Sodom* is defined by placing it at the
bottom of an ascending scale. Libertine discourse is not objectionable *per se*, but
it requires those qualities of artistic genius that favourable critics would find in
Rochester:

> Hadst thou the Pow'r as well as bold Design
> To outdo Nero's Pimp and Aretine,
> Or that fam'd Spanish Whore—
> Who shews how far her Sex can Conquest boast
> Ore ours both acting and describing Lust;
> 'T had bin Heroick, and deserv'd our Praise,
> 'Tis something to be great in Wickedness. (MS p. 84)

It *would have been* heroic to emulate the *Satyra Sotadica of Aloisia Sigea*, just as
Rochester's Corinna would have been heroic had she launched into unconditional
promiscuity; Oldham's aphorism ' 'Tis something to be great in Wickedness' clearly
matches his mentor's line 'There's something generous in mere Lust'. The author of
Sodom's 'nauseous Rhymes', on the other hand, has failed to live and write up to the
standard of energetic transgression established by Petronius and Aretino but
brought to sublime fruition by Aloisia Sigea; he must be a sexless creature, a 'Weak
feeble strainer at meer Ribaldry' whose 'Impotent' Muse must be 'whipt to Lechery'
(*Poems*, 342). Addressed in the intimate or contemptuous *thou* form, the *Sodom*-
writer 'covetst to be lewd, but want'st the Might' (MS p. 92).

The dominance of the 'famed Spanish Whore'—a phrase that makes Sigea de
Toledo sound like the celebrated courtesan-authors of her own period—proves that
this writerly 'Might' cannot simply be equated with phallic prowess.[71] As in Pallavicino's *Retorica delle puttane* (Ch. 2, sect. 1 above), the abject 'whore' can achieve a
certain 'nobility' by turning her sexuality into a *disegno*. Sigea's 'bold Design'
and powerful writing stand at the opposite extreme from *Sodom*, leading the
'Heroick' or high-libertine line that stretches back to antiquity. Oldham constructs
a neoclassical canon by combining Milton's allusion to Petronius and Aretino
in *Areopagitica* with the genealogy that Chorier's Aloisia-figure claims for herself
when she lists those authors among her companions in Elysium, or when Tullia
traces the history of sexual representation back through Aretino to Elephantis and
Sappho (Ch. 1, sect. 2, Ch. 4, sect. 4 above). The high-libertine tradition thrives on
action and excess, each author aspiring to 'outdo' or 'outwrite' whoever came

[71] Though cf. 'If ere thy long-frig'd Fancy chance to rise | Next Line like a Spent Tarse it flags and lies'
(MS p. 98).

before.[72] Oldham alternated these verbs in various drafts, but the figure of Aloisia makes this split vocabulary unnecessary, since she 'outdoes' men in deeds as well as words. He might celebrate 'uncontrolled' or 'masterless' erections in his Latin poem (*indomiti nervi*), but in this passage—as in Chorier's own text—they must acknowledge their *domina* and her 'Conquest'.

Speaking as both a censorious male and an identifying author, Oldham abjects and exalts Sigea in the same breath. She is whorish but famous, lustful but heroic, wicked but great. He indulges the misogynistic urge to violate the norms of modesty and reveal women as creatures of unbounded lust, but at the same time projects a fictitious female bursting with energy and self-confidence, enjoying an unusually close relationship between discourse and action. Oldham blames the *Sodom*-poet for writing pornography that fails to come up to the standard set by this supposedly female author, who outdoes/outwrites the male sex 'both acting and describing Lust' and who thereby transcends the conflict of *faire* and *dire* that troubles Molière's Dom Juan and 'real-life' contemporaries like John Sheffield, Earl of Mulgrave:

> But now, alas! for want of further force
> From action we are fallen into discourse.[73]

In this realm beyond Nature and beyond infamy, moreover, to emulate Sigea's 'further force' (whether successfully or not) has the consequence of feminizing the author.

As in the character of a foul speaker, Oldham equates sexual discourse with anatomical inversion, with the grotesque intermingling of face and genitals. But in the *Sodom*-poem he adds the twist of gender reversal. Butler accuses the ribald of 'expos[ing]' that with his Tongue which Nature gave Women Modesty ... to cover',[74] and Rochester turns Corinna into a Magritte-like hybrid with a 'Cunt' for a mouth. Oldham develops these hints into a portrait of the male artist as talking vulva: virtually born with 'Thy Tongue a Clitoris, thy Mouth a Cunt', his poetic inspiration flows like menstrual blood.[75] Paradoxically, the aspiring author's sex is cancelled and dislocated while his vulgar text regains a kind of masculinity; after passing through the hands of whores who use it as a masturbation device— compare the *gaude mihi* formed by Le Petit's equally aggressive sonnet to the 'Prétieuses' (Ch. 3, sect. 5 above)—it ends up 'bugger[ing] wiping Porters' who use it in the public toilet.[76] Like the priapic epigrams of Martial or Beccadelli, or like *L'Escole des filles* 'standing' and 'disgracing' the other books in Pepys's library, *Sodom*

---

[72] Cf. MS pp. 82, 83 (another cancelled passage, which assumes that 'the Design' of *Sodom* was to 'outdo Fiends in daring Villany'); for 'outdoing' in lewd art, see also *Poems*, 336, 349.

[73] 'The Appointment' (also known as 'The Perfect Enjoyment'), in *The Gyldenstolpe Manuscript Miscellany*, ed. Bror Danielsson and David M. Vieth (Stockholm, 1967), 234; Molière, *Dom Juan*, ii. iv ('il faut faire et non pas dire').

[74] *Characters*, 247.

[75] *Poems*, 343 (the insult is qualified by the idea that Nature 'meant at least t'have don't', recycling the Rochesteroid rhyme on *cunt* and *done [i]t* from the draft on Sigea).

[76] Ibid. 344 (from the 1680 'Rochester' version). The idea of a rival's work becoming toilet paper was a common trope (cf. 'relics of the Bum' in Dryden's *Mac Flecknoe*), but Oldham adds the priapic detail himself.

is imagined with a *mentula* of its own. By analogy, Oldham's own text continues the Roman tradition of expressing vigorous disapproval as punitive penetration, sodomizing *Sodom*.

Oldham's loathing for *Sodom*, in those drafts that retain the 'Heroick' alternative of emulating Aloisia Sigea, is provoked not by its lewdness but by its plebeian social status. Phallic vigour can only flourish in the gutter, as Rochester assumes when he denounces his former priapism as the adventures of a 'Hector' or street hooligan. Oldham turns the entire diatribe into a Grub Street satire like Dryden's *Mac Fleck-noe*, a poem that he had carefully transcribed and preserved in this very manuscript: the ribald bungler should rest content with being Poet to Smithfield or Moorfields, an entertainer at Bartholomew Fair, a writer of commercial jingles, a City laureate. Father Garasse had applied the same social belittlement to Théophile de Viau, attacking him for 'stable boy' grossness in contrast to the transgressions of classical authors, which 'slide sweetly in by favour of their beautiful inventions' (782). Oldham now proposes a modern-classic status for Aloisia Sigea, exempting her from a moral critique that consists largely of class prejudice and revulsion at the aspiring author's coarseness. But at whom is this distaste addressed, and from what position?

Interestingly, Oldham castigates the would-be Rochester who wrote *Sodom* in exactly the same terms he flung against his own poetic presumptions, and assigns him to a social position very similar to his own—a misfit among the lewd and confident earls who had temporarily adopted him, yet scornful and apprehensive of the Grub Street career more suitable to his humble origins and professional status. He warns the poetaster that his 'brave Works' (in the plural) will 'be lent | To wipe some Porter's shitten Fundament', and he warns himself, in the voice of Spenser, that his deathless verses will 'Wipe Porters Tails' (MS p. 91; *Poems*, 241). He calls his own poetic ambition a 'vile and wicked lust' or venereal infection, imagines his Muse interchangeably as a jilting whore or 'clapped' actress, and equates his own literary failures with impotence:

> As a dry Lecher pump'd of all my store,
> I loath the thing, 'cause I can do't no more.[77]

When inspiration returns, he is 'Tickled' with an autoerotic pleasure that he 'think[s] a secresie to all mankind'—an unmistakable echo of a Dryden prologue which had identified the young poet's debut with his discovery of masturbation ('some Sport which he alone does find, | And thinks a secret to all Humane kind').[78] The 'long-frigged Fancy' of the *Sodom*-poet definitely resembles Oldham's own.

Anthony à Wood sensed, when reading the compact version of 'Upon *Sodom*' published under the name of Rochester, that the same author could well have written both the obscene burlesque and the 'piercing' satire against it.[79] Oldham's fuller rough drafts confirm this impression. The 'Smithfield' version, for example,

---

[77] *Poems*, 151, 544–5, 153.   [78] 'Prologue to *The Wild-Gallant*, Reviv'd' (*Works*, viii. 6).
[79] *RCH* 172 (Wood had no access to Oldham's papers and considers Rochester himself as the author of both, following the title pages of clandestine print editions).

collapses into a series of fragments that apply equally to the 'Sodomite' and to him-self. After a particularly noisome image he breaks off with an exclamation ('Enough! fond scribbling Fool enough for shame!') that closely resembles the pas-sionate speeches he makes 'against my self' in the autobiographical 'Letter from the Country' ('Enough, mad rhiming Sot, enough for shame').[80] The following lines—'Go and in gawdy Rhimes some Princess wed, | Be Gossip to some Goddess brought to bed'—resume the theme and rhetorical pattern of the *Sodom* draft (the addressee is to 'Go and . . .' perform some commonplace poetic task), and continue the asso-ciation with 'low' female discourse and birthing rituals. The self-reference is almost explicit here, for Oldham actually *had* just completed his serious ode on the 1677 marriage of Princess Mary and William of Orange, which *does* end with a luscious blessing on her future pregnancy and child-bed (*Poems*, 281). Draft sheets of the Princess Mary ode were also used for the *Sodom* poem, so that on some pages neatly written stanzas of official praise alternate with obscene denunciations of the 'arrant bungler at meer Ribaldry', written in a looser and more jagged hand—a vivid graphological expression of Oldham's divided attitude (Fig. 13). As in Claude Le Petit's equally obscene poem on the 'auteur foutu' of *L'Escole des filles* (Ch. 3, sect. 2 above), Oldham may well be praising-by-vituperation his own work.

Aloisia Sigea's 'Power' and 'bold Design' are supposed to lift the libertine author above all this squalor, above the grotesque femininity of the midwife and the over-done masculinity of the street bully. But can the 'Heroick' pornographer escape the problem of feminization posed by her 'Conquest'? Even if *Sodom* had succeeded, Oldham goes on, the writer would still only serve as a mouthpiece for 'female' desire, a splendid yet menial servant in a court where the monarch is always a queen. If Sigea speaks 'Cunt' through her mouth (like Rochester's Corinna), then the male pornographer acts as her ventriloquist. Speaking for all his fellow-libertines, indeed for masculine public opinion in general, Oldham makes literal what is implied in all (pseudo)feminocentric erotica, all representations of the formative oral culture of women as the excluded male imagines it; men's voicing of these voices must, by de-finition, be obtained through the disguised presence of the solitary spy, who aban-dons his masculine company and obliterates his identity to gain mastery over this secret female discourse. If the English poet *had* 'perform'd that high design' in *Sodom*, if he *had* achieved something in the heroic vein, 'We' would have 'canonized' him, certainly. But this literary, quasi-ecclesiastical preferment would give him a dubious title:

> We'd canoniz'd thee (if thou couldst have don't)
> The high and mighty Secretary to a C——. (MS p. 91)

Playing out yet again the paradox formulated by Secundus, the feminine 'sex' always already occupies the position that can only be gendered masculine. The *cunnus* would still dominate even if *Sodom* had succeeded, and at best the libertine poet can only aspire to be its 'Secretary', at once the keeper and betrayer of its secrets.

---

[80] MS p. 85; *Poems*, 152 (though both passages continue with the identical line, Brooks-Selden do not transcribe this MS fragment among the abandoned passages of 'A Letter', 542–5).

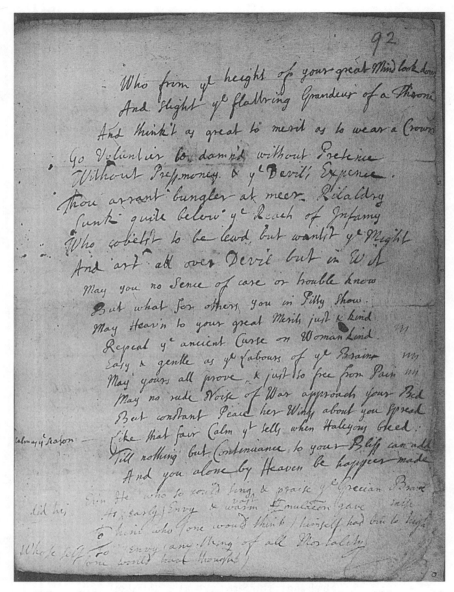

13. Oldham, drafts of 'Upon *Sodom*' and 'Upon the Marriage of the Prince of Orange with the Lady Mary' (MS p. 92)

In these heated meditations on the sexualization of literature, Oldham's response to the 'famed Spanish Whore' mingles with anxieties about his own career—as a writer in an age dominated by the spectacular sexual display of the aristocracy and the unprecedented influence of the King's mistresses. In Chorier's convincing author-effect the would-be English Juvenal encounters a double embodiment of his fears, a Messalina with a pen in her hand. Reading Aloisia Sigea puts him into a kind of gender panic, in which he identifies his own authorship simultaneously with female sexuality and with a hyper-masculine phallicism. He compares his literary debut to the initiation of a 'young wanton Girle' into pleasing sin, fusing Chorier's Octavia and Rochester's Artemiza, and he dismisses the author of *Sodom* as a 'Gossip' or midwife's assistant—exactly the feminized role he gives himself when he strains to produce courtly celebrations of royal weddings (*Poems*, 544; MS p. 85). As Oldham contemplates his future career he imagines himself 'spending' his royalties between the thighs of an actress, and his images of noble authors who 'spend at Quill' or 'squirt' themselves onto paper equally describe his own efforts: in his 'Satyr upon a Woman' he claims that 'My Ink unbid starts out and flies on her', and on another page of the manuscript drafts he complains that 'I . . . all my Vigour loose | In service on that worst of Jilts a Muse.'[81]

By a splendid irony, this image of depletion is written across the first fragment of the poem on 'Aloisia Sigea' (Fig. 14). Here spending at quill becomes a reality, for the Latin fragment breaks off in a great spurt of ink, precisely at the syllable '*jac*'— suggesting either a faulty nib or a burst of nervous energy generated by the subject of the poem itself. The 'outdoing' and 'outwriting' Sigea is endowed with the 'ravishing' power emblematized in Fig. 7, the hand of the *sçavante* artist. Confronted with a woman who controls sex by her command of language—to us a patent fabrication of male desire, to the seventeenth-century reader an awesome embodiment of female sexual and discursive authority—Oldham's pen slips out of control. Like the bridegroom in the *Satyra* and the peer in *The Imperfect Enjoyment* he dissolves into venereal liquid, bringing a blot on infamy.

3. *SODOM AND GOMORAH* IN THE CONTEXT OF 'LIBERTINE' TRANSLATION

The vicious circle of Rochester and Oldham seems to have produced both direct and indirect attempts to 'canonize' Aloisia Sigea and thereby to canonize her English secretaries. We shall see that in the various anthologies that emanate from that group, relations of emulation, direct borrowing, and actual translation constitute the same kind of triangle that Oldham struggled to articulate in his rough drafts— a three-way connection among Rochester, Chorier's female author-surrogate, and the *Sodom*-author, mirror of his own ambivalent aspiration. First, however, I would like to trace the preoccupations of those unpublished drafts in the text of *Sodom* itself, which Oldham explicitly pairs with the dialogues of Aloisia Sigea. In Oldham's construction of canonicity *Sodom* and the *Satyra* form the polar extremes, identical in aspiration but diametrically opposite in achievement. I suggest that

---

[81] MS p. 86; *Poems*, 81, 151, 156–7, 240 ('squirting' poets so 'filthy' that ''Tis scandal to be of the Company'), 545. For noblemen who 'spend at Quill' (69), see p. 283 above.

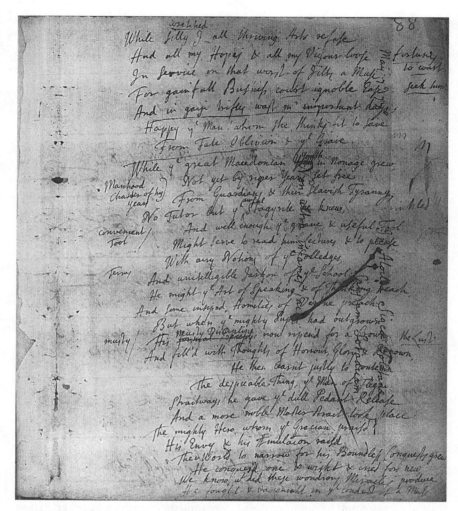

14. Oldham, abandoned fair copy of 'In Aloisiae Sigeae Toletanae Satyram Sotadicam' (MS p. 88)

Sodom not only prompts his speculations on 'Heroick' obscenity and its abject simulacrum, but incorporates, albeit in fragmentary form, a cultural translation of the canon that culminates in Chorier.

Oldham's speciality—the metacritical commentary on sexual representation, the obscene rant against obscenity, the impersonation of a reckless libertine that both pillories and exemplifies his excess—places him much closer to *Sodom* than to the 'great witty bawdy peer' he admired and abhorred. His 'Ode' in the persona

of a Rochester-like 'Court Hector', the energetic, overwrought parody in the
Pindaric style that reportedly amused its subject so much that he went to
Croydon to seek him out, actually shares more features with the *Sodom* drafts and
'Sardanapalus' than with Rochester's own poetry. Though he imitates Rochester's
coruscating obscenity and borrows individual phrases from him, Oldham's
poetic manner is quite different: he prefers flashy exercises in obscene Pindaric to
the tight lyric forms that Rochester mastered, and his powerful but ponderous
couplets are often hobbled by forced rhymes and laboured conceits. (This technical
roughness is famously captured by Dryden in his poem on Oldham's early
death.) Oldham's masturbatory heat and frenzied indignation make him seem high
where Rochester is cool. The flamboyant 'Pindarique' ode (published, like the
Sodom poem, as the work of Rochester himself) uses as its epigraph Juvenal's
comment on the crimes of a 'powerful matron' and eunuch-fancier: nowadays one
must 'dare something worthy of exile or prison in order to *be* something' (I. 73–4)—
a predicament that could equally be applied to the 'daring' artist. If Oldham knew
that Rubens had adopted the same Juvenal phrase *Aude aliquid* ('Dare something')
as his personal motto, removing it from the context of ignominy, this could only
reinforce the sense of identity between the transgression of the Rochester-figure,
the 'bold Design' of the libertine tradition culminating in Aloisia Sigea, and the legitimate aspirations of the artist 'designing' something heroic in words or paint.[82]
Though the poem on Sigea itself is lost, the surviving fragments (as we have seen)
show Oldham attempting the same heady mix of emulation and expostulation
in Latin.

We concluded from the drafts of Oldham's (mock?) condemnation that *Sodom*
embodies his own shameful aspiration to be great in wickedness; his attacks on the
would-be-libertine drama echo expostulations with himself for inappropriate
poetic ambitions, for effeminacy and lack of aristocratic assurance. *Sodom* itself
(which survives in several manuscripts associated with Oldham and Rochester, in a
three-act version called *Sodom and Gomorah* and in longer versions) confirms this
identification both in style and content. The scene-directions strive to outdo
Aretino (a motif that recurs in Oldham's canonical poems), the songs mutate into
mock-Pindarics whose free form supposedly represents the metamorphic desire of
the insatiable woman, and the death-defying bravado of the depraved monarch, an
obvious parody of heroic drama, resembles Oldham's simulation of the Court
Hector in the 'Aude aliquid' ode and the sex-crazed ruler in 'Sardanapalus'. The
attention-grabbing effect of these songs can be gauged from the 1707 prosecution of

---

[82] The immediate source of the idea that Oldham should write on the 'Aude aliquid' line was the Duke
of Buckingham (son of Rubens's English patron), according to Selden, 'Rochester and Oldham', 90; the
tradition of applying the line to artistic licence is presumably influenced by Horace's *Ars Poetica*, line 10,
'Quidlibet audendi semper fuit aequa potestas' (see Ch. 8 n. 23 below for its application to obscene
poetry). For a deconstructive reading of this ode see Rose A. Zimbardo, *At Zero Point: Discourse,
Culture, and Satire in Restoration England* (Lexington, Ky., 1998), 69–80, 126.

Sodom, which chooses the ode-like 'Unhappy cunt, oh comfortless' from Act II as its sole illustrative passage.[83]

The authorship of *Sodom* cannot be determined, and might well be a group effort—a product of the kind of 'salty' Bacchic community that Oldham boasts about in his Latin letter to Rochester. Harold Love suggests, ingeniously, that Oldham's mock-hostile 'Upon *Sodom*' was a 'burlesque commendatory epistle' for some projected edition.[84] But the drama's most striking stylistic markers confirm an even closer affinity to Oldham's obscene writings on obscenity, as the poet himself hinted in the drafts he suppressed. The main characters also exhibit a distinctly Oldhamesque tendency to state rather than perform the tenets of high, intellectualized libertinism. Courtiers urge King Bolloxinian to be 'as boundless in your pleasures as your will', the aspiration of the speaker in the 'Aude aliquid' ode. Buggeranthes, 'Whose vertues are to dare and not to feare', likewise recalls the 'Dare something' motto of that poem. Pockenello, dimly echoing Lucian's linkage of sodomy to the philosophic mind and Rochester's subordination of right reason to the senses, claims that

> Wee the kind Dictates of our sense pursue:
> Wee study pleasures still and find out new.[85]

This eroto-didactic programme—explicitly designed to distinguish human multiplicity from the monotony of animal sexuality—applies 'study' to 'pleasure' and thereby creates an onstage equivalent to the erudite-prurient reader that Oldham constitutes in his draft poem ('Studied he was in Sodom . . .').

These statements of heroic aspiration that punctuate *Sodom* do not mean that the characters, or the play, actually achieve 'greatness' in transgression or Rochesterian 'right reason', following the 'dictates of their sense'. On the contrary, they rarely rise above what the modern film critic calls the 'teenage gross-out' mode: in this 'study'-scene, for example, the courtiers make up culinary dishes of 'Cunts' garnished with crablice or infected vaginal discharges, and discuss the pleasures of 'Turkey's arse' (322–3/143–4). Buggeranthes is called 'daring' by his (disappointed) mistress Cuntagratia, but he himself bows out of her invitation to put his audacious 'virtues' into action, pleading impotence brought on by sexual exhaustion. He ascribes his earlier prowess to 'your Cunt's omnipotence' (321/141), anticipating Casanova's solution of Secundus' paradox by ascribing absolute power to the *cunnus*.

The libertine curriculum 'studied' and tentatively 'canonized' in Oldham's commentary also informs *Sodom* itself, though by echo more than by direct citation. As

---

[83] London, Public Record Office, KB 28/24/8; *Sodom*, 306/132–3 (see Abbreviations above for the texts cited).

[84] Rochester, *Works*, 675. Though he does not pursue Oldham's involvement further, Love's introduction to the variant texts he edits, and his article 'But Did Rochester *Really* Write *Sodom*?', *Papers of the Bibliographical Society of America*, 87 (1993), 319–36, demonstrate the extreme unlikeliness of Rochester's authorship, a popular myth that persists in Paddy Lyons's edition and in Chernaik, *Sexual Freedom*, 60–79 (a full account of thematic resemblances to Rochester).

[85] 304/129 (text from Princeton MS AM 14401 p. 40), 321/141, 323/143; see Introd. n. 33 above, for the Lucianic formulation of 'philosophical' pederasty. In the short A-text version Bolloxinian experiences 'Warre twixt my reason and its pleasing sence' when he considers 'Buggering the Gods from hence' (312).

Oldham's rough drafts imply, the burlesque drama strives to sum up a whole tradition of sexually transgressive discourse, a common stock of obscene topoi. It begins
in 'an Antichamber hung with Aretine's postures' (303/129) and ends with the motif
that Aretino himself chose to begin his sonnet-sequence on those postures (n. 59
above): confronting death by persisting in some damnable sexual practice or by de-
fiantly flinging rude words in the face of the gods. This topos had been elaborated
by the French *libertins*, first in the anthology associated with Théophile and then in
the second-generation imitations of Claude Le Petit, who exclaims 'fuck the fire' and
'fuck the thunder' much as King Belloxinian would later do.[86] The character of the
'King of Sodom' had already been adopted by Le Petit's contemporary Saint-Pavin,
and a misogynistic 'Italian' secret society supposedly flourished in the French
Court.[87] Generically, *Sodom* belongs with other ribald travesties of heroic drama
like the *Comédie galante* (featuring the notorious comtesse d'Olonne) which circulated as the work of another scandal-mongering aristocrat, Bussy-Rabutin (in later
fiction credited with having translated *Sodom* into French).[88] Like *L'Escole des filles*
and the Secundus poem, this exercise in mock-heroic transgression formed part of
an anthology entitled *La Bibliothèque d'Aretin* or Aretino's Library (Ch. 7, sect. 1
below), just as *Sodom*, Oldham's mock-heroic ode, and the earliest translation of
Chorier were gathered into an anthology for English readers.

In its attempt to achieve the 'quintessence of debauchery', *Sodom* also echoes the
specific texts defined in this book as the core curriculum of sexual representation.
The subject announced in the title invites particular comparison with Rocco's pro-
sodomitical *Alcibiade fanciullo a scola* (even though most of the play involves not
buggery but heterosexual excess and female insatiability). I have already linked
Sodom's epigrammatic assertion that 'Man delights in various ways to swive' and
Rocco's argument that human nature, in contrast to that of the animals, demands
the maximum variety of diet and sexual modes—an argument already adopted in
heterosexual form by *L'Escole des filles* and now returned to the sodomitical fold
(Ch. 2, sect. 2, Ch. 3, sect. 4 above). Rocco's theory of cognitive transfer by spermatic
insertion resurfaces in Bolloxinian's method of communication with his favourite
('In roapy seed my Spirrit shall be sent | With joyfull tideings to his fundament',
306/132), a phrase repeated with variation in the shorter draft. Rocco's biblical-
critical explanation of Isaiah—who warns against taking up with 'foreign boys'
rather than one's own—suggested the climactic scene in which the King of Gomor-
rah sends a diplomatic consignment of boys to satisfy Bolloxinian's taste for 'strange

---

[86] Frédéric Lachèvre, *Le Libertinage devant le Parlement de Paris: Le Procès du poète Théophile de Viau*
(Paris, 1909), i. 417, 'Approche, approche ma dryade'; Le Petit, *Œuvres* 107 (and cf. 110, where he urges
Apollo and all the deities 'Branlez, boujaronnez, foutez').

[87] *La France devenue italienne*, published as a continuation of Bussy-Rabutin's *Histoire amoureuse des
Gaules*; see Paul Boiteau's edn. of Bussy's work. *Suivie des Romans historico-satiriques du XVIIe siècle*, ed.
Charles-Louis Livet, iii (Paris, 1868), 345–509. Maurice Lever stretches the evidence by treating it as a historical account of a group of 'homosexuals', in *Les Bûchers de Sodome: Histoire des 'infâmes'* (Paris, 1985),
156–62.

[88] The muddled library catalogue in *La Cauchoise* includes 'Le Roi de Sodome, tragi-comédie en prose
et en 5 actes, traduite de l'anglais par Bussi-Rabutin'; see BnF Enfer 679, *L'Histoire de Marguerite, fille de
Suzon, niece de D** B*****, suivie de La Cauchoise* (Paris, 1784), 273–4.

flesh' (325/146). And Rocco's reinterpretation of the original Sodom story (the Is-raelite army turned to boys during the desert crossing because all the women withered up in the harsh climate) might explain why *Sodom* goes out of its way to describe the soldiers taking happily to buggery (323–4/144), and why it misses no opportunity to depict the female body as grotesquely as possible. Amplifying the misogyny still further, the cause of this physical decay is now given as excessive desire and the use of chemicals to fabricate virginity, rather than external hardship; the ugly detail of the 'Cunt washt with Allom' has been imported from Aretino and *La retorica delle puttane*, as if to confirm the doctrine that men cling to one another because all women are whores.[89]

From *L'Escole des filles* the English burlesque derives its homely kitchen im-agery—crablice as buttered shrimps, sperm 'like the white of eggs' or jelly, mastur-bation with a chicken neck—and its recurrent emphasis on the 'vertues' of the hand, which loomed so large in the French original (318–19/138–9). In this more resentful text, however, touch leads inevitably to *ejaculatio praecox* and accusations of 'ruin-ing' the penis (320/140, 328/149–50). Rochester covers Corinna's entire body with his 'clammy joys', but in *Sodom* the seed always falls on the ground. In the shorter ver-sion, which seems closer to a working draft, premature ejaculation is also experi-enced by the King himself as he contemplates his homosexual lovers and by a dildo; even inanimate objects feel the neurotic 'fear' of the vagina that pervades the play (312, 308). The masturbatory preoccupation is announced in the earliest prologue, which describes how the pubescent girl 'Begins with little finger' and then 'teaches by Degrees whole hand to sin' (302), and it continues to flourish even in the final scene: in the three-act version Bolloxinian murders his Queen with a poisoned dildo as they 'frig' together—a prosthetic version of *Hamlet*—and in the longer ver-sion the unrepentant King threatens to 'bugger all the Gods' and at the same time to 'drain' their 'Cods' by giving them an uncontrollable desire to 'rubb' or 'frig [themselves] out of imortallity' (313, 329/150). The heteronormative Epilogue (332–3/320–1) in which Fuckadilla urges the male audience to return to vaginal in-tercourse, assumes that they have been using the hand (not the anus) as their prin-cipal alternative, making the *Roi de Sodome* sound more like Chorier's 'Prince of Masturbators'.[90] In fact, *Onan* would make a more suitable title than *Sodom*.

Above all, both Oldham's expostulation and the burlesque drama can be seen as emulations of Aloisia Sigea's 'bold Design', imitating her drive-to-excess by piling on the obscenity. Tullia too had explained the male turn to buggery as a result of vagi-nal stretching, though this ugly and misogynistic theme plays only a small part in her argument (*Satyra*, VI. 206). The Roccoesque defence of sodomy in the courtier's speeches could also derive from Tullia's learned lectures in Colloquium VI (Ch. 4, sect. 3 above). Tullia and Octavia reach orgasm within the dialogue in tribute to each other's narrative power; the prologues and epilogues added to *Sodom* elaborate the

---

[89] 302/320; cf. *Ragionamenti*, II. i. 217 [226] ('allume'), *RP* 80 ('acque ristrettive').

[90] p. 218 above; Saint-Pavin also asserts, in a poem cited in Collins, 'Pleasure's Artful Garb', 184, that by solitary masturbation ('Ma main est la bien aymée') he will 'keep the name that everyone gives me', i.e. King of Sodom.

idea of not only the reader/viewer but the author becoming uncontrollably aroused by the text itself, engendering a masturbatory frenzy that paradoxically 'disturbs' rather than satisfies his Muse (679). The Sodomite Queen and her ladies-in-waiting bring each other to orgasm by friction, like the two cousins in Chorier, but the English drama adds some gratuitous violence ('You do't as if you were afraid to hurt') and makes the women dependent on the gigantic dildo, an instrument that Tullia prides herelf on not using.[91] As in Chorier, characters talk about male homosexual intercourse without actually performing it on stage, whereas the heterosexual and lesbian-masturbatory versions happen as an integral part of the action.

Chorier's central theme, the sexual education of the ingénu(e) by a teacher-lover (who might also be a close relative), generates an entire incestuous subplot. In a central scene of the longer version, Princess Swivia introduces her 14-year-old brother Pricket to the genitals and their use—fusing elements from the lesbian initiation of Octavia by her cousin and the instruction-seduction of the 14-year-olds Jocondus and Robertus. Octavia had praised her friend Lucretia's bottom as 'a soft pillow for cradling Cupid, and at the same time the proper anvil for forging the human race' (*incubanti dulci pulvinar Cupidini, et eidem humanam procudenti sobolem aptam incudem*, VII. 230). In this cruder and more compressed eroto-didactic scene, Swivia presents her own vulva with the boast that 'On such soft anvills all mankind was made'—perhaps the clearest example of direct translation from 'Aloisia Sigea' (317/137).

The most concentrated emulation of the 'famed Spanish Whore' occurs in the shorter version of the play, the uncirculated text entitled *Sodom and Gomorah* found only in a manuscript associated with both Oldham and Chorier. The two versions diverge at the point where female masturbation is introduced, and the shorter text then focuses almost entirely on the wild excesses of Queen Cuntagratia during a separation from her husband that ends in their murderous 'frigging' reunion, an explosive combination of sex and death far closer to Oldham's 'Sardanapalus' than to the finale of *Sodom* in the longer version.

By a covert etymological pun, generating a new version of female libertine transgression involves multiplying the perversion; as in Chorier's seventh dialogue, this means adding the anus, breast, and (above all) mouth to the 'treasury' of orifices that define the 'woman' (Ch. 4, sect. 5 above). In Cuntagratia's representation of Fuckadilla, for example, the lady-in-waiting 'offers' the King all these receptacles for his royal 'jelly' (308, and cf. 313). In seventeenth-century libertine writing, only 'Aloisia Sigea' includes this array of alternative acts. The male response (still narrated by the Queen) matches this extremity: Bolloxinian tears out her pubic hair—like the sadistic priest Theodorus in Chorier's Colloquium V. 146—and then applies his hands and mouth to her labia. To supply a motive for this reckless if infantile behaviour (and a rhyme for 'sucks them like a teat') Cuntagratia concludes that he does all this 'to be magnificently great' (308).

---

[91] 315/134 (and cf. the recurrence of the dildo theme in 325/145–6, 328/149–50).

This 'greatness' can only partly be explained as a mock-heroic satire on Court politics.[92] In a generic way, the King's predilection refers to the Declaration of Indulgence, the open anus the submissiveness of male courtiers, and excessive 'frigging' the independence of royal mistresses. Queen Cuntagratia is certainly advised (by the redundantly named Clitoris) that she 'should Pr—'s great prerogative controul' (308), and in the closing speech of *Sodom and Gomorah* the new King Pockenello inscribes polymorphous penetration as a national tradition by assigning various responsibilities to his ministers: as he 'sways the great Scepter' he appoints Buggeranthes 'my humane C—t' and orders that 'Lady Officina shall my sperme devour' (314). But the impulse to be 'magnificently great', in Cuntagratia's interpretation, seems to escape any such referential net and to spiral off into a sexual version of the heroic absolutism that sustained the heroic drama that *Sodom* travesties.[93] Her own motives are similarly sublime: 'love of Glory' inspires her campaign of demented promiscuity, in which she will 'spend at each melting pore', deliberately and not accidentally; she 'grew strong' during these Messalina-like exploits because her soul 'admits no feare' (309, 312). (Whereas Chorier's Tullia outdoes Messalina in the *number* of ejaculations she receives (Ch. 4, sect. 4 above) Cuntagratia competes with her in the *location*; Clitoris reports that 'I frigd her twice . . . in publique streets', while crowds cheered her on (310).) Thus the central protagonists, female as well as male, explicitly confirm the principle that Oldham gives to Rochester and the 'Heroick' disciples of Aloisia Sigea: 'dare something', combine the 'great' and the 'bawdy', because ' 'Tis something to be great in Wickedness.'

But the logic of escalation demands that the English author 'outdo' predecessors like Sigea and Rochester, and not merely copy them. Combining the tribadism of Colloquium II with the fellatio of Colloquium VII, *Sodom and Gomorah* creates an unprecedented description of lesbian cunnilinctus, complete with showers of 'roapy sperme' that fill the submissive partner's 'longing mouth'.[94] (It adds a hint of Robertus-style *heteropaedophilia* when Cuntagratia compares her lady-in-waiting's tongue to 'Pricke | Of Charming boy', while the ugly kitchen-image that follows— 'or bloudy neck of Chick' (308)—evokes and belittles the giant organ 'like a goose's neck' that haunted the anatomy treatises, especially since the licker's name actually *is* Clitoris.) Oral sex is almost unheard of in early modern libertine discourse, and even Chorier refrains from describing cunnilinctus on the occasions that he mentions it (*Satyra*, VII. 240, 245); the only other text to go further than Aloisia Sigea in this speciality is Oldham's character of the lecher 'studied in Sodom', imagined as a

---

[92] A common critical approach; see my *Libertines and Radicals*, 327 n. 14.

[93] Numerous echoes, starting with the first line of Dryden's *Conquest of Granada*, are noted in Love's notes, in Zimbardo, *Zero Point*, 127–31, and in nn. 95, 97 below.

[94] 308; for heterosexual cunnilinctus cf. 318, where male dancers are displayed 'kissing and tonging' their partners' vulvas (in Lyons's text, 136, only 'touching' them). The A-text *Sodom and Gomorah* (available in microfilm and typescript for many years before Harold Love published it) undermines such generalizations as Harold Weber, *Paper Bullets: Print and Kingship under Charles II* (Lexington, Ky., 1996), 119 ('the play never imagines the possibility of women satisfying each other'), or Cameron McFarlane, *The Sodomite in Fiction and Satire, 1660–1750* (New York, 1997), 91 ('*Sodom* is incapable of imagining the possibility that any satisfying erotic activity might take place between the women themselves. Indeed this *cannot* be imagined').

devotee of this 'slavering' pleasure (sect. 2 above), and even there the occasion is presumed to be heterosexual. Throughout his portrait of the *Sodom*-author Oldham plays games with bodily secretions and inverted, Arcimboldesque minglings of face and genitalia; in *Sodom and Gomorah* itself Cuntagratia appears 'dropping Sperme for teares', since her 'eyes are C—ts and every glance a haire' (312). In yet another variation on *The Conquest of Granada*, the look/cunt equation in Rochester's *Imperfect Enjoyment* is here elaborately even pedantically, 'outdone'.

But how can this competition-in-extremity end? Rather than polarizing Eros and Thanatos, as Chorier does towards the close of his final dialogue, *Sodom and Gomorah* combines them into the Oldham-style finale, when King and Queen expire at the climax of their toxic masturbation. In the widely circulated longer version, the 'Fire and Brimstone' promised by the biblical story appear in a farcical parody of the Don Juan legend, with demons from Shadwell's *Libertine* and jog-trot verses warning the King that his 'Bollocks' will be 'singed' (331 and notes). The short version, in contrast, makes the deadly fire a purely internal phenomenon—lust, poison, and syphilis boiling out uncontrollably—and anticipates this pyrotechnic-hydraulic ending from early on. Cuntagratia determines in Act II to 'control Prick's great prerogative' by selecting a new lover to 'Fuck to heaven'; outperforming all his efforts and achieving greater 'Glory', she will first 'charge his thrust, spend at each melting pore,' then 'melt him to pox', and finally 'fire the world'. Act I, common to both versions, had already given a sexual meaning to the 'Soveraignes Prerogative', but this second instance steers the whole play closer to Oldham's 'Sardanapalus', where another erotomaniac monarch is led by 'thy Sovereign Pr—k's Prerogative' to a fiery grave that is also a gigantic orgasm. In the shorter but not the longer version the final act returns to 'the antichamber . . . hung with Aretines Postures', recalling the posture-emblazoned funeral pyre in 'Sardanapalus', which 'Show'd the choice Artist's Mastery and Design | And far surpast the Wit of modern *Aretine*'.[95]

Oldham's Sardanapalus dies in a state only fleetingly represented in our previous examples of the *every pore* effect in Milton and Rochester,

> Revelling in Fire,
> At every Pore dripping out Scalding Lust,
> With all thy Strength collected in one Thrust.[96]

At the climactic end of *Sodom and Gomorah*, likewise, the 'heat of Lust' opens all the Queen's 'pores' and liquefies her into a state that she associates with sublime elevation as well as total genitalization. Renewed desire for her husband has 'inspir'd me, Charm'd my vitall powers', and 'Raised me to heights', making her 'all sperme, all C—t'—a direct translation of Chorier's *tota cunnus*. As the poison works, transferred from the dildo to 'Her hands annoynted with the king' and then to the monarch himself in a bizarre replay of the coronation ritual, the royal pair become

---

[95] 309, 306; Oldham, *Poems*, 347, 349. For 'prerogative' a common source may be the Emperor in Dryden's *Aureng-Zebe*, II. i (xii. 180).

[96] *Poems*, 350; earlier in Act III, *Sodom and Gomorah* uses the idea of 'spen[ding] all o're' and the *fire/expire* rhyme that terminates Oldham's poem (311).

ironic Petrarchan lovers. She turns to ice, her sperm freezing to hail as 'in hight of Lust shee dyes'; he feels 'fire | Strike to his heart and kill him with desire', and soon achieves the terminal condition we have been anticipating:

> Thou hast infus'd a seareing, killing heat—
> I spend from Eyes and dy in spurting sweat.[97]

This grotesque *Liebestod* pushes *Sodom and Gomorah* 'beyond infamy', beyond Chorier and Rochester, into a new realm of libertine (anti)canonicity.

The gathering and dissemination of the transgressive texts studied in this chapter, in book-length manuscript anthologies and clandestine reprints of them, allow us to see libertine canonization in action. As in life, so in these surreptitious collections, Oldham's and Rochester's lewd poems form a scandalous 'Company' (alongside works by other cronies and rivals like Dorset or Mulgrave), and in several cases *Sodom* is brought into the same gathering.[98] In 1680 one of these anthologies found its way into print as the *Poems* of Rochester, with a false Antwerp imprint, and this often-reprinted text fixed Oldham's libertine verse in the most intimate family relationship to his adopted poetic father: the 'daring' ode and the withering 'Upon the Author of the Play call'd *Sodom*' now appeared as the voice of the 'witty bawdy peer' who formed their point of reference, subsumed into his transgressive canon. Four years later *Sodom* itself came out with the identical false place and opportunistic ascription to Rochester.

These Rochesteroid (and Oldhamesque) volumes in turn stuck closely to the Continental texts forming the libertine canon that Oldham himself reviewed, as we learn from various sweeps by secret agents of the Stationers' Company. One in March 1688 netted four 'Rochesters Poems', six 'School of Venus', and two 'Tullia and Octavia', a single shop in Pall Mall offering the translations of *L'Escole* and *Satyra Sotadica* side by side. One 1688 prosecution shows the same Rochester–*L'Escole*–Chorier triad under investigation, and in the following year the publishers of the translations were hauled in for 'Sodom, or the Quintessence of Debauchery'; the same Benjamin Crayle who published Jane Barker's poems (Ch. 5 n. 7 above) thus produced *The School of Venus*, a version of Chorier known as *A Dialogue between a Married Lady and a Maid*, and the English *Sodom*, precisely the three texts that are first mentioned together in Oldham's rough drafts.[99] One print of a book auction (Introd. n. 79 above) shows *Sodom* on sale next to Aretino and Rochester, on the same stall where *Tullia and Octavia* and *The School of Venus* appear side by side. A 1707 indictment finds one publisher producing both *Sodom* and 'The School of Love containing severall dialogues between Tullia and Octavia'; printer and prosecutor alike treat the two texts as a pair, a double-barrelled instrument of

---

[97] 311, 312–13 ('spercing'); several details in this fire-and-ice death-scene parody Dryden's *Aureng-Zebe*, v. i (e.g. xii. 233, 240, 247).

[98] In London, Victoria and Albert Museum, MS Dyce 43, *The Farce of Sodom* is preceded by several correctly ascribed Rochester poems and by Mulgrave's 'Injoyment' (p. 132), and joined later by Oldham's 'Sardanapalus' (pp. 333–40).

[99] Foxon, plates I and II, pp. 11, 13.

iniquity.[100] These publications were in turn retranscribed into manuscript, and thus survive the destruction of all printed copies.[101]

One manuscript anthology in particular bears witness to the circular self-defining or merging of identities among Oldham, Chorier, and the anonymous obscenity. The collection (now in Princeton) begins with the two different texts of *Sodom*, each complete in itself but veering off in opposite directions; though this could result from later botching of an uncompleted fragment, such twinning of irreconcilable versions characterizes Oldham's working drafts, as we saw in the case of 'Upon *Sodom*'. The short three-act text, closest to Oldham's reading of Aloisia Sigea's 'great' transgression and Sardanapalus' fiery consummation, is in fact unique to this manuscript. Immediately after *Sodom* comes Oldham's 'Aude aliquid' ode— the dramatic monologue in the persona of Rochester that brought about the unlikely meeting of the Earl and the Latin teacher—followed by the first known translation of Chorier into any language: 'The Duell, Being a translation of one of the dialogues in Satyra Sotatica [*sic*] De Arcanis amoris et Veneris. Anno Domini 1676.'[102] After this long Chorier extract the compiler slips in a topical political poem and only then transcribes the apologetic 'Epilogue' that Oldham appended to his anti-virtue ode, closing the sequence that began by fastening 'Aude aliquid' to the 'Epilogue' of the burlesque tragedy; he even adds a note referring the reader forward to that 'Apology for these Pindariques' (p. 135), the plural form suggesting that *Sodom and Gomorah* might be included in that dramatic-poetic category. This accurate but hasty translation of Chorier's Colloquium IV is thus embedded in a context that ties it closely to Oldham, to *Sodom*, and to the clandestine world of the Restoration Court Wits.

This English version of Chorier's *Duellum* is obviously done by an expert Latinist with time on his hands and the opportunity to fulfil a private commission. It is quite possible that Rochester, who sought out the unknown school usher on reading the ode that explicitly parodies his libertine ranting, commissioned the translation from Oldham himself. The title date '1676' fits within the apogee of his fascination with libertine excess, from the Rochesteroid pindaric of 'July 1676' to the Sigea poem (dated '7 May 1677'), the *Sodom* drafts intertwined with the Royal Wedding poem, and the Latin letter of 5 November 1677—almost certainly to Rochester—which apologizes for that solemn effort and boasts of 'saltier' effusions from his convivial group. Where *The Duell* departs from the original, it reveals an affinity with the boisterous rhyming and gratuitous violence of Oldham's own translations at this time.

---

[100] The two Queen's Bench indictments of John Marshall, KB 28/24/8 and 9, are almost identical in date and length.

[101] Three of the seven MSS identified in A. S. G. Edwards, 'Libertine Literature in Restoration England: Princeton MS AM 14401', *Book Collector*, 25 (1976), 354–68, and Larry D. Carver, 'The Texts and the Text of *Sodom*', *Papers of the Bibliographical Society of America*, 73 (1979), 19–40, transcribe the title page of an actual publication that can be matched to the records of prosecution; significantly, MS texts that seem independent of the publications of 1684 and 1689 (and which may pre-date them) do *not* ascribe the farce to Rochester even though they take every opportunity to announce his authorship of other anthology pieces.

[102] Princeton MS AM 14401, pp. 137–204; for a description of the MS and a breakdown of its contents, none dating from later than 1676, see Edwards, 'Libertine Literature'.

Like Rochester and Dryden, Oldham participated in the debate between literal and loose translation that raged in the 1670s, and helped to pioneer the mode of 'Imitation' that finds a racy modern equivalent for the Latin original. Setting out his theory and practice in a published preface, Oldham announces that his own versions of Horace exemplify this 'libertine way'. In contemporary usage, the freedoms taken by translators who modernize and adapt the classics, the wild leaps sanctioned by the Pindaric mode, and the intrinsic licence of poetry itself, could all be conveyed by the word 'libertine'—and thus strongly associated with sexual transgression.[103] When the subject is erotic, this double meaning results in 'imitations' that brazenly spell out the sexual details conveyed more decorously in the original; immediately after the text of *Sodom* in some manuscripts, for example, a short Aesopic fable about a widow is expanded into a poem of blistering obscenity.[104] This genre includes Dryden's version of Lucretius IV, which subtly augments the genital realism without recourse to gutter vocabulary, but which still (as we have seen) provoked his enemies to equate it with 'the translation of Aloisia Sigea'.

Oldham's autograph drafts contain a vivid example of this 'libertine' revisionism, which seems to pun on two meanings of that word—*free in translation* and *sexually explicit*. Taking a Greek distich that literally means 'What is life, what is sweet, if golden Cypris fails? | Let me die when the care of Venus dies for me', Oldham replaces the euphemism of the original with English bluntness: 'What joy without dear C. has life in store? | Let me not live when I can Sw. no more' (MS p. 216). In a strikingly similar vein, the translator of *The Duell* alters an erudite little poem that Chorier weaves into the dialogue. Tullia's distich, which she had delicately 'transmuted' from Virgil's epic (*immutasti*, as Octavia puts it), becomes a self-consciously vulgar burlesque ('Soe you once travesty'd modest Virgil'). In the Latin Tullia converts the young Euryalus' noble contempt for death on the battlefield into the *cunnus*' defiance of the enemy's weapon, but in the English she defines herself in much commoner terms and shifts the emphasis from bravery to injury:

> Heere, heere the Wench that dreads not force of Tarse,
> Tho' mighty Prick should split my Cunt to Arse.[105]

This favourite rhyme of the Restoration lampoonist—used many times in *Sodom*, especially in the shorter version unique to this manuscript—links penis and anus in a rending assault on the female sex. The new (per)version of the couplet, obscene and thoroughly Oldhamesque, enacts in miniature what Oldham proposes at greater length in the rough drafts of 'Upon *Sodom*': it represents yet another attempt

---

[103] Oldham, preface to *Poems and Translations*, in *OED* s.v. 'libertine', B.3.b, alongside relevant citations from Cowley and Walpole; the previous entry, B.3, records Sir William Temple's opinion that 'there is something in the Genius of Poetry, too libertine to be confined to so many Rules'. Dryden defines the 'libertine way' of imitation in his 1680 preface to *Ovid's Epistles*, but warns that it is too extreme.

[104] V&A MS Dyce 43, pp. 163–5; Vienna, Österreichische Nationalbibliothek, MS 14090, pp. 169–71.

[105] Princeton MS, p. 195, translating *Satyra*, IV. 68 (discussed Ch. 7, sect. 1 below); the actual text says 'Soe you one travesty'd modest virgin', suggesting that the scribe was copying from a hard-to-read MS. Of the frequent (t)arse rhymes in *Sodom*, seven appear in scenes only found in the short version (308, 310, 312–13).

to 'outdo' the erotic classic, to convert Tullia into one of the grotesque caricatures of female desire that inhabit the burlesque drama, to *Sodom*ize the 'Heroick' work of the 'famed Spanish Whore' Aloisia Sigea.

'Libertine' translation—in both senses of that word—will form the subject of Chapter 7. These two violently licentious couplets, one from Oldham's inky autograph and one from the earliest translation of Chorier's pseudo-female dialogues, epitomize in miniature the problems to be explored in this next stage, involving 'traduction' as much as transmission. After 1680 the network of clandestine allusions and fitful imitations, studied in the current chapter, will be supplemented by a series of book-length, published adaptations in French and English, disseminating the libertine canon to a wider public that included prosecuting magistrates. Their distortions and amplifications continue the work of outdoing and undoing that seems inseparable from canon-formation.

The Loose Canon

Translations and (Per)versions of Libertine Literature, 1676–1700

Oh! mon petit cher, quel livre court secrètement par Paris! l'*Escole des Filles*, bagatelle! *Arétin*, livre honeste! il ni a point de vestale, je l'en desfie, fût-elle vestale mille fois, qui puisse tenir contre, qui ne rompe son vœu et en diligence encore! il est écrit en latin . . .

(François de Maucroix)

Oh! dear boy, what a book is secretly going the rounds of Paris! *L'Escole des filles*, a trifle! *Aretino*, a respectable book! I bet there is no vestal virgin, even if she were a vestal a thousand times over, who could hold out against it, who wouldn't break her vow of chastity, with all haste too! It's written in Latin . . .

To understand the 'translation' of Pallavicino, *L'Escole des filles*, and Chorier, it is necessary to trace the network of cultural expectations into which the new text must fit, the grid or lattice of generic cross-references that keeps the reader's mind on the subject. To adapt a metaphor common to Margaret Cavendish and *Venus in the Cloister*, we should make visible the 'grille' that limits and intensifies desire. The acts of reading and citation studied so far in Part II set the terms for the longer imitations, anthologizing reprints, and full-length vernacular versions explored in this chapter. But these fresh texts always enjoy a problematic relation with their original, raising the question of what theory of translation is at work: faithful transcription or the 'libertine way' defined by Oldham? homage or competition? disciplining or 'imitation'? compromising or 'outdoing'? Though this chapter deals mainly with literal translations—including the English *Whores Rhetorick* and *Aretinus Redivivus*, and the French *Academie des dames* (after Chorier's Latin)—I will frame it between two episodes from French reception-history that establish, not only the critical response to individual texts, but the *idea of a canon*. Both Maucroix (who supplies my epigraph) and Barrin (in *Vénus dans le cloître*) set Chorier into a curriculum, a series of texts arranged according to the principle of advancement or escalation. Oldham's sketchy, conditional account of libertine 'canonization' already captures the drive essential to canon-formation—a progression in 'daring', a graduated movement towards the goal of proving oneself a writer 'great in wickedness'.

Chorier introduced into sexual discourse, and acted out in the dissolute form of his dialogues, the idea of a graduated and continuous progression from the simplest to the most complex kinds of sexual figuration. And Chorier's restructuring of the libertine text as a propulsive, escalating series is replicated in contemporary comments on the newly emerging canon. In the breathless, gossipy letter cited as my epigraph, Maucroix captures the restless movement of illicit discourse, 'running secretly through Paris' and at the same time striving to surpass its predecessors in wickedness and therefore in seductive power.[1] Maucroix amplifies reactions like those of Pepys ('worse than *Puttana errante*') or Wycherley's Horner, who provokes his faux-respectable audience with a series of increasingly shocking citations that culminate in a suggestive dash: 'I have brought over not so much as a Bawdy Picture, new Postures, nor the second Part of the *Escole de Filles*; Nor——' (Ch. 5 above). Like Horner, Maucroix creates a crescendo-effect, a rising scale of transgression that announces the gossip-writer's own breadth of knowledge and height of worldly discretion. By a happy coincidence this canon-builder was himself a canon of the Church (like Ferrante Pallavicino) as well as a minor libertine writer, whose epigrams flaunt his knowledge of *L'Escole des filles* and the priapic poems that surround it. It was Maucroix, in fact, who compressed libertine theory into the pithiest couplet, urging his beautiful female readers to 'fuck' because 'virtue is nothing but language'.[2]

Maucroix launches his exponential series by defining *L'Escole des filles* as a 'bagatelle', a graceful and sophisticated trifle; Chorier's speakers had identified their own discourse as *eruditae nugae*—the Renaissance-humanist dismissal of one's own highest achievement as a trifle—but here *bagatelle* becomes the minor term in a dichotomy that always posits something more serious and solid. As in Oldham's reaction to Chorier, each item in this canon 'outwrites' its predecessor. Though *L'Escole* continued to be cited, published, and prosecuted in England and in France (as we have seen in Chapters 3 and 5), it did remain under the rubric of the minor classic. In the most visible incarnation of the French text, it formed the first item in an often-reprinted pocket anthology, along with other bagatelles like the prose *Putain errante*, the French and Latin versions of Secundus' epigram on the feminine phallus, obscene burlesque dramas like *La Comédie galante*, and clusters of faintly wicked lyrics like Maucroix's own; *L'Escole* becomes a liminary text, a warm-up act, its forematter now inviting 'Belles et curieuses Demoiselles' into the entire corpus and not just into the dialogue itself. The earliest version of this handy collection even bore the title *La Bibliothèque d'Aretin*, as if that author had established an erotic book club in the afterlife—perhaps in the corner of the Elysian Fields to which Chorier's Aloisia Sigea had consigned him.[3]

---

[1] Letter to Favart, 4 Feb. 1682, in *Lettres, édition critique, suivie de poésies inédites*, ed. Renée Kohn (Paris, 1962), 146; cf. Leibacher-Ouvrard, 'Transtextualité et construction de la sexualité: La *Satyra Sotadica* de Chorier', *L'Esprit créateur*, 35/2 (Summer 1995), 52, 64–5 n. 8.

[2] *Lettres*, 220 (cited in Introd. above), and see Ch. 3 n. 30 above.

[3] For this title (preserved on a detached title page in the Bodleian, 'Cologne', n.d.) see Foxon, 30, and Pascal Pia, *Les Livres de l'Enfer* (Paris, 1978), cols. 120 and 142; the same collection appears as *Le Cabinet d'Amour et de Vénus, contenant les pieces marquées à la table suivante* ('Cologne', dated by the BL *c*.1690), frequently reprinted. Jean Mainil is clearly wrong to assert of *L'Escole* that 'nobody read it any more'; *Dans les règles du plaisir* (Paris, 1996), 58 (245 n. 34 recognizes but downplays its citation in the late-18th-century *La Cauchoise*).

By using Aretino as the middle term in his catalogue of the surpassed, Maucroix places him somewhere between notoriety and obsolescence. (In Chorier's own text, Tullia praises him as 'divini vir ingenii *Petrus Aretinus*', an important predecessor in writing 'beautiful Dialogues on these amusements', but the fictional author herself, while noting his presence in Elysium, marks him as a primitive, goatish figure.[4]) Both the heteronormative *Escole des filles* and the homonormative *Alcibiade fanciullo* were casually ascribed to Aretino when they appeared, and titles like the *Bibliothèque* or *Histoire et vie de l'Arretin* continued to add perverse glamour to reissues of the standard prose canon, associating it with the engraved 'figures of Aretino';[5] in England, *The School of Venus* appeared 'adorned with Twenty four curious plates designed from Aretenez's postures', and the translation of *L'Academie des dames* (after Chorier) was sold under the title *Aretinus Redivivus*. But Aretino finds himself depotentiated in these acts of canon-formation. Oldham's libertine, 'studied' in Rochester, *L'Escole*, 'Heloisas', and *Sodom*, cannot find a text of Aretino that he can read (Ch. 6, sect. 2 above). In *The Parliament of Women* Aretino, identically placed between '*Eschole defilles*' and Aloisia Sigea, drops out of the French mistress's reading because she does not understand Italian—increasingly irrelevant in an age of French hegemony? (1684, 30–1). Maucroix's airy declaration that the generic *Arétin* is a mere 'livre honnête' compared to Chorier draws on a trope that we might call the Benchmark Overthrown or the Extremist Outdone: the present subject is declared so outrageous that he, or more often she, makes Aretino seem 'dull' (as in Killigrew's imaginary convent) or 'modest' (as in Wycherley's *Hero and Leander* or attacks on Milton's libertinism).[6] His choice of *honnête* as a synonym for timid respectability will in turn be surpassed by the time he reaches the end of the *Satyra*, since Chorier (as we saw in Chapter 4) actually redefines *honestas* to make it compatible with the most advanced synthesis of sexual awareness and social 'formation'.

Canon de Maucroix, the *Parliament of Women*, and *Vénus dans le cloître* all assume that girls will be reading the new text, contrary to everything we believe about pornography but consonant with the internal fantasies of these books themselves. (Ironically, the canon's heterosexist reading occurs in a letter to his *petit cher*, an address roughly equivalent to 'dear boy'.) Maucroix's remark about 'Vestals'—a *galant* periphrasis that suggests both virgins in general and nuns in particular—transplants Chorier's text into the overheated atmosphere of the female institution, despite its Latinity.[7] Like an ardent seducer the new book will besiege the virgin who 'holds out against it', break down her fortress, and convert her 'vow' of chastity into an equally intense 'diligence' in the pursuit of immediate pleasure; Maucroix gives it the irresistible power that Rochester ascribed to poetry (Ch. 6, sect. 1 above), the power to

---

[4] *Satyra*, 6, 7, 9 ('barbam longam, hirciniam *Aretinus* laeva mulcebat'), VI. 214, VII. 279 ('his de ludicris amoena conscripsit Colloquia').

[5] Ch. 2, sect. 2, Ch. 3 nn. 1, 104 above.

[6] See passages referenced in Ch. 1 n. 63, Ch. 2 n. 93, Ch. 5 n. 44, and Jonson, *Alchemist*, II. ii. 37.

[7] Chorier calls the lesbian Mother Superior 'magni inter Vestales nominis' (VII. 281), and cf. Pope, *Eloisa to Abelard*, line 4, 'What means this tumult in a Vestal's veins?'

kindle such a fire
Betwixt declining Virtue and Desire,
Till the poor vanquish't Maid dissolves away. (72)

Similarly, the nuns in *Vénus dans le cloître* (as we shall see in section 4 below) review the texts that Maucroix cites and rate them according to the same criteria of extremity and power to arouse, while the *Parliament of Women* creates a new curriculum out of precisely the same triad, exempting '*Aloysia Sigea*, *L'Eschole de fils*, and *Peter Aretines* discourses' from the 'General Massacre' of all other books. Just as in Maucroix, the lady speaker (reviewing her memory of learning French in boarding school) ranks them in order of efficacy, 'melting' over *L'Escole* but losing her virginity to Chorier's 'ravishing', 'absolute and perfect' dialogue. Like Maucroix she defines virgin schoolgirls as the primary target ('were it translated there would not be a Virgin in the Town, by that time a Girl had read her Primmer out'), but unlike Maucroix she opposes the seductive and educational agency of the book to that of flesh and blood men, a 'contemptible' and now unnecessary substitute for textual pleasure.[8]

What gives Chorier's *Satyra* the edge over other erotic fictions, and ensures it the privileged place in the illicit canon given by Oldham or Maucroix, is its fabrication of a female erudite voice, reduplicated in the speakers of the dialogue and the supposed author. Combining the rhetorical sophistication of Pallavicino's bawd-preceptor and the classical learning of Rocco's philosopher-seducer, Aloisia Sigea can be seen as 'outdoing' all previous author-transgressors because she commands the frontiers of knowledge. Tullia acts as the 'Oedipus' who unlocks the mysteries of Eros promised in the original title, and sums up the scandalous erudition of the ancients in the jocoserious spirit of the late Renaissance; future generations then cite the characters and the author interchangeably as authorities on actual sexual practice (as I shall show in the Epilogue). Chorier's Latinity and erudition undoubtedly contributed to this privileged status. Both Maucroix and the *Parliament of Women* assume that the classical language (which is also 'the Language of the Whore') does nothing to impede its allure for women readers: though her French teacher admits that Latin is 'beyond her Spheare', the avid schoolgirl 'enquir'd after a Woman that understood Latin, and money that finds out all things soon found me an Interpreter' (31). The future Parliamentarian inverts the achievement of real-life classicists like Lucy Hutchinson, who translated all of Lucretius except the parts more fit for a midwife.

Translation and canon-formation evidently involve 'libertine' emulation, even violation, of the original, especially when that author(ity) is perceived as female. We have seen in Chapter 6 that Oldham (or ghostly contemporaries who resemble him) competes with Sigea to produce images of transgression, which despite these efforts tend to reveal his 'gender panic' rather than his sophistication. For this would-be aristocrat of extremity, we saw, 'canonization' can bring on feminization or even envagination, as the author becomes what he calls a 'Secretary to a Cunt'; Oldham

---

[8] 32, 136–7; for copies of *L'Escole* planted on young women see Ch. 3, sect. 1 above.

reminds us that 'Heroick' and abject emulation can converge, that the anti-canonical negative exemplum (*Sodom*) can resemble the yardstick used to beat it ('Aloisia Sigea'). Furthermore, once the canon has been defined as an escalating series of transgression, once reviewers like Maucroix show their sophistication by dismissing all previous pornography as a *bagatelle*, the emulator must decide how to trump his predecessor.

1. TRANSLATION AS EXPROPRIATION: *THE DUELL*, *ARETINO'S LIBRARY*, AND *THE WHORES RHETORICK*

The translations analysed in the next three sections—*The Whores Rhetorick*, *L'Academie des dames*, *Les Sept Entretiens galants d'Alosia*, *The Duell*, *The School of Love*, *Aretinus Redivivus*, *A Dialogue between a Married Lady and a Maid*—represent various solutions to this dilemma, which can be summed up as either the 'outdoing' or the 'taming' strategy. The first possibility, followed by *Sodom and Gomorah* in the seventeenth century and by the marquis de Sade in the eighteenth, is to outperform the ancestral competitor in extremity, to escalate the escalation but at the same time to preserve the predecessor as the benchmark to be overthrown. Attempting once and for all to terminate the series begun by the likes of Maucroix, Sade does in fact cite *L'Académie des dames* (and thereby admit its canonicity) as an example of timidity.[9] (This lofty dismissal conceals his debt to the flagellation-scenes of Chorier's Colloquium V, which even in this French adaptation are almost as revolting as his own inventions.[10]) The other possibility—in its way just as contrary to the unfolding plot of the *Satyra Sotadica*—is to domesticate and modernize sexual representation, to bring it under the discipline of companionate marriage or proto-Enlightenment naturalism.

We saw at the close of Chapter 6—introducing *The Duell*, the 1676 version of Colloquium IV that I associate with Oldham—that multiple models of translation compete even in the same text. Chorier's 'original' Latin dialogue (Tullia's description of her wedding-night and thus the first extended account of phallic penetration) is itself supposedly translated from Sigea's Spanish by Meursius and augmented in the process; in contrast to this prestigious (and wholly fictitious) model of humanist translation, Chorier quietly incorporates, and surpasses, Susanne's domestic narrative in the first part of *L'Escole des filles*. To show its lofty classical pedigree Colloquium IV displays embedded quotations 'immuted' from

[9] *Histoire de Juliette*, part 3, in *Œuvres*, Bibliotheque de la Pléiade, iii, ed. Michel Delon and Jean Deprun (Paris, 1998), 590–1.
[10] Cf. Patrick J. Kearney, *A History of Erotic Literature* (1982), 44, and Carole F. Martin, 'From the Mark to the Mask: Notes on Libertinage and Utopianism', in Catherine Cusset (ed.), *Libertinage and Modernity*, special issue, *Yale French Studies*, 94 (1998), 103, 105, 108, who places the flogging-scenes of 'Chorier' (in fact *L'Académie*) at the 'center of seventeenth-century libertinage' because they anticipate Sade; this anachronistic or teleological tendency is magnified in Mainil's *Règles du plaisir*, chs. 2–3 *passim*, and in Jean-Pierre Dubost's various attempts to pass off a highly abbreviated French adaptation as Chorier's work, e.g. *L'Académie des dames, ou La Philosophie dans le boudoir du Grand Siècle* (Arles, 1999).

Virgil's *Aeneid*, as Octavia puts it. Under the shadow of compulsory heterosexuality, Octavia and Tullia reinforce their Sapphic-intellectual bond by exchanging Virgilian lines wittily misapplied to the epic of defloration. In most cases the words are kept intact, but in the instance discussed in Chapter 6—closely related to Oldham's theory and practice of 'libertine' translation—Octavia cites from memory a rewrite that Tullia must have composed for their amusement earlier: Virgil's Euryalus declares his willingness to die in battle, scornful of quotidian daylight and ready to exchange life for *honor*; Tullia scorns the 'javelin' and sacrifices her *cunnus* for the sake of *amor*.[11] Yet the result is not burlesque, for Octavia does conceive her own imminent wedding night as a daunting epic battle, and this citation from the famous episode of Nisus and Euryalus preserves, indeed augments, the homoerotic pathos of the original. The 1676 translator follows the text faithfully for the most part, but at this point switches modes by substituting 'travesty'd' for *immutasti*, clearly thinking of Scarron's *Virgile travesty*. His own invention *Sodom*izes the Latin quotation into a crude couplet on splitting anus and vulva. The body of the text is mutilated as well as travestied.

These two models of translation—refined 'mutation' and violent 'travesty'—sometimes correspond to the different expressive means of prose and poetry. Already in Aretino the explosive, concentrated *sonetti lussuriosi* alternate with the discursive and descriptive prose dialogues, and in France the *Parnasse satyrique* tradition had created a body of 'pointed' obscenity to rival the ancient Roman epigram. (We recall from Chapter 2 how Father Garasse concentrates on a single 'sodomite sonnet' in the anthology attributed to Théophile de Viau.) Claude Le Petit 'transmutes' *L'Escole des filles* into a commendatory poem so aggressive that it threatens to 'fuck' the work it supposedly epitomizes (Ch. 3, sect. 2 above), and even Chorier juxtaposes his erudite *Satyra*, where literary quotation is integrated into the dialogue, with the vituperative 'Birthday Poem for Tubero'—a Martialesque catalogue of sexual malpractices closer to *Sodom* and the Restoration lampoon than to the text it accompanies.[12]

In successive adaptations of Chorier the prose becomes more decorous and indirect, but (as in the 1676 *Duell*) the fragments of inserted verse are treated as occasions for violent obscenity. We shall see in section 2 that the French versions tone down the frank *cunnus* and *futuo* of the original and excise all quotations from classical erotic poetry, but then supplement this denuded text with modern verse fragments from the *satyrique* anthologies. To take a conspicuous example, the *Academie des dames* 'mutates' the Latin distich of Secundus at the close of the sixth dialogue into a poetic threat: if the grammarian fails to answer the riddle about the masculinity of *cunnus*, if he 'stops short' in a kind of hermeneutic impotence, then 'every

---

[11] *Aeneid*, IX. 205–6, *Satyra*, IV. 68; for other citations in Colloquium IV see pp. 54 (*Aeneid*, IV. 317–18), 72 (IX. 744, I. 218), 75 (VI. 122), borrowing passages that involve the betrayal of Dido, mourning for lost comrades, and the chance to revisit a dead brother.

[12] *Satyra*, 315–18; *Sodom*'s disgusting obsession with 'the whites' (leucorrhoea) is matched in Chorier's poem by the image of Cotytto ('alba tabe conspuit femora', 'she spewed white discharge onto her thighs') (316).

(294)

toute nuë sous son amant? d'estre comme a demy estouffée sous la pesanteur de son corps? Qui y a t'il de plus sensible que de repaître ses yeux d'un si tendre objet? Que veux tu de plus voluptueux, que de le manier par tout, de luy mettre la langue dans la bouche, & d'expirer amoureusement entre ses bras? Pour moy je croy que c'est la le comble de la felicité, car je ne vois rien qui puisse flatter davantage la passion de l'un ou de l'autre que les mouvements lascifs de tous deux. Ah! qu'il est doux Tullie, de se regarder mourir l'un & l'autre, & de resusciter un moment aprés. Celuy qui s'amuse au Derriere n'a qu'un seul plaisir, mais celuy qui ayme le Devant gouste tous les plaisirs ensemble. *Tull.* On perd souvent l'appetit a une table bien garnie, on y quitte des mets Delicieux pour se rassasier de viandes communes, ce qui faict que l'on cherche le plaisir dans le changement, & qu'un homme qui qui aura une belle femme la méprisera souvent pour s'abandonner a une vilaine. Trop de biens nous causent ordinairement du dégoust, nous nous plaisons a la diversité, & nous avons du panchant pour les choses qui nous sont defendües. Mais pandant que nous causons ainsi, nous passons la nuict sans dormir, reposons un peu Octavie, baile moy mon cœur & t'endors, que Venus te puisse tousiours favoriser?

E.P.

(295)

EPIGRAMMA.

Dicite Grammatici cur Mascula
nomina Cunnus,
Et cur Fœmineum Mentula nomen
habet.

EPIGRAMME.

Dites moy Docteurs de Grammaire,
Pourquoy le Vit chez vous est d'un
nom Feminin,
Et que le Con paroît du Genre Masculin?
On ne sçait ce qu'on en doit croire,
Mais si vous ne sçavés expliquer ce
Mistere,
Et qu'avec vostre bel esprit
Vous demeuriés tout court, sans pouvoir passer outre,
Vous merités sans contredit,
Que toute Femme qui sçait Foutre,
Vous coupe Rasibus le Vit.

SEPT.

15. Jean Nicholas(?) after Nicolas Chorier, *L'Academie des dames, divisée en sept entretiens satiriques* ('A Ville-Franche, chez Michel Blanchet', 1680), i.294–5 (British Library, PC 31.b.30)

Woman who knows how to Fuck should cut your Prick clean off' (Fig. 15). This 'Epigramme' circulated simultaneously in the *Bibliothèque d'Aretin* anthology, falsely claiming to be a 'translation' of Secundus' Latin; in this circumstance, the French word 'Traduction' might more appropriately be read as impeachment or betrayal.[13]

[13] *Academie*, i. 295 (for the word 'rasibus' cf. *Escole*, II. 95, on Turkish eunuchs); BL Cup. 800.a.48, *Le Cabinet d'Amour et de Vénus* (identical to the *Bibliothèque d'Aretin*, as I show in n. 3 above), 322 (a garbled text that reads 'mentez' for 'méritez'); cf. Littré, s.v. 'Traduire', 1, 'Traducteur', H.

Had Casanova read this French (per-)version rather than the Latin of 'Meursius' he would surely have found something sinister in the Englishman's challenge to interpret Secundus.

Throughout the period of libertine canon-formation, individual motifs migrate from verse to prose and back again, mutating into autonomous poetic gestures. Take, for example, what I call the trope of biomorphic voluntarism, the desire to transform the structure of the body by the assertion of sexual will. The wish to become 'all prick, to slip entirely inside', migrates from the sonnets of Aretino to the prose *Puttana errante* and then to *L'Escole des filles*, where it confirms the Cartesian idea of total fusion with the love object (Ch. 3, sect. 4 above). In Chorier, this fantasy embodies the key principle of Tulia's erotology, *Mutari amat Proteus Amor*: her friend Aloisia describes herself as 'all cunt' at the moment of arousal, and her lover thrusts as if he could 'put in his whole body', or at least convert 'all his longings, needs, desires, thoughts and loving soul' into sperm (pp. 186, 187 above). We have seen variants on this self-genitalization topos in Rochester and in Oldham, who imagine the extreme condition of 'spending at every pore'. In the brief lyric called 'The Wish' or 'Insatiate Desire', later included among Rochester's poems, an anonymous English libertine extends this regressive-transformative urge to the birthing process, and adds a typical air of swaggering misogynistic violence:

> O that I could by any Chymick Art
> To sperme convert my spirit and my heart,
> That at one thrust I might my soul translate,
> And in the womb my self regenerate,
> There steep'd in lust nine months I would remain,
> Then boldly f— my passage back again.[14]

The bizarre image of interuterine incest had already been incorporated into Rocco's *Alcibiade fanciullo*, where as part of naturalizing the 'unnatural' he posits that certain fetuses assume a position in the womb that allows their father's penis to sodomize them, endowing them with unusual receptivity in that orifice (83). Migrating back into heterosexual discourse, this unimaginably obscene topos inspires an epigram by the Duke of Buckingham, apparently directed against his cousin the Duchess of Cleveland, the mistress of Charles II generically portrayed as Fuckadilla in *Sodom*; as in Rocco, the 'exquisite whore' is imagined copulating in the womb with her own father. This epigram too joins 'The Wish' in the *Works* of Rochester, while an almost identical poem appears on the other side of the Channel, in that comprehensive collection *La Bibliothèque d'Aretin*.[15]

---

[14] *The Second Part of Merry Droilery* (1661), 31 ('Insatiate Desire'), with some readings from 'The Wish' in [Edmund Curll (ed.),] *The Works of the Earls of Rochester, Roscomon, Dorset, Etc.*, '4th' edn. (1714), i. 112 (as by Rochester); see also David M. Vieth, *Attribution in Restoration Poetry: A Study of Rochester's 'Poems' of 1680* (1963), 33, 490.

[15] Christine Phipps (ed.), *Buckingham, Public and Private Man: The Prose, Poems and Commonplace Book of George Villiers, Second Duke of Buckingham (1628–1687)* (1985), 154 (attribution uncertain but 'possible'); *The Works of the Earls*, i. 112 ('Written under Nelly's Picture'); *Cabinet d'Amour et de Vénus*, 326 ('Ci git l'impudique Nannon. | Qui dans le ventre de la Mére | Se rangeoit si bien dans son con, | Qu'elle y foutoit avec son Pére').

Within the covers of this single anthology, in fact, can be found an entire catalogue of the genital transformation trope. In this 'Library' presided over by the founding figure of Aretino, the pseudo-Aretine *Putain errante* provides the simplest statement of the desire to be engulfed in the other body, and *L'Escole des filles* a more complex philosophic elaboration of the same idea. The technological approach is represented by *Nouvelles Leçons du commerce amoureux, par la sçavante T****, a prose advice manual allegedly by one of Louis XIV's mistresses, which concludes with cynically practical tips about alum washes and reusable contraceptive pessaries (briefly mentioned in *L'Escole des filles*, Ch. 3, sect. 4 above).[16] In verse, Secundus' distich provides the theoretical basis for separating biological sex, grammatical gender, and hierarchical position, while the accompanying French 'Traduction' proposes the most violent surgical intervention as a way of cancelling biology completely. A set of mock-epitaphs play with the conjunction of sex, birth, and death, and present the grotesque image of incestuous copulation in the womb. But the most elaborate versification of Protean biomorphic fantasy comes in the mock-heroic drama already mentioned as an analogue for *Sodom*, the *Comédie galante de Monsieur de Bussy*—a doubtful and scandalous attribution to Bussy-Rabutin, though his more genuine verse 'Maximes d'amour' are also included in this anthology.

This dramatization of Bussy's *Histoire amoureuse des Gaules* replaces his icily polite prose with the full *satyrique* vocabulary, and converts his detached narrative into another ventriloquistic voicing of 'female' desire. In her opening outburst, the comtesse d'Olonne wishes that the genitals could take on the qualities of the hand, multiplex and infinitely controllable. Her unacknowledged source here is St Augustine, who speculated that before the fall Adam and Eve would have had precisely this ability to manipulate the genitals at will, like the hands. But whereas Augustine's prelapsarian state would have reduced sexuality to a controlled and moderate delight, the d'Olonne character loses herself in a vision of perpetual orgasm:

> Oui, je voudrois bien, tant j'aime le déduit
> Que chaque doigt de l'homme eût pris forme de V...
> Et qu'au lieu du bas ventre, où nos C... sont sans grace,
> La paulme de la main fût desormais leur place.
> Et tout temps, en tout lieu, lors fort commodement
> Nous aurions toûjours nôtre contentement.
> Qui finissant d'ailleurs aussi-tôt qu'il commence,
> Auroit enfin par là, plus longue subsistance,
> Un doigt relevant l'autre, il ne le verroit pas,
> Que ces vigoureux V... devinssent jamais las.[17]

---

[16] *Cabinet d'Amour et de Vénus*, 281–300, esp. 298; the same text appears independently as *Leçons du commerce amuoreux* [sic] *adressées par la sçavante Madame la E.H.C.U.O.T. aux plus fameuses de sa profession* (1684), BL PC 31.b.20.

[17] *Cabinet d'Amour et de Vénus*, 256–7. The question of Bussy-Rabutin's authorship remains open; one 19th-century sales catalogue records a Paris, 1667, edn. attributed to 'M de B' (cf. *Sodom*, published as by the 'E of R'), according to Lemonnyer (Ch. 3 n. 32 above), who notes both Bussy and Blessebois as putative authors.

Yes, I love the pleasure so much that I would really like every finger on the man's hand to take the form of a prick, and the palm of the hand to be at the bottom of the belly instead of our graceless cunts. At all times, in every place, with the utmost ease, we would always obtain our happiness. And that way, finally, it would subsist for longer, ending at the same moment that it starts; one finger taking over from another, these vigorous pricks would never seem to grow tired.

As if to emphasize the inventiveness of this attempt to 'outdo' the limits of biology and literary history, the *Bibliothèque d'Aretin* makes these lines available in two different formats. Elsewhere in the anthology, prominently placed at the head of the 'Vers gaillards et satiriques', the ode-like dramatic reverie is compressed into a six-line epigram and 'transmuted' from the female voice to the male—bringing out its latent misogyny. In this portable form, as we shall see, this articulation of 'Insatiate Desire' is reincorporated into the libertine dialogue; as part of its modernization of Chorier, *L'Academie des dames* gives it to the triumphant husband on the wedding night.[18]

The multifarious processes of translation—anthologizing, reincorporation, genre mutation, travesty, 'imitation', competition for authority—operate even in texts that purport to transmit the original directly, like the 1683 *Whores Rhetorick, Calculated to the Meridian of London, and Conformed to the Rules of Art*. It shares the title of Pallavicino's *Retorica delle puttane*, and takes its localizing effect from the Italian text too; Pallavicino had explained that his work was cast, like a horoscope, 'for the meridian of Venice' (*RP* 110). Nevertheless, the English adaptor changes more than the 'meridian' and the lexical base. In the first place, the form itself has been transmuted, making the text less regular despite the 'Rules of Art' announced in the title. *The Whores Rhetorick* reduces or abandons many of Pallavicino's structural devices, such as the systematic naming of rhetorical-sexual 'figures' and the fifteen-part lunar lecture-cycle, recasting *La retorica delle puttane* rather clumsily into the dialogue form of *L'Escole des filles*, *The Wandring Whore*, and *L'Academie des dames*. The 'rhetoric' trope—already a popular running joke in English whore-biographies—becomes one theme among many, fragmented and transformed into a multiplicity of discourses and metaphoric sequences. Long stretches of intellectual ingenuity are cut, and the space filled with extracts from Aretino's *Ragionamenti*, topical allusions to the London sexual underworld, and satire against the Puritans. Pallavicino's unnamed teacher-figure becomes the bawd Mrs Cresswell, whose name had been on Tory satirists' lips since her trial in 1681 supposedly revealed Presbyterian City leaders among her regulars. Pallavicino had introduced an element of social satire when he encouraged upper-class refinement in the prostitute (she must not sound and move like a porter), but this class-awareness is now sharpened by specifically English references, to the sexual adventures of Charles II

---

[18] *Cabinet d'Amour et de Vénus*, 321 ('Tant j'aime l'amoureux deduit | Que chaque doigt fût un gros vit | Vous en feriez bien plus contente, | Outre qu'il n'arriveroit pas, | Que ces vits fussent jamais las | A vous payer chacun sa rente)'; it is hard to determine whether this or the *Academie* citation (p. 324 below) came first.

and Monmouth at one end of the social spectrum, to the dangers of Bridewell at the other. Topicality invades the body-as-simulacrum; even the precepts for vaginal hygiene receive local colour, using as metaphor the slippery steps of a Thames boat-landing.[19]

Sexuality is still subject to 'method' and 'Conformed to the Rules of Art', as the title page of the new version proclaims—echoing the English translation of *L'Escole*, which had promised 'the Ladies delight reduced into Rules of Practice'. But 'art' now encompasses a broader range of those modern disciplines that had been transformed by Cartesian rationality. Military metaphors, for example, associate sexual adventure with the new science of siege warfare perfected by Vauban: Mrs Cresswell compares herself to a battle-scarred veteran like Wycherley's Horner or Rochester's disabled debauchee, and the author himself (now given the comic name 'Philo-Puttanus') claims that, if 'the bawdy Science' can be 'made hereby more regular and methodical, both Combatants, the Masculine besieger and the besieged Female, are informed of one anothers designs, and so by easy consequence to shun the danger and hazzard of a Battel'.[20] But despite this aspiration to turn 'bawdy' into 'science', the didactic programme of transforming sexual practice into art is much curtailed. The 'Italian' fascination with sodomy—for Pallavicino the goal and test of erotic art, the instrument on which the courtesan plays her toccata, the prime instance of 'translation' and self-mutation—is either removed completely or explicitly rejected: the old teacher reverses the recommendation of *La retorica*, rejecting '*Aretin*'s Figures' because 'they are calculated for a hot Region a little on this side *Sodom*, and are not necessary to be seen in any Northern Clime' (*WR* 171). The adaptor seems torn between the need to disparage 'unnatural' sexual arts and the need to advertise his own expertise in 'Aretino'. Mrs Cresswell dismisses the 'Six and Thirty Geometrical Schemes' (evidently thinking of the numbered lists in the pseudo-Aretine *Puttana errante*), but goes out of her way to mention the 'Four and Twenty rough draughts' currently available on the London market.

As part of its modernizing discourse on method, *The Whores Rhetorick* bristles with 'philosophical' observations that evoke the experimentalism of the Royal Society. Restoration 'imitation' demands topicality even when the classic text is written only forty years previously, and contemporary humour often linked the new 'bawdy science' and the new 'Natural Philosophy' that was currently defending itself against the charge of being 'a carnal knowledge'.[21] (In *Sodom*, for example, the dildo-maker is called Virtuoso and speaks loftily of 'the Philosophicall dimension' or 'demonstration'.[22]) Mrs Cresswell often 'talks Philosophically', and admits that, rather than 'contain my self within the bounds of a Rhetorick, my vain curiosity transported me into the wild and impassible mazes of Philosophy, and to dive too far into secrets of

---

[19] *WR* 37, 122, 182; for the social context (including anti-Puritan allusions to 'Mother Cresswell') see my *Libertines and Radicals in Early Modern London* (Cambridge, 2001), chs. 5–6 and epilogue *passim*.

[20] *WR* fo. B2ᵛ, 25, but cf. fo. A10–ᵛ, which *contrast* the life-enhancing art of sex to the destructive 'Military Art' (for the original in Montaigne, see Ch. 1, sect. 1 above).

[21] Thomas Sprat, *The History of the Royal-Society* (1667), 27.

[22] 327 (and variant in Lyons 148).

natural Philosophy to gratifie my own fantastical and giddy nature' (71, 20). Unfortunately she regrets this tendency to 'out-do' herself and move higher in the curriculum, leaving it to the reader to guess what these advanced studies might involve. Whereas contemporary French dialogues like Chorier's try to construct sexuality itself on philosophical lines, the English satire focuses on the prostitute's lechery and cunning, her understanding of the masculine foibles she must learn to exploit. 'Bawdy science' amounts to a simple joke about physical quantity: 'Mr. *Hobbs*, Child, says well, that Wisdom is nothing but experience; so by consequence the Bawd must surpass all mankind in point of Wisdom. . . . She has read more Men than any mortal has Books' (85).

Hobbes does, however, provoke the idea that 'the whole series of carnal satisfaction does purely consist in fancy', which in turn yields the principle that 'the World, and so all men in it, are governed by fancy and opinion: good and evil are therefore little understood as they are in themselves, but rather as they come represented to Mens various and often vitiated palates.' This 'Philosophical' subjectivism then sharpens the satire on masculine solipsism, suggesting an epistemic countermeasure for the courtesan to adopt. If things and feelings are only true 'as they come represented', then she must direct the representation. If 'Men are oft of opinion, that Women were made only for their enjoyment', if they 'force their Mistresses to dissolve in pleasure . . . in regard their own fancies are high and elevated', 'believing these amorous pangs created by themselves', then she must retain control of the script by fashioning herself according to what men think *they* have fashioned. This is a dangerous game, like the controlling deceptions practised by Chorier's Sempronia: men violently reject 'as nauseous' any sexual expertise in women, 'unless it be when they may conclude themselves the Authors and Instructers'. To retain her power as 'Author' the trainee courtesan must *simulate* ignorance, or at least ascribe her inventiveness to 'nature' as Montaigne had done. Provided she learns to maintain this unlearned façade, she should put her trust in man's gullibility. Mrs Cresswell assures her pupil Dorothea that the typical client 'will pay for a Dutchess, and over-act himself in that Faith; yet all the while he imbraces (I cannot say a Cloud, because there is so much dirt) yet at best but her imaginary Grace'.[23]

The topical elements in *The Whores Rhetorick* bring to fruition the decade-long cross-pollination or mutual reinforcement of theatre and pornography. Restoration comedy frequently cites the scandalous text on stage and thereby contributes to the formation of a libertine canon.[24] Wycherley, as we have seen in Chapter 5, creates a eunuch-libertine who blurts out the name of *L'Escole des filles* and seems ready to go on to worse. In turn, Wycherley appears so often in *The Whores Rhetorick* that one begins to suspect his hand in the translation. Dorothea expresses her enthusiasm for *The Plain-Dealer* and *The Country-Wife*, Cresswell recommends 'Modern Comedies' and drags in anecdotes about the very actor who created Horner: hired to

[23] WR 113–14, 45–6, 167–8, 174–5; cf. Antonio Cavallino?, *Tariffa delle puttane di Venegia* (1535), ed. Guillaume Apollinaire (Paris, 1911), 112, where customers who think they are sleeping with 'la signora' are tricked by substituting 'La Fornaia' (the baker's wife).

[24] Cf. Introd. n. 82 above and sect. 3 below.

impersonate a rejected noble suitor, he comes straight from the stage to rant like Dryden's Almanzor in *The Conquest of Granada*, 'still full of the Hero he there represented'.[25] Like Horner in his opening scene, she equates midwifery with procuring and proclaims her sexual expertise in the mountebank's phrase '*probatum est*' (26, 94). Philo-Puttanus himself adopts the ponderous epigrammatic sarcasm of Wycherley and borrows extensively from the dedication to *The Plain-Dealer*, itself an imitation of Pallavicino's original text; like Wycherley, he refers to the author as 'poetical Dawber', compares the brothel to the theatre, avows 'Plain-dealing', denounces flattery and Latin verse quotation, and praises the prostitute for her public virtues—'though I never had the honour to receive any marks of your favour'.[26]

The English (per)version of *La retorica delle puttane*, then, turns Pallavicino's single-minded master-trope of rhetoric into an unstable constellation of genres, a fragmentary mix of epistemology, theatre, politics, philosophy, 'Novel', and 'Romance'. Weaving *The Whores Rhetorick* as a 'new modelled Fabrick' (221) involves a kind of internal anthologizing or pastiche. We have seen in Chapter 2 that, in her English incarnation, the courtesan creates herself as the heroine of Romance, using what we would call novelistic realism to 'unfold' a character of sincere passion. More topically, Mrs Cresswell remarks that the sexual adventures of Charles II and his son Monmouth might 'afford matter for a Novel' and obviate the need for 'translating daily such numbers of *French* ones, that are in my mind fitter for the necessary House than the Closet' (182–3). Aphra Behn realized this possibility almost immediately, when she fabricated *Love-Letters between a Nobleman and his Sister* out of the scandals of Monmouth and his co-conspirator Lord Grey.

Alongside these modernizing allusions, the adaptor imports a number of 'pornodidactic' routines that go back to the origins of the genre. A dream-sequence gives the older woman a chance to display her hermeneutic skills. A catechistic question-and-answer session calms the fears of the virgin as she plans her career as a whore. A running mercantile metaphor reviews Dorothea's sexual assets as if they were the jewels that she keeps in her 'shop'. The pupil explicitly acknowledges the educational trope when she exclaims 'I wonder, Mother, you do not set up a School, I am sure you would have a multitude of Scholars!' In every case, these inset passages are plagiarized directly from Aretino's *Ragionamenti*.[27] Paradoxically, updating Pallavicino means incorporating an earlier libertine tradition. By a process that Julia Kristeva wittily calls *père-version*, the rebellious modern pornographer turns to embrace the founding father.[28]

---

[25] WR 189, 150, 97–9 (almost certainly an in-house anecdote about the actor Charles Hart); note that *Sodom* and *WR* both play pornotropic variations on the grandiose *Conquest of Granada*.

[26] WR fos. A2, A3ʳ–4ᵛ, A6–7.

[27] WR 129–34, 195, 38, 202; *Ragionamenti*, II. ii. 229–30 [239–40], II. i. 216 [225], 166–7 [173], 184–5 [192] (cited Ch. 1, sect. 1 above). Note that *L'Escole* and Chorier also import unacknowledged translations from Aretino: cf. Ch. 3 nn. 50, 86, and *Satyra*, IV. 53–5, a dream-interpretation sequence modelled on *Ragionamenti*, II. ii. 229–30 [239–40].

[28] *Histoires d'amour*, Folio Essais (Paris, 1983), 253; Kristeva coins the term to describe the psychology of Dom Juan, but I am transferring the concept to the relation between texts.

2. 'ALOISIA' AND L'ACADEMIE DES DAMES (1680)

The very title of *L'Academie des dames*—sometimes attributed to Jean Nicolas junior, son of the Grenoble publisher who sold Chorier's *Satyra* to local notables[29] —announces its relationship to *L'Escole des filles, ou La Philosophie des dames* and thus to the emergent vernacular-libertine canon. As we have seen when juxtaposing the pornographic *Escole* to Margaret Cavendish's oppositional *Female Academy*, the faux-educational trope mocks women's exclusion from the official academies of Louis XIV's France, eroticizes the private intellectual gatherings where they influenced *philosophie*, and belittles the teacher-training institutions set up by the new orders of Dames to 'police' the family (Ch. 3, sect. 5 above); as Lise Leibacher-Ouvrard rightly suggests, the French title also evokes the equestrian Academy or riding school (a pun flogged to death in Claude Le Petit's *Université d'amour*).[30] In many ways *L'Academie* 'conforms' Chorier's metamorphic and excessive text to the world of the *bonnes bourgeoises* so efficiently captured in *L'Escole*. This is done, not by large-scale importation of topicality and satire *à la Whores Rhetorick*, but by a kind of plastic surgery, by nipping, tucking, and inserting discreet pieces of alien, synthetic material. Above all, this cosmetic smoothing suppresses the female erudite voice that impressed and alarmed readers of the Latin. We shall see, however, that vestiges of this vanished erotic-didactic fusion return to haunt the new 'Academy'.

The first change to astonish the reader in *L'Academie des dames, divisée en sept entretiens satiriques* ('A Ville-Franche, chez Michel Blanchet', 1680)[31] is that it strips off the Latin supporting scaffold and expunges all mention of Aloisia Sigea's supposed authorship: the reader plunges directly into the 'Premier entretien academique' between Tullie and Octavie, without the slightest preparation or mediation. Only one word remains from Chorier's title. the 'satiriques' that signals us not to take the following 'academic discourse' at face value. Significantly, however, the various abbreviated translations that circulated in the following decade restore a ghostly shadow of the fictional author, cutting her surname and her historical specificity but leaving her first name—as if the original title page, where ALOISLÆ is set in heavier type (Fig. 8), had been glimpsed through a myopic mist. Just as Chorier's text passed under the decoy title *Johannis Meursii Elegantiae*, so this abridged version shows up as *Aloysia, ou L'Académie des dames, Les Sept Entretiens d'Aloysia*, or any combination of these, and the police sometimes identify it merely as *D'aloisia*.[32] In effect, a

---

[29] Foxon, 39 (following a MS note in the flyleaf of BL PC 30.i. 9).

[30] 'Pseudo-féminocentrisme et ordre (dis)simulé: La *Satyra sotadica* (1658–1678) et l'*Académie des dames* (1680)', in Roger Duchêne and Pierre Ronzeaud (eds.), *Ordre et contestation au temps des classiques* (Paris, 1992), 201 (confirmed by *Academie*, i. 232, which adds to the spur-image in *Satyra*, VI. 182 a pun on 'Exercises Academiques'); for Le Petit's *Manège* or riding school see Ch. 1, sect. 3 above. Elizabeth Susan Wahl, *Invisible Relations: Representations of Female Intimacy in the Age of Enlightenment* (Stanford, Calif., 1999), 220–5, links *L'Academie* to anti-précieuse texts like Chappuzeau's *Académie des femmes*.

[31] BL PC 31.b.30, the first and most complete translation (Foxon, 39–40, plate VIII).

[32] Foxon, 40; Anne Sauvy, *Livres saisis à Paris entre 1678 et 1701* (The Hague, 1972), entries 539, 540, 974; Margaret Jacob, 'The Materialist World of Pornography', in Lynn Hunt (ed.), *The Invention of*

new character of female extremity has been created by this titling. 'Aloisia' remained the commonest way of referring to the vernacular text, even as late as Diderot's *Bijoux indiscrets* (where the 14-year-old masturbator 'perfects himself' after 'reading *Aloysia*', as I showed in the Introduction above). In the same year that versions of the *Academie* started to 'run through Paris'—as Maucroix would later say of the Latin original—a putative sexual biography of Mme de Montespan seems to exploit the notoriety of 'Aloisia', and to merge the truth-claims of the libertine dialogue and the *roman à clef*, by adopting the title *Alosie*.[33] This effect is amplified in the English translation: *Aloisa, or The Amours of Octavia, Englished*.

Titling, naming, and even diction corroborate the genre-convergence exploited in this Aloisia-effect. Though they remain dialogues and not 'novels', the French adaptations rename their characters to suggest the contemporary *chronique scandaleuse*, where genteel romance names coexist ironically with scabrous subject matter. Bussy-Rabutin slanders the comtesse d'Olonne as 'Ardelise', Pierre-Corneille Blessebois populates *Le Rut* with 'Céladon' and 'Dorimène', and the French *Academie* changes Chorier's antique-sounding Callias and Lampridius to 'Oronte' and 'Cléante'. To some extent Chorier himself precipitated this change by hinting at an *à clef* reading: the preface to the *Satyra* promises *narratiunculae* (that is, the 'historiettes' that Blessebois and Tallemant call their scandals) and identifies Sigea's targets as the 'Duchesses, Marchionesses, and Countesses' of her own circle; just as Blessebois describes orgies in explicit localized detail and showers sexual abuse on the *noblesse de robe* of Alençon, 'the Sodom of Normandy', so Chorier's later Colloquia could be interpreted as a secret history of the Dauphiné.[34]

But Chorier maintains the Renaissance-humanist setting to support the fiction of Sigea's authorship, whereas the *Academie* reduces most of its characters to the present tense of gossip. (The 'Stoics' become cheekily anticlerical 'Fathers', and the historical Juan Luis Vives becomes the decontextualized, generic 'Patrice'.) At times, *L'Academie* also tries to modify its 'satyric' diction to match this updated *galanterie*. *Aloisa*, for example, tries to reconcile the stylistic reticence of Bussy with the explicit genital realism of Chorier, the *cunnus* becoming 'that place which it is more natural to touch, than modest to name', the *mentula* 'some thing more powerful, which she could not resist', and pregnancy 'the evil she feared'.[35] Likewise Nicolas replaces the physical particularity of lesbian copulation—'Ut committis cunnum cunno!' 'How you put cunt to cunt!'—with more generic lan-

---

Pornography (New York, 1993), 167. Critics who cite later versions of the *Académie*—fraudulently presented as the original in recent editions by Michel Camus and Jean-Pierre Dubost—generally fail to acknowledge that they are using an abridgement, twice removed from Chorier's text.

[33] For *Alosie, ou Les Amours de Madame de M.T.P.* (1680) and earlier versions alluding to Montespan, see Foxon, 40; for its context see Kathryn A. Hoffmann, *Society of Pleasures: Interdisciplinary Readings of Pleasure and Power during the Reign of Louis XIV* (New York, 1997), 153 and ch. 8 *passim*.

[34] For *narratiunculae* and *à clef* gossip cf. Ch. 4, sect. 1 above and Blessebois, *Le Rut, ou La Pudeur éteinte*, in *Œuvres satyriques*, i (Paris, 1866), esp. 62 ('Cette seconde petite partie d'une historiette'), 115 ('la Sodome normande').

[35] (1681), 9, 12, 15; cf. *Alosie*, ed. Marc de Montifaud ('London', 1880), 50, 52, 54–5 (the ascription to Blessebois in this edn. seems unfounded, but Apollinaire does include the original 1668 version *Lupanie* in his Paris, 1912, edn. of Blessebois's *Œuvre*).

guage ('ah comme nos deux parties sont ointes l'une a l'autre!'). *L'Academie* makes Octavia more passive by giving the exclamation to Tullia, and further reduces role ambiguity by suppressing her question about 'shadow' and 'body', absent husband and present lover.[36]

Though the differences between *L'Academie* and Chorier are frankly more interesting than the continuities, I should acknowledge that long passages have been translated literally, and that occasionally the modernizing language adds a new flair to Chorier's point. When Octavie calls her vulva *esclatante* she imparts a kind of vivaciousness to the labia, which resonates with a later passage in which Tullie imagines the noise of copulation *esclatant* through the bedroom walls and windows—as if erotic energy streams from that source into the wider world (i. 7). When female speakers exclaim how excited they are by their *entretien* (their 'conversation' in the carnal and verbal sense), or how 'nos entretiens' bring back the fleeting pleasures of the body, the reader can identify self-referentially, since the word 'Entretien' now prefaces each of the colloquia.[37] Sometimes the new vocabulary narrows the distance between Chorier and *L'Escole des filles*, as when Tullie explains that all women love girls who are *douillettes*, soft and dainty (a word that Susanne applied both to the skin of the penis and to Fanchon's thighs), or when she erupts with desire for Octavie because she narrates her wedding night so *naïvement*.[38]

Much of the *Satyra*'s scandalous content remains in the vernacular work: Tullie still thrusts her 'adulterous finger' into Octavie (i. 66), monogamous marriage still dissolves into a priapic festival under the direction of Sempronie, multiple male athletes still perform *ad nauseam* in the sixth dialogue, only to be superseded by the play of mental images, the literary and artistic canon as primary erotic object. Tullie still recounts and marginalizes the history of male homosexuality (as a gloss on the hetero-sodomite impulses of her fellow Italians), and the polymorphous seventh dialogue still dissolves the idea of a single normative mode; this all-important final section is actually tied more tightly to the earlier parts, since the 'manuscript' gaps have been cleverly smoothed over and the characters' names homogenized to play down the shift in locale from Italy to Spain. The crudely phallocratic wedding-night scenes, with their accompanying doctrines of wife as possession and penis as source of 'mind', still fall in the first quarter of the work, and the hyper-masculine figures of the later *Entretiens* are still mortified by comparison with the romantic-utopian education of Robertus, now renamed Alexis to suggest the beloved youth in

---

[36] *Satyra*, V. 88; *Academie*, i. 86. For other toning down cf. *Academie*, i. 89–90 (cuts the intense kissing of mother and daughter in *Satyra*, V. 90–1), 237 (*Satyra*, VI. 186), ii. 6–7 (but contrast i. 109, Ch. 1 n. 110 above).

[37] i. 189, ii. 6, translating the passage on 'salty wit', 'erudite libido', and 'remembering pleasure' (*Satyra*, VII. 220) frequently cited in Ch. 4 above.

[38] *Escole* I. 19, II. 65; *Academie*, i. 20, ii. 76; by cutting Tullia's intervening citation from Ovid (*Satyra*, II. 36–7), *L'Academie* makes Octavie's first arousal (21) seem an immediate response to the word *douillette*. For *naïvement*, *naïveté*, etc., referring to the aphrodisiac effect of vivid representation, see *Academie*, i. 12, 38 (translating 'ad vivum' in *Satyra*, V. 88), 189, 260, and ii. 91; on the *naïf* as a positive aesthetic quality in *L'Escole* and contemporary usage, see Ch. 3 n. 92 above.

Virgil's second eclogue.[39] The sexual initiation of a tender youth still constitutes 'la veritable honnesteté' and places him 'in the world' (ii. 68, 80). And the erotic bond of the two cousins, rekindled by the arousing *naïveté* of their discourse, still forms the vivid foreground; the entire work still ends with Tullie and Octavie locked in a kiss that looks as if it will 'never end'.

Nevertheless, passages have been cut from almost every page, and these cuts work to enforce an ideology of anti-intellectual domesticity. Tullie may still be reputed 'sçavante dans l'Histoire et dans les langues estrangeres' but she gets less opportunity to display it; once Sigea has been expelled from the Academy there remains no reason to make Tullia a scholarly libertine like her. *L'Academie* drives a wedge between *libido* and the *erudita*. When Octavie bewails the confusion caused by awakening desire she can no longer compare her plight with the sympathetic description of Byblis in Ovid, which Tullia holds up to her like a mirror. When Tullie explains the universality of lesbian desire to her freshly seduced cousin, she no longer mentions Sappho, Philaenis, or the ancient literature on *tribadas* and *subagitatrices*; since Nicolas also cuts the personal account of Tullia's initiation by her friend Pomponia, lesbianism is left with no empowering history, no founding ancestress to support a counter-tradition, no story of origins, and no classificatory vocabulary. Renamed 'Angelique', Pomponia still shows up frequently in the heterosexual scenes, but her secret and ironizing lesbian identity has been expunged.[40]

As the *Academie* cuts most of the classical allusions from female speakers—in contrast to Patrice/Vives, who still adorns his desire with comparisons to Ganymede and Hylas—they become more stupid. Tullia's self-identification as 'Oedipus' disappears (i. 28). Pomponia is stripped of her intellect as well as her bisexuality, since *L'Academie*, i. 41 translates her *ingenium* (*Satyra*, IV. 56) as 'ce certain je ne sçay quoi, qui gaigne tous les cœurs', and completely omits Tullia's praise of her 'literary studies' (69). The connection of writerly and erotic 'acumen' in Laura (Ch. 4, sect. 2 above) is reduced to generic praise: she 'ecrit fort bien' and is 'tendre' and 'spirituelle', i. 257). When Octavia gets Robertus alone in her bedroom Tullia recites the 'Io Paean' lines from the *Ars Amatoria* (VII. 269), but in the *Academie* Tullie merely murmurs 'Ah Dieu! il me semble que j'y suis' (ii. 65). In *L'Academie*, ii. 6, the paradigmatic sentence 'Eruditae libidini prospere omnia cedunt'—'everything yields happily to erudite desire' (*Satyra*, VII. 220)—is simply dropped from an otherwise well-translated speech.

By removing the network of mock-heroic Virgilian quotation from the defloration narratives (n. 11 above), Nicolas takes away the resource through which the two women strengthen their own bond and undermine husbandly pretensions. By dropping Lucretius' recommendation of quadruped-style coupling, the missionary

---

[39] Mentioned by Tullie in *Entretien* VI (i. 271, translating *Satyra*, VI. 204); cf. David Robinson, 'To Boldly Go Where No Man Has Gone Before: The Representation of Lesbianism in Mid-Seventeenth- to Early Eighteenth-Century British and French Literature', Ph.D. dissertation (Berkeley, 1998), 341 n. 74.

[40] i. 2, 9–10, 22–3, and cf. *Satyra*, I. 24, I. 28, II. 38–9. For the conservative implication of removing classical erudition from the early Sapphic dialogues, see Wahl, *Invisible Relations*, 223–4 and Robinson, 'To Boldly Go', 185–6 (contrast Jacob, 'Materialist World of Pornography', 171).

position is made to seem more definitive (i. 293). (Oddly, a few patches of decorative erudition do survive, for example in Tullie's allusions to the Milesian women using dildos and the nuptial gods that helped the bridegroom penetrate the virgin; it is as if the phallus still deserved, or required, the kind of gilding now denied to alternative forms of libido.[41]) Deep cuts are made even in the basic exposition of anatomy, excising not only the learned synonyms and etymologies but the description of the *mons veneris*, labia, nymphae, clitoris, vagina, and cervix—together with Octavia's tribute to Tullia's Comenian brilliance as a teacher, which lets her see these secret organs *quasi ob ocula posita*. Even in the original the clitoris is precarious, since Tullia admits that it almost slipped her mind ('de *clitoride* me fugit dicere'); but where Chorier had included a scene of Callias playing with that organ and catching Tullia's ejaculate in his hand, in *L'Academie* all mention of it has vanished. Nicolas has performed a radical clitoridectomy on the text.[42]

Almost as if compensating for this abrasion of the classical base, after the two wedding-night scenes Nicolas begins to retain fragments of Chorier's Latin. Beginning with (and thus exemplifying) the phallepistemic doctrine that *Qui aperit vulvam aperit et mentem*, 'he who opens the vulva also opens the mind' (i. 91), the most memorable sentences of Alois a Sigea and Joannes Meursius now stand italicized within the text like ruins of a wiser antiquity, marble monuments along the Via Appia of sexual understanding:

> *Sine Testibus non agitur*
> Nothing can take place without Witnesses (or Testicles)
>
> *Palam vive omnibus, clam et in tuto tibi*
> live publicly for everyone, live secretly and safely for yourself
>
> *Ut Caeca Mentula sic et surda est*
> The Penis is as deaf as it is Blind
>
> *Mutari amat Proteus Amor*
> Love is a Proteus who loves metamorphosis
>
> *Mulier matula est*
> Woman is a chamber-pot.[43]

From the sublime to the abject, the entire contradictory range of Chorier's ideology is now memorialized. The original attains instant classic status, preserved by the same aura of Latinity that preserved Secundus' epigram in *The School of Venus*, in

---

[41] i. 23 (from *Satyra*, II. 39), i. 97–8 (from *Satyra*, V. 96); *Entretien* VI keeps significantly more of the classical allusion (though not the verse quotation), both in the heavily heterosexual orgies (e.g. the Danaë scenario on i. 229) and in the lecture on sodomy.

[42] *Academie*, i. 25, and cf. *Satyra*, III. 44–5; Mainil (*Règles du plaisir*, 105) notes the absence of the clitoris in the (abbreviated) *Académie* but not its presence in Chorier.

[43] i. 95, 127, ii. 69, 74, 75 (*Satyra*, V. 94, 113, VII. 274, 278, 282); in a few cases Nicolas actually adds Latin phrases that are not in Chorier (e.g. *Sceptrum Mentula est*, ii. 99). Maucroix's letter of 1682 (epigraph above) shows that the *succès de scandale* of the Latin original was not eclipsed by the French adaptations. Latin, having no articles, also confers the 'effect of universality' and the 'archaizing patina' that Charlotte Schapira finds in certain French maxims of the period (*La Maxime et le discours de l'autorité* (Paris, 1997), 58, a ref. I owe to Alfred Bruckstein).

Casanova's memoir, and in this very *Academie*. Chorier himself now stands to the *entretiens d'Aloysia* as Ovid, Virgil, Lucretius, and Petronius once stood to the *erudita libido* of Tullia and Octavia.

Though the surgical cuts and implants of *L'Academie* involve the dialogic prose as well as the cited verse, its handling of poetry forms the most conspicuous example of 'traduction'. Chorier's Latin verse quotations are translated only once (i. 120, from the *Priapea*), and in every other case Nicolas borrows from *libertin* tradition or invents *a novo*. He adds a couplet about *cocuage* to the expanded discussion of infidelity (i. 36)—a passage influenced by Molière's *École des femmes*, as I suggested in Chapter 5—and a sonnet about 'dying' together to the orgy-scene (i. 207). Striving to seem modern and classic at the same time, *L'Academie* introduces the French (per)version of Secundus (pp. 311–12 above), which converts humanist paradox into bantering violence and enlarges the masculine *cunnus* into a threatening Everywoman ready to castrate any male reader not already equipped with the knowledge encrypted in the Latin distich. And Nicolas supplements his proto-Enlightenment naturalism with the *Italian* text of the famous Golden Age chorus from Tasso's *Aminta*, leaving the motto 's'EI PIACE EI LICE' in capitals (i. 131): 'if it pleases, then it is lawful.'

In the narration of Tullia's frightful wedding night, where Octavia endorses her courage with a faux-Virgilian citation and where the first English translator had substituted an injurious 'travesty', the French *dames* quote no verse at all. But a few lines earlier the *husband* Oronte is made to spout the poem first uttered by the comtesse d'Olonne in the *Sodom*-like burlesque attributed to Bussy, and then trimmed into an epigram. (We have encountered both versions in the *Bibliothèque d'Aretin* anthology, section 1 above.) Oronte wishes his painful attempts at defloration to last for ever, his penis transformed into an open hand, exclaiming (in the words of *Aretinus Redivivus*)

> O Heavens how I love these Amorous Tricks,
> I wish by Jove my Fingers turn'd to P—ks
> And ever Constant to the Feats of Love
> May they ne're weary of their duty prove
> But ever ready for the Task design'd
> Their Tribute pay your C—t and please your Mind.[44]

Already transferred to the male voice and augmented with an economic metaphor—'spending' becomes an enforced 'Tribute', or 'rent' in the French version—this sadistic little verse now introduces the forcible entry of 'Priapus triumphant'. Setting this epigram in a dialogic context creates certain ironies, however. Tullie immediately protests and puts her alternative perspective, rather than acquiescing in this male fantasy of female insatiability. Furthermore, the man's urge to transcend detumescence makes him resemble the lesbian, whose 'adulterous fin-

---

[44] *Aretinus Redivivus or The Ladies Academy*, partial transcription in 1745 indictment of John Leake, London, PRO, KB 28/176/21, from p. '45' (according to marginal note); the French text (*Academie*, i. 50, amplifying the original where he fondles Tullia with his hand but recites no poetry (IV.61–2)) is verbally identical to that in the *Cabinet*, n. 18 above.

gers' are always ready to perform. Tullie evidently tries to refashion masculinity according to this biomorphic ideal when she plans the orgy in dialogue VI; the two men are required to provide exactly twenty penetrations, the number of their fingers and thumbs. In these repeated 'translations' of the comtesse d'Olonne's fantasy the phallus is digitalized and endlessly replicable.

The new poems thus make good the promise of 'entretiens satiriques', delivering a small explosive charge of obscenity instead of the web of classical allusion. In one case the inserted verses actually do derive from the 1622 *Quintessence satyrique*, one of the anthologies denounced by Father Garasse at that founding moment of French libertinism. (Like the Secundus epigram and the finger poem, it can also be found in the *Bibliothèque d'Aretin*.) In La Porte's original poem—'De la Docte Alizon, touchant le souverain bien'—the 'beautiful and learned' female philosopher discovers that 'the *summum bonum* consists only in fucking well'; now, in the post-educational *Academie*, that insight is given to a male thinker (who has tried all the 'postures' himself) and conveyed by a male 'author of our own time' (Fig. 16).[45] Exit the erudite Tullia and the lecherous philosopher Juan Luis Vives; enter 'Alexius Cunnilogus' or 'Cunnicola', a comic sexual pedant like the Philo-Puttanus invented for *The Whores Rhetorick*. (Since Chorier clearly does give his philosophical speakers the doctrine that sexual fulfilment is the 'summum bonum' (*Satyra*, VII. 219), Nicolas probably alludes to him under the figure of Cunnilogus, the modern writer of postures with the Latin/Greek name.) Once again, the new 'Academy' resembles the old *Escole*, where Le Petit's commendatory poem had likewise reduced erotic philosophy to one nutty aphorism, *bien foutre est bien vivre*. As if to enforce this principle and emulate the satyric poet, the French author now uses 'le souverain bien'—supreme good, *summum bonum*—as a direct and concrete synonym for Octavie's vulva (i. 18).

The modernizing 'transmutation' of Chorier also involves additions that emulate the libertine prose canon and update its materialist philosophy. Augmented passages on the joys of cuckoldry and the 'covering' function of the husband recall *L'Escole des filles* as well as *L'École des femmes*; when Tullie expresses a fear of pregnancy, for example, her pupil turns the tables by assuring her that 'whatever happens, marriage will hide everything'.[46] When Octavie adds her account of a medal that she has seen 'in Florence', celebrating the union of Jove and Ganymede under the motto '*Amori Vera Lux*' (Ch. 4 n. 81 above), she evokes the 'Loves of the Gods' theme in Italian pro-sodomitic literature from Vignali's *Cazzaria* to Rocco's *Alcibiade*, where Ganymede serves to define the ephebic hero that everyone desires. (The idea of linking 'True Light' to homosexual love might derive from Vignali's mock-learned treatise-title, *Lumen Pudendorum* or *The Light of the Pudenda*.[47]) Pallavicino could have suggested Tullie's addition of 'a Figure of Rhetorick called

---

[45] i. 292, supplementing the praise of Aretino. Titian, and 'Carace' carried over from *Satyra*, VI. 214; for the 1622 poem see Ch. 3 n. 43 above.

[46] i. 209 ('arrive ce qui poura, le mariage cachera tout'), added to *Satyra*, VI. 168; cf. *Escole*, II. 139 ('le mary sert de couverture à tout').

[47] *La cazzaria*, ed. Pasquale Stoppelli, introd. Nino Borsellino (Rome, 1984), 82; links to Renaissance sodomic literature are obscured, however, when Tullia's allusion to della Casa's *Forno* is fictionalized as *Gli gusti spherici*, by 'Hydaspe' (ii. 76).

(292)

venté douzes extremement luxurieufes pour l'homme & pour la femme. De noftre temps *L'Aretin*, ce Divin efprit en a expolé trente cinq dans fes Colloques, que Titian & Care ce fameux Peintres ont enfuitte tirées & depeintes d'apres nature. Le Dernier de ceux qui nous en ont laiffé, quelque chofe par efcrit eft *Alexius* furnommé *Cunnilogus* par quelques uns, a caufe des traittés qu'il a faicts fur cette Matiere, & appellé par d'autres *Cunnicola* a raifon d'une infinité de poftures qu'il n'a point expolées qu'apres les avoir luy mefme mifes en ufage. Voicy ce q'un autheur du temps a dit de luy dans un ouvrage qu'il a faict à fa loüange.

> *Platon, Ariftote, Heraclite,*
> *Zenon, Socrate, & Demecrite,*
> *Tous Grands Docteurs fans Controuver.*
> *Par le moyen de leur eftude*
> *N'ont encor jamais pû trouver*
> *En quoy gift la Beatitude.*
> *Alexis fans comparaifon*
> *Plus fçavant dans cette Science,*
> *Se moque d'eux avec raifon,*
> *Se fondant fur l'experience,*
> *Et dit que le fouverain Bien,*
> *Ne confifte, qu'à Foutre bien.*

Ce n'eft pas Octavie il faut que je t'avoüe qu'il y a beaucoup de poftures entre celles qu'on nous a laiffées dont on ne fçauroit fe fervir, un Homme Lubrique en peut inventer
plus

(293)

plus milles fois qu'il n'en pourra executer, quoy qu'on ne faffe que les effayer elles donnent toufiours beaucoup de plaifir, & ne laiffent pas d'efchauffer l'imagination de ceux qui les efprouvent.

Octav. A quoy bon tant de raffinement? ou il y a plufieurs Venus ou il n'y en à qu'une, s'il y en à plufieurs pourquoy tout le Monde n'en convient t'il pas? s'il n'y en à qu'une pourquoy tant de chemins pour y aller? Pour moy je croy que tous ces détours que la Lubricité des hommes & des Femmes ont inventés font mal-honneftes.

Tull. Quelques uns difent que la Pofture la plus naturelle eft quand on chevauche la femme a la maniere des autres Animaux, c'eft-a-dire quand elle fe met a quatres pieds, d'autant que dans cette fituation, le Membre de l'homme entre bien plus avant, & la femence coule avec plus de facilité dans la Matrice. Quelques autres font pour la pofture commune, quand l'homme s'eftend fur la femme ventre fur ventre, poitrine contre poitrine, bouche contre bouche, les Medecins difent que la premiere pofture, eft moins propre pour la generation, parce qu'elle convient moins avec les parties generatives. Quoy quil en foit ma chere Octavie j'ayme beaucoup qu'on me le faffe a la commune maniere.

Octav. Pourquoy ne l'aymerois tu pas? Qui y a t'il je te prie de plus doux que d'eftre
N 3   toute

16. *L'Academie des dames*, i.292–3

Antonomasia' to her otherwise minimal list of names for the penis.[48] Like Mrs Cresswell flaunting her knowledge of 'Six and Thirty Geometrical Schemes' and 'Four and Twenty rough draughts', Nicolas displays his expertise in literary illustration; though the Latin text never associates Aretino with precise numeration, the *Academie des dames* informs us that '*L'Aretin*, ce Divin esprit', has 'exhibited thirty-

---

[48] *Aretinus Redivivus*, '27', glossing *Academie*, i. 28.

five Postures in his Colloquies', a clear allusion to the apocryphal prose *Puttana errante*.[49]

Some of Nicolas's additions amplify the philosophical ambition, others destroy it. The new figure of the 'incomparable Alexis' or Alexius bases his philosophy solely on 'experiment', and 'mocks' all his predecessors for failing to locate the *souverain bien* in sexual monomania. Tullie now takes over Vives's function by lecturing somewhat mechanically on the seat of the soul; like Susanne in *L'Escole* she applies the Cartesian agenda to the new sexology, but like Alexius she reviews the ancient philosophers by name before settling on a narrowly genital solution—'the true seat of the soul is in the Testicles of man and woman', and Nature therefore acts wisely in limiting our capacity to ejaculate.[50] Theodore the monk also flirts with Cartesian ideas when he describes the Stoics' ideal passionless man as 'a Statue without pulse or movement' (ii. 19). Fragments of philosophic naturalism and proto-Enlightenment social critique can be culled from throughout the text, some added—like the definition of Honour as a mere 'Culte', with all its laws made up by men to serve their own interests (i. 130)—and some already in Chorier.[51] But they relate quite uneasily to the main project, making Chorier's women stupid: Octavie actually interrupts Tullia's seat-of-the-soul speech by exclaiming 'in God's name Tullie that's enough, what you're saying is too *sçavant* for me, drop all this philosophy garbage' (*tous ces fatras de philosophie*), reducing the intellectual-erotic quest to farce (i. 65).

Nicolas attempts to salvage the status of philosophy at the very end, however, after the grim narrative of Mme de Chateaubriand's execution by her own husband. Replacing the baroque contrast of abject and sublime in the original ending, which praises the 'fervent *conatus* of the mind' but declares the uneducated subservient woman nothing but a 'chamber-pot', Octavie and Tullie now join in a litany of Enlightenment belief. Cultural relativity leads to the principle that 'nothing is Just or Unjust in itself, nothing good or evil in Morals'—except the 'Tyranny of evil custom' and 'idiotic opinions', which must now be overthrown. Where the *Whores Rhetorick* promises sexuality 'Conformed to the Rules of Art', Tullie now calls for a life of 'natural needs examined by the rule of right reason' and 'conformed to what pure and innocent Nature demands of us'—a programme uncannily similar to Rochester's earlier vision of 'right reason' subordinated to the 'Rules' of sensuality.[52] This naturalizing, modernizing conclusion has been cleaned up and at the same time dissociated. By suppressing the dialectic of erotically charged 'mind' and inert

---

[49] i. 292, adapting *Satyra*, VI. 214 on *figurae* (the passage is visible in Fig. 16); this borrowing from the pseudo-Aretine posture-list is noted in Carolin Fischer, *Éducation érotique: Pietro Aretinos 'Ragionamenti' im libertinen Roman Frankreichs* (Stuttgart, 1994), 246 (a study marred by using the corrupt and abbreviated Camus text as if it were the original).

[50] i. 63–5; contrast *Satyra*, VII. 292, and cf. Jacob, 'Materialist World of Pornography', 171–3.

[51] i. 124 for example, defining religion as a political arrangement with no basis in nature, exactly translates *Satyra*, V. 112; Fischer bases her analysis of *L'Académie* entirely on progressive-sounding extracts like these.

[52] ii. 110–11 ('examinant a la reigle d'une droite raison les necessités naturelles . . . nous devons . . . conformer ensuitte nôtre vie a ce que la Nature pure et innocente demande de nous'); for Rochester see Ch. 6, sect. 1 above, and for contradictions between this Enlightenment-naturalist ending and the rest of *L'Academie* see Robinson, 'To Boldly Go', 201–3.

excremental matter, Nicolas leaves standing the earlier and far more misogynistic statement that it qualifies: *Mulier matula est*, 'Woman is a chamber-pot', isolated from the transforming power of intellect.

Even small differences in translation can signal large ideological shifts. Tullia's conditional negotiation of freedom in marriage—'if you would like obsequiousness, keep me in slavery, if you want honour, set me free'—becomes her abject submission: 'I would receive whatever laws you want to impose on me, whether you treat me as a slave or a free woman' (i. 56, cf. *Satyra*, IV. 66). Tullia's injective orgasm, which entitles her to claim that she has 'done the deed' or 'perfected the *opus*' with Octavia, has been reduced to a mere 'wetting' (i. 20). The lesbian *furores* of Sempronia become the trivial-sounding *badineries*, the playful word used in the *Academie* for all kinds of sexual contact that do not conform to the vaginal-ejaculative norm enforced with equal vigour by the Church and by libertine discourse. Just as Maucroix arranged the libertine canon on a scale from *bagatelles* to serious shockers, so Nicolas brackets the perversions as *bagatelles* or *badineries*; this chic but insubstantial category includes lesbianism, sodomy, fellatio, adolescent masturbation, and even the hasty fully clothed copulation that Sempronie allows her daughter on the morning of her wedding. Several times, when the Sapphic theme recurs in the closing dialogue, Nicolas frames and distances it with the word *plaisant*, ordering us to be amused rather than aroused or impressed.[53]

It seems, then, that the new Académie des Dames teaches a more advanced grade of heteronormativity and subtracts intellectual seriousness from '(per)verse' alternatives like Sapphism. Conceptually, the lesbian bond of the two protagonists is stripped of its erudition and reduced to *badinage*. On the other hand, some of the alterations in *L'Academie* increase the titillating details of woman–woman sex. Octavie participates more actively in Tullie's seductive-instructive 'research', and her consent is now conceived as an expression of her 'power' (even if sadly 'limited' because it brings about no metamorphosis).[54] In *Entretien* III Octavie takes a more commanding role in her tutorial inspection of Tullie's genitalia, becoming so aroused at her teacher's 'luxurieuse' and 'lubrique' bottom that she starts kissing and biting it (i. 27). And at the crucial moment in *Entretien* V when the narration of past heterosexual coupling rekindles the present lesbian desire of the narrators, Nicolas scripts extra lines to make her more active and responsive; just before orgasm she exclaims 'who could have imagined that this *badinage* could lead to such sweet pleasure?' (i. 87). *Badinerie* comes to connote inexhaustible and irrepressible ludicity

---

[53] *Academie*, i. 127 (Tullie explains to Octavie that 'I have suffered [your mother's] *badineries* just as you have endured mine', translating *Satyra*, V. 113), ii. 75 (the medal of Sappho as *plaisant*), 84; for *badin(age)* see esp. i. 43, 83, 87, ii. 31, 47, and for *bagatelles* i. 232 (translating *nugis*, VI. 182). Robinson notes the belittling effect of this vocabulary in 'To Boldly Go', 174, 186–7, though it could also connote aristocratic grace: when Yorick arrives in Paris (in Sterne's *Sentimental Journey*) a nobleman takes him aside and shows him how to make his cravat more '*badinant*'.

[54] i. 14–15, 18, and contrast *Satyra*, II. 33, 35; Octavie expands the original 'Quae voles, maxime volo' into 'ta volonté te peut servir de regle dans toutes tes recherches', perhaps echoing the *règles du plaisir* in *Escole*, I. 23.

rather than mere frivolity, and at the very end it seems to outlast the heterosexual 'solidity' that supposedly replaces it. Octavie will 'never tire' of her days and nights of *entretien* with Tullie, never wants to separate from her, and demands a final kiss; Tullie's last exclamation before saying goodbye—'Ah que tu es badine? je croy que tu ne veux finir' ('I believe you never want to finish')—fixes the kiss in the ongoing present tense and not the conclusive past (ii. 112). This Sternean sexual-textual pun is itself the ultimate *badinerie*: the word FIN cuts off the demonstration that Octavie will 'never finish' making love to Tullie as a tribute to her erotic-didactic enlightenment.

The changes made in *L'Academie* may even multiply the sites of Sapphic 'playfulness'. In tidying up Colloquium VII, for example, Nicolas gives more prominence to another lesbian episode, in which the ferocious Judith, set as a spy to catch Lucie, falls in love with her instead; in Chorier this tale is exceptionally broken-backed (since the lesbian denouement occurs in a fragment many pages after the first episode), whereas *L'Academie* rejoins the two halves and thus makes the entire story earlier and more coherent.[55] Nicolas renders Octavie's romance with the teenage boy more polymorphous by using the pronoun 'elle' for Alexis in her disguise as Diana (ii. 58–9). In Chorier, as we have seen, Octavia boasts of her affair with Diana to conceal the fact that 'she' is really Robertus—a kind of reversed closeting. *L'Academie* turns this Sapphic alibi into an actual affair with a new lover, Felice (ii. 83–4), adding a touch of neoclassical grandeur by keeping in Latin *Lusimus* [*Lucta*] *Cupidinea Sappho et Andromede*, 'we played Sappho and Andromeda in Amorous Combat'. This story now forms a logical sequence, leading directly to the scene where Ferdinand 'interjects' himself into his sister's lesbian seduction of Melitte, a paradigm of the male author's dependence on the (per)version he tries to belittle as 'une plaisante affaire'.

The most spectacular injections of new material in *L'Academie* help to dilate the anus as erotic site, to preserve sodomy as an area of intellectual-prurient interest. In marked contrast to his treatment of lesbianism—where the erudition is removed even as the action-sequences are expanded—Nicolas's discussion of anal penetration, heterosexual and homosexual, leaves intact the panoply of classical learning that Chorier had given his erudite libertine heroine.[56] In this specialized arena, defined in Aretino and *La retorica delle puttane* as the courtesan's expertise par excellence, 'philosophical' knowledge need not conjure up the spectre of female autonomy and can therefore be indulged more freely in the surrogate voice. The orgy-scene in *Entretien* VI, for example, adds precisely the kind of *femmes savantes* jokes that had been cut from the earlier marital episodes: one of the Florentines expresses mock-surprise that Tullie 'refuses to do what many Roman girls do for us', since 'you have so much *esprit*, and you've cultivated it so much by studying *belles lettres*' (in the original she is just *ingeniosa*); the other man then breaks in with the

---

[55] Contrast *Academie*, ii. 45–50 and *Satyra*, VII. 254–6, 289–91; on the masculinized representation of Judith, see Robinson, 'To Boldly Go', 174–7.

[56] Though a few names (and all the Latin verse quotations) are cut, *Academie* actually adds some examples to the list of famous Greek authors (i. 270–1, cf. *Satyra*, VI. 203).

impatient command not to 'faire la pretieuse' (i. 220). The description of penetration itself is fortified with military jokes from the *Université d'amour* (involving 'half-moons' and 'capturing the rear') and plumped out with details of the 'great pleasure' that Tullie received, the 'play of Fabrice's member about my Buttocks', the 'frequent entries and exits he made in my Derriere', all of which forces her to conclude that she could 'grow accustomed to this *badinage*' (i. 221–2). Octavie meanwhile underlines the 'infinite pleasure' she received from this description, the 'witty turn' that hides the 'deformity' of the story—as if she had been reading Pallavicino on the 'sublime' art of creating ecstasy from the abominable (Ch. 2, sect. 1 above).

Thereafter the titillating possibility of hetero-sodomy is kept simmering throughout both main scenes of the sixth dialogue, the Villa Orsini orgy that Tullie relates and Octavie's present-tense performance with two 'athletes'. In the middle of her reassuringly Gallo-vaginal return to the French Acaste (Chorier's Turrianus or La Tour) Tullie breaks off to wonder if the two Florentines are returning to the fray (i. 281, not in *Satyra*, VI. 211); in both versions the Frenchman wins her heart by constantly declaring that he will *not* sodomize her. Anality thus becomes the significant exclusion that focuses (and legitimizes) all the other perversions. In her later lecture on the infinite multiplicity of postures Tullie adds a list of her own favourite 'foretastes' that includes 'the Whip' ('I like it when a young man torments me') and excludes only one prohibited mode: she permits everything 'provided that he doesn't turn against my Derriere' (i. 291).

Nicolas adds to this already interminable sequence a number in which the two men adore Octavie's buttocks, pose her for sodomitic penetration, but then proceed to 'enconner par Derriere'. When Tullie launches what turns out to be a massive historical and philosophical vindication of sodomy, she embroiders her account of Venus Callipyga with a specific connection to this episode with Octavie—had she been alive then, she would have been venerated 'for the same subject'—and recommends her to try this way of intensifying pleasure 'provided that, after coming and going a few times in your Derriere, he takes his Prick out and retreats to the ordinary place'. When both women recount their husbands' attempts to perform this *badinage*, Tullie adds an entirely new episode in which Oronte, 'entirely spoiled' after a business trip to Florence, actually succeeds in penetrating her anally and giving her a 'horrible enema'.[57]

The 'philosophical' discussion as well as the 'pornographic' action is augmented in this Academy of Sodomy. Chorier had already given Tullia a powerful naturalist argument for non-procreative sex (later unconvincingly refuted), ascribing to Socrates and Plato the idea that Nature gives us an abundance of sperm for all kinds of pleasure just as she creates a cornucopia of seeds and grains for consumption as well as procreation (Ch. 4, sect. 3 above). But Nicolas takes it further. He cuts the remark that the Socratic arguments are 'false' (though he also removes Tullia's anatomical demonstration that *women* eject surplus seed as well as men), and he brings out the full bisexual implications of 'natural' desire, which gives men '*more* of

---

[57] i. 248–9, 262–3, 265–6, added to *Satyra*, VI. 190, 197–8, and 200 respectively.

a penchant for our sex than their own' and *more* appetite for the vagina than 'other places of our bodies' (my emphasis); spelling out the Latin *propensiores*, this expanded phrasing declares both vaginal and non-vaginal desires innate, varying only in relative intensity (i. 267–8). Having thus strengthened the substrate of 'natural' arguments, *L'Academie* can then endorse sodomy even less ambiguously than Chorier had done, evaluating it almost wholly as a source of physical and aesthetic pleasure.

Translating Chorier's double-edged disparagement of the French for failing to develop 'le bon goust pour ce volupté', the Italian Tullie adds that they (we?) are becoming 'a little more sensitive' to this pleasure, and that such preferences cannot be called wrong. Like Rocco, Chorier had already theorized sodomy in anatomical-geographical terms, pointing out its advantages (from the penetrator's point of view) in countries warmer than France where vaginas are looser; Tullie not only repeats this misogynist and xenophobic 'explanation' in full, but expands its luscious description of the pleasure the *mentula* derives from being 'pressed and sucked to the last drop' by the compliant anus.[58] Octavie again doubles as cheerleader for sodomy, interjecting to express her pleasure at Tullie's brilliance but now disagreeing when her mentor switches tack to denounce the arguments she earlier reported. Tullie's condemnation is considerably shortened in Nicolas's version (by cutting Chorier's description of the injuries inflicted on women by anal violation), and he makes no attempt to hide the obvious contradiction in Tullie's argument from design: if the vagina is naturally accommodated to the penis, unlike the anus, why was so much ink and blood spilled describing painful and violent deflorations, foot-long 'clubs' breaking into microscopic slits?[59]

In contrast to these reductions in the anti-sodomitic case, Octavia's brief reminder that long-established custom and the example of 'great men throughout history' support it is expanded into a full refutation. Octavie shifts the focus from heterosexual sodomy to homosexual pairing, rejects all Tullie's 'reasons' for condemnation, argues that since 'love is born from resemblance' it is therefore 'more perfect between two boys than between a man and a girl', and concludes that 'we should not be surprised if men despise our embraces and search for a more perfect pleasure in their *semblables*', because the '*agreable*' is 'preferable to the *utile*'.[60] Incongruously, the straighter and more conventional spokeswoman now recapitulates the 'anti-natural' and 'philosophical' tradition. The similarity-argument is

---

[58] i. 273–4, and cf. *Satyra*, VI. 206 ('Comprimi et exsugi gaudet mentula'). In Chorier and in *L'Academie* Tullia's first stance on sodomy is to call it 'ridiculous' rather than wicked (*Satyra*, VI. 197; *Academie*, i. 261), but in the French version the word 'ridicule' is further applied to the narrowly procreational argument (268) and to the motions of heterosexual copulation (288).

[59] Cf. *Satyra*, VI. 174–5 ('the massacre of your front virginity cost you more' suffering than anal penetration would) and Mainil, *Règles du plaisir*, 111 (but Mainil draws from the anality discussion several unsupportable generalizations, e.g. that Tullie simply opposes sodomy to Nature, that woman's *jouissance* disappears and becomes 'impossible' or that 'the male body' becomes the sole subject and object of pleasure).

[60] i. 279 (expanding *Satyra*, VI. 209); for slippage between the anatomical practice of anal penetration (of women or boys) and the historical phenomenon of ancient man–boy love, 'as if the transition were completely "natural" or no transition at all' see Robinson, 'To Boldly Go', 191.

virtually translated from Rocco's *Alcibiade* (Ch. 2, sect. 2 above), though Octavie transfers it from the hierarchic teacher–pupil bond to the mutual embrace of 'deux garçons'. And the aesthetic argument—equating sodomy with art and reproductive heterosexuality with mere necessity—comes from one of Rocco's most important sources, the (pseudo)Lucianic *Erōtes*. Tullie herself had just cited this very text as an example of balanced, non-judgemental appraisal.

The idea of packaging Nicolas's (per)version as the voice of 'Aloysia' might have been suggested by the self-referential discussion that initiates the final dialogue. Here Leonor incites the newly-wed Aloisia to recount her first sexual experience, thus continuing the cycle begun by Tullie and Octavie in the earlier dialogues, and she does so by promoting the durable delights of *entretien* over the fleeting pleasures of 'practice'. Adopting the worldly style of de Rochefoucauld, she declares that

il y en a mesme qui trouvent dans l'esperance, ou dans le souvenir de la volupté, la volupté mesme, et j'en connois qui ressentent de plus douces émotions en parlant de Venus, qu'en la mettant en pratique. Avouë donc Aloïsia, que cet agreable passe-temps qui ne dure qu'un moment devient long par nos entretiens. (ii. 5–6)

There are people who find the essence of pleasure itself in the hope or memory of pleasure, and I know some who feel sweeter emotions in talking about Venus than in putting it into practice. So, Aloisia, you must admit that this agreeable pastime which lasts but a moment is lengthened by our dialogues.

Passing time and detumescent pleasure can thus be made 'long' by *entretiens* like these, and 'Aloisia' can stand in for the whole process of 'talking about Venus', the whole *mise en discours* of sexuality. Like Tullia herself, Aloisia evolves from an obedient wife into a kind of Pallavicinian bawd-preceptor, fully expert in the arts of erotic 'translation' and 'transmutation into Ganymede'. The character who 'admits' becoming wholly envaginated—*tota cunnus* in the original—is thus qualified to apply for the position that Oldham defined as 'Secretary to a Cunt'.

In this new author-effect the eroticized *aveu* of Aloisia will 'make it long' for the reader and generate fresh scenes that, like the closing kiss of the dialogue-partners, seem 'never to finish'. We shall see an example of this in *Vénus dans le cloître* (section 4 below), when the two nuns dwell on the 'unnatural' yet irresistible brilliance of *Les Sept Entretiens satyriques d'Aloïsia*; since they particularly mention the Florentine homoerotic medal with its motto *Amori Vera Lux*—an episode that occurs neither in Chorier nor in the surviving abridgements of *Aloisia*—it is clear that the full Nicolas text circulated under this title and performed the work of canon-formation. Ironically, however, Leonor's vision of the *longue durée* is contradicted by the surviving texts of the *Aloisia* version, which lop off three-quarters of the seventh dialogue where Aloisia comes into her own. This truncation of the real *Academie des dames*, making it culturally less significant and more deserving of Sade's contemptuous dismissal of its timidity, is further compounded by those twentieth-century critics who ignore the crucial finale completely.[61]

Imposing arbitrary cuts (in the seventeenth as in the twentieth century) carves out a different work, suppressing troublesome anomalies and throwing a different emphasis on what remains. In the sixth dialogue, for example, the largest abridgements in the short version seem designed to contain the anal (per)version and to avoid the mingling of categories. Sodomy still gets ample treatment in the orgy-scenes and in the historical discussion, but the abridger cannot tolerate the idea of husbands and wives experimenting with such pleasures. He drops an entire page that explored gender confusion in ancient marriage, wives winning husbands back from their favourite boys, and Jupiter enjoying the same favours from Juno and Ganymede, and removes more than three pages on husbandly attempts to sodomize Tullie and Octavie—clearly a systematic censoring rather than the small-scale cutting that compresses the text throughout.[62] Also vanished is the relativistic version of the argument from Nature, in which desire focuses 'more' on the vagina but still pursues other parts of the body, in boys as well as girls.

In the worst of these reprints the foreign-language quotations have been further bowdlerized or garbled, reinforcing the idea that any erudition taught in the 'Académie des Dames' must be worthless.[63] It is particularly sad, then, that the latest and most corrupt of all these abbreviations has been chosen as the basis for modern editions. Critics and editors have colluded in this traduction by concocting spurious arguments for its originality, blinding future readers to much of what makes *L'Academie des dames* significant. The vast omissions from this version make it especially inappropriate for the critic to praise it as a full manifestion of Eros, citing Racine's famous phrase 'Vénus toute entière à sa proie attachée'.[64]

The debilitating cuts are particularly cruel in the seventh dialogue, altering the entire complexion of the work. The abridger keeps the lengthy (and pedantic) discussion of ideal beauty (ii. 1–16), but starts pruning frantically the moment that Octavie begins to describe married couples experimenting with the breasts and the mouth. Fellatio and lesbianism still appear, but shorn of their tenticular narrative complexity and reduced to the briefest episode—the degree zero of (per)version. (Putting two eggs in one basket, he keeps the scene in which Leonor, kissing Octavie in bed, teases her about what she might have sucked and Tullie tells the version of the Prometheus myth that explains the 'natural affinity' of penis and mouth; the

---

[61] Cf. (e.g.) Fischer, *Éducation érotique* 246 and Mainil, *Règles du plaisir*, 111 (referring to VI as 'le dernier dialogue'), 100 (asserting incorrectly that VII can be ignored because not added until 1678, even though he cites it to prove a point about fellatio, 109–10).

[62] Compare the text in Michel Camus (ed.), *Œuvres érotiques du XVIIe siècle*, L'Enfer de la Bibliothèque nationale 7 (Paris, 1983), 585–6, 589, with *L'Academie*, i. 263–7, 271–2 (and cf. Epilogue n. 20 below, where Baudelaire cites one of these dropped passages in the original Latin).

[63] In BnF Enfer 277 ('Venise, Chez Pierre Arretin', obviously late 18th century) the Italian text of the Tasso quotation is even more mangled than the Latin, ending with 's'EIPTAGE EILIGE' (165), followed precisely in Camus, *Œuvres érotiques*, 497 (reprinting this worst edition under the fraudulent claim that it is the 'first', 393).

[64] Mainil, *Règles du plaisir*, 241 n. 52.

story connects to nothing, however, since none of the other oral scenes survives.[65])
Some of the fabliau-like tales are retained (the gardener in the nunnery, the priest at
the keyhole, the teenage lovers discovered by Judith), but once the discussion turns
to 'philosophic' speculation and erotic connoisseurship the adaptor abandons the
Academy almost completely. Dropping the second half of the dialogue increases the
effect of morbidity at the very end, even though many sadistic scenes have been cut:
the subject lurches from Priapus to Death without the slightest attempt at logical transition, which throws the one remaining episode (the tragic romance of
Clémence and Victor) into greater relief; and though it drops the final story of the
royal mistress slaughtered by a jealous spouse, the short version keeps (without context) the ominous passage about the dangers of discovery in which Octavie declares
that she would rather commit Roman-style suicide than be killed by her husband.[66]

Even a brief catalogue reveals how much of what makes Chorier interesting has
been retained in the original *Academie des dames* but destroyed in this taming or
'traduction' of the longer text. Massive cutting begins when Tullie and Octavie start
to speculate about the varieties of genital formation and whether size matters (a
preoccupation Tullie dismisses as worthy only of 'Geometres d'Amour' (ii. 54)). In
Chorier and Nicolas this brings in the long recurrent narrative of the seduction of
Robertus/Alexis, which softens the violent 'satyra sotadica' into erotic romance, and
which in turn allows digressions into philosophy, art, and history. Nicolas translates
the 'Alexis' episodes in full, while cutting the brutal episode of sex-as-execution or
'putting death into the body' which forms a deliberate contrast to the tenderness of
the Robertus-scenes (Ch. 4, sect. 5 above).[67] But in the abbreviated text we have no
Alexis at all.

The abridged pseudo-*Academie* thus traduces its two sources by obliterating
their most important episode. Future readers fooled by the substitution encounter
no *ephebe* handed from one powerful woman to another, no dreamlike transsexual
masquerades, no painful loss of male virginity, no 'becoming a man' by learning
vraie honnêteté, no debates on the folly of legislating sexual frequencies and postures, no visits to the Senate by Messalina, no male voyeur projecting himself
into the lesbian embrace and no 'Diana' as transvestite disguise or lesbian alibi,
no Patrice acting as *instituteur libertin* to his brightest pupils of both sexes, no
simulation of beleaguered virginity to deceive a gullible mother, no defence of nudity in art, no 'figures of Venus' with their history stretching back to Sappho and
Elephantis, no medals of Sappho and Ganymede showing public approval of

---

[65] BL PC 31.b.29, *L'Académie des dames, ou Les Sept Entretiens galants d'Alosia* [sic] ('A Venise, Chez
Pierre Arretin'), 283–4 (Camus, *Œuvres érotiques*, 619–20), retaining *Academie*, ii. 33–4, after skipping
everything from p. 22 onwards.

[66] *Sept Entretiens galants d'Alosia*, 308–9 (Camus, *Œuvres érotiques*, 634), jumping from *Academie*, ii.
53 to 100. Mitchell Greenberg, who consults only the unscholarly Camus edn. and the 1910 translation by
'Villeneuve' (likewise silently abridged), concludes that 'Nicholas Chorier's *L'Académie des dames*'
'refus[es]' to end and avoids the subject of death completely (*Baroque Bodies: Psychoanalysis and the
Culture of French Absolutism* (2001), 67, 104–6).

[67] Contrast *Satyra*, VII. 265 and *Academie*, ii. 61; Nicolas adds one year to Robertus' age and perhaps
puns on his own title when Sempronie gets him into the 'Academie' (ii. 56).

every sexual variant, no *Mutari amat Proteus Amor*.[68] Enlightenment polemic had already started to dwindle when the monk-seducer Theodore was trimmed to a minimum, and now it vanishes entirely—leaving stranded the perfunctory remarks on Custom and Right Reason at the very end. Without Alexis the lines of gender and age are drawn more tightly. *L'Academie des dames* loses its most important counterweight to the grotesque phallic gigantism, and suppression of women's agency, that still constitutes what is ludicrously called 'adult' pornography. Nicolas's *Academie* had already excised the clitoris, the *gaude mihi* or *mépris des hommes*. Now the abbreviated *Entretiens galants d'Alosia* removes that other kind of ladies' delight, the femme Ganymede or clitoral boy.

3. ARETINUS REDIVIVUS, OR ALOISIA SIGEA IN ENGLAND

Rumours of a libertine translation boom ran through London much as Maucroix described Aloisia Sigea running through Paris, setting off a chain reaction of emulation. *The School of Venus* established the selling power of titles that promise sexual education, and *The Whores Rhetorick*, as we have seen, echoes its claim to have reduced the ladies's delight to Rules of Art. In Edward Ravenscroft's popular farce *The London Cuckolds*, the censorious alderman, clucking over the depravity of the young, reports having seen two 12-year-old girls reading 'that beastly bawdy translated book *The Schoole of Women*'—leading the audience (and some modern scholars) to imagine that they have missed some hot new translation of *L'Academie des dames*.[69] In fact, no actual work of this title exists; through a haze of wishful thinking, prudery, and half-remembered expertise, these comic characters apparently take Molière's play to be pornography. The in-joke is particularly appropriate since Ravenscroft specialized in translations of Molière, though *The London Cuckolds* itself derives not from *L'École des femmes* but from its source, Scarron's *Précaution inutile*.

L'Escole des filles was certainly translated by the date of Ravenscroft's play (1682, two years after the first prosecution records of *The School of Venus*), whereas in *The Parliament of Women* of 1684 the 'female' protagonists still lament the lack of an available translation of 'Aloisia Sigea'; in an elaborate fantasy of female cultural power intersecting with the power of the text, one Parliamentarian recalls commissioning her own crib from a woman skilled in Latin, and claims that if it *were* translated into a 'Primer' there would not be a single virgin left in primary school (n. 8 above). (The assembly then promulgates Aretino, *L'Escole*, and *Aloisia Sigea* as official textbooks.) By 1688, on the other hand, Tom Brown could attack the lusciousness of Dryden's Lucretius by associating it with 'Culpepper's Midwife, or the

---

[68] Mainil's assertions that 'possibilities for Sapphic relations completely disappear' after *Entretien* III, and that sodomy 'ne peut se dire' after the Florentines exit in VI (*Règles du plaisir*, 105, 106) are true, if at all, only of this tamed abridgement.

[69] (1682), 2; Ravenscroft's feint (like his borrowing from Scarron) seems to have escaped the attention of scholars, even Foxon (6, 41).

English translation of Aloysia Sigea', both assumed to be degraded forms of 'female' sexual discourse.[70] 'Tullia and Octavia' and *A Dialogue between a Married Lady and a Maid* mingled in the market place with *The School of Venus* and native products like *Sodom*, as we saw in our discussion of Oldham and Chorier (Ch. 6, sect. 3 above). As if confirming Tom Brown's categorization, Culpepper's midwifery manual and 'Tulliae Octavia' are shown freely on sale together in a print as disreputable-looking as the activity it represents, an open-air book auction where the libertine canon is laid out for viewing.[71]

Judging from what survives, the English translations of this canon continue the work of containment and abridgement—with brief eruptions of topical satire and intensified obscenity to match the Restoration taste. *The School of Venus*, as we saw in Chapter 3, embroiders its literal translation of *L'Escole des filles* with impudent scriptural quotations, low-style characterization ('as cunning and deep a Whore as any in the Nation'), and riotous military imagery: 'Be not afraid of having thy Quarters beaten up, though the Prick be never so big.' *The Whores Rhetorick* adapts Pallavicino to the meridian of London by abolishing the complex interrelation of rhetoric and anal 'perversion'. *The Duell*—the manuscript translation of Chorier's fourth Colloquium that antedates *L'Academie* by four years—likewise augments the language of battle and fortification already prominent in Chorier, and gives a contemporary raciness to the Latin.

We have already seen how, for the sake of the rhyme, this Oldhamesque translation 'splits the Cunt to Arse' and turns the noble Tullia into a 'Wench'. Callias now storms the 'halfe moone' rather than just the *castrum*, while Tullia now steers his 'battering Ram' to her 'Gate'. Laughter becomes 'Drollery' and the salty or *salsa* Octavia a 'Witty Slut' like Nell Gwyn. In one of Tullia's 'transmuted' classical quotations the *rabies* or fury strengthened by repression becomes 'Letchery by modesty restrayn'd'. Octavia approaches her defloration not with a 'deliberate' but with a 'philosophicall mind'. The *narrationes* that trigger the mutual arousal of narrator and listener—so strong that in both versions Octavia must beg her 'sister' to 'take away that adulterous finger'—now become 'your leacherous memoires', anticipating Delariviere Manley and Fanny Hill.[72] Yet despite these accretions of fashionably sluttish wit, *The Duell* constricts the work of 'Aloisia Sigea' by choosing a single colloquium as representative of the whole—selecting, in fact, the dialogue most narrowly focused on conventional heterosexuality and the violent triumphalism of the wedding night.

Subsequent translations of Chorier play variations on these effects. As we saw with the Tarse/Arse couplet in *The Duell*, verse tends to be translated more licentiously than prose—a tendency taken to extreme lengths in 'The Delights of Venus, from Meursius', an attempt to condense the whole of Colloquium IV into Rochesteroid couplets. The obscene vocabulary is so concentrated that, when it was

---

[70] Foxon, 6, and see Ch. 6, sect. 2 above.

[71] 'The Compleat Auctioner', described in Introd. n. 79 above.

[72] Princeton University Library, MS AM 14401, pp. 147, 158, 163, 165, 195, 210, 218, 232 (translating *Satyra*, IV. 55, 59, 60–1, 66, 72, 74, 76).

published in Curll's anthology *The Cabinet of Love*, the effect of unbridled lewdness was ruined by the need to turn every significant word into a blank. As in *The Duell*, this translator restricts the range by chosing only the marital fourth dialogue, but then spices it up by imitating lines from the more risqué *Imperfect Enjoyment*:

> Naked I lay clasp'd in my *Callus*'s Arms,
> Dreading, yet longing for his sweetning Charms. . . .
> His —— bore forward with such Strength and Pow'r,
> That 'twould have made a ——, had there been none before.

This Anglo-Latin hybrid ends with a totally un-Chorieran scene in which Tullia penetrates Octavia with a 'D—', dutifully identified as a poor substitute for the real thing, the ——.[73] Meanwhile, prose translation seems to have reduced the pungency. The 1684 prosecution of the *Dialogue between a Married Lady and a Maid*, searching for a single sentence to convince the court of its irredeemable wickedness, found only this: 'He took his pricke out finding it all wet with my spending, and having wiped it and me, he immediately put it in again and began to thrust with great vigour.'[74] The identical sentence—not in the original Latin, and apparently written to link two excerpted passages—appears in the only printed text to have survived, a cleaned-up reduction of Chorier's original, dated 1740, with the same title as the 1684 version; though we cannot reconstruct the full seventeenth-century text, it is certainly the source of this 1740 abridgement.[75] The bland title of this *Dialogue* in turn suggested the subtitle for a new reissue of *The School of Venus . . . In two Dialogues between Frances, a married Lady, and Kitty, a young Maiden*.

Another faux-didactic work claiming affinity with Chorier, the *School of Love* prosecuted in 1707, contained 'severall dialogues between Tullia and Octavia', but again only one passage survives. Though it does not correspond to any one line in Chorier, it resembles those repeated moments that direct the reader's response by showing a character aroused by the narrative itself. Tullia actually reaches orgasm in one sentence ('my sweet Oct. you give so pleasing an account, that every Particle of my Cunt itches so, that I spend in abundance with hearing you'), and Octavia caps this by boasting of her husband's didactic and masturbatory prowess: he 'is not only furnished with as large a Prick as most men, but is as well vers'd in the various manners of Fucking and Frigging, as the Captain of the Virtuosa's'.[76]

The new name of Octavia's husband ('my lovely Phil.') corresponds to 'Philander' in the *Dialogue* of 1740—and presumably also of 1684, when the name would evoke the main character of Behn's scandalous *Love-Letters*. The Captain of the Virtuosas

---

[73] Separated paginated appendix to *The Works of the Earls*, 7–16 (in later reprints integrated into the pagination); for the Rochester lines echoed here, see Ch. 6, sect. 1 above.

[74] Cited from Middlesex Sessions Roll MJ/SR 1653/26 in Roger Thompson, 'Two Early Editions of Restoration Erotica', *Library*, 32 (1977), 27.

[75] BL PC 16.h.1 (microfilm of the unique copy in Munich), 45; Foxon (who had not encountered this 1684 record at the time of writing *Libertine Literature*) assumes that it is 'impossible' to tell whether the 17th- and 18th-century versions are the same (41), but this link (not noted by Thompson) increases the likelihood.

[76] London, Public Record Office, KB 28/24/9, Queen's Bench prosecution of John Marshall (partially noted in Foxon, 13).

must be some heroine of the London bawdy houses, her title further suggesting the affinity between the Royal Society and sexual experimentation exploited by *The Whores Rhetorick*. The philosophical but ineffective dildo-maker in *Sodom* was named Virtuoso, and this nickname shows that the word had already been inflected into the feminine. The husband 'versed' in female masturbatory techniques also recalls the ambiguous figure of 'The Tartar'—either a lady-in-waiting or the publisher of *The School of Venus*—famous in Restoration lampoons for teaching women 'to frig with their toes' (Ch. 5 n. 19 above). As a male reappropriating the instructor's role he recalls Robinet in *L'Escole des filles*, who teaches Fanchon the 'various manners' or *modi*, except that his expertise lies in 'Frigging' as much as 'Fucking'. His most direct antecedent is therefore the monk in Aretino's *Ragionamenti* who teaches Nanna the precise place on her 'fox' where her finger will produce the most feeling (Ch. 1 n. 6): Philander likewise 'told me, which I have since found true, that rubbing ones finger upon the Extremity of the Clitoris, did far exceed the common way of putting ones finger into the Cunt'. Here we can measure how far these purported translations have drifted from Chorier's text; in the *Satyra* Tullia's husband fondles her clitoris and receives sperm in his hand (III. 44), but there is no implication that he is teaching her something she did not know.

As in *The Whores Rhetorick*, in *The School of Love* and other Chorier translations we see citations from the 'ancient' Aretino used to modernize the seventeenth-century text. Some versions of the truncated *Alosia* had sported the fictitious imprint 'Venise, Chez Pierre Arretin', and its English derivative bore the title *Aretinus Redivivus or The Ladies Academy*. Though this text translates *L'Academie des dames* very closely (as far as we can tell from the fifty-two pages extracted in the King's Bench records), it still catches the reader's eye with an elaborate title page that suggests affinities with the entire canon. 'Aretinus' is 'Redivivus' by augmenting the dialogue with twenty-four pictures, by inventing a mock-pedantic author like Alexius Cunnilogus or 'Philo-Puttanus' ('Philo-Cunnus, Posture-professor in the University of Paphos'), and by adding a verse epigraph about the secret desires of nuns, monks, and prudes—not a central theme in Chorier, but dominant in *Venus in the Cloister* and the first day of Aretino's *Ragionamenti*. The translation itself finds vivid English equivalents for *L'Academie*'s modern phrasing: the *esclatante* vulva is now 'a little red pouting Slit', the lesbian love-object 'a young Girl Beautifull Soft Tender and Genteel'; Octavia (genteelly renamed Olivia) is now called 'little wanton Rogue' rather than merely *badine* when she interrupts. At the climax of the first defloration-sequence, where Chorier had mentioned the husband's *ultimo conatu*, the French *Academie* uncharacteristically *adds* a classical reference to 'Priape glorieux et triomphant'. *Aretinus Redivivus* makes this sound even more heroic by echoing the death-throes of Oldham's Sardanapalus: 'at the fourth Thrust having collected all his Strength, he drove his Priapus glorious and Triumphant into a place so well defended.'[77]

---

[77] *Aretinus Redivivus* (KB 28/176/21), transcription of title page, pp. '8', '18', '40' (from Octavie's interruption in *Academie*, i. 43, an episode not in *Satyra*, IV. 57–8 and probably borrowed from the prose *Puttana errante*), '50' (cf. *Sardanapalus*, Ch. 6, sect. 3 above, 'With all thy Strength collected in one Thrust').

A Dialogue between a Married Lady and a Maid, then, represents at once the most complete of these surviving translations and the most egregious example of taming 'Aloisia Sigea' by truncation and domestication. It achieves this by simply obliterating every mention of every sexual encounter that takes place outside marriage (together with any extra-vaginal adventures between husband and wife), reassembling the remaining fragments into three dialogues that culminate with Octavia's wedded bliss. In *L'Escole des filles*, as we saw in Chapter 3, marriage is nothing but a 'couverture' and sexual pleasure belongs wholly to the illicit side; in French *galant* fiction like *Alosie*, and in burlesque dramas like *La Comédie galante de Bussy*, the idea of having sex with one's husband is treated with repugnance and indignation.[78] In contrast, the English *School of Venus* turns Fanny's lover into her husband, and the *Dialogue* continues this maritalizing trend.

Chorier had already eroded the traditional barrier separating *amour* from marriage, going far beyond the licence allowed by the epithalamium by turning the wedding night into a full-scale pornographic narrative, complete with ideological statements about the husband's absolute rule; this marital-aid portion of the *Satyra* forms a dummy conclusion to the early dialogues, a false front systematically demolished by the following three-quarters of the work. Later adaptors, however, cut the wedding sections off and make in effect an autonomous work, as the King's Bench scribe does by stopping his transcript of *Aretinus Redivivus* after Tullia—renamed 'Charlotte' to fit better into the eighteenth-century drawing room—describes to 'Olivia' her total submission to her husband's 'Priapus triumphant' and the mutual, simultaneous orgasm that follows. Some twentieth-century critics performed a similar adulterectomy when they mistook the defloration-sequence for the whole work, or discussed the husband's 'authority' as if it remains unchallenged.[79] The marital-domestic turn may be accidental in these cases, but in the *Dialogue* of 1684/1740 it is carried out deliberately and consistently.

In contrast to the violent exaggerations of Restoration verse, this English prose version drastically reduces Chorier's tendency to metamorphosis and excess. Some trimming and tidying had begun with the first *Academie des dames* of 1680, which closed the gaps in Colloquium VII, homogenized the characters' names, and cleaned up some of the extreme imagery; the shorter recension of the *Academie* further removes ambiguity as well as bulk, though it still demolishes the edifice of monogamy and leaves the reader with the ominous possibility of the wife's suicide or execution at the hands of her husband. The cuts and additions in the *Dialogue between a Married Woman and a Maid*, however, take conceptual neatness so far that wedlock remains unbreached. Despite its Dunbar-like title, the English work conveys no hint of satire, marital trickery, or illicit love, much less sublime morbidity

---

[78] *Aloisa, or The Amours of Octavia*, 1; similar expressions of shock and anger (by the lover) can be found throughout Bussy-Rabutin's *Histoire amoureuse des Gaules*. The only French genre to represent marital sex in a positive light is the popular medical manual, e.g. Nicholas Venette's *Tableau de l'amour conjugal*.

[79] Cf. Cryle, Ch. 4 n. 105 above, and Mainil *Règles du plaisir*, 88 (identifies 'the object of education' with 'the authority of the husband').

and enlivening perversity. Libertine discourse is now wholly contained within a form of romance—not the French novel of extramarital initiation, but the distinctly English attempt to combine the frank avowal of passion with the celebration of amorous companionate marriage. This new redaction of Chorier could almost have appeared under the title of Venette's popular manual for married couples, *Le Tableau de l'amour conjugal*. The adaptor does not simply stop at the first simultaneous orgasm, like the legal archivist, or select a single dialogue as a sample (like the author of *The Duell*), but carefully excises all earlier hints of an alternative: the eru- . dition that shows classical precedent for irregular desires, the lesbian 'initiation' that recurs so often that it cannot be dismissed as a mere adolescent phase or rehearsal, the dream that allows Tullia to predict Octavia's spectacular career of adultery even *before* the wedding narratives begin—all these are rigorously expunged.[80] The 'Protean' element has vanished from both form and content.

The English *Dialogue* still shocked its prosecutors by its explicit representation of sexuality, and certainly confirms the fear of moralists like John Evelyn, who warned his son against turning his own wedding night into a Chorier-style feast of the senses, attempting 'lewd postures' and boasting about 'how frequently they can be brutes in one night'.[81] Evidently the category-confusion of marriage and pornography had already invaded reality. Evelyn insisted that newly-weds should not 'incite your fancy with nakednesses'; here they gaze at each other 'almost naked', leave the candles burning, and repeat their endeavours several times (though less than in the original). Fearing the revival of Aretino, Evelyn particularly discourages 'unnatural figures and usages of your selves': Philander clearly begins to emulate 'the figures of Aretine' when 'he put his P—ck into my Left-hand, desiring me to hold it fast, and convey it to its beloved Place' (37). This translator even amplifies the 'delight to feede and satisfie your Eyes' that fills Evelyn with distaste; Tullia appreciates her husband's white body, 'here and there, upon the Breast and Belly, shaded with some light brown Hair' (18), while he plays with her pubic hair and 'admired the pretty Effects of its Shade upon a white Skin' (20–1).

After consummation they talk freely about their pleasures, another practice condemned by Evelyn; passages about ideal female beauty, similar to those at the end of *L'Escole* and in the libertine conversations of Colloquium VII, are removed from their adulterous context and anchored in the marital situation. Mothers continue to play an active part in the defloration, and Tullia's friend Pomponia likewise intervenes in the bedroom, receives 'roguish' remarks from the bridegroom, and watches him 'jogging on'—an extreme version of the horseplay that normally took place at weddings (25–6). Octavia's mother still allows the young couple a quick standing number during the wedding day itself, while the guests are arriving downstairs; she still bursts in, rejoices in the son-in-law's dimensions ('*Gemini*! . . . What a Monster is this!'), and keeps the stained petticoat as a 'Relick' (33, translating *Satyra*, V. 84–5).

---

[80] Tullia does once insert a 'wicked Finger' into Octavia, who simply asks her to take it out because 'it hurts me' (14, and contrast 8, where the adaptor *cuts* the 'fear and horror' she first feels on touching semen, in *Satyra*, I. 28).

[81] Letter cited Introd. n. 52 above.

The naive directness of the language would also have offended Evelyn, who warned against 'uncomely and filthy expressions'. The female organ, shorn of its learned etymology and privileged connection to the intellect, becomes a mere 'C—t'. Sperm 'leaps two Foot or more' (an effect more easily observed in the solitary garret than in the marriage-bed). When a man comes, 'his Eyes turn in his Head'. His 'Member' or 'P—ck' when not in action 'hangs loose, bobbing here and there', but when aroused becomes a 'terrible Foe', an 'Engine' so large that it can be 'raised only with Machines' (12, 15, 22, 31, 43).

Any attempts to lift the language or the sexual sophistication above this basic level must be channelled within the conventional narrative of the wedding night, now the climax rather than the pretext of sexual narrative. Instead of Chorier's *conatus* or drive towards ever more complicated transgressions, the whole book is now subordinated to its romantic ending, when the happy married couple swoon together into a perfect orgasm followed by a gentle sleep. Descriptive inventiveness is only lavished on those forms of pleasure that anticipate this end. Each wifely orgasm is presented on a velvety cushion of language that anticipates the raptures of Fanny Hill: 'the Extasy, at last, is such, that in some, it comes near Pain, by being so ravishingly delightful' (27); 'I felt the very utmost Parts of my Body contract themselves with convulsive Pleasures, and at last, I lay as unmoved as a Stone, as dissolved in Joys . . . all my Person was seized with a strange, and not before felt Extasy, for I was almost out of myself' (45–6). Such elaborate verbal provocations may be allowed their metanarrative effect on the hearer-reader. When Octavia tells her mother about the first penetration, 'as I made the Description her Eyes sparkled, her Veins swelled, and embracing me, she almost fell away in my Arms, with the Sense of my Pleasure' (33), and Tullia is later driven 'mad with thy Descriptions, they are so natural, and the Image of thy Pleasures create such in me, as comes very near thy own' (45). (This self-referential tribute to the power of description comes just before the sentence that struck the prosecutor so forcibly that he wrote it into the indictment.) Such puffs are the nearest our heroines get to mutual climax—'Sure this Bout had something in it Divine, for you are transported even at the Remembrance of it, and make me ready to die with the Description' (46)—but unlike the protagonists of *L'Escole des filles* or *The School of Love* no one actually 'discharges' in the present tense of the dialogue. The English contractor never suggests that discourse and image could rival, or even supersede, the pleasures of physical intercourse.

One striking interpolation sums up the affective turn that modifies baroque libertine discourse for the age of sensibility. In contrast to the *Academie*, the *Dialogue* not only retains Chorier's description of the clitoris but embellishes it; rubbing this 'Thing they call *Clitoris*' causes it to ejaculate, plunging women into 'a Trance, as if we were dying, all our Senses being lost and as it were summed up in that one Place, and our Eyes shut, our Heads languishing on one Side, our Limbs extended', followed by 'a dissolving of our whole Person, and melting in such inexpressible Joys, as none but those who feel them can express or comprehend'. Aloisia in Chorier's Colloquium VII becomes 'all in her cunt' (*in cunno tota eram*), but now the female erotic subject is 'summed up' in a different 'place'. I argued above that *L'Academie* performs a radical clitoridectomy on the Sigea text; here, the clitoris becomes more resplendent and representative. Instead, the organ removed is the brain. The French translator had cut Tullia's erudition strategically, according to whether it accentuates the new ideology of glorious phallus and abject, distended vagina: he keeps the insulting reference to Curtius leaping into Tullia's chasm, for example, but removes the recognition that Octavia is joking. In the corresponding passage of the *Dialogue*, Octavia is still 'very pleasant' (that is, *plaisant*), but her pleasantry about Curtius' exchange has evaporated; she merely remarks that she could 'thrust my whole Hand in almost'.[82] These cuts are carried out globally, leaving not a shred of ancient wisdom or cultural relativism to interrupt the 'Head's languishing'.

In comparison with the original, even with *L'Academie des dames*, the *Dialogue of a Married Woman and a Maid* seems intellectually stunted and ideologically univocal. It retains the maternal insistence that 'thy Wit and Understanding will clear up with thy Enjoyments, for that very Engine that opens our Bodies will do the same to our Minds' (33), but in fact the mind never opens. Stripped of her lesbian authority and libidinous erudition, Tullia virtually disappears. The mentalized eroticism that lifts sex above the physical, the cognitive interchange that allows some reciprocity between male and female, are confined to one husbandly lecture:

Most Women are in that Error, that they think they ought to hide [their] Joys from us, but it is the greatest Mistake in the World, for our Pleasures consist more in theirs, than our own. These Delights in Men of Wit and Understanding please not only the Body, but charm the Mind, and so our whole Enjoyment is made up of being pleas'd in pleasing, and none but Brutes can be delighted only with that unusual Evacuation of easing themselves.[83]

This attractive theory of mutuality, closer to *L'Escole des filles* than to Chorier, is confounded by the illustration that follows; sounding like Molière's Dom Juan with an added drop of sadism, Philander defines the quintessence of male pleasure as 'to see a delicate Creature, whose Modesty struggles with her very Senses, be forced, in our Arms, to give up all her Reserve' (37).

Discourse does complicate the pleasures of the marriage-bed, but only to reinforce the subordination of the female to the male ideal and to close the gap between representation and reality. As Philander describes his ideal mate, in terms borrowed partly from Chorier's Colloquium VII and partly from domestic conduct books, Octavia conforms herself 'with great pleasure' to his 'Description': 'as he went on, I still viewing myself, and making Reflections upon every Part, found that I had most, if not all these Perfections mentioned' (40). Only in one instance does male authority seem undermined by irony, when Philander declares his 'Member stiff and red' to be 'the best Instructor, and as long as you take Lessons from him, you will never fail to please'; Octavia asks him with a smile 'whether he would always be in a

---

[82] 13 (orig. 'Hearts languishing'), 15 (cf. *Satyra*, III. 44, 47).

[83] 36–7; romanticized mutuality is even transcribed into genital physiology, e.g. the *glans penis* 'of a delicate Sense, so as [men] feel us when we spend upon it' (16). Cf. Hobbes, *Humane Nature* (1650), 106–7: lust 'consisteth of two appetites together, to *please*, and to *be pleased*; and the delight men take in delighting, is not Sensual, but a pleasure or joy of the minde consisting in the imagination of the power they have so much to please'.

Condition to teach, when I had a Mind to learn' (43). Otherwise, the subversive 'salt'
of Chorier's original vanishes completely, while the wooden statements of male
supremacy are left standing unqualified. Tullia is 'extreamly pleased' to be a virgin
for her husband, now given the dashing name Horatio (18). Gushings like 'Oh,
what it is to feel my Love! My Horatio!' (25) once again anticipate Fanny Hill's
exclamations over Charles, who likewise represents the fusion of libertine fantasy
with romantic marriage.

By a paradox perhaps endemic to the process of cultural translation, this extreme
example of domestic moderation—the 'taming' rather than the 'outdoing' approach to the canonical predecessor—takes on a Sadean tinge, where intensified
sentiment and ideological subjection converge. Octavia tells her mother that 'any
Pain which would procure him Pleasure would be a Delight to me', and Philander,
overhearing this, hugs her and thanks her for 'that pretty Thought!' (34)—evidently
a paradigm of the intended reader's response. The adaptor does his best to turn
Philander into a man of refinement, like Elisabeth Rowe's 'philosophical libertine'
or the 'rational pleasurist' who educated Fanny Hill. Milton's *Areopagitica* imagined
Court libertines discussing 'the choisest delights and criticisms of sin' (Ch. 1, sect. 2
above); the voluptuary husband now becomes 'an excellent Critick in the Charms
which make a Woman lovely' (38–9), 'one of those Men, who being great Observers,
and having a refined Imagination, manage the Pleasure of Enjoyment with extreem
Niceties, . . . much surpassing the ordinary Rate of Men, who do only brutishly satisfy their own Lusts in us' (42). But *sensibilité* comes at a steep price, accentuating the
polarization of gender. When Tullia warns that men of 'refined Imagination' easily
grow disgusted, Octavia dutifully responds 'For that, I suppose, we must blame
none but ourselves'; agreeing wholeheartedly, Tullia explains that men's heads are
full of business when they come home, and women's duty is to make them forget
their cares and relax them for pleasure 'by our Softness' (42–3). It is hard to share the
judgement that the passive Tullia of the English reduction is 'more natural', that its
conduct-book didacticism is 'charming', or that the three-part *Dialogue*, stripped of
its transgressive form and content, represents a great improvement over the 'hypertrophic' discourse of Chorier.[84]

4. 'THE GRILLE TURNS UP THE HEAT': *VENUS IN THE
   CLOISTER, OR THE NUN IN HER SMOCK* (1683)

The simultaneous canonization and repudiation of *L'Escole des filles* and *Aloisia* can
be seen most prominently in *Vénus dans le cloître, ou La Religieuse en chemise,
Entretiens curieux*, generally attributed to Father Jean Barrin, which appeared in
1683 and was expanded with additional dialogues during the following decades. The

---

[84] Foxon, 41–2; Peter Naumann, *Keyhole und Candle* (Heidelberg, 1976), 36–43, and cf. 50–2. Naumann
criticizes Chorier for breaking the rules of the 'Hetärendialog' or prostitute-dialogue, and praises the
English abridgement because it restores the 'true nature' of that genre—a bizarre conclusion since it deals
with nothing but married sex.

leitmotifs of the libertine canon—hermetic exclusion from the world to concentrate on sexual awakening, proto-Enlightenment social critique and natural
philosophy, voyeuristic deployment of lesbianism and flagellation—are woven
throughout the three dialogues of the original 1683 version, so that when the two
nuns Angélique and Agnès discuss their reading it forms an appropriate climax to
the whole work. We shall see that, like Maucroix, the two libertine reader-surrogates
arrange *L'Escole* and *L'Academie des dames* in an escalating series (with *Vénus dans
le cloître* itself forming the third term, by implication). But the older mentor and the
younger ingénue then disagree over how to evaluate that progression, bringing out
the contradictory status of 'Nature' in the philosophy of Eros, and dramatizing the
divergent possibilities that the canon holds out: excess or moderation, 'taming' or
'outdoing'.

Vénus dans le cloître rapidly entered both the French and the English canon,
perhaps because its anticlerical and gendered title predisposed the reader to find
erotic spectacle in the acceptable guise of satire. We have seen how the cloister
provoked fevered speculations about female 'Sodomy' in authors like Killigrew, how
Maucroix felt compelled to imagine the effect of Chorier on the 'Vestales', and how
the English publisher adorned *Aretinus Redivivus* with gratuitous allusions to
monks and nuns; indeed, the prototype of all libertine space is the nunnery in
Aretino's *Ragionamenti*, where centuries of Boccaccian comic narrative are con-
densed into hard-core routines. Aloisia Sigea in the sixteenth century had envisaged
the cloister as a calm, Paradisal space where women could 'enjoy colloquia with God
and philosophize fearlessly about the universe';[85] barely a hundred years later Nicolas Chorier impersonates her voice to describe a lesbian nunnery whose abbess 'phi-
losophizes' just as fearlessly about the natural force of Eros. (Chorier had included
two convents of 'Vestals' in his encyclopedic seventh dialogue, one this crucible of
'unnatural' lusts, the other the stamping-ground for a disguised gardener straight
out of Boccaccio.) As we saw with *The Nunns Complaint against the Fryars*, Louis
Varet's report on the convent besieged by monks bearing copies of *L'Escole des filles*
(Ch. 3, sect. 1 above), anxieties about the eruption or intrusion of sexuality easily
slide into titillated fascination.

It is no accident that cloistral pornography expanded when convents were becoming increasingly brilliant centres of culture. Together with the uncloistered but
celibate communities of teaching Dames, they provided schooling and shelter for a
great range of women; they were places of autonomy, patronage, educational and
'philosophical' advancement, and their activities included petitioning for recognition, voting on their own membership, designing their own premises and the ceremonies that take place there, writing and performing their own music and drama.[86]

---

[85] *Dialogue de deux jeunes filles sur la vie de cour et la vie de retraite/Duarum Virginum Colloquium de
Vita Aulica et Privata* (1552), ed. and tr. Odette Sauvage (Paris, 1970), 269 ('cum Deo colloquuntur et de
universo philosophantur intrepide', the words of the ascetic Blesilla so not necessarily Sigea's personal
view).

[86] Judith C. Brown, *Immodest Acts: The Life of a Lesbian Nun in Renaissance Italy* (New York, 1986), Ch.
2; for nuns as playwrights see Beatrice del Sera, *Amor di virtù: Commedia in cinque atti, 1548*, ed. Elissa

When Margaret Cavendish wishes to assert women's creativity and criticize male sexualization of their intellect, she sets the action in a 'Convent of Pleasure' as well as a 'Female Academy' framed by a quasi-monastic 'grille'.[87] More explicitly than *L'Escole des filles*, Barrin's religious-didactic fantasy recalls, by parody, the important expansion of teaching orders in France, often led by aristocratic women (Ch. 3, sect. 5 above). Angélique—herself the sister of a *comte*—follows the vocation of 'schoolmistress', as she reveals when she admits to flogging an attractive 13-year-old pupil purely for the 'satisfaction' it gave her (I. 30, 33). Though nuns, like other 'Collegiate Ladies', were accused of every kind of transgression—with men, with books, with crucifixes, with other nuns—the lesbian aura grew so strong that the marquise de Maintenon, founder of the most famous girls' school of the seventeenth century, is made to declare (in a novel by Delariviere Manley) that 'in *France*, where our young Ladies are that Way debauch'd in their *Nunnery* Education, . . . few People of Quality care now to have their Daughters brought up in those Places'.[88]

Barrin's erotic dialogue and its sequels ride on the enormous success of convent literature purporting to capture the true voice of female passion. *Vénus* can be understood as a bastard cousin of the fictional *Lettres* of the Portuguese nun or the historical letters of Héloïse, eagerly devoured in England as well as France. (Oldham had already conflated Héloïse with Aloisia Sigea, as we saw in Chapter 6.) An English three-dialogue *Venus in the Cloister* appeared almost simultaneously with the French original, and a five-dialogue text was translated and published by Curll in 1725; this version became famous in fiction as the jewel of Shamela's library and in legal history as the proof-text of prosecutions for obscenity. (The judge in Curll's trial complained that *Venus* threatened public order because it 'goes all over the kingdom', extending Maucroix's image of the lewd book 'running through Paris'.[89]) *Vénus dans le cloître* may be the first explicitly erotic work documented in a lady's library, since Mary Wortley Montagu certainly owned the French version.[90]

Three genres converge in *Venus in the Cloister*, the soft-core narrative of sex in holy orders, the 'University of Love' with its facetious curriculum and library catalogue, and the two-woman dialogue of initiation and seduction. In *Vénus*, as in *L'Escole* and Chorier, the scenario is explicitly didactic and ideological: the

Weaver (Ravenna, 1990), and Weaver, *Convent Theatre in Early Modern Italy: Spiritual Fun and Learning for Women* (Cambridge, 2002). Music by nuns (esp. Chiara Margarita Cozzolani) is increasingly being recorded and performed, e.g. by The Newberry Consort, 11–13 Jan. 1996, 30 Apr. 1999, and Magnificat, 2–4 Feb. 2001, 2 June 2002.

[87] Robinson, 'To Boldly Go', 134–56, 3.7–29, brings out parallels between Cavendish's comedy *The Convent of Pleasure* and *Vénus dans le cloître*; see Ch. 1, sect. 4 above for her *Female Academy*.

[88] *The Rival Dutchess*, cited in Ros Ballaster, '"The Vices of Old Rome Revived": Representations of Female Same-Sex Desire in Seventeenth and Eighteenth Century England', in Suzanne Raitt (ed.), *Volcanoes and Pearl Divers: Essays in Lesbian Feminist Studies* (1995), 30; the fictional Maintenon asks that other educator (and suspected lesbian), Abigail Masham, 'does that Female Vice, which is the most detestable in Nature, Reign among you, as it does with us?' and Masham replies, 'O, Madam, we are arriv'd to as great Perfection in sinning that Way as you can pretend to.'

[89] See Foxon, 14–15, Thomas, 42–50, and Ian Hunter, David Saunders, and Dugald Williamson, *On Pornography: Literature, Sexuality and Obscenity Law* (New York, 1993), esp. 51 (citing Justice Reynolds).

[90] Isobel Grundy, 'Books and the Woman: An Eighteenth-Century Owner and her Libraries', *English Studies in Canada*, 20 (1994), 16.

'bibliothèque' of erotic texts, cited within the erotic text, will allow the younger woman to 'perfectionner ton esprit et te rendre telle que tu dois être', *devoir* replacing *jouir* as the main verb; like Diderot's 14-year-old courtier, the 16-year-old novice will 'perfect herself' by conversation with 'Aloisia' (II. 76–7). (The names of the enlightened Angélique and the naive but intelligent Agnès certainly suggest the heroines of Molière, not to mention the two Arnauld sisters who presided over the nuns of Port-Royal, but their immediate source is *L'Academie des dames*, where the worldly Pomponia is renamed Angelique and the nun who loves the gardener becomes Agnes.) As in Chorier too, the pseudo-educational format creates intellectually self-conscious 'female' protagonists who nevertheless remain hermetically sealed within their double cloister, the physical nunnery and the conceptual prison of male-defined sexuality. These two enclosures become one, in fact, when the Abbess organizes the male clergy into the chivalric Order of the Grille, celebrating the grid that separates, frames, and intensifies their desire; its emblem is St Lawrence burning on his gridiron, and its motto *Ardorem craticula fovet*, 'the Grille turns up the heat' (II. 60–2). Margaret Cavendish would understand.

Among many other contradictions, *Venus in the Cloister* embodies two incompatible theories of the origins of discursive authority: is it 'born in the blood' or produced by books? do women or men generate it primarily? Like Chorier, Father Barrin abdicates the narrator's role and invents a pair of female dialoguists, endowing them with a sophisticated literary awareness (in marked contrast to the whores of Aretino or the simple hedonists who speak in *L'Escole des filles*). And like Chorier, Barrin prefaces the dialogue proper with an elaborate fiction of female origin: the 'Abbé du Prat' reports in a cover-note to the Abbess of Beaulieu that he has obeyed her command to 'reduce' the conversations of her nuns to writing, however difficult it has been to 'rendre à la voix et aux actions le beau feu dont elles ont été animées', to capture their beautiful animating 'fire' (3). Though the *fonction-auteur* has been ascribed to a male, his role is reduced to what Oldham calls 'Secretary to a Cunt', subservient to a powerful patroness and aware of how inadequately he has approximated his incandescent original.

Almost immediately, however, the text is marked by intrusive signs of satirical intention, starting with an arch reinterpretation of the nun's vows: poverty is shown by stripping to her shirt, chastity by following the rule of 'la nature toute pure', obedience by sexual 'docility' (5). Whenever this anticlerical wit reappears in the dialogue, it reminds us of the ventriloquizing male author. Angélique similarly negates the vow of chastity, by defining continence as a pure gift of God that human laws can do nothing about. (Agnès responds that '*libertinage* can often furnish us with reasons to damn ourselves', prompting her teacher to defend the innocence of her pleasures and to distinguish 'liberty' from 'licence' (II. 90–2).) Angélique's 'libertine' misapplications of Scripture recall Rocco's outrageous theological defences of sodomy (Ch. 2, sect. 2): as in Rocco, the command to 'Love God and thy neighbour' entails *eros* rather than *agapē* (I. 25). The Rabelaisian titles of Agnès's library likewise evoke the tradition of exclusionary, misogynistic humour exemplified in the *Université d'amour*. Furthermore, all these books are literally brought into the convent by some male mentor, abbé or monk, as if 'female' knowledge has to be supplied by a man, or (as Chorier puts it) *mens* can only derive from *mentula*.[91]

Intellectual and didactic initiative is thus presented inconsistently, as a compulsory gift from outside and as the self-affirming *conatus* of the nuns themselves. At the height of her seduction of Agnès, Angélique presents herself as a fully autonomous source of the sexual *cogito*, a Cartesian philosopher who strips off 'the sentiments of others', 'disengages' herself from 'the stupid thoughts of the vulgar', and sees things 'according to their origins, envisaging them in their simple nature'. (The English translator adds a bawdy twist by having Angelica 'consider things from their Rise, view them in their pure naturals'.) 'Nature' in these proto-Enlightenment declarations denotes both a state of sexual experience and a reliable epistemic touchstone, a guide who never did betray the heart that loved her. The occasion of this burst of confidence—and the narrative device that leads directly to the review of *L'Escole des filles* and *L'Academie des dames*—is the description of Sister Dosithée, the nun who simultaneously bursts her hymen and her mental dependence on Christian doctrine by the 'force' of her own autoeroticism, gaining enlightenment without the help of any *mentula*: 'pure nature' emerges from within her sex and submits her to its 'laws'. Angélique flaunts her grasp of the new science by explaining how Dosithée's self-flagellation causes the purest parts of the blood to flow into the affected part—a close paraphrase of Meibomius and Descartes—and then turns the physiology lecture into a demonstration of new, 'Florentine' kissing techniques.[92] Before this, however, she acted as a deferential teaching assistant, handing her pupil over to a team of male instructors who will 'make you more *savante* in a quarter of an hour' than in a week of woman-to-woman conversation (I. 29).

Even in the third and final dialogue Angélique fawns over the expertise of these tutors, the fetishistic monk and 'our Abbé' (who seems identical to the author du Prat, suitor of the Abbess de Beaulieu and leading Knight of the Grille). These male preceptors are educated in 'all the sweetest manners' or *modi* of love, 'savants dans toutes les pratiques les plus secrètes', which they have learned in Italy; the Abbé even introduces her to the 'glass instrument', emblem of all the knowledge he has brought back from that country, duplicating the scene in Aretino's *Ragionamenti*, I. i, where a monk delivers a basket of Murano-glass dildos to the nunnery. (Like Wycherley's Horner, Barrin assumes that libertine literature and expertise must be 'brought over' from a hotter and more advanced country.) Male authority embodies all the *arcana Veneris et amoris* promised in Chorier's title, and brings them into the hermetic world of the convent, but its origin still comes from outside—from Italy,

---

[91] Ch. 4, sect. 2 above; Agnès's personal 'library' (II. 77) was provided by the priestly tutors that Angélique arranged for her.

[92] *Vénus*, III. 111–16, *Venus in the Cloister* (1633), 149; see Johann Heinrich Meibom[ius], *De Flagrorum Usu in Re Veneria et Lumborum Renumque Officiis* (Leiden, 1643), for a blood-flow theory of arousal (during flagellation) that anticipates Descartes's explanation of love (Ch. 3, sect. 4). The Dosithée episode is crucial to those historians who emphasize the teleological, pre-Enlightenment aspect of libertine discourse, e.g. Robert Darnton, 'Sex for Thought', *New York Review of Books*, 22 Dec. 1994, 69, and Fischer, *Éducation érotique*, 269–70.

source of all imported wisdom, and from 'the bad books from which they draw their light'.[93]

Books therefore play the crucial role in undermining the figure of female intellectual agency made possible by Cartesian erotics. The works in Agnès's 'library' certainly help to constitute libertine discourse as a 'self-reflexive and self-authenticating referential system' (as one critic puts it),[94] but at the same time they emphasize the intellectual passivity of the nun, the necessity to import sexual knowledge from outside. These 'livres curieux' mirror the 'entretiens curieux' announced in the subtitle of *Vénus* itself, endorsing the erotic yet innocent 'curiosité' that inspires Angélique to gaze at Agnès's smarting bottom and to run her hand into 'that place which is *nature itself*' (I. 27–8, II. 61). Yet they are not *produced* by that curiosity; though Barrin shows us the power of the Abbess as patron and Angélique as thinker, he never invents a female author-figure like Chorier's Tullia or Aloisia Sigea. Every title is supplied and applied *to* the nuns, either by the dildo-importing Abbé or by the monk of the reformed Cistercian Feuillant order; in one scene we see this 'application' in action, when the monk seduces Agnès by presenting her with a book entitled *Soft and Easy Remedies against Dangerous Swelling* and feeding her contraceptive jam. (Agnès's monk-teacher not only hoards book-learning but also wears a fetishistic 'Reliquary of the Holy Beard' containing pubic hair from all his mistresses.[95]) Confirming the same logic of origination, the canonical works reviewed in the closing scene have likewise been introduced by the abbé-preceptor. The Abbé du Prat has been working hard to stoke the 'fires' of pseudo-spontaneous 'female' dialogue, even though in his preface he had abdicated originality and defined authorship as nothing more than impotent transcription.

As the two female dialoguists review their predecessors in the genre, *L'Escole des filles* is placed decisively in the minor category, the *bagatelle* position to which Maucroix had also assigned it. They recognize the earlier book's intellectual claim by paraphrasing its subtitle as 'cette infâme *philosophie*'—the English version asks 'what canst thou say of the *School of Venus*, and that *Infamous Phylosophy*?'—but they remain quite unimpressed by its 'philosophie des dames'. From the start Agnès challenges her mentor by taking the position of Milton's *Areopagitica*, that no book can be forbidden to the *savant* and that none is evil in itself; she concedes, however, that *L'Escole* might be a waste of time. Its philosophy is nothing but 'fade et insipide' (the criterion being flavour rather than consistency), while its 'forts raisonnements' can only persuade 'low and vulgar Spirits' or 'half-corrupted women'. All the nuns' critical attention is then focused on another imported book, which 'handles almost the same matter but with far more *adresse* and *spiritualité*': Angélique spells out the

---

[93] II. 56–9, III. 119–21 ('les mauvais livres où ils puisent leur lumière').

[94] Domna C. Stanton, 'Erotic Pleasure and Sacred Law: The Tensions of *Vénus dans le cloître*', unpublished MLA conference paper, 5; this phrase is not retained in the published version, 'Sexual Pleasure and Sacred Law: Transgression and Complicity in *Vénus dans le cloître*', *Esprit créateur*, 35/2 (Summer 1995), 67–83, which submits *Vénus* to Bataillian and Foucauldian theories of stimulating prohibition.

[95] *Vénus*, II. 66 (and 76 for the same title, *Remèdes contre l'embonpoint dangereux*, in the library 'catalogue'), 67–8; *Venus in the Cloister* (1683), 83.

work in question, '*The Academy of Ladyes: Or the Seven Satyrical Dialogues of Aloisia*', a composite title that retains the fullest version of Nicolas's translation but adds the faux author's name.[96]

The younger Agnès enthuses about these *Entretiens satyriques d'Aloïsia*, recently given to her by the Abbé who had previously provided *L'Escole des filles*; evidently the seducer-confessor has chosen the 'female-authored' version rather than the anonymous first edition to infiltrate the female space of the cloister. Angélique reproves her pupil, insisting that Chorier is worse than *L'Escole* because of its greater influence on *les mœurs* or 'manners'. (The 1725 Curll translation expands this to 'forming of Peoples Manners', ascribing a didactic social and educational function to the erotic dialogue—the same power to define the 'Subject' or 'breed women up in Venus' School' that early feminists denounced.[97]) 'The purity of its style and its easy Eloquence . . . the Flame and the briskness which sparkle there in many places' only make the poison go down more sweetly. Angélique's disapproval clearly functions as a recommendation to the reader, just as her frequent exclamations of horror at the possibility of being secretly observed increase the reader's sense of pleasurable intrusion: she denounces *L'Academie* for its extreme sensibility, for the dangerous *brillant* of its style, and for the 'imagination corrompüe' that endorses all the bizarre perversions of the ancient world. Chorier can only 'inspire Debauchery'—a term of opprobrium in libertine fiction, which purports to represent a high, refined, yet somehow also natural voluptuarism. Angélique/Angelica distinguishes herself, rather indignantly, from the 'Libertinisme' of those readers 'who never enjoy perfect Pleasures unless they go seek them in the lessons of a Corrupted Imagination, beyond the most inviolable bounds of Nature, and even into the most dissolute Licentiousness of past Fables'—the Greek and Roman belief-systems constantly evoked in Chorier's text, and retained in *L'Academie* (as we have seen) in those passages that deal with sodomy and fellatio. With enemies prepared to select such fascinating details to condemn, *Aloisia* hardly needs friends.

By criticizing *L'Academie*'s tendency to drive 'beyond' the bounds of Nature, Angélique clearly places it in the 'outdoing' rather than the 'taming' line, and legitimizes her own discourse by situating it *within* those bounds: here and elsewhere, she stands for 'liberty' rather than 'licence', 'innocence' rather than 'crime', 'Nature' rather than 'Corrupted Imagination'. Denouncing Chorier, the authority-figure here preaches a sort of proto-Enlightenment moderation, urging her pupil to shun 'toutes les extrémitez' in pleasure and to respect 'les bornes les plus inviolables de la nature'; like a good Augustan, she exhorts her disciple to follow 'Nature', 'Prudence', and the 'middle Way'. In his preface du Prat defined Chastity as following the purity and innocence of (sexual) Nature, and throughout the dialogue this concept serves

---

[96] This review passage (also cited in the following paragraphs) appears on *Vénus*, III. 121–5, *Venus in the Cloister* (1683), 155–60. No copy called '*L'Académie des Dames, ou Les Sept Entretiens satyriques d'Aloïsia*' (III. 122) has actually survived, but the wording of the title, and the inclusion of the Florentine medal episode, indicates a work much closer to the first edn. than to the abridgements.

[97] *Venus in the Cloister* (1725), 126. The Curll text (but not the original or the 1683 tr.) is briefly discussed in Bradford K. Mudge, *The Whore's Story: Women, Pornography, and the British Novel, 1684–1830* (New York, 2000), 168, 170.

as a universal signifier. 'Pure' or 'simple nature' becomes a physical disposition, a 'right' that overrides the artificial rules of the convent, an epistemological criterion, a euphemism for Agnès's desirable genital organs, a secular equivalent to the evangelical desire for 'primitive' sanctity. 'The state of nature' and 'innocence' refer interchangeably to the young nun's state of pure Eve-like nudity, kissing passionately on the bed or emerging from the bath.[98]

Barrin's Angélique and Chorier's Tullia both stand in for what Montaigne called the 'schoolmaster nature', showing by the ingenuity and persistence of their arguments that the natural does not in fact come naturally, that it requires a full didactic apparatus. In Chorier 'Nature' is intermittently evoked as the ideal, the 'bounds' within which conventional gender roles should be played out, but its authority is continually undermined by philosophical inconsistency and by examples from the culture and literature of antiquity. Angélique, on the other hand, strives to maintain her naturalism throughout the dialogue, insisting on the artificiality of forced cloistering and the 'innocence' of the pleasure she takes with Agnès (fingering her *nature*, appreciating the 'vermillion' of the welts on her buttocks, receiving a vigorous whipping, and training her in deep 'Florentine kisses'). In this climactic review of *L'Academie des dames*, she brings all her nature-arguments to a head.

Despite all this preparation, however, Angélique's apparently definitive condemnation of *Aloisia* falls apart—in two directions at once. Firstly, she implies a higher canonical value for Chorier's text when she recalls how she herself had been initiated into its mysteries by a male tutor, who had explained its difficult passages over an eight-day period; access to a potentially alarming 'female' discourse comes once again under the control of male authority. She particularly mentions his exegesis of the homosexual medal of Jove and Ganymede—a highly favourable representation of the 'unnatural'—which finds a message coded by anagram in its motto *Amori Vera Lux*.[99] Secondly, the junior and supposedly more natural Agnès sticks to her enthusiasm for the 'nouveaux plaisirs', 'appetits extravagans', and 'viandes inconnües' recommended in *Aloisia*. The dialogue form inverts the roles of ingénue and authority-figure. On first mentioning the *Academie* Agnès had exclaimed 'Lord, Lord, how ingenious it is in inventing new Pleasures for a satiated and disgusted mind!', ascribing to Chorier's text precisely the function that Tullia claims for her imagination—to replace the *Veneris nausea* with a cerebral 'invented' eroticism. She adores its 'extravagant Appetites', 'Strange Objects', and 'unknown Meats', and celebrates its ability to cure the 'satiated and disgusted mind', to 'revive that Lust that is the most lulled asleep, the most languishing, nay and that which is no longer able!' Angélique seems too conventional when she reproves this aspiration to forbidden knowledge (and to what Rochester would call 'Love rais'd to an extream'). Instead of

[98] *Vénus*, I. 10, 14, 23, 28, II. 78, III. 116; the sexual interpretation of Edenic nudity is a frequent preoccupation of François Chavigny de La Bretonnière, the contemporary author of *Eve resuscitée* and *L'Adamite, ou Le Jésuite insensible* (reprinted with the six-dialogue *Vénus*), which may explain why *Vénus* has sometimes been ascribed to him.

[99] III. 123; a footnote in Kearney, *History of Erotic Literature*, 183, attempts to explain this as 'Amor e luxuria' or 'Love from excess'. The idea of an 'eight-day' crash course derives from Aretino, *Ragionamenti*, II. i. 184–5 [192], cited p. 34 above.

obeying her mentor, Agnès refutes her with her own naturalistic doctrine: attacking *L'Academie* is tantamount to 'Preaching Reformation', a futile operation since 'We are not responsible for the freaks, fancies, propensities and inclinations that [Nature] gives us.'

At this high point of her enlightenment, the younger nun now translates almost verbatim from the high point of libertine (un)naturalism. Rocco's philosopher-seducer had persuaded Alcibiade that pederasty fulfils a 'natural inclination', and the new star pupil persuades her teacher that 'Nous ne sommes pas responsables des fantaisies, du penchant, et des inclinations que [la nature] nous donne', and that consequently everything is blameless. This revelation so delights her mentor that the couple dissolve into a lesbian embrace, concluding their lesson in *baisers à la florentine*—precisely the sort of 'unknown meat' that the allegedly immoral and unnatural Chorier had introduced into the erotic dialogue. Aloisia is thus *rediviva* in the very text that purports to expel her.

The return of Aloisia, and the hegemony of *L'Academie des dames*, are even more dramatically expressed by the fourth dialogue, the first of three *post hoc* accretions that eventually inflated *Vénus dans le cloître* to the six-part structure of Aretino's *Ragionamenti*. Here the familiar philosophical themes reappear—Angélique launches an Enlightenment attack on prejudice and custom, calling for a life of pleasure based on 'droite raison' and 'la Nature toute pure et innocente'—but the two nuns seem strangely focused on narratives about third parties beyond the convent wall. The bulk of the dialogue is taken up with Angélique's account of watching a hitherto unknown friend, Alios, being flogged by the sadistic priest Théodore to purify her before marriage. Angélique introduces a fresh batch of faux-learned titles, but the only author cited directly (in a brief discussion comparing two forms of sexual pleasure) is Lucian. By the end—Agnès once again kissing her beloved teacher, who declares 'I think you will never finish!'—the feeling of *déjà lu* has become overwhelming.

Most of this added fourth dialogue is indeed a barefaced and incompetent plagiarism from *L'Academie des dames*.[100] We recall that, at a crucial moment in the discussion of sodomy, Octavie interrupts to point out that Tullie has forgotten to say whether she approves or disapproves of anal penetration; her mentor utters a perfunctory condemnation, then returns to her non-committal stance by citing pseudo-Lucian's even-handed comparison of women and boys. The *Vénus* pastiche steals this entire exchange but gives no indication of the context, literally reducing the discussion of 'two pleasures' to nonsense. The theft of the final sermon on Nature and 'right reason' might be a little more plausible, since Angélique in the original dialogue does reject all religious superstitions, raise Nature to the universal touchstone or signifier, and espouse a Rochesterian programme of reason devoted to enhanced hedonism: 'When our minds are cleared of those clouds of Darkness . . . there is not a moment in our whole lives but what affords us some

---

[100] IV. 149–59, 160–2; for the corresponding passages in *L'Academie* see sect. 2 above, esp. n. 52.

pleasures.'[101] All that can be said for the expropriation of the flogging-scenes, however, is that it mitigates some of the voluptuary, proto-Sadean wound-licking of
Chorier's original. At considerable risk to plausibility, Chorier had introduced
two flogging-scenes with Father Theodorus; in the first, just before the wedding,
Octavia believes that she is being purged of impurities to guarantee the salvation
of her future children, and feels nothing but pain and repugnance; in the return
bout the goal is unequivocally redefined as sexual pleasure—clearly a pretext for
collusive eroticism between reader and author, who lingers on the details of the tortured body and insists that the victim's pain turns into delight. The earlier parts of
Vénus, where 'female' characters flagellate themselves and comment on the result,
are equally lurid. But the added fourth dialogue transcribes only the first of
Chorier's episodes, maintaining a clearer boundary between anticlerical satire and
vicarious sadism.

Chorier's vast and deliberately hypertrophic sequence of dialogues had established the *conatus* as literary form, each new narrative bringing a corresponding increase in contradiction and (per)version. Whether in its Latin form or in the full
Academie, this escalation-effect posed a challenge to the critic like Maucroix, who
must adjust his threshold of outrage to each new provocation or 'blasphemy'. The
various 'taming' strategies reviewed in the latter part of this chapter all involve large-
scale cutting as the principal technique of control, whether or not they also bring in
the new 'soft and genteel' language of sensibility. In the fifth and sixth dialogues of
the pseudo-*Vénus*, in contrast, accretion is put in the service of normalization. The
entire fifth dialogue is taken up with the lusty young man in disguise who is given
free run of the convent, another variant on the Boccaccian theme already milked
dry by Chorier, reinforcing the most traditional elements in the libertine narrative.
The sixth, in contrast, reviews that entire tradition and turns it around. Clearly
added in the early eighteenth century,[102] *Entretien* VI introduces two new speakers
who seem to have migrated from the original *Vénus dans le cloître*, and who first
rehearse, then dissolve, its premisses.

Much of Barrin's text had been given over to the loves of Father Raucourt and
Virginie, and she now achieves her own voice. The new dialoguists first perform an
arresting lesbian number modelled on Chorier's Tullia and Octavia. Virginie's raptures over Séraphique's 'members as dainty as those of a Helen or a Cleopatra', particularly the 'little labyrinth of jade, coral, and alabaster' which she describes as she
explores it with her fingers, are considerably more explicit and articulate than those
of Agnès and Angélique, which tend to peter out into discussion.[103] Once our attention has been riveted, however, the entire voluptuary pretence begins to unravel. We
are led into a very different kind of labyrinth.

---

[101] *Vénus*, III. 117, *Venus in the Cloister* (1683), 149.

[102] VI. 214 refers to the papacy of Clement XI (1700–21); the idea of bringing in new speakers might
derive from Aretino, who had done so in *his* sixth dialogue.

[103] As Emma Donoghue argues in *Passions between Women: British Lesbian Culture 1668–1801* (1993),
198–200, though wrongly asserting that the nuns never get beyond kissing; Donoghue is not aware of
Vénus, VI. 205–6 ('membres douillets comme ceux d'une Hélène ou d'une Cléopâtre . . . petit labyrinthe
de jais, de corail et d'albâtre').

First, in a blatantly ideological move the two nuns declare that 'the essential thing is missing', that 'we must aim for the solid and renounce the *bagatelle*', that lesbian-ism is a mere 'shadow' of heterosexual penetration (VI. 206–7). Tullia had made similar statements early in the *Satyra*, but they were then ironized by the counter-assertion of female autonomy and the superiority of *narratio* to *actio*; in this sixth dialogue added to *Vénus*—as later in Cleland's *Memoirs* of Fanny Hill—the 'essen-tial' is unequivocally embodied in the two male 'lovers' who await in coaches at the garden gate. Scandalously, these anonymous young men will take them not to some Lovelacean house of bondage but to the delights of conventional marriage, another anticipation of Cleland's domestic-sentimental ending. Thus the 'strange meats' and 'unnatural appetites' of Aloisia give way to the simplicities of a different 'school'—not the rampant adulteries of the original *L'Escole des filles*, but the faux-pornographic trick of the 1658 *Escole*, which lured the reader into an intensely liber-tine text, then switched to a sermon on true Christian marriage (Ch. 3, sect. 2 above). And this domestic turn then brings with it a reforming turn. The anti-monastic rhetoric, formerly the pretext to bring on another flagellant or autoerotic number, now gathers into a full-fledged Huguenot polemic against the papacy, a ringing call for a 'second reformation' in France. *Vénus*' erotic naturalism always had an evangelistic tinge, establishing the equivalence of sexual awakening, 'primi-tive' innocence, direct access to Scripture, and Cartesian understanding of physical nature (I. 21–2, II. 65, II. 78, III. 116). But now the sexual tenor becomes the vehicle, the pretext for Protestant discipline and holy matrimony.

The Erotics of Literary Response

Chorier and Rochester in the Critical Mainstream

The short and true state of the Case is this: all depends upon the Genius and Art of the Writer, for an obscene Thought, if it be not livelily painted, will have but a small or perhaps no effect upon the Mind of the Reader. . . . For a further Proof of this, when [the Critick's] squeamish Fit is over, I wou'd recommend to his Perusal *Aloisia Sigea*, or if that be too hard for him because 'tis writ in Latin, let him read *L'Escole des Filles*, and if the obscene Words and Descriptions he will meet with there do not raise his Appetite, the World will be apt to conclude it, not only very dull, but absolutely dead; and as bad as his Poetry is, his Reader will be better entertain'd than his Mistress.

(Robert Wolseley, preface to Rochester's *Valentinian*)

Principalmente rendesi sublime l'arte in questo tropo, quando per arrecare maggior piacere ponsi l'anima de' gusti ove la natura collocò note d'abbominevole disprezzo.

(Pallavicino, *La retorica delle puttane*)

The courtesan's art becomes sublime principally by means of this trope [of anal 'translation'], when to obtain greater pleasure the soul derives its tastes from the very place where Nature has collected signs of abominable disgrace.

WE saw in Chapter 7 that, by the 1680s, publicists like Canon Maucroix and rival erotica like *The Parliament of Women* and *Venus in the Cloister* had established Chorier's Latin text as the best of books and the worst of books. *Aloisia Sigea* makes the libertine canon *citable*, and establishes the possibility of a modern erotic classic. Later reception-history assigns the *Satyra Sotadica* a paradoxical position, defining the upper and the lower limit of possibility, representing Art in a realm largely defined as Nature. Whereas the publisher of *L'Escole* could defend it as 'a bit free but still all natural', Chorier's dialogue was prosecuted as 'a pernicious, wicked, scandalous, vicious, and illicit book',[1] and yet at the same time distinguished as the supreme artistic expression of eroticism, the touchstone of stylistic elegance. As we have just seen in Chapter 7, the rigged discussion in *Vénus* dramatizes both these poles, as Agnès's readerly enthusiasm prevails over Angélique's initial condemnation. *Aloisia*, still ostensibly received as a female-authored work, comes to represent

---

[1] Pia, 181; Roger Thompson, 'Two Early Editions of Restoration Erotica', *Library*, 32 (1977), 47.

both the extreme of fantastic perversion and the definitive textbook of sexuality, the standard source of enlightenment: for Casanova (as I showed in my Introduction) the whole of 'theory' can be discovered here; for Diderot, *Aloysia* formed the penultimate stage in the 'self-perfecting' of the aristocratic male, and even that final stage—becoming an *honnête homme* by an affair with an experienced woman, as Robertus does with Octavia—is already envisaged within the mistress-text.

It seemed that a 'Genius' had emerged who could transform the most shamefully pornographic subjects, a modern Petronius who could sanction a new kind of writer, brilliant yet obscene. *Obscenité*, we learn from Molière's *Critique de L'École des femmes*, was a brand-new concept in the seventeenth century, associated as much with *précieuse* innovation as with libertine transgression. Then as now it provoked theoretical speculation on language and sexuality, representation and concealment. Defenders and attackers of 'obscenity' alike assumed that they were witnessing a powerful fusion of erotic explicitness and literary expressivity. The interaction of sexual practice and literary theory often took a comic form, as in the sonnet-sequence that Antonio Malatesti presented to Milton: the peasant-poet can 'heighen his style' because Tina causes his phallic *stilo* to rise.[2] But it goes beyond a joke, in the elaborate systems of Pallavicino's *Retorica delle puttane* and in the exponential, encyclopedic dialogues of *Aloisia Sigea*. As I show in the Epilogue below, this synthesis continued to reverberate in eighteenth-century debates over literary decorum and in the nineteenth-century aesthetic movement: Baudelaire cites from 'Meursius' in his proposal for a museum of erotic art 'sanctified by genius', and translates Tullia and Octavia into the most dissolute characters of *Les Fleurs du mal*; Huysmans enshrines Aloisia Sigea in the library of the ultimate connoisseur, the duc Des Esseintes.

This closing chapter returns to the most prominent example of the lubricious-sublime author in the later seventeenth century, the Earl of Rochester. We have already examined Rochester's own relation to Chorier and the attempt to link him during his lifetime to *Aloisia Sigea* and *Sodom*, the poles of abjection and sublimity in erotic writing (Chapter 6 above). To conclude, I explore in detail two episodes in his canonization, from the decade after his death in 1680. Here we pass from the clandestine or 'pornographic' substratum to the mainstream of literary culture. The first section establishes the critical ambience of the later seventeenth century, which adopts the aphrodisiac as a measure of literary quality and promotes an alternative classic tradition dominated by Petronius, Chorier, and Rochester. Section 2 analyses Robert Wolseley's articulate preface to Rochester's posthumous and much-acclaimed play *Valentinian* (1685). As my first epigraph shows, Wolseley fully embraced the libertine 'obscenity' of his friend's poetry, vindicating it by evoking a concept of transformative 'genius' that anticipates Baudelaire's and Flaubert's by 160 years. Wolseley turns sexual arousal into a theoretical model of literary excellence, and explicitly invites the critic to use *L'Escole des filles* and *Aloisia Sigea* as

---

[2] *La Tina: Equivoci rusticali in cinquanta sonetti*, ed. Giovanni Lami (n.d. [*c*.1860]), 44 ('Sopra l'alzar lo stile').

touchstones—the most prominent allusion to the libertine classics in the medium of sanctioned print.

Section 3 switches genders to explore the figure of Rochester, and the theory of erotic poetics, in Aphra Behn. Behn does not allude directly to the libertine canon— apart from her impudent translation of Cantenac's poem on impotence—but the best-documented library of erotic classics was owned by her closest friend, John Hoyle, and she engages conceptually with all the issues it raises. Her emotionally intense poems on the death of Rochester proclaim a new passion-centred conception of literary value and prepare the way for Wolseley's warm, homoerotic tribute to his late friend. The speakers of Behn's odes, and the oversexed protagonists of her novel *Love-Letters between a Nobleman and his Sister*, embrace in all seriousness the 'sublimity' and 'nobility' that Pallavicino had half-ironically imagined as the ultimate achievement of the courtesan expert in perversity (my second epigraph). Behn and her fellow-poet Anne Wharton, Rochester's close relative, define a form of female desire compatible with elevation, breaking out of the tradition of 'pornographic' debasement. Wolseley, like other male followers of Rochester, conceives literary sublimity in phallocentric terms, which Behn attempts to replace with an equally sexualized poetics based on arousal and susceptibility rather than performative 'Vigour'. She promotes the ineffable, the 'infinite', the dissolution of narrow confines and 'rules' in favour of a state of excited exaltation that can be felt but not expressed. Behn's 'strange something more' (I show in a final section) completes the revaluation of women's arousal and women's creativity initiated—or at least simulated— in *L'Escole*'s Susanne and Chorier's Tullia. Molière had slyly denigrated female literary response by equating it with the *je ne sais quoi* of prurience; Behn fully accepts this liaison but reverses the consequences, turning disparagement into celebration and amorous sensibility into 'genius'.

1. GENIUS AND NAUSEA

As my first epigraph shows, the core libertine curriculum that culminates in *Aloisia Sigea* served in England as the mapping-system to place the meteoric new poet Rochester, who combined art and indecency at the highest level. No longer confined to the clandestine or scandalous contexts studied so far, published criticism of Rochester frequently evokes Chorier as a reference point for evaluating the Earl's disorientingly 'Original' achievement, and for exploring the issues raised by a self-consciously obscene art. The reputations of Rochester and Chorier twine together whenever critics want to evoke the *ne plus ultra*, the isolated peaks of erotic discourse that transcend its ignominy. In Rochester's own lifetime (as we saw in Chapter 6) the poet John Oldham equates 'our great witty bawdy Peer' and 'that fam'd Spanish Whore' at the 'Heroick' end of the spectrum; the twentieth-century satirist, parodying some exquisitely decadent English disciple of Des Esseintes, specifies that his guest bedroom contains 'the *Elegancies of Meursius* (Rochester's copy)'.[3]

---

[3] Cyril Connolly (taking off Aldous Huxley) in *Parodies: An Anthology from Chaucer to Beerbohm and After*, ed. Dwight Macdonald (1961), 231.

Later seventeenth-century embodiments of this bibliophilia bring into the public sphere metacritical questions that had already been raised within the clandestine texts that they cite. Is bodily response a legitimate effect of literature? Can high stylistic sophistication lift and transform abject material? Is representation a compensation or an enrichment of experience?

These issues are vividly raised in an anonymous essay reprinted in several editions of Rochester, purporting to be a private letter from the seigneur de Saint-Évremond to the duchesse de Mazarin—old *roués* exiled from the French court who ended their lives in London. This simulation of the gallant and worldly reader praises the 'peculiar Beauties' of Rochester's libertine pieces even though they are 'too obscene for the Ladies' Eyes, . . . indeed too dangerous to peruse'. Luckily the critic himself has braved this perilous combination of beauty and obscenity, and now reconstructs the effect for the very 'Ladies' whose eyes were supposed to be protected. Rochester 'alarms the Fancy, and rouzes the Blood and Appetite more than all the Medicaments of *Cleopatra*'. A directly physical aphrodisiac response, accompanied by an 'alarming' assault on the imagination, is here offered as evidence of the highest literary quality. Obscenity and physical provocation need not be hostile to art, but they require unusual creative energy; in 'a Genius less powerful' than Rochester, erotic subject matter would have been 'nauseous' rather than arousing. Only three authors have ever managed to combine explicit sexual discourse with sufficient expressive 'Beauty' and imaginative 'Strength' to transcend or set aside morality, giving 'a Sort of Merit to Lewdness'. Rochester belongs with 'two Books in *Latin* that seem to be wrote with my Lord's Spirit, the Satyr of *Petronius Arbiter*, and *Meurcius* a Modern'.[4] Among contemporaries, then, Chorier and Rochester stand alone as definitive exemplars of the art of arousal. Even the cross-reference to the 'Medicaments of *Cleopatra*' derives from Chorier, since Cleopatra's prescriptions to provoke and cool desire were included in all editions of 'Meursius'.[5]

The pseudo-Saint-Évremond here distils, for public consumption, several generations of libertine speculation on the limits of literary decorum. When he ascribes 'peculiar Beauties' to his 'looser' writing, he recalls not only Rochester's own defence of scurrilous lies in his conversation with Burnet—'Ornaments that could not be spared without spoiling the beauty of the *Poem*' (*RCH* 54)—but Father Garasse on those *libertins* who identify 'Extravagances' with 'la beauté des Esprits' (fo. e1). And by frankly admitting the aphrodisiac 'danger' he echoes the self-promotion of the erotic text itself. The critic's testimony of arousal matches the 'Bulle Orthodoxe' in *L'Escole des filles* that orders both male and female readers to *spermatizer*, or those exemplary scenes in *L'Escole* and '*Meurcius*' where one speaker 'discharges' in direct response to the other's vivid description (Ch. 3, sect. 2, Ch. 4, sect. 2 above).

By casting this physiological provocation in the respectable aesthetic language of *spirit*, *power*, and *genius*, 'St Evremont' builds a conceptual bridge to the higher forms of emotional persuasion and passionate rapture defined by rhetorically

---

[4] 'Memoirs of the Life of . . . Rochester', in *The Miscellaneous Works of the Right Hon. the Late Earls of Rochester and Roscommon* (1707), fos. 36ᵛ–7; parts of this essay are included in *RCH* (see Abbreviations above) 184–5.

[5] See Ch. 1 n. 88 above.

inflected poetics, just as Aretino had done when he defended his lascivious sonnets, inspired by 'the same *spirit* that moved Giulio Romano' to create his images of spectacular copulation (my emphasis). Aretino also established arousal as an artistic criterion, literally inviting his reader to 'touch himself in the codpiece' to prove the effectiveness of what he has seen and read; in his role as art adviser to the courts of Europe he made this erotic response acceptable, encouraging patrons and followers to appreciate the 'lustful thoughts' and 'stirring of the blood' provoked by artists like Titian.[6] The equation of erection and 'elevated style' might be comic in the mouth of a Tuscan peasant, but it could be taken more seriously. Before 'St Evremont', *La retorica delle puttane* had thoroughly explored the analogies of sexual arousal and rhetorical persuasion, and Pallavicino had identified his own talent as 'lascivious genius' (Ch. 2, sect. 1 above). In the Latin ascribed to 'Meurcius' Chorier had identified erotic susceptibility with literary invention and had used the phrase 'indulgere genio' for the intercourse of aristocratic lesbians (*Satyra*, VII. 286). And Oldham makes the same assumptions in his unpublished thoughts on the same configuration that preoccupied 'St Evremont'—Chorier, Petronius, Rochester, and (his own?) failed attempts to imitate their peculiar beauties.

Like the later critic of Rochester, Oldham sets up a polarity between the 'nauseous Rhymes' of *Sodom* and the potent achievement of Petronius, Aretino, and Aloisia Sigea; if the aspiring libertine author had mustered

> the Pow'r as well as bold Design
> To outdo Nero's Pimp and Aretine
> Or that fam'd Spanish Whore

he would have achieved something 'Heroick', but his present efforts reveal him as flaccid in his penis as his pen (Ch. 6, sect. 2 above). In a mirror-image of this speculation, 'St Evremont' avers that 'what would have render'd [Rochester's obscenities] nauseous, if they had been written by a Genius less powerful, in him alarms the Fancy and rouzes the Blood'. Behind both lies Chorier's revelation that *Veneris nausea* lurks in the heart of arousal itself, the inseparable double of extreme desire: two sisters appear symmetrically after their wedding night, one 'nauseated' unto death and the other awakened to infinite libidinous pleasure; after her four-man orgy Tullia herself succumbs to 'the nausea of Venus', which prompts her to create still more 'figures' that leave the body behind, generated by her 'cogitatio exsultabanda et intemperans', her 'exultant and disordering intellect' (VI. 214–15, VII. 235).

The figure of Petronius runs through all these displays of eroto-critical expertise. Milton's *Areopagitica* (like the 'St Evremont' essay) singles out Petronius as the one ancient who might be coupled with the salient example of illustrious obscenity in modern literature; these aristocrats of depravity must be considered essential reading because they produce, not commonplace bawdy, but 'the choisest delights and

---

[6] *Lettere*, ed. Francesco Erspamer (Parma, 1995–   ), i. 655, 39, *Modi* sonnets, Epilogo 1 (attribution questionable), and cf. Lodovico Dolce, letter to Alessandro Contarini, in Mark Roskill, *Dolce's 'Aretino' and Venetian Art Theory of the Cinquecento* (New York, 1968), 216.

criticisms of sin'—voluptuarism selected and heightened by critical intellect, as in Rochester's own theory that 'Reason' should intensify the senses and 'keep them more in vigour', or the husbandly 'Critick' of pleasure in the English adaptation of Chorier, or Elisabeth Rowe's 'philosophick libertine', who 'made critical reflections on every enjoyment'.[7] Chorier himself invites comparison with his Roman ancestor Petronius, by direct citation within the text, by titles such as *Satyra* and *Tribadicon* that echo the *Satyricon*, and by the general air of worldly, stylish appreciation of what conventional judgement brands as perverse. When the Council of Trent excuses ancient erotica from the Counter-Reformation ban on lewd books because of their 'elegancies' (Ch. 1 n. 84), or when publishers of 'Aloisia Sigea' conceal her behind the title *Elegantiae*, Petronius the 'Arbiter Elegantiarum' is not far away. Pairing Petronius and Chorier, as a double-barrelled, ancient-modern name to quash all moral objection, continued into the eighteenth century: Ralph Griffiths asserted in his review of Fanny Hill's *Memoirs* (which he had himself published) that they 'must be allowed to be the best executed and the most picturesque of any work of the kind, not excepting that of *Petronius*, and the celebrated Dialogues of Meursius'.[8]

The core of the pseudo-Saint-Évremond defence is the promotion of Petronian elegance over moral criteria of decorum, summed up in the paradoxical assertion that 'the Beauty of the Expression, and the Strength of the Spirit and Fancy, have given a Sort of Merit to Lewdness'. This bracing oxymoron sums up a rhetorical tactic often employed when promoting the aesthetic over the pornographic, inventing figures in which morality and obscenity break their polar opposition and recombine in new ways. 'Meritorious lewdness' recalls Pallavicino's *lascivio genio*, the paradoxes of Honour in *L'Escole des filles* and *The Country-Wife*, Chorier's *ingeniosa procacitas* or 'brilliant impudence', Rochester's 'Mannerly Obscene', or the fictional educator's euphemism for the lesbianism rampant in English boarding schools: 'Perfection in sinning'.[9] The sober concept of 'Merit' jars against the despicable associations of 'Lewdness', forcing us to separate the criteria that govern civil behaviour and literary expression; as Pepys explains when he conceals (and preserves) his copy of Rochester's poems in a separate drawer, the dead poet 'is past writing any more so bad in one sense', but 'I despair of any man surviving him to write so good in another'.[10] When a poet-critic like Oldham takes up this oxymoron, the plain language of 'merit' and 'goodness' mutates into fanciful panegyric—'glorious infamy', 'Heroick' obscenity, 'our great witty bawdy Peer' (and compare the 'magnificently great' perversions of *Sodom and Gomorah*). Rochester's comment on promiscuous *behaviour*—'There's something gen'rous in meer Lust'—is converted by the clerkly Oldham into a goal for *writing*: ''Tis something to be great in Wickedness.'

'St Evremont's' certificate of arousal prompts us to consider important questions

---

[7] Ch. 1, sect. 2 (Milton, *CPW* ii. 518) Ch. 6 n. 13, Ch. 7, sect. 3, Introd. n. 68 above.

[8] *Monthly Review* (Mar. 1750), 431 (for the authorship of this review, see Foxon, 57 n. 5).

[9] Delariviere Manley, cited Ch. 7 n. 88 above, and cf. *RP* 117, Ch. 5 nn. 63–4, Rochester, 72.

[10] Letter of 2 Nov. 1680, in *Letters and the Second Diary*, ed. R. G. Howarth (1933), 105. The concealed object is presumably Pepys Library 810 in Magdalene College, Cambridge, an exemplar of the 'Antwerp' *Poems* (1680) bound with additional MS verse.

about the proper response to literature and the interrelation of aesthetics and sexuality. Like other eulogies of great-spirited lewdness, it tends to collapse the distinction between sexual action and sexual representation, provided they are mediated by art. Francis Bacon disapproved of courtesans because they turn sin into art (*peccatum in artem conversum est*),[11] but that is precisely what the libertine counter-culture claimed to value. Chorier's preface promises the reader that Aloisia Sigea will 'salt' her exposé of wickedness with 'arte et procacitate ingeniosa' (3), combining *procacitas* (nymphomaniac 'lewdness' or 'impudence'), 'art' (the same *ars et ratio* that Tullia requires of her pupils in bed), and *ingenium* or wit—the same 'fervent exertion of the mind' that lifts women above the abject. To combine Chorier's and Pallavicino's terms, 'brilliant lewdness' becomes 'lascivious genius' through 'art'.

As we have seen, however, the negative connotations of 'Art' evoke compensatory artifice, prosthesis, crutches for an exhausted libido. Readers of this Rochester edition might remember the real Saint-Évremond as 'a little old man in a black coif, carried along Pall Mall' to visit his beloved Duchess, and this essayist probably hints at personal reasons for his expertise in the medicaments of Cleopatra; the pseudonymous critic is not only an expert in Rochester and his literary peers, but an exemplification of Rochester's 'Ancient Person' whose 'frozen' members require 'all that Art can add to Love' (30). At the threshold of French libertine literature, the opening poem of *Le Cabinet satyrique* particularly addresses readers who 'only have something flaccid in their breeches', recommending this book as the best way to 'get back the taste'—just as 'St Evremont' equates Rochester (and Chorier) with dangerously effective aphrodisiac medicines.[12] The combined eulogy and condemnation of Chorier in *Venus in the Cloister*, which anticipates the ideas and phrases of this essay on Rochester, likewise associates artistic representation with impotence; Angélique denounces the *Satyra* for the stylistic 'purity' and 'easy Eloquence' that make the text 'infinitely dangerous', arousing 'those that are the least susceptible', while Agnès celebrates its ability to cure the 'satiated and disgusted mind', to 'revive' even 'that Lust which is no longer able!' (155–6, 157). We have seen in Chapter 5 how easily Wycherley's Horner can turn his connoisseurship of books and other 'Effigies' into prima facie evidence for his impotence, and Restoration literature abounds with tales of men 'bawdy only in pictures'. The Earl of Mulgrave, Rochester's detested rival for the title of great bawdy witty peer, had equated language itself with impotence; in a pornographic idyll ironically titled *The Perfect Enjoyment*, Mulgrave laments the moment when

> alas! for want of further force
> From action we are fallen into discourse.[13]

To reverse the sense of 'St Evremont's' key word, advertising a work's aphrodisiac power is itself 'dangerous', since it draws attention to the fatal equation of art and incapacity, the inverse relation of 'action' and 'discourse'.

---

[11] *New Atlantis*, Ch. 2 n. 53 above.

[12] Cited in Yves Citton, *Impuissances* (Paris, 1994), 80 n. 2; for a Victorian description of Saint-Évremond in the 1690s, see Ruth Perry, *The Celebrated Mary Astell: An Early English Feminist* (1986), 152–3.

[13] Humphrey Prideaux cited in Foxon, 7; John Sheffield, Earl of Mulgrave, 'The Appointment' (cited Ch. 6 n. 73 above).

2. 'LET HIM READ *ALOISIA SIGEA* . . .': ROBERT WOLSELEY'S DEFENCE OF ROCHESTER

The most prominent defence of Rochester's libertinism within the paradigm set by *L'Escole* and Chorier, and the primary source of later introductions like the 'St Evremont', is the preface that Robert Wolseley wrote for the Earl's posthumous, much-publicized, and often-reprinted revision of Fletcher's tragedy *Valentinian* (1685). Even the title page advertises this 'Preface by One of his Friends', and Wolseley frequently evokes that personal connection as he vindicates the memory of the *libertin maudit* five years after his death. Rochester's bachelor 'Friend' (who presents himself more like a lover) came from a higher social class than Oldham, but their joint experience as intimates and protégés might explain the similarity between their critiques of good and bad obscenity. Oldham had occasionally conflated moral and aesthetic criteria ('What Honour is't how well soe're thou write?') but retained some sense of the alternative possibility, achieving 'Heroick' status by writing 'well' on a bad subject; Wolseley follows this line to its conclusion, radically separating artistic from social-ethical criteria and making Rochester the fulfilment of this libertine promise, alongside 'Aloisia Sigea' and 'Petronius Arbiter'.[14] Oldham had likewise contrasted the heroic libertine author with the 'Weak feeble strainer at meer Ribaldry' who 'covets to be lewd, but wants the Might', and we shall see that Wolseley attacks Rochester's enemy Mulgrave in exactly the same terms.

A large proportion of Wolseley's spirited preface is devoted to refuting Mulgrave's disparagement of Rochester in the anonymous *Essay on Poetry*, a refutation that culminates with the triumphant citation of *Aloisia Sigea* as the test or 'Proof' that the malignant Critick fails. Mulgrave had argued (with the help of Dryden) that 'obscene words' are 'too gross to move desire', that Rochester's 'barefac'd' expression defeated his aphrodisiac intention and 'pall'd the appetite he meant to raise'. Ironically, the same nobleman had suggested in his erotic poetry that *all* linguistic expression serves as a feeble substitute for physical 'appetite' ('alas! for want of further force | From action we are fallen into discourse'). Wolseley exorcizes this spectre of intrinsic impotence by transferring it to Mulgrave himself, while exalting Chorier and Rochester as true embodiments of 'the Genius and Art of the Writer' (158).

Even before he turns to the specific attack on Mulgrave, Wolseley angles his appreciation of Rochester towards the issues of erotic poetics. Proving him 'the Delight and the Wonder of Men, the Love and Dotage of Women', Wolseley fabricates a kind of Ganymede, a hermaphroditic conflation of conventionally female attributes ('the uncommon Graces of his Fashion . . . the becoming gentleness, the bewitching softness of his Civility') with a hyperphallic power to penetrate that recalls the all-dissolving thunderbolt in *The Imperfect Enjoyment*. Rochester's pen was as 'pricking' as a sword and as 'weighty' as the club of Hercules—classic figures for the phallus used *ad nauseam* in Chorier—and its well-directed thrusts 'did the World as much good . . . as he hurt himself by a wrong pursuit of Pleasure' (141); the

---

[14] *RCH* 151, 155 (all subsequent citations of Wolseley's essay will give the page of *RCH*); for Oldham see Ch. 6, sect. 2 above, and for Wolseley's violent bachelor life see *DNB*, 'Wolseley, Sir Charles (1630?–1714)'.

parallel could hardly be more explicit. His satire never 'stabs into the Wounds of fallen Virtue', but equally never 'prostitutes his Sence' or daubs him with cosmetics. For those who conversed with him 'Enjoyment did but increase Appetite', as they received that Wit 'whose Edge cou'd ease by cutting, and whose Point cou'd tickle while it prob'd'.[15]

Wolseley testifies to his late friend's potency by assuming the role of mistress or catamite, perhaps taking his cue from the images of classical pederasty and eunuch-love that Rochester had added to the original play.[16] Simulating sexual passivity is a surprisingly common reaction to the erotic classic, as we have seen: Father Garasse excuses rude authors like Martial or Petronius whose 'beautiful inventions' let them 'slip more sweetly' into the mind, *glisser doucement à faveur de leurs belles inventions* (782 and cf. 1016); the narrator of Cantenac's impotence-poem, as we saw in Chapter 6, feels '*Loves dart*' gliding into his heart 'with slippery sweetness'. Other eulogists of Rochester went even further, echoing the phallic bravado of *The Imperfect Enjoyment* with embarrassing fidelity: 'Thro all he pierc'd . . . Into a Breast how nimbly would he glide, | And through and through the heart tryumphant ride!'[17] But in Wolseley's account the recipient of Wit is also the one who actively *enjoys* Rochester, over and over, without the usual male loss of 'appetite'. This vivid portrait of the author as polymorphous seducer—later explicitly defined as 'a Man whose Person I was ever naturally inclin'd to love'—prepares us for the literary-critical turn in the essay; Rochester's poetry in fact 'has every where a Tincture of that unaccountable Charm in his Fashion and Conversation . . . that drew the Eyes and won the Hearts of all who came near him' (159, 143).

This eroticization of the author's 'Person' is reinforced by a sensuous vocabulary of literary connoisseurship, often drawn from the fine arts. Wolseley hovers on the edge of *double entendre*, choosing words sometimes identical to the moral critique he claims to render irrelevant. At the very beginning he disarms criticism of Rochester's unfinished draft revision by comparing it to 'the loosest Negligence of a great Genius' or 'the rudest Drawings of famous Hands', even if it might lack the 'Grace-strokes and finishing Touches' of his extant writing (137–8); Pallavicino, as we have seen, had already brought out the erotics of 'touch', particularly when instructing the courtesan to perform a toccata with every organ of her body (Ch. 2, sect. 1 above). For Wolseley, Rochester's poetry may lack the density and 'Force' of Dorset's but surpasses it in the 'Grace' and 'delicacy' of 'Touches that are more affecting'; to analyse its 'thousand irresistible Beauties' would be as redundant as 'to describe to a Lover the Lines and Features of his Mistress's Face', since 'every Body is so well acquainted with it, by the effect it has had upon 'em' (142–3). It is the reader who now occupies the masculine position, responding to Rochester's charm as an 'effect' at once ineffable and corporeal, a discipline born in the blood and felt by

---

[15] 139; Wolseley's amorous-surgical image influenced Dryden's 1693 tr. of Persius, I. 116–17 (Horace could 'tickle, while he gently prob'd the Wound', *Works*, iv. 275).

[16] Loc. cit. Ch. 2 n. 70 above.

[17] Author unknown, 'An Elegy on Ossory, Rochester, and Bedlow', ed. Paul Hammond, *Restoration*, 17 (1993), 86 (not in *RCH*).

'every Body'. 'Spirit' and 'liveliness', the crucial qualities that distinguish the Genius from the plodder, likewise become a quasi-biological infusion that 'warms and animates every Part', a 'plastick Heat' and 'vivifying Power' that can 'beautifie the vilest Dirt' (143, 148); though Wolseley proves his point here by citing the 'masterly Strokes' in Virgil's *Georgics*, we recall Tullia's 'fervent *conatus*' of the libertine mind, which transforms women from 'mud' and excrement. (The sexual implications of Wolseley's phrase can be gauged from the moralist's complaint that 'our *Modern Plays*' show 'Prophaneness, Irreligion, and Unlawful Love made the masterly Stroaks of the *fine Gentleman*'.[18]) 'True Genius', which 'will enter into the hardest and dryest thing' to 'infuse' it with beauty (148), sounds less like Rochester's Dart of Love than Rocco's pedagogic phallus, infusing brilliance with its liquid warmth.

The erotics of literary 'Genius' become even more blatant when Wolseley defines the failed writer and the incompetent critic. Rochester's supporters instinctively *feel* his tickling warmth, and therefore his enemies ('Criticks' in the negative rather than the voluptuary sense) can only be 'Men who have got the *Form* of Poetry without the *Power*, . . . Men who like old Lovers are curst with a strong Inclination and weak Abilities', whose unhappy efforts 'do but betray the Impotence of their Wit' (143–4). This comic portrait of the impotent poet/critic/lover stands at the threshold of the personal assault on Mulgrave, thus forming the exact counterpart to the passage that closes it (my first epigraph, where Wolseley stages something like a congress-trial of his adversary's erotic-poetic capacity by having him perform on *L'Escole des filles* or *Aloisia Sigea*. Mulgrave is here hoist with his own petard. His attack on Rochester's 'barefaced bawdry' and 'nauseous Songs', which 'pall'd the appetite he meant to raise', assumes precisely the reverse of the twentieth-century distinction between art and pornography; literature should play a provocative and seductive role (conveying 'warm thoughts of the transporting joy'), but Rochester *fails* to move desire, lacking the crucial element of 'Wit' (*RCH* 42–3).

Mulgrave turns on Rochester the insult that Oldham heaped on the 'Impotent' *Sodom*-author, and Wolseley turns it back on Mulgrave tenfold; applying the phallic criterion to the Critick as well as the poet, he pretends to interpret the attack on words 'too gross to move desire' as a confession. This 'barefaced' genitalization of wit throws its aura over the entire discourse. The common vocabulary of aesthetic disapproval ('flat', 'cold', 'dead', 'liveless', and above all 'dull') inevitably suggests penile collapse, in Wolseley's essay as in Oldham's abusive poems against himself, while conversely 'power' and 'force' (Mulgrave's own word for sexual ability) cannot be separated from potency. The various meanings of Dullness—Wolseley's favourite insult, as it was Rochester's and would be Pope's—struggle to stay ahead of the 'obscene' meaning that threatens to engulf them. Lack of taste, lack of wit, lack of energy, lack of talent, all appear as symptoms of the fundamental sexlessness that becomes explicit in the Chorier citation: 'if the obscene Words and Descriptions he

---

[18] Josiah Woodward, *Some Thoughts Concerning the Stage, in a Letter to a Lady* (1704), 5. Though the term *genius* often means little more than character or disposition, Wolseley clearly talks of 'True Genius' in the full-blown Romantic sense, and his phrase 'poetical Daemonianism' is practically Shelleyan (148).

will meet with there do not raise his Appetite, the World will be apt to conclude it, not only very dull, but absolutely dead; and as bad as his Poetry is, his Reader will be better entertain'd than his Mistress' (158). Literary prowess has been wholly assimilated to sex, but a kind of sex that already resembles a public performance (or a critical debate in print)—sex on parade, visible to 'the World'.

The arousal-model of literary endeavour thus runs throughout Wolseley's essay—as it does through other writings like his gallant address to Rochester's niece Anne Wharton. (Wolseley praises the erotic-poetic 'Softness' and 'Power' of her complimentary verse, even calling it an aphrodisiac or 'strong Philtre'.[19]) This poses several theoretical problems when he launches his main attack on Mulgrave's ideas. Wolseley assaults his enemy's position from several directions: sometimes he narrows the target material by asserting that many of Rochester's obscene poems intended to satirize rather than stimulate sexual 'Appetite' (157); sometimes he argues that supreme art transcends its subject matter and gains more glory the more its raw material is trivial or abject. But asexual or anti-sexual aesthetics could not defend Rochester against accusations of sexual failure and lack of wit—a double charge that is really one in Wolseley's mind. To take the high critical ground without contradicting his seductive account of Rochester's person and poetry, Wolseley has to negate and exalt 'obscene' sexuality at the same time, somehow assigning it the lowest and the highest place in the hierarchy of literary values.

One step in Wolseley's theoretical argument has attracted most attention because it seems to anticipate a post-rhetorical, proto-Kantian conception of disinterested and autonomous art. 'All depends upon the Genius and Art of the Writer.' Poetic value has nothing whatever to do with the intrinsic value of the subject matter, and consists only in the 'manner of treating': connoisseurs pay vast sums for pictures of 'Lazars' and tortured flesh; the *Georgics* infuse true genius into 'unlovely' things like 'the Working of Ants' or 'the Lust of Horses and Boars' (148–50). Artistic power is manifested by a kind of alchemy or 'poetical Daemonianism' that transfigures the material—indeed it appears all the more brilliantly 'the baser, the emptier, the obscurer, the fouler, and the less susceptible of Ornament the Subject appears to be' (148). This certainly anticipates Baudelaire's assertion that 'genius' cleanses and transfigures what would otherwise be 'revolting obscenity' (a doctrine inspired by Chorier himself, as we shall see in the Epilogue), or Flaubert's famous dictum that 'everything in art depends on execution: the story of a louse can be as beautiful as the story of Alexander.'[20] But it should be interpreted as a distillation from the seventeenth-century libertine dialogue rather than a glimmering of modernity.

In the very act of setting aside the sexual element, paradoxically, Wolseley locates himself in the core of libertine theory. In his proof-text *Aloisia Sigea*, for example, Tullia is particularly impressed (and excited) by Octavia's narrative of Robertus,

---

[19] In *The Surviving Works of Anne Wharton*, ed. G[ermaine] Greer and S[usan] Hastings (Stump Cross, 1997), 298–9.

[20] Cited in Julian Barnes, *Flaubert's Parrot* (1984), 136; for an earlier argument that decorum depends not on the content but on the 'manière de conter', cf. Anne Birberick, *Reading Undercover: Audience and Authority in Jean de La Fontaine* (1998), esp. 87.

which proves her a supreme *artifex* because she can generate such vast pleasure from an object in itself so trifling. In *L'Academie des dames* Octavie pays a similar tribute to Tullie's description of being sodomized, truly 'spiritual' because it 'hides the deformity' of the subject; for Wolseley true Wit or Genius, which 'infuses dignity and breathes beauty' into the 'empty, obscure, and foul', at the same time 'can hide all the natural deformities', 'supply all the wants with his own plenty', and create 'Roses out of Dunghils'.[21] In the other book that Wolseley cites as a test case, Claude Le Petit locates the 'glory' of *L'Escole des filles* in its prose style, which 'fucks' the reader right in the eyes ('ce qui te rendra pour jamais glorieux, | C'est que . . . Ta prose nous fout par les yeux,' Ch. 3, sect. 2 above). Before that, Pallavicino had claimed for his own *Retorica delle puttane* the 'glorious' status of the artist who creates an admirable painting of a 'deformed' and ugly subject; as in Wolseley (and Flaubert), everything depends on the 'operazione perfettamente eseguita', the 'perfect execution'. Pallavicino's preface maintains a certain detachment between the writer's glory and the prostitute's abjection, but in the body of the text sexual acts themselves become 'sublime' artefacts, proving that 'i eccessi medesimi di lascivia sono contrasegni di gloria': 'even the excesses of lasciviousness are signs of glory' (122). Within a few years this extraordinary idea had passed into Cartesian erotics and thence into high culture. Descartes himself conceived the 'most excessive' desire as a vehicle of perfection, and the *Discours sur les passions de l'amour* sometimes attributed to Pascal declares that this 'excess' render erotic passion 'beautiful': 'la passion ne peut pas être belle sans cet excès.'[22]

Just as the Wolselean artist 'infuses dignity and breathes beauty' into a dark, filthy emptiness (reminding us of Rocco as well as Pallavicino), so the Ganymedic art of the courtesan in *La retorica delle puttane* endows copulation with *nobiltà*, grandeur, elevation. Pallavicino reconfigures the aesthetic argument to propose, not the annulment of sex, but its intensification: the move from abomination to art—explicitly called 'sublime', as my second epigraph reminds us—takes place within the realm of bodily pleasure, as the anus is transformed into the drinking cup of the gods (6, 57, 122–3, and cf. Ch. 2, sect. 1 above). The English translator shrinks back from the 'Italian' rectal element but expands upon the 'glory' passage in words that exactly anticipate Wolseley's. Inspired by the venereal sharpness that he contracts from the courtesan herself, the artist can 'infuse such a lively, brisk and vigorous Spirit into the mass of matter, as may in all points correspond to the vivacity of the Ladies Soul'. Like Wolseley's favourite word *lively*, briskness and vigour inevitably denote sexual energy in Restoration English, and in this context the imagery of alchemical infusion also takes on an erotic aura. Wolseley compares true genius to the philosopher's stone (148), but *The Whores Rhetorick* had already claimed this vivifying and transmuting power for the pornographer: 'a judicious writer, like an expert

---

[21] *RCH* 148; cf. pp. 218–19 above and *Academie*, i. 222 ('la description que tu viens de faire de ces dernieres attaques, m'a infiniment plû, et le tour que tu as donné a l'histoire pour en cacher la deformité, m'a semblé fort spirituel').

[22] Descartes, *Les Passions de l'âme* (1648), ed, Geneviève Rodis-Lewis (Paris, 1966), art. 139 (Ch. 1 n. 122 above); Blaise Pascal, *Œuvres complètes*, ed. Jacques Chevalier, Bibliothèque de la Pléiade (Paris, 1954), 545.

Chymist, will so order the most abject, the most indisposed matter, as to extract thence both pleasure and advantage' (fo. A8).

This tradition of libertine aesthetics, with its radical separation of sexual-energetic and moral criteria, allows Wolseley to sidestep the attack on Rochester's obscenity and to coin a new definition of poetic 'Wit', theoretically removed from conventional questions of virtue and value. Trenchantly insisting that 'Decency is one thing, and Poetry and Painting, or the skill of Drawing and Describing, is another', he concedes that Rochester's effusions can be branded 'libertine, unjust, ungrateful, and every way immoral', but declares such questions entirely irrelevant to literary quality. This cleavage of the moral and the aesthetic resonates with Pepys's private opinion that Rochester was the worst writer in one sense and the best in another—a dichotomy that will echo in 'St Evremont' praising Rochester's 'Merit in Lewdness', in Defoe appreciating his 'brightness of Fancy' or the 'Life' and 'Beauty' of criminality in *Moll Flanders*, and eventually in the title of *Les Fleurs du mal*. To be 'good' in the aesthetic sense, the artist must achieve 'a true and lively expression of Nature'. Defining 'Nature' in a way that removes any normative or judgemental implication, Wolseley reinterprets Horace's strictures against inventing incongruous and monstrous figures as a licence to depict anything that actually might exist, indeed an obligation to exert 'power' and 'daring' in doing so ('Quidlibet audendi semper fuit aequa potestas').[23] The emphasis in Wolseley's definition falls on the persuasive-seductive effect, on what 'gains' the mind and the body, rather than on imitation *per se*: '*true* this expression of Nature must be that it may gain our Reason, and *lively* that it may affect our Passions' (152). He then ingeniously blends this vitalistic-affective theory with Dryden's definition of True Wit as '*a Propriety of Thoughts and Words—Or Thoughts and Words elegantly adapted to the Subject*' (153–4). Propriety equals truth and elegance equals liveliness. Since the key term *lively*—the opposite of *dull*—has been so thoroughly imbued with erotic asociation, we see here another link to the 'elegance' of Petronius and Meursius.

Separating literary 'Propriety' and 'elegance' from social 'Decency' allows Wolseley a further strengthening concession, moreover. He freely admits that Rochester's loose poems might 'offend Age and corrupt Youth' (while dismissing the issue as irrelevant) but then insinuates their acceptability, by characterizing them as effusions of youthful energy appropriate for that season of life ('carry'd away with the precipitancy of that *Liber spiritus*, as *Petronius* calls it'), by contrasting these sallies with the gross obscenity of street hooligans and bullies, and by insisting that Rochester kept his writings within a closed circle of élite males (like the critic himself) who could enjoy 'a skilful Imitation of any thing that was natural with the freedom and the reflexion of Philosophers'. Here he translates, almost verbatim, from Tullia's philosophical justifications of erotic representation and private pleasure

---

[23] *RCH* 149–50, 152, 154; Defoe is cited from *RCH* 186 and the preface to *Moll Flanders* (where he also repeats the term 'Brightness'). Wolseley's use of Horace's *Ars Poetica*, line 10, an interjection qualified by Horace himself, echoes Renaissance debates about artistic licence, e.g. *Trattati d'arte del cinquecento fra manierismo e controriforma*, ed. Paola Barocchi, ii (Bari, 1961), 3, 15–16 (a point I owe to Martha Pollak); for 'daring' as an aesthetic goal see Ch. 6, sect. 2 above (esp. n. 82).

behind the veil of decorum, and from Aretino's most articulate pupil in art theory, who excused the Giulio Romano *Modi* because their inventor 'did not publish them in city squares and churches'.[24]

The slippery concept of 'Propriety' disguises the central difficulty of Wolseley's two-tier definition: how do the criteria of 'truth' and 'liveliness' relate to one another? Does truth-to-the-object involve its intrinsic properties, or does everything emanate from the artist (who 'supplies all the wants with his own plenty')? Must it also involve truth to the *affect* of the object? This last question leads Wolseley to a major contradiction, since his 'disinterested' argument depends on dismissing sex *per se* as repulsive and 'unlovely' (like the lust of boars in Virgil's *Georgics*), even though his eulogy of Rochester and Chorier depends on glamorizing erotic energy. To borrow the polarized terms that Wolseley himself borrows from Dryden, is a text like *Aloisia Sigea* or *The Imperfect Enjoyment* a painting of a 'Lazar' or a 'Venus' (149)? When the subject matter is sexual, does that count as another example of the trivial and worthless, or does it constitute the supreme topic, the best opportunity to align attractive matter with potent manner (thus breaking down the supposed divide between them)?

The tensions within Wolseley s argument are strongly felt whenever he enriches his point with concrete examples from art and literary history. Far from downplaying the erotic, the passages that lead up to his theoretical formulation attempt to drown Mulgrave under the sheer volume and prestige of sexual literature and art (including a detailed catalogue of the nudities in Italian painting and Roman sculpture, 'the Glory of ancient Artists'). Wolseley organizes a kind of Grand Tour of classical and Renaissance erotica that includes the very painters singled out by Tullia in her praise of sexual figuration (Titian and Carracci), even evoking the Aretino/ Giulio Romano *Modi* when he insists that the very greatest artists have depicted 'Men or Women in *Postures* and with Parts obscene' (150, my emphasis). Rochester was an even greater artist than all these, since 'none of 'em knew how to show indecent and ill-favour'd Objects after a more agreeable and delightful manner, nor have any of 'em grac'd their obscene Representations with a bolder strength or a fuller Life'. Likewise the most canonical classical poets—those exempted by the censors of the Church, though they would soon be kicked out of Parnassus in the eighteenth-century revolution of taste—elicit a rapture uncannily similar to the 'Charm' exerted by the late Earl: 'our Understandings still own the truth of their instructive sence, and all our Passions feel the Charm of their Versification, when we find the kindest propensions of Nature and all the sensibility of our Souls waking at the Call of that celestial Musick . . . our Pains intermitted by the unaccountable Magick of their powerful Descriptions' (151).

The authority of ancient literature now reinforces the erotic response to

[24] *RCH* 146, 152, 154–5 ('those Painters I mention'd before, tho' they liv'd in Popish Countreys, did not, I suppose, intend their obscene Pieces for the service of the Church, or to be set up at the Market-Cross'); Roskill, *Dolce's 'Aretino'*, 162–4 (spoken by a fictional version of Aretino). For the aesthetics of the Restoration hooligan, see my *Libertines and Radicals in Early Modern London* (Cambridge, 2001), Ch. 6.

Rochester, just as the listing of distinguished names—to which Wolseley adds the 'free-spirited' Petronius and the sublime theorist Longinus—helps to prepare for the naming of canonical libertine texts at the end. And the lush language of appreciation, while maintaining the parallel of Understanding and Passion, mingles them into a single eroto-didactic complex, a synthesis most fully expressed in the very works he cites as the final touchstone of his argument. As in Chorier, mind and body converge towards a unified 'exertion' of the *mentula-mens* or *cunnus*-consciousness. As in Rochester's own *Satyr against Mankind*, the same root-word denotes (and therefore mediates between) the 'instructive sence' of the mind, the 'sensibility' of the soul, and the 'certainty of Sence' that derives from feeling *all* the Passions, including 'the kindest propensions of Nature'—an unmistakable euphemism for sexual desire (151, 152). It is from this very passage, in fact, that Wolseley derives his ostensibly disinterested definition of Wit as 'true' and 'lively' expression. Artistic criteria may be fundamentally different from ethical criteria, but here they seem fundamentally identical to the erotic.

Wolseley slides from the cold or neutral form of his argument (that sexuality *may* be depicted, like any other subject, because subject matter is in itself indifferent) to the inverse or perverse form articulated by Pallavicino (that art is the more glorious the more disgusting its material) and finally to the full-blown, hot version that reverses Mulgrave's objection entirely: that Bawdry Barefaced is in fact the supreme example, the defining instance of creative Wit—provided that it is created by a Chorier or a Rochester ('much the best that ever was seen of the Kind'). He brings back the arousal-model of literary connoisseurship together with the idea of intrinsic affective properties, while cleverly noting that, if Mulgrave were right about the antaphrodisiac effect of Rochester, the moral objection would vanish for good (155–6).

Wolseley's antagonist had described Rochester's songs as 'nauseous' and his *satyrique* vocabulary as 'too grosse to move Desire'; he responds by generalizing the linguistic and rhetorical issues. Wolseley does not dismiss the possibility of *nausea*, any more than Chorier or Oldham had done, but he defines it as a vector of that 'provocation' essential to all the arts that persuade by moving the passions, virtuous as well as vicious. Mulgrave 'might say with as much sence that pious Words are too good to move Devotion'. Coarse, random obscenities, like the meaningless godly language of the Puritans, 'will provoke indeed the wrong way, and nauseate instead of affecting; but if a man of Wit has the ranging and applying of the one, and a man of Learning and Judgement the other, both will operate according to their natural tendency.' Closing the semiotic gap between 'force' and 'discourse' that Mulgrave lamented in his own erotic poetry (and embodies in his impotent criticism), Wolseley theorizes obscenity as language fully immanent in physical reality and so fully exemplifying 'Propriety': ''tis impossible that any Words shou'd come too near the nature of the things they are to represent, when the design is to touch our Passions by that representation, for if there be an attraction of any sort in the nature of the things, the more truly they are describ'd to us, the more is that attractive virtue drawn forth and made to exert it self' (157). By defining 'the design to touch our Passions' as the goal shared by pornography and devotional literature, Wolseley links erotica to the mainstream genres of 'instructive' persuasion (the same *disegno* that underlies Pallavicino, but in a less whorish context). Rhetoric and poetics both urge the writer to 'move' by means of an authentic passion that he himself feels; if Wolseley's 'lively painting' recalls the 'life of learning' that Milton associates with Petronius and Aretino and the 'precious life blood' preserved in even the most shocking text, then his parallel of religious and sexual 'provocation' recalls the language of 'incitement', 'fuel', 'infusion', and 'inflammation' in *Of Education* and in Milton's autobiographical account of reading erotic literature (Ch. 1, sect. 2 above).

The truth-criterion and the passion-criterion, kept apart in Wolseley's definition of true art, are now dissolved into the idea of a 'natural tendency' or 'attractive virtue' intrinsic to the object—its aphrodisiac power dressed up in the modern, Newtonian concept that brought occult influences back into a science that had threatened to sever all sensory responses to the object as mere secondary qualities. 'Nausea' results only when the artist's failure blocks this approach to the 'nature of things' and sends Attraction 'the wrong way'. Like Oldham condemning the clumsiness of *Sodom* while praising the heroic achievements of Aloisia Sigea, or *The Whores Rhetorick* eulogizing the pornographer's ability to 'order the most indisposed matter', Wolseley locates the crucial difference in the ability to 'range and apply'; expropriating Mulgrave's own image of a choking fire, he shows that everything depends on having the wood 'regularly laid and artificially pil'd up' (158). No longer arguing for the indifference of the subject matter, in this pyrotechnic ending he assumes that the 'natural' purpose of erotic art is a good blaze.

In the final twist of his argument, Wolseley confronts the core of Mulgrave's objection head on. He embraces the full obscenity of his beloved poet and makes it the ultimate proof of his literary potency. For the reader truly capable of receiving his tickling probe, Rochester's obscenity is nothing less than 'attractive virtue drawn forth', desire 'made to exert it self; so that what [Mulgrave] calls *grossenesse* is here the chief power, the main weight and stamp of the Poet's Expression' (157). As in Le Petit, the very roughness of the language authenticates the 'power' and the 'glory' of a writer who can truly 'fuck us in the eyes'. The hapless critic who denies this somewhat brutal arousal merely confesses his own sexual-textual incapacity. It is in this context that Wolseley orders Mulgrave to test his critical equipment against the acknowledged standard:

> when his squeamish Fit is over, I wou'd recommend to his Perusal *Aloisia Sigea*, or if that be too hard for him because 'tis writ in Latin, let him read *L'Escole des Filles*, and if the obscene Words and Descriptions he will meet with there do not raise his Appetite, the World will be apt to conclude it, not only very dull, but absolutely dead. (158)

Like the fumbling cuckolds and *fausses précieuses* of Restoration comedy, the lecherous student in Oldham, or the ingénu(e)s at Casanova's dinner table, Mulgrave is jeered for his ladylike 'squeamish fit', his inability to negotiate Latinity, his ignorance of a contemporary classic, and his sexual-textual inability to perform upon the (feminized) reader or mistress. (With the same tutorial condescension that he assumed when explaining the erotic masterpieces of Rome, Wolseley adds that the French *Escole* for girls might do, if he cannot rise to the hardness of Latin.) Held up to the newly emergent canon of 'obscene Description', the Earl of Mulgrave and future Duke of Buckinghamshire becomes a pathetic, declassed, depotentiated figure, a quasi-Popean embodiment of Dullness.

3. APHRA BEHN'S ROCHESTER AND THE FEMINIZATION OF POETIC AROUSAL

Wolseley's emotional yet theoretically incisive panegyric soon became a rallying point for authors loyal to Rochester, a quarry for new critical appraisals, and a proof-text in discussions of the larger aesthetic issue, whether major art can derive from indecent or negligible matter. It earned him a position within another circle of Rochester's acolytes, distinct from the club of masculine wits; Aphra Behn and Anne Wharton (Rochester's niece, adoptive sibling, and reputed lover) had woven a series of funeral elegies and commendatory poems around his memory, and Wharton extended this poetic embrace to Wolseley when his essay 'stretched the bounds of Love beyond the grave'.[25] (This is the poem that affected Wolseley like a 'strong philtre'.) 'St Evremont' and others adopt Wolseley's vocabulary of 'Genius', 'Spirit', 'Beauty', and arousing 'Power' as well as his comparisons with Petronius and Chorier. The schoolboy poet Samuel Wesley justifies his collection of witty poems on trifling subjects by citing 'the Authority of the ingenious Preface to the *Valentinian*'; Wolseley's account of genius transforming 'the working of ants' and 'the lust of boars' presumably authorized Wesley to write poems about kisses and 'Maggots'. As we saw in Chapter 6, Wesley testifies that Chorier's Latin text circulated in his dissenting academy even though 'our tutors' did not mention it; Wolseley's impressive public allusion clearly provided an alternative way of learning about the existence and the 'Authority' of the pornographic classic, as well as a model for similar exculpatory citations.[26]

Yet despite its sophistication and its wide influence, Wolseley's promotion of Rochester, *L'Escole*, and *Aloisia Sigea* must strike us as tediously phallic. As in Chorier himself, the ultimate judge of beauty is the *mentula*; for Wolseley the same organ seems to constitute 'the chief power, the main weight and stamp of the Poet's Expression', even 'the Genius and Art of the Writer'. He extends the classical tradition, most famously expressed in Catullus and Martial, which declared that poems on sexual subjects 'cannot please without a prick' and are worthless *nisi pruriant*— literally 'unless they itch', but clearly referring to both the feeling and the power to

---

[25] *RCH* 160, and cf. 97, 108, 101–10, 132–3. Greer and Hastings provide a better biography of Wharton than *RCH*: orphaned hours after her birth in 1659, she was raised by Rochester's mother and according to her unstable brother-in-law Goodwin Wharton 'lay a long time by her uncle Rochester' after being debauched at Court (*Surviving Works of Anne Wharton*, 19 n. 93).

[26] *Maggots, or Poems on Several Subjects, Never Before Handled* (1685), fo. A6; for Wesley's recollections of Chorier at school, see Ch. 6 n. 3 above.

induce *pruritis* in the venereal sense. Because of the patrician association of manliness, *Romanitas*, and sexual plain-speaking, this poetic arousal was almost exclusively imagined as masculine, even though the physical form can obviously be experienced and caused by either sex. The Roman epigram was supposed to be *mentulata*, and thus capable of 'fucking us in the eyes' (in Le Petit's gallant phrase); though Beccadelli created poems that he called 'Hermaphrodite', priapism remained the default mode for sexual discourse, medical as well as literary.[27]

In Restoration England, the narrow phallocentrism or erection-fetishism that bonds Wolseley to Rochester and Le Petit to *L'Escole des filles* threatened to become the default image for authorship and 'wit' in general. At least among male authors the 'power' and 'fire' of literary genius were increasingly equated with phallic vigour: according to the future Lord Bolingbroke, for example, Dryden enjoys all the 'wishing Muses' like a Sultan in his harem (while shunning the 'stale thing' of a 'Poetick Wife', which might put out his 'Fire'); since these nine mistresses 'no decay, no want of vigour find', Bolingbroke infers that 'Sublime your Fancy, boundless is your Mind'.[28] In this crude reversal of Renaissance womb-imagery, the bright poets and critics 'fuck' and the dull ones cannot; women seem excluded entirely from the creative and interpretative process.

We have already noticed, however, a certain shifting of roles between active and passive, writer and reader. Wolseley puts the recipient of Wit in the catamite position, but he also equates the Critick with the ancient lover, smitten with the 'Form' of poetry but lacking the 'Power' to possess her. Even straightforward-seeming images of impotence have a tendency to confuse the gender positions. Rochester himself, for example, declared in an epilogue that

> Poets and Women have an Equal Right
> To hate the Dull, who Dead to all Delight
> Feel pain alone, and have no Joy but spite.[29]

This highly public allusion to 'Impotence' and flagellation not only grants women an 'Equal Right' (albeit the 'right to pleasure' that often serves as a slur on their supposed insatiability), but reverses the conventional gendering of author and reader, putting the poet in the 'female' position of demanding to be *bien baisée* by a well-disposed critic. Simultaneously, it puts Rochester himself in the category of the dull, since his own cult of 'Love rais'd to an extream' defines him as one who 'feels pain alone' because 'pain can ne're deceive' (28). And if erection *were* the entire 'source

---

[27] Cf. Martial, I. iv, I. xxxv (cited by Sinibaldi (Ch. 4 n. 19 above), XI. xx (and V. lxxviii for dancing-girls 'sine fine prurientes'); Catullus, XV.; Antonio Beccadelli, *Hermaphroditus*, in *L'Œuvre priapique des anciens et des modernes* (Paris, 1914), *passim* (in II. xxxvii, for example, the book is told to visit a favourite brothel, where Galla will 'put her hand on your prick or on your cunt, since you have both').

[28] Quoted in James and Helen Kinsley (eds.), *Dryden: The Critical Heritage* (1971), 76–7. For the contrary (though no less male) imagery of creativity as pregnancy, see Katharine Eisaman Maus, 'A Womb of his Own: Male Renaissance Poets in the Female Body', in James Grantham Turner (ed.), *Sexuality and Gender in Early Modern Europe: Institutions, Texts, Images* (Cambridge, 1993), 266–88.

[29] 122, probably a direct source of Wolseley's image of Mulgrave since the next line explains that ' 'Twas Impotence did first this Vice [of Malicicus Criticks] begin'.

and goal and test of art', what would this make the author? When he rouses the blood and appetite of the male reader, does he penetrate a passive recipient in an act of 'slippery sweetness', or does he entice him like a prostitute? Rochester compares Wits to courtesans quite sympathetically, in the *Satyr* and in speeches made for agreeable female personae who express much of his own mind; Artemiza's recognition that 'Whore is scarce a more reproachfull Name | Than Poetess' makes her all the more eager to write, stimulated by 'the Contradiction and the Sin' (Ch. 6, sect. 1 above). Even in the highest flush of Wolselean panegyric, Rochester is compared to the made-up prostitute as well as the 'stabbing' rapist, to 'the lines of a mistress's face' as well as the point that tickles as it probes. The poetics of arousal makes susceptibility—the capacity to soften and let the sweetness slip in—just as important as erection. It involves the entire 'blood and Appetite', and though the phallus certainly comes into play it is never securely attached.

In this context it is significant that Chorier's Sigea—still thought to be the authentic female author of the *Satyra Sotadica*—should be invoked as the touchstone of erotic art. Wolseley's citation of '*Aloisia Sigea*' as the ultimate proof-text reminds us of the power ascribed to the (pseudo)female in libertine discourse. His dismissal of Mulgrave seems to endorse a masculine definition of authorship as it moves from bed to verse: 'bad as his Poetry is, his Reader will be better entertain'd than his Mistress.' In fact, however, Wolseley gives the male only an intermediary place in the hierarchy. Submitting to the poet, the reader must be pleased (or disappointed) in the same way as his mistress, but in turn the writer must authenticate his prowess by submission to the mistress-text, either in the junior version ('the School for Girls') or in the full-grown form of Sigea—Oldham's 'famed Spanish Whore' who effortlessly 'outdoes' men 'both acting and describing lust', and who thereby blends together what Mulgrave polarizes into 'action' and 'discourse'.

According to 'St Evremont' (himself quoting from some edition of '*Meurcius*'), Rochester 'alarms the Fancy, and rouzes the Blood and Appetite more than all the Medicaments of *Cleopatra*', but it is still Cleopatra who provides the standard and holds the patent for the medicine. In *The Whores Rhetorick* the author's 'lively, brisk and vigorous Spirit' clearly betokens his sexual performance, but it means nothing unless it 'corresponds to the vivacity of the Ladies' Soul'. Within libertine fiction itself, as we have seen, the 'Ladies' Soul' takes over all the seductive agency and 'vivifying' power conventionally attributed to the potent male. Killigrew's nuns make Aretino 'dull', and Chorier's Laura displays the kind of 'invention' as a letter-writer that proves her brilliance in bed; dullness in *Aloisia Sigea* is explicitly connected to the Stoic who despises erotic pleasure (*hebes et corruptus*) and to those few 'stolid, stony' women who cannot feel lesbian desire. Chorier offers plenty of phallic boasting, but attaches still greater importance to authorial kinds of sexuality that belong more to the female characters than the male, exertions of the erotic will that make them *artifices* and lift them above 'abject' domesticity.[30]

---

[30] For Killigrew see Ch. 2, sect. 2, for Chorier Ch. 4 *passim*, esp. *Satyra*, VII. 232, II. 35–6; for his use of *abjecta* in association with household duties, see p. 377 below.

Women authors could be 'suffocated' by this (mis)representation of their vast literary-erotic capacity—as Aloisia Sigea puts it in a fictional confrontation with Chorier–or they could expropriate it.[31] For Aphra Behn (as for numerous contemporaries in England and France) it provided a pretext for launching her own literary claims. The notion that women 'outdo' men in this area, that they are inherently more susceptible to desire and therefore 'more apt' to express it in writing (as Chorier said of his Sigea), dominated the gallant world of the later seventeenth century and even penetrated the 'philosophical' *salon* (Ch. 3, sect. 5 above), but it clearly carried an ugly implication: women were insatiable or 'nymphomaniac' in the sexual-discursive realm and incompetent in any other. Pinchwife in Wycherley's *Country-Wife* expresses the abject version of this commonplace—'Why should Women have more invention in love than men? It can only be, because they have more desires, more solliciting passions, more lust, and more of the devil' (IV. ii. 311)—but Behn converts it to sublimity.

Smarting from sexist criticisms of her comedy *Sir Patient Fancy* (1678), Behn defends women's writing in an epilogue intriguingly spoken by 'Mrs Gwin', assuming a provocative and distinctly libertine equation of sex and art:

> That we have Nobler Souls than you, we prove
> By how much more we're sensible of Love;
> Quickest in finding all the subtlest waies
> To make your Joys—why not to make you Plays?[32]

Women had for too long heard that their 'Sex', and specifically their sexuality, *prevented* them from achieving the 'Sublime Fancy' and 'boundless Mind' that Bolingbroke praises in Dryden as if they flowed directly from his testicles; the representative of masculinism in the 1683 *Triumphs of Female Wit*, for example, blindly asserts that women cannot be educated—and cannot write in '*Masculine* Pindarick Strains'—because 'Your Sex. that prison of your Souls, | Your rational unbounded Mind controuls' (Ch. 3 n. 160 above). Behn appears to accept this prison sentence, but then finesses it into a promotion.

In a less playful and more 'unbounded' poetic form, a commendatory ode for Thomas Creech's translation of Lucretius, Behn explains her own female constitution according to the materialist atomism that Creech had just made available to non-Latinists. She would like to emulate Lucretius' heroic achievement,

> But I of feebler Seeds design'd,
> While the slow moveing Atoms strove
> With Careless Heed to Form my Mind,
> Compos'd it all of softer Love:

---

[31] Antoine Gachet d'Artigny, *Relation de ce qui s'est passé dans une assemblée tenue au bas du Parnasse* (The Hague, 1739), 95.

[32] *Works*, vi. 79. Scholars assume that Anne Quin spoke this epilogue and not Behn's patroness the retired actress and royal mistress Nell Gwyn, but the odd spelling of her name with a G would certainly have created a profitable confusion at the time; the epilogue's knowing remarks about 'our' expertise in the sexual 'ways' or *Modi* would fit Gwyn better than Quin, not notable for fornication.

> In Gentle Numbers all my Songs are drest:
> And when I would Thy Glories sing,
> What in Strong Manly Verse should be exprest
> Turns all to Womanish Tenderness within.

What seems like self-deprecation rapidly mutates into a higher claim, however. Others merely 'admire' Creech, but Behn—precisely because of her erotic 'softness'—kindles into an authentic 'Fire' that generates 'this newer way' of writing, paying him an even greater tribute.[33] The rest of the poem bears this out, in the ambitious 'Pindarick' mode that women were thought incapable of achieving.

Behn transfers to the young translator the most 'ravishing' features of the late Rochester, as portrayed by herself and Anne Wharton in their funeral poems—a much-publicized intervention which guaranteed that Rochester's memory would not be owned by an exclusively male clique. Since Creech went to the same Oxford college as Rochester, the Pindaric mode allows Behn to compare them: '*Strephon* the great', who 'writ, and Lov'd and Lookt like any God', whose death has reduced the Muses to 'Love sick Maids' and the Cupids to limp figures 'Weeping their Rifled Power', has been reincarnated in this young '*Daphnis*, whom every Grace, and Muse inspires; | Scarce *Strephon*'s Ravishing Poetick Fires | So kindly warm, or so Divinely Cheer.' Behn reconstructs the male genius as a figure like herself, in whom poetic and amorous qualities merge in fluid continuity (Strephon writ/loved/looked in the same divine way, Daphnis caresses 'muse and mistress' in the Elysian grove of his own success). Here and in the funeral poems, Behn locates the 'ravishing' or 'kindly warming' element in manifestly feminine qualities, producing the same heteropaedophile mélange of boy and girl that she explores in 'To the fair Clarinda, who made Love to me, imagin'd more than Woman'. Anticipating and perhaps authorizing Wolseley's lush vocabulary, she remembers Strephon/Rochester as 'soft' (eight times), 'lovely' (three times), and 'charming' (seven times), as well as 'Gay and Great'. He embodied, and fused together, 'all the charms of Poetry and Love'. His beam was 'piercing' and 'pointed', but only like the sun's. In his role as satirist and literary mentor, education and seduction blended into a 'dear instructing Rage', so that, when he lashed, the 'chastising stroke' was 'kind and gentle'. Rochester devoted himself to the ladies, but was so 'soft' and fragile that he exhausted himself and expired as Beauty's victim (the fate that Octavia fears for Robertus in *Aloisia Sigea*). He died like a rose, 'softly falling' so that the scattered petals—that is, literary tributes such as Behn's own poem—allow us to sense 'How lovely 'twas when whole, how sweet, how fair'.[34]

The death of Rochester in 1680, like Princess Diana's in 1997, released a flood of voluptuous, transsexual mourning that can still be heard in Wolseley's tribute.

---

[33] 'To the Unknown Daphnis on his Excellent Translation of Lucretius' (Jan. 1683), *Works*, i. 25; for a thorough reading of this ode, see Margaret A. Doody, 'Gender, Literature, and Gendering Literature in the Restoration', in Steven N. Zwicker (ed.), *The Cambridge Companion to English Literature, 1650–1740* (Cambridge, 1998), 64–6. Behn makes a strong case for the liberating effect of this translation for women, but seems unaware that Lucy Hutchinson had already composed a full version in MS.

[34] *Works*, i. 27–8, 56–7, 161–3 (the poems on Rochester's death are also in *RCH* 101–6); for the 'Clarinda' poem, now conventionally labelled 'lesbian' even though Behn clearly locates erotic charm in youthful ambiguity, see i. 288.

Oldham, like the 'Ravisht' Behn, adopted the Hellenistic lovesick mode when he modelled his elegy on Moschus' lament for Bion. Like all his personal acquaintance, Oldham emphasizes the fusion of the erotic and the didactic, the charismatic seducer who 'taught [us] how to sing, and how to love'. Rochester's 'all-teaching tongue', his 'Voice which could all hearts command' (as the thunderbolt is supposed to do in *The Imperfect Enjoyment*), seduces not only all the Shepherdesses but 'all the Herdsmen', who mope and carve his name in the barks of trees just as Oldham does in this poem.[35] The exchange of poems between Wharton and Behn embodies this transgendered stimulus.

An interlocking series of poetic addresses connects Wharton, Behn, and the late Rochester into a kind of literary love-triangle. Behn pays tribute to the conjunction of eroticism and didactic gift in Rochester, while Wharton's own elegy bewails the loss of her brother-uncle's 'useful kinde instructing Tongue' and recreates, not only his nurturing of her 'Infant Muse', but his precocious childhood—which 'flam'd with Poetick rage' just as the prospect of joining him in heaven 'inflames' the sibling-poet's mind to 'extasie'. At the same time Wharton wrote a fervent epistle 'To Mrs. A. Behn, on what she Writ of the Earl of *Rochester*', though her respectable male friends advised her to have nothing to do with that abominable woman. Just as she later commended Wolseley for 'stretching the bounds of love beyond the grave'—a compliment that Wolseley returned by declaring her both the 'Executrix' of Rochester's Wit and the 'Philtre' that stimulates his—so here she responds to Behn's 'Inticing Strain', which 'excites my Art'. In the first line she confesses herself 'In pleasing Transport rap't' (apparently 'raped' as well as rapt) and in the last she blesses her fellow-poet with considerable tenderness: 'may your Numbers ever flow, | Soft as the Wishes that I make for you.' What are these wishes, exactly? As well as commemorating Rochester, Wharton wants Behn to emulate and vindicate Sappho, enhancing her 'Glory' while eliminating 'Shame' and 'low desire'.[36]

Behn responded to Anne Wharton's epistle with an explosion of grateful rapture, pretending to believe (on her sickbed) that the young woman poet was not a blood relative but Rochester himself, 'very very he'. Of course this vision is no more 'he' than Behn herself (who adopts the role of 'All-Ravisht Swain'), but it conveys the identical qualities that she had praised in her Strephon—'His Softness all, his Sweetness everywhere', correcting her literary faults and 'School[ing her] loose Neglect' in the same 'gentle Voice' that softly penetrated the 'Known Paths' of her soul.[37] Finding these qualities now incarnate in Rochester's niece/sister obeys a certain

[35] 'Bion, a Pastoral, in Imitation of the Greek of Moschus, bewailing the Death of the Earl of Rochester', *RCH* 94–101; in this poem Oldham claims to have derived all his poetic gifts from Rochester (Ch. 6, sect. 3 above), though his influence also creates anxiety (the God Pan himself now fears to be 'outdone' (97), the same word that Oldham applies to Aloisia Sigea).

[36] *Surviving Works*, 140–3, 189; cf. 292 for William Atwood's contrast between the pure Wharton and 'counterfeit *Astraea*'s lustful Rage', and 351–2 for Gilbert Burnet's attempt to separate her from the 'abominably vile . . . odious and obscene' Behn. Wolseley's preface borrows several details from Wharton's elegy, including the idea that Rochester was 'useful' and the contrasting image of poetry as a prostitute (not in the bowdlerized published version, *RCH* 107–8).

[37] 'To Mrs. W[harton] on her Excellent Verses (Writ in Praise of some I had made on the Earl of Rochester) Written in a Fit of Sickness' *Works*, i. 56–8.

logic, since they were so feminine to start with. Behn undoubtedly had access to the hard-core canon of libertine dialogues (since her close friend John Hoyle owned them all), but we do not need to posit direct influence to appreciate the parallels in this real-life dialogue of women. Like Tullia and Octavia, they strengthen their own bond by cultivating a revisionist history of Sappho even while 'sharing' a mutually adored but absent man. In this Behn–Wharton collaboration over Rochester we see a *femme* version of the homoerotic bonding that Eve Sedgwick detects in male dialogues about women, or perhaps (on the model of the princess's statue in *L'Escole des filles*) two women giving each other pleasure by sharing a life-sized effigy of the male, 'soft' in all the appropriate parts. Now, however, the liquid that gushes on command is tears rather than milk.

The posthumous performance of *Valentinian* in 1684 (sponsored by Wharton herself) revived this eroticized cult of Rochester, and thus prepared the way for Wolseley's preface. Behn wrote the prologue for the first night, comparing the inevitable success of this Fletcher–Rochester collaboration to the irresistible seductiveness of a confident beauty. Only 'Great *Strephon*'s soft and powerful Wit' would dare revise Fletcher's classic play. Speaking over the heads of the male critics, who chatter witlessly about the price of whores, the actress delivering Behn's lines appeals directly to the women in the audience: Virgins will appreciate Rochester's fusion of erotics and poetics ('The Gods of Love and Wit inspir'd his Pen') and Ladies can now celebrate him 'Without a scandal on your spotless Fame'. The second-night prologue (for the same actress) takes up the themes of Wolseley's forthcoming preface, recreating Rochester's presence as lover and satirist while defending his transcendent 'obscenity' against Mulgrave's insult. On the third night a new prologue for Elizabeth Barry sums up the Behn–Wharton line by declaring Rochester 'a *Genius* as sublime' as any in Augustan Rome or Jacobean England, engaging 'every Passion' and combining 'sharp' satire with 'sweet' love-poetry. To prove his classic status in these two genres ('As soft his Love, and as divine his Rage') she appeals, not to the text, but to the bodies of the audience—and by implication to her own. Oldham had lamented the voice 'Whose pow'r no Shepherdess could e're withstand', in generic pastoral terms, but Barry, acknowledged mother of Rochester's bastard daughter, concretizes this in the face-to-face of the theatrical prologue, where the sexual bond between actress and audience became flirtatiously real: 'Some Beauties here I see——'—breaking off for a suggestive pause that allows all heads to turn and follow her gaze—'Though now demure, have felt his pow'rful Charms.' Transferring the softness of 'his Love' from the literary to the literal, Barry dispels all ambiguity by insisting that these omnipresent ex-mistresses 'languish'd in the Circle of his Arms'.[38]

Far from excluding women writers, then, the 'pleasing contradictions' and aestheticized 'sin' of Rochester's memory encouraged them. Once he was safely dead,

---

[38] *RCH* 132–6, and cf. Wharton, *Surviving Works*, 87, 90. One detail in the anonymous third prologue might suggest that Behn wrote it too: it associates Rochester's tragic death with Lucretius ('So fatal is it vastly to excel; | Thus young, thus mourn'd, his lov'd *Lucretius* fell'), a linkage found in the Creech poem but not in the other elegies.

the plasticity of desire could refashion him as an Aloisia-like teacher-seducer, at once 'soft' and 'piercing'. For better or worse, the Rochester-cult endorsed a passion-centred definition of literature for which women were supposedly 'more apt', more 'sensible', more inventive, 'Quickest in finding all the subtlest ways'. Behn herself came to be used as a touchstone of literary-seductive power and a passepartout to slip between the rigid categories imposed on women. Jane Barker, who opposed the 'Deluge of Libertinism' by espousing the idealistic erotics of Romance, and who associated her own literary genius with her personal vow of chastity, still found herself praised for her Behnish sexiness: partially breaking the usual virgin–whore polarity, one admirer declares her writing 'more than *Orinda*'s chast' but 'more than *Astraea*'s soft'; since she exceeds even Astraea/Behn in this exciting softness, future generations will '*Bless, Bless* the *Author* of [their] soft desire'.[39]

Nor was this purely a masculine trope. The impeccably virtuous Anne Finch, Countess of Winchilsea, still manages to recuperate Behn into her literary practice and theory. 'The Introduction' continues Behn's spirited attack on the enemies of women's writing. (Her complaint against disparaging women's intellects and restraining them to 'the dull manage of a servile house' resembles, though it cannot possibly echo, Chorier's praise of Sigea for rejecting 'abjecta et stupida animi demissione' and 'sordida rei familiaris cura' (1), the abject, mind-destroying, and sordid management of household affairs.[40]) And in 'The Circuit of Apollo' (93–5) she mourns the late Behn in terms that recall, not only the sisterhood's lament for their soft-cum-powerful mentor and Wolseley's reclamation of his 'obscenity', but Rochester's own approval of poetry's power to 'dissolve' without forcing blushes.[41] Anne Finch's Apollo laments for the incomparable Behn and makes light of her alleged obscenity. Though he 'owned that a little too loosely she writ' the error seems venial, given the defining centrality of arousal to the entire poetic enterprise: 'the art of the Muse is to stir up soft thoughts, | Yet to make all hearts beat without blushes or faults.'

Behn's critical polemic, like Wolseley's, polarizes writers and critics into the rule-bound hack, sexually and poetically 'Dull', and the true genius—infinite in her erotic capacity or 'quickness' of feeling and therefore free to invent new forms beyond the conventional limits of 'art', like Laura in Chorier's *Aloisia Sigea*. Literary success cuts across gender boundaries, as we see in Behn's feminized Rochester and her Rochesterized Wharton, deriving not from male-only phallic 'vigour' but from

[39] *Poetical Recreations* (1688), ii. 32, a commendatory poem for Crayle's projected publication of the very romance in which Barker denounced Libertinism (Ch. 5 n. 7 above); for Barker's linkage of poetry and chastity, see Magdalen College, Oxford, MS 343, fos. 75ᵛ–76 (I am grateful to Alison Shell for transcripts) and Germaine Greer et al. (eds.), *Kissing the Rod: An Anthology of 17th-Century Women's Verse* (1988), 360.

[40] Katherine M. Rogers and William McCarthy (eds.) *The Meridian Anthology of Early Women Writers* (New York, 1987), 78–9; a probable common source for Finch and Chorier is Mlle de Scudéry, who attacked the domestic definition of women very strongly (cf. Ch. 1 n. 112 above).

[41] 72 (the 'mannerly Obscene . . . can stir Nature up by springs unseen, | And without forceing blushes warm the Queen').

those internal fires (common to both sexes if stronger in the female) that inspire the writer to defy the mechanical servitude of neoclassical correctness. (Rochester used similar terms in *A Ramble in St James's Park* when he attacks 'Rote' learning and 'abortive Imitation'.) In the preface to *The Dutch Lover* Behn creates a vividly contemptuous image of the foppish critic who dismisses her play because of her sex—this 'long, lither, phlegmatick, white' smelt-like creature with a hole for a mouth makes an unimpressive spokeman for phallocracy—and then goes on to disparage all 'their musty rules of Unity'. In the epilogue to *Sir Patient Fancy*, where 'Mrs Gwin' provocatively equates literary creativity with 'Quick' inventiveness in bed, Behn again attacks her male critics in terms that fuse their literary theory and their sexual pretensions. Men's 'dull Fopperies', 'saucy Love', and 'worse than womanish Affectation' are as absurd as their 'way of Writing':

> Method and Rule you only understand;
> Pursue that way of Fooling, and be damn'd.

Women will now create a new kind of literature free of Method and independent of the Unities, ranging from 'unlabour'd Farce' to an erotic poetics of unprecedented vitality and refinement.[42]

The methodized critic-seducer, in contrast, is reduced to 'A Glass'—a passive reflective device emblematic of vanity—'by which the admiring Country Fool | May learn to dress himself *en Ridicule*'. Both the town-fop and his reflection, the mirror-image having turned both into simulacra, 'strive who shall most ingenious grow | In Leudness, Foppery, Nonsense, Noise and Show'; all the qualities that misogyny associates with women are here thrown back as the symptoms of 'worse than womanish Affectation' (vi. 79). (Behn's attack on the fop's 'ingenious lewdness' seems to disparage *ingeniosa libido* itself, but her other writings prove her faith in erotic poetics; here she clearly satirizes the impotent striving for effect rather than the desired result.) In time, male critics came to associate this transcendent rejection of rules with 'The Female Wits', first sarcastically and then earnestly. Matthew Prior, for example, would soon praise a woman playwright who abandons the 'dull forms' of female reticence: 'Let Critics follow *Rules*, she boldly writes | What N*ature* dictates, and what L*ove* indites.'[43]

Behn's campaign against constraint would have been interpreted as *libertine* in every sense of the word: the sexual cult of 'free love' merges with the stylistic transgression described by Pierre Corneille, who used the word *libertin* for dramas that abandon the Unities, or Sir William Temple, who declared that 'there is something in the Genius of Poetry too libertine to be confined to so many Rules'.[44] The erotic-discursive nexus is spelled out in Behn's version of *The Golden Age*, a more sympathetic impersonation of the male seducer persona. Adapting the Tasso

---

[42] *Works*, v. 162–3, vi. 79; for Rochester on abortive imitation see Ch. 6, sect. 1 above.

[43] 'The Female Wits: A Song by a Lady of Quality' (1685), in Alastair Fowler (ed.), *The New Oxford Book of Seventeenth-Century Verse* (Oxford, 1992), 776–7; Prior, *Literary Works*, ed. H. Bunker Wright and Monroe K. Spears, 2nd edn. (Oxford, 1971), 689.

[44] Corneille, *Œuvres complètes*, ed. André Stegmann, L'Intégrale (Paris, 1963), 76, 845–6; Temple cited in *OED*, s.v. 'libertine' B.3 (and see Ch. 6 n. 103 above for other literary applications).

chorus that Tullie in *L'Academie des dames* uses for the same purpose, the speaker woos 'Sylvia' by disparaging false Honour and transferring its 'glory' to the erotic realm. Golden Age freedom is defined in a string of negatives—love was 'uncontroul'd', no 'Politick Curbs [would] keep man in', no tight hairnet would impose a 'stinted order' on women's coiffure—and scornfully opposed to method and prescription: 'Who but the Learned and dull moral Fool | Could gravely have forseen, man ought to live by Rule?' Constraints on sexuality translate immediately into cramps upon expression, likewise blamed on

> Honour! that put'st our words that should be free
> Into a set Formality.
> Thou base Debaucher of the generous heart,
> That teachest all our Looks and Actions Art.

In a neat alliterative package, 'Glorious Love should be confest' as opposed to 'confin'd'. But *confession* produces another version of *confinement*, a genteel version of the pansexual ideology that runs throughout *L'Escole des filles* and *Aloisia Sigea*; human beings were 'form'd for love alone', and should take 'Pride' in nothing else.[45]

According to her rhetorical needs, Behn uses the contrast of 'boundless' sublimity and 'dull' method with rapturous assent or critical suspicion. High Pindaric odes like 'On Desire' exalt female libido (while recognizing its 'inconvenient' unpredictability) and purge it of the whorish associations that literary rivals were all too ready to pin on the author herself. She also seems sincerely committed to a romance hero like Oroonoko, whose impossible amorous intensity derives from the innate 'greatness' of his soul and from 'some new and till then unknown Power [that] instructed his Heart and Tongue in the Language of Love'; both its scale and its ineffability link this version of erotic education to contemporary theories of the sublime.[46] But Behn is equally aware that the discourse of infinity can serve as a rationale for male fickleness and exploitation. Far from interpreting Don Juanism as a generous urge or a universal aspect of the human condition, she sees it as a specifically male neurosis with disastrous consequences for women. 'Alexis' had written a philosophical poem on the vanity of fruition, inspired by Montaigne: reversing Rochester's valuation of bad reason and good sensuality in the *Satyr against Mankind*, he laments (or boasts) that 'our boundless vast desires' drive us from one hollow satisfaction to another. Behn responds by challenging this sublime conception, suggesting that it is the 'feebleness' rather than the vastness of man's libido, the coldness of responses that 'like lightning flash and are no more', that make him abandon mistress after mistress. The ethos of libertine conquest is a social construct, moreover, acquired rather than innate: ' 'tis a fatal lesson he *has learn'd*, | After fruition ne're to be concern'd' (my emphasis), and like all lessons learned by rote it

---

[45] *Works*, i. 30–5 (and cf. *Academie*, i. 134); even careful readings like Warren Chernaik, *Sexual Freedom in Restoration Literature* (Cambridge, 1995), 136–8, treat this male-persona-poem as an expression of Behn's view, whereas it belongs more with Oldham's pindaric impersonations of the extreme sensualist.

[46] *Oroonoko, or The Royal Slave*, ed. Catharine Gallagher with Simon Stern (Boston, 2000), 44, 45 (but contrast 75, where the hero *resents* love and craves 'Actions great enough for his large Soul').

is then mechanically repeated. Far from liberating the vastness of desire for women, the *larghezza* that Tullia d'Aragona recognizes even in the illicit form of love, the contradictory prejudices of the double standard impose claustrophic limits: 'all our joys are stinted to the space | Of one betraying enterview.' Chorier's Tullia might declare sexual fruition the *summum bonum*, but Behn discovers at the heart of libertine eroticism a philosophical principle that displaces the erotic: 'Inconstancy', rather than enjoyment, is 'the good supream'.[47]

The polarity of 'sublime' and 'dull' erotics, in both its sincere and its hypocritical manifestation, plays a central role in Behn's *Love-Letters between a Nobleman and his Sister*, the political scandal novel that (as Mrs Cresswell recommended in *The Whores Rhetorick*) turns the rebellious circle of the Duke of Monmouth into a hotbed of erotic transgression. In this thinly disguised fictionalization of Lord Grey's affair with his sister-in-law, the ill-fated lovers write of 'Glorious ruine', 'vast heights of Love', 'excess of joy far above dull sense or formal thinking', 'the flights of thy generous Love … elevated above what we have seen yet on Earth', and the 'awfull ceremony' of copulation; extremity and excess are the supreme good, dullness and confinement the greatest evil. In what seems at first a mutual discourse, the incestuous couple elevate their forbidden desires into a glamorous and sublime transgression:

HE: Your Beauty shou'd . . . force all obligations, all laws, all ties even of Nature's self: You, my lovely Maid, were not born to be obtained by the dull methods of ordinary loving. . . . Let us (born for mightier joys) scorn the dull *beaten road*, . . . let us look forward to Pleasures vast and unconfin'd.

SHE: I cannot fall more gloriously . . . I will be brave in Love, and lavish all. . . . If there be no boldness like that of love, nor courage like that of a lover, sure there never was so great a Heroine as *Sylvia*. Undaunted, I resolve to stand the shock of all; . . . it is below the dignity of my mighty passion to justifie it farther.[48]

These sentiments may be ironized by the perfidy of the characters who speak them, but they correspond closely to Behn's *propria persona* voice. In her praise of Thomas Creech's Lucretius, for example, she looks forward to the translator's success in 'Poetry and Love' as an orgiastic explosion of constraint, when his erotic and poetic life runs 'loose, | Unfetter'd, Unconfin'd by any other Muse' (i. 28). The author and her villain share a contempt for 'the dull methods of ordinary loving'.

The Cartesian erotics of *L'Escole des filles* sought to realize sexuality through 'méthode', but this more baroque conception of Eros soars beyond 'Method and Rule', which are consigned to the dismal categories of dullness and constraint; ironically, Behn plays Descartes's own conception of erotic 'excess' against his most important philosophical legacy. In the voice of Sylvia and Philander she comes closer to Tullia's doctrine, in the later dialogues of *Aloisia Sigea*, of a Spinozan 'fervent *conatus*' that pushes beyond the limits of the material and transforms the

---

[47] *Works*, i. 281, 272–3; both Alexis's poem and the answer appear in *A Miscellany of New Poems*, appended to Behn's *Lycidus* (1688), 127–31, and Richard Quaintance suggests that Behn herself might have written both ('Passion and Reason in Restoration Love Poetry', Ph.D. dissertation (Yale, 1962), 141).

[48] *Works*. ii. 44–5, 86, 70, 99, 11–12, 28, 69, 84 (further citations from *Love-Letters* are from this volume).

abject condition of women. As a corollary of this hostility to Method, 'philosophy' takes on a negative connotation in Behn's novel. Far from giving the highest rank to what Elisabeth Rowe would call the 'philosophick libertine', who combines 'critical reflection' and sensuous arousal in a mutually heightening fusion, Behn equates the philosophical with the methodical, with the calculating 'Arts and Politicks of Love', the cynical but realistic analysis that the high-born libertines, male and female, share with their servants. Behn splits the seducer-role between the sublime Philander, who pretends to set himself above 'the dull methods of ordinary loving', and his sinister valet Brilliard, who like Wycherley's Horner 'fancy'd himself a very *Machiavel*' (155). The 'Philosophy' of Brilliard (shared by his master in secret) represents the lower stratum of sexual understanding, in contrast to the high rhetoric of 'immense passion' and ecstatic excess that Sylvia and Philander present to each other (151, 185). To the extent that the rake becomes heroic in this fiction, it is by embracing the libertine sublime and concealing the 'philosophy' that dictates fickleness and new conquests for the man, dissimulation and survival for the woman. It is especially ironic, then, that Behn herself should be associated with the corrupt 'arts' of sexual enhancement. One lampoon against the tragic actress Elizabeth Barry— mistress of Rochester and public defender of his 'Genius sublime' in her prologue to *Valentinian*—declares her 'Expert in all the arts of thriving sin | From Posture Moll to Machiavellian Behn'.[49]

In a positive sense, however, Behn's *Love-Letters* does share the 'philosophical' scepticism of a Machiavelli or a Pallavicino. In their initial frenzy the lovers speak of the breathless 'Rhetorick of Love' or 'Rethorick in looks' as if it were utterly spontaneous, but that term carries undertones of calculation that later come to the fore.[50] The unfolding narrative of seduction and betrayal does indeed reveal the discourse of sublimity as a mere whore's rhetoric, at first self-deluding but later staged to exploit the world. When Philander celebrates the transcendence of his 'mighty passion' (59) he is compensating for a fit of impotence, like Rochester in *The Imperfect Enjoyment*. (Like the boyish lover of the comtesse d'Olonne, in Bussy-Rabutin's *Histoire amoureuse des gaules*, his absurdity is increased by being caught dressed as a maid.) The libertine sublime, for Behn, may be a genuinely heroic attempt to transcend the 'arts and politics of love', or else it may be a façade to hide predation and deceit. The distinction is rooted in her sense of the inequalities of gender. In the opening flurry of letters both Sylvia and Philander translate their passion into sublime terms, and both are eventually perceived as wilful and corrupt. But their trajectories, and our sympathies, move quite differently.

The man at first seems authentically passionate and heroic, and potentially appreciative of such heroism in women: he could have found his wife's affair with Monmouth 'bold' and 'noble', if she had 'generously' acknowledged it and not sunk

---

[49] 'Satire on Bent[inck]', in John Harold Wilson (ed.), *Court Satires of the Restoration* (Columbus, Oh., 1976), 220 (and 223–4 for 'Posture Moll', a brothel-keeper famous in the 1690s for *tableaux vivants* that presumably recreated 'Aretino's Postures').

[50] 33, 37; cf. Bradford K. Mudge, *The Whore's Story: Women, Pornography, and the British Novel, 1684–1830* (New York, 2000), 130.

to dissimulation (18). Philander's declaration recalls Pallavicino's discovery of *no-biltà* in the most absolute whore, Chorier's elevation of *procacitas* or boldness in the aristocratic nymphomaniac, and Rochester's half-ironic assertion that 'there's something generous in mere lust'; he even anticipates Sylvia's own commitment to throw herself into ruin 'generously' (69). But his credibility is rapidly undermined by farcical episodes of impotence and transvestite disguise, and by his political rebellion (detested by the Tory Behn). Sylvia, on the other hand, only gradually builds up a heroic image of her transgression, as she struggles with the alternative heroism of traditional virtue, and only gradually loses her dignity after her betrayal. (The treacherous Philander abandons her for another intrigue within a few months, leaving her to make her way as a courtesan with the 'philosophical' Brilliard as her pimp-husband.) Behn never lets us forget the different situations of the man and the woman. Sylvia is inspired by an egalitarian vision of the love-bond between 'two souls touched with equal passion' and 'equal judgments', a higher relationship in which 'both undertake to take and pay' whereas in marriage 'I've nought to do, but dully give a cold consenting affirmative' (112); but at the same time she knows that she is going to her ruin, and her lover does indeed abandon her for the masculine-libertine principle of variety. As in the case of Alexis, Inconstancy becomes the 'good supreme'.

4. BEYOND EXPRESSION: THE *JE NE SAIS QUOI* AND THE END OF DESIRE

It might seem ludicrous to suggest that the entire tradition of libertine representation tends towards the *je ne sais quoi*, as if this massive expenditure of discourse and cognition, this School of Venus with its graduated curriculum and its canon of intense dialogues and rapturous odes, finally acknowledges that it can neither know nor speak the ultimate Eros towards which it aspires. But this is precisely the logical outcome of introducing *sublimità* and *nobiltà* into the most 'abominable' kind of sexuality (as Pallavicino did), or redefining excess as a virtue in heroic passion (like Pallavicino and Descartes), or locating the highest truth in 'Love raised to an extreme' (as Rochester put it). The sublime tends toward ineffability, inexpressibility, an excess of sensibility over any 'method and rule' that language can comprise. Veiling sexual transgression in the unknowable gives it the kind of glamorous 'vastness' that thrills Sylvia and Philander as they write up their incestuous amours, a feeling of moving across the edge of the known categories. Thus Chorier's Tullia finds the *nescio quid*—literally, 'I don't know what'—in the unfamiliar sensation of anal penetration or the 'unrepresentable supplement of libidinous excess' that overflows any attempt to systematize or enumerate the postures (pp. 191, 204 above).

In all philosophies of the *honnête homme* the *je ne sais quoi* stands for that undefinable grace that distinguishes the aristocrat from the pretender and allows free interchange between the personal and the aesthetic. Thus Wolseley praises the 'uncommon Graces' of Rochester's manner, the 'inimitable Turns of his Wit', the 'unaccountable Charm' that tinges his presence and his poetry alike, inseparable from the 'unaccountable Magick' of classic literature; sexual charisma becomes the mark of his character *and* the test of his writings, both of which exude the 'inimitable' that can be felt but not captured by discourse (*RCH* 139, 143, 151). It is the very vagueness of '*something* generous in mere lust' that allies it with '*something* in the genius of poetry too libertine to be confined to so many rules', or with 'some unknown power' that transforms Orooncko from warrior to lover. For Pallavicino the sublimity of art 'translates' the most disgraceful orifices (as in my second epigraph), and the '*non so che* of resemblance' allows him to translate freely between rhetoric and corporeality.[51]

The (non)concept of the *je ne sais quoi* is at once mysteriously vast and unmistakably concrete. Just as *double entendre* only means one thing, so everybody knows the *je ne sais quoi*, especially when it refers to what Behn called 'that which I dare not name' and Rochester (also speaking in a female voice) called the 'nobler parts which but to name | In our Sex would be Counted shame'—an ironic concession to modesty since Tullia and Octavia name them *ad nauseam*.[52] In Molière we recognize the *je ne sais quoi* perfectly even when it is obscure to the speaker herself, whether it 'trickles through' the sublimating *précieuse* Philaminte (Ch. 3 n. 167 above) or 'moves inside' the earthy, naive Agnès (Ch. 5, sect. 3). Similarly the *Academie des dames*, as part of its campaign to domesticate Chorier's original text, translates the woman writer's *ingenium* as 'ce certain je ne sçay quoi, qui gaigne tous les cœurs'— concealing the eroticized mind, rather than the anatomy of arousal, behind that inscrutable phrase.[53] Here the equation of literary and amorous sensibility has a levelling, demystifying effect, intended to reduce the former to the latter. Behn takes the same nexus and reverses it in an upward direction, promoting her own erotic-poetic 'fire' in the Lucretius poem and the 'Quickness' of women playwrights in the critical epilogue to *Sir Patient Fancy*; by a syllogism that Pallavicino would have recognized, women's intenser 'sensibility' not only generates 'the subtlest waies' in bed and the liveliest plays on stage, freed from the dullness of 'Method and Rule', but proves 'that we have Nobler Souls than you'.

One purpose of the discourse of sublimity is to enforce the separation of the higher Eros from the 'dull beaten road' of common routine and to exalt the creative act, the moment when sex becomes art. Behn expresses this fully in her ode 'On the Death of Mr Greenhill, the Famous Painter', a poem that closely resembles the Rochester elegy and which first appeared as the work of Rochester himself, in the scandalous 1680 *Poems*. Like Rochester, the painter is transformed into an idealized bisexual love-object, 'manly' and 'soft' at the same time, whose beautiful body and 'Large' soul

[51] *RP* 75 ('Ha l'orazione, come composto artificiale, non so che di somiglianza co' corpi'), and contrast *WR*, which translates this feebly as 'no small resemblance' (107) but later adds a recommendation to call the genitals '*Je ne sçaiquois*' or 'What do ye Call'ums' (114). For the *je ne sais quoi* in French conduct theory see Domna C. Stanton, *The Aristocrat as Art: A Study of the Honnête Homme and the Dandy in Seventeenth- and Nineteenth-Century France* (New York, 1980), 207–11, 273–4.

[52] Behn, *Works*, v. 185 (but cf. i. 6 for a slightly earlier version in a male voice); Rochester, 30.

[53] i. 41, altering *Satyra*, IV. 56, on the erudite and bisexual Pomponia.

supplied the model for his canvases. But though he personally 'had all that cou'd adorn a Face, | All that cou'd either Sex subdue', his aphrodisiac art arouses an elevated form of Eros, a 'Vertuous Heat' rather than 'the course road of Common Love'. (Behn profits from the fact that *coarse* and *course* had not yet separated, making her praise of Greenhill's erotic refinement another polemic against dull method.) This uncommon heat is then recreated for the reader by an intense ecphrastic description of his painterly 'touches', a *toccata virtuosa* in which Behn renders arousal-in-language almost as immediate as in *L'Escole* or the dialogues of Tullia and Octavia. The painter's hand—a powerful emblem of female creativity in Fig. 7 above—is now celebrated by a female connoisseur. The movement of Greenhill's living hand, inferred from the painted surface or remembered from studio visits, merges with the nude body depicted, which in turn comes alive under the brush:

> So bold, yet soft, his touches were,
> So round each part, so sweet and fair,
> That as his Pencil mov'd men thought it prest
> The Lively imitating rising Breast,
> 　　Which yields like Clouds ... [54]

The variant reading in which the passively 'imitated' breast begins actively 'imitating' the painter's touch, rising and yielding in the same moment, only increases the pleasurable metamorphic confusion. (Behn makes the painter's technique 'soft' and 'round' as if already anticipating the shape and texture of the breast.) Pygmalion is the unspoken model here, but who is the artist—Greenhill, or Behn herself?

This question is thoroughly answered in Behn's most intricate meditation on the representation of sexuality and the sexuality of representation, the ode 'To Damon, to inquire of him if he cou'd tell me by the Style, who writ me a Copy of Verses that came to me in an unknown Hand' (i. 269–71). Astonished by the aphrodisiac effect of this anonymous love poem, which her critical intellect recognizes as a mere 'form' or conventional compliment, Behn asks her coterie friend to discover the author and so release her from infatuation. But this detective work still would not answer the driving question of the poem: what creates this arousal-effect? At first Behn herself follows the form by declaring it the work of 'the wanton God' testing his 'Power'; since she received the paper in complete solitude no concrete person or 'human thing' could have caused her excitement, nor did she recall any 'Dream' or 'Idea' to her mind. Next she assumes that the poem itself was the 'Philter' that 'darted pain | Thrô every pleas'd and trembling vein' (the same compliment that Wolseley paid to Anne Wharton, but without an identifiable author). Behn seems to create a gender-reversed variant of the Laura episode in Chorier, when Tullia and Octavia infer a 'quick', aroused, inventive sexual subject from the text of a letter; precisely because Laura writes 'without literary art or order'—in what Mme de Sévigné and her

---

[54] *Works*, i. 43 (with some variants from the 1680 'Rochester' text, which reads 'imitated' breast). Was Behn aware of a tradition of 'female' art criticism? Tullia d'Aragona in Speroni's *Dialogo d'amore* praises Titian at length for his '*non so che* of divinity'; see Mary Pardo, 'Artifice as Seduction in Titian', in Turner, *Sexuality and Gender*, 58.

contemporaries would call a *libertin* style—the female preceptor-critic can feel the immediate presence of her erotic *acumen* and *ingenium*.[55] But in fact Behn can tell nothing 'by the Style', infer no person behind the text, since in itself it expresses nothing but routine, method, 'form and compliment', 'all those usual flatteries | To me as common as the Air', things written as a matter of 'course' to display 'wit' rather than 'esteem'. This charming but mechanical product of gallant convention (or 'set Formality' as she witheringly called it in *The Golden Age*) seems to come from one of those men described by Wolseley 'who have got the *Form* of Poetry without the *Power*', and should have been quite impotent to provoke desire. And yet the 'abortive imitation' stirred what Diotima in Plato's *Symposium* called a 'birth in beauty'.

Finally, Behn can only explain textual-erotic agency by invoking her version of the *nescio quid*, the *non so che*, the *je ne sais quoi*; this flood of desire can only be attributed to the 'strange somthing more'. But in the moment of articulating this inexpressible cause of her unaccountable feeling, she realizes that she herself has created the 'dear Idea'. Somewhere between exultation and regret, she repeats three times that 'I drew him': *she creates him*, just as generations of male love-poets had claimed to create their literary mistresses—and just as Behn herself projected the living Rochester into Anne Wharton's congratulatory poem. Now she can take on herself the full prestige of the classical myth that previously ennobled male creativity:

> *Pigmalion* thus his Image form'd,
> And for the charms he made, he sigh'd and burn'd. (271)

Equating the ineffable 'something' of Eros with her own *conatus* of mental fervour, her own *ingenium* or literary imagination, Behn recognizes how deeply fiction suffuses even the intimate corners of the body where Nature supposedly reigns. She extends to her perfectly irresistible paper lover the implication of the brilliant phrase in her impotence-poem 'The Disappointment'—where she calls the organ of Priapus 'Fabulous' in every sense (68).

Generations of male authors had invented female sexual speakers for their own disciplinary purposes, culminating in Chorier's Aloisia Sigea. In Behn's own lifetime male flatterers began to recognize, and eroticize, poets like Jane Barker as the 'Author' of future readers' 'soft desire'. But Behn authors her own desire. Like the princess in *L'Escole des filles*, she pleasures herself with the effigy of her own contriving. 'All depends upon the Genius and Art of the Writer'.

---

[55] *Satyra*, VI. 195 (cf. Ch. 4, sect. 2 above). Octavia's observation that Laura's letter is 'Litterae nulla exaratae arte, nullo ordine' (194) may sound like a typical put-down of women's 'natural' spontaneity, but it resembles the self-designated 'libertine' disorder of several aristocratic writers including Sévigné; see my 'Lovelace and the Paradoxes of Libertinism', in Margaret Anne Doody and Peter Sabor (eds.), *Samuel Richardson: Tercentenary Essays* (Cambridge, 1989), 75–6, 79.

Epilogue

Les Fleurs du mal
Afterlife and Retrospect

Le génie sanctifie toutes choses, et si ces sujets étaient traités avec le soin et le recueillement nécessaires, ils ne seraient point souillés par cette obscénité révoltante, qui est plutôt une fanfaronnade qu'une vérité.

(Baudelaire, *Salon de 1846*)

Genius sanctifies everything, and if these subjects were treated with the necessary care and discrimination they would not be soiled by that revolting obscenity, which is more parade than truth.

THE scenes of reading that opened this book allow us to reconceive the history of sexuality, not as an unfolding teleology but rather as a genealogy, a neoclassical engagement with the seventeenth-century libertine canon which itself revived the erotic culture of antiquity. 'Reception' is too passive a term for this history, which I have presented as an active *deployment* or creative *use* of the mighty lewd book. Pepys exploits *L'Escole des filles* both directly, as a prompt to 'décharger', and indirectly to 'inform' himself and his categories of sexual experience. Diderot imagines his accomplished courtier 'perfecting himself' with '*Aloysia*', and imitates Chorier directly by adding a Latin passage to *Les Bijoux indiscrets*, a novel that itself emulates Chorier's ambition to capture the authentic, unmediated voice of female desire; in *La Promenade du sceptique* Diderot describes an erotic library where 'Meursius' is honoured with a sculptured bust crowned with myrtles.[1] And Casanova's memoirs repeatedly re-enact the primal scene where he triumphs by applying the 'theory' he derived from Chorier. In a typical episode involving two nuns, he selects books and plates from the secret convent library—the *Puttana errante* containing the codified 'Postures of Aretino', illustrations for 'Meursius or Aloisia Sigea Toletana', the French translation *L'Académie des dames*—and borrows these images for his own performance. Like Tullia in 'Meursius', he establishes the rules for an orgy by specifying a target number of orgasms. Opening up *L'Académie* at the lesbian section, Casanova asks the two nuns to recreate the loves of Tullie and Octavie, joining them in a polymorphic orgy where 'we all became of

---

[1] *Bijoux indiscrets*, ch. 47 (commissioned by Diderot from another writer?); *Œuvres complètes*, ii: *Philosophie et mathématique*, ed. Robert Niklaus et al. (Paris, 1975), 141 (the other three canonical amorists are Marguerite de Navarre, Boccaccio, and La Fontaine).

the same sex in all the trios we performed'.[2] Textuality and sexuality change places continually.

An equally direct translation from book to flesh makes *L'Escole des filles* not a stimulant or pictorial programme but a contraceptive manual. For the modern reader, who takes for granted the availability of efficient birth control and who barely remembers the stigma attached to it, *L'Escole* offers a dangerous combination of soft-focus hedonism and sperm-fetishism, certain to cause the very ignominy it discounts. Nevertheless, though it seems criminally casual about the technical means of separating pleasure and procreation, mentioning coitus interruptus and linen pessaries only in passing (II.126), contemporaries could read this 'mighty lewd book' as an agent of that very separation. The idea and practice of contraception had begun to cross the boundary from the prostitutional underworld to the marriage-bed, and those who found such transgression sinful associated it directly with this text. The publisher and entrepreneur John Dunton—who presents himself as a militant moralist and staunch proponent of women's education (as we saw in Chapter 3)—accuses a London clergyman of practising with his mistress 'UN-NATURAL WAYS OF ENJOYMENT a long Time, on purpose to prevent Mrs. E——'s proving with Child. So that that lewd, vile and abominable Book call'd *The School of Venus*, seems to be a meer Novice to Mr. L—— for teaching and practising Diversity of Lewdness.'[3] As in Killigrew's vision of the convent girls who outstrip Aretino and put Ovid to school (Chapter 2 above), Dunton imagines the erotic-didactic text itself becoming a pupil, overreached in the ability to conceive and perform 'Diversity of Lewdness'.

These and countless other eighteenth-century echoes reinforce the central conclusion that emerges from all my readings of the seventeenth-century hard core: the idea of sexual education reached its definitive form. Organized around a philosophical engagement with physical Eros, a partnership of cognition and arousal, the sexual *cogito* matches that of Descartes. By a kind of reverse irony the erotic-didactic trope, ostensibly burlesqued and rendered scandalous by these books, imprints itself on the consciousness of the period. Formative traces of the schooling text can therefore be found even in those whose pedagogy vehemently opposes it. The voluminous writings of the marquise de Maintenon, constituting the rules and manners of her school at Saint-Cyr, seem quite aware that her 'method'—like Susanne's in *L'Escole des filles*—might produce 'une troupe de libertines'. (In this context the word means 'naughty girls' rather than sexual rebels, but it must resonate with her own life experience-turning to high moral education after a career of sexual adventure that led from the *libertin* circle of her first husband Scarron—patron of the original *Escole*—to the bedroom of the King himself.) Maintenon wrote dramatic dialogues and Moliéresque mini-comedies for the Saint-Cyr girls to perform, illustrating and rehearsing the dangers of the outside world; perhaps

---

[2] *Histoire de ma vie*, Édition intégrale, iv (Wiesbaden, 1960), 57, 65–70, 77, 118–20 (and cf. 201, where he gets into trouble for owning a 'petit livre des postures lubriques de l'Arétin').

[3] *Athenianism* (1710), 2nd pagination, 229–30 (referring specifically to coitus interruptus and chemical abortions).

significantly, she gives the names Suzanne and Fanchon to flighty servant characters, as if establishing distance from a text that might have tainted her early years as
a *bonne bourgeoise*. Her regulating letters, dialogues, and maxims reveal that she has
reappropriated Susanne's erotic pedagogy for the cause of virtue: the Dames must
'open' their girls' minds by a 'method' based upon 'the way of love and abandon',
'attracting' them towards a piety not severe but 'gay, sweet, and free'; the pupils must
'learn to be secret' and must 'love to give pleasure, . . . which is the greatest of all
pleasures'.[4] In turn, hostile satire interprets Mme de Maintenon's institution-
building as an extension of the original *Escole des filles* into Court society: to revive
the flagging desires of the impotent Louis XIV, she is imagined searching out the
most alluring girls from Saint-Cyr—the ultimate educational experiment by the ultimate *maîtresse en titre*.[5]

I have emphasized throughout *Schooling Sex* the founding role of Chorier's Latin
dialogues in establishing the idea of erudite libido, the *conatus* or will-to-knowledge
that drives sexual discourse from plain facts of life to complicated passions. Classical authors like Martial and Renaissance satirist-humanists like Antonio Beccadelli
and Pietro Aretino had deplored, celebrated, or joked about most of the
'perversions', and Counter-Reformation theologians like Thomas Maria Sanchez
and Lodovico Maria Sinistrari had categorized the precise degrees of sexual deviance for the benefit of confessors—much to the delight of later *philosophes*.
(Sanchez, in an encyclopedic work that catalogues virtually every sexual variant
later found in secular pornography, became famous for posing questions like: if a
husband sodomizes his wife but finishes by ejaculating in her vagina, is this mortal
sin?[6]) The pseudo-Aretine *Puttana errante* described multiple and perverse cou-
plings and enumerated the 'Postures', but with minimal philosophical or narrative
elaboration. *L'Escole des filles* provided a model for the philosophical interlocutor
and the metamorphic fluidity of gender, but largely confines itself to two-person
heterosexual intercourse (and a simple two-dialogue structure). It was Chorier who
combined the 'pornographic' focus, the encyclopedic Menippean form, and the
philosophical approach, building them into an erotology appropriate for the age of
intellectual systems. This Comenius of the genitals refashions libertine knowledge
into a *curriculum sexualis* leading to universal improvement or deeper damnation,
according to one's position. Eighteenth-century libertines such as Casanova or
Richardson's Lovelace conceive themselves in this mould. When Lovelace contemplates his future life, for example, he imagines himself torn between a good angel
who wants him to remain a bachelor and a bad angel who urges him to marry; in

---

[4] Françoise d'Aubigné, marquise de Maintenon, *Lettres sur l'éducation des filles*, ed. Théophile
Lavallée (Paris, 1854), 98, 23, 39–40, 65, 100, 369; *Conseils et instructions aux demoiselles pour leur conduite
dans le monde*, ed. Lavallée (Paris, 1857), esp. vol. ii, *Proverbes*, pp. II, XVI, XXXVIII.

[5] *Le Tombeau des amours de Louis le Grand*, cited in Kathryn A. Hoffmann, *Society of Pleasures: Interdisciplinary Readings of Pleasure and Power during the Reign of Louis XIV* (New York, 1997), 156–7.

[6] *De Sancto Matrimonii Sacramento Disputationum Tomi Tres* (1602; Viterbo and Venice, 1737), iii. 166
(the Latin passage in Diderot's *Bijoux indiscrets*, ch. 47, links 'Amatoria Sanchesii' to 'festivas Aretini
tabulas'). For Sinistrari see Ch. 3 n. 123 above.

Clarissa as in *Aloisia Sigea*, marriage forms the initiatory gateway that will lead him from the 'simple sins' he currently enjoys to increasingly 'complex transgressions'.[7]

Tullia's philosophical-didactic-seductive project strives to combine the categories of Art and Truth, the *volonté de savoir* and the pleasures of connoisseurship. In subsequent reception-history, the *Satyra Sotadica* operates in two epistemic fields that the original dialogue tried to keep in synthesis: evoked as 'Aloisia Sigea' or 'the Sotadic' it belongs to science and scholarship; evoked as 'Meursius' it belongs to literature, typifying the 'elegance' that exempts the best erotica from moral censure. The twin channels of Chorier's reception give rise to the two legal defences of 'pornography', the one appealing from 'artistic merit' and the other from 'social usefulness'—the 'information' of the sober man, as Pepys would put it.

L'Escole provoked in Pepys both lust and rationalization, pleasure and information sitting awkwardly side by side; he never seeks to synthesize the two responses or soften them by evoking literary quality, and resolves the conflict by burning the book. *Aloisia Sigea*, in contrast, provided an aesthetic mantle, especially in its original Latin form. Chorier-Sigea-Meursius formed the test case for authors whose undoubted literary prowess conflicted with the requirements of decorum and *politesse*. Antoine Gachet d'Artigny's *Assemblée au bas du Parnasse*—the first printed work to name Chorier as the author and confront him with the real Sigea—simultaneously preserves his historic memory and expels him from the new polite canon along with all the other classics that require castration.[8] We saw in Chapter 8 that '*Petronius* and the celebrated Dialogues of Meursius' became touchstones of exculpatory elegance, in Ralph Griffiths's self-interested review of *Fanny Hill* (p. 359 above) and in similar justificatory parallels of Cleland and 'Meursius'.[9] Eighteenth-century editions are marked by a similar desire to incorporate Chorier into the republic of polite letters, identifying the author by name, introducing a rational order into the text, and justifying a translation that restores all the passages bowdlerized in *L'Academie des dames* and yet matches contemporary ideals of refinement; the 1749 *Nouvelle Traduction du Mursius*, 'reviewed, corrected, and restored', claims to have 'purged it of obscene terms without weakening in any way the power of its ideas'— making it the quintessence of scholarly equanimity and genteel sophistication, yet at the same time advertising its undimmed aphrodisiac power.[10] Cleland's novel itself originated as an attempt to rewrite *L'Escole des filles* without the rude words,[11] and evolved into a genteel and sentimental revision of Chorier: the *Memoirs of a Woman of Pleasure*, like the *honesta lupanar* or 'academy' where Fanny learns every trick in

---

[7] *Clarissa*, ed. Angus Ross (Harmondsworth, 1985), 518 (letter 152).

[8] *Relation de ce qui s'est passé dans une assemblée tenue au bas du Parnasse* (The Hague, 1739), 94–100 (authors dismissed include Martial, Petronius, Boccaccio, Aretino, Rabelais, Théophile de Viau, and Bussy-Rabutin, but La Fontaine is permitted to stay though the *Contes* earn him expulsion).

[9] e.g. William Rider, *A Historical and Critical Account of the Lives and Writings of the Living Authors of Great-Britain* (1762), 16.

[10] BL PC 31.i.27, title page.

[11] James Boswell's journal cited in John Cleland, *Memoirs of a Woman of Pleasure*, ed. Peter Sabor (Oxford, 1999), p. xiv (but originally written '[blank] des filles'); if the earlier parts were written in Cleland's youth and the latter part nearer to the date of publication, as Boswell records him saying here, the *Memoirs* recapitulate the 17th-century evolution from *L'Escole* to *Aloisia Sigea*.

the book, aims at 'reconciling even all the refinements of taste and delicacy with the most gross and determinate gratifications of sensuality', creating a space where 'decency made no intrenchment upon the most libertine pleasures'.[12]

Chorier attempted to constitute the female body as a *thesaurus* or encyclopedic 'treasure-house' of male desire, but in time his text replaced the body in this function, focusing the fantasies of solitary thinkers and training generations of school-boys like Casanova. Latinity authorized and camouflaged the *Satyra Sotadica*, allowing it to be treasured in princely libraries[13] (while *L'Escole des filles* was consigned to the flames) and cited in quasi-scientific treatises on sexuality, historical and medical. In his obsessively learned study of sexual practice in the ancient world, the Dutch scholar Adriaan Beverland elaborates Tullia's erudition and alludes to 'Aloisia Sigea', together with Aretino, as 'modern' authors who rival the obscenity of those books enjoyed in bed by the most sensual of the emperors; echoing Tullia's own account of the tradition in which she works (Ch. 4, sect. 4 above), he links the ancient posture-series invented by Elephantis and Philaenis to the erotic images of Titian and the Carracci.[14] Martin Schurig, compiling his 'historico-medical' encyclopedias of female sexuality in the 1720s, emulates Tullia with long dissertations on the names given to the genitals, and slyly includes 'Aloysia Sigaea Toletana' as an authority alongside Harvey, de Graaf, and the *Proceedings of the Royal Society*. This form of citation suggests that he took the pornographic dialogue as reportage and the author, the *auctoritas*, as Aloisia Sigea herself. I suggested in Chapter 4 that Chorier's Latin dialogue derives in part from medical treatises like Vesalius' *Fabrica* and Sinibaldi's *Geneanthropeia*; Schurig now reverses the process by absorbing the erotic fiction into his documentation. His eager adoption of the seventeenth-century term 'nymphomania', meaning a discursive-genital inflation of female desire, surely predisposed him to read (pseudo)female sexual discourse as authentic.[15]

Continuing this attempt to fuse sex and science, the philosopher and librarian Friedrich Karl Forberg, in the early nineteenth century, uses the *Satyra* as the principal basis for an encyclopedic classification of sexual perversions, a vital link between the 'Sotadic' scholarship of Beverland and the pseudo-objective taxonomies of Krafft-Ebing and Havelock Ellis. The title of Forberg's book-length *De Figuris Veneris*, the appendix to his scholarly edition of Beccadelli's *Hermaphroditus*, comes explicitly from Chorier's Tullia. His opening page borrows her phrase *ingeniosa li-*

---

[12] *Memoirs*, 111, 94.

[13] *Catalogus Librorum Bibliothecae . . . Principis Eugenii de Sabaudia*, vol. ii, Vienna, Österreichische Nationalbibliothek, MS 13964, p. 742.

[14] *De Prostibulis Veterum* (c.1680), Leiden University Library, MS BPL 1994, fos. 32, 47ᵛ. In the preface to *De Stolatae Virginitatis Jure* (Leiden, 1680), fo. A1, Beverland compares his own research favourably to Aretino and the 'Sotadic writings' that prurient readers might expect; he may also have reprinted Giovanni della Casa's sodomitical *Capitolo del forno* in a pamphlet entitled *Satyrae Sotadicae Diversorum Authorum Compositae* (n.p., n.d.), All Souls College, Oxford, mm. 17.3.

[15] *Muliebra Historico-Medica* (Dresden and Leipzig, 1729), 2, 385; *Gynaecologia Historico-Medica* (Dresden and Leipzig, 1730), 3, 419; in *Parthenologia Historico-Medica* (Dresden and Leipzig, 1729) he even includes 'Sigaea' in the alphabetical *Syllabus Autorum* (fo. Ccc1). For *nymphomania* see Ch. 4 n. 21 above.

bido and cites her declaration that 'quot inflexiones, quot corporis conversiones, tot sunt Veneris figurae', the number of Venus' figures is equivalent to the inflexions and conversions of the body; in this crucial passage, we recall from Chapter 4, Tullia had abolished the Virgilian maxim that 'Love is the same for all', promoting the infinite variability of individual taste.[15] Yet despite his airy allusion to 'a thousand modes of Venus' in this opening passage, Forberg does submit to arithmetic when he draws up his final list of precisely ninety-five postures.

In *De Figuris Veneris* the fifteenth-century Italian humanist epigram, the seventeenth-century French *libertin* dialogue, and nineteenth-century German scholarship are superimposed in transparent layers, forming a single exhaustive body of sexual knowledge. Forberg makes massive use of Chorier, both in the notes to Beccadelli's text and in the *Figures of Venus*, while always maintaining the gallant pretence that Aloisia Sigea herself wrote the work, exerting her authority as 'Mistress of pleasures': the 'Magistra voluptatum Aloisia' provides at least forty extracts, some—like Tullia's erudite lecture on sodomy—running for many pages and glossed with a scholarly apparatus of their own (i. 138, 140, 144–77). Chorier's *ars amatoria* thus evolves into a taxonomic *scientia sexualis*, confounding the supposed opposition of these two modes and reinforcing the truth-claim of the original text. Though Forberg's ostensible goal, like Beverland's, is to clarify the allusions in classical literature, in the text itself he frequently addresses a Casanova-like reader intent on trying every pleasure and going beyond the benchmark set by Chorier. One variant is recommended 'if you want to enter the woman in a different way from Tullia's'—*in alia ratione ac Tulliana*, literally 'Tullian reasoning'—and this advice is confirmed by referring to 'a most delightful image of this figure, which could excite the organ even of a chaste Hippolytus' (i. 30–2). Forberg's Latin word *jucundissima* unites science and art, echoing Sinibaldi's defence of his own eroto-didactic 'jocundity' and Jocundus, the name of Sempronia's boy trainee in Chorier.

Forberg places himself directly in the great erotic tradition of Philaenis and Elephantis, as Chorier had done in the guise of Sigea (i. 6–8). And his justificatory preface—which begins with a Pepysian claim to provide scholarly information and an owlish tribute to the 'respectable pricks of Coberg' (4–6), inexperienced in the adventures that Tullia describes—mutates into pure literary appreciation. Forberg's praise of Chorier's festive, elegant, perfumed, jewelled, antique style, and his prodigious gift of endowing 'one thing' with the maximum variety, anticipates his eulogy of Aloisia Sigea's unsurpassed ability to express sex 'vividly, charmingly, elegantly' (*vivide, lepide, laute, ut nihil posset supra*)—the very terms that Chorier showered on Aloisia and Tullia on Octavia.[17] Finally, the ascetic librarian defines his ideal readers as those who embrace humanity and nature through sexuality, who emerge from darkness and 'dare to live', who achieve the golden mean by pursuing the full

---

[16] *Manual of Classical Erotology (De Figuris Veneris), Latin Text and Literal English Translation* (1884), i. 2–4 (citing *Satyra*, VI. 214). Since Forberg became court librarian to the House of Saxe-Coburg after his career as a philosophy professor, he may here met Queen Victoria on her state visit in 1845.

[17] *Manual/De Figuris*, i. 18–20, 62. As late as 1913, the Leipzig editor of *Satyra Sotadica* praised it for 'salibus atque leporibus' (fo. 5ᵛ).

pleasures of love without flaunting them in public. Forberg tells us that he abandoned the chaos of post-Hegelian philosophy for the surer rewards of erotic philology, but in this glowing tribute to sexual enlightenment he rediscovers a philosophical vocation by adopting, almost verbatim, the doctrines of Tullia and Octavia (4, 20).

We saw in Chapter 4 that the first recorded use of *pornographique* as a literary classification—an 1806 dictionary of prohibited books intended to justify censorship and provoke abhorrence (rather than curiosity) for the libertine canon—offers that new word as a synonym for the established term 'sotadique', clearly echoing the title of the *Satyra Sotadica*; Chorier's classicizing label easily fits the modern activities of the *pornographe*, the nocturnal investigator invented by Restif de La Bretonne who combines elements of the social scientist, the detective, and the whoremonger. As the historical anthropology of perversion developed in the hothouse atmosphere of the nineteenth century, supplementing the literary erudition of a Beverland or a Forberg with first-hand investigation and global speculation, the old term nevertheless stuck with it. When Sir Richard Burton writes up his rigorous research into the boy-brothels of Karachi for the colonial Civil Service, he anticipates modern historians by relating sexual mores to different regional cultures—but his nomenclature looks back to Chorier. Discovering from his travels and his reading that a worldwide belt of tolerated pederasty runs from the Mediterranean to South-East Asia, he calls it the Sotadic Zone. The essay where he expounds this theory, appended to his translation of the Arabian Nights, is culturally if not literally translated from Tullia's sodomy lecture—complete with rolling lists of Greek names and literary allusions—and further adorned with erudite bibliographical citations of Forberg and *Alcibiade fanciullo a scola*. Burton even steals Rocco's blasphemous interpretation of the Old Testament, alleging that *pueris alienis adhaeserunt* ('they adhered to foreign boys') refers to pederastic brothels of the kind he himself investigated on foreign service.[18]

During the same period, the cultural memory of the *Satyra Sotadica* contributed to the growing taste for luxurious aestheticism and literary-erotic connoisseurship. The authorizing presence of Chorier haunts Baudelaire's influential *Salon de 1846*, for example. In a 'reverie' prompted by the 'obscene book' and the 'libertine print', Baudelaire imagines the poet and the *philosophe* constructing a definitive Love Museum that contains everything from the ecstasy of St Teresa to the 'serious debauches of the Age of Boredom'. His rationale—cited as my epigraph above—sounds uncannily like the late-seventeenth-century defences of Chorier and Rochester that form the subject of Chapter 8. Since 'genius sanctifies everything', since aesthetic care and selectivity removes the taint of 'revolting obscenity', this

---

[18] *The Sotadic Zone* (New York, n.d. [*c.*1930]), 15–16, 30–1, 43, 62 (see Ch. 2 n. 80 above for Rocco's interpretation of the same biblical line). Burton's geographical method has survived the colonial era that he personifies; for an overview of the 'two world-wide systems for organizing homosexual behavior', varying by period and region, see Randolph Trumbach, *Sex and the Gender Revolution*, i: *Heterosexuality and the Third Gender in Enlightenment London* (1998), 4–6 and notes.

canonical collection will display even the most explicit texts and images, starting with the *Modi* of Giulio Romano that founded the entire genre of erotic representation in the Renaissance.[19]

Baudelaire begins to construct this parallel museum of 'philosophical' literature and graphic art in the essay itself, describing a print by the artist under review and matching it to a weighty Latin quotation. In this scene of modern sophistication a cross-dressed woman 'lifts the skirt' of her lover in drag, a reversal of agency as well as dress-code that confirms the text cited in the erudite-looking footnote: recalling that 'in the brothels the boys dressed as girls underneath, and the girls fixed their clothing and faces to look like boys, each sex appearing from under the other,' the citation concludes with the biblical phrase 'all flesh had corrupted [God's] way'. The authority named in this conspicuous note, which appears to set an official seal on the idea of savouring sexual configurations as museum pieces, is not, however, the Vulgate Bible (impudently misapplied) but the Moses of secular-erotic scripture, 'Meursius'. Baudelaire has mined these words from Tullia's lecture on sodomy in Chorier's sixth dialogue, and elevated them to a classical quotation.[20] In Baudelaire as in Robert Wolseley, the idea of a 'genius' that transcends obscenity combines with the elevation of Chorier into an *auctoritas*.

In one of the most notorious poems of *Les Fleurs du mal*, the dialogue between the lovers Delphine and Hippolyte that begins 'A la pâle clarté des lampes languissantes', Baudelaire translates an even more recondite passage from the discussion of fellatio and Socratic folly in the seventh dialogue. Tullia insists that seeking to reconcile sexual pleasure and conventional *honestas* is as futile as looking for darkness in the light ('Honestatem qui quaerit in voluptate tenebras et quaerat in luce'); Delphine lays a curse on the dreamer who tries 'Aux choses de l'amour mêler l'honnêteté', which is tantamount to combining 'l'ombre avec la chaleur, la nuit avec le jour'. The entire poem recreates Tullia's 'tribadic' seduction of Octavia just before her wedding, but Baudelaire transforms the two women's dialogue into something doom-laden and infernal, as the title 'Femmes damnées' implies. Ironically, the nineteenth-century aesthete proves less amoral than his seventeenth-century model: since the consciousness of evil must be retained in Baudelaire's transgressive aesthetic, he also withholds from his lesbian seducer the further twist in Tullia's argument, that 'nothing is immoral to libido when it rages and foams'.[21] In another of the poems suppressed from the first edition of *Les Fleurs du mal*, provocatively titled 'Les Bijoux', the beloved mistress or courtesan 'was trying out various postures' or

---

[19] *Œuvres complètes*, ed. Claude Pichois, Bibliothèque de la Pléiade, ii (Paris, 1976; repr. 1985), 443–4.

[20] Ibid. 444; Chorier, *Satyra*, VI. 204. Tullia (and therefore Baudelaire) cheekily quotes a rearrangement of Genesis 6: 12 in the Vulgate, 'Corruperat omnis caro viam suam' (wrongly identified in the Pléiade notes), which originally referred to God's decision to destroy the world in the Flood; this blasphemy was evidently too much for Forberg, who omits it from a passage that otherwise he cites in full (*Manual*, i. 170–2), and note that the *entire* passage is cut from the abridgement of *L'Academie des dames* (Ch. 7 n. 62 above).

[21] *Œuvres complètes*, ed. Pichois, i (Paris, 1975), 152–5; Chorier, *Satyra*, VII. 232; cf. Otto Görner, 'Baudelaire und Aloisia Sigea', *Zeitschrift für französische Sprache und Literatur*, 56 (1932), 330–2.

'essayait des poses, | Et la candeur unie à la lubricité | Donnait un charme neuf à ses métamorphoses';[22] back in his familiar heterosexual twilight, the poet can now translate the seventeenth-century conception of erotic metamorphosis into the detached, voyeuristic mode of the 'Museum'.

Chorier's pastiche of Aloisia Sigea's sexual erudition and Meursius' Latinity thus gained the same privileged place in the nineteenth-century *Musée d'amour* that it enjoyed in the libertine canon of the 1680s. Baudelaire's citation in the *Salon de 1846* clearly served as a stamp of approval. The luxurious quasi-scholarly editions and translations produced in Paris by Isidore Liseux brought Rocco, Chorier, and Forberg to the attention of 'decadent' taste; a 1881 review of *Aloisia Sigea* by Octave Uzanne, for example, praises Chorier in terms that make him sound like Gustave Moreau, gushing over 'l'étincellement de son style diapré, relevé de broderies et de tons chatoyants'.[23] Huysmans's duc Des Esseintes, the ultimate nineteenth-century aesthete whose library defines a counter-canon that exalts Petronius and Baudelaire while utterly rejecting the conventional ancient and modern classics, admits Chorier into this rarefied company.

Des Esseintes has no trouble finding an ancient author to match his exalted contemporaries Baudelaire and Flaubert: Petronius was always the 'other' classic, expelled from Parnassus as a direct outcome of the eighteenth-century debate provoked by Chorier and for that very reason valued in a library from which the likes of Cicero and Virgil have been contemptuously ejected. But who carries this torch across the dark ages, keeping alive the possibility of canonizing the most lubricious details of the *ars erotica* in a style whose extreme elegance banishes any thought of moral condemnation? Since Des Esseintes fastidiously excludes almost all writing from the tenth to the mid-nineteenth centuries, the exceptions are particularly striking, an intense distillation of the *discours de la sexualité*: his library treasures a few of the confessor's manuals that deal most explicitly with recondite sexuality, and two versions of the erotic classic central to the present book—Forberg's *De Figuris Veneris* and its major source, 'the dialogues of Meursius'.[24] Standing in this library, Michel Foucault would see side by side the confessionals that supply, and the libertine classics that destroy, the central thesis of his 'history of sexuality' *La Volonté de savoir*. But all pretence to truth-value has now receded, and Aloisia Sigea stands almost alone as the epitome of perverse genius.

By framing this afterlife as a brief retrospect rather than a heroic progress, I hope to challenge the ruling assumption among historians of sexuality and literature, expressed in the title of essay collections such as Lynn Hunt's *The Invention of Pornography: Obscenity and the Origins of Modernity* or Catherine Cusset's *Libertinage and*

---

[22] *Œuvres complètes*, i. 158.

[23] Cited in André Berry's introduction to *Les Secrets de l'amour et de Vénus: Satire sotadique de Luisa Sigea de Tolède* (Paris, 1959), p. xxix.

[24] Joris-Karl Huysmans, *À rebours*, ch. 3; as Lise Leibacher-Ouvrard points out (private communication), Marc Fumaroli misses this allusion to Chorier in his 1977 edn. of *À rebours*, citing instead the real Meursius' 1631 *Roma luxuriens* (not a dialogue).

Modernity. My hard-core texts have not exactly been neglected in recent scholarship, but I would argue that they have been weakened by anachronistic assimilation into genres like 'pornography' and 'the novel'. There is nothing decisively modern about the tense synthesis of lust and intellect, body and artefact, that I reveal in these seventeenth-century dialogues. Just as it evolved from Italian courtesan and pederast literature by performing a domestic or intellectual turn (sometimes both at once), so the discourse of sexuality evolves from the baroque counterpoint of Chorier towards the stylized extremity of Rochester and the rococo sentimentality of Fanny Hill and *Thérèse philosophe*. But evolution does not mean teleology. In particular, it does not oblige us to install the marquis de Sade as the benchmark of significance, and to note only those aspects of *L'Escole des filles* and *L'Académie des dames* that look like 'charmingly unfinished' and less 'radical' fragments of Sade.[25]

Abundant evidence shows that the seventeenth-century canon remained current and citable. The anthologies and reprints discussed in Chapter 7 often expanded to include illustrations, of the kind that Casanova converted into performative routines. Lists of confiscated books include Rocco's *Alcibiade*, Pallavicino's *Retorica delle puttane*, and Piccolomini's *Rafaella*, as well as the central neo-Latin and French texts.[26] Library-scenes from d'Argens's *Thérèse philosophe* to Sade's *Juliette* continue the canonizing project of *Venus in the Cloister* (a work that itself appears in Henry Fielding's parodic *Shamela*, along with 'Rochester's poems').[27] I argued in Chapter 7 that this torrent of citation and emulation ran into two divergent channels, *Sodome*sque or Sadean 'outdoing' and domestication or 'taming'. But perhaps escalation-in-extremity is no more than a variety of taming? Innovation requires the presence of the ancestor. Sade revives the centuries-old dialogue form and its erotic-didactic project as he turns *La Philosophie des dames* into *La Philosophie dans le boudoir, ou Les Instituteurs libertins*, recuperating the strident male voice submerged in Susanne, Tullia, and 'Aloisia Sigea'; he evokes the whole 'schooling' tradition when he attaches to *Les 120 Journées de Sodome* the subtitle *L'École de libertinage*. Clinging tenaciously to the Oldhamesque injunction—'Dare something', 'be great in wickedness'—he seems fixed in a retrospective attitude of dependence on the past he professes to scorn.

I can certainly point to modern moments in libertine literature of the Grand Siècle: delirious gay sex in Rocco's *Alcibiade*; Pallavicino's arguments for the moral 'indifference' of erotic pleasure, beyond good and evil; mutual reassurance in *L'Escole des filles* and *A Dialogue between a Married Lady and a Maid*; Chorier's appeal to individual taste; Wolseley's theory of transformative genius. But these flashes of recognition are not the main story. I would rather emphasize connections and contradictions specific to the period, developing in the sixteenth and culminating

[25] Cf. Jean-Pierre Dubost (ed.), *L'Académie des dames, ou La Philosophie dans le boudoir du Grand Siècle* (Arles, 1999), 27, 25, and Ch. 6 n. 10 above.

[26] See Armando Marchi, 'Obscene Literature in Eighteenth-Century Italy: An Historical and Bibliographical Note', in Robert Purks Maccubbin (ed.), *'Tis Nature's Fault: Unauthorized Sexuality during the Enlightenment* (Cambridge, 1983), 255.

[27] *Joseph Andrews and Shamela*, ed. Douglas Brooks-Davies, rev. Thomas Keymer (Oxford, 1999), 332, 317.

in the seventeenth century: the imbrication of sexuality with 'nobility' and 'sublimity', hierarchic spaces and heroic poses; the special liberties conferred by Latin; Proteus Amor, or the metamorphic body becoming an artefact; the secret affinity of
libertinage and *préciosité*; the Pygmalionesque pleasure of 'fashioning' an acolyte of
variable sex. I show the emergence of a full-fledged *ars amatoria* just when Foucault
least predicted it, and I suggest that fictional voicings of female libido—no doubt
intended to belittle—can escape their handlers and inflict damage on patriarchal
power. I trace the crucial effect of the educational revolution and its contradictory
demands, to incorporate physical experience into the learning process but to guarantee intellectual advancement for women by freeing them from corporealizing
prejudice, from the prison-house of sex. Confronting libertine and feminist visions
of the Female Academy reveals both the narrow 'room' of sex-obsession and the
breadth of utopian imagination. Little remains of the original Montaignean separation between artificial male book-learning and natural female instinct, the discipline born in the blood.

Index